Fundamentals of Management

ESSENTIAL CONCEPTS AND APPLICATIONS

Canadian Edition

Stephen P. Robbins

David A. De Cenzo

Robin Stuart-Kotze

Prentice Hall Canada Inc.
Scarborough, Ontario

Canadian Cataloguing in Publication Data

Robbins, Stephen P., 1943-
    Fundamentals of management

Canadian ed.
Includes index.
ISBN 0-13-502295-9

1. Management. I De Cenzo, David A.
II. Stuart-Kotze, Robin. III. Title.

HD31.R5643 1996   658   C95-932245-0

© 1996 Prentice-Hall Canada Inc., Scarborough, Ontario
A Viacom Company

ALL RIGHTS RESERVED

No part of this book may be reproduced in any form without permission in writing from the publisher.

Prentice-Hall, Inc., Englewood Cliffs, New Jersey
Prentice-Hall International (UK) Limited, London
Prentice-Hall of Australia, Pty. Limited, Sydney
Prentice-Hall Hispanoamericana, S.A., Mexico City
Prentice-Hall of India Private Limited, New Delhi
Prentice-Hall of Japan, Inc., Tokyo
Simon & Schuster Asia Private Limited, Singapore
Editora Prentice-Hall do Brasil, Ltda., Rio de Janeiro

ISBN 0-13-502295-9

Acquisitions Editor: *Patrick Ferrier*
Developmental Editor: *Lesley Mann*
Copy Editor: *Dianne Broad*
Production Editor: *Mary Ann Field*
Production Coordinator: *Anita Boyle-Evans*
Permissions/Photo Research: *Marijke Leupen*
Cover Design: *Monica Kompter*
Cover Image: *The Image Bank/Laurie Rubin*
Page Layout: *Paul Sneath*

Original edition published by Prentice Hall Inc.
A division of Simon & Schuster.
Englewood Cliffs, New Jersey
Copyright © 1995 by Prentice Hall Inc.

    2 3 4 5   C   00 99 98 97 96

Printed and bound in The United States

Every reasonable effort has been made to obtain permissions for all articles and data used in this edition. If errors or omissions have occurred, they will be corrected in future editions provided written notification has been received by the publisher.

BRIEF CONTENTS

PART 1 INTRODUCTION
  1 • Managers and Management   1
  2 • The Changing Face of Management   25

PART 2 PLANNING
  3 • Foundations of Planning   53
  4 • Planning Tools and Techniques   78
  5 • Foundations of Decision Making   103

PART 3 ORGANIZING
  6 • Foundations of Organizing   124
  7 • Organization Design for the Twenty-first Century   148
  8 • Human Resource Management   173
  9 • Managing Change and Innovation   203

PART 4 LEADING
  10 • Foundations of Behaviour   224
  11 • Understanding Groups and Teams   248
  12 • Motivating Employees   268
  13 • Leadership and Supervision   293
  14 • Communication and Conflict Management   319

PART 5 CONTROLLING
  15 • Foundations of Controlling   344
  16 • Control Tools and Techniques   366

Appendix: The Evolution of Management   397
Scoring Keys for Self-Assessment Exercises   411
Endnotes   419
Glossary   437
Illustration Credits   447
Index   449

CONTENTS

PART 1 INTRODUCTION

Preface xvi

Chapter 1
Managers and Management 1

Who Are Managers and Where Do They Work? 3

    What common characteristics do all organizations have? 3

    How are managers different from operative employees? 3

    How are managers classified? 4

What Is Management and What Do Managers Do? 4

    How do we define management? 5

    What are the four functions of management? 5

    What are management roles? 7

    How are these roles evident in managers' jobs? 7

    Are effective managers also successful managers? 9

    Details on a Management Classic: Mintzberg's Roles 10

    Is the manager's job universal? 11

    Is managing the same in profit and not-for-profit organizations? 12

    Is the manager's job any different in a small organization than in a large one? 13

    Are management concepts transferable across national borders? 14

    How much importance does the marketplace put on managers? 14

    Do all managers make six-figure incomes? 15

Why Study Management? 16

How Do We Study Management? 16

    What is the process approach? 16

    Managers Who Made a Difference: Pierre Beaudoin at Bombardier 17

    How can a systems approach integrate management concepts? 18

    What's a contingency approach to management? 19

Summary 20

Review and Discussion Questions 21

Self-Assessment Exercise: How Strong Is Your Motivation to Manage in a Large Organization? 21

Class Exercise: Class Expectations 22

Key Terms 22

Case Application: Small To Big 22

Video Case: Skyfreight Takes Off 24

Chapter 2
The Changing Face of Management 25

The Increasingly Dynamic Environment 27
  What is the environment? 27
  Is there a global village? 28
  Why are the big guys laying off? 32
  Details on a Management Classic: Hofstede's Cultural Variables 32
  Why is the future of business with small business? 34
  What will the workforce of 2001 look like? 35
  Why the increased concern with quality? 35
  What responsibility, if any, do managers have to the larger society? 37
  Managers Who Made a Difference: Douglas Hallett at ELI Eco Logic 40
  How is social responsibility extended to women in the workplace? 40
  Why must managers think in terms of quantum changes rather than incremental change? 42
  Developing Management Skills: Guidelines to Protect a Company from Sexual Harassment Charges 42
New Challenges for Managers 44
  How do managers turn from bosses into coaches? 44
  How do managers motivate today's workers? 45
  How do managers improve their ethics? 46
  What's more important: stability or flexibility? 47
  How do we make people in organizations more sensitive to cultural diversity? 47
Summary 48
Review and Discussion Questions 49
Self-Assessment Exercise: What Are Your Personal Value Preferences? 49
Class Exercise: The International Culture Quiz 50
Key Terms 51
Case Application: Xerox of Mexico 51
Video Case: The Automotive Business in Canada 52

PART II PLANNING

Chapter 3
Foundations of Planning 53

Planning Defined 54
  Managers Who Made a Difference: Sonia and Gordon Jones at Peninsula Farms 55
Purpose of Planning 56
Planning and Performance 56
Types of Plans 56
  How does strategic planning differ from operational planning? 57
  In what time frame do plans exist? 57
  What's the difference between specific and directional plans? 57
Contingency Factors Affecting Planning 58
  Does planning differ by one's level in the organization? 58
  How are plans and the life cycle of the organization related? 58
  How does the degree of environmental uncertainty affect planning? 60
  What effect does the length of future commitments have on planning? 60
Management by Objectives 61
  What is MBO? 61
  Are there common elements to an MBO program? 62
  Details on a Management Classic: Peter Drucker's Management by Objectives 63

Contents

The Importance of an Organizational Strategy 64

The Strategic Management Process 64
- How does the strategic management process operate? 65
- What are the primary steps in the strategic management process? 66
- **Ethical Dilemmas in Management: Is "Going Bankrupt" an Unethical Strategy? 67**
- How do you reassess the organization's mission and objectives? 67
- How do you formulate strategies? 68
- **Details on a Management Classic: Michael Porter's Generic Strategies 69**
- How do you implement the strategic management process? 69

Strategy Is Part of Every Manager's Job 70
- **Developing Management Skills: Steps in Goal Setting 70**

TQM as a Strategic Weapon 71

Entrepreneurship: A Special Case of Strategic Planning 72
- What is entrepreneurship? 73
- Do entrepreneurs possess similar characteristics? 73
- How do entrepreneurs compare to traditional managers? 74

Summary 74
Review and Discussion Questions 75
Self-Assessment Exercise: Are You a Good Planner? 75
Class Exercise: Your School's Mission 76
Key Terms 76
Case Application: Topps Trading Cards 76
Video Case: The Reichmann Empire 77

Chapter 4
Planning Tools and Techniques
78

Assessing the Environment 79
- What is environmental scanning? 80
- How does competitive intelligence help? 80
- **Managers Who Made a Difference: Allen and Philip Fracassi at Philip Environmental "Treating Waste as a Resource" 81**
- Is there any way to help predict the future? 82
- What are the different types of forecasts? 82
- How can benchmarking help? 83
- **Ethical Dilemmas in Management: When Does Competitive Intelligence Become Espionage? 84**

Budgets 85
- Why are budgets so popular? 85
- What are the primary types of budgets? 85
- **Details on a Management Classic: Texas Instruments's Zero-Based Budgeting Technique 86**

Operational Planning Tools 88
- What is scheduling? 88
- How do you use a Gantt chart? 88
- What is a PERT network analysis? 89
- What is break-even analysis? 92
- What is linear programming and what kinds of problems lend themselves to it? 93
- What is queuing theory and when is it useful? 94
- **Developing Management Skills: Five Steps to Better Time Management 96**

Summary 97
Review and Discussion Questions 97
Self-Assessment Exercise: Are You an Entrepreneur? 98
Class Exercise: PERTing a Term Paper 98
Key Terms 99
Case Application: Freight Haulers 99
Video Case: Knowing Your Competition and Your Market 100

Chapter 5
Foundations of Decision Making
101

Planning and Decision Making 102
The Decision-Making Process 103
- What defines a decision problem? 103
- What is relevant in the decision-making process? 104

Why does the decision maker need to weight the criteria? 104

What determines the "best" choice? 106

What is decision implementation? 106

Why evaluate decision effectiveness? 106

Rational Decision Making 107

What is rationality? 107

To what extent is rationality limited? 107

Ethical Dilemmas in Management: Should Social Responsibility Play a Factor in the Decision to Relocate a Plant or Headquarters' Office? 108

If managers can't be rational, what do they do? 108

Details on a Management Classic: Herbert Simon and Bounded Rationality 109

Decision Making: A Contingency Approach 109

How do problems differ? 109

What's the difference between programmed and nonprogrammed decisions? 110

What are procedures, rules, and policies, and where are they best used? 110

Managers Who Made a Difference: Yasuyo Kikuta of Fujitsu Ltd. 111

What do nonprogrammed decisions look like? 112

How can you integrate problems, types of decisions, and level in the organization? 112

Group Decision Making 113

What are the advantages to group decision making? 113

What are the disadvantages to group decision making? 114

When are groups most effective? 114

Details on a Management Classic: Irving L. Janis and Groupthink 115

Developing Management Skills: Conducting a Group Meeting 116

How can you improve group decision making? 116

The Effect of National Culture on Decision-Making Styles 118

Summary 119

Review and Discussion Questions 120

Self-Assessment Exercises: What's Your Intuitive Ability? 120

Class Exercise: Contrasting Individual and Group Decision Making 121

Key Terms 122

Case Application: Adidas vs. Nike 122

Video Case: The Realities of Decision Making 123

PART III ORGANIZING

Chapter 6
Foundations of Organizing 124

What Is Organization Structure? 126

Basic Organization Design Concepts 126

Details on a Management Classic: Max Weber and the Ideal Structure: Bureaucracy 127

What is division of labour? 127

What is the unity of command? 129

What is authority and responsibility? 129

Details on a Management Classic: Stanley Milgram and Following Orders 130

Ethical Dilemmas in Management: Should You Follow Orders with Which You Don't Agree? 133

What is the span of control? 134

Developing Management Skills: Building a Power Base 135

Can you identify the five ways to departmentalize? 136

The Contingency Approach to Organization Design 138

Contents

How is a mechanistic organization different from an organic organization? 139

What contingency variables affect organization design options? 140

Managers Who Made a Difference: Monte Peterson at Thermos 142

Organization Structures Reflect Cultural Values 143

Summary 143

Review and Discussion Questions 144

Self-Assessment Exercise: How Power Oriented Are You? 145

Class Exercise: How Is Your School Organized? 145

Key Terms 146

Case Application: The General Hospital 146

Video Case: How Real Is Bureaucracy? 147

Chapter 7
Organization Design for the Twenty-first Century 148

Traditional Organization Designs 150

What is the simple structure? 150

Developing Management Skills: Empowering Employees 151

What is the functional structure? 151

What is the divisional structure? 152

Designs for a Changing World 153

What is the matrix structure? 154

Managers Who Made a Difference: Percy Barnevik, CEO of ABB 154

How does the network structure work? 156

Can mechanistic and organic structures be combined? 158

Why is there movement toward a boundary-free organization? 159

So what's the key to organization design? 162

TQM and Structural Design 162

Ethical Dilemmas in Management: Do Matrix Structures Create Schizophrenic Employees? 163

Organization Culture and Structural Design 163

What is organization culture? 164

How can cultures be assessed? 164

Where does an organization's culture come from? 165

Does culture influence structure? 165

Job Design Options 165

What is the job characteristics model? 166

Details on a Management Classic: J. Richard Hackman and Greg R. Oldham: The Job Characteristics Model 167

What guidance can the JCM offer managers in designing jobs? 167

Summary 168

Review and Discussion Questions 169

Self-Assessment Exercise: Is an Enriched Job for You? 169

Class Exercise: What Kind of Organization Design Do You Want To Work For? 170

Key Terms 171

Case Application: Magna International 171

Video Case: Process Engineering Restructures Organizations 172

Chapter 8
Human Resource Management 173

Managers and Human Resource Management 175

The Human Resource Management Process 175

Important Environmental Factors Affecting HRM 176

Strategic Human Resource Planning 177

How does an organization conduct an employee assessment? 177

How are future employee needs determined? 178

Recruitment and Selection 179

Is there a basic premise to selecting job candidates? 180

Managers Who Made a Difference: Mike Haner at Saskatoon Chemicals 181
Are there selection devices that every manager should use? 183
Ethical Dilemmas in Management: Is It Wrong to Write a "Creative" Resume? 184
Developing Management Skills: Interviewing Skills 187

Orientation and Training 188
How do we introduce new hires to the organization? 188
What is employee training? 189

Career Development 190
Do all employees progress through career stages? 191
How can you apply the career-stage model? 192

Labour-Management Relations 192
Why are good labour-management relations important? 192
Details on a Management Classic: John P. Wanous and the Realistic Job Preview 193
What is the collective bargaining process? 194

HRM and Workforce Diversity 195
Summary 197
Review and Discussion Questions 197
Self-Assessment Exercise: How Do You Define Life Success? 198
Class Exercise: Decruitment 200
Key Terms 200
Case Application: Edgar's Supermarkets 200
Video Case: Retraining Canada's Workers 202

Chapter 9
Managing Change and Innovation 203

What Is Change? 205
Forces for Change 205
What are the external forces creating a need for change? 206
What are the internal forces creating a need for change? 207
How can a manager serve as a change agent? 207

Two Different Views on the Change Process 208
What is the "calm waters" metaphor? 208
What is the "white water rapids" metaphor? 209
Details on a Management Classic: Coch and French: Resistance to Change 210
Does every manager face a world of constant and chaotic change? 211

Organizational Change 211
Why do people resist change? 212
What are some techniques for reducing resistance to organizational change? 213
Developing Management Skills: Overcoming Resistance to Change 213

Change and TQM 213
Stimulating Innovation 215
How do creativity and innovation differ? 215
Managers Who Made a Difference: Colin Patey at the Waterford Hospital 216
How can a manager foster innovation? 217
Ethical Dilemmas in Management: What Would You Do if You Had Details on a Competitor's Trade Secret? 218

Summary 219
Review and Discussion Questions 220
Self-Assessment Exercise: How Ready Are You for Managing in a Turbulent World? 220
Class Exercise: The Celestial Aerospace Company 221
Key Terms 222
Case Application: Change in the Big Accounting Firms 222
Video Case: Pressures to Change 223

Contents   xi

PART IV LEADING

Chapter 10
Foundations of Behaviour 224

Toward Explaining and Predicting Behaviour 225

    What is the focus of organizational behaviour? 226

    What are the goals of organizational behaviour? 226

Attitudes 227

    Does an individual's attitude and behaviour need to be consistent? 227

    What is cognitive dissonance theory? 228

    Details on a Management Classic: Leon Festinger and Cognitive Dissonance Theory 228

    How can managers be kept informed about employee attitudes? 230

    How can an understanding of attitudes help managers be more effective? 230

Personality 231

    Can behaviour be predicted from personality traits? 231

    Managers Who Made a Difference: John Forzani 232

    How do we match personalities and jobs? 234

    How can an understanding of personality help managers be more effective? 235

    Do personality attributes differ across national cultures? 235

Perception 236

    What influences perception? 236

    How do managers judge employees? 236

    What is attribution theory? 237

    Can attributions be distorted? 238

    What shortcuts do managers use in judging others? 239

    How can an understanding of perceptions help managers be more effective? 240

Learning 240

    What is operant conditioning? 240

    What is social learning theory? 241

    How can managers shape behaviour? 242

    Developing Management Skills: Shaping Behaviour Skills 242

    Ethical Dilemmas in Management: Is Shaping Behaviour a Form of Manipulative Control? 243

    How can an understanding of learning help managers be more effective? 243

Summary 244

Review and Discussion Questions 244

Self-Assessment Exercise: Who Controls Your Life? 245

Class Exercise: Salary Increase Request 245

Key Terms 246

Case Application: Binney & Smith (Canada) 246

Video Case: Men and Women Working Together 247

Chapter 11
Understanding Groups and Teams 248

Understanding Group Behaviour 250

    What is a group? 250

    Why do people join groups? 250

    What are the basic concepts for understanding group behaviours? 251

    Details on a Management Classic: Solomon Asch and Group Conformity 253

Building Real Teams 255

    What are work teams? 256

    Managers Who Made a Difference: Ken Ball at Imperial Oil 256

    Why use teams? 257

    What common characteristics exist in effective teams? 258

    Developing Management Skills: Building Trust Among Team Members 259

What challenges do teams present for managers? 260

Ethical Dilemmas in Management: Should Managers Agree with Their Boss When They Don't? 261

Teams and TQM 263

Summary 264

Review and Discussion Questions 265

Self-Assessment Exercise: How Trustworthy Are You? 265

Class Exercise: Building an Airplane 266

Key Terms 266

Case Application: Ford Electronics Manufacturing 266

Video Case: Saskatchewan Oil 267

Chapter 12
Motivating Employees 268

Motivation and Individual Needs 270

Early Theories of Motivation 271

    What is Maslow's hierarchy of needs theory? 271

    What is McGregor's Theory X and Theory Y? 272

    What is Herzberg's motivation-hygiene theory? 273

Contemporary Theories of Motivation 275

    What is McClelland's three-needs theory? 275

    Details on a Management Classic: David McClelland and the Three-Needs Theory 276

    How does Adams' equity theory help explain employee motivation? 277

    Ethical Dilemmas in Management: The Ethics of CEO Compensation 278

    Why is Vroom's expectancy theory considered a comprehensive theory of motivation? 280

    How can we integrate the contemporary theories of motivation? 283

    Are theories of motivation transferable across national cultures? 284

    Developing Management Skills: Getting the Most from Employees 285

Motivating a Diversified Workforce 286

    Managers Who Made a Difference: Hubert Saint-Onge at CIBC 286

Summary 287

Review and Discussion Questions 288

Self-Assessment Exercise: What Needs Are Most Important to You? 288

Class Exercise: How Can We Motivate Others? 290

Key Terms 290

Case Application: Lincoln Electric 290

Video Case: Reward and Motivation 292

Chapter 13
Leadership and Supervision 293

Managers versus Leaders 295

Trait Theories of Leadership 295

Behavioural Theories of Leadership 296

    What was the importance of the Ohio State studies? 297

    What were the leadership dimensions of the University of Michigan studies? 297

    Managers Who Made a Difference: Guy Saint-Pierre at SNC-Lavalin 298

    What is the managerial grid? 299

    What did the behavioural theories teach us about leadership? 300

Contingency Theories of Leadership 300

    What is the Fiedler model? 300

    How does path-goal theory operate? 302

    Details on a Management Classic: Fred Fiedler and the Fiedler Contingency Model of Leadership 302

    What is the leader-participation model? 304

    Is leadership ever irrelevant? 305

Emerging Approaches to Leadership 306

    What is charismatic leadership theory? 306

    How do transactional leaders differ from transformational leaders? 308

Contents

A Special Case of Leadership: First-Line Supervision 308

Ethical Dilemmas in Management: Is It Unethical to Create Charisma? 309

Why are supervisors considered first-level managers? 309

What's unique about being a supervisor? 310

How is the supervisor's role different? 310

How is the supervisor's role changing in today's organizations? 312

Developing Management Skills: Coaching Skills 313

Summary 314

Review and Discussion Questions 315

Self-Assessment Exercise: What Kind of Leader Are You? 315

Class Exercise: The Pre-Post Leadership Assessment 316

Key Terms 316

Case Application: Sue Reynolds 317

Video Case: Visionary of the North 318

Chapter 14
Communication and Conflict Management 319

Understanding Communication 321

What is communication? 321

Managers Who Made a Difference: Burgess Oliver at Northern Telecom 321

How does the communication process work? 323

What is oral communication? 325

Are written communications more effective? 325

How do nonverbal cues affect communications? 326

Is the wave of communication's future in electronic media? 326

What barriers exist to effective communication? 327

Ethical Dilemmas in Management: Is It Unethical to Purposely Distort Information? 328

How can managers overcome communication barriers? 329

Developing Management Skills: Developing Effective Active Listening Skills 331

Cross-Cultural Insights into Communication Processes 331

Conflict Management Skills 332

What is conflict? 333

Can conflict ever be positive? 333

What is your underlying conflict-handling style? 334

Which conflicts do you handle? 335

Who are the conflict players? 335

What are the sources of the conflict? 335

Details on a Management Classic: Kenneth W. Thomas and Conflict-Handling Techniques 336

What tools can you use to reduce conflict? 337

How does a manager stimulate conflict? 337

Summary 339

Review and Discussion Questions 340

Self-Assessment Exercise: Conflict-Handling Style Questionnaire 340

Class Exercise: Active Listening 341

Key Terms 341

Case Application: WordPerfect 341

Video Case: Red Cross and the Canadian Blood Supply 343

PART V CONTROLLING

Chapter 15
Foundations of Controlling 344

What Is Control? 345
The Importance of Control 346
The Control Process 346
- What is measuring? 346
- How do managers determine variations between actual performance and planned goals? 349
- What managerial action can be taken? 350

Types of Control 351
- What is feedforward control? 351
- When is concurrent control used? 352
- Why is feedback control so popular? 353
- **Developing Management Skills: Providing Feedback 353**

Qualities of an Effective Control System 354
- **Managers Who Made a Difference: Paul Clough at Imperial Parking 356**

Contingency Factors of Control 357
Adjusting Controls for National Differences 359
The Dysfunctional Side of Controls 359
- **Ethical Dilemmas in Management: Control and Employees' Right to Privacy 360**

Summary 361
Review and Discussion Questions 361
Self-Assessment Exercise: How Willing Are You to Give Up Control? 362
Class Exercise: Paper Plane Corporation 363
Key Terms 364
Case Application: Mayor Barnes 364
Video Case: Is Franchising the Shortcut to Success? 365

Chapter 16
Control Tools and Techniques 366

Information Control Systems 368
- What is a management information system (MIS)? 368
- Why are end-users replacing centralized systems? 369
- How can MIS enhance planning? 370
- **Ethical Dilemmas in Management: What's Wrong with Pirating Software? 371**
- What effect does MIS have on decision making? 371
- **Managers Who Made a Difference: Robert Cullen at Mount Sinai Hospital 372**
- How does MIS affect an organization's structure? 373
- Does MIS change communication patterns in organizations? 374
- What effect does MIS have on controlling? 374

Operations Controls 374
- What is the transformation process? 374
- How can managers control costs? 375
- How can managers minimize purchasing costs? 376
- What is maintenance control? 378
- Are TQM and quality control the same thing? 379

Financial Controls 381
- What are the more popular ratio analyses? 382
- What role does cost-benefit analysis play in control? 383
- What is activity-based accounting? 384

Behavioural Controls 384
- What is a performance appraisal? 385
- What is discipline? 387
- Are there substitutes for direct behavioural control? 387
- **Developing Management Skills: Disciplining Employees 389**

Summary 390
Review and Discussion Questions 391

Contents

Self-Assessment Exercise: Testing Your Understanding of Computers 391
Class Exercise: Financial Controls 392
Key Terms 394
Case Application: Harley-Davidson 394
Video Case: Software Sells at Home 396

Appendix
The Evolution of Management 397

Historical Background 398
- What was Adam Smith's contribution to the field of management? 398
- How did the Industrial Revolution influence management practices? 398

A Period of Diversity 399
Scientific Management 399
- What contributions did Frederick Taylor make? 399

Details on a Management Classic: Frederick Taylor 400
- Who else, besides Taylor, were major contributors to scientific management? 401
- Why did scientific management receive so much attention? 402

General Administrative Theorists 402
- What did Henri Fayol and Max Weber contribute to management thought? 402
- What were the general administrative theorists' contributions to management practice? 404

Human Resource Approach 404
- Who were some early advocates of the human resource approach? 405
- For what is Hugo Munsterberg best known? 405
- What contributions did Mary Parker Follet make to management? 405
- Who was Chester Barnard? 405
- What were the Hawthorne studies? 406
- Why was the human relations movement important to management history? 406

Details on a Management Classic: Hawthorne Studies 407
- What was the common thread that linked advocates of the human relations movement? 408
- Who were the behavioural science theorists? 408
- What can be concluded from the human resource contributors? 408

The Quantitative Approach 408
- What are the quantitative techniques and how have they contributed to current management practice? 409
- How has the quantitative approach contributed to management practice? 409

Key Terms 409

Scoring Keys for Self-Assessment Exercises 411

Endnotes 419

Glossary 437

Illustration Credits 447

Index 449

PREFACE

To the Instructor

There is an old adage that says "you can't judge a book by its cover." That cliché just might hold true here. As you undoubtedly deduced from the title, this is an introductory management text. Sure, you're thinking, we need another introductory management text about as much as we need another football game on New Year's Day. This book, we think, is authentically different. We believe that it meets a need that has gone untapped.

There is no shortage of excellent introductory management texts in the market. Almost every major college publisher offers one or more attractive, two-colour, comprehensive introductory texts. For many instructors, these books perfectly meet their needs. But a number of instructors tell us they're looking for something different. Maybe you're like them. Do you ever wonder how you'll get through your introductory text, with its 20-plus chapters and 800 pages, in a one-term course? Do you ask yourself if you really need all the material that's in these texts? Would your students be better served by a text that covered the essential concepts in management, provided a sound foundation for understanding the key issues, had a strong practical focus, yet also covered the latest research studies in the field?

We have taught introductory management courses for many years (actually nearly 60 years between us). But we found that, in a typical semester, we couldn't get through the text we'd assigned. So what did we do? We omitted a number of topics and eliminated some of the chapters from the syllabus. We still found that in a one-term course, we were able to cover no more than about 16 or 17 chapters. This recurring experience led us to think about developing a more "manageable" management textbook.

In the same way that organizations have become more "lean and mean," we've designed this book to be a lean and mean version of the larger introductory texts. The market tells us that organizations recognize and respond to consumer differences. For example, automobile manufacturers offer full-size cars with all the extras, while simultaneously selling economy versions that emphasize value. College textbook publishing should be no different. For instance, probably the most observable change you'll recognize in this book is that we have collapsed the number of chapters on planning and control from the more typical seven or eight to four. We felt that topics such as strategy, production and operations management, management information systems, and operations research could be covered in a much more focused and relevant presentation. The result from our streamlining is the book you have in front of you—Fundamentals of Management: Essential Concepts and Applications.

Now let's take a closer look at what's in this reengineered text. In doing so, we'll answer three basic questions:

Preface

xvii

    (1) What assumptions guided the development of this book?
    (2) What important features are in the text?
    (3) How does the book encourage understanding for the reader?

Assumptions

Every author who sits down to write a book has a set of assumptions—either explicit or implied—that guide what is included and what is excluded. We want to state ours upfront.

    Management is an exciting field. The subject matter encompassed in an introductory management text is inherently exciting. We're talking about the real world. We're talking about how Microsoft, a company that fifteen years ago had annual sales of less than $10 million, can grow into an enterprise so valuable that it made its co-founder and CEO the richest man in America; how to redesign an entire company to cut waste, control costs, and increase productivity; and techniques that can make a university more efficient and responsive to its students. A good management text should capture this excitement. For nowhere is it written that a textbook has to be dry and boring! If its subject matter is exciting, the text should reflect that fact. It should include lots of examples and visual stimuli to make concepts come alive, capture the excitement of the field, and convey this excitement to the reader.

    Management should not be studied solely from the perspective of "top management" or "billion-dollar corporations." The subject matter in management encompasses everyone from the lowest supervisor to the chief executive officer. The content should give as much attention to the challenges and opportunities in supervising fifteen clerical workers as those in directing a staff of MBA-educated vice-presidents. Similarly, not everyone wants to work for a large company. Readers who are interested in working in small businesses or not-for-profit organizations should find the descriptions of management concepts applicable to their needs.

    Content should emphasize relevance. Before authors commit something to paper and include it in their text, it should meet the "So what?" test. Why would someone need to know this fact or that? If the relevance isn't overtly clear, either the item should be omitted or its relevance should be directly explained.

    Additionally, content must be timely. We live in dynamic times. Changes are taking place at an unprecedented pace. A textbook in a dynamic field like management must reflect this fact by including the latest concepts and practices.

    To reflect these changes that are occurring around us, we have built this book around the four functions of management and supplemented that material with current issues affecting the field. For example, we take the reader through the Changing World Managers Face (Chapter 2), look at organization designs for the twenty-first century (Chapter 7), and integrate throughout the text such relevant topics as reengineering, empowerment, work teams, and total quality management . The text is divided into five parts: Part I: Introduction; Part II: Planning; Part III: Organizing; Part IV: Leading; and Part V: Controlling. There are a total of sixteen chapters; plus an appendix that describes the evolution of management thought.

    Bringing an introductory management text in at sixteen chapters required us to make some difficult decisions regarding the cutting and reshaping of material. After a lot of review and considerable discussion, we believe we've identified the essential elements students need in an introductory management course. Of course, the choice of "right topics" is a judgment call. We ask you, however, to take a look at our Table of Contents. We think you'll find that the critical issues that you typically expect in an introductory management text are included.

The Important Features In the Book

Classic research studies. Achieving our goal of writing a "lean and mean" version of the 800-page hardback texts required some major changes. In addition to cutting material that we considered to be marginally relevant to the introductory students, we concluded that much of the research that is covered in the "big books" was not as critical for introductory students. In fact, we cut through the theory where possible and emphasized a more practical approach to discussing management. But we respect the fact that there are classic studies that most authors include as part of the body of the text and that many instructors want their students to know about. Unfortunately, most students aren't as interested as text authors and instructors in the details behind these classics. In response, we've created boxed vignettes called "Details on A Management Classic." Although the research implications are discussed in the body of the text, the background on the research is reserved for the "Details" boxes. For example, in Chapter 6, in our discussion of authority and power, conclusions based on Milgram's Obedience study are presented. In an accompanying box, we provide details on how Milgram got his results. This approach allows you—the instructor—a choice of emphasizing research findings or leaving them out; whichever best facilitates your course objectives.

There are a number of issues that cut across issues in management. These include management skills, ethics, and practical applications.

Management Skills. We recognize that today's student is unlikely to end up as a CEO of a Fortune 500 company. Rather, he or she is likely to be an entrepreneur, a senior executive in a small business, a manager in a not-for-profit organization, or a mid-level manager in a large company. Success in these jobs will require practical skills. Therefore, we have included skill boxes throughout the text, which provide a step-by-step basis for handling a particular facet of managing. We call these "Developing Management Skills."

Ethics. Business educators now recognize the importance of including ethics in all key business areas. Consistent with that, we have included "Ethical Dilemmas in Management" boxes. To increase student awareness of the broad range of ethical issues managers face, we pose ethical dilemmas for students to address throughout the text.

Practical applications. Our experience has led us to conclude that students like to see and read about people who have had a significant influence on their organization's performance. Consequently, we have included "Managers Who Made a Difference" boxes. Almost all of the managers described in these boxes are from organizations.

Encouraging Understanding With In-Text Learning Aids

Just what do students need to facilitate their learning? We began to answer that question by pondering some fundamental issues: could we make this book both "fun" to read and pedagogically sound? A book that motivates students to read on and that helps them to learn? Our conclusion was that an effective textbook should teach as well as present ideas. Toward that end, we designed this book to be a quality learning tool. Let us specifically point out some pedagogical features that we included to help students better assimilate the material presented.

Headings designed around questions. We have introduced major topic areas with main headings in each chapter. But within these headings are a series of questions to

Preface

guide the reader in his or her learning. How many times have you had a student approach you and say that he or she is reading the material, but still not performing well on tests? From our experience, we think a lot of students confuse reading with understanding. We know they're not the same. To help students improve their understanding, we have created subheadings that read as questions. This allows readers to identify what important concept they should have gotten from that section; or where they can go to get the answers to something they failed to grasp.

Chapter objectives. Before you start a trip, it's valuable to know where you're headed. That way, you can minimize detours. The same holds true in reading a text. To make learning more efficient, each chapter of this book opens with a list of learning objectives that describe what the student should be able to do after reading the chapter. These objectives will focus students' attention on the major issues within each chapter.

Chapter summaries. Just as objectives clarify where one is going, chapter summaries remind you where you've been. Each chapter of this book concludes with a concise summary organized around the opening learning objectives.

Review and discussion questions. Every chapter ends with a set of eight to ten review and discussion questions. If students have read and understood the contents of a chapter, they should be able to answer the review questions. These review questions are drawn directly from the material in the chapter.

The discussion questions go beyond the content of the chapter. They require the reader to integrate, synthesize, or apply management concepts. The discussion questions will allow students to demonstrate that they not only know the facts in the chapter, but also can use those facts to deal with more complex issues.

Key terms. Every chapter includes a number of key terms that students will need to know. These terms are highlighted in bold print when they first appear, are defined at that time in the adjoining margin, and are listed at the end of each chapter for quick reference and reinforcement. These same terms, and their definitions, are also grouped together at the end of the book in the Glossary.

Self-assessment exercises. Our experience is that students like to get feedback about themselves that they then can use in their development. Toward this end, we have included a self-assessment in each chapter. These self-assessments will focus on some managerial aspect from the chapter in which they are contained.

Class-exercises. Today's students are tomorrow's employees, who will undoubtedly work in teams. To help facilitate teamwork, we've included a number of in-class group exercises, which are also tied to content in their respective chapters.

Case applications. Each chapter contains a recent, realistic, and in almost all chapters, an actual case of an organization that has experienced some dilemma. These end-of-chapter cases give students an opportunity to use one or more concepts discussed in the chapter, and apply them to actual problems faced by managers.

Video case. Each chapter also includes a video case. These are based on videos from the CBC *Venture* series. The write-up of these video cases could also be used as stand-alone case applications for those not wanting to show the video.

Supplements package. Although this book may be smaller than the competition, our supplements package is not. This book is accompanied by the full complement of support material that you expect. For example, adopters of this text can obtain the following classroom aids especially tailored for this text.

Instructor's manual and video guide. This package contains suggestions on how to use the text effectively. It also includes transparency masters, suggested lecture outlines, answers to end-of-chapter questions, as well as answers to video case study questions.

Test item file/Computerized test item file. This test bank contains five types of questions for examination purposes: fill in the blank, multiple choice, true/false, short answer, and essay style. A computerized version, PH Custom Test, is also available. It uses a state-of-the-art software program, which provides fast, simple, and error-free test generation.

Financial Post student supplement. The Financial Post and Prentice Hall Canada have joined together to produce a student edition of *The Financial Post*, tailored to management students. These specially-chosen, time-senstive articles, which are updated annually, demonstrate the vital connection between what is learned in the classroom and what is happening in Canada and the world. This free supplement comes shrinkwrapped to the text.

Electronic transparencies. Overhead masters of selected graphic illustrations have been chosen from the text for use in the classroom. They include lecture notes with page references. These transparencies are also available in full-colour Powerpoint electronic format.

CBC videos. Prentice Hall Canada and the CBC have worked together to bring you a comprehensive Canadian video package that you can use to enhance your classes. These CBC video clips present substantial content and are hosted by well-versed, well-known anchors.

Acknowledgements

Writing a textbook is often the work of a number of people whose names generally never appear on the cover. Yet without their help and assistance, a project like this would never come to fruition. We'd like to recognize some special people, who gave so unselfishly to making this book a reality.

Thanks first to the people at Prentice-Hall of Canada. Maurice Esses, our Senior Development Editor, showed amazing patience managing the book over four time zones and two continents. And Pat Ferrier, Executive Editor, who was understanding of the idiosyncracies of a constant traveller.

Each of us has some special people we'd like to recognize. From Steve's corner, there are all those people and organizations that allow me to so intensely focus on my writing. Special thanks to the Del Mar Cleaners; Hoehn Porsche; the Window Cleaning Co.; Holly Hobbs; Clemento Salazar and Associates; Domino Pizza; the Del Mar Cafe; Double Happiness; Frogs; Professional Travels; San Diego Office Supply; my lawyers and accountants; and the others who have freed me from the hassles of everyday life.

From Dave's. I'd like to recognize some special individuals—my family. The joy that closeness can bring cannot be described. Yet, we must remember how fragile that feeling might be, and how quickly it may disappear. To Teri, my lovely bride of 12 years, I am so glad you're still around. Life wouldn't have been fun without you. Besides, who else would put up with my maniacal writing habits? To Mark, Meredith, Gabriella, and Natalie—the twinkles of my life. I only hope that when you read this when the book is out, and for years to come, you feel the love in which it was written.

Preface

From Robin's: My warmest thanks and deepest admiration to my marvellous son Gavin who did all the Canadian groundwork so incredibly well—over *eiight* time zones and sometimes three continents. I never could have done it without you, Gavin. I hope this is the start of a lot of joint writing ventures.

To the Students

Now that our writing chores are over, we can put out feet up on the table and offer a few brief comments to those of you who will be reading and studying this book. First, this text provides you exposure to the fundamentals of management. As you'll see in our first chapter, fundamentals implies coverage of the basic functions of management. We've made every effort to give you the essential information a student will need to solidly build a knowledge foundation about this dynamic, exciting, and often chaotic field. A knowledge base, however, is not easily attained unless you have a text that is straightforward, timely, and interesting to read. We have made every effort to achieve these goals with a writing style that tries to capture the conversational tone that you would get if you were personally attending one of our lectures. That means logical reasoning, clear explanations, and lots of examples to illustrate concepts.

A book, in addition to being "enjoyable" to read and understand, should help you learn. Reading for reading's sake, without comprehension or understanding what you've just read, is a waste of your time and effort. So, we've developed a structure for this text that should serve as a learning aid. We've introduced major topic headings in each chapter. These you'll find as headings in the red boxes. Those number-one heads, as they are called, provide exposure to a broad management concept. Within most of these number-one heads, we follow with questions. Each of these "question" headings were carefully chosen to reinforce understanding of very specific information. Accordingly, as you read each of these sections, material presented will address the question posed. Thus, after reading a chapter (or a section for that matter), you should be able to return to these headings and "respond" to the question. If you do, congratulations. You're one step closer to adding to your knowledge base. If you can't, or are unsure of your response, you'll know exactly what sections need to be reread, reviewed, or where more of your effort needs to be placed. All in all, this format provides a self-check on your reading comprehension.

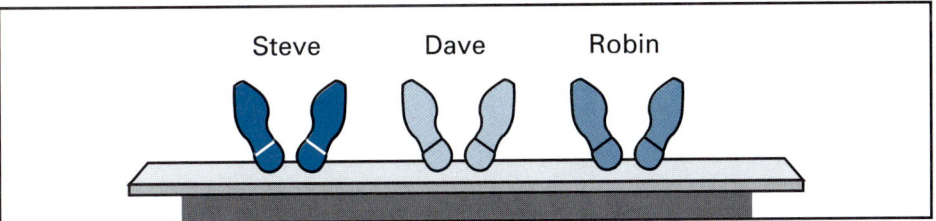

We've also added other check points that you should find useful. Our review and discussion questions are designed to reinforce the chapter learning objectives from two perspectives. First, review questions focus on material covered in the chapter. These are another way to reinforce the important concepts in the chapter. The discussion questions require you to go one step further. Rather than recite facts, discussion questions require you to integrate, synthesize, or apply a management concept. True understanding of the material is revealed when you can deal with these more complex issues.

There is another element of this text that we hope you'll share our excitement about. These are our "Developing Management Skills" boxes. Practicing management today requires sound competencies; competencies that can be translated into specific skills. In chapters 2-16, we've taken a major concept and developed a series of specific steps (skills) that if followed (and mastered), can make you more effective as a manager. We hope that you carefully review each of these, focus on the central behaviours we are explaining, and keep these handy for later reference in you career.

Good luck this semester and we hope you enjoy reading this book as much as we enjoyed writing it.

Steve Robbins   Dave De Cenzo   Robin Stuart-Kotze

Managers and Management

Learning Objectives

WHAT WILL I BE ABLE TO DO AFTER I FINISH THIS CHAPTER?

1. Differentiate managers from operatives.
2. Define management.
3. Distinguish between efficiency and effectiveness.
4. Identify the roles performed by managers.
5. Differentiate the activities of successful managers from effective ones.
6. Explain whether the manager's job is generic.
7. Explain the value of studying management.
8. Distinguish between the process, systems, and contingency approaches.

Managers in organizations fit no specific profiles. They come in all sizes, shapes, colours, and in both genders. They work in organizations whose goal is to produce a profit and in those who are attempting to achieve some social good. Irrespective of who they are, or where they work, these individuals share a common goal—to get their job done through the efforts of others. Take Jim Moore for example.[1]

Jim Moore is the director of technical support at Delrina Inc., a Toronto data communications and fax software manufacturer. When he joined Delrina in April 1993, he inherited a huge problem. The company was growing faster than its ability to handle questions from customers, and customer service, as measured by customer satisfaction, was awful. Delrina was short-staffed and customers who called on the help lines faced either very long waits or busy signals. The company's automatic call-distribution system was inadequate for handling the customer queues that were being created. There was a clear danger of annoying customers to the extent of losing them. The explosive growth of the company (from $48.6 million in 1993 to $102.4 million in 1994) was putting tremendous demands on customer service.

But the job of a manager is, as we said, to get his or her job done through the efforts of others. So Jim began the task of creating the right mentality and structure for a support call centre. He then began to add staff, effectively doubling the number of people in the centre from seventy to 150. His second task became to *keep* the staff he had hired and trained because there was a high demand throughout the company for people with a detailed understanding of all its products. Other departments were taking his people almost as fast as he could get them. His third challenge was to instal a customer management system that could record details of customer calls — essential for product development. Knowing what customers want from products and what bugs they have encountered forms the basis for effective product development.

Jim Moore in the customer service area of Delrina Inc.

This book talks about the sorts of problems Jim faced: creating the right culture and structure; hiring the right people; working with other departments and groups to solve problems; and planning and scheduling the installation of systems and processes.

Jim was able to handle all of these problems and more. In December 1994, he won the industry's most prestigious award for customer support — the Software Support Professional Association's Star Award. And one of Delrina's customers was so excited with the level of service that he named his new daughter Delrina Marie.

As Jim Moore demonstrates, successful managers don't fit a mould. Managers can be found from under age eighteen to over eighty. Nowadays, they are as frequently women as they are men.[2] They manage large corporations, but also small businesses, government agencies, hospitals, museums, schools, and such nontraditional organizations as cooperatives. Some hold positions at the top of their organizations, while others are first-line supervisors. These people can also be found doing their managerial work in every country.

This book is about the work activities that Jim Moore and the tens of millions of other managers like him do. In this chapter, we want to introduce you to managers and management by answering, or at least beginning to answer, these questions: Who are managers and where do they work? What is management and what do managers do? And why should you spend your time studying management?

Who Are Managers and Where Do They Work?

Managers work in an organization. Therefore, before we can identify who managers are, it is important to clarify what we mean by the term organization.

An **organization** is a systematic arrangement of people to accomplish some specific purpose. Your college or university is an organization. So are fraternities, government agencies, churches, the Wal-Mart Corporation, your neighbourhood gas station, the Canadian Medical Association, the Toronto Blue Jays baseball team, and the United Way. These are all organizations because they all have three common characteristics.

What Common Characteristics Do All Organizations Have?

First, each organization has a distinct purpose. This purpose is typically expressed in terms of a goal or set of goals. Second, each is composed of people. Third, all organizations develop a systematic structure that defines and limits the behaviour of its members. This would include, for example, creating rules and regulations, identifying some members as managers and giving them authority over other members, or writing job descriptions so that members know what they are supposed to do. The term organization therefore refers to an entity that has a distinct purpose, includes people or members, and has a systematic structure.

How Are Managers Different from Operative Employees?

Managers work in organizations, but not everyone in an organization is a manager. For simplicity's sake, we can divide organizational members into two categories: **operatives** or managers. Operatives are people who work directly on a job or task and have no responsibility for overseeing the work of others. The people who attach fenders in an automobile assembly line, cook your hamburger at Wendy's, or process your licence renewal appli-

organization
A systematic arrangement of people to accomplish some specific purpose.

How does an organization like the Toronto Blue Jays become successful? By having in place a systematic arrangement of quality people all focused on achieving some goal—like winning the World Series.

operatives
People who work directly on a job or task and have no responsibility for overseeing the work of others.

**Exhibit 1-1
Organizational Levels**

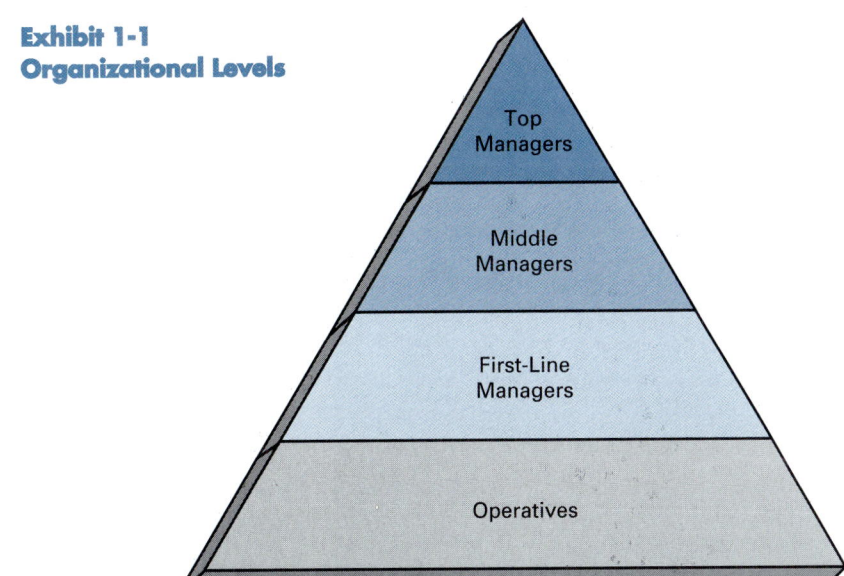

managers
Individuals in an organization who direct the activities of others.

cation at the motor vehicles office are all operatives. In contrast, **managers** direct the activities of other people. They are shown in the coloured areas in Exhibit 1-1. Managers may also have some operative responsibilities; for example, an insurance claims' supervisor may also have basic responsibilities to process insurance claims in addition to overseeing the activities of the other claims clerks in the department. However, our definition presumes that a manager has subordinates. Also, as shown in Exhibit 1-1, we typically classify managers as either first-line, middle, or top.

How Are Managers Classified?

first-line managers
Supervisors; the lowest level of management.

Identifying exactly who the managers are in an organization is often not a difficult task, although you should be aware that managers come packaged in a variety of titles. **First-line managers** are usually called supervisors. They are responsible for directing the day-to-day activities of operative employees. Middle managers may have titles such as department or agency head, project leader, unit chief, district manager, dean, bishop, or division manager. These individuals manage other managers (like a first-line supervisor) and are responsible for translating the goals set by top management into specific details that other managers can perform. At or near the top of an organization, managers typically have titles such as vice-president, president, chancellor, managing director, chief operating officer, chief executive officer, or chairperson of the board. It is these people who have the responsibility for establishing the direction of the organization.

What Is Management and What Do Managers Do?

Just as organizations have common characteristics, so do managers. In spite of the fact that their titles vary widely, there are common characteristics to their jobs—regardless of whether the manager is a supervisor in the mailroom at Alcan who oversees a staff of seven or the chairperson of the board of Barrick Resources. In this section, we define management, present the classical functions of management, review recent research on managerial roles, and consider the universal applicability of managerial concepts.

This Xerox worker helped increase the company's market share to 17 per cent by focusing on the efficiencies of his job.

Managers and Management

How Do We Define Management?

Management refers to the process of getting activities completed efficiently with and through other people. The process represents the functions or primary activities engaged in by managers. These functions are typically labelled planning, organizing, leading, and controlling. We elaborate on these functions in the next section.

Efficiency, a vital part of management, means doing the thing right. It refers to the relationship between inputs and outputs. For instance, if you get more output for a given input, you have increased efficiency. Since managers deal with input resources that are scarce—money, people, equipment—they are concerned with the efficient use of these resources. Management, therefore, is concerned with minimizing resource costs.

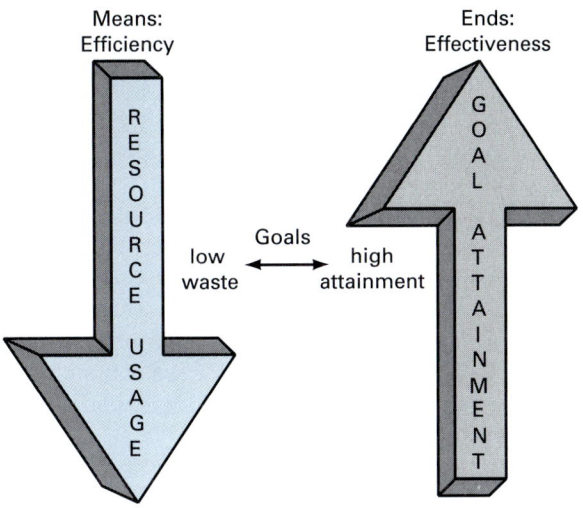

Exhibit 1-2 Management Seeks Efficiency and Effectiveness

It is not enough simply to be efficient. Management is also concerned with getting activities completed; that is, it seeks **effectiveness.** Effectiveness, then, is doing the right thing. In an organization, this means achieving organizational goals (see Exhibit 1-2).

Efficiency and effectiveness are interrelated. For instance, it is easier to be effective if one ignores efficiency. Seiko could produce more accurate and attractive timepieces if it disregarded labour and material input costs. Some federal agencies have been regularly attacked on the grounds that they are reasonably effective but extremely inefficient; that is, they get their jobs done but at a very high cost. Management is therefore concerned not only with getting activities completed (effectiveness), but also with doing so as efficiently as possible.

Can organizations be efficient and yet not be effective? Yes, by doing the wrong things well! A number of colleges and universities have become highly efficient in processing students. Through the use of computer-assisted learning, large classes, and heavy reliance on part-time faculty, the administrators have significantly cut the cost of educating each student. Yet some of these colleges have been criticized by students, alumni, and accrediting agencies for failing to educate students properly. Of course, high efficiency is associated more typically with high effectiveness. And poor management is most often due to both inefficiency and ineffectiveness or to effectiveness achieved through inefficiency.

management
The process of getting activities completed efficiently with and through other people.

efficiency
Doing the thing right. Concerned with the relationship between inputs and outputs, seeks to minimize resource costs.

effectiveness
Doing the right thing. Goal attainment.

What Are the Four Functions of Management?

In the early part of this century, a French industrialist named Henri Fayol wrote that all managers perform five management functions: They plan, organize, command, coordinate, and control.[3] In the mid-1950s, two professors at UCLA used the functions of planning, organizing, staffing, directing, and controlling as the framework for a textbook on management that for 20 years was unquestionably the most widely

management functions
Planning, organizing, leading, and controlling.

sold text on the subject.⁴ The most popular textbooks still continue to be organized around **management functions,** though these have generally been condensed to the basic four: planning, organizing, leading, and controlling (see Exhibit 1-3). Let's briefly define what each of these functions encompasses. Although we'll look at each as an independent function, keep in mind that managers must be able to perform all four functions simultaneously and that one function has an effect on the others. That is, these functions are interrelated and interdependent.

If you don't have any particular destination in mind, any road will get you there. Since organizations exist to achieve some purpose, someone has to define that purpose and the means for its achievement. Management is that someone. The **planning** function encompasses defining an organization's goals, establishing an overall strategy for achieving these goals, and developing a comprehensive hierarchy of plans to integrate and coordinate activities. Like Jim Moore, setting goals keeps the work to be done in its proper focus.

planning
Includes defining goals, establishing strategy, and developing plans to coordinate activities.

Managers are also responsible for designing an organization's structure. We call this function **organizing.** It includes determining what tasks are to be done, who is to do them, how the tasks are to be grouped, who reports to whom, and where decisions are to be made.

organizing
Determining what tasks are to be done, who is to do them, how the tasks are to be grouped, who reports to whom, and where decisions are to be made.

Every organization contains people, and it is management's job to direct and coordinate these people. This is the **leading** function. When managers motivate employees, direct the activities of others, select the most effective communication channel, or resolve conflicts among members, they are engaging in leading.

leading
Includes motivating employees, directing others, selecting the most effective communication channels, and resolving conflicts.

The final function managers perform is **controlling.** After the goals are set, the plans formulated, the structural arrangements delineated, and the people hired, trained, and motivated, something may still go amiss. To ensure that things are going as they should, management must monitor the organization's performance. Actual performance must be compared with the previously set goals. If there are any significant deviations, it is management's job to get the organization back on track. This process of monitoring, comparing, and correcting is what we mean when we refer to the controlling function.

controlling
Monitoring activities to ensure that they are being accomplished as planned and correcting any significant deviations.

The continued popularity of the functional approach is a tribute to its clarity and simplicity. But is it an accurate description of what managers actually do?⁵ Following the functional approach, it is easy to answer the question, What do managers do? They plan, organize, lead, and control. But is this really true of all managers? Fayol's original functions were not derived from a careful survey of thousands of managers in hundreds of organizations. Rather, they merely represented observations based on his experience in the French mining industry.

Exhibit 1-3 Management Functions

Planning	Organizing	Leading	Controlling		
Defining goals, establishing strategy, and developing subplans to coordinate activities	Determining what needs to be done, how it will be done, and who is to do it	Directing and motivating all involved parties and resolving conflicts	Monitoring activities to ensure that they are accomplished as planned	Lead to	Achieving the organization's stated purpose

What Are Management Roles?

In the late 1960s, Henry Mintzberg undertook a careful study of five chief executives at work.[6] What he discovered challenged several long-held notions about the manager's job. For instance, in contrast to the predominant views at the time that managers were reflective thinkers who carefully and systematically processed information before making decisions, Mintzberg found that his managers engaged in a large number of varied, unpatterned, and short-duration activities. There was little time for reflective thinking because the managers encountered constant interruptions. Half of these managers' activities lasted less than nine minutes. But in addition to these insights, Mintzberg provided a categorization scheme for defining what managers do based on actual managers on the job.

These quality inspectors are ensuring that McDonald's french fries are properly prepared.

Mintzberg concluded that managers perform ten different but highly interrelated roles. The term **management roles** refers to specific categories of managerial behaviour. These ten roles, as shown in Exhibit 1-4, can be grouped under three primary headings—concerned with interpersonal relationships, the transfer of information, and decision making.

management roles
Specific categories of managerial behaviour.

How Are These Roles Evident in Managers' Jobs?

All managers are required to perform duties that are ceremonial and symbolic in nature, which require **interpersonal roles.** When the president of a college hands out diplomas at commencement or a factory supervisor gives a group of high school students a tour of the plant, he or she is acting in a *figurehead role*. All managers have a role as a *leader*. This role includes hiring, training, motivating, and disciplining employees. The third role within the interpersonal grouping is the *liaison role*. Mintzberg described this activity as contacting external sources who provide the manager with information. These sources are individuals or groups outside the manager's unit and may be inside or outside the organization. The sales manager who obtains information from the personnel manager in his or her same company has an internal liaison relationship. When that sales manager has contacts with other sales executives through a marketing trade association, he or she has an outside liaison relationship.

interpersonal roles
Roles that include figurehead, leader, and liaison activities.

All managers will, to some degree, receive and collect information from organizations and institutions outside their own. Performing these activities is part of **informational roles.** Typically, this is done through reading magazines and talking with others to learn of changes in the public's tastes, what competitors may be planning, and the like. Mintzberg called this the *monitor* role. Managers also act as a conduit to

informational roles
Roles that include monitor, disseminator, and spokesperson activities.

decisional roles
Roles that include those of entrepreneur, disturbance handler, resource allocator, and negotiator.

transmit information to organizational members. This is the *disseminator* role. When they represent the organization to outsiders, managers also perform a *spokesperson* role.

Finally, Mintzberg identified four roles that revolve around the making of choices—**decisional roles.** As *entrepreneurs,* managers initiate and oversee new projects that will

ROLE	DESCRIPTION	IDENTIFIABLE ACTIVITIES
Interpersonal		
Figurehead	Symbolic head; obliged to perform a number of routine duties of a legal or social nature	Greeting visitors; signing legal documents
Leader	Responsible for the motivation and activation of subordinates; responsible for staffing, training, and associated duties	Performing virtually all activities that involve subordinates
Liaison	Maintains self-developed network of outside contacts and informers who provide favours and information	Acknowledging mail; doing external board work; performing other activities that involve outsiders
Informational		
Monitor	Seeks and receives wide variety of special information (much of it current) to develop thorough understanding of organization and environment; emerges as nerve centre of internal and external information about the organization	Reading periodicals and reports; maintaining personal contacts
Disseminator	Transmits information received from other subordinates to members of the organization—some information is factual, some involves interpretation and integration of diverse value positions of organizational influencers	Holding informational meetings; making phone calls to relay information
Spokesperson	Transmits information to outsiders on organization's plans, policies, actions, results, etc.; serves as expert on organization's industry	Holding board meetings; giving information to the media
Decisional		
Entrepreneur	Searches organization and its environment for opportunities and initiates "improvement projects" to bring about change; supervises design of certain projects as well	Organizing strategy and review sessions to develop new programs
Disturbance handler	Responsible for corrective action when organization faces important, unexpected disturbances	Organizing strategy and review sessions that involve disturbances and crises
Resource allocator	Responsible for the allocation of organizational resources of all kinds—in effect, the making or approval of all significant organizational decisions	Scheduling; requesting authorization; performing any activity that involves budgeting and the programming of subordinates' work
Negotiator	Responsible for representing the organization at major negotiations	Participating in union contract negotiations

Exhibit 1-4 Mintzberg's Managerial Roles
Source: Henry Mintzberg, *The Nature of Managerial Work* (New York: Harper & Row, 1973), pp. 93–94. Copyright © 1973 by Henry Mintzberg. Reprinted by permission of Harper & Row, Publishers, Inc.

improve their organization's performance. As *disturbance handlers,* managers take corrective action in response to previously unforeseen problems, like Jim Moore's handling of the unexpected crises at Delrina. As *resource allocators,* managers are responsible for allocating human, physical, and monetary resources. Last, managers perform as *negotiators* when they discuss and bargain with other groups to gain advantages for their own units. (If you want to learn more about managers' roles, see Details on a Management Classic.)

Whenever a manager, like John McLennan, president of Bell Canada, represents the company to the community at large, that individual is performing what Mintzberg called the spokesperson role.

Are Effective Managers Also Successful Managers?

Fred Luthans and his associates looked at the issue of what managers do from a somewhat different perspective.[7] They asked the question, Do managers who advance most quickly in an organization do the same activities and with the same emphasis as those managers who do the best job? You would tend to think that those managers who were the most effective in their jobs would also be the ones who were promoted the fastest. But that's not what appears to happen.

Luthans and his associates studied more than 450 managers. What they found was that these managers all engaged in four managerial activities.

▶ 1. *Traditional management:* Decision making, planning, and controlling
▶ 2. *Communication:* Exchanging routine information and processing paperwork
▶ 3. *Human resource management:* Motivating, disciplining, managing conflict, staffing, and training
▶ 4. *Networking:* Socializing, politicking, and interacting with outsiders

Managers studied spent 32 per cent of their time in traditional management activities, 29 per cent communicating, 20 per cent in human resource management activities, and 19 per cent networking. However, the amount of time and effort that different managers spent on these four activities varied a great deal. Specifically, as shown in Exhibit 1-5, managers who were successful (defined in terms of the speed of promotion within their organization) had a very different emphasis than managers who were effective (defined in terms of the quantity and quality of their performances and the satisfaction and commitment of their subordinates). Networking made the biggest relative contribution to manager success, while human resource management activities made the least relative contribution. Among effective managers, communication made the largest relative contribution and networking the least.

This study adds important insights to our knowledge of what managers do. On average, managers spend approximately 20 to 30 per cent of their time on each of the four activities of traditional management, communication, human resource management, and networking. However, successful managers don't give the same emphasis to activities as do effective managers. In fact, they do almost the opposite. This challenges the historical assumption that promotions are based on performance, vividly illustrating the importance that social and political skills play in getting ahead in organizations.

Details on a Management Classic

MINTZBERG'S ROLES

A number of follow-up studies have tested the validity of Mintzberg's role categories across different types of organizations and at different levels within given organizations.[8] The evidence generally supports the idea that managers—regardless of the type of organization or level in the organization—perform similar roles. However, the emphasis that managers give to the various roles seems to change with hierarchical level.[9] Specifically, the roles of disseminator, figurehead, negotiator, liaison, and spokesperson are more important at the higher levels than at the lower ones. Conversely, the leader role is more important for lower-level managers than it is for either middle- or top-level managers.

Have these ten roles, which are derived from actual observations of managerial work, invalidated the more traditional functions of planning, organizing, leading, and controlling? Do they diminish the importance placed on these functions or negate the reasons we study them? No! First, the functional approach still represents the most useful way of conceptualizing the manager's job. "The classical functions provide clear and discrete methods of classifying the thousands of activities that managers carry out and the techniques they use in terms of the functions they perform for the achievement of organizational goals."[10] Second, although Mintzberg may offer a more detailed and elaborate classification scheme of what managers do, these roles are substantially reconcilable with the four functions.[11] Many of Mintzberg's roles align smoothly with one or more of the functions. Resource allocation is part of planning, as is the entrepreneurial role. All three of the interpersonal roles are part of the leading function. Most of the other roles fit into one or more of the four functions, but not all of them do. The difference is substantially explained by Mintzberg's intermixing management activities and pure managerial work.[12]

All managers do some work that is not purely managerial. The fact that Mintzberg's executives spent time in public relations or raising money attests to the precision of Mintzberg's observational methods but shows that not everything a manager does is necessarily an essential part of the manager's job. This may have resulted in some activities being included in Mintzberg's schema that should not have been.

Do the comments above mean that Mintzberg's role categories are invalid? Not at all! Mintzberg has clearly offered new insights into what managers do. The attention his work has received is evidence of the importance attributed to defining management roles. Future research comparing and integrating Mintzberg's roles with the four functions will continue to expand our understanding of the manager's job. ▼

Managers and Management

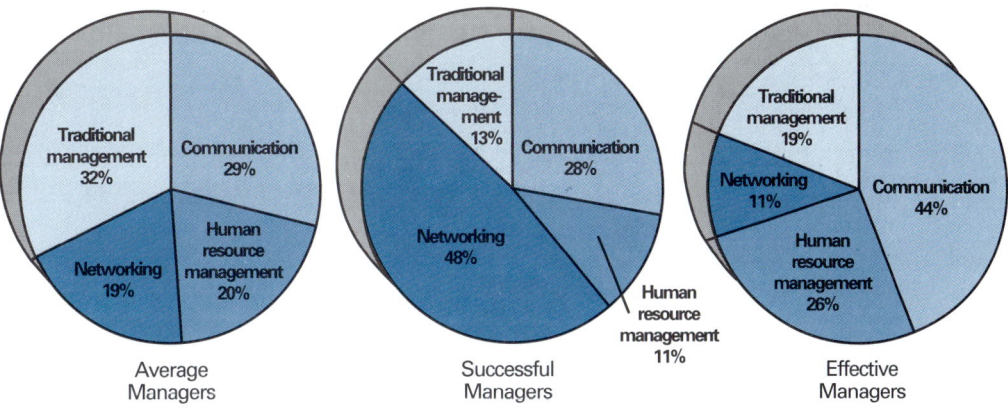

**Exhibit 1-5
Distribution of Time per Activity by Average, Successful, and Effective Managers**
Source: Based on Fred Luthans, Richard M. Hodgetts, and Stuart A. Rosenkrantz, *Real Managers* (Cambridge, Mass.: Ballinger Publishing, 1988).

Is the Manager's Job Universal?

We have previously mentioned the universal application of management. To this point, we have discussed management as if it were generic; that is, a manager is a manager regardless of where he or she manages. If management is truly a generic discipline, then what a manager does should be essentially the same regardless of whether he or she is a top-level executive or a first-line supervisor; in a business firm or a government agency; in a large corporation or a small business; or located in London, England, or London, Ontario. Let's take a closer look at the generic issue.

We have already acknowledged that the importance of managerial roles varies depending on the manager's level in the organization. But the fact that a supervisor in a research laboratory at du Pont doesn't do exactly the same things that the president

This first-line supervisor is showing his operative employees how to assemble parts in their manufacturing process.

Exhibit 1-6 Distribution of Time per Function by Organizational Level

Source: Adapted from T.A. Mahoney, T.H. Jerdee, and S.J. Carroll, "The Job(s) of Management," *Industrial Relations,* Vol. 4, No. 2 (1965), p. 103.

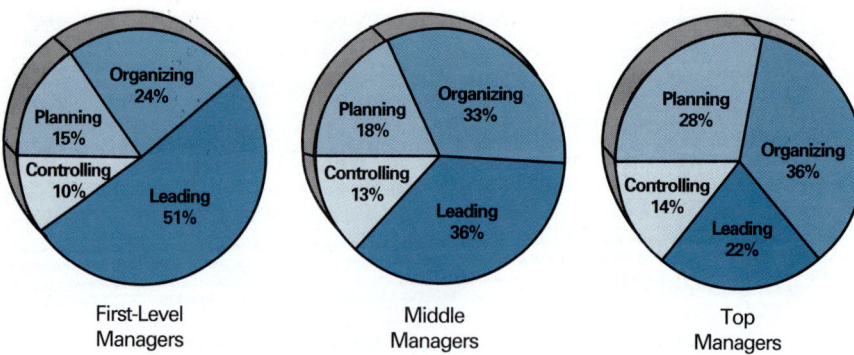

of du Pont does should not be interpreted to mean that their jobs are inherently different. The differences are of degree and emphasis, but not of function.

In functional terms, as managers move up the organization, they do more planning and less direct supervising. This is visually depicted in Exhibit 1-6. All managers, regardless of level, make decisions. They perform planning, organizing, leading, and controlling functions. But the amount of time they give to each function is not necessarily constant. Additionally, the content of the managerial functions changes with the manager's level. For example, as we'll demonstrate in Chapter 7, top managers are concerned with designing the overall organization, while lower-level managers focus on designing the jobs of individuals and work groups.

Even though we recognize that all managers perform some degree of the four basic functions of management, a more crucial question becomes, What are the critical skills that are related to managerial competence? In the 1970s, management researcher Robert L. Katz attempted to answer that question.[13] What Katz and others have found is that managers must possess four critical skills. These are conceptual, human, technical, and political skills.

Conceptual skills refer to one's mental ability to coordinate all of the organization's interests and activities. **Human skills** address the manager's ability to work with, understand, and motivate other people. **Technical skills** require one to use the tools, procedures, and techniques of a specialized field. Finally, **political skills** refer to one's ability to enhance one's power, build a power base, and establish the "right" connections. Undoubtedly, as we are becoming more "skills" oriented in our pursuit of organizational goals, it becomes crystal clear that possessing and demonstrating these skills are important to one's success as a manager.

Is Managing the Same in Profit and Not-For-Profit Organizations?

Does a manager who works for Revenue Canada or a public library do the same things that a manager in a business firm does? Put another way, is the manager's job the same in both profit and not-for-profit organizations? The answer is, For the most part, yes.[14] Regardless of the type of organization a manager works in, there are commonalities to his or her job. All make decisions, set objectives, create workable organization structures, hire and motivate employees, secure legitimacy for their organization's existence, and develop internal political support in order to implement programs. Of course, there are some noteworthy differences. The most important is measuring performance. Profit, or the "bottom line," acts as an unambiguous measure of the effectiveness of a business organization. There is no such universal measure in not-for-profit organizations. Mea-

conceptual skills
A manager's ability to coordinate the organization's interests and activities.

human skills
A manager's ability to work with people.

technical skills
A manager's ability to use procedures and techniques of a specialized field.

political skills
A manager's ability to build a power base.

suring the performance of schools, museums, government agencies, or charitable organizations, therefore, is made considerably more difficult. Managers in these organizations generally don't face the market test for performance.

Our conclusion is that, while there are distinctions between the management of profit and not-for-profit organizations, the two are far more alike than they are different. Both are similarly concerned with studying the role of decision makers as they plan, organize, lead, and control.

Is the Manager's Job Any Different in a Small Organization Than in a Large One?

This question is best answered by looking at the job of managers in small business firms and comparing them to our previous discussion of managerial roles. First, however, let's define small business and the part it plays in our society.

There is no commonly agreed-upon definition of a small business because of different criteria used to define "small"—for example, number of employees, annual sales, or total assets. For our purposes, we'll call a **small business** any independently owned and operated, profit-seeking enterprise that has fewer than 500 employees.

Rebecca Matthias, owner of Mothers' Work, Inc., has built a $14-million mail-order business by selling upscale maternity clothes.

Small businesses may be little in size, but they have a very large impact on our society. Statistics tell us that small businesses comprise about 97 per cent of all nonfarm businesses; they employ over 60 per cent of the private work force; they dominate such industries as retailing and construction; and they will generate a significant majority of all new jobs during the next decade. Moreover, small businesses are where the job growth has been in recent years. Between 1980 and 1993, Fortune 500 companies cut several million jobs. But companies with fewer than 500 employees created more than 13 million jobs during that same period.[15]

small business
An independently owned and operated profit-seeking enterprise having fewer than 500 employees.

Now to the question at hand: Is the job of managing a small business different from that of managing a large one? A study comparing the two found that the importance of roles differed significantly.[16] As illustrated in Exhibit 1-7, the small business manager's most important role is that of spokesperson. The small business manager spends a large amount of time doing such outwardly directed things as meeting with customers, arranging financing with bankers, searching for new opportunities, and stimulating change. In contrast, the most important concerns of a manager in a large organization are directed internally—toward deciding which organizational units get what available resources and how much of them. According to this study, the entrepreneurial role—looking for business opportunities and planning activities for performance improvement—is least important to managers in large firms.

Compared with a manager in a large organization, a small business manager is more likely to be a generalist. His or her job will combine the activities of a large corporation's chief executive with many of the day-to-day activities undertaken by a first-line supervisor. Moreover, the structure and formality that characterize a manager's job in a large organization tend to give way to informality in small firms. Planning is less likely to be a carefully orchestrated ritual. The organization's design will be less complex and structured. And control in the small business will rely more on direct observation than on sophisticated computerized monitoring systems.[17]

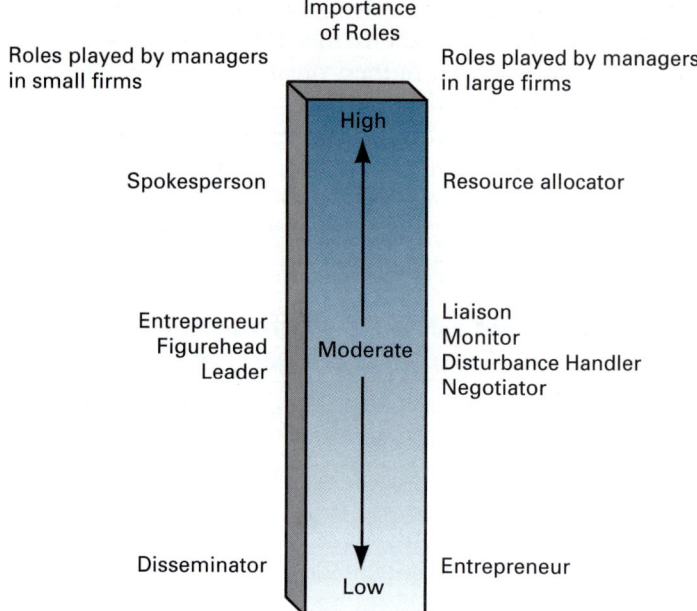

Exhibit 1-7 Importance of Managerial Roles in Small and Large Firms
Source: Adapted from Joseph G.P. Paolillo, "The Manager's Self Assessments of Managerial Roles: Small vs. Large Firms," *American Journal of Small Business,* January-March 1984, pp. 61–62.

Again, as with organizational level, we see differences in degree and emphasis, but not in function. Managers in both small and large organizations perform essentially the same activities; only how they go about them and the proportion of time they spend on each are different.

Are Management Concepts Transferable Across National Borders?

If managerial concepts were completely generic, they would apply universally, regardless of economic, social, political, or cultural differences. Studies that have compared managerial practices between countries have not generally supported the universality of management concepts. In Chapter 2, we'll examine some specific differences between countries. At this point, it is sufficient to say that most of the concepts we'll be discussing in future chapters apply to the United States, Canada, Great Britain, Australia, and other English-speaking democracies. However, we would have to modify these concepts if we wanted to apply them in India, China, Chile, or any other country whose economic, political, social, or cultural environment differs greatly from that of the so-called free-market democracies.

How Much Importance Does the Marketplace Put on Managers?

Good managers can turn straw to gold. Poor managers can do the reverse. This realization has not been lost on those who design compensation systems for organizations. Managers tend to be more highly paid than operatives. As a manager's authority and responsibility expand, so typically does his or her pay. Moreover, many organizations willingly offer extremely lucrative compensation packages to get and keep good managers.

If you were privy to the compensation paid to employees at such large public accounting firms as Price Waterhouse and Arthur Andersen, you would discover an interesting fact. Their best accounting specialists rarely earn more than $75,000 a year. In contrast, the annual income of their senior managing partners is rarely less than $125,000 and, in some cases, may exceed $750,000. The fact that these firms pay their managers considerably more than their nonmanagers is a measure of the importance placed on effective management skills. What is true at these accounting firms is true in most organizations. Good managerial skills are a scarce commodity, and compensation packages are one measure of the value that organizations place on them.

Do All Managers Make Six-Figure Incomes?

All managers don't make six-figure incomes. Such salaries are usually reserved for senior executives. What could you expect to earn as a manager? The answer to this question depends on your level in the organization, your education and experience, the type of business the organization is in, comparable pay standards in the community, and how effective a manager you are. Most first-line supervisors earn between $25,000 and $45,000 a year. Middle managers start near $35,000 and top out at around $90,000. Senior managers in large corporations can earn $1 million a year or more. In 1994, for instance, Conrad Black, chairman and CEO of Hollinger, earned $1,179,880 in salary plus a bonus of $934,904; David Radler, president and COO, earned $1,161,728 in salary and $813,210 in bonus. Richard Currie, president of Loblaw Cos. Ltd. had a 1994 salary of $1,050,000 plus a bonus of $1 million.

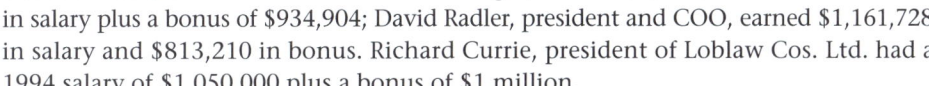

Masoto Mizuno uses specific management skills learned in college and tailored to his homeland in Osaka to build his nearly $2-billion sporting goods empire.

However, while the average cash compensation (salary plus bonus) for chief executives at the 200 largest publicly held corporations was $3.2 million in 1992, Canadian executives are generally compensated on a much lower scale. For instance, in 1994 Galen Weston, chairman and president of George Weston Ltd., earned $990,000 in salary and bonus, while Robert Kidd, the senior vice-president and chief financial officer earned $461,900. And Hollis Harris, chairman, chief executive, and president of Air Canada, one of the world's major airlines, took a 10 per cent pay cut in 1994. His salary was $495,000, plus a bonus of $654,220. Management salaries reflect the market forces of supply and

Conrad Black, chairman and CEO of Hollinger, is among the highest paid executives in Canada, with a 1994 combined salary and bonus of $2,114,784.

demand. Management superstars, like superstar athletes in professional sports, are wooed with signing bonuses, interest-free loans, performance incentive packages, and guaranteed contracts.

Why Study Management?

The first reason for studying management is that we all have a vested interest in improving the way organizations are managed. Why? Because we interact with them every day of our lives. Does it frustrate you when you have to spend three hours in a department of motor vehicles office to get your driver's licence renewed? Are you perplexed when none of the salespeople in a department store seem interested in helping you? Are you angered when you call an airline three times and their representatives quote you three different prices for the same trip? These are all examples of problems caused by poor management. Organizations that are well managed—including Wal-Mart, McCain Foods, Motorola, The Body Shop, Merck Pharmaceuticals, Siemens, and Toys "R" Us—develop a loyal constituency, grow, and prosper. Those that had been poorly managed—for example, General Motors or IBM—found themselves with a declining customer base and reduced revenues. Eventually, the survival of poorly managed organizations becomes threatened. Thirty years ago, Canadian Breweries, IAC, and Massey-Ferguson were thriving corporations. They employed tens of thousands of people and provided goods and services on a daily basis to hundreds of thousands of customers. But weak management did them in. Today these companies no longer exist.

The second reason for studying management is the reality that once you graduate and begin your career, you will either manage or be managed. For those who plan on careers in management, an understanding of the management process forms the foundation upon which to build their management skills. But it would be naive to assume that everyone who studies management is planning a career in management. A course in management may only be a requirement for a degree you want, but that needn't make the study of management irrelevant. Assuming that you will have to work for a living and recognizing that you will almost certainly work in an organization, you will be a manager and/or work for a manager. If you plan on working for a manager, you can gain a great deal of insight into the way your boss behaves and the internal workings of organizations by studying management. The point is that you needn't aspire to be a manager to gain something valuable from a course in management.

How Do We Study Management?

Prior to the mid-twentieth century, a number of diversified approaches to management were suggested (see Appendix, p. 397). In recent years, however, we have witnessed the establishment of a framework for integrating the various approaches to organizing the subject matter of management. These are the process, systems, and contingency approach.

What Is the Process Approach?

In December 1961, Professor Harold Koontz published an article in which he carefully detailed the diversity of approaches to the study of management and concluded that

Managers Who Made a Difference

Pierre Beaudoin at Bombardier

Good managers can have a major effect on an organization. Take the case of Pierre Beaudoin, president of Sea-Doo/Ski-Doo, in Valcourt, Quebec.[18]

In 1985, Pierre Beaudoin accepted a challenge from his father, Laurent Beaudoin, to revive a product that is now part of the motorized consumer products group (MCPG) at Bombardier Inc.—the Sea-Doo. The Sea-Doo was developed by Bombardier in 1968 as a counter-seasonal product to help balance sales of the Ski-Doo. But it didn't have much success in the marketplace, was plagued by design problems, and was eventually shelved. Pierre Beaudoin believed that the product was good and could be made to work, so, as project leader for Sea-Doo, he and his team redesigned it. But when he brought it to Valcourt in 1985 to integrate it with the manufacturing operations there, he encountered all the resistance of a large bureaucracy. His response was to take his team back to Quebec City and spend two years perfecting a prototype. At that juncture he brought it back to Valcourt for mass production, and Bombardier had a product that both worked well and fit the needs of the marketplace perfectly. The only competitor was a stand-up machine from Kawasaki that was more difficult to operate. The Sea-Doo was a sit-down machine, and this easy-to-use aspect helped it take 43 per cent of the North American personal watercraft market. As well, Yamaha had introduced a sit-down machine one year before Bombardier.

It was also very profitable and helped to more than triple the profits of the MCPG division. In 1995, MCPG earned $117.1 million, about 34 per cent of Bombardier's total pre-tax profit, and as a stand-alone company it would be among Canada's 100 most profitable. ▼

there existed a "management theory jungle."[19] Koontz conceded that each of the diverse approaches had something to offer management theory but then proceeded to demonstrate that (1) the human resources and quantitative approaches were not equivalent to the field of management, but rather were tools to be used by managers, and (2) a process approach could encompass and synthesize the diversity of the day. The **process approach,** originally introduced by Henri Fayol, is based on the management functions we discussed earlier. The performance of these functions—planning, organizing, leading, and controlling—is seen as circular and continuous (see Exhibit 1-3).

Although Koontz's article stimulated considerable debate, most management teachers and practitioners held fast to their own individual perspectives.[20] But Koontz had made a mark. The fact that most current management textbooks follow the process approach is evidence that it continues to be a viable integrative framework.

process approach
Management performs the functions of planning, organizing, leading, and controlling.

How Can a Systems Approach Integrate Management Concepts?

systems approach
A theory that sees an organization as a set of interrelated and interdependent parts.

closed systems
Systems that are neither influenced by nor interact with their environment.

open systems
Dynamic systems that interact with and respond to their environment.

The mid-1960s began a decade in which the idea that organizations could be analysed in a systems framework gained a strong following. The **systems approach** defines a system as a set of interrelated and interdependent parts arranged in a manner that produces a unified whole. Societies are systems, and so too are automobiles, animals, and human bodies. The systems perspective, for instance, has been used by physiologists to explain how animals maintain an equilibrium state by taking in inputs and generating outputs.

There are two basic types of systems: closed systems and open systems. **Closed systems** are not influenced by and do not interact with their environment. In contrast, an **open systems** approach recognizes the dynamic interaction of the system with its environment (see Exhibit 1-8). Today, when we talk of organizations as systems, we mean open systems; that is, we acknowledge the organization's constant interaction with its environment.

An organization (and its management) is a system that interacts with and depends upon both its specific and general environments (closed and open systems). Exhibit 1-9 shows a diagram of this perspective. For a business firm, inputs would be material, labour, and capital. The transformation process would turn these inputs into finished products or services. The system's success depends on successful interactions with its environment; that is, those groups or institutions upon which it depends. These might include suppliers, labour unions, financial institutions, government agencies,

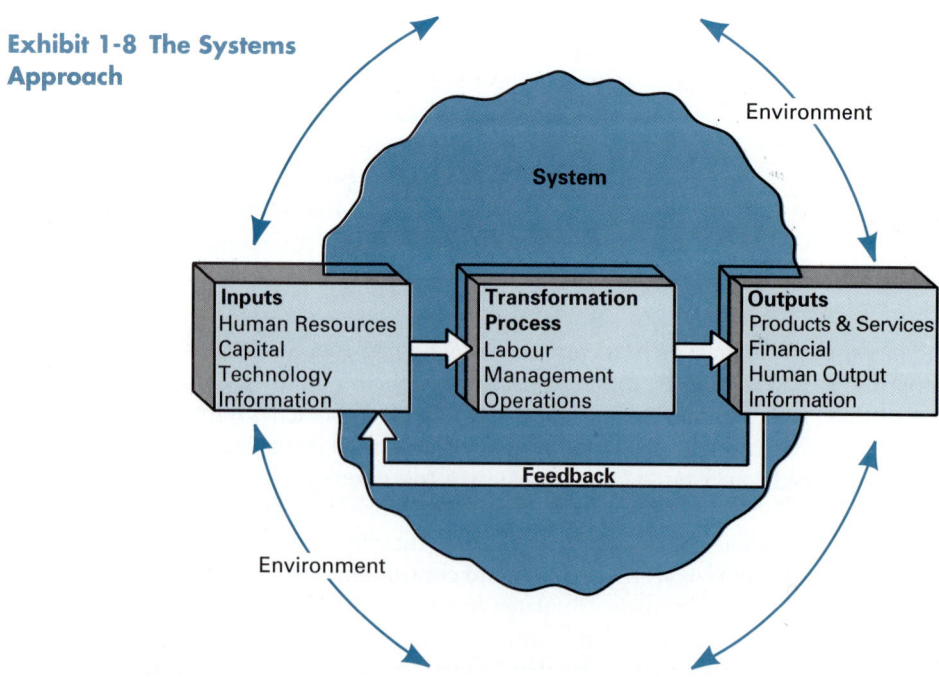

Exhibit 1-8 The Systems Approach

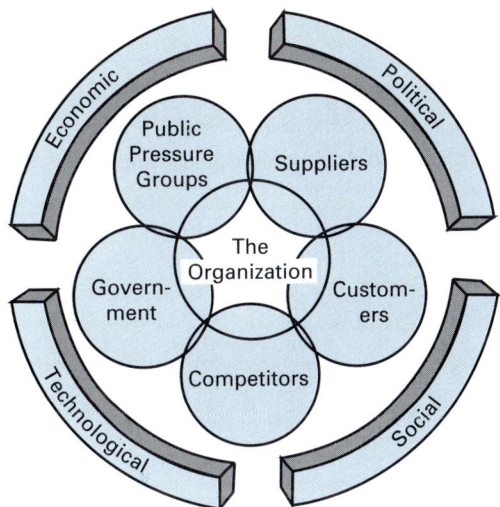

Exhibit 1-9 The Organization and Its Environment

and customers. The sale of outputs generates revenue, which can be used to pay wages and taxes, buy inputs, repay loans, and generate profits for stockholders. If revenues are not large enough to satisfy environmental demands, the organization shrinks or dies. Management must understand its environment and the constraints that environment imposes.

What's a Contingency Approach to Management?

Management, like life itself, is not based on simplistic principles. Insurance companies know that everyone doesn't have the same probability of being in an auto accident. Factors such as age, gender, past driving record, and number of miles driven per year are contingencies that influence accident rates. Similarly, you can't say that students always learn more in small classes than in large ones. An extensive body of research tells us that contingency factors such as course content and the teaching style of the instructor influence the relationship between class size and learning effectiveness. It's not just a coincidence that college courses in introductory psychology are often taught in mass lectures—the course content lends itself well to the straight lecture format. The **contingency approach** (sometimes called the situational approach) has been used in recent years to replace simplistic principles of management and to integrate much of management theory.[21]

A contingency approach to the study of management is intuitively logical. Since organizations are diverse—in size, objectives, tasks being done, and the like—it would be surprising to find that there would be universally applicable principles that would work in all situations. But, of course, it is one thing to say, "It all depends" and another to say what it depends upon. Management researchers, therefore, have been trying to identify these "what" variables. Exhibit 1-10 describes four popular contingency variables. This list is not comprehensive—there are at least 100 different variables that have been identified—but it represents those most widely in use and gives you an idea of what we mean by the term contingency variable.

contingency approach
Recognizing and responding to situational variables as they arise.

> **Organization Size.** The number of people in an organization is a major influence on what managers do. As size increases, so do the problems of coordination. For instance, the type of organization structure appropriate for an organization of 50,000 employees is likely to be inefficient for an organization of fifty employees.
>
> **Routineness of Task Technology.** In order for an organization to achieve its purpose, it uses technology; that is, it engages in the process of transforming inputs into outputs. Routine technologies require organizational structures, leadership styles, and control systems that differ from those required by customized or nonroutine technologies.
>
> **Environmental Uncertainty.** The degree of uncertainty caused by political, technological, sociocultural, and economic changes influences the management process. What works best in a stable and predictable environment may be totally inappropriate in a rapidly changing and unpredictable environment.
>
> **Individual Differences.** Individuals differ in terms of their desire for growth, autonomy, tolerance for ambiguity, and expectations. These and other individual differences are particularly important when managers select motivation techniques, leadership styles, and job designs.

Exhibit 1-10 Popular Contingency Variables

Summary

This Summary is organized by the chapter opening learning objectives found on page 1.

1. Managers are individuals in an organization who direct the activities of others. They have such titles as supervisor, department head, dean, division manager, vice-president, president, and chief executive officer. Operatives are nonmanagerial personnel. They work directly on a job or task and have no responsibility for overseeing the work of others.

2. Management refers to the process of getting activities completed efficiently with and through other people. The process represents the functions or primary activities of planning, organizing, leading, and controlling.

3. Effectiveness is concerned with getting activities completed—that is, goal attainment. Efficiency is concerned with minimizing resource costs in the completion of those activities.

4. Henry Mintzberg concluded from his study of five chief executives that managers perform ten different roles or behaviours. He classified them into three sets. One set is concerned with interpersonal relationships (figurehead, leader, liaison). The second set relates to the transfer of information (monitor, disseminator, spokesperson). The third set deals with decision making (entrepreneur, disturbance handler, resource allocator, negotiator).

5. Fred Luthans and his associates found that successful managers—those who got promoted most quickly—emphasized networking activities. In contrast, effective managers—those who performed best—emphasized communication. This suggests the importance of social and political skills in getting ahead in organizations.

6. Management has several generic properties. Regardless of level in an organization, all managers perform the same four functions; however, the emphasis given to each function varies with the manager's position in the hierarchy. Similarly, for the most part, the manager's job is the same regardless of the type of organization he or she is in. The generic properties of management are found mainly in the world's English-speaking democracies, and it is therefore dangerous to assume that they are universally transferable outside so-called free-market democracies.

7. People in all walks of life have come to recognize the important role that good management plays in our society. The study of management, for those who aspire to managerial positions, provides the body of knowledge that will help them to be more effective managers. For those who do not plan on

careers in management, the study of management can give them a great deal of insight into the way their bosses behave and into the internal activities of organizations.
8. A unifying framework for management began in earnest in the early 1960s. The process approach was proposed as a way to synthesize the diversity. Managers plan, organize, lead, and control according to the process approach. The systems approach recognizes the interdependency of internal activities in the organization and between the organization and its external environment. The contingency approach isolates situational variables that affect managerial actions and organizational performance.

Review and Discussion Questions

1. What is an organization? Why are managers important to an organization's success?
2. Are all effective organizations also efficient? Discuss.
3. What four common functions do all managers perform? Briefly describe them.
4. Contrast the four functions with Mintzberg's ten roles.
5. What are the four managerial activities identified by Luthans? Contrast the emphasis placed on these four activities by average, successful, and effective managers.
6. How does a manager's job change with his or her level in the organization?
7. Is your instructor a manager? Discuss in terms of both Fayol's managerial functions and Mintzberg's managerial roles.
8. In what ways would the mayor's job in a large city and the president's job in a large corporation be similar? In what ways would they be different?
9. Some so-called managers oversee only assembly line robots or a roomful of computers. Can they really be managers if they have no subordinates?
10. How might the job of an owner-manager of a small business compare with the job of president of a large corporation?
11. How is the process approach integrative?
12. Explain how practising managers can benefit by using the contingency approach.

Self-Assessment Exercise

How Strong Is Your Motivation to Manage in a Large Organization?

The following questions evaluate your motivation to manage in large and complex organizations. They are based on seven established role dimensions in the manager's job. For each question, circle the number that best describes the strength of your motivation.

	Weak						Strong
1. I have a desire to build positive relationships with my superiors.	1	2	3	4	5	6	7
2. I have a desire to compete with peers in games and sports.	1	2	3	4	5	6	7
3. I have a desire to compete with peers in work-related activities.	1	2	3	4	5	6	7
4. I have a desire to behave in an active and assertive manner.	1	2	3	4	5	6	7
5. I have a desire to tell others what to do and to impose sanctions in influencing others.	1	2	3	4	5	6	7
6. I have a desire to stand out from the group in a unique and highly visible fashion.	1	2	3	4	5	6	7
7. I have a desire to carry out the routine duties often associated with managerial work.	1	2	3	4	5	6	7

Turn to page 411 for scoring directions and key.

Source: Based on John B. Miner and Norman R. Smith, "Decline and Stabilization of Managerial Motivation Over a 20-Year Period," *Journal of Applied Psychology,* June 1982, p. 298.

Class Exercise

One of the more unnerving aspects of beginning a new semester is gaining an understanding of what is expected in each class. By now, your instructor has probably provided you with a course syllabus that gives you some necessary information about how the class will function. Understandably, this information is important to you. Yet, there is another component—giving your instructor some indication of what you want/expect from the class. Specifically, there are some data that can be useful for providing insight into your taking of this class. To help collect these data, you'll need to answer some questions. First, take out a piece of paper and place your name at the top; then respond to the following:

1. What do I want from this course?
2. Why is this important to me?
3. How does this course fit into my career plans?
4. How do I like an instructor to "run" the class?
5. What is my greatest challenge in taking this class?

When you have finished answering these questions, pair up with another class member (preferably someone you do not already know) and exchange papers. Get to know one another (using the information on these sheets as a starting point). Prepare an introduction of your partner, and share your partner's responses to the five questions with the class and your instructor.

Source: The idea for this exercise was derived from Barbara K. Goza, "Graffiti Needs Assessment: Involving Students in the First Class Session," *Journal of Management Education,* Vol. 17, No. 1 [February 1993], pp. 99–106.

Key Terms

Key terms are listed in the order in which they appear in the chapter.

organization	management functions	informational roles	process approach
operatives	planning	decisional roles	systems approach
managers	organizing	conceptual skills	closed systems
first-line managers	leading	human skills	open systems
management	controlling	technical skills	contingency approach
efficiency	management roles	political skills	
effectiveness	interpersonal roles	small business	

Case Application

Small to Big

Ray Merton and his wife Janet bought a licenced restaurant in 1992. It was located in a small town and had a loyal clientele. When they bought it, it was losing money. The problems they first encountered seemed to include almost everything. On the food side, there was a lot of wastage. Orders for fresh vegetables, fruit, and baked goods sometimes resulted in large amounts going bad or stale, and sometimes resulted in the restaurant running out of important ingredients, like lettuce, during busy meal times. Staffing levels were also a problem. Sometimes the restaurant was very busy and there were not enough staff to cope, leaving customers waiting for their food. At other times, the restaurant was virtually empty and the wait and kitchen staff sat around with nothing to do. When Ray and Janet first looked at the books, they found it almost impossible to determine which items made a profit or a loss, which were the most important sources of revenue and costs, or even simple things like the ratio of staff cost to food cost. The former owner had spent little time in the restaurant and there had been a series of managers.

Over the following three years Ray and Janet turned the restaurant into a profitable business. Janet managed the financial side of the business and the ordering of food and beverage. Ray managed the kitchen and the front of the house. The restaurant employed twelve people.

In 1995, a chain offered to buy the restaurant and at the same time offered Janet a position in the company as regional financial officer, and offered Ray a job as regional head of staffing and staff development. The price offered for their restaurant was good and they knew they would realize a good profit on their investment if they sold. Also, the jobs they had been offered paid well and were interesting and challenging to them. Now they had to make a decision.

Questions

1. As owners of their own restaurant, what management functions did Ray and Janet have to perform?
2. As employees of the restaurant chain, how would their jobs differ in terms of the sorts of things they would need to do to manage effectively?
3. In terms of Mintzberg's roles, how would their jobs change?
4. Moving from their own restaurant with twelve employees to a chain with several hundred employees in the region seems like a big change. Is it really? Will there be a major difference between how they managed a small business and how they manage in a large one? What do you see as the major differences?
5. From what you know about management and management effectiveness, how successful do you think Ray and Janet will be if they take the new jobs offered?
6. Do you know anyone who has moved from working in a small organization to working in a large one, or vice versa? Interview them and get them to compare their roles in the two situations.

Skyfreight Takes Off

The things this book talks about — the fundamentals of management — are well illustrated by Michael Talker, the founder and head of Skyfreight, an air courier company focusing on servicing the market for same-day delivery of packages from Toronto to Ottawa and Montreal. Michael Talker started Skyfreight in 1994. He is an engineer and, having lost his job in 1993, decided to start his own business. Buying an airplane for $70,000 was only the beginning.

As you read through this book, you will be able to reflect back on Michael Talker and the issues he faced as he began his business. Perhaps the one that hit Talker first was planning. On March 1, 1994, Skyfreight appeared to be ready to launch its business. It had 10,000 advertising flyers printed to announce a March 7th opening. But a large problem arose: Transport Canada had to check the pilots and review the procedures of companies like Skyfreight — and the inspectors were very busy and booked up for about a month ahead. No inspection, no flying. And no flying, no business. Talker had failed to plan ahead and was forced to delay his opening. In the third week of March, he had to cancel the scheduled inspection because two of his pilots had quit. On April 13th, when Skyfreight was ready to start flying, another obstacle appeared — the National Transport Agency (NTA), which grants charter licenses, required Skyfreight to have more insurance.

As Mintzberg says, managers play a number of roles, one of which involves negotiation. Skyfreight's strategy was based on providing a service that significantly undercut its giant competitors, Air Canada and Canadian Airlines. But while Skyfreight advertised a rate of $29, its customers, land-based couriers, needed a higher price to make their profit margins, so Talker had to work out a pricing strategy compromise. He was also involved in negotiations with his customers, government agencies, and even his competitors. As a fall-back strategy, Skyfreight used Air Canada to deliver packages that the company was unable to handle.

Now much of Talker's time is taken up with talking to customers and potential customers, and dealing with the various government bodies that regulate air services, with staff, and with the banks. His training is as an engineer. But as a manager, he needs to know how to plan, organize, lead, motivate, communicate, schedule, and control. Starting Skyfreight was a tremendous task and a huge challenge. Making it work successfully is an even greater one.

Questions

1. Is formal training in management necessary to be successful in business? If you were starting up an air courier service like Michael Talker's, what sorts of skills would you want to develop? List the 10 most important things you feel you would need to know about, or skills you would like to have.
2. Looking at Mintzberg's roles, which were the most important ones for Michael Talker to master (a) during the start-up of Skyfreight, and (b) running the ongoing business? Explain your selections.
3. What characteristics do you need to have to be a successful manager? List what you feel are the five most important ones and explain your choices.

Video Resource: "Skyfreight," *Venture* 486 (May 1, 1994).

2

The Changing Face of Management

Learning Objectives

WHAT WILL I BE ABLE TO DO AFTER I FINISH THIS CHAPTER?

1. **Explain the importance of viewing management from a global perspective.**
2. **Contrast multinational and transnational corporations.**
3. **Describe why corporations downsize.**
4. **Explain why small business concepts are being found in large companies.**
5. **Describe the workforce of 2001.**
6. **Identify the five primary components of TQM.**
7. **Define social responsibility and social responsiveness.**
8. **Differentiate between incremental change and quantum change.**
9. **Explain the increased popularity of managers performing a coaching role.**
10. **Define ethics.**
11. **Describe why managers are more concerned with stimulating innovation and change.**
12. **Explain the workforce diversity implications for managers.**

What would you say about the managers in a company that had achieved sales over the $1 billion mark, made considerable profit, then decided to redo how the company was operated? Crazy? Poor management? Neither of these! Rather, this activity typifies a trend in business today. That is, there is movement among today's managers to rethink how their organizations operate in an effort to make their companies more quality oriented.

This is exactly what Union Carbide Corporation did.[1] Called reengineering, companies like Union Carbide are looking at making "radical changes in business processes to achieve breakthrough results."[2] This means that in these organizations, management and employees alike are evaluating all aspects of the operations—not just to fine-tune but to overhaul how the work gets done, if it gets done at all. And this applies to successful organizations as well as ones with problems. Reengineering boldly attacks the belief that "if it ain't broke, don't fix it!"

For many of these corporations, reengineering has paid off handsomely. Union Carbide, for

Workers at Union Carbide celebrate the success of reengineering their plant.

instance, cut more than $400 million out of fixed costs; Mutual Benefit Life Insurance reduced costs and cycle time by about 80 per cent; and GTE eliminated several inefficiencies in their processes, resulting in almost a 30 per cent increase in productivity.[3]

Succeeding in today's business environment is difficult at best. Faced with global competition, a need for better quality products and services, diversity in the workforce, and more concerns for better treatment of the environment, managers have had to make sweeping changes in the way they do business. For those companies like Union Carbide that do, this results in both higher quality output and improved productivity from employees—and ultimately increased profitability. In the current dynamic business environment, managers need to rethink many of their old and established practices.

A generation ago, successful managers valued stability, predictability, and efficiency achieved through economies of scale. But many of yesterday's stars have faded. For instance, in Exhibit 2-1, we have identified a number of industries, the 1960s star, and the current leader in the market.

What common factors characterize the 1990s' stars? They're lean, fast, and flexible. They are dedicated to quality, work around teams, and minimize hierarchical overhead. Furthermore, employees in these organizations understand what is the right thing to do, as many of these companies stress the importance of managing the business in an ethical manner.

In this chapter, we'll establish a foundation for understanding this changing world of work. No successful organization can operate without understanding and dealing with the dynamic environment that surrounds it.

The Changing Face of Management

The Increasingly Dynamic Environment

As our 1960s stars in Exhibit 2-1 demonstrated, organizations that remain stagnant and highly bureaucratic are increasingly fading from the limelight. Why? Because one of the biggest problems in managing an enterprise today is trying to hold on to the past. Our world has changed, resulting in concerns for dealing with an international market, restructuring of our companies, and more emphasis being placed on the small business and entrepreneur. And if that isn't enough, our workforce has changed drastically over the past two decades. In this section, we'll explore some of the more important forces that are making the environment in which managers must operate more challenging.

What Is the Environment?

The recognition that no organization is an island unto itself was a major contribution of the systems approach to management (see Chapter 1). Anyone who questions the impact of the external environment on managing should consider the following:

▶ In the summer of 1993, Aloro Foods of Mississauga had just shipped its biggest order ever, $100,000 worth of frozen pizzas, to Tengelmann, the German supermarket company, when they received a phone call from the buyer. The European Union had just changed its meat inspection laws and all the pizzas with pepperoni (about two-thirds of the shipment) had been barred from entering Germany.

▶ In 1995, when the Mexican peso plunged dramatically, the Bank of Nova Scotia's $102-million investment in Grupo Financiero Inverlat SA, Mexico's fourth-largest bank, lost much of its value. Peter Godsoe, the bank's chairman was quoted as saying, "Obviously our investment just ain't what it used to be." Scotiabank plans to have its investment for the long term and says that it's prepared to weather the storm.

▶ The provinces across Canada earn a significant amount of revenue from sports lottery tickets. They have proved to be a strong growth market. But a cancellation of the 1994-95 hockey season would cost the provinces about $75 million in lost profits. The baseball strike cost Ontario $6 million in profits. But it cost Labatt $13 million in the three months from August to October in 1994.

As these examples show, there are forces in the environment that play a major role in shaping managers' actions. The term **environment** refers to institutions or forces that are outside the organization and affect the organization's performance. As

environment
Outside institutions or forces that potentially affect an organization's performance.

Exhibit 2-1 Corporate Stars: 1960s versus 1990s

INDUSTRY	1960s STAR	1990s STAR
Automobiles	General Motors	Toyota
Brewing	Canadian Breweries	Labatt
Broadcasting	CBS	CNN
Cameras	Bell & Howell	Minolta
Computers	IBM	Gateway 2000
Cosmetics	Revlon	Mary Kay
Film	Eastman Kodak	Fuji
Food	Dominion Stores	Loblaws
General Retailing	Sears	Wal-Mart

one writer put it, "Just take the universe, subtract from it the subset that represents the organization, and the remainder is environment."[4] But it's really not that simple. To help make some sense of this quotation, let's consider an organization's environment consisting of two areas, the general and the specific environments.

The general environment includes everything outside the organization, such as economic factors, political conditions, the social environment, and technological factors. It encompasses conditions that may affect the organization but whose immediate effect is not readily clear. The specific environment, on the other hand, is part of the environment that is directly relevant to the achievement of an organization's goals. It consists of the critical components that can positively or negatively influence an organization's effectiveness. The specific environment, then, is unique to each organization and may change with conditions. Elements of each environment that affect business are illustrated in Exhibit 2-2.

Although such a depiction as Exhibit 2-2 can provide a general overview, one point should be made. That is, the environmental factors that one organization is dependent upon and that have a critical bearing on its performance may not be relevant to another organization at all, even though they may appear at first glance to be in the same type of business. For example, Humber College and the University of Toronto are both institutions of higher education, but they do substantially different things and appeal to different segments of the higher education market. Subsequently, the administrators in each institution face different constituencies in their specific environments. What's the point of this defining of the environment? The elements in the environment are undergoing rapid change and are imposing new demands on organizations. As such, managers must respond—or see their organization decline or even go bankrupt.

Even North American cars are products of a global village. For example, this Ford Crown Victoria contains parts from Mexico, Japan, Germany, and England.

Is There a Global Village?

Part of the rapidly changing environment managers face is the globalization of business. Management is no longer constrained by national borders. Burger King is owned by a British firm, and McDonald's sells hamburgers in Moscow. Toyota makes cars in

The Changing Face of Management

Exhibit 2-2 General versus Specific Environments

Kentucky, General Motors makes cars in Brazil, and Toyota and General Motors jointly own a plant that makes cars in California. Parts for Ford Motor Company's Crown Victoria come from all over the world: Mexico (seats, windshields, and fuel tanks); Japan (shock absorbers); Spain (electronic engine controls); Germany (antilock brake systems); and England (key axle parts). These examples illustrate that the world has become a **global village** and that effective managers need to adapt to cultures, systems, and techniques that are different from their own.

In the 1960s, Pierre Trudeau described Canada's proximity to the United States as analogous to sleeping with an elephant: "You feel every twitch the animal makes." In the 1990s, we can generalize this analogy to the entire world. A rise in interest rates in Germany instantly affects managers and organizations throughout the globe. The fall of communism in Eastern Europe and the collapse of the Soviet Union create

global village
The production and marketing of goods and services world-wide.

unlimited opportunities for business firms throughout the free world. Alcan is a very good example. Prior to the fall of the Berlin Wall, Alcan enjoyed strong demand and firm prices for aluminum. As a result they added to their capacity. Alcan has a highly sophisticated strategic planning process, but it was unable to predict the fall of the Iron Curtain and the resulting flood of aluminum on the market from the former Soviet countries.

International businesses have been with us for a long time. Siemens, Remington, and Singer, for instance, were selling their products in many countries in the nineteenth century. By the 1920s, some companies, including Fiat, Ford, Unilever, and Royal Dutch/Shell, had gone multinational. But it wasn't until the mid-1960s that **multinational corporations (MNCs)** became commonplace. These corporations—which maintain significant operations in two or more countries simultaneously, but are based in one home country—initiated the rapid growth in international trade.

> **multinational corporations (MNCs)**
> Companies that maintain significant operations in more than one country simultaneously but manage them all from one base in a home country.

One way to grasp the changing nature of the global environment is to consider the country of origin for ownership of some familiar companies. Take a look at the following list and check which ones you think are Canadian owned. Write down the name of the country where the primary owners of each of these companies reside.

1. Rothmans Inc. (tobacco)
2. Jaguar (automobiles)
3. DuPont Canada (chemicals)
4. Canada Dry Beverages (soft drinks)
5. Shell Oil (oil & gas)
6. Alcan (aluminum)
7. Union Gas (natural gas)
8. Nestlé Canada Inc. (food products)
9. Husky Oil (oil & gas)
10. Connaught Laboratories Ltd. (pharmaceuticals)

There are only two Canadian-owned companies on the list: Alcan and Union Gas. Connaught Laboratories is French owned; Husky Oil—Hong Kong; Nestlé—Switzerland; Shell—Netherlands; Canada Dry—United States; DuPont—United States; Jaguar—United States (it's owned by Ford); Rothmans—United Kingdom.

The global village is extending the reach and goals of MNCs to create an even more generic organization—the **transnational corporation (TNC)**. This type of organization doesn't seek to replicate its domestic successes by managing foreign operations from home. Rather, decision making in TNCs takes place at the local level. Nationals typically are hired to run operations in each country. And the products and marketing strategies for each country are uniquely tailored to that country's culture. Nestlé, for example, is a transnational. With operations in almost every country on the globe, it is the world's largest food company, yet its managers match their products to their consumers. Thus, Nestlé sells products in parts of Europe, for instance, that aren't available in Canada or Latin America.

> **transnational corporation (TNC)**
> A company that maintains significant operations in more than one country simultaneously and decentralizes decision making in each operation to the local country.

We should point out that while managers of multinational and transnational organizations have become increasingly global in their perspectives and accept the reality that national borders no longer define corporations, politicians and the public have been slower to accept this fact. The United States has had a love/hate relationship with Japan for years. During the 1992 recession the cry was "Buy American." The irony is that many of the so-called Japanese products that critics were attacking were made in the United States. As a case in point, Honda employs more than 10,000 Americans at four plants in central Ohio and is now actually exporting Accords to Japan. Moreover, a number of those so-called American cars sitting in Chrysler showrooms, cars with Dodge and Plymouth

The Changing Face of Management

insignias, were made by Japanese workers employed by Mitsubishi Motors Corporation. Similarly, most Sony televisions sold in the United States are made in California, while "American" manufacturer Zenith's TVs are made in Mexico. The message from these examples should be obvious: A company's national origin is no longer a very good gauge of where it does business or the national origin of its employees.

Just a few years ago, international competition would be described in terms of country against country: the United States versus Japan, France versus Germany, Mexico versus Canada. In the 1990s, global competition is being reshaped by the creation of regional cooperation agreements. The most notable of these are the sixteen-nation European Union, and the North American Free Trade Agreement (NAFTA). These regional cooperative arrangements among countries are essentially designed to stimulate trade among members by removing tariffs and other barriers. We have summarized these alliances in Exhibit 2-3.

The European Union	The formation of the sixteen-nation European Union (Belgium, Denmark, France, Greece, Ireland, Italy, Luxembourg, Netherlands, Portugal, Spain, the United Kingdom, Austria, Sweden, Finland, Norway, and Germany) united 330 million people. By combining into a single market, the European Union is now one of the world's single richest markets.
North American Free Trade Agreement (NAFTA)	With the passage of NAFTA, a free trade zone from the Yukon to the Yucatan has been created. Encompassing Canada, the United States, and Mexico, NAFTA consolidates 360 million consumers into a $6-trillion market.

Exhibit 2-3 Trading Alliances

Furthermore, with the Cold War over, communism is on the retreat, and capitalism is spreading throughout the world. In the last several years, Germany has been reunited; countries like Poland and Romania have introduced democratic governments; and the former Soviet Union has become a set of independent states trying to implement market-based reforms. With a few exceptions, such as Cuba, the world is opening up to free markets and profit-seeking enterprises.

In terms of the changing global environment, the spread of capitalism makes the world a smaller place. Business has new markets to conquer. Additionally, well-trained and reliable workers in such countries as Hungary, Slovakia, and the Czech Republic provide a rich source of low-cost labour. The implementation of free markets in Eastern Europe further underscores the growing interdependence between countries of the world and the potential for goods, labour, and capital to move easily across national borders.

A boundary-free world introduces new challenges for managers. One specific challenge is managing in a different national culture. You know that your environment will differ from the one at home, but how? What should you look for?

Anyone who finds himself or herself in a strange country faces new challenges.

cultural environments
The attitudes and perspectives shared by individuals from a specific culture, or country, that shape their behaviour and the way they see the world.

These result from the legal-political, economic, and **cultural environments.** It is beyond the scope of this book to go into every detail on these environments. Suffice it to say, using an old adage—When in Rome, do as the Romans! That is, whenever you go to another country, you must understand their legal, political, economic, and cultural systems. Failing to do so may result in one not succeeding in that assignment—or worse, even death!

One definitive study of the differences of cultural environments was conducted by Geert Hofstede.[5] By analysing various dimensions of a country's culture, Hofstede was able to provide a framework for understanding and insight into what one might find when he or she goes to work in the global village (see Details on a Management Classic).

Why Are the Big Guys Laying Off?

downsizing
An activity in an organization designed to create a more efficient operation through extensive layoffs.

Pick up any recent newspaper and you're almost assured of finding a common story in the business section—organizations are laying off workers, an action called **downsizing.** For example, in March 1995, Bell Canada announced that it would cut 10,000 jobs over three years; the Canadian Armed Forces will also cut 8,000 jobs over the next three years, starting in 1995; and we've seen company after company, including giant firms like IBM, General Motors, Air Canada, and the banks, all cutting staff by the thousands. Why? Because to maintain some flexibility to deal with the changes around them, companies had to create flatter structures and redesign the way work has been traditionally

Details on a Management Classic

HOFSTEDE'S CULTURAL VARIABLES

To date, the most valuable framework to help managers better understand differences between national cultures has been developed by Geert Hofstede.[6] He surveyed over 116,000 employees in forty countries who worked for a single multinational corporation. What did he find? His huge database indicated that national culture had a major impact on employees' work-related values and attitudes. More important, Hofstede found that managers and employees vary on four dimensions of national culture: (1) individualism versus collectivism, (2) power distance, (3) uncertainty avoidance, and (4) quantity versus quality of life.[7]

individualism
A cultural dimension in which people are supposed to look after their own interests or those of their immediate families.

Individualism refers to a loosely knit social framework in which people are supposed to look after their own interests and those of their immediate family. This is made possible because of the large amount of freedom that such a society allows individuals. Its opposite is **collectivism,** which is characterized by a tight social framework in which people expect others in groups of which they are a part (such as a family or an organization) to look after them and protect them when they are in trouble. In exchange for this, they feel they owe absolute loyalty to the group.

Power distance is a measure of the extent to which a society accepts the fact that power in institutions and organizations is distributed unequally. A high power distance society accepts wide differences in power in organizations. Employees show a great

The Changing Face of Management

deal of respect for those in authority. Titles, rank, and status carry a lot of weight. In contrast, a low power distance society plays down inequalities as much as possible. Superiors still have authority, but employees are not fearful or in awe of the boss.

A society that is high in **uncertainty avoidance** is characterized by an increased level of anxiety among its people, which manifests itself in greater nervousness, stress, and aggressiveness. Because people feel threatened by uncertainty and ambiguity in these societies, mechanisms are created to provide security and reduce risk. Their organizations are likely to have more formal rules, there will be less tolerance for deviant ideas and behaviours, and members will strive to believe in absolute truths. Not surprisingly, in organizations in countries with high uncertainty avoidance, employees demonstrate relatively low job mobility, and lifetime employment is a widely practised policy.

Quantity versus **quality of life,** like individualism and collectivism, represents a dichotomy. Some cultures emphasize the quantity of life and value things like assertiveness and the acquisition of money and material goods. Other cultures emphasize the quality of life, the importance of relationships, and show sensitivity and concern for the welfare of others.

Into which countries are Canadian managers likely to fit best? Which are likely to create the biggest adjustment problems? All we have to do is identify those countries that are most and least like Canada on the four dimensions.

Canada is strongly individualistic but low on power distance. This same pattern was exhibited by Great Britain, Australia, the U.S., the Netherlands, and New Zealand. Those least similar to Canada on these dimensions were Venezuela, Colombia, Pakistan, Singapore, and the Philippines.

Canada scored low on uncertainty avoidance and high on quantity of life. This same pattern was shown by Ireland, Great Britain, the Philippines, the U.S., New Zealand, Australia, India, and South Africa. Those least similar to Canada on these dimensions were Chile and Portugal.

These results empirically support part of what many of us suspected—that the American manager transferred to London, New York, Melbourne, or a similar Anglo city would have to make the fewest adjustments. In addition, the results further identify the countries in which "culture shock" is likely to be greatest and the need to modify one's managerial style most imperative. ▼

collectivism
A cultural dimension in which people expect others in their group to look after them and protect them when they are in trouble.

power distance
A cultural measure of the extent to which society accepts the unequal distribution of power in institutions and organizations.

uncertainty avoidance
A cultural measure of the degree to which people tolerate risk and unconventional behaviour.

quantity of life
A national cultural attribute describing the extent to which societal values are characterized by assertiveness and materialism.

quality of life
A national cultural attribute that reflects the emphasis placed upon relationships and concern for others.

---

carried out. This means fewer levels of management between employees and senior management, greater use of outside firms for providing necessary products and services, and redesigning work processes to gain increased productivity. Are we implying that big companies are disappearing? Absolutely not! But how they operate has changed.

Big isn't necessarily inefficient. Companies such as 3M, Johnson & Johnson, GE, Wal-Mart, and Microsoft have managed to blend large size with agility. But they typically divide their organization into smaller, more flexible units. Few managers today accept the notion that large organizations should automatically produce at lower cost because of economies of scale. In the steel industry, for example, many of Nucor's minimills are 20 to 60 per cent more efficient than the larger plants of Dofasco and Stelco.

As noted above, management is cutting layers out of their organizations and widening the number of employees reporting to each manager. The twenty-one people who make up the staff of Nucor's headquarters, including the board chair and administrative assistants, look after twenty-two steel plants across the United States. In place of

Once, when you had a job with IBM, you had one for life. But difficult times have required the company to take some Draconian measures, including laying off thousands of employees.

rigid departments, managers are using teams that cut across functions. And the guiding organizational concept is focusing on the needs of the customer or work process. The 1,500 Eastman Kodak employees who make black and white film are now organized horizontally. This means that these employees don't work in departments but in what they call "the flow." A twenty-five member leadership team watches the flow. Within the flow are "streams" defined by customers. And within these streams, most employees work in semiautonomous teams.

Why Is the Future of Business with Small Business?

In Chapter 1, we introduced the small business in terms of differences in managing in a small business versus a large one. Although some differences were noted, the issue before us is one of size. As more and more companies downsize, the trend is for them to emulate the small business. Why? Generally speaking, small businesses are faster to respond to a changing environment. Because the owner/manager is involved in the day-to-day operations, that individual is usually closer to the customer.

The small business also has several other attributes that are welcomed in today's larger organizations. First, the owner/manager is usually the main decision maker, and all employees report to him or her. Accordingly, this is a flat organization containing very few, if any, layers of hierarchy. Second, individuals who manage these businesses often possess unique characteristics. They are independent workers who tend to take calculated risk, while at the same time accept the fact that mistakes occur.[8]

entrepreneurs
A manager who is confident in his or her abilities, seizes innovative opportunities, and capitalizes on surprises.

In business, people who demonstrate these characteristics are often called **entrepreneurs.** Some organizations today have witnessed the benefits of having managers possess these characteristics because it has helped increase the speed through which work gets done. Does this imply then that entrepreneurs can exist in large, established organizations? The answer to that question depends on one's definition of entrepreneur. The noted management guru, Peter Drucker, for instance, argues that they can.[9] He describes an entrepreneurial manager as someone who is confident in his or her abilities, who seizes opportunities for innovation, and who not only expects surprises but capitalizes on them. He contrasts that with the traditional manager who feels threatened by change, is bothered by uncertainty, prefers predictability, and is inclined to maintain the status quo.

intrapreneurship
Creating the entrepreneurial spirit in a large organization.

Drucker's use of the term entrepreneurial, however, is misleading. By almost any definition of good management, his entrepreneurial type would be preferred over the traditional type. Moreover, the term **intrapreneurship** is now widely used to describe the effort to create the entrepreneurial spirit in a large organization.[10] Yet intrapreneurship can never capture the autonomy and riskiness inherent in true entrepreneurship. This is because intrapreneurship takes place within a larger organization; all financial risks are

The Changing Face of Management

Jerry Jones, owner of the Dallas Cowboys, has used his entrepreneurial skills to build one of the more dominant football teams in the National Football League.

carried by the parent company; rules, policies, and other constraints are imposed by the parent company; intrapreneurs have bosses to report to; and the payoff for success is not financial independence but rather career advancement.[11] We'll come back to entrepreneurs in the next chapter.

What Will the Workforce of 2001 Look Like?

The bulk of the pre-1980s workforce in North America consisted of male Caucasians, working fulltime to support a nonemployed wife and school-aged children. Such employees are now true minorities in organizations. Today's organizations are characterized by **workforce diversity**—that is, workers are more heterogeneous in terms of gender, race, and ethnicity. But diversity includes anyone who is different: the physically disabled, gays and lesbians, the elderly, and even those who are significantly overweight.

Until very recently, we took a "melting pot" approach to differences in organizations. We assumed that people who were different would somehow automatically want to assimilate. But we now recognize that employees don't set aside their cultural values and lifestyle preferences when they come to work. The challenge for managers, therefore, is to make their organizations more accommodating to diverse groups of people by addressing different lifestyles, family needs, and work styles. The "melting pot" assumption is being replaced by the recognition and celebration of differences.[12]

workforce diversity
Employees in organizations are heterogeneous in terms of gender, race, ethnicity, or other characteristics.

Why the Increased Concern with Quality?

There is a quality revolution taking place in both business and the public sector.[13] The generic term that has evolved to describe this revolution is **total quality management,** or TQM for short. It was inspired by a small group of quality experts, the most prominent of them being the late W. Edwards Deming.

An American, Deming found few managers in the United States interested in his ideas. Consequently, in 1950, he went to Japan and began advising many top Japanese managers on how to improve their production effectiveness. Central to his management methods was the use of statistics to analyse variability in production processes. A well-managed organization, according to Deming, was one in which statistical control reduced

total quality management (TQM)
A philosophy of management that is driven by customer needs and expectations.

> 1. Intense focus on the *customer*. The customer includes not only outsiders who buy the organization's products or services, but also internal customers (such as shipping or accounts payable personnel) who interact with and serve others in the organization.
> 2. Concern for *continual improvement*. TQM is a commitment to never being satisfied. "Very good" is not good enough. Quality can always be improved.
> 3. Improvement in the *quality of everything* the organization does. TQM uses a very broad definition of quality. It relates not only to the final product but also to how the organization handles deliveries, how rapidly it responds to complaints, how politely the phones are answered, and the like.
> 4. Accurate *measurement*. TQM uses statistical techniques to measure every critical variable in the organization's operations. These are compared against standards or benchmarks to identify problems, trace them to their roots, and eliminate their causes.
> 5. *Empowerment of employees*. TQM involves the people on the line in the improvement process. Teams are widely used in TQM programs as empowerment vehicles for finding and solving problems.

Exhibit 2-4 What Is Total Quality Management?

variability and resulted in uniform quality and predictable quantity of output. Deming developed a fourteen-point program for transforming organizations. (We'll look closer at this program in Chapter 16 when we discuss control techniques.)

Today, Deming's original program has been expanded into TQM—a philosophy of management that is driven by customer needs and expectations[14] (see Exhibit 2-4). Importantly, however, the term "customer" in TQM is expanded beyond the traditional definition to include everyone who interacts with the organization's product or service either internally or externally. So TQM encompasses employees and suppliers, as well as the people who buy the organization's products or services. The objective is to create an organization committed to continuous improvement.

TQM represents a counterpoint to earlier management theorists who believed that low costs were the only road to increased productivity. The automobile industry, in fact, represents a classic case of what can go wrong when attention is focused solely on trying to keep costs down. Throughout the 1970s and 1980s, companies like GM, Ford, and Chrysler ended up building products that a large part of the car-buying public rejected. Moreover, when the costs of rejects, repairing shoddy work, recalls, and expensive controls to identify quality problems were factored in, the North American manufacturers actually were less productive than many foreign competitors. The Japanese demonstrated that it was possible for the highest-quality manufacturers also to be among the lowest-cost producers. Only recently have North American auto manufacturers realized the importance of TQM and implemented many of its basic components, such as quality control groups, process improvement, teamwork, improved supplier relations, and listening to the needs and wants of customers. TQM, or at least the recognition that the continuous improvement in quality is necessary for an organization to compete effectively, is not just a fad. It is here to stay!

What Responsibility, If Any, Do Managers Have to the Larger Society?

The issue of corporate **social responsibility** drew little attention before the 1960s when the activist movement began questioning the singular economic objective of business. For instance, were large corporations irresponsible because they discriminated against women and minorities, as shown by the obvious absence of female and minority managers at that time? Was the Canadian pulp and paper industry ignoring its social responsibilities by clear-cutting areas of British Columbia forest large enough to be seen by the naked eye from the space shuttle?

Before the 1960s, few people asked such questions. Even today, there are good arguments that can be made for both sides of this issue (see Exhibit 2-5). Arguments aside, times have changed. Managers are now regularly confronted with decisions that have a dimension of social responsibility—philanthropy, pricing, employee relations, resource conservation, product quality, and operations in countries with oppressive governments are some of the more obvious. To help managers make such decisions, let's begin by defining social responsibility.

Few terms have been defined in as many different ways as social responsibility. Some of the more popular meanings include "profit making only," "going beyond profit making," "voluntary activities," "concern for the broader social system," and "social responsiveness."[15] Most of the debate has focused at the extremes. On one side, there is the classical—or purely economic—view that management's only social responsibility is to maximize profits. On the other side stands the socioeconomic position, which holds that management's responsibility goes well beyond making profits to include protecting and improving society's welfare.

Imperial Oil Ltd. is an outstanding example of a Canadian company that regards ethics and social responsibility as being of the first order of importance. Its charitable donations from 1980 to 1994 have totalled $107 million. Its environmental initiatives include enhanced oil spill clean-up capabilities, reduced plant emissions, and the development of gasoline formulas that decrease pollution. It also supports programs of employee involvement in community volunteer activities, as well as programs for health, safety, and environmental protection.[16]

How Can an Organization Go from Obligations to Responsiveness? Now it's time to narrow in on precisely what we mean when we talk about social responsibility. It is a business firm's obligation, beyond that required by the law and economics, to pursue long-term goals that are good for society.[17] Note that this definition assumes that business obeys the law and pursues economic interests. We take as a given that all business firms—those that are socially responsible and those that aren't—will obey all laws that society imposes. Also note that this definition views business as a moral agent. In its effort to do good for society, it must differentiate between right and wrong.

We can understand social responsibility better if we compare it with two similar concepts: social obligation and social responsiveness.[18] **Social obligation** is the foundation of business's social involvement. A business has fulfilled its social obligation when it meets its economic and legal responsibilities and no more. It does the minimum that the law requires. A firm pursues social goals only to the extent that they contribute to its economic goals. In contrast to social obligation, both social responsibility and social responsiveness go beyond merely meeting basic economic and legal standards.

Social responsibility adds an ethical imperative to do those things that make society better and not to do those that could make it worse. **Social responsiveness** refers

social responsibility
An obligation, beyond that required by the law and economics, for a firm to pursue long-term goals that are good for society.

social obligation
The obligation of a business to meet its economic and legal responsibilities.

social responsiveness
The capacity of a firm to adapt to changing societal conditions.

The major arguments supporting the assumption of social responsibilities by business are:

▶ 1. **Public expectations.** Social expectations of business have increased dramatically since the 1960s. Public opinion in support of business pursuing social as well as economic goals is now well solidified.
▶ 2. **Long-run profits.** Socially responsible businesses tend to have more secure long-run profits. This is the normal result of the better community relations and improved business image that responsible behaviour brings.
▶ 3. **Ethical obligation.** A business firm can and should have a conscience. Business should be socially responsible because responsible actions are right for their own sake.
▶ 4. **Public image.** Firms seek to enhance their public image to gain more customers, better employees, access to money markets, and other benefits. Since the public considers social goals to be important, business can create a favourable public image by pursuing social goals.
▶ 5. **Better environment.** Involvement by business can solve difficult social problems, thus creating a better quality of life and a more desirable community in which to attract and hold skilled employees.
▶ 6. **Discouragement of further government regulation.** Government regulation adds economic costs and restricts management's decision flexibility. By becoming socially responsible, business can expect less government regulation.
▶ 7. **Balance of responsibility and power.** Business has a large amount of power in society. An equally large amount of responsibility is required to balance it. When power is significantly greater than responsibility, the imbalance encourages irresponsible behaviour that works against the public good.
▶ 8. **Stockholder interests.** Social responsibility will improve the price of a business's stock in the long run. The stock market will view the socially responsible company as less risky and open to public attack. Therefore, it will award its stock a higher price-earnings ratio.
▶ 9. **Possession of resources.** Business has the financial resources, technical experts, and managerial talent to provide support to public and charitable projects that need assistance.
▶ 10. **Superiority of prevention over cures.** Social problems must be dealt with at some time. Business should act on them before they become more serious and costly to correct and take management's energy away from accomplishing its goal of producing goods and services.

The major arguments against business assuming social responsibility are:

▶ 1. **Violation of profit maximization.** This is the essence of the classical viewpoint. Business is most socially responsible when it attends strictly to its economic interests and leaves other activities to other institutions.
▶ 2. **Dilution of purpose.** The pursuit of social goals dilutes business's primary purpose: economic productivity. Society may suffer as both economic and social goals are poorly accomplished.
▶ 3. **Costs.** Many socially responsible activities don't pay their own way. Someone has to pay these costs. Business must absorb these costs or pass them on to consumers in higher prices.
▶ 4. **Too much power.** Business is already one of the most powerful institutions in our society. If it pursues social goals, it would have even more power. Society has given business enough power.
▶ 5. **Lack of skills.** The outlook and abilities of business leaders are oriented primarily toward economics. Business people are poorly qualified to cope with social issues.
▶ 6. **Lack of accountability.** Political representatives pursue social goals and are held accountable for their actions. Such is not the case with business leaders. There are no direct lines of social accountability from the business sector to the public.
▶ 7. **Lack of broad public support.** There is no broad mandate from society for business to become involved in social issues. The public is divided on the issue. In fact, it is a topic that rarely fails to generate a heated debate. Actions taken under such divided support are likely to fail.

The Changing Face of Management

Who is singlehandedly regarded as the individual who helped build the quality into Japanese products? It's W. Edwards Deming, an American professor whose ideas on quality were originally rejected by American businessmen. Some fifty years later, however, Deming's concepts began to catch on and quickly spread in American corporate cultures. Before his death in December 1993, Deming gained the respect in America that he had held for half of a century in Japan.

to the capacity of a firm to adapt to changing societal conditions.[19]

As Exhibit 2-6 describes, social responsibility requires business to determine what is right or wrong and thus seek fundamental ethical truths. Social responsiveness is guided by social norms. The value of social norms is that they can provide managers, like Doug Hallett, with a more meaningful guide for decision making. The following makes the distinction clearer.

When a company meets pollution control standards established by the federal government or doesn't discriminate against employees over the age of forty in promotion decisions, it is meeting its social obligation and nothing more. The law says that the company may not pollute or practice age discrimination. In the 1990s, when Magna provides on-site child care facilities for employees, Procter & Gamble declares that Tide "is packaged in 100 per cent recycled paper," and the head of the world's largest tuna canner says, "StarKist will not purchase, process or sell any tuna caught in association with dolphins," these firms are being socially responsive. Why? Pressure from working mothers and environmentalists make such practices pragmatic. Of course, if these same companies had provided child care, offered recycled packaging, or sought to protect dolphins back in the early 1970s, their actions probably would have been accurately characterized as socially responsible.

◀ **Exhibit 2-5 Arguments for and against Social Responsibility**

Source: Based on R. Joseph Monsen, Jr., "The Social Attitudes of Management," in Joseph M. McGuire, ed. *Contemporary Management: Issues and Views* (Englewood Cliffs, N.J.: Prentice-Hall, Inc., 1974), p. 616; and Keith Davis and William Frederick, *Business and Society: Management, Public Policy, Ethics,* 5th ed. (New York: McGraw Hill, Inc., 1984), pp. 28–41.

Managers Who Made a Difference

Douglas Hallett at ELI Eco Logic

Douglas Hallett left the civil service in Canada in 1986 to turn his energies to developing a process that would destroy hazardous wastes safely and efficiently. Although we think of Canada as a clean country with wide open spaces, we produce more garbage per capita than any other nation in the world and have the highest energy consumption per capita of any nation in the world. With weak legislation on pollution, Canada is, in fact, very dirty, with municipalities dumping raw sewage into lakes, rivers and oceans, and companies doing things that would get them prosecuted in the United States. As Hallett says, "The reason we think we are clean is that we don't know we are dirty."

But Doug Hallett is doing something about it. He has developed a chemical process to destroy hazardous wastes such as PCBs. In 1991, sediment containing coal tar and PCBs from Hamilton harbour was fed into his mobile destructor unit, which destroyed them 99.9999%. In 1992 he replicated the results for the Environmental Protection Agency (EPA) in the United States. His company, ELI Eco Logic Inc., has the technology to destroy a wide number of hazardous wastes—without incinerating them and without uncontrolled emissions. And it can do it at a price that is competitive with incineration and with a technology that can be easily transported to the pollution site.

Doug Hallett won a United Nations Silver Medal for Environmental Stewardship in the 1980s. He was senior scientific advisor and chairman of the government's toxic chemicals program in 1986 when he gave it all up to make a major contribution to the world's pollution problems. He's a manager who has made a difference![20] ▼

How Is Social Responsibility Extended to Women in the Workplace?

What about an organization's responsibility to its employees—especially women? Over the past few years there has been a major concern over the issue of sexual harassment in our organizations. How did this come about?

Professor Anita Hill's widely publicized allegations of sexual harassment against the U.S. Supreme Court nominee Clarence Thomas in the fall of 1991 single-handedly moved the topic of sexual harassment to the top of many organizations' education agendas.[21]

The Changing Face of Management

The record industry shows its social responsiveness by repackaging compact disks. The 6 by 12 inch longbox cardboard packaging was designed to thwart shoplifters and to fit neatly into pre-existing album bins. But the longbox consumed twice as much paper as it needed. In response to vocal environmentalists, the industry developed less wasteful packaging.

Sexual harassment that is work-related has been defined by the Violence Against Women Survey conducted by Statistics Canada in 1993[22] as the following unwelcome actions by co-workers, bosses, customers, patients or students:

sexual harassment
Behaviour marked by sexually suggestive remarks, unwanted touching and sexual advances, requests for sexual favours, or other verbal or physical conduct of a sexual nature.

▶ making a woman uncomfortable by commenting inappropriately about her body or sex life

▶ making her uncomfortable by repeatedly asking for a date and refusing to take no for an answer

▶ leaning over her unnecessarily, getting too close, or cornering her

▶ hinting that she could lose her job, or that her employment situation might suffer, if she is unwilling to have a sexual relationship

The Statistics Canada survey is the first national survey of its kind to be conducted anywhere in the world. It reported that almost 25 per cent of Canadian women over 18 have been sexually harassed on the job. The most frequent assailants were co-workers and bosses. The least severe forms of harassment were the most prevalent, with 77 per cent of the women who reported being harrassed saying that a man had made inappropriate comments about their body or sex life, while 18 per cent reported being pressured to have sex

	SOCIAL RESPONSIBILITY	SOCIAL RESPONSIVENESS
Major consideration	Ethical	Pragmatic
Focus	Ends	Means
Emphasis	Obligation	Responses
Decision framework	Long-term	Medium- and short-term

Exhibit 2-6 Social Responsibility versus Social Responsiveness
Source: Adapted from Steven L. Wartick and Philip L. Cochran, "The Evolution of the Corporate Social Performance Model," *Academy of Management Review*, October 1985, p. 766.

Developing Management Skills

GUIDELINES TO PROTECT A COMPANY FROM SEXUAL HARASSMENT CHARGES

1. Issue a sexual harassment policy describing what constitutes sexual harassment and what is inappropriate behaviour.
2. Institute a procedure (or link to an existing one) to investigate sexual harassment charges.
3. Inform all employees of the sexual harassment policy. Educate these employees about the policy and how it will be enforced.
4. Train all supervisory personnel how to deal with sexual harassment charges and what responsibility they have to the individual and the organization.
5. Investigate all sexual harassment charges immediately.
6. Take corrective action as necessary. Discipline those doing the harassing, and "make-whole" the harassed individual.
7. Continue to follow up on the matter to ensure that no further sexual harassment occurs or that retaliation does not occur.
8. Periodically review turnover situations to determine if a potential problem may be arising.
9. Don't forget to privately recognize individuals who bring these matters forward. Without their courageous effort, the organization might have been faced with a serious liability.

Sources: Adapted from Clifford M. Keon, Jr., "Sexual Harassment Claims Stem from a Hostile Work Environment," *Personnel Journal,* August 1990, pp. 97–98; Martha E. Eller, "Sexual Harassment: Prevention, Not Protection," *The Cornell H.R.A. Quarterly,* February 1990, p. 87; Maureen P. Woods and Walter J. Flynn, "Heading Off Sexual Harassment," *Personnel,* November 1989, p. 48; and Jacqueline F. Strayer and Sandra E. Rapoport, "Sexual Harassment: Limiting Corporate Liability," *Personnel,* April 1986, pp. 32–33.

---

under the threat that their job might suffer. The more severe forms of sexual harassment such as unwanted sexual touching and being forced into having sex, were reported by 5 per cent and 1 per cent of the respondents respectively.[23]

In the United States, AT&T has advised all employees that they can be fired for making repeated unwelcome sexual advances, using sexually degrading words to describe someone, or displaying sexually offensive pictures or objects at work. From management's viewpoint, not only is sexual harassment morally wrong, it also interferes with job performance and can be the subject of legal action.

Why Must Managers Think in Terms of Quantum Changes Rather than Incremental Change?

Although TQM is a positive start in many of our organizations, it focuses on continuous improvement or ongoing incremental change. Such action is intuitively appealing—the constant and permanent search to make things better. Many of our companies, however, live in a time of rapid and dynamic change. And as the elements around them change ever so quickly, a continuous improvement process may keep them behind the times.

The problem with continuous improvements is that it provides a false sense of security. It makes managers feel like they're actively doing something positive, which is somewhat true. Unfortunately, ongoing incremental change avoids facing up to the possibility that what the organization may really need is radical or quantum change, commonly referred to as **reengineering**.[24] Continuous change may make managers feel like they're taking progressive action, while at the same time, avoiding having to

reengineering
Radical, quantum change in the organization.

The Changing Face of Management

The roller skate versus the in-line skate. Which is more representative of reengineering? Although the roller skate may be improved, the in-line skate reveals a "start-from-scratch" approach to manufacture a "better" product.

implement quantum changes that will threaten organizational members. The incrementalism approach in continuous improvement, then, may be the 1990s version of rearranging the deck chairs on the Titanic.

If you've been reading this chapter closely up until now, you may be asking yourself, Aren't these authors contradicting what they said a few pages ago about TQM? On the surface, it may appear so, but consider this. While TQM is important for organizations and can often lead to improvements, TQM may not always be the right thing initially. For example, if what you are producing is outdated, a new improved version of the product may not be helpful to the company. Rather, in a number of instances, major change is required. After that has occurred, then continually improving it (TQM) can have its rightful place. Let's see how this may be so.

Assume you are the manager responsible for implementing some type of change in your roller skate manufacturing process. If you took the continuous improvement approach, your frame of reference would be a high-top leather shoe on top of a steel carriage, with four wooden wheels. Your continuous improvement program may lead you to focus on things like using a different grade of cowhide for the shoe, adding speed laces to the uppers, or using a different type of ballbearing in the wheels. Of course, your skate may be better than you previously made, but is that enough? Compare your action to that of a competitor who reengineers the process.

To begin, your competitor poses the following question: How does she design a skate that is safe, fun, fast, and provides greater mobility? Starting from scratch, and not being constrained by her current manufacturing process (à la reengineering), she completes her redesign with something that looks like today's popular in-line skates. Instead of leather and metal skates, you are now competing against a moulded boot, similar to that used in skiing. Your competitor's skate is better than one made from leather and has no laces to tie. Additionally, it uses four to six high-durability plastic wheels, which are placed in-line for greater speed and mobility.

In this contrived example, both companies made progress. But which do you believe made the most progress given the dynamic environment they face? It's a moot point, but it clearly reinforces why companies like Union Carbide, GTE, or Mutual Benefit Life opted for reengineering as opposed to incremental change.[25] It is imperative in today's business environment for all managers to consider the challenge of reengineering their organizational processes. Why? Because reengineering can lead to "major gains in cost, service, or time."[26] And these kinds of gains will take companies well into the twenty-first century.

New Challenges for Managers

If you stop for a moment and digest what you've been reading in this chapter, you've got to be thinking that managers as we described them in Chapter 1 no longer exist. That is, it may be no longer appropriate to accept the status quo and manage the company from a traditional, hierarchical position. The fact is managers, too, must change with the times. In this section, we'll explore some of the implications of these changes on managers.

How Do Managers Turn from Bosses into Coaches?

Frederick Taylor, the "Father of Scientific Management" (see appendix), argued for the division of work and responsibility between management and workers. He wanted managers to do the planning and thinking. Workers were just to do what they were told. That prescription might have been good advice at the turn of the century, but today's workers are far better educated and trained than they were in Taylor's day. In fact, because of the complexity of many jobs, today's workers are often considerably more knowledgeable than their managers about how best to do their jobs. This fact has not been ignored by management. Managers are transforming themselves from bosses into team leaders. Instead of telling people what to do, an increasing number of managers are finding that they become more effective when they focus on motivating, coaching, and cheerleading. Managers also recognize that they can often improve quality, productivity, and employee commitment by redesigning jobs in order to increase the decision-making discretion of workers. We call this process empowering employees.[27]

empowerment
Increasing the decision-making discretion of workers.

Empowerment builds on ideas originally made by early management writers who promoted the well-being of employees. For many years, a lot of organizations stifled the capabilities of their workforce. They overspecialized jobs and demotivated employees by treating them like unthinking machines. Recent successes at empowering employees in companies across Canada suggest that the future lies in expanding the worker's role in his or her job rather than in practising Taylor's segmentation of responsibilities.

The empowerment movement is being driven by two forces. First is the need for quick decisions by those people who are most knowledgeable about the issues. That requires moving decisions to lower levels. If organizations are to successfully compete in a global village, they have to be able to make decisions and implement changes quickly. Second is the reality that the large layoffs in the middle-management ranks during the late 1980s and early 1990s have left many managers with considerably more people to supervise than they had a decade earlier. The same manager who today oversees a staff of thirty-five can't micromanage in the ways that were possible when he or she supervised ten people. The letting go and stretching process required to manage extended groups of people can be likened to a sports team **coach.**

coach
A manager who motivates, empowers, and encourages his or her employees.

Consider the job of head coach of a football team. This individual is the one who establishes the game plan for an upcoming game and readies the players for the task. Even though the plans and the players are prepared, the fact remains that the coach cannot go out on Saturday and play the game. Instead, it is the players who execute the game plan. So what does the coach do during the game? It depends on how well the plan is working. When the competition is doing something that is counter to the game plan, new plans are quickly formulated to give the players another competitive advantage. Thus, the coach deals with the exceptions. And regardless of the game's outcome,

The Changing Face of Management

as the players play the game, the coach becomes one of the major cheerleaders—recognizing outstanding performance toward fulfilling the plan, and boosting player morale. So, too, must today's managers!

How Do Managers Motivate Today's Workers?

As recently as twenty years ago there were plenty of semi-skilled jobs in the steel, automobile, rubber, and similar manufacturing industries that paid solid middle-class wages. A young man in Hamilton, for example, could graduate from high school and immediately get a relatively high-paying and secure job in a local steel plant. That job would allow him to buy a home, finance a car or two, support a family, and enjoy other lifestyle choices that come with a middle-class income. But that's ancient history.[28] A good portion of those manufacturing jobs in first-world industrialized countries are gone—either replaced by automated equipment, reconstituted into jobs requiring considerably higher technical skills, or taken by workers in other countries who will do the same work for a fraction of the wages. What's left can best be described as a **bi-modal workforce**—where employees tend to perform either low-skilled service jobs for near-minimum wages or high-skilled jobs that provide the means to maintain a middle-class or upper-class lifestyle.

bi-modal workforce Employees tend to perform either low-skilled service jobs for near-minimum wage or high-skilled, well-paying jobs.

Exhibit 2-7 illustrates this bi-modal phenomenon, which has been created by the massive decline of blue-collar, manufacturing jobs that pay $25,000 to $35,000 a year in current dollars.

Most organizations' employee practices were designed to keep and motivate well-paid manufacturing employees and high-paid skilled workers. They don't, however, seem to be working very well with the low-skilled, low-paid service workers in the left curve of Exhibit 2-7.

At wages of $4.50 to $6.00 per hour, today's low-skilled workers can't come close to moving into the middle class. Moreover, their promotion opportunities are limited. This leads to a major challenge for managers: How do you motivate individuals who are making very low wages and have little opportunity to increase their pay significantly either in their current jobs or through promotions? Can effective leadership make a difference? Can these employees' jobs be redesigned (empowered) to make them more challenging? Does management have an ethical responsibility to raise these wages so they can provide employees with an adequate income? Should management target these jobs for elimination? These are questions that, until twenty years ago, managers didn't have

Cindy Ransom, factory manager at Clorox, knows what it's like to become a coach. She gave her employees the opportunity to redesign their work operation. Assisting where necessary, Ransom saw her employees establish training programs for the group, develop work rules and enforcement procedures, and reorganize themselves into a more customer-focused group. Because of these changes, Ransom's unit was recognized as the most improved division. With a lot of managerial duties now handled by her employees, what does Ransom do? She now spends most of her time meeting with customers and suppliers.

Exhibit 2-7 Wages for Low-Skilled and High-Skilled Labour

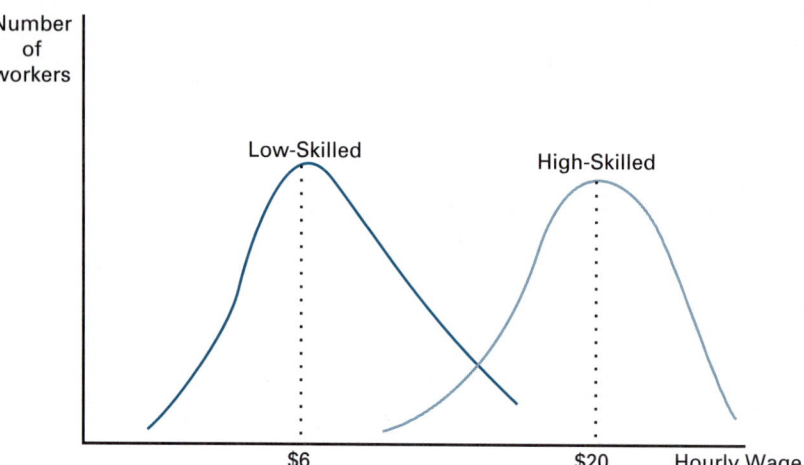

to concern themselves with. Today, however, they may lead to answers that are long overdue. (We'll come back to motivation in Chapter 12.)

How Do Managers Improve Their Ethics?

Many observers believe that we are currently suffering an ethics crisis. Behaviours that were once thought reprehensible—lying, cheating, misrepresenting, covering up mistakes—have become, in many people's eyes, acceptable or necessary practices. Managers profit from illegal use of insider information.

Concern over this perceived decline in ethical standards is being addressed at two levels. First, ethics education is being widely expanded in college and university curriculums. For instance, the primary accrediting agency for business schools now requires all its member programs to integrate ethical issues throughout their business curriculum. Second, organizations themselves are creating codes of ethics and introducing ethics training programs. Let's look closer at this issue of ethics.

Is it ethical for a salesperson to offer an expensive gift to a purchasing agent as an inducement to buy? What if the gift comes out of the salesperson's commission? Does that make it any different? Is it ethical for someone to understate his or her educational qualifications to get a job during hard times if that person would ordinarily be considered overqualified for the job? Is it ethical for someone to use company gasoline for private use? How about using the company telephone for personal long-distance calls? Is it ethical to ask a company employee to type personal letters?[29]

Ethics commonly refers to the rules or principles that define right and wrong conduct.[30] But understanding ethics may be difficult depending on the view that one holds of the topic. We have presented the three views of ethical standards[31] in Exhibit 2-8.

Regardless of one's view of ethics, whether a manager acts ethically or unethically will depend on a number of factors. These factors range from one's morality, individual differences, the organization's culture, and the issue that is being called into question.[32] People who lack a strong moral sense are much less likely to do the wrong things if they are constrained by rules, policies, job descriptions, or strong cultural norms that frown on such behaviours. Conversely, very moral people can be corrupted by an organizational structure and culture that permits or encourages unethical practices. For example, you are in a class where a copy of the final exam is being sold for $50. Rumours

ethics
Rules and principles that define right and wrong conduct.

The Changing Face of Management

abound in the department, but nothing is done. Do you buy a copy because without it you'll be disadvantaged, or do you do without it and try your best? If the faculty member suspects a copy is floating and does nothing and then gives no curve on the exam because the grades are so high (mainly due to those who had a copy of the exam), the professor is doing little to dissuade cheating. In that case, you may rationalize getting a copy for yourself.

The example above illustrates how ambiguity about what is ethical can be a problem for employees. Codes of ethics are an increasingly popular response for reducing that ambiguity.[33] For instance, nearly 90 per cent of Fortune 1,000 companies have a stated code of ethics.[34] A **code of ethics** is a formal document that states an organization's primary values and the ethical rules it expects employees to follow. It has been suggested that codes be specific enough to guide employees in what they're supposed to do—like make decisions—yet loose enough to allow for freedom of judgment.[35]

code of ethics
A formal statement of an organization's primary values and the ethical rules it expects its employees to follow.

What's More Important: Stability or Flexibility?

The organizational world that existed when early management theorists wrote no longer exists. Managers now confront an environment in which change is taking place at an unprecedented rate; new competitors spring up overnight and old ones disappear through mergers, acquisitions, or failure to keep up with the changing marketplace. Constant innovations in computer and telecommunications technologies combined with the globalization of product and financial markets have created chaos. As a result, many of the past "principles of management" guidelines—created for a world that was far more stable and predictable—no longer apply. The successful organizations of the 1990s and beyond will be flexible, able to respond quickly, and led by managers who can effectively enact massive and revolutionary changes.

As you'll see in later chapters of this book, the need for innovation and change is requiring many organizations to reinvent themselves. Managers are restructuring their organizations by eliminating unnecessary levels of overhead, cutting redundant functions, and eliminating low-performing units.

How Do We Make People in Organizations More Sensitive to Cultural Diversity?

Recognizing that the workforce of 2001 will be considerably different than that of two decades ago, management must implement programs to create more sensitivity for cultural diversity. In doing so, managers must recognize that workforce diversity will carry with it important implications for their practice. They will have to shift their philosophy from treating everyone alike to recognizing differences and responding to these differences in ways that will ensure employee retention and greater productivity. At the same time, they must not illegally discriminate against their employees.

A number of organizations are providing sophisticated diversity training programs for their managers to help them better communicate, motivate, and lead. These training programs are designed to raise diversity consciousness among current employees, and

General Electric has made an impressive commitment to high ethical standards by its employees. For instance, GE employees can tap into specially designed interactive software on their personal computers to get answers to ethical questions. Additionally, the company has seminars and videos that encourage employees to report any wrongdoing. Nevertheless, GE recently pleaded guilty and paid $70 million to settle charges that it punished employees who reported wrongdoing. Employees claimed they were fired for following the company's compliance procedures.

address racial, ethnic, and gender stereotypes. In addition, a number of companies have instituted special mentoring programs to deal with the reality that lower-level females and minorities have few role models with whom to identify.

Utilitarian View of Ethics	Refers to a situation in which decisions are made solely on the basis of their outcomes or consequences. The goal of utilitarianism is to provide the greatest good for the greatest number. On one side, utilitarianism encourages efficiency and productivity and is consistent with the goal of profit maximization. On the other side, however, it can result in biased allocations of resources, especially when some of those affected lack representation or voice.
Rights View of Ethics	Refers to a situation in which the individual is concerned with respecting and protecting individual liberties and privileges, including the rights to privacy, freedom of conscience, free speech, and due process. The positive side of the rights perspective is that it protects individuals' freedom and privacy. But it has a negative side in organizations: It can present obstacles to high productivity and efficiency by creating an overly legalistic work climate.
Theory of Justice View of Ethics	Refers to a situation in which an individual imposes and enforces rules fairly and impartially. A manager would be using a theory of justice perspective in deciding to pay a new entry-level employee $1.50 an hour over the minimum wage because that manager believes that the minimum wage is inadequate to allow employees to meet their basic financial commitments. Imposing standards of justice also comes with pluses and minuses. It protects the interests of those stakeholders who may be underrepresented or lack power; but it can encourage a sense of entitlement that reduces risk taking, innovation, and productivity.

Exhibit 2-8 Three Views of Ethics

Source: Gerald F. Cavanaugh, Dennis J. Moberg, and Manual Valasquez, "The Ethics of Organizational Politics," *Academy of Management Journal,* June 1981, pp. 363–74.

Summary

This Summary is organized by the chapter opening learning objectives found on page 25.

1. Competitors are no longer defined within national borders. New competition can suddenly appear anytime, from anywhere in the world. Managers must think globally if their organizations are to succeed over the long term.
2. Multinational corporations have significant operations functioning in two or more countries simultaneously, but primary decision making and control is based in the company's home country. Transnationals also have significant operations in multiple countries, but decision making is decentralized to the local level.
3. Corporate downsizing in North America has occurred in response to global competition. Downsizing was an attempt to make the companies more responsive to customers and more efficient in operating.
4. Small business concepts are being used in larger companies to help them respond faster to a changing environment.
5. The workforce of 2001 will witness heterogeneity of gender, race, and ethnicity. It will also include the physically disabled, gays and lesbians, the elderly, and those who are significantly overweight.
6. TQM focuses on the customer, seeks continual improvement, strives to improve the quality of work, seeks accurate measurement, and empowers employees.

The Changing Face of Management

7. Social responsibility refers to an obligation, beyond that required by law and economics, for a firm to pursue long-term goals that are good for society. Social responsiveness is the capacity of the firm to adapt to changing societal conditions.
8. Incremental change refers to change that is constant and continuous. Quantum change, or reengineering, is radical change in determining new processes for the organization.
9. Managers today can no longer manage in the classic sense. Through downsizing, managers are supervising more and more employees. Thus, managers must allow these employees freedom to act within the confines of the overall unit's goals. The coach, then, provides the structure for the employees and encourages employees to succeed.
10. Ethics refers to rules or principles that define right or wrong conduct.
11. Managers have become increasingly concerned with stimulating innovation and change because the environment in which organizations exist has become very dynamic. Successful organizations will be flexible, able to respond quickly, and led by managers who can effectively enact massive and revolutionary changes.
12. Because of workforce diversity, managers will have to shift their philosophy from treating everyone alike to recognizing differences and responding to these differences in ways that will ensure employee retention and greater productivity.

Review and Discussion Questions

1. Why must managers pay attention to the global village?
2. What is the difference between a multinational corporation and a transnational corporation?
3. "Corporate downsizing for better customer service and more efficiency was just a ruse by large companies to reduce their payrolls and increase their profits." Do you agree or disagree with this statement? Explain.
4. Given that all different kinds of people will comprise tomorrow's organizations, what managerial implication will this diversity bring about?
5. "TQM includes contributions from all management approaches." Do you agree or disagree with this statement? Discuss.
6. In what ways do you think the changing face of management has changed or will change the way in which a company selects and trains managers?
7. "Coaching will never replace traditional managers. There's too much at stake to be left up to coaching techniques." Do you agree or disagree with this statement? Explain.
8. Would you prefer to work in a company that has a good salary but no reward for your performance or one in which your base salary is lower but you have an opportunity to more than double your yearly earnings based on your performance? Discuss.
9. Over the past twenty years, has business become less willing to accept its societal responsibility? Explain.
10. While Playboy Enterprises has a woman president, the magazine it publishes contains photographs and stories that may be regarded as exploitive. With this in mind, discuss the following: "Companies that promote women are acting ethically, but those that exploit women are acting unethically." Could Playboy be both?

Self-Assessment Exercise

What Are Your Personal Value Preferences?

Listed below are eighteen values. Indicate their importance to you by rank—ordering them from one to eighteen. Place a "1" next to the value that has the greatest importance as a guiding principle in your life, a "2" next to the one with the second highest importance, and so forth.

Values	Rank	Values	Rank
ambitious (hard-working, aspiring)	____	logical (consistent, rational)	____
broadminded (open-minded)	____	loving (affectionate, tender)	____
capable (competent, effective)	____	obedient (dutiful, respectful)	____
cheerful (light-hearted, joyful)	____	polite (courteous, well-mannered)	____
clean (neat, tidy)	____	responsible (dependable, reliable)	____
courageous (standing up for your beliefs)	____	self-controlled (restrained, self-disciplined)	____
forgiving (willing to pardon others)	____	Turn to page 411 for scoring directions and key.	
helpful (working for the welfare of others)	____		
honest (sincere, truthful)	____		
imaginative (daring, creative)	____		
independent (self-reliant, self-sufficient)	____		
intellectual (intelligent, reflective)	____		

Source: Based on William C. Frederick and James Weber, "The Values of Corporate Managers and Their Critics: An Empirical Description and Normative Implications," in W.C. Frederick and L.E. Preston, eds. *Business Ethics: Research Issues and Empirical Studies* (Greenwich, Conn.: JAI Press, 1990), pp. 123–44.

Class Exercise

The International Culture Quiz

How knowledgeable are you about customs, practices, and facts regarding different countries? The following multiple-choice quiz will provide you with some feedback on this question. First, take the test by yourself. Then in groups of four to five class members, discuss your answers. Did your group develop any consensus on the questions? If so, what? After seeing the correct responses, what has this exercise taught you about international culture? What might this indicate for anyone considering to work abroad? How about for individuals who will stay in Canada but work with individuals from other countries?

1. In which country would Ramadan (a month of fasting) be celebrated by the majority of people?
   a. Saudi Arabia
   b. India
   c. Singapore
   d. Korea
   e. All of the above

2. On first meeting your prospective Korean business partner, Lo Kim Chee, it would be best to address him as:
   a. Mr. Kim
   b. Mr. Lo
   c. Mr. Chee
   d. Bud
   e. Any of the above are readily accepted

3. In Brazil, your promotional material should be translated into what language?
   a. French
   b. Italian
   c. Spanish
   d. No need to translate it
   e. None of the above

4. In Japan it is important to:
   a. Present your business card only after you have developed a relationship with your Japanese host
   b. Present your business card with both hands
   c. Put your company name on the card, but never your position or title
   d. All of the above
   e. None of the above

5. Which one of the following sports is the most popular worldwide?
   a. Basketball
   b. Baseball
   c. Tennis
   d. Soccer
   e. Golf

6. For a Canadian businessperson, touching a foreign businessperson would be least acceptable in which one of the following countries?
   a. Japan
   b. Italy
   c. Slovenia
   d. Venezuela
   e. France

7. Which of the following would be an appropriate gift?
   a. A clock in China
   b. A bottle of liquor in Egypt
   c. A set of knives in Argentina
   d. A banquet in China
   e. None of the above would be appropriate

8. Which one of the following countries has the most rigid social hierarchy?

The Changing Face of Management

   a. United Kingdom   d. India
   b. United States   e. Germany
   c. Japan
9. Traditional western banking is difficult in which of the following countries because their law forbids both the giving and taking of interest payments?
   a. Brazil   d. India
   b. Saudi Arabia   e. Greece
   c. Mongolia

10. The capital of Germany is:
    a. Berlin   d. Cologne
    b. Bonn   e. Munich
    c. Frankfurt

Turn to page 412 for scoring key only after your group has reached consensus.

Source: Professor David Hopkins, University of Denver, 1991. With permission.

Key Terms

Key terms are listed in the order in which they appear in the chapter.

environment
global village
multinational corporations (MNCs)
transnational corporation (TNC)
cultural environments
individualism
collectivism
power distance
uncertainty avoidance

quantity of life
quality of life
downsizing
entrepreneurs
intrapreneurship
workforce diversity
total quality management (TQM)
social responsibility
social obligation

social responsiveness
sexual harassment
reengineering
empowerment
coach
bi-modal workforce
ethics
code of ethics

Case Application

Xerox of Mexico

Paul Dubord grew up in Montreal and received his degree in business administration from Concordia in 1986. Upon graduation, Paul took a job with Xerox Canada in Toronto as a human resource specialist. During his first two years, he divided his time between recruiting on university campuses and establishing a training program for maintenance engineers. In 1988, Paul was seconded to Xerox Corporation's training centre in Leesburgh, Virginia. In 1990, he was promoted to Assistant Manager for Human Resources back in Xerox Canada.

Paul's annual performance appraisals were consistently high. The company believed he had strong advancement potential. Though Paul was ambitious and made no attempt to hide his desire to move into higher management, even he was a bit surprised when, in 1993, he was offered the position of Director of Human Resources for Xerox of Mexico. If he accepted the position, Paul would oversee a staff of twenty people in Mexico City and be responsible for all human resource activities—recruiting, hiring, compensation, labour relations, and so on—for the company's Mexican operations. He was told that the combination of his outstanding job performance ratings and his ability to speak Spanish as well as French led the company to select him for the promotion.

Paul accepted the offer. Why not? It was an important promotion, meant a large increase in pay, and provided an opportunity to live in a foreign country.

Questions

1. Describe Mexico's national culture.
2. How does Mexico compare with the culture Paul grew up in?
3. Based on the discussion in Chapter 1 of what managers do, and the differences in culture between Canada and Mexico, what changes to you think Paul will need to make in his management style?

The Automotive Business in Canada

Traditionally, car and truck manufacturing has been a main driver of the Canadian economy. When the manufacturing companies — General Motors, Ford, and Chrysler — expand production, the ripples are felt throughout the country. One in every eight jobs in Canada is associated with the automotive business, either with vehicle manufacturers, parts manufacturers, or the service and repair sector. But over the last five years, the vehicle manufacturers have cut 17,000 jobs, and now, in spite of buoyant markets and increasing production, they aren't adding any new jobs.

In 1974, Chrysler Canada built the Plymouth Satellite largely by hand. Windshields were installed by lowering them with ropes, positioning and then sealing them. Seats were put in by hand, and springs had to be clamped to the car frame. The production line was manned by hundreds of workers. But the world of manufacturing has changed tremendously in 20 years and now the successor to the Satellite, the Chrysler LHS, is built by computer-controlled robots. The company makes two and a half times the number of cars it did when it manufactured the Satellite in 1974, but it does it with fewer people. A Rip van Winkel who slept for 20 years between visits to a car or truck plant wouldn't recognize the place today.

The buyers for many of the vehicles aren't Canadian, they're American. NAFTA means that Canadian companies are now competing in a much more global marketplace and for the first time in five years, manufacturers are finding that they can't keep up with demand. But, because keeping costs under control and increasing productivity and efficiency are essential in order to remain competitive, the companies are operating very differently than they used to. Where will it end? Will factories soon be run entirely without people?

Questions

1. What effect has the quality movement had on the changes in the big car makers?
2. How is a manager's job changing in a company like Ford of Canada? Are managers still needed? Why?
3. Investment by the Big Three in automobile manufacturing in Canada has doubled in the last two years. Will that make jobs more stable or less stable? Explain your view and your arguments for either possibility.

Video Resource: "Auto Sector Recovery," *Venture* 487 (May 8, 1994).

3

Foundations of Planning

Learning Objectives

WHAT WILL I BE ABLE TO DO AFTER I FINISH THIS CHAPTER?

1. Define planning.
2. Explain the potential benefits of planning.
3. Distinguish between strategic and operational plans.
4. State when directional plans are preferred over specific plans.
5. Identify four contingency factors in planning.
6. Explain the commitment concept.
7. Define Management by Objectives and identify its common elements.
8. Explain the importance of Strategic Planning.
9. Outline the steps in the strategic management process.
10. Explain SWOT analysis.
11. Compare how entrepreneurs and bureaucratic managers approach strategy.

Is planning really worth the time it takes? We made the point in Chapter 2 that business needs to think in terms of quantum changes. How does this fit with the slow and deliberate concept of planning? An analogy is taking a trip. First, you need to know where you want to end up; then you figure out how to get there. You may wish to go the quickest way, the most interesting way, the safest way, the cheapest way, etc. In fact, you have to *plan* the trip. And if it's a trip across town, for instance, it's a good idea to take a number of factors like traffic flows, construction, and accidents into account. Just going the same way every time may not be best—a lesson some large companies have learned the hard way.

One of the best examples of the power of planning is the largest consumer electronics company in the world—Matsushita. Like many successful companies, Matsushita began with an idea. In 1918, when Konosuke Matsushita started in business, most houses with electricity in Japan only had one ceiling outlet. Matsushita developed a double-ended socket that allowed for extension cords, and more importantly meant that electric devices other than lighting could be used. The company developed an electric iron that, by 1929, had gained a 50% market share. It also developed radios and other electric-powered devices for the rapidly growing market, moving into TV sets, stereos, tape recorders, and so on in the 1950s.

Thirty years ago the market for television sets was dominated by domestic giants like RCA, GE, and Zenith. What chance did a company from Japan have against these giants? Now, when you go shopping for a TV you come across brands like Panasonic, Quasar, Sylvania, Magnavox—all made by Matsushita, the largest manufacturer of television sets in the world. How did this occur?

One of the elements in the success of Matsushita is planning. On May 5th, 1932, Konosuke Matsushita announced a 250-year plan. Yes, 250 years! But broken into 25-year segments. "I, myself and you assembled here," he told his employees, "are to carry out the first 25 years. Our successors will carry on exactly the same for another 25 years, and so on." In the early 1950s, Matsushita established a goal to dominate the U.S. television market. Over the 25-year period, every one of his U.S. competitors retired from the business — either bankrupt or acquired by foreign interests.

This chapter presents the basics of planning. In the following pages, you'll learn the difference between formal and informal planning, why managers plan, the various types of plans that managers use, the key contingency factors that influence the types of plans that managers use in different situations, and the important role that strategic planning plays in promoting better organizational performance.

Planning Defined

As we stated in Chapter 1, planning encompasses defining the organization's objectives or goals, establishing an overall strategy for achieving these goals, and developing a comprehensive hierarchy of plans to integrate and coordinate activities. It is concerned, then, with ends (what is to be done) as well as with means (how it is to be done).

Planning can be further defined in terms of whether it is informal or formal. All managers engage in planning, but it might be only the informal variety. In informal planning, nothing is written down, and there is little or no sharing of objectives with others in the organization. This describes planning in many small businesses; the owner-manager has a vision of where he or she wants to go and how he or she expects to get there. The planning is general and lacks continuity. Of course, informal planning exists in some large organizations, and some small businesses have very sophisticated formal plans.

Foundations of Planning

When we use the term planning in this book, we are implying formal planning. Specific objectives are formulated covering a period of years. These objectives are written down and made available to organization members. Finally, specific action programs exist for the achievement of these objectives; that is, management clearly defines the path it wants to take to get from where it is to where it wants to be. (See Managers Who Made a Difference.)

Managers Who Made a Difference

SONIA AND GORDON JONES AT PENINSULA FARMS

You've tasted one yogurt, you've tasted them all, right? Well, the people in the Maritimes seem to think differently because they love Peninsula Farm yogurt—and they're willing to pay a premium price for it. Peninsula Farm is based in Lunenburg, Nova Scotia, and owned and run by Sonia and Gordon Jones, who began producing yogurt in 1976 for local health food stores with the excess milk from a cow they owned. In 1995 the company had sales of more than $2.5 million, and enjoyed a 25% share of the markets they serve. How they do this is even more impressive when you realize what they *don't* have going for them. They don't have economies of scale like the big producers, nor do they have the power to buy shelf space like their large competitors. They use costly premium ingredients—fresh frozen strawberries, blueberries, and raspberries—while the competition uses prepared fruits from food companies. Their advertising budget consists of one $65 advertisement in the Lunenburg High School yearbook. And they compete in the small Maritime market.

But they are fanatic about quality. And their distribution system is superb, matching supply and demand very closely. As a result, Peninsula Farm loses less than 2% of its product due to expiry date, which is many times less than competitors' losses. And when the product gets to the store, part-time merchandisers record the sales by individual product and fax the numbers back to Lunenburg where the computer system plans exact orders for each store. The third "arm" of the system is the trucking fleet that Peninsula Farm runs. Yogurt is a very sensitive product and can go bad easily. Hence the trucks are refrigerated and are each driven by just one driver, who, in many cases, customizes their trucks to suit their needs. Employees have a very high degree of autonomy. Only one out of 42 has fixed work hours; the others work out the best scheduling among themselves. As a result, there is a high level of commitment to the firm and it is not unusual to find employees pitching in to deal with emergencies or problems. And it must all be working because sales continue to rise.[1] ▼

Purpose of Planning

Managers should engage in planning because it gives direction, reduces the impact of change, minimizes waste and redundancy, and sets the standards to facilitate control.

Planning establishes coordinated effort. It gives direction to managers and non-managers alike. When all concerned know where the organization is going and what they must contribute to reach the objective, they can begin to coordinate their activities, cooperate with each other, and work in teams. A lack of planning can foster "zigzagging" and thus prevent an organization from moving efficiently toward its objectives.

By forcing managers to look ahead, anticipate change, consider the impact of change, and develop appropriate responses, planning reduces uncertainty. It also clarifies the consequences of the actions managers might take in response to change.

Planning also reduces overlapping and wasteful activities. Coordination before the fact is likely to uncover waste and redundancy. Further, when means and ends are clear, inefficiencies become obvious.

Finally, planning establishes objectives or standards that facilitate control. If we are unsure of what we are trying to achieve, how can we determine whether we have achieved it? In planning, we develop the objectives. In the controlling function, we compare actual performance against the objectives, identify any significant deviations, and take the necessary corrective action. Without planning, there can be no control.

Planning and Performance

Do managers and organizations that plan outperform those that don't? Intuitively, you would expect the answer to be a resounding yes. Reviews of the evidence are generally affirmative, but that shouldn't be interpreted as a blanket endorsement of formal planning. We cannot say that organizations that formally plan always outperform those that don't.

Dozens of studies have been undertaken to test the relationship between planning and performance.[2] They allow us to draw the following conclusions. First, generally speaking, formal planning is associated with higher profits, higher return on assets, and other positive financial results. Second, the quality of the planning process and the appropriate implementation of the plans probably contribute more to high performance than does the extent of planning. Finally, in those studies in which formal planning hasn't led to higher performance, the environment is typically the culprit. When government regulations, powerful labour unions, and similar environmental forces constrain management's options, planning will have less of an impact on an organization's performance. Why? Because management will have fewer choices for which planning can propose viable alternatives. For example, planning might suggest that a manufacturing firm produce a number of its key parts in Asia in order to compete effectively against low-cost foreign competitors.

Developer Olympia & York's multibillion-dollar Canary Wharf project in London stands only partially finished. O&Y's management failed in their long-range planning to anticipate the dramatic collapse of the commercial real estate market in the early 1990s.

Types of Plans

The most popular ways to describe plans are by their breadth (strategic versus operational), time frame (short- versus long-term), and specificity (specific versus directional). However, these planning classifications are not independent of one another. For instance, there is a close relationship between the short- and long-term categories and the strategic and operational categories. Exhibit 3-1 lists all these types of plans according to category.

Foundations of Planning

Exhibit 3-1 Types of Plans

CATEGORIZED BY	TYPES
Breadth	• Strategic • Operational
Time Frame	• Short-term • Long-term
Specificity	• Specific • Directional

How Does Strategic Planning Differ from Operational Planning?

Plans that apply to the entire organization, that establish the organization's overall objectives, and that seek to position the organization in terms of its environment are called **strategic plans.** Plans that specify the details of how the overall objectives are to be achieved are called **operational plans.** Strategic and operational plans differ in their time frame, their scope, and whether they include a known set of organizational objectives.[3] Operational plans tend to cover shorter periods of time. For instance, an organization's monthly, weekly, and day-to-day plans are almost all operational. Strategic plans tend to include an extended time period—usually five years or more. They also cover a broader area and deal less with specifics. Finally, strategic plans include the formulation of objectives, whereas operational plans assume the existence of objectives. Operational plans offer ways of attaining these objectives.

In What Time Frame Do Plans Exist?

Financial analysts traditionally describe investment returns as short and long term. The short term covers less than one year. Any time frame beyond five years is classified as long term. Managers have adopted the same terminology to describe plans. For clarity, we'll emphasize **short-term plans** and **long-term plans** in future discussions.

What's the Difference Between Specific and Directional Plans?

It seems intuitively correct that specific plans are always preferable to directional, or loosely guided, plans. **Specific plans** have clearly defined objectives. There is no ambiguity, no problem with misunderstandings. For example, a manager who seeks to increase his or her firm's sales by 18 per cent over a given twelve-month period might establish specific procedures, budget allocations, and schedules of activities to reach that objective. These represent specific plans.

However, specific plans are not without drawbacks. They require clarity and a sense of predictability that often does not exist. When uncertainty is high, which requires management to maintain flexibility in order to respond to unexpected changes, then directional plans are preferable[4] (see Exhibit 3-2). **Directional plans** identify general guidelines. They provide focus but do not lock management into specific objectives or specific courses of action. Instead of a manager following a specific plan to cut costs by 8 per cent and increase revenues by 5 per cent in the next six months, a directional plan might aim at improving corporate profits by 6 to 12 per cent during the next six months. The flexibility inherent in directional plans is obvious. This advantage must be weighed against the loss in clarity provided by specific plans.

strategic plans
Plans that are organization-wide, establish overall objectives, and position an organization in terms of its environment.

operational plans
Plans that specify details on how overall objectives are to be achieved.

short-term plans
Plans that cover less than one year.

long-term plans
Plans that extend beyond five years.

specific plans
Plans that are clearly defined and leave no room for interpretation.

directional plans
Flexible plans that set out general guidelines.

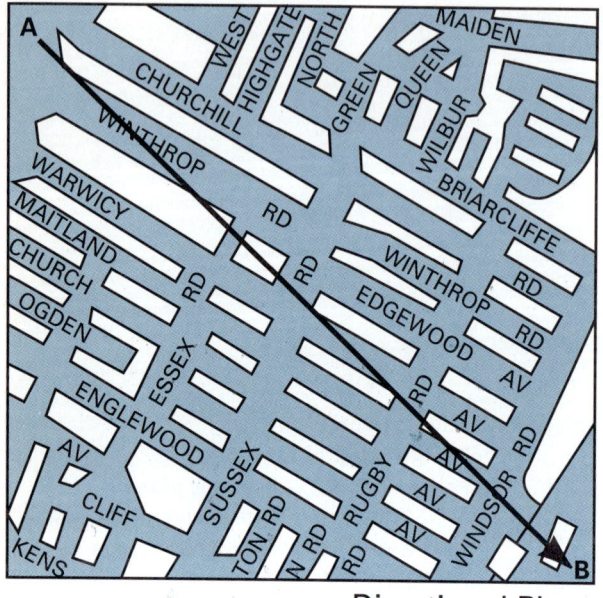

Exhibit 3-2 Directional versus Specific Plans

Contingency Factors Affecting Planning

In some cases, long-term plans make sense, in others they do not. Similarly, in some situations, directional plans are more effective than specific ones. What are these situations? In this section, we identify several contingency factors that affect planning.[5]

Does Planning Differ by One's Level in the Organization?

Exhibit 3-3 illustrates the general relationship between managerial level in an organization and the type of planning that is done. For the most part, operational planning dominates the planning activities of lower-level managers. As managers rise in the hierarchy, their planning role becomes more strategy oriented. The planning effort by the top executives in large organizations is essentially strategic. In a small business, of course, the owner-manager needs to do both.

How Are Plans and the Life Cycle of the Organization Related?

Organizations go through a life cycle. Beginning with the formative stage, organizations then grow, mature, and eventually decline. Planning is not homogeneous across these stages. As Exhibit 3-4 depicts, the length and specificity of plans should be adjusted at each stage. If all things were equal, management would undoubtedly benefit most by developing and using specific plans. Not only would this provide the clearest direction, it would also establish the most detailed benchmarks against which to compare actual performance. However, all things aren't equal.

Foundations of Planning

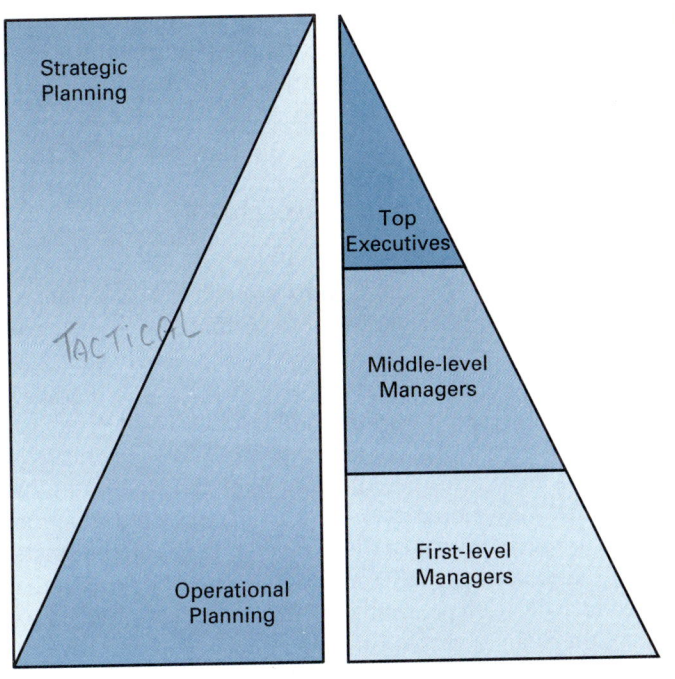

Exhibit 3-3 Managerial Level and Plans

When an organization is mature, predictability is greatest. It is at this stage in the life cycle, therefore, when specific plans are most appropriate. Managers should rely more heavily on directional plans in an organization's infancy. It is at precisely this time that high flexibility is desired. Objectives are tentative, resource availability is more uncertain, and the identification of clients or customers is more in doubt. Directional plans, at this stage, allow managers to make changes as necessary. During the growth stage, plans become more specific as objectives become more definite, resources more committed, and loyalty of clients or customers more developed. The pattern reverses itself on the downward swing of the cycle. From maturity to decline, plans need to move from specific to directional as objectives are reconsidered, resources reallocated, and other adjustments made.

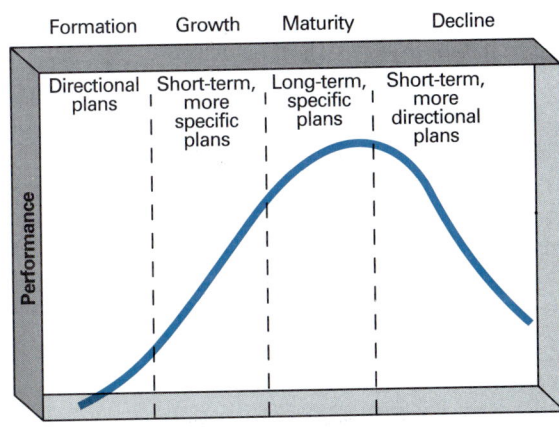

Exhibit 3-4 Plans and the Organization Life Cycle

The length of planning should also be related to the life cycle. Short-term plans offer the greatest flexibility and therefore should be more prevalent during the formative and decline stages. Maturity is the time when stability is greatest and long-term plans can pay the biggest dividends.

How Does the Degree of Environmental Uncertainty Affect Planning?

The greater the environmental uncertainty, the more plans should be directional and emphasis placed on the short term. If rapid or important technological, social, economic, legal, or other changes are taking place, well-defined and precisely chartered routes are more likely to hinder an organization's performance than aid it. When environmental uncertainty is high, specific plans have to be altered to accommodate the changes—often at high cost and decreased efficiency. For example, in the late 1980s, when intense rate wars were raging among airlines on major cross-country routes, the airlines should have moved to more directional plans concerning price setting, number and size of aircraft allocated to routes, and operating budgets. Moreover, the greater the change, the less likely plans are to be accurate. For example, one study found that one-year revenue plans tended to achieve 99 per cent accuracy in comparison to 84 per cent for five-year plans.[6] Therefore, if an organization faces rapidly changing environments, management should seek flexibility.

What Effect Does the Length of Future Commitments Have on Planning?

commitment concept
Plans should extend far enough to see through current commitments.

The final contingency factor again relates to the time frame of plans. The more that current plans affect future commitments, the longer the time frame for which management should plan. This **commitment concept** means that plans should extend far enough to see through those commitments that are made today. Planning for too long or for too short a period is inefficient.

Since its beginning as a small Texas commuter airline in 1971, Herb Kelleher has built Southwest Airlines into the eighth-largest airlines by successfully employing directional plans.

Managers are not planning for future decisions. Rather, they are planning for the future impact of the decisions that they are currently making. Decisions made today become a commitment to some future action or expenditure. Tenure decisions in colleges and universities provide an excellent illustration of how the commitment concept should work.

When a college gives tenure to a faculty member, it is making a commitment to provide lifelong employment for that individual. The tenure decision must therefore reflect an assessment by the college's administration that there will be a need for that faculty member's teaching expertise through his or her lifetime. If a college awards tenure to a 30-

Foundations of Planning

year-old sociology instructor, it should have a plan that covers at least the 30 to 40 or more years this instructor could be teaching in that institution. Most important, the plan should demonstrate the need for a permanent sociology instructor through that time period.

Management by Objectives

L. Perrigo is a manufacturer of over-the-counter drugs and beauty aids.[7] When William Swaney took over as president, he found that the company relied on traditional objective setting. Managers had vague objectives, including "maintaining client communications" and "reviewing performance periodically." He wanted an objective-setting program that would specify exactly what his managers and employees were expected to accomplish and that would motivate rather than intimidate. What he installed was a system of participatory objective setting. Each employee identified no more than ten critical changes that would make a difference in his or her job performance. Then each set specific, quantitative objectives for which he or she would be personally responsible. Examples included "submit budgets within two weeks of contract ratification" and "deliver the project within three per cent of the budgeted cost."

William Swaney is using **management by objectives (MBO)**. It is a system in which specific performance objectives are jointly determined by subordinates and their superiors, progress toward objectives is periodically reviewed, and rewards are allocated on the basis of this progress. Rather than using goals to control, MBO uses them to motivate.

What Is MBO?

Management by objectives is not new. The concept goes back forty years.[8] Its appeal lies in its emphasis on converting overall objectives into specific objectives for organizational units and individual members.

management by objectives (MBO)
A system in which specific performance objectives are jointly determined by subordinates and their superiors, progress toward objectives is periodically reviewed, and rewards are allocated on the basis of this progress.

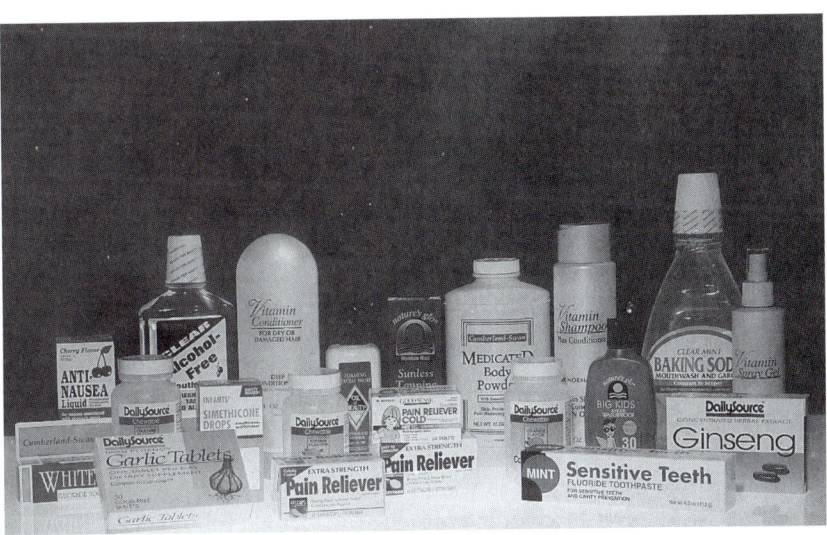

L. Perrigo, a manufacturer of over-the-counter drugs and beauty aids, uses management by objectives (MBO).

Exhibit 3-5 Cascading of Objectives

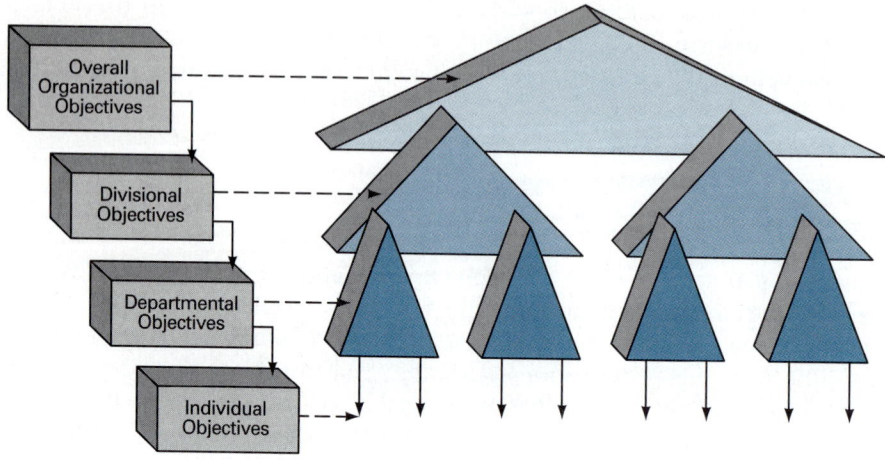

MBO makes objectives operational by devising a process by which they cascade down through the organization. As depicted in Exhibit 3-5, the organization's overall objectives are translated into specific objectives for each succeeding level—divisional, departmental, individual—in the organization. Because lower-unit managers jointly participate in setting their own goals, MBO works from the "bottom up" as well as from the "top down." The result is a hierarchy that links objectives at one level to those at the next level. For the individual employee, MBO provides specific personal performance objectives. Each person therefore has an identified specific contribution to make to his or her unit's performance. If all the individuals achieve their goals, then their unit's goals will be attained, and the organization's overall objectives will become a reality.

Are There Common Elements to an MBO Program?

There are four ingredients common to MBO programs. These are goal specificity, participative decision making, an explicit time period, and performance feedback.

The objectives in MBO should be concise statements of expected accomplishments. It's not adequate, for example, merely to state a desire to cut costs, improve service, or increase quality. Such desires have to be converted into tangible objectives that can be measured and evaluated. To cut departmental costs by 7 per cent, to improve service by ensuring that all telephone orders are processed within twenty-four hours of receipt, or to increase quality by keeping returns to less than 1 per cent of sales, are examples of specific objectives.

In MBO the objectives are not unilaterally set by the boss and assigned to subordinates, as is characteristic of traditional objective setting. MBO replaces these imposed goals with participatively determined goals. The manager and employee jointly choose the goals and agree on how they will be achieved (see also Details on a Management Classic).

Each objective has a concise time period in which it is to be completed. Typically, the time period is three months, six months, or a year.

The final ingredient in an MBO program is feedback on performance. MBO seeks to give continuous feedback on progress toward goals. Ideally, this is accomplished by

Details on a Management Classic

PETER DRUCKER'S MANAGEMENT BY OBJECTIVES

Several decades ago, management professor Peter Drucker developed a system called management by objectives. Often the main question raised about MBO is, Does it work? Assessing the effectiveness of MBO is a complex task. Let's then briefly review a growing body of literature on the relationship between goals and performance.[9] If factors such as a person's ability and acceptance of goals are held constant, evidence demonstrates that more difficult goals lead to higher performance. Although individuals with very difficult goals achieve them far less often than those with very easy goals, they nevertheless perform at a consistently higher level.

Moreover, studies consistently support the finding that specific hard goals produce a higher level of output than do no goals or generalized goals such as "do your best." Feedback also favourably affects performance. Feedback lets a person know whether his or her level of effort is sufficient or needs to be increased. It can induce a person to raise his or her goal level after attaining a previous goal and can inform a person of ways in which to improve his or her performance.

The results cited above are all consistent with MBO's stress on specific goals and feedback. MBO implies, rather than explicitly states, that goals must be perceived as feasible. Research on goal setting indicates that MBO is most effective if the goals are difficult enough to require the person to do some stretching.

But what about participation? MBO strongly advocates that goals be set participatively. Does the research demonstrate that participatively set goals lead to higher performance than those assigned by a superior? Interestingly, the research comparing participatively set and assigned goals on performance has not shown any strong or consistent relationships.[10] When goal difficulty has been held constant, assigned goals frequently do as well as participatively determined goals, contrary to MBO ideology. Therefore, it is not possible to argue for the superiority of participation as MBO proponents advocate. One major benefit from participation, however, is that it appears to induce individuals to establish more difficult goals.[11] Thus, participation may have a positive impact on performance by increasing one's goal-aspiration level.

Studies of actual MBO programs confirm that MBO effectively increases employee performance and organizational productivity. A review of seventy programs, for example, found organizational productivity gains in sixty-eight of them.[12] This same review also identified top management commitment and involvement as important conditions for MBO to reach its potential. When top management had a high commitment to MBO and was personally involved in its implementation, the average gain in productivity was found to be 56 per cent. When commitment and involvement were low, the average gain in productivity dropped to only 6 per cent. ▼

giving ongoing feedback to individuals so they can monitor and correct their own actions. This is supplemented by periodic formal appraisal meetings in which superiors and subordinates can review progress toward goals and further feedback can be provided. MBO is used, in a variety of forms, by many organizations in Canada, from government departments to charities, from manufacturers to marketing companies.

The Importance of an Organizational Strategy

Before the early 1970s, managers who made long-range plans generally assumed that better times lay ahead. Plans for the future were merely extensions of where the organization had been in the past. However, the energy crisis, deregulation, accelerating technological change, and increasing global competition, as well as the other environmental shocks of the 1970s and 1980s, undermined this approach to long-range planning.[13] These changes in the rules of the game forced managers to develop a systematic means of analysing the environment, assessing their organization's strengths and weaknesses, and identifying opportunities where the organization could have a competitive advantage. The value of strategic planning began to be recognized.

A recent survey of business owners found that 69 per cent had strategic plans, and, among those owners, 89 per cent responded that they had found their plans to be effective.[14] They cited, for example, that strategic planning gave them specific goals and provided their staffs with a unified vision. Today, strategic planning has moved beyond the private sector to include government agencies, hospitals, and educational institutions. For example, the skyrocketing costs of a college education, cutbacks in federal aid for students and research, and the decline in the absolute number of high school graduates have led many university administrators to assess their colleges' aspirations and identify a market niche in which they can survive and prosper.[15]

The Strategic Management Process

strategic management process
A nine-step process encompassing strategic planning, implementation, and evaluation.

When an organization attempts to develop its strategy, senior management goes through an activity called the **strategic management process.** The strategic management process, as illustrated in Exhibit 3-6, is a nine-step process that involves strategic planning, implementation, and evaluation. While strategic planning encompasses the first seven steps, even the best strategies can go awry if management fails either to implement them properly or to evaluate their results. Let's look at the various steps in the strategic management process.

These senior Data Point managers spend considerable time each year setting the strategy for their software design company, establishing goals, and planning their future direction.

Foundations of Planning

Exhibit 3-6 The Strategic Management Process

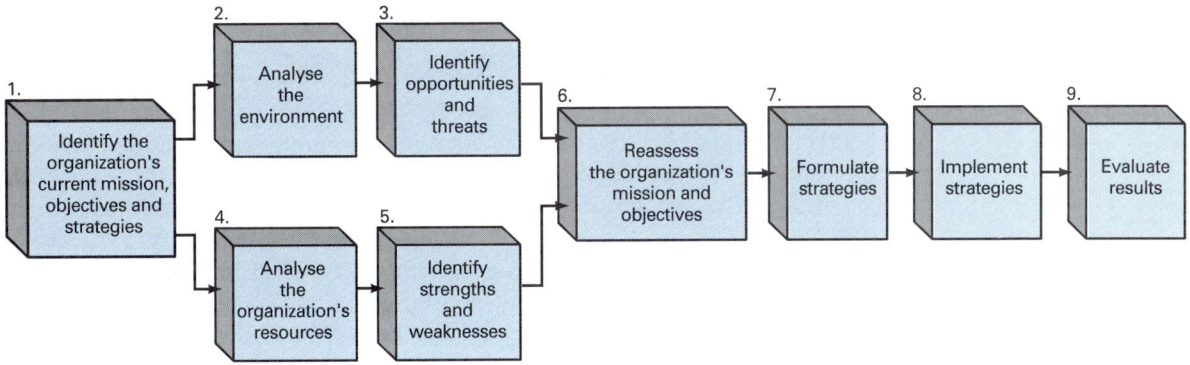

How Does the Strategic Management Process Operate?

In order to develop its strategy, the first step for organizational members is to identify the organization's current mission, objectives, and strategies. Every organization has a **mission** that defines its purpose and answers the question, What business or businesses are we in? Defining the organization's mission forces management to identify the scope of its products or services carefully. It has been argued, for instance, that the decline of the railways was due to their misdefining the business they were in. During the 1930s and 1940s, if the railways had considered themselves to be in the transportation business instead of the railway business, their fate might have been quite different.

mission
The purpose of an organization.

Determining the nature of one's business is as important for not-for-profit organizations as it is for business firms. Hospitals, government agencies, and colleges must also identify their missions. For example, is a college training students for the professions, training students for particular jobs, or educating students through a well-rounded, liberal education? Is it seeking students from the top 5 per cent of high school graduates, students with low academic grades but high aptitude test scores, or students in the vast middle ground? Answers to questions such as these clarify the organization's current purpose (see Class Exercise). Once classified, the organization can begin to look outside the company to ensure that its strategy aligns well with the environment.[16] As a case in point, Panasonic is a major producer of home entertainment systems. But beginning in the mid-1980s, technological breakthroughs in miniaturization and the social trend toward living in smaller homes dramatically increased the demand for powerful, but highly compact, sound systems. The success of Panasonic's home-audio strategy depends on understanding the technological and social changes that are taking place in its environment.

An organization like Panasonic must continue to strive to understand the technology and social changes it faces in order to produce products customers want.

Management of every organization needs to analyse its environment (step 2). It needs to know, for instance, what its competition is up to, what pending legislation might affect the organization, and what the supply of labour in locations where the organization operates is like. Step 2 of the strategy process is complete when management has an accurate grasp of what is taking place in its environment and is aware of important trends that might affect its operations.

What Are the Primary Steps in the Strategic Management Process?

After analysing the environment, management needs to evaluate what it has learned in terms of opportunities that the organization can exploit and threats that the organization faces (step 3).[17] Keep in mind that the same environment can present opportunities to one organization and pose threats to another in the same industry because of their different resources. In 1993, the long recession had created a weak Canadian economy. Business bankruptcies were at postdepression highs (see Ethical Dilemmas in Management). Especially hurt were businesses—like home-furnishing retailers—that sold large-ticket items whose purchase could be easily postponed. However, several large, prosperous, and well-managed chains of home-furnishing retailers saw this situation as an opportunity. They were able to buy inventories of former competitors at bargain prices and to selectively take over these competitors' better locations. The result—a consolidation among the larger and more prosperous furniture retailers. So what an organization considers an opportunity or a threat depends on the resources that it controls.

Next, in step 4, we move from looking outside the organization to looking inside. That is, we are evaluating our internal resources. What skills and abilities do the organization's employees have? What is the organization's cash position? Has it been successful at developing new and innovative products? How does the public perceive the organization and the quality of its products or services?

This fourth step forces management to recognize that every organization, no matter how large and powerful, is constrained in some way by the resources and skills it has available. A smaller automobile manufacturer, like Alfa Romeo, isn't able to move into making minivans simply because management sees opportunities there. Alfa Romeo doesn't have the resources to successfully enter the minivan market against the likes of Chrysler, Ford, Toyota, and Nissan.

The analysis in step 4 should lead to a clear assessment of the organization's strengths and weaknesses (step 5). Management can then identify the organization's **distinctive competence,** or the unique skills and resources that determine the organization's competitive weapons. Black & Decker, for instance, bought General Electric's small appliances division—which made coffee makers, toasters, irons, and the like—renamed them, and capitalized on Black & Decker's reputation for quality and durability to make these appliances far more profitable than they had been under the GE name.

An understanding of the organization's culture and the strengths and liabilities it offers management is a crucial part of step 5 that has only recently been getting the attention it deserves.[18] Specifically, managers should be aware that strong and weak cultures have different effects on strategy and that the content of a culture has a major effect on the content of the strategy.

In a strong culture, for instance, almost all employees will have a clear understanding of what the organization is about. This should make it easier for management to convey to new employees the organization's distinctive competence. A department store chain like Marks and Spencer, which has a very strong culture that embraces service and customer satisfaction, should be able to instil its cultural values in new employees in a much shorter time than can a competitor with a weak culture. The negative side of a strong culture, of course, is that it is more difficult to change. A strong culture may act as a significant barrier to acceptance of a change in the organization's strategies. In

distinctive competence
The unique skills and resources that determine the organization's competitive weapons.

Ethical Dilemmas in Management

IS "GOING BANKRUPT" AN UNETHICAL STRATEGY?

Dow Corning, the company that developed and marketed silicone breast implants, has a list of 19,000 lawsuits facing it, with the litigants including some 10,000 Canadian women. Dow and the other two large producers of the implants negotiated a $4.2-billion (U.S.) fund to settle world claims. Dow's share was $2 billion over 30 years. However, it became clear that this amount would not be enough to cover all the claims being made against the company and on May 15th, 1995, it sought bankruptcy protection under Chapter 11 of the U.S. Bankruptcy Code. The effect of this action is to freeze all lawsuits and turn the claimants into creditors who will be asked to negotiate a settlement as part of the company's efforts to restructure its finances. Canadian women have been outraged by the action.

But the law of the U.S. allows companies to use Chapter 11 to nurse themselves back to financial health, continuing operations and keeping managers and staff employed—whether they are bankrupt or not. In other words, a company can file for reorganization without being bankrupt, and Chapter 11 has become a strategic option. The discretionary nature of the law has allowed organizations, almost at will, to escape from undesirable financial obligations.

Texaco, for instance, was found to have interfered in Pennzoil's attempt to buy Getty Oil. The courts gave Pennzoil a $10.5 billion judgment against Texaco. Texaco's management responded by filing for bankruptcy even though the company was enormously profitable. The strategy allowed Texaco to cut its obligation to Pennzoil down to $3 billion.

Is it wrong for managers to use bankruptcy as a strategy? It does allow the company to continue to operate and thus save employees' jobs. It can, in the longer term, even create enhanced value for stockholders. But it can place an undue hardship on creditors and other claimants. Creditors may have to settle claims for just a few cents on the dollar. Landlords may be left with broken leases, and unions may be left with unenforceable labour agreements. And innocent customers who endured pain, suffering, or even death as a result of a company's negligence may be unable to achieve anything near an equitable financial settlement. When bankruptcy is used to evade responsibility and liability, is management acting unethically?

---

fact, the strong culture at Wang Labs undoubtedly kept top management from perceiving the need to adopt a new corporate strategy in the 1980s in response to changes in the computer industry. Successful organizations with strong cultures can become prisoners of their own past successes.

How Do You Reassess the Organization's Mission and Objectives?

A merging of steps 3 and 5 results in an assessment of the organization's opportunities (step 6) (see Exhibit 3-7). This is frequently called SWOT analysis because it brings together the organization's strengths, weaknesses, opportunities, and threats in order to identify a niche that the organization can exploit.

In light of the SWOT analysis and identification of the organization's opportunities, management needs to reevaluate its mission and objectives. Are they realistic? Do they need modification? If changes are needed in the organization's overall direction, this is where they are likely to originate. On the other hand, if no changes are necessary, management is ready to begin the actual formulation of strategies.

The culture in Marks & Spencer creates a sense of belonging that retains employees. The senior executives have spent their lives in M&S.

How Do You Formulate Strategies?

Strategies need to be set for all levels in the organization (step 7). Management needs to develop and evaluate alternative strategies and then select a set that is compatible at each level and will allow the organization to best capitalize on its resources and the opportunities available in the environment.

This seventh step is complete when management has developed a set of strategies that will give the organization a competitive advantage. That is, management will seek to position the organization so that it can gain a relative advantage over its rivals. This requires a careful evaluation of the competitive forces that dictate the rules of competition within the industry in which the organization operates.

One of the leading researchers into strategy formulation is Michael Porter of Harvard's Graduate School of Business.[19] His competitive strategies framework demonstrates that managers can choose among three generic strategies (see Details on a Management Classic). According to Michael Porter, no firm can successfully perform at an above-average level by trying to be all things to all people. Rather, Porter proposed that management must select a strategy that will give its organization a competitive advantage. Management can choose from among three strategies: **cost-leadership** (low-cost producer), **differentiation** (uniqueness in a broad market), and *focus* (uniqueness in a narrow market). Which strategy management chooses depends on the organization's strengths and its competitors' weaknesses. As such, management should avoid

cost-leadership strategy
The strategy an organization follows when it wants to be the lowest-cost producer in its industry.

differentiation strategy
The strategy a firm follows when it wants to be unique in its industry along dimensions widely valued by buyers.

Exhibit 3-7 Identifying an Organization's Opportunities

Foundations of Planning

a position in which it has to slug it out with everybody in the industry. Rather, the organization should put its strength where the competition isn't. Success, then, depends on selecting the right strategy, the one that fits the complete picture of the organization and the industry in which it is a part. This will enable organizations to gain the most favourable competitive advantage.

This cost-leading company has been successful in the highly competitive hardware business by offering low-priced goods and quality customer service.

Details on a Management Classic

MICHAEL PORTER'S GENERIC STRATEGIES

According to Michael Porter, when an organization sets out to be the low-cost producer in its industry, it is following a cost-leadership strategy. Success with this strategy requires that the organization be the cost leader and not merely one of the contenders for that position. Additionally, the product or service being offered must be perceived as comparable to that offered by rivals, or at least acceptable to buyers.

How does a firm gain such a cost advantage? Typical means include efficiency of operations, economies of scale, technological innovation, low-cost labour, or preferential access to raw materials. Examples of firms that have used this strategy include Wal-Mart, Gallo wines, and Southwest Airlines.

The firm that seeks to be unique in its industry in ways that are widely valued by buyers is following a differentiation strategy. It might emphasize high quality, extraordinary service, innovative design, technological capability, or an unusually positive brand image. The key is that the attribute chosen must be different from those offered by rivals and significant enough to justify a price premium that exceeds the cost of differentiating. There is no shortage of firms that have found at least one attribute that allows them to differentiate themselves from competitors. Intel (technology), Maytag (reliability), Mary Kay cosmetics (distribution), and L.L. Bean (service) are a few.

focus strategy
The strategy a company follows when it pursues a cost or differentiation advantage in a narrow industry segment.

The first two strategies sought a competitive advantage in a broad range of industry segments. The **focus strategy** aims at a cost advantage (cost focus) or differentiation advantage (differentiation focus) in a narrow segment. That is, management will select a segment or group of segments in an industry (such as product variety, type of end buyer, distribution channel, or geographic location of buyers) and tailor the strategy to serve them to the exclusion of others. The goal is to exploit a narrow segment of a market. Of course, the feasibility of a focus strategy depends on the size of a segment and whether it can support the additional cost of focusing. Stouffer's used a cost-focus strategy in its Lean Cuisine line to reach calorie-conscious consumers seeking both high-quality products and convenience. ▼

How Do You Implement the Strategic Management Process?

The next-to-last step in the strategic management process is implementation (step 8). No matter how effective strategic planning has been, it cannot succeed if it is not implemented properly. Top management leadership is a necessary ingredient in a successful strategy. So, too, is a motivated group of middle- and lower-level managers to carry out senior management's specific plans. And finally, results must be evaluated (step 9). How effective have our strategies been? What adjustments, if any, are necessary? In Chapter 15, we'll review the control process. The concepts and techniques that we introduce in that chapter can be used to assess the results of strategies and to correct significant deviations.

Strategy Is Part of Every Manager's Job

Have you ever attended a symphony or watched a play? Did you ever give much thought to what made the event successful? One of the key ingredients is that all members must work together in harmony. So, too, must organizational members.

Strategies in an organization provide that direction. These goals indicate to all members where the organization is going and what it takes to be successful. Furthermore, strategic planning serves as a catalyst that drives every other activity in the organization. For example, when a company sets its goals, it identifies which specific human resources are needed to accomplish its objectives. (See Developing Management Skills.) Therefore, employees are selected (either internally or recruited from the outside) based on their

Developing Management Skills

▼
STEPS IN GOAL SETTING
▲

▶ **1. Identify an employee's key job tasks.** Goal setting begins by defining what it is that you want your employees to accomplish. The best source for this information is each employee's job description.

▶ **2. Establish specific and challenging goals for each key task.** Identify the level of performance expected of each employee. Specify the target for the employee to hit.

▶ **3. Specify the deadlines for each goal.** Putting deadlines on each goal reduces ambiguity. Deadlines, however, should not be set arbitrarily. Rather, they need to be realistic given the tasks to be completed.

▶ **4. Allow the employee to actively participate.** By allowing employees to participate, acceptance of the goals increases. However, it must be sincere participation. That is, employees must perceive that you are truly seeking their input, not just going through the motions.

▶ **5. Prioritize goals.** When someone is given more than one goal, it is important for you to rank the goals in order of importance. The purpose of prioritizing is to encourage the employee to take action and expend effort on each goal in proportion to its importance.

▶ **6. Rate goals for difficulty and importance.** Goal setting should not encourage people to choose easy goals. Instead, goals should be rated for their difficulty and importance. In doing so, individuals can be given credit for trying difficult goals, even if they don't fully achieve them.

▶ **7. Build in feedback mechanisms to assess goal progress.** Feedback lets employees know whether their level of effort is sufficient to attain the goal. Feedback should be both self and supervisor generated. In either case, feedback should be frequent and recurring.

▶ **8. Link rewards to goal attainment.** It's natural for employees to ask, "What's in it for me?" Linking rewards to the achievement of goals will help to answer that question.

Foundations of Planning

possession of the required skills, knowledge, and abilities necessary to successfully complete the jobs. As such, a major focus of hiring should be the fulfilment of company goals.

There is another important aspect of strategic planing that must be recognized—its filtering-down effect. When senior managers set the strategic direction for the company, they establish the overall goals for the corporation. But it is not at this level that the actual work takes place. Thus these goals must be pushed downward. In essence, corporate goals are achieved through the collective activities in each division or department. By translating these strategic goals into more specific plans, each successive level in management in turn will identify specific work activities of the unit's employees. And finally, strategy aids all managers in their decision-making process. Any decisions made should be supportive of the company's objectives.

TQM as a Strategic Weapon

An increasing number of organizations are applying Total Quality Management as a way to build a competitive advantage. As we discussed in Chapter 2, TQM focuses on quality and continuous improvement. To the degree that an organization can satisfy a customer's need for quality, it can differentiate itself from the competition and attract and hold a loyal customer base. Moreover, constant improvement in the quality and reliability of an organization's products or services can result in a competitive advantage others can't steal.[20] Product innovations, for example, offer little opportunity for sustained competitive advantage. Why? Because usually they can be quickly copied by rivals. But incremental improvement, which is an essential element of TQM, is something that becomes an integrated part of an organization's operations and can develop into a considerable cumulative advantage. To illustrate how TQM can be used as a strategic tool, let's look at four companies—AMP of Canada Ltd., Cargill Limited, Pratt & Whitney Canada Ltd., and Steelcase Canada Limited.[21]

AMP, a manufacturer and distributor of electric and electronic connecting products to original equipment manufacturers of computers and telecommunications equipment, has created an environment that is organized around processes rather than functions and it has done this by not filling vacancies as they arise in the workforce. This forces people to wear more than one hat and focus their activities on what the *customer* wants rather than what the function wants. A cross-functional team that exemplifies this flexibility and customer focus is the "on-time delivery" team, made up of people from quality, inside sales, warehouse, and inventory control departments. They have achieved 98 to 99 per cent delivery "as promised."

Pratt & Whitney Canada, a manufacturer of small gas turbines for corporate aircraft, commuter aircraft, and helicopters, and auxiliary power units for jumbo jets, has integrated the efforts of marketing, engineering, manufacturing, procurement, customer support, and finance to cut the product development cycle from five years to two-and-a-half years.

Steelcase Canada is a manufacturer and distributor of office furniture and equipment. Its "focus factories," which integrate all functions in production, inventory, ordering, procurement, and production scheduling, have cut cycle times of eight to ten weeks down to four weeks and decreased inventory by 50 per cent in two manufacturing areas. Their "Quick Ship" program ensures delivery of items in twelve days or less.

Cargill is a diversified agricultural company with operations across Canada in grain, fertilizers, and farm chemicals, livestock and feed and seed. By linking a computer to the finished goods scanning system to tell the meat fabrication line when orders from sales for any given cut of meat have been filled, a 15 to 20 per cent improvement in production accuracy has been achieved.

However, the record of TQM attempts has not been good overall. A *Canadian Business Review* article in the winter of 1992 documents a U.S. survey showing that only 13 per cent of CEOs reported that TQM efforts resulted in higher profits or operating income. A British study showed that in the U.K. 80 per cent of TQM efforts fail. A Canadian study showed that while 80 per cent of Canadian companies are making some effort at implementing total quality programs, only a third have achieved tangible positive results.

Entrepreneurship: A Special Case of Strategic Planning

You've heard the story dozens of times. With only an idea, a few hundred dollars, and use of the family garage, someone starts what eventually becomes a multimillion-dollar corporation. In the case of Dell Computer, the only deviation is that Michael Dell began his business in his university bedroom.[22] Michael Dell had been fascinated by computers since junior high. As an eighteen-year-old freshman at the University of Texas in 1983, he started selling disk drives and other components that he bought from dealers who had surplus inventory. His first customers were friends and fellow students at the university. Then Dell found that he could buy stripped-down versions of IBM PCs and add components that would significantly increase their power. By early 1984, Dell was selling $50,000 to $60,000 worth of customized computers and computer parts each month. That summer, he decided to quit school and devote his full attention to his computer business. He specialized in building complete PC systems for doctors, lawyers, and small businesses. In his first month of business, he sold $180,000 worth of equipment. Each month thereafter, sales grew exponentially. After nine months, he had sales of $6 million and thirty-nine employees working for him.

What differentiates Dell Computer Corporation from its competitors? High-quality hardware, comprehensive service and technical support, and low prices. Dell sells to customers through the mail and other direct-marketing techniques, bypassing dealers. Also, Dell can custom-design a personal computer system precisely to a customer's needs, build it, and ship it within three days. In 1992, Dell's 800 number was handling over 8,000 sales and service phone calls a day. Annual sales were close to $2 billion in fiscal 1992. And Michael Dell is a wealthy man, holding more than $150 million worth of stock in his company.

Strategic planning carries a "big business" bias. It implies a formalization and structure that fits well with large, established organizations that have abundant resources. But the primary interest of many students is not in managing large and established organizations. Like Michael Dell, Dave Thomas of Wendy's, or Fred Smith of Federal Express, they're excited about the idea of starting their own businesses from scratch—an action that is called entrepreneurship.

Karl Brackhaus is an example of somebody who did just that. He finished a PhD in engineering physics at the University of British Columbia in 1976 and started a firm to help companies apply programmable industrial-control technology. Three years later he produced a colour graphics display system, called the Grafix Terminal, which was quickly bought by breweries, mines, and sawmills, principally in British Columbia. Brackhaus's company, Dynapro Systems Inc., was off and running.

Foundations of Planning

Except for a hitch. Allen-Bradley, a subsidiary of the giant Rockwell International, became interested in entering the field. However, instead of trying to compete head-to-head with Allen-Bradley, Karl Brackhaus did a deal with them whereby Allen-Bradley bought 50 per cent of Dynapro Systems, and became its major customer. Sales have risen an average of 50 per cent a year since 1983, surpassing the $40 million mark in 1994. [23]

What Is Entrepreneurship?

There is no shortage of definitions of *entrepreneurship*.[24] Some, for example, apply it to the creation of any new business. Others focus on intentions, claiming that entrepreneurs seek to create wealth, which is different from starting businesses merely as a means of income substitution (that is, working for yourself rather than working for someone else). When most people describe entrepreneurs, they use adjectives such as bold, innovative, venturesome, and risk taking. They also tend to associate entrepreneurs with small businesses. We'll define entrepreneurship as a process by which individuals pursue opportunities, fulfilling needs and wants through innovation, without regard to the resources they currently control.[25]

It's important not to confuse managing a small business with entrepreneurship. Why? Because not all small business managers are entrepreneurs.[26] Many don't innovate. A great many managers of small businesses are merely scaled-down versions of the conservative, conforming bureaucrats who staff many large corporations and public agencies.

Do Entrepreneurs Possess Similar Characteristics?

One of the most researched topics in entrepreneurship has been the search to determine what, if any, psychological characteristics entrepreneurs have in common. A number of these characteristics have been found. These include hard work, self-confidence, optimism, determination, and a high energy level.[27] But three factors regularly sit on the top of most lists that profile the entrepreneurial personality. Entrepreneurs have a high need for achievement, believe strongly that they can control their own destinies, and take only moderate risks.[28]

Michael Dell is a successful entrepreneur. His company, Dell Computer, began in a college dorm room. In only ten years, company sales reached nearly $2 billion.

The research allows us to draw a general description of entrepreneurs. They tend to be independent types who prefer to be personally responsible for solving problems, for setting goals, and for reaching these goals by their own efforts. They value independence and particularly don't like being controlled by others. While they're not afraid of taking chances, they're not wild risk takers. They prefer to take calculated risks where they feel that they can control the outcome.

The evidence on entrepreneurial personalities leads us to two obvious conclusions. First, people with this personality makeup are not likely to be contented, productive employees in the typical large corporation or government agency. The rules, regulations, and controls that these bureaucracies impose on their members frustrate entrepreneurs. Second, the challenges and conditions inherent in starting one's own business mesh well with the entrepreneurial personality. Starting a new venture, which they control, appeals to their willingness to take risks and determine their own destinies. But because entrepreneurs believe that their future

	TRADITIONAL MANAGERS	ENTREPRENEURS
Primary motivation	Promotion and other traditional corporate rewards such as office, staff, and power	Independence, opportunity to create, financial gain
Time orientation	Achievement of short-term goals	Achievement of five- to ten-year growth of business
Activity	Delegation and supervision	Direct involvement
Risk propensity	Low	Moderate
View toward failures and mistakes	Avoidance	Acceptance

Exhibit 3-8 Comparing Entrepreneurs and Traditional Managers

Source: Based on Robert D. Hisrich, "Entrepreneurship/Intrapreneurship," *American Psychologist,* February 1990, p. 218.

is fully in their own hands, the risk they perceive as moderate is often seen as high by nonentrepreneurs.

How Do Entrepreneurs Compare to Traditional Managers?

Exhibit 3-8 summarizes some key differences between entrepreneurs and traditional bureaucratic managers. While the latter tend to be more custodial, entrepreneurs actively seek change by exploiting opportunities. When searching for these opportunities, entrepreneurs often put their personal financial security at risk. The hierarchy in large organizations typically insulates traditional managers from these financial wagers and rewards them for minimizing risks and avoiding failures.

Summary

This Summary is organized by the chapter opening learning objectives found on page 53.

1. Planning is the process of determining objectives and assessing the way these objectives can best be achieved.
2. Planning gives direction, reduces the impact of change, minimizes waste and redundancy, and sets the standards to facilitate controlling.
3. Strategic plans cover an extensive time period (usually five or more years), cover broad issues, and include the formulation of objectives. Operational plans cover shorter periods of time, focus on specifics, and assume that objectives are already known.
4. Directional plans are preferred over specific plans when uncertainty is high and when the organization is in the formative and decline stages of its life cycle.
5. Four contingency factors in planning include a manager's level in the organization, the life stage of the organization, the degree of environmental uncertainty, and the length of future commitments.
6. A manager should plan just far enough ahead to see through those commitments he or she makes today.
7. Management by objectives is a system in which specific performance objectives are jointly determined by employees and their bosses, progress toward objectives is periodically reviewed, and rewards are allocated on the basis of the progress. The four ingredients common to MBO programs are goal specificity, participative decision making, explicit time periods, and performance feedback.
8. In a dynamic and uncertain environment, strategic planning is important because it can provide man-

Foundations of Planning

agers with a systematic and comprehensive means for analysing the environment, assessing their organization's strengths and weaknesses, and identifying opportunities in which their organization could have a competitive advantage.

9. The strategic management process is made up of nine steps: (1) Identifying the organization's current mission, objectives, and strategies; (2) Analysing the environment; (3) Identifying opportunities and threats in the environment; (4) Analysing the organization's resources; (5) Identifying the organization's strengths and weaknesses; (6) Reassessing the organization's mission and objectives based on its strengths, weaknesses, opportunities, and threats; (7) Formulating strategies; (8) Implementing its strategies; and (9) Evaluating results.

10. SWOT analysis refers to analysing the organization's internal strengths and weaknesses as well as external opportunities and threats in order to identify a niche that the organization can exploit.

11. Entrepreneurs approach strategy by first seeking out opportunities that they can exploit. Bureaucratic managers approach strategy by first determining the availability of their resources.

Review and Discussion Questions

1. Contrast formal with informal planning.
2. How does planning affect an organization in terms of performance?
3. Describe the six different types of plans discussed in this chapter.
4. How does the planning done by a top executive differ from that performed by a supervisor?
5. How does environmental uncertainty affect planning?
6. Compare an organization's mission with its objectives.
7. Describe the nine-step strategic management process.
8. What is a SWOT analysis?
9. How would you describe Wal-Mart's competitive advantage in its industry?
10. All managers are involved in the strategic planning process. Describe how this happens.
11. How can TQM provide a competitive advantage?
12. Are all small business managers entrepreneurs? Explain your answer.

Self-Assessment Exercise

Are You a Good Planner?

Instructions: Answer either Yes or No to each of the following eight questions:

	Yes	No
1. My personal objectives are clearly spelled out in writing.	___	___
2. Most of my days are hectic and disorderly.	___	___
3. I seldom make any snap decisions and usually study a problem carefully before acting.	___	___
4. I keep a desk calendar or appointment book as an aid.	___	___
5. I make use of "action" and "deferred action" files.	___	___
6. I generally establish starting dates and deadlines for all my projects.	___	___
7. I often ask others for advice.	___	___
8. I believe that all problems have to be solved immediately.	___	___

Turn to page 412 for scoring directions and key.

Source: Ted Pollack, "Are You a Good Planner," *Supervision,* January 1980, pp. 26–27; "How Good a Planner Are You?" *Supervision,* July 1983, p. 24; and "How to Be a Good Planner," *Supervision,* April 1984, pp. 25–26. Reprinted by permission of © National Research Bureau, P.O. Box 1, Burlington, Iowa 52601-0001.

Class Exercise

Your School's Mission

Often we lose sight of our college's goals and objectives as we pay more attention to our studies. Even so, your school must also be prepared to carve out its niche in an effort to provide something of value to its students. For this exercise, your professor will put you into small groups. The charge of each small group is to prepare responses to the following questions and present its findings to the class.

1. What do you think is your school's mission?
2. How would you describe your school's environment?
3. What are the strengths and weaknesses of your school? Its competitive advantage?
4. What resources does your school have that support its mission?
5. Given your perception of your school, what strategic suggestions would you make?

Key Terms

Key terms are listed in the order in which they appear in the chapter.

strategic plans	directional plans	distinctive competence
operational plans	commitment concept	cost-leadership strategy
short-term plans	management by objectives (MBO)	differentiation strategy
long-term plans	strategic management process	focus strategy
specific plans	mission	

Case Application

Topps Trading Cards

Since the 1950s, Topps Company has been one of the world's leading trading card manufacturers. Their success in trading cards has allowed Topps' senior management to diversify the company. For example, in addition to selling sports cards, Topps manufactures Bazooka bubble gum. It also publishes comic books, competing in a market dominated by Marvel Comics. Although these other areas were making profits, the main revenue generator for Topps remained sports cards.

By 1980, sales in the sports card business hovered around the $50 million mark. Topps' success was virtually assured, given the frenzy of the baby boom generation toward collecting complete sets of baseball cards of their favourite team. But what happened next sent Topps' management reeling.

During the 1980s and culminating in 1992, sales of sports trading cards shot off the charts. By 1992, sales in this industry reached $1.2 billion. Sales were no longer made to sports-oriented 10-year-olds, but to a large group of 30- to 40-year-olds. As the baby boom generation got older, their desire for these cards grew. The excitement, however, was not to get pictures of your favourite team. Rather, sports trading cards became a major investment prospect. For example, Mickey Mantle's baseball card that was packaged with other cards and sold for a nickel in 1952 brought almost $50,000 at an auction some forty years later. There didn't appear to be an end to this craze, and Topps couldn't have been happier. Then the party ended. Sales in 1993 fell 20 per cent from the prior year. Topps' profits declined almost 65 per cent during those same twelve months. And if that weren't enough, their stock tumbled more than 35 per cent. This new environment forced Topps' managers to think quickly if the company was to stay afloat.

Questions

1. Develop a strategy to help Topps cope with the changing environment it faces.
2. Michael Porter identified three generic strategies that companies follow. Which one of the three do you believe Topps should use? Discuss and support your choice.

Source: Elizabeth Lesley, "A Burst Bubble at Topps," *Business Week*, August 23, 1993, p. 74.

The Reichmann Empire

One success or one failure isn't enough to measure a company's or an individual's effectiveness. Success over the longer term makes the difference. The Reichmanns, well known in Canada through their former company, Olympia & York, which failed in the recession of the early 1990s when property values fell dramatically, are long-term thinkers and strategists. They built their wealth over 30 to 40 years after World War Two, and the downturn that lost them O&Y, while it caused them significant losses, has not changed their strategic perspective on property development.

Paul Reichmann is a great visionary, and many of his developments stand as monuments to that vision. Canary Wharf in London, England, and First Canadian Place in Toronto, Ontario, are landmarks that set standards that others have followed. So where are the Reichmanns now? Mexico. In the heart of Mexico City, to be exact, developing the centrepiece of a huge project called Santa Fe, which is turning an old gravel mine into 2,000 acres of modern buildings. The Reichmanns' project consists of 25 acres in the core, and includes office, residential, and recreational development.

The Reichmanns spend time looking around the world, seeking out areas where there is a need for what they do; they focus on their distinctive competence; they analyse the environment; they assess risks and opportunities; and they develop a strategy that attempts to manage risk and maximize opportunity. In England, Canary Wharf failed when the market dropped because it was unable to attract tenants. There was a lot of alternative decent office space in London at the time; there is very little good office space in Mexico City. The location of Canary Wharf was difficult — historically on the "wrong side" of town; in Mexico City, the Santa Fe project is on the "right" side of town. While Canary Wharf was a massively huge project, the Reichmanns' Santa Fe project is being built in small steps. And finally, in England, the Reichmanns didn't have allies who could help them through the crisis, while in Mexico they have teamed up with Latin America's largest construction company, and have the billionaire financier George Soros working with them. They are also politically well connected. President Salinas personally asked Monte Kwinter, an Ontario MPP, to bring the Reichmanns to Mexico to discuss involvement in Santa Fe. Is this enough to make the Santa Fe project succeed?

Questions

1. What is the Reichmanns' distinctive competence?
2. The Reichmanns aren't the only developers in Mexico. While there is a shortage of office space in Mexico City now, what happens if supply outruns demand and too much has been built? If you were helping them develop a strategic plan, what factors would you list as (a) their strengths, (b) their weaknesses, (c) the risks, and (d) the opportunities?
3. In Michael Porter's terms, what sort of strategy are the Reichmanns following? Explain your answer.

Video Resource: "Reichmann Revival," *Venture* 480 (March 20, 1994).

4

Planning Tools and Techniques

Learning Objectives

WHAT WILL I BE ABLE TO DO AFTER I FINISH THIS CHAPTER?

1. Describe techniques for scanning the environment.
2. Contrast quantitative and qualitative forecasting.
3. Explain why budgets are popular.
4. List two approaches to budgeting.
5. Differentiate Gantt and load charts.
6. Identify the steps in a PERT network.
7. State the factors that determine a product's break-even point.
8. Describe the requirements for using linear programming.
9. Discuss how queuing theory can be a planning tool.

Jimmy Lai is a modern-day rags-to-riches story.[1] Born in China in 1948, his early life was filled with poverty and despair. At age 12, he had to leave his family and flee to Hong Kong. Because Jimmy had little formal education, the only work he could find was labouring in sweat shops, making such garments as sweaters and gloves.

Although Jimmy was unknowingly learning the clothing business, his low-paying job didn't provide him with enough money to purchase the basic necessities of life. He was often caught sleeping on work premises, for he couldn't afford a place to live. But Jimmy didn't let such difficulties get the best of him. After all, he had only one way to go, and that was up! Instead, he looked at this as an opportunity to better himself. He spent many of those long, cold, lonesome nights teaching himself English. His fluency with the language years later opened the doors for Lai to move up to manager of the garment factory. As a manager, Jimmy was able to travel abroad, gaining more insight about the knitwear business.

Then in 1981, Jimmy Lai started his own business—Giordano Holdings Ltd. In just twelve years, his business has grown to over 600 shops (about 150 that he still personally manages), selling a variety of expensive tee and polo shirts, sweaters, and jeans in Hong Kong, Japan, Southwest Asia, and China. Company sales rose in 1993 to $260 million, netting Jimmy about $20 million profit.

How did Jimmy succeed in all these retail shops spread out over many miles? Lai has a system. That is, he knows when inventories need to be replaced. He understands how many employees are needed to staff each store, with extra personnel on hand for peak sales periods. Jimmy also recognizes that each outlet store must maintain its profitability. He assists each store in this area by developing budgets and implementing controls to ensure that budgets are adhered to. And finally, Lai must forecast. He needs to be able to predict with some certainty what trends he'll face in the next fashion season.

Jimmy Lai reminisces about his rags-to-riches life.

Through it all, and keeping tabs on the pulse of the day-to-day operations of his business, Jimmy Lai has come a long way. This young lad, born into poverty, is now worth better than $200 million.

In this chapter, we'll discuss a number of basic planning tools and techniques. We'll begin by looking at three planning techniques to assist managers in assessing their environment—environmental scanning, forecasting, and benchmarking. We'll review the most popular planning tool used by managers: budgets. We'll then discuss scheduling, break-even analysis, and other operational planning tools. Finally, we'll conclude this chapter by offering some ideas to help you in your personal, day-to-day planning.

Assessing the Environment

In our last chapter, we introduced planning and the strategic management process. In this section, we want to review several techniques that have been developed to help managers with one of the most challenging aspects of this process: assessing their organization's environment. Twenty years ago, environmental analysis was an informal endeavour based

Where does Goodyear look to see what its biggest competitor is doing next? It scans Michelin's operations in France and Japan because these products typically show up shortly in Canada.

on intuitive judgments. Today, using structured techniques such as environmental scanning, forecasting, and benchmarking, a manager's ability to accurately analyse an organization's environment has improved measurably.

What Is Environmental Scanning?

Poco Petroleums, of Calgary, Alberta, has developed from a small producer and marketer of gas to one of the top three non-aggregator exporters to the United States, along with Shell and Mobil (non-aggregators principally sell the gas they produce: aggregators sell gas they acquire). It accomplished this by carefully scanning the environment and recognizing the changes needed to survive and prosper. By understanding the changes taking place in the market, the regulation changes affecting pipelines, the evolving relationships with customers and the opportunities to buy and sell gas in either the Canadian or U.S. market wherever prices warranted, Poco has developed a strong customer base and knowledge and relationships within the exceedingly complex world of gas marketing that now makes it very difficult for competitors to catch up.

Managers, like Allen and Philip Fracassi (see Managers Who Made a Difference), in both small and large organizations, are increasingly turning to environmental scanning to anticipate and interpret changes in their environment.[2] The term, as we'll use it, refers to screening large amounts of information to detect emerging trends and create a set of scenarios.

The importance of environmental scanning was first recognized (outside of the national security establishment) by firms in the life insurance industry in the late 1970s.[3] Life insurance companies found that the demand for their product was declining. Yet all the key environmental signals they were receiving strongly favoured the sale of life insurance. The economy and population were growing. Baby boomers were finishing school, entering the labour force, and taking on family responsibilities. The market for life insurance should have been expanding, but it wasn't. What the insurance companies had failed to recognize was a fundamental change in family structure in Canada.

Young families, who represented the primary group of buyers of new insurance policies, tended to be dual-career couples who were increasingly choosing to remain childless. The life insurance needs of a family with one income, a dependent spouse, and a houseful of kids are much greater than those of a two-income family with few, if any, children. That a multibillion-dollar industry could overlook such a fundamental social trend underscored the need to develop techniques for monitoring important environmental developments.

How Does Competitive Intelligence Help?

competitor intelligence
Environmental scanning activity that seeks to identify who competitors are, what they're doing, and how their actions will affect the focus organization.

One of the fastest-growing areas of environmental scanning is **competitor intelligence**.[4] It seeks basic information about competitors: Who are they? What are they doing? How will what they're doing affect us? Accurate information on the competition can allow managers to anticipate competitor actions rather than merely react to them.

One expert on competitive intelligence emphasizes that 95 per cent of the competitor-related information an organization needs to make crucial strategic decisions is available and accessible to the public.[5] In other words, competitive intelligence isn't

Managers Who Made a Difference

ALLEN AND PHILIP FRACASSI AT PHILIP ENVIRONMENTAL "TREATING WASTE AS A RESOURCE"

The Fracassi brothers, Allen and Philip, started a waste disposal business in the 1970s hauling foundry sand from the Canron Inc. foundry in Hamilton.[6] Because they had to pay tipping fees to a landfill site, they used to dump the last load in their yard, remove the scrap by hand and then reload the sand, thereby having to dump less and pay a smaller tipping fee. They also acquired scrap that they could sell elsewhere. This was their first venture into a value-added approach to waste disposal. They now operate a business that had 1994 revenues of more than $570 million and is one of the largest integrated environmental services companies in North America.

Canada and the United States generate more than 400 million tons of non-hazardous waste a year, of which about 50 per cent comes from industry. In addition, 186 million tons of hazardous waste is produced. In the past three years, Philip Environmental has bought some 20 companies, growing to twenty times its size four years previously. It generates about 50 per cent of its revenue in the United States. And its goal is to become a sort of one-stop shop for environmental services. It handles everything from recycling paint-sludge, wire and cable scrap, to operating water and sewage treatment plants.

The challenge now is to integrate the companies it has acquired and actually cross-sell their services—in other words, provide a complete environmental waste management service. As one part of the company receives and treats waste, it may send parts of it on to another plant where it will be treated for the removal of different elements. For instance, Waxman Resources, one of its companies, will send any tin-plated copper scraps it picks up from its brass-mill customers to Metal Recovery Industries Inc, another subsidiary, for de-tinning. Aluminum scrap can be sent to Recyclage Cote-Nord Inc. in Quebec, where aluminum is recycled for reuse by industry.

Starting from zero, and through hard work and vision, the Fracassis, who immigrated to Canada in the 1960s, have built one of the fastest-growing businesses in the country, and one that is helping to tackle a major problem. ▼

organizational espionage. Advertisements, promotional materials, press releases, reports filed with government agencies, annual reports, want ads, newspaper reports, and industry studies are examples of readily accessible sources of information. Trade shows and the debriefing of your own sales staff can be other good sources of information on competitors. Many companies even regularly buy competitors' products and have their own employees evaluate them to learn about new technical innovations.

But sometimes these practices escalate and upset the parties involved. In December 1994, a mini-war of words erupted between Future Shop, an international retailer of electronic equipment and computers with 53 stores in Canada and 10 in the U.S., and A & B Sound, a regional electronics and music retailer with eight stores in British Columbia and three in Alberta. A & B accused Future Shop of sending their staff into A & B's stores to disrupt service and occupy their sales staff's time. Future Shop did not deny having its staff check pricing and sales at A & B. Peter de Verteuil, Future Shop's manager of advertising, says, "Shopping the competition is a common practice in all parts of the retail industry. In the end it's good for the customer." Bob Hitchcock, director of marketing for

A & B Sound says, "It's retail terrorism. Everybody likes to know what is going on on the sales floor of their competitors. But if they are disrupting business, it's not fair. " Where is the line between gathering competitive intelligence and guerilla-style tactics?[7]

Is There Any Way to Help Predict the Future?

scenario
A consistent view of what the future is likely to be.

revenue forecasting
Predicting future revenues.

A **scenario** is a consistent view of what the future is likely to be. If, for instance, scanning uncovers increasing interest in Congress for raising the national minimum wage, Burger King could create a multiple set of scenarios to assess the possible consequences of such an action. What would be the implications for its labour supply if the minimum were raised to $5.00 an hour? How about $5.50 an hour? What effect would these changes have on labour costs? How might competitors respond? Different assumptions would lead to different outcomes. The intention of this exercise is not to try to predict the future but to reduce uncertainty by playing out potential situations under different specified conditions.[8] Burger King could, for example, develop a set of scenarios ranging from optimistic to pessimistic in terms of the minimum-wage issue. It would then be better prepared to initiate changes in its strategy to gain and hold a competitive advantage.

What Are the Different Types of Forecasts?

Environmental scanning creates the foundation for forecasts. Information obtained through scanning is used to form scenarios. These, in turn, establish premises for forecasts, which are predictions of future outcomes. Probably the two most popular outcomes for which management is likely to seek forecasts are future revenues and new technological breakthroughs. However, virtually any component in the organization's general and specific environment can receive forecasting attention.

Sara Lee's sales level drives purchasing requirements, production goals, employment needs, inventories, and numerous other decisions. Similarly, BCIT's income from tuition and government grants will determine course offerings, staffing needs, salary increases for faculty, and the like. Both of these examples illustrate that predicting future revenues—**revenue forecasting**—is a critical element of planning for both profit and not-for-profit organizations.

Technological forecasting has become a necessity for organizational survival. Had companies like Columbia Records and MCA not adapted to technological changes and consumer preferences for CDs, their ability to compete in today's markets may have been significantly hampered.

Where Does Management Get the Data for Developing Revenue Forecasts?
Typically, management obtains data for developing revenue forecasts by reviewing historical revenue figures. For example, what were last year's revenues? This figure can then be adjusted for trends. What revenue patterns have evolved over recent years? What changes in social, economic, or other factors in the general environment might alter the pattern in the future? In the specific environment, what actions can we expect from our competitors? Answers to questions like these provide the basis for revenue forecasts.

Between 1986 and 1990, some firms, including Columbia and MCA, saw one of their basic products—vinyl long-playing records—almost disappear. Consumers still wanted to listen to music, but they preferred a new technology: compact discs. The record companies that successfully forecasted this technology and foresaw its impact on their business were able to convert their production facilities, adopt the technology, and beat their competition to the record store racks. Ironically, CDs are already under attack from digital tape technology. Again, those in the music business who accurately forecast when, or if, this technology will become the preferred music medium are likely to score big in the market.

What Is Technological Forecasting?
Technological forecasting attempts to predict changes in technology and the time frame in which new technologies are likely to be

Planning Tools and Techniques

economically feasible. The rapid pace of technological change has seen innovations in lasers, biotechnology, robotics, and data communications dramatically change surgery practices, pharmaceutical offerings, the processes used for manufacturing almost every mass-produced product, and the practicality of cellular telephones. Few organizations are exempt from the possibility that technological innovation might dramatically change the demand for their current products or services. The environmental scanning techniques discussed in the previous section can provide data on potential technological innovations.

What Are the Different Types of Forecasting Techniques? Forecasting techniques fall into two categories: quantitative and qualitative. **Quantitative forecasting** applies a set of mathematical rules to a series of past data to predict future outcomes. These techniques are preferred when management has sufficient "hard" data from which to work. **Qualitative forecasting,** on the other hand, uses the judgment and opinions of knowledgeable individuals. Qualitative techniques typically are used when precise data are scarce or difficult to obtain.

Exhibit 4-1 lists some of the better-known quantitative and qualitative forecasting techniques.

quantitative forecasting
Applies a set of mathematical rules to a series of past data to predict future outcomes.

qualitative forecasting
Uses the judgment and opinions of knowledgeable individuals to predict future outcomes.

How Can Benchmarking Help?

Another planning tool is **benchmarking.** This is the search for the best practices among competitors or noncompetitors that lead to their superior performance.[9] The basic idea underlying benchmarking is that management can improve quality by analysing and then copying the methods of the leaders in various fields. As such, benchmarking is a very specific form of environmental scanning (see Ethical Dilemmas in Management).

benchmarking
The search for the best practices among competitors or noncompetitors that lead to their superior performance.

TECHNIQUES	DESCRIPTION	APPLICATION
Quantitative		
Time-series analysis	Fits a trend line to a mathematical equation and projects into the future by means of this equation	Predicting next quarter's sales based on four years of previous sales data
Regression models	Predicts one variable on the basis of known or assumed other variables	Seeking factors that will predict a certain level of sales (for example, price, advertising expenditures)
Econometric models	Uses a set of regression equations to simulate segments of the economy	Predicting change in car sales as a result of changes in tax laws
Economic indicators	Uses one or more economic indicators to predict a future state of the economy	Using change in GNP to predict discretionary income
Substitution-effect	Uses a mathematical formulation to predict how, when, and under what circumstances a new product or technology will replace an existing one	Predicting the effect of microwave ovens on the sale of conventional ovens
Qualitative		
Jury of opinion	Combines and averages the opinions of experts	Polling all the company's personnel managers to predict next year's college recruitment needs
Sales-force composition	Combines estimates from field sales personnel of customers' expected purchases	Predicting next year's sales of industrial lasers
Customer evaluation	Combines estimates from established customers of expected purchases	Surveying of major dealers by a car manufacturer to determine types and quantities of products desired

Exhibit 4-1 Forecasting Techniques

Ethical Dilemmas in Management

▼ WHEN DOES COMPETITIVE INTELLIGENCE BECOME ESPIONAGE? ▲

Texas Instruments hires a senior engineering executive from Motorola. While the new executive is certainly well qualified for his new position, so were a dozen or so other candidates. However, they didn't work for Motorola and have up-to-date knowledge of what new microchip products Motorola was developing. Is it unethical for Texas Instruments, one of Motorola's primary microchip competitors, to hire this executive? Is it acceptable to hire this executive but unacceptable to question him about Motorola's plans?

The vice-president at a major book publishing company encourages one of her editors to interview for an editorial vacancy at a competing book publisher. The editor isn't interested in the position. The sole purpose of the interview will be to gain as much information as possible on the competitor's near-term publishing list and relay that information back to the vice-president. Is going to such an interview unethical? Is asking a subordinate to engage in this intelligence mission unethical?

Neither of these situations involves obtaining publicly available information. Yet tactics like these are practised by organizations in a number of highly competitive businesses. When does competitive intelligence become espionage? Does any effort to conceal one's real motives when attempting to gather information automatically brand that action as unethical? What do you think?

These German autoworkers, producers of Volkswagens, will benchmark their product lines against the industry leaders in an effort to regain their world-class standing.

Xerox undertook what is widely regarded as the first benchmarking effort in North America in 1979. Up until then, the Japanese had been aggressively copying the successes of others by travelling around, watching what others were doing, and then applying their new knowledge to improve their products and processes. Xerox's management couldn't figure out how Japanese manufacturers could sell midsize copiers for considerably less than Xerox's production costs. So the company's head of manufacturing took a team to Japan to make a detailed study of their competition's costs and processes. They got most of their information from Xerox's own joint venture, Fuji-Xerox, which knew its competition well. What the team found was shocking. Their Japanese rivals were light-years ahead of Xerox in efficiency. Benchmarking those efficiencies marked the beginning of Xerox's recovery in the copier field. Today, in addition to Xerox, companies such as Magna, Bombardier, Ford, and Motorola use benchmarking as a standard tool in their quest for quality improvement.

To illustrate its use in practice, let's look at its application at Ford Motor Company. Ford used benchmarking in the early 1980s in developing its highly successful Taurus. The company compiled a list of some 400 features its customers said were the most important and then set about finding the car with the best of each. Then it tried to match or top the best of the competition. When the Taurus was updated in 1992, Ford benchmarked all over again. For instance, the door handles on the latest Taurus were benchmarked against the Chevrolet Lumina, the easy-to-change taillight bulbs against the Nissan Maxima, and the tilt steering wheel against the Honda Accord.

The Waterford hospital in St. John's began its plan to become a leading psychiatric hospital in Canada by looking at all of its departments and processes, then identifying which hospital in Canada had the best example of these departments or processes, visiting each hospital to find out what they were doing and how they were doing it, identifying the elements that contributed to being the best, and then focusing on doing these things as well, or, in most cases, better than they were being done elsewhere. Benchmarking allows an organization to take established best practices and develop them further.

Budgets

Few of us are unfamiliar with budgets. Most of us learned about them at an early age, when we discovered that unless we allocated our "revenues" carefully, we would consume our weekly allowance before half the week was out. A **budget** is a numerical plan for allocating resources to specific activities. Managers typically prepare budgets for revenues, expenses, and such capital expenditures as machinery and equipment. It's not unusual, though, for budgets to be used for improving time, space, and the use of material resources. These latter types of budgets substitute nondollar numbers for dollar terms. Such items as person-hours, capacity utilization, or units of production can be budgeted for daily, weekly, or monthly activities. However, we'll emphasize dollar-based budgets.

budget
A numerical plan for allocating resources to specific activities.

Why Are Budgets So Popular?

Budgets are popular probably because they are applicable to a wide variety of organizations and units within an organization. We live in a world in which almost everything is expressed in monetary units. Dollars, pesos, francs, yen, and the like are used as a common denominator within a country. Even human life has a monetary value. Insurance actuaries regularly compute the value of a lost eye, arm, or leg. While most people argue that life is priceless, Canadian insurance companies and juries regularly convert the loss of human body parts or life itself into dollars and cents. It seems logical, then, that monetary budgets make a useful common denominator for directing activities in such diverse departments as production and marketing research or at various levels in an organization. Budgets are one planning device that most managers, regardless of level in the organization, help to formulate.

What Are the Primary Types of Budgets?

There is no shortage of items or areas for which budgets can be used. The following—revenue budgets, expense budgets, profit budgets, cash budgets, capital expenditure budgets, fixed and variable budgets—represent the ones managers are most likely to use. Exhibit 4-2 provides an overview of each.

Revenue Budget:	A budget that projects future sales.
Expense Budget:	A budget that lists the primary activities undertaken by a unit and allocates a dollar amount to each.
Profit Budget:	A budget used by separate units of an organization that combines revenue and expense budgets to determine the units.
Cash Budget:	A budget that forecasts how much cash an organization will have on hand and how much it will need to meet expenses.
Capital Expenditure Budget:	A budget that forecasts investments in property, buildings, and major equipment.
Fixed Budget:	A budget that assumes a fixed level of sales or production.
Variable Budget:	A budget that takes into account those costs that vary with volume.

Exhibit 4-2 Types of Budgets

incremental budget
A budget that allocates funds to departments according to allocations in the previous period.

zero-based budgeting (ZBB)
A system in which budget requests start from scratch, regardless of previous appropriations.

How Do Incremental Budgets Differ from Zero-Based Budgets? There are essentially two approaches managers can take to budgeting. By far the most popular approach is the incremental or traditional budget. But in recent years, managers in some organizations have been trying to make budgets more effective by experimenting with the zero-based budget. Let's look at each of these approaches.

The **incremental** (or traditional) **budget** has two identifying characteristics. First, funds are allocated to departments or organizational units. The managers of these units then allocate funds to activities as they see fit. Second, an incremental budget develops out of the previous budget. Each period's budget begins by using the last period as a reference point. Only incremental changes in the budget request are reviewed. Each of these characteristics, however, creates a problem.

When funds are allocated to organizational units, it becomes difficult to differentiate activities within units. Why? Because organizational units typically have a multiple set of goals and hence engage in a number of activities. Incremental budgets don't take this diversity of activities into consideration. They focus on providing funds for units rather than for activities within the units. Given that units have multiple goals, it seems reasonable to conclude that (1) some goals are more important than others, and (2) unit managers have varying degrees of success in achieving these multiple goals. Incremental budgets throw everything into the same pot. Thus, as planning devices, they lack sufficient focus and specificity.

Zero-based budgeting (ZBB), originally developed by Texas Instruments, requires managers to justify their budget requests in detail from scratch, regardless of previous appropriations.[10] It's designed to attack the second drawback we mentioned in incremental budgets: activities that have a way of becoming immortal. Once established, organizational activities can take on lives of their own. This is especially true in public organizations.

ZBB shifts the burden of proof to the manager to justify why his or her unit should get any budget at all. The ZBB process reevaluates all organizational activities to see which should be eliminated, funded at a reduced level, funded at the current level, or increased (see Details on a Management Classic).

Why Isn't Zero-Based Budgeting Appropriate for All Organizations? The difficulty and expense of implementing ZBB suggest that it is not for every organization.

Details on a Management Classic

TEXAS INSTRUMENTS'S ZERO-BASED BUDGETING TECHNIQUE

When Texas Instruments was developing its budgeting system, the company decided on a three-part process. These three steps consisted of the following:

▶ 1. Each discrete departmental activity is broken down into a decision package.
▶ 2. The individual decision packages are ranked according to their benefit to the organization during the budget period.

Planning Tools and Techniques

▶ **3.** Budget resources are allocated to the individual packages according to preferential rank in the organization[11] (see Exhibit 4-3).

The decision package is a document that identifies and describes a specific activity. Usually prepared by operating managers, it includes a statement of the expected result or purpose of the activity, its costs, personnel requirements, measures of performance, alternative courses of action, and an evaluation of the benefits from performance and consequences of nonperformance from an organizationwide perspective. In more specific terms, each package lists a number of alternative methods of performing the activity, recommends one of these alternatives, and delineates effort levels. These effort levels identify spending targets—for instance, how the activity would be completed at 70, 90, and 110 per cent of the current budget level. Any large organization that adopts ZBB will have literally thousands of these packages.

Once departmental managers have completed the decision packages, the packages are forwarded to the top executive group, which determines how much to spend and where to spend it. This is done by ascertaining the total amount to be spent by the organization and then by ranking all packages in order of decreasing benefits to the organization. Packages are accepted down to the spending level. When properly executed, the ZBB process carefully evaluates every organizational activity, assigns it a priority, and results in either the continuation, modification, or termination of the activity.

ZBB is no panacea. Like incremental budgeting, it has its own set of drawbacks.[12] It increases paperwork and requires time to prepare; the important activities that managers want funded tend to have their benefits inflated; and the eventual outcome rarely differs much from what would occur through an incremental budget. ▼

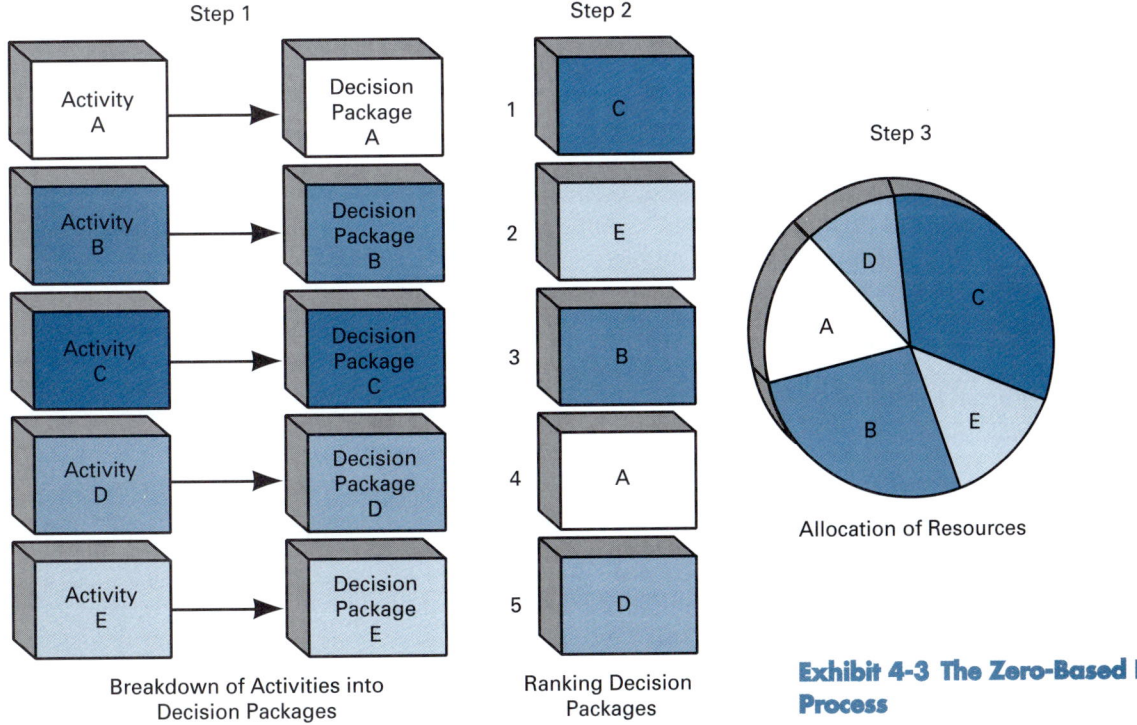

Exhibit 4-3 The Zero-Based Budget Process

The politics of large organizations often undermine any potential gain that ZBB might produce. It is possibly most effective in smaller public organizations, in supporting staff units in business firms, or in declining organizations. For example, because the resource requirements of staff units in business firms, which include areas like market research and human resource management, are rarely related directly to the firm's output, it's difficult to determine whether their budgets are realistic or denote efficient operation. Thus, for this type of unit, ZBB may be a valuable planning and control device. Also, ZBB is compatible with managing declining resources.[13] When organizations face cutbacks and financial restraints, their managers particularly look for devices that allocate limited resources effectively. ZBB can be just such a device.

Operational Planning Tools

What Is Scheduling?

If you were to observe a group of supervisors or department managers for a few days, you would see them regularly detailing what activities have to be done, the order in which they are to be done, who is to do each, and when they are to be completed. The managers are doing what we call **scheduling.** In the material that follows, we will review some useful scheduling devices.

How Do You Use a Gantt Chart?

The **Gantt chart** was developed around the turn of the century by Henry Gantt (see the Appendix), a protégé of Frederick Taylor. The idea is inherently simple. It is essentially a bar graph with time on the horizontal axis and the activities to be scheduled on the vertical axis. The bars show output, both planned and actual, over a period of time. The Gantt chart visually shows when tasks are supposed to be done and compares that to the actual progress on each. It is a simple but important device that allows managers to detail easily what has yet to be done to complete a job or project and to assess whether it is ahead of, behind, or on schedule.

A modified version of the Gantt chart is called a **load chart.** Instead of listing activities on the vertical axis, load charts list either whole departments or specific resources. This allows managers to plan and control for capacity utilization. In other words, load charts schedule capacity by work stations. An example of a load chart for six production editors from the same firm is shown in Exhibit 4-4.

What Is a PERT Network Analysis?

Gantt and load charts are helpful as long as the activities or projects being scheduled are few in number and independent of each other. But what if a manager had to plan

How do you run a successful restaurant? You provide customers with quality value meals. You also make sure you have enough people scheduled to meet customer demand.

scheduling
A listing of necessary activities, their order of accomplishment, who is to do each, and time needed to complete them.

Gantt chart
A graphic bar chart that shows the relationship between work planned and completed on one axis and time elapsed on the other.

load chart
A modified Gantt chart that schedules capacity by work stations.

Planning Tools and Techniques

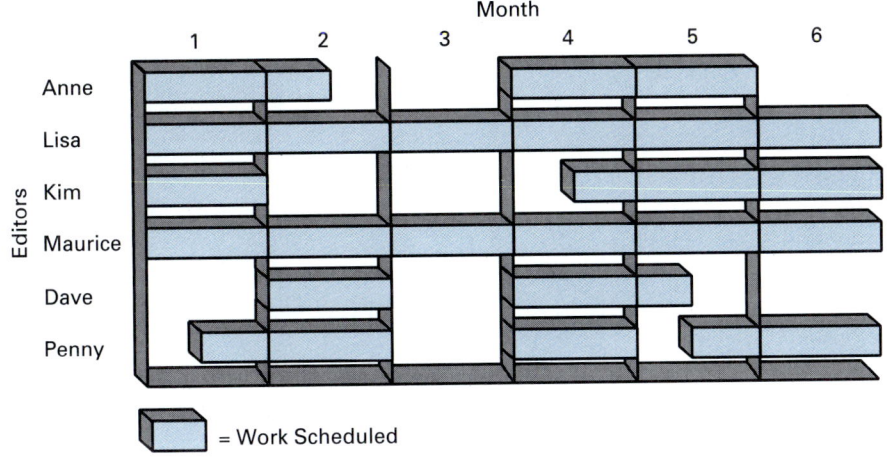

Exhibit 4-4 An Example of a Load Chart

a large project such as a reorganization, the launching of a cost-reduction campaign, or the development of a new product that required coordinating inputs from marketing, production, and product design personnel? Such projects require coordinating hundreds or thousands of activities, some of which must be done simultaneously and some of which cannot begin until earlier activities have been completed. If you're constructing a building, you obviously can't start erecting walls until the foundation is laid. How, then, can you schedule such a complex project? You could use the Program Evaluation and Review Technique.

The **Program Evaluation and Review Technique**—usually just called PERT or PERT network analysis—was originally developed in the late 1950s for coordinating the more than 3,000 contractors and agencies working on the Polaris submarine weapon system.[14] This project was incredibly complicated, with hundreds of thousands of activities that had to be coordinated. PERT is reported to have cut two years off the completion date for the Polaris project.

A **PERT network** is a flowchartlike diagram that depicts the sequence of activities needed to complete a project and the time or costs associated with each activity. With a PERT network, a project manager must think through what has to be done, determine which events depend on one another, and identify potential trouble spots (see Exhibit 4-5). PERT also makes it easy to compare the effects alternative actions will have on scheduling and costs. Thus, PERT allows managers to monitor a project's progress, identify possible bottlenecks, and shift resources as necessary to keep the project on schedule.

What Are the Key Components of PERT? To understand how to construct a PERT network, you need to know three terms: events, activities, and critical path. Let's define these terms, outline the steps in the PERT process, and then develop an example.

Events are end points that represent the completion of major activities. Sometimes called milestones, events indicate that something significant has happened (like receipt of purchased items) or an important component is finished. In PERT, events represent a point in time. **Activities,** on the other hand, are the actions that take place. Activities consume time, which represents the time or resources required to progress from one event to another. The **critical path** is the longest or most time-consuming sequence

Program Evaluation and Review Technique (PERT)
A technique for scheduling complicated projects comprising many activities, some of which are interdependent.

PERT network
A flowchartlike diagram showing the sequence of activities needed to complete a project and the time or costs associated with each.

events
End points that represent the completion of major activities in a PERT network.

activities
The time or resources needed to progress from one event to another in a PERT network.

critical path
The longest sequence of activities in a PERT network.

To coordinate some 3,000-plus subcontractors in the building of this submarine, a PERT chart was used. In doing so, two years were cut off the completion date for the project.

of events and activities required to complete the project in the shortest amount of time. Let's work through a simplified example.

Assume that you are the superintendent for a residential home builder. You have been assigned to oversee the construction of a custom home. Because time really is money in your business, you must determine how long it will take to put up the house. You have carefully dissected the entire project into activities and events. Exhibit 4-6 outlines the major events in the construction project and your estimate of the expected time required to complete each activity. Exhibit 4-7 depicts the PERT network based on the data in Exhibit 4-6.

**Exhibit 4-5
Developing PERT Charts**

Developing a PERT network requires the manager to identify all key activities needed to complete a project, rank them in order of dependence, and estimate each activity's completion time. This can be translated into five specific steps:

▶ **1.** Identify every significant activity that must be achieved for a project to be completed. The accomplishment of each activity results in a set of events or outcomes.

▶ **2.** Ascertain the order in which these events must be completed.

▶ **3.** Diagram the flow of activities from start to finish, identifying each activity and its relationship to all other activities. Use circles to indicate events and arrows to represent activities. This results in a flowchart diagram that we call the PERT network.

▶ **4.** Compute a time estimate for completing each activity. This is done with a weighted average that employs an optimistic time estimate (t_o) of how long the activity would take under ideal conditions, a most-likely estimate (t_m) of the time the activity normally should take, and a pessimistic estimate (t_p) that represents the time that an activity should take under the worst possible conditions. The formula for calculating the expected time (t_e) is then

$$t_e = \frac{t_o + 4t_m + t_p}{6}$$

▶ **5.** Finally, using a network diagram that contains time estimates for each activity, the manager can determine a schedule for the start and finish dates of each activity and for the entire project. Any delays that occur along the critical path require the most attention because they delay the entire project. That is, the critical path has no slack in it; therefore, any delay along that path immediately translates into a delay in the final deadline for the completed project.

Planning Tools and Techniques

Exhibit 4-6 Major Events in Building a House

EVENT	DESCRIPTION	TIME WEEKS	PREDECESSOR ACTIVITY
A	Approve Design and Get Permits	3	None
B	Perform Excavation/Lot Clearing	1	A
C	Pour Footers	1	B
D	Erect Foundation Walls	2	C
E	Frame House	4	D
F	Instal Windows	.5	E
G	Shingle Roof	.5	E
H	Instal Brick Front and Siding	4	F, G
I	Instal Electrical, Plumbing, and Heating A/C Rough Ins	6	E
J	Instal Insulation	.25	I
K	Instal Sheetrock	2	J
L	Finish and Sand Sheetrock	7	K
M	Instal Interior Trim	2	L
N	Paint House (Interior and Exterior)	2	H, M
O	Instal All Cabinets	.5	N
P	Instal Flooring	1	N
Q	Final Touch Up and Turn Over House to Homeowner	1	O, P

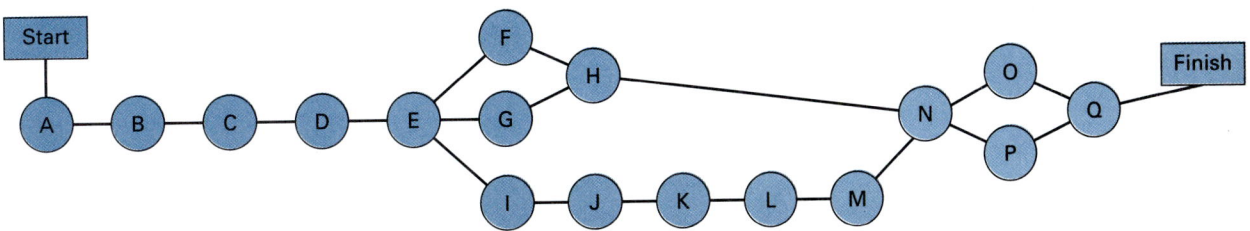

Exhibit 4-7 A PERT Network for Erecting a House

Your PERT network tells you that if everything goes as planned, it will take just over thirty-two weeks to complete the house. This is calculated by tracing the network's critical path: A-B-C-D-E-I-J-K-L-M-N-P-Q. Any delay in completing the events along this path will delay the completion of the entire project. For example, if it took six weeks instead of four to frame the house (event E), the entire project would be delayed by two weeks (or the time beyond that expected). Conversely, a delay of one week on installing the brick front and siding (event H) would have little effect because this event is not on the critical path. Now back to our critical path dilemma.

Notice how the critical path passes through activities N-P-Q. Looking at just these three activities, we notice from our PERT chart (Exhibit 4-6) that it takes four weeks. Wouldn't path N-O-Q be faster? In fact, the PERT network shows that it takes 3.5 weeks to complete this. So why isn't N-O-Q on the critical path? Because activity Q cannot begin until both activities O and P are completed. Although activity O takes one-half

slack time
The difference between the critical path time and the time of all other paths.

week, activity P takes one full week. Thus, the earliest we can begin Q is after one week. So what happens to the difference between the critical activity (activity P) and the non-critical activity (activity O)? The difference, in this case one-half week, becomes **slack time**. Slack time, then, is the time difference between the critical path and all other paths. And what use is there for slack? If the project manager notices a possible slippage on a critical activity, quite possibly slack time from a noncritical activity can be borrowed and temporarily assigned to work on the critical one.

How Is PERT Both a Planning and a Control Tool? Not only does PERT help us to estimate the times associated with scheduling a project, it also gives us clues about where our controls should be placed. Because any event on the critical path that is delayed will delay the overall project (not only making us late, but probably also over budget), our attention needs to be focused on them at all times. For example, if in our house-building example activity H (installing the brick front and siding) is delayed by a week because supplies have not arrived, that is not a major issue. But if activity O (installing cabinets) is delayed from one-half week to one week, the entire project will be delayed by one-half week. As such, anything that has the immediate potential for delaying a project (critical activities) must be monitored very closely.

What Is Break-Even Analysis?

Companies like Kinko's and Carla's Photocopying Service use break-even analysis to determine the relationship among revenues, costs, and profits.

How many units of a product must an organization sell in order to break-even—that is, to have neither profit nor loss? A manager might want to know the minimum number of units that must be sold to achieve his or her profit objective or whether a current product should continue to be sold or be dropped from the organization's product line. **Break-even analysis** is a widely used technique for helping managers to make profit projections.[15]

Break-even analysis is a simplistic formulation, yet it is valuable to managers because it points out the relationship among revenues, costs, and profits. To compute the break-even point (BE), the manager needs to know the unit price of the product being sold (P), the variable cost per unit (VC), and total fixed costs (TFC).

break-even analysis
A technique for identifying the point at which total revenue is just sufficient to cover total costs.

An organization breaks even when its total revenue is just enough to equal its total costs. But total cost has two parts: a fixed component and a variable component. Fixed costs are expenses that do not change, regardless of volume. Examples include insurance premiums and property taxes. Fixed costs, of course, are fixed only in the short term because, in the long run, commitments terminate and are thus subject to variation. Variable costs change in proportion to output and include raw materials, labour costs, and energy costs.

The break-even point can be computed graphically or by using the following formula:

$$BE = \frac{TFC}{P - VC}$$

This formula tells us that (1) total revenue will equal total cost when we sell enough units at a price that covers all variable unit costs, and (2) the difference between price and variable costs, when multiplied by the number of units sold, equals the fixed costs.

Planning Tools and Techniques

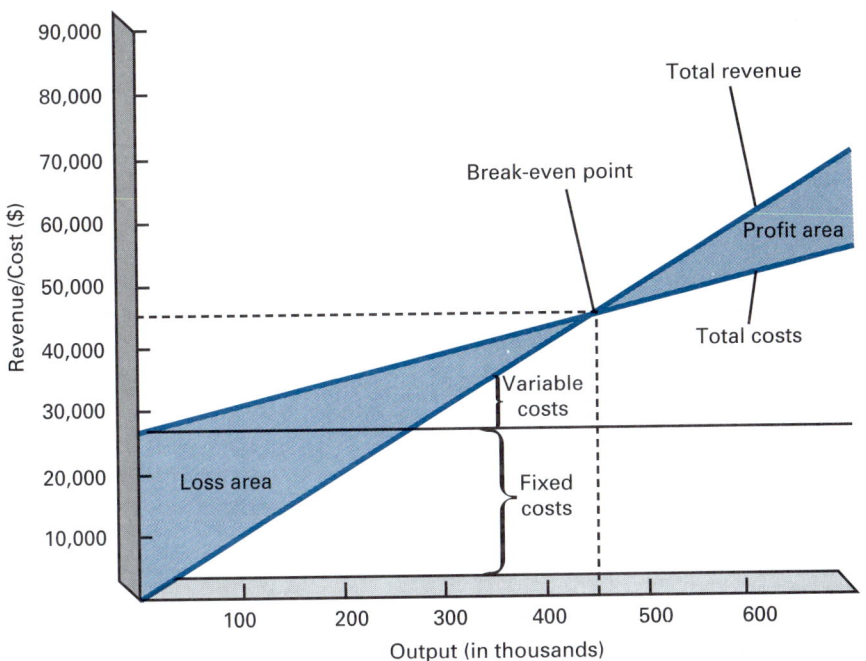

Exhibit 4-8 Break-Even Analysis

When Is Break-Even Useful? To demonstrate, assume that Carla's Photocopying Service charges $0.10 per photocopy. If fixed costs are $27,000 a year and variable costs are $0.04 per copy, Carla can compute her break-even point as follows: $27,000 / ($0.10 − $0.04) = 450,000 copies, or when annual revenues are $45,000. This same relationship is shown graphically in Exhibit 4-8.

How Can Break-Even Serve as a Planning Tool? As a planning tool, break-even analysis could help Carla to set her sales objective. For example, she could establish the profit she wants and then work backward to determine what sales level is needed to reach that profit. Break-even analysis could also tell Carla how much volume has to increase to break-even if she's currently operating at a loss or how much volume she can afford to lose and still break-even if she's currently operating profitably. In some cases, such as the management of professional sports franchises, break-even analysis has shown the projected volume of ticket sales required to cover all costs to be so unrealistically high that the best action for management to take is to sell or close the business.

What Is Linear Programming and What Kinds of Problems Lend Themselves to It?

Paul Adams has a manufacturing plant that produces two kinds of music players: compact disc players and laser disc players. Business is good. He can sell all of the music players he can produce. This is his dilemma: Given that both players go through the same production departments, how many of each type should he make to maximize his profits?

A closer look at Paul's operation tells us that he can use a mathematical technique called **linear programming** to solve his resource allocation dilemma. As we'll show, linear programming is applicable to Paul's problem, but it can't be applied to all resource

linear programming
A mathematical technique that solves resource allocation problems.

allocation situations. Besides requiring limited resources and the objective of optimization, it requires that there be alternative ways of combining resources to produce a number of output mixes. There must also be a linear relationship between variables.[17] This means that a change in one variable will be accompanied by an exactly proportional change in the other. For Paul's business, this condition would be met if it took exactly twice the amount of raw materials and hours of labor to produce two of a given music player as it took to produce one.

Many different types of problems can be solved using linear programming. For instance, selecting transportation routes that minimize shipping costs, allocating a limited advertising budget among various product brands, making the optimum assignment of personnel among projects, and determining how much of each product to make with a limited number of resources are just a few. To give you some idea of how linear programming is useful, let's return to Paul's problem and see how linear programming could help him to solve it. Fortunately, Paul's problem is relatively simple, so we can solve it rather quickly. For complex linear programming problems, there is computer software that has been designed specifically to help develop solutions.

First, we need to establish some facts about Paul's business. Paul has computed the profit margins on the music players at $100 for the compact discs and $180 for the laser discs. He can therefore express his objective function as: maximum profit = $100R + $180S, where R is the number of compact discs produced and S is the number of laser discs. Additionally, Paul knows the time each compact disc must spend in each department and the monthly production capacity (1,200 hours in manufacturing and 900 hours in assembly) for the two departments (see Exhibit 4-9). The production capacity numbers act as constraints on his overall capacity. Now Paul can establish his constraint equations:

$$2R + 4S \leq 1,200$$
$$2R + 2S \leq 900$$

Of course, since neither music player can be produced in a volume less than zero, Paul can also state that $R \geq 0$ and $S \geq 0$.

Paul has graphed his solution as shown in Exhibit 4-10. The shaded area represents the options that don't exceed the capacity of either department. This area represents his feasibility region. Paul's optimal resource allocation will be defined at one of the corners within this feasibility region. Point C is the farthest from the origin and provides the maximum profits within the constraints stated. At point A, profits would be zero. At points B and D, profits would be $54,000 and $45,000, respectively. At point C, however, profits would be $57,000.

Why do organizations like this grocery store have only a few cash registers open? Because employing queuing theory has shown them that they can balance the cost of waiting in line against the cost of maintaining that line.

What Is Queuing Theory and When Is It Useful?

queuing theory
A technique that balances the cost of having a waiting line against the cost of service to maintain that line.

You are a supervisor for a 24-hour supermarket. One of the decisions you have to make is how many of the eighteen cash registers you should keep open at any given time. **Queuing theory,** or what is frequently referred to as waiting-line theory, could assist you with this problem.

Whenever a decision involves balancing the cost of having a waiting line against

Planning Tools and Techniques

DEPARTMENT	NUMBER OF HOURS REQUIRED (PER UNIT)		MONTHLY PRODUCTION CAPACITY (IN HOURS)
	COMPACT DISCS	LASER DISCS	
Manufacturing	2	4	1,200
Assembly	2	2	900
Profit per unit	$100	$180	

Exhibit 4-9 Production Data for Music Players

the cost of service to maintain that line, it can be made easier with queuing theory. This includes such common situations as determining how many gas pumps are needed at gas stations, tellers at bank windows, or check-in lines at airline ticket counters. In each situation, management wants to minimize cost by having as few stations open as possible, yet not so few as to test the patience of customers. Referring back to our supermarket example, during rush hours you could open all eighteen registers and keep waiting time to a minimum, or you could open only one, minimize staffing costs, and risk a riot.

The mathematics underlying queuing theory is beyond the scope of this book. But you can see how the theory works in a simple example. Assume that you're a bank

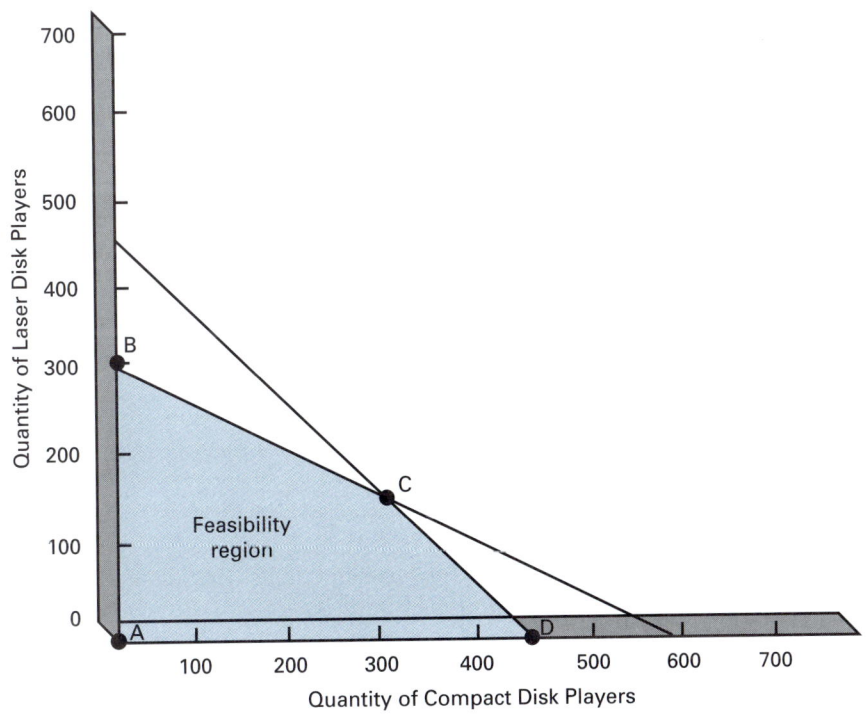

Exhibit 4-10 Graphical Solution to Paul Adams' Linear Programming Problem

Developing Management Skills

FIVE STEPS TO BETTER TIME MANAGEMENT

The essence of time management is to use your time effectively. This requires that you know the objectives you want to accomplish, the activities that will lead to the accomplishment of those objectives, and the importance and urgency of each activity. We've translated this into a five-step process.

▶ 1. **Make a list of your objectives.** What specific objectives have you set for yourself and the unit you manage? If you're using management by objectives, these objectives are already in place.

▶ 2. **Rank the objectives according to their importance.** Not all objectives are of equal importance. Given the limitations on your time, you want to make sure you give highest priority to the most important objectives.

▶ 3. **List the activities necessary to achieve your objectives.** What specific actions do you need to take to achieve your objectives? Again, if you're using MBO, these action plans are already laid out.

▶ 4. **For each objective, assign priorities to the various activities required to reach the objective.** This step imposes a second set of priorities. Here, you need to emphasize both importance and urgency. If the activity is not important, you should consider delegating it to someone below you. If it's not urgent, it can usually wait. This step will identify activities that you must do, those you should do, those you'll get to when you can, and those that can be delegated to others.

▶ 5. **Schedule your activities according to the priorities you've set.** The final step is to prepare a daily plan. Every morning, or at the end of the previous workday, make a list of the five or so most important things you want to do for the day. If the list grows to ten or more activities, it becomes cumbersome and ineffective. Then set priorities for the activities listed on the basis of importance and urgency.

supervisor. One of your responsibilities (see Developing Management Skills) is assigning tellers. You have five teller windows, but you want to know whether you can get by with only one window open during an average morning. You consider twelve minutes to be the longest you would expect any customer to wait patiently in line. If it takes four minutes, on average, to serve each customer, the line should not be permitted to get longer than three deep (12 minutes @ 4 minutes per customer = 3 customers). If you know from past experience that during the morning people arrive at the average rate of two per minute, you can calculate the probability that the line will become longer than any number (n) customers as follows:

$$P_n = \left(1 - \frac{\text{arrival rate}}{\text{service rate}}\right) \times \left(\frac{\text{arrival rate}}{\text{service rate}}\right)^n$$

where n = 3 customers, arrival rate = 2 per minute, and service rate = 4 minutes per customer. Putting these numbers into the above formula generates the following:

$$P_3 = \left(1 - \frac{2}{4}\right) \times \left(\frac{2}{4}\right)^3 = \left(\frac{1}{2}\right)\left(\frac{8}{64}\right) = \frac{8}{128} = .0625$$

What does a P_3 of .0625 mean? It tells you that the likelihood of having more than three customers in line during the morning is one chance in sixteen. Are you willing to live with four or more customers in line for 6 per cent of the time? If so, keeping one teller window open will be enough. If not, you'll need to add windows and assign additional personnel to staff them.

Planning Tools and Techniques

Summary

This Summary is organized by the chapter opening learning objectives found on page 78.

1. Techniques for scanning the environment include reading newspapers, magazines, books, and trade journals; reading competitors' ads, promotional materials, and press releases; attending trade shows; debriefing sales personnel; and analysing competitors' products.
2. Quantitative forecasting applies a set of mathematical rules to a set of past data to predict future outcomes. Qualitative forecasting uses judgments and the opinions of knowledgeable individuals to predict future outcomes.
3. Budgets are popular planning devices because money is a universal common denominator that can be used in all types of organizations and by managers at all levels.
4. The most popular approach to budgeting is the traditional, or incremental, budget, which is based on past allocations. However, its drawbacks have led to increased interest in zero-based budgets, which make no reference to past allocations.
5. Gantt and load charts are scheduling devices. Both are bar graphs. Gantt charts monitor planned and actual activities over time; load charts focus on capacity utilization by monitoring whole departments or specific resources.
6. The five steps in developing a PERT network are (1) identifying every significant activity that must be achieved for a project to be completed; (2) determining the order in which these activities must be completed; (3) diagramming the flow of activities in a project from start to finish; (4) estimating the time needed to complete each activity; and (5) using the network diagram to determine a schedule for the start and finish dates of each activity and for the entire project.
7. A product's break-even point is determined by the unit price of the product, its variable cost per unit, and its total fixed costs.
8. For linear programming to be applicable, a problem must have limited resources, constraints, an objective function to optimize, alternative ways of combining resources, and a linear relationship between variables.
9. Queuing theory can be used as a planning tool when the cost of having a waiting line is balanced against the costs incurred in maintaining that line.

Review and Discussion Questions

1. How is scanning the environment related to forecasting?
2. Assume that you manage a large fast-food restaurant in downtown Calgary and you want to know the amount of each type of sandwich to make and the number of cashiers to have on each shift. What type of planning tool(s) do you think will be useful to you? What type of environmental scanning, if any, would you likely do in this management job?
3. What is a scenario and how does competitor intelligence help managers to formulate one?
4. How can benchmarking improve the quality of an organization's products or processes?
5. What is a budget? Must it always be based on monetary units?
6. "Budgets are both a planning and a control tool." Explain this statement.
7. Develop a Gantt chart for writing a college term paper.
8. What is the significance of the critical path in a PERT network?
9. What is the value of break-even analysis as a planning tool?
10. How can queuing theory serve to make an operation more efficient?

Self-Assessment Exercise

Are You an Entrepreneur?

Instructions: This quiz is designed to see if you have the traits associated with highly successful entrepreneurs. Rate yourself on each of the characteristics using a -2 to +2 scale as described at the top of the scale.

−2 I don't really have this characteristic
−1 I don't have very much of this characteristic
 0 Neutral or don't know
+1 I have this characteristic a little bit
+2 This characteristic is very strong in me

Characteristic	−2	−1	0	+1	+2	Characteristic	−2	−1	0	+1	+2
Self-confidence	___	___	___	___	___	Resourcefulness	___	___	___	___	___
Energy, diligence	___	___	___	___	___	Need to achieve	___	___	___	___	___
Ability to take calculated risks	___	___	___	___	___	Initiative	___	___	___	___	___
Creativity	___	___	___	___	___	Independence	___	___	___	___	___
Flexibility	___	___	___	___	___	Foresight	___	___	___	___	___
Positive response to challenges	___	___	___	___	___	Profit orientation	___	___	___	___	___
Dynamism, leadership	___	___	___	___	___	Perceptiveness	___	___	___	___	___
Ability to get along with people	___	___	___	___	___	Optimism	___	___	___	___	___
Responsiveness to suggestions	___	___	___	___	___	Versatility	___	___	___	___	___
Responsiveness to criticism	___	___	___	___	___	Knowledge of product and technology	___	___	___	___	___
Knowledge of market	___	___	___	___	___						
Perseverance, determination	___	___	___	___	___						

Turn to page 412 for scoring directions and key.

Source: Robert Marx, Todd Jick, and Peter Frost, *Management Live! The Video Book* (Englewood Cliffs, N.J.: Prentice-Hall, Inc., 1991), p. 291.

Class Exercise

PERTing a Term Paper

Have you ever thought much about how you write a term paper for a course, or how long it takes? Often we just begin the project and work on it until it is finished. But that may not be the most effective way. For this exercise, you'll need to consider the following. The term paper was assigned in week one of a fifteen-week class, and it is due by the end of week fourteen. Your instructor has also included in the syllabus the following requirements. A draft of the paper must be completed by week ten. Furthermore, it must be at least twenty-five pages, and contain twenty-five sources.

Identify the activities that need to be completed to attain your objective. Estimate times associated with each activity. Draw a PERT network of your activities and determine the critical path.

When you have completed this, answer the following:

1. How much alike or different is this process you've developed from the typical way you have written a term paper?
2. How could you use this plan to better facilitate completing the term paper assignment? For getting a better grade on the assignment?
3. How can PERT be used as a means of managing one's time? Explain.

Planning Tools and Techniques

Key Terms

Key terms are listed in the order in which they appear in the chapter.

- competitor intelligence
- scenario
- revenue forecasting
- quantitative forecasting
- qualitative forecasting
- benchmarking
- budget
- incremental budget
- zero-based budgeting (ZBB)
- scheduling
- Gantt chart
- load chart
- Program Evaluation and Review Technique (PERT)
- PERT network
- events
- activities
- critical path
- slack time
- break-even analysis
- linear programming
- queuing theory

Case Application

Freight Haulers

Freight Haulers, a regional trucking company, is having profitability problems as a result of deregulation in the trucking industry. Management wants to decrease driver turnover and reduce the use of its own trucks by hiring more independent owner-operators to haul products and materials. Subsequently, management has launched a program to recruit owner-operators. The project manager responsible for achieving this goal has identified the following activities that will be required for such a program.

Activities to decrease turnover of all drivers (company and owner-operator)

A. Establish terminal facilities for drivers (food, showers, parking, and so on)
B. Implement terminal facility standards
C. Design a diesel fuel purchase program
D. Implement the diesel fuel purchase program

Activities to recruit the desired number of owner-operators

E. Advertise for owner-operators
F. Establish a bonus system for employees who recommend new owner-operators who are placed under contract
G. Revise procedures, train staff to sign up new owner-operators, and begin sign-ups

After careful thought, the project manager has concluded that some activities must be completed before others can begin. The sequencing requirements among all activities are shown in Exhibit CA4-1. The director has also computed estimates of the activity times for the driver program. They are shown in Exhibit CA4-2.

ACTIVITY	PRECEDING ACTIVITY
A. Establish terminal facility standards	None
B. Implement terminal facility standards	A
C. Design fuel program	None
D. Implement fuel program	C
F. Establish bonus system	B,D
E. Advertise	B,D
G. Sign up owner-operators	F,E

Exhibit CA4-1 Sequencing of Activities

ACTIVITY	OPTIMISTIC TIME t_o	MOST LIKELY TIME t_m	PESSIMISTIC TIME t_p
A	$2\frac{1}{2}$	$6\frac{1}{2}$	$7\frac{1}{2}$
B	15	20	37
C	2	4	6
D	5	$6\frac{1}{2}$	11
E	3	5	7
F	$\frac{1}{2}$	2	$3\frac{1}{2}$
G	5	6	7

Exhibit CA4-2 Activity Time Estimates for Driver Program (in weeks)

Source: Adapted from Charles N. Greene, Everett E. Adam, Jr., and Ronald J. Ebert, *Management for Effective Performance* (Englewood Cliffs, N.J.: Prentice-Hall, 1985), pp. 736–37. With permission.

Knowing Your Competition and Your Market

The shoe and boot industry in Canada has gone through a major decline over the last 20 years. In the first three years of this decade alone, 1,000 retail shoe stores closed. Canadian manufacturers at the low and medium end of the market have been driven out of business by low-priced imports from Brazil, while at the high end where fashion, good looks, high quality, careful finish and high detail is important, Italian shoes own the market. So what's left? Only about 20 per cent of the shoes sold in Canadian stores and Canadian made. And they're largely in one specific area, the one area where Canadians know the business better than anyone else: winter boots, or to be more specific, waterproof boots.

Canadian manufacturers know winter. Ninety per cent of the toe rubbers made in Canada, for instance, come from the Acton Rubber Plant in Actonville, Quebec. Waterproof boots are a competitive niche that is dominated by Canadian producers, 65 of whom are in the province of Quebec. It's an $850-million industry in Canada, and employs 12,000 people — only 4,000 less than it did 25 years ago, which, considering the degree of sophisticated automation that has been introduced, is a good indicator of growth in this segment of the market. Acton Rubber employs more than 300 people and exports more than 30 per cent of its production.

The waterproof boot producers keep a keen eye on their competition, but they maintain an edge no producer in Asia can match — they live in climates of –30° C and they know what works and what doesn't. They also maintain a constant environmental scan, and have uncovered markets as far away as Texas where it also snows and slushes on occasion. And they have invested in modern technology and processes that have made them more responsive to changing market demands. Manufacturers can now ship a product three to four weeks after having ordered the raw materials, whereas 10 years ago it took three to four months.

Questions

1. What sort of information would an environmental scan by a Canadian waterproof boot manufacturer look for? What areas would it scan?
2. How important is competitive intelligence for manufacturers in this sector? What do they need to know?
3. If you were to run a boot manufacturing plant in Canada, what would you benchmark, and against whom would you make the comparisons?

Video Resource: "Boots," *Venture* 474 (February 6, 1994).

Foundations of Decision Making

Learning Objectives

WHAT WILL I BE ABLE TO DO AFTER I FINISH THIS CHAPTER?

1. Outline the steps in the decision-making process.
2. Define the rational decision maker.
3. Explain the limits to rationality.
4. Describe the perfectly rational decision-making process.
5. Describe the bounded rational decision-making process.
6. Identify the two types of decision problems and the two types of decisions that are used to solve them.
7. Identify the advantages and disadvantages of group decisions.
8. Describe four techniques for improving group decision making.

A retailing trend that is attracting a lot of attention (and a lot of customers) is what the industry calls Big Box stores—the megastores like Price Club-Costco that sell a mix of goods that includes groceries, garden and office furniture, inflatable rubber rafts, shower stalls, paint, jewelry, CD players, cordless phones, sporting goods, car accessories, refrigerators and ranges, tools and countless other items. Several things make them stand out as being very different. First, they're huge, often the size of one or two football fields. And second, they don't do a lot of things that other retailers do, like offer service, advertise, or have in-store specials or comforting atmospheres. And to top it all off, they charge a membership fee for the privilege of shopping. But despite going against all these accepted retail practices, Price Club-Costco has attracted 300,000 members in British Columbia alone.

Vast changes have swept the retail industry over the last forty years. Some of the great names in Canadian retailing have disappeared. Supermarkets have been succeeded by superstores; companies like Wal-Mart have swept less efficient competitors aside; specialist outlets like Starbuck's and the Body Shop have established loyal clienteles. Retailing is a constantly changing mosaic, and it is one of the most exciting and challenging areas of business in Canada today. So how successful will the Big Box stores be, and how long will the success last? Diane Brisebois, president of the Retail Council of Canada says that "is the $10-million answer to the $10-million question."[1]

By 2000, more than 50 per cent of Canadians will be over 50, and whether they will continue to want to shop in no-service stores for case lots of groceries, or whether they will return to retailers who offer more convenience and service, albeit at a higher price, is an element around which investment decisions in the retailing industry must be made. The stakes are high. The wrong decision can be extremely costly. As is the case most of the time in organizations, the data are not clear, we don't have all of the facts, and yet a decision still has to be made. How do we make decisions? In this chapter, we examine the foundations of "decision making."

They're not beautiful—inside or out—but "Big Box" megastores are taking a lot of customers away from the competition.

Planning and Decision Making

The previous two chapters discussed how companies plan—both for the long-term survival of the organization, and the short-term day-to-day operations. Implied in those planning activities were the decisions managers make. Plans don't just come out of thin air. They are the result of careful analyses. After weighing the advantages and disadvantages of various alternatives, managers select the ones that will best serve the interests of the company. This selection process is called decision making. What kinds of planning decisions do our managers make? We've listed a few in Exhibit 5-1.

What are the organization's long-term objectives?
What strategies will best achieve these objectives?
What should the organization's short-term objectives be?
What is the most efficient means of completing tasks?
What might the competition be considering?
What budgets are needed to complete department tasks?
How difficult should individual goals be?

Exhibit 5-1 Examples of Planning Function Decisions

The Decision-Making Process

Decision making is typically described as "choosing among alternatives." But this view is overly simplistic. Why? Because decision making is a process rather than the simple act of choosing among alternatives. Exhibit 5-2 illustrates the **decision-making process** as a set of eight steps that begins with identifying a problem, moves to selecting an alternative that can alleviate the problem, and concludes with evaluating the decision's effectiveness. This process is as applicable to your personal decision about where you're going to take your summer vacation as it is to PepsiCo's decision to introduce Crystal Pepsi. The process can also be used to describe both individual and group decisions. Let's take a closer look at the process in order to understand what each step encompasses.

decision-making process
A set of eight steps that include identifying a problem, selecting an alternative, and evaluating the decision's effectiveness.

What Defines a Decision Problem?

The decision-making process begins with the existence of a **problem** (step 1) or, more specifically, a discrepancy between an existing and a desired state of affairs.[2] Let's develop an example that illustrates this point and that we can use throughout this section. For the sake of simplicity, let's make the example something to which most of us can relate: the decision to buy a new car. Take the case of an Office Depot regional manager whose car just blew its engine. Again, for simplicity's sake, assume that it's not economical to repair the car and that public transportation is unavailable. So now we have a problem. There is a disparity between the manager's need to have a car that runs and the fact that her current one doesn't.

After carefully analysing a set of alternatives, PepsiCo made a decision to market its new Crystal Pepsi product.

Unfortunately, this example doesn't tell us much about how managers identify problems. In the real world, most problems don't come with neon signs identifying them as such. While a blown engine might be a clear signal to the manager that she needs a new car, few problems are so obvious. Problem identification is subjective. Furthermore, the manager who mistakenly solves the wrong problem perfectly is likely to perform just as poorly as the manager who fails to identify the right problem and does nothing. Problem identification is neither a simple nor an unimportant part of the decision-making process.[3] How do managers become aware that they have a discrepancy? Managers have to make a comparison between their current state of affairs and some standard. What is that standard? It can be past performance, previously set goals, or the performance of some other unit

problem
A discrepancy between an existing and a desired state of affairs.

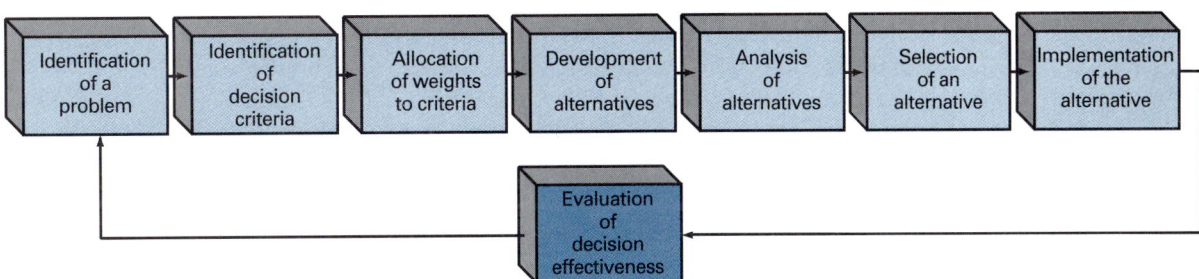

Exhibit 5-2 The Decision-Making Process

within the organization or in other organizations. In our car-buying example, the standard is a previously set goal—having a car that runs.

What Is Relevant in the Decision-Making Process?

Once a manager has identified a problem that needs attention, the **decision criteria** that will be important in solving the problem must be identified (step 2).

In our car-buying example, the store manager has to assess which factors are relevant in her decision. These might include criteria such as price, model (two-door or four-door), size (compact or intermediate), manufacturer (foreign or domestic), optional equipment (automatic transmission, air conditioning, passenger air bag, and so on), and repair records.

decision criteria
Criteria that define what is relevant in a decision.

These criteria reflect what she thinks is relevant in her decision.

Whether explicitly stated or not, every decision maker has criteria that guide his or her decision. Note that in this step in the decision-making process, what is not identified is as important as what is. If the store manager doesn't consider fuel economy to be a criterion, then it will not influence her final choice of car. Thus, if a decision maker does not identify a particular criterion in this second step, then it's treated as irrelevant to the decision maker.

Sure, it would be easy to identify problems if they all jumped out at us like this. Unfortunately, in real life, problems are not this discernible.

Why Does the Decision Maker Need to Weight the Criteria?

The criteria listed above are not all equally important. It's necessary, therefore, to weight the items listed in step 2 in order to give them their relative priority in the decision. We call this step allocating weights to the decision criteria (step 3).

A simple approach is merely to give the most important criterion a weight of ten and then assign weights to the rest against this standard. Thus, in contrast to a criterion that you gave a five, the highest-rated factor would be twice as important. The idea is to use your personal preferences to assign a priority to the relevant criteria in your decision as well as to indicate their degree of importance by assigning a weight to each.

Exhibit 5-3 lists the criteria and weights that our store manager developed for her car-replacement decision. Price is the most important criterion in her decision, with such factors as performance and handling having low weights. The next step requires the decision maker to list the viable alternatives that could succeed in resolving the problem (step 4). No attempt is made in this step to appraise these alternatives, only to list them. Let's assume that our manager has identified twelve cars as viable choices. They are Buick Century, Chevrolet Cavalier, Ford Escort, Geo Prism, Honda Civic, Hyundai Excel, Mazda Protégé, Nissan Sentra, Plymouth Acclaim, Pontiac Grand Am, Toyota Corolla, and Volkswagen Golf.

Once the alternatives have been identified, the decision maker must critically analyse each one (step 5). The strengths and weaknesses of each alternative become evident as they are compared with the criteria and weights established in steps 2 and 3. Each alternative is evaluated by appraising it against the criteria. Exhibit 5-4 shows the assessed values that the plant manager put on each of her twelve alternatives after

Foundations of Decision Making

she had test-driven each car. Keep in mind that the ratings given the twelve cars shown in Exhibit 5-4 are based on the assessment made by the store manager. Again, we are using a one-to-ten scale. Some assessments can be achieved in a relatively objective fashion. For instance, the purchase price represents the best price the manager can get from local dealers, and consumer magazines report data from owners on frequency of repairs. But the assessment of handling is clearly a personal judgment. The point is that most decisions contain judgments. They are reflected in the criteria chosen in step 2, the weights given to the criteria, and the evaluation of alternatives. This explains why two car buyers with the same amount of money may look at two totally distinct sets of alternatives or even look at the same alternatives and rate them differently.

CRITERIA	WEIGHT
Initial price	10[a]
Interior comfort	8
Durability	5
Repair record	5
Performance	3
Handling	1

Exhibit 5-3 Criteria and Weight in Car-Buying Decision

[a] In this example, the highest rating for a criterion is 10 points.

Exhibit 5-4 represents only an assessment of the twelve alternatives against the decision criteria. It does not reflect the weighting done in step 3. If one choice had scored 10 on every criterion, you wouldn't need to consider the weights. Similarly, if the weights were all equal, you could evaluate each alternative merely by summing up the appropriate lines in Exhibit 5-4. For instance, the Honda Civic would have a score of 44, and the Toyota Corolla a score of 43. If you multiply each alternative assessment against its weight, you get Exhibit 5-5. To illustrate, the Nissan Sentra scored a 40 on durability which was determined by multiplying the weight given to durability (5) by the manager's appraisal of Nissan on this criterion (8). The summation of these scores represents an evaluation of each alternative against the previously established criteria and weights. Notice that the weighting of the criteria has changed the ranking of alternatives in our example. The Honda, for example, has gone from first to third. From our analysis, both initial price and interior comfort worked against the Civic.

ALTERNATIVES	INITIAL PRICE	INTERIOR COMFORT	DURABILITY	REPAIR RECORD	PERFORM-ANCE	HANDLING	TOTAL
Buick Century	2	10	8	7	5	5	37
Chevrolet Cavalier	9	6	5	6	8	6	40
Ford Escort	8	5	6	6	4	6	35
Geo Prism	9	5	6	7	6	5	38
Honda Civic	5	6	9	10	7	7	44
Hyundai Excel	10	5	6	4	3	3	31
Mazda Protégé	4	8	7	6	8	9	42
Nissan Sentra	7	6	8	6	5	6	38
Plymouth Acclaim	9	7	4	4	4	5	33
Pontiac Grand Am	5	8	5	4	10	10	42
Toyota Corolla	6	5	10	10	6	6	43
Volkswagen Golf	8	6	6	5	7	8	40

Exhibit 5-4 Assessment of Car Alternatives

ALTERNATIVES	CRITERIA						TOTAL
	INITIAL PRICE (10)	INTERIOR COMFORT (8)	DURABILITY (5)	REPAIR RECORD (5)	PERFORMANCE (3)	HANDLING (1)	
Buick Century	2 20	10 80	8 40	7 35	5 15	5 5	195
Chevrolet Cavalier	9 90	6 48	5 25	6 30	8 24	6 6	223
Ford Escort	8 80	5 40	6 30	6 30	4 12	6 6	198
Geo Prism	9 90	5 40	6 30	7 35	6 18	5 5	218
Honda Civic	5 50	6 48	9 45	10 50	7 21	7 7	221
Hyundai Excel	10 100	5 40	6 30	4 20	3 9	3 3	202
Mazda Protégé	4 40	8 64	7 35	6 30	8 24	9 9	202
Nissan Sentra	7 70	6 48	8 40	6 30	5 15	6 6	209
Plymouth Acclaim	9 90	7 56	4 20	4 20	4 12	5 5	203
Pontiac Grand Am	5 50	8 64	5 25	4 20	10 30	10 10	199
Toyota Corolla	6 60	5 40	10 50	10 50	6 18	6 6	225
Volkswagen Golf	8 80	6 48	6 30	5 25	7 21	8 8	212

Exhibit 5-5 Assessment of the Twelve Alternatives against the Decision Criteria

What Determines the "Best" Choice?

The sixth step is the critical act of choosing the best alternative from among those enumerated and assessed. Since we have determined all the pertinent factors in the decision, weighted them appropriately, and identified the viable alternatives, we merely have to choose the alternative that generated the highest score in step 5. In our car example (Exhibit 5-5), the decision maker would choose the Toyota Corolla. On the basis of the criteria identified, the weights given to the criteria, and the decision maker's assessment of each car's achievement on the criteria, the Toyota scored highest (225 points) and thus became the "best" alternative.

What Is Decision Implementation?

While the choice process is completed in the previous step, the decision may still fail if it is not implemented properly (step 7). Therefore, this step is concerned with putting the decision into action. **Implementation** includes conveying the decision to those affected and getting their commitment to it. As we'll demonstrate later in this chapter, groups or committees can help a manager achieve commitment. If the people who must carry out a decision participate in the process, they are more likely to endorse enthusiastically the outcome.

implementation
Conveying a decision to those affected and getting their commitment to it.

Why Evaluate Decision Effectiveness?

The last step in the decision-making process appraises the result of the decision to see whether it has corrected the problem. Did the alternative chosen in step 6 and implemented in step 7 accomplish the desired result? The evaluation of such results is detailed in Chapters 15 and 16 of this book, where we look at the control function.

Rational Decision Making

Managerial decision making is assumed to be **rational.** By that we mean that managers make consistent, value-maximizing choices within specified constraints.[4] In this section, we want to take a close look at the underlying assumptions of rationality and then determine how valid these assumptions actually are.

rational
Describes choices that are consistent and value-maximizing within specified constraints.

What Is Rationality?

A decision maker who was perfectly rational would be fully objective and logical. He or she would define a problem carefully and would have a clear and specific goal. Moreover, the steps in the decision-making process would consistently lead toward selecting the alternative that maximizes that goal. Exhibit 5-6 summarizes the assumptions of rationality.

To What Extent Is Rationality Limited?

Managerial decision making can follow rational assumptions. If a manager is faced with a simple problem in which the goals are clear and the alternatives are few, in which the time pressures are minimal and the cost of seeking out and evaluating alternatives is low, for which the organizational culture supports innovation and risk taking, and in which the outcomes are relatively concrete and measurable, the decision process is likely to follow the assumptions of rationality.[5] But most decisions that managers face don't meet all these tests.

Hundreds of studies have sought to improve our understanding of managerial decision making.[6] Individually, these studies often challenge one or more of the assumptions of rationality. Taken together, they suggest that decision making often veers from the logical, consistent, and systematic process that rationality implies.

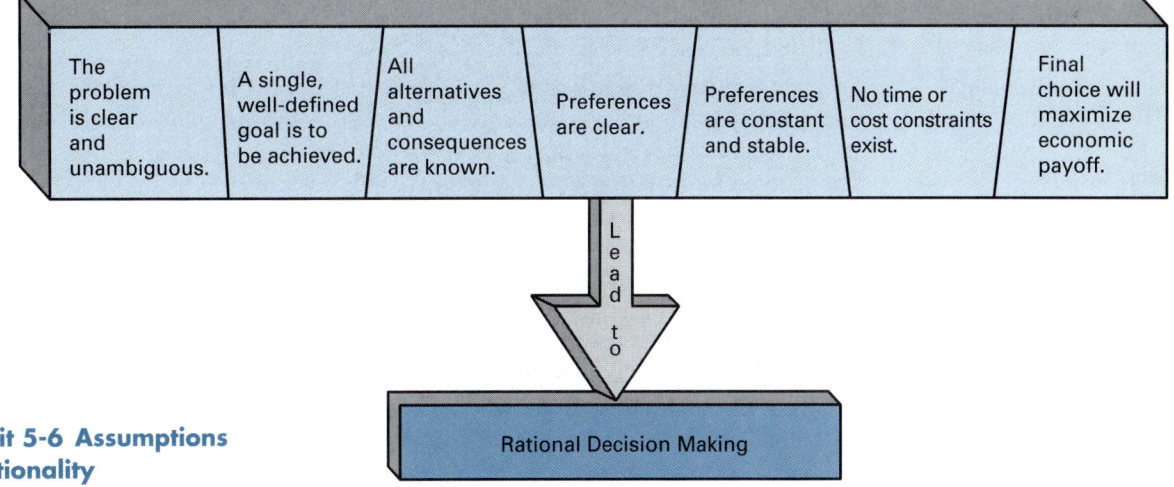

Exhibit 5-6 Assumptions of Rationality

Ethical Dilemmas in Management

▼

SHOULD SOCIAL RESPONSIBILITY BE A FACTOR IN THE DECISION TO CLOSE A PLANT, MINE OR OFFICE?

▲

Procter & Gamble announced in July 1993 that it planned to cut 13,000 jobs worldwide as part of a global restructuring. P&G had six plants in Canada—five in Ontario and one in Quebec at the time. Closing or relocating plants and corporate headquarters can be devastating to small towns and even to large cities if the organization is a major employer. Many communities incur very high expenditures to entice and appease large employers. They build roads, schools, and hospitals for corporations and their personnel. They provide police and fire protection. Other businesses, of course, open up to service the needs of the corporation, its workers, and their families. Management can respond by arguing that it brought more to the relationship than the community gave back—specifically, high-paying jobs that allowed the community to grow and prosper—and that, in today's global economy, hometown loyalties cannot override economic considerations. But global economies don't cut much ice when 1,000 people lose their jobs in a town when a plant or mine or mill closes.

Should social responsibility play a part in management's decision to relocate a plant or headquarters office? What do *you* think?

If Managers Can't Be Rational, What Do They Do?

Do the limits to rationality mean that managers ignore the eight-step decision process we described at the beginning of this chapter? Not necessarily. Why? Because in spite of the limits to perfect rationality, managers are expected to appear to follow the rational process.[7] Managers know that "good" decision makers are supposed to do certain things: identify problems, consider alternatives, gather information, and act decisively but prudently (see Ethical Dilemmas in Management). Managers can thus be expected to exhibit the correct decision-making behaviours. By doing so, managers signal to their bosses, peers, and employees that they are competent and that their decisions are the result of intelligent and rational deliberation.

How many managers proceed through this process is often best explained by an alternative model—one in which a manager operates under the assumptions of **bounded rationality**.[8] In bounded rationality, managers construct simplified models that extract the essential features from the problems they face without capturing all their complexity. Then, given information-processing limitations and constraints imposed by the organization, managers attempt to behave rationally within the parameters of the simple model. The result is a satisficing decision rather than a maximizing one; that is, a decision in which the solution is "good enough."

The implications of bounded rationality on the manager's job cannot be overlooked. In situations in which the assumptions of perfect rationality do not apply (including many of the most important and far-reaching decisions that a manager makes), the details of the decision-making process are strongly influenced by the decision maker's self-interest, the organization's culture, internal politics, and power considerations (see Details on a Management Classic).

bounded rationality
Behaviour that is rational within the parameters of a simplified model that captures the essential features of a problem.

Details on a Management Classic

HERBERT SIMON AND BOUNDED RATIONALITY

Management theory is built on the premise that individuals act rationally, and the essence of their job revolves around the rational decision-making process. However, the assumptions of rationality are rather extreme. Few people actually behave that way. Given this fact, how do managers make decisions if it's unlikely that they are perfectly rational? Herbert Simon has the answer. Simon found that within certain constraints, managers do act rationally. Since it's impossible for human beings to process and understand all the information necessary to meet the test of rationality, what they do is construct simplified models that extract the essential features from problems without capturing all their complexities.[9] Consequently, they can behave rationally (the rational decision-making model) within the limits of the simplified or bounded model.

So how do managers' actions within these boundaries differ from those within the rational model? Once a problem is identified, the search for criteria and alternatives begins. But this list of criteria is generally limited and made up of the more conspicuous choices. That is, Simon found that the decision maker will focus on easy-to-find choices—those that tend to be highly visible. In many instances, this means developing alternatives that vary only slightly from decisions that have been used in the past to deal with similar problems.

Once this limited set of alternatives is identified, the decision maker will begin reviewing them. But that review will not be exhaustive. Rather, the manager will proceed to review the alternatives only until he or she identifies an alternative that is sufficient, or good enough to solve the problems at hand. Thus, the first alternative to meet the "good enough" criterion ends the search, and the decision maker can then proceed to implement this acceptable course of action. ▼

Decision Making: A Contingency Approach

The type of problem a manager faces in a decision-making situation often determines how that problem is treated. In this section we present a categorization scheme for problems and for types of decisions. Then we show how the type of decision a manager uses should reflect the characteristics of the problem.

How Do Problems Differ?

Some problems are straightforward. The goal of the decision maker is clear, the problem familiar, and information about the problem easily defined and complete. Examples might include a supplier being late with an important delivery, a customer wanting to return a purchase to a retail store, a newspaper having to respond to an unexpected and fast-breaking news event, or a college's handling of student who seeks to have a grade changed. Such situations are called **well-structured problems.** They align closely with the assumptions underlying perfect rationality.

well-structured problems
Straightforward, familiar, easily defined problems.

ill-structured problems
New problems in which information is ambiguous or incomplete.

Many situations faced by managers, however, are **ill-structured problems.** They are new or unusual. Information about such problems is ambiguous or incomplete. The selection of a new product design is one example. So too is the decision to invest in a new, unproven technology.

What's the Difference between Programmed and Nonprogrammed Decisions?

Just as problems can be divided into two categories, so too can decisions. As we will see, programmed, or routine, decision making is the most efficient way to handle well-structured problems. However, when problems are ill-structured, managers like Yasuyo Kikuta must rely on nonprogrammed decision making in order to develop unique solutions (see Managers Who Made a Difference).

A waiter in a fine restaurant spills a drink on a customer's dress. What does the manager do? There is probably some standardized routine for handling the problem. For example, if it is the waiter's fault, if the damage is significant, and if the customer has asked for a remedy, the manager offers to have the dress cleaned at the restaurant's expense. This is a **programmed decision.**

programmed decision
A repetitive decision that can be handled by a routine approach.

Decisions are programmed to the extent that they are repetitive and routine and to the extent that a definite approach has been worked out for handling them. Because the problem is well-structured, the manager does not have to go to the trouble and expense of working up an involved decision process. Programmed decision making is relatively simple and tends to rely heavily on previous solutions. The "develop-the-alternatives" stage in the decision-making process is either nonexistent or given little attention. Why?

Having customers return previously purchased items is generally an easy problem to deal with. The problem is clear, familiar, and straightforward.

Because once the structured problem is defined, its solution is usually self-evident or at least reduced to very few alternatives that are familiar and that have proven successful in the past. In many cases, programmed decision making becomes decision making by precedent. Managers simply do what they and others have done in the same situation. The spilled drink on the customer's dress does not require the restaurant manager to identify and weigh decision criteria nor develop a long list of possible solutions. Rather, the manager falls back on a systematic procedure, rule, or policy.

What Are Procedures, Rules, and Policies and Where Are They Best Used?

procedure
A series of interrelated sequential steps that can be used to respond to a structured problem.

A **procedure** is a series of interrelated sequential steps that a manager can use for responding to a structured problem. The only real difficulty is in identifying the problem. Once the problem is clear, so is the procedure. For instance, a purchasing manager receives a request from engineering for five computer assisted design (CAD) software packages. The purchasing manager knows that there is a definite procedure for handling

Managers Who Made a Difference

YASUYO KIKUTA OF FUJITSU LTD.

Yasuyo Kikuta is something of a renegade.[10] She refuses to accept that something is impossible. For instance, she set her mind on a career in computer programming. Her father tried vigorously to get Yasuyo to change her mind. She refused. After she graduated from Ochanominzu Women's University, few companies would even accept that a woman was applying for a computer job. However, Fujitsu Ltd. took a chance, but with one condition—Kikuta could not call on a customer. And although pressure to quit was applied by coworkers, once again, Yasuyo refused to bend. That decision turned out to be a windfall for Fujitsu.

Now twenty years later, Kikuta is the company's general manager of systems development engineering. She has worked extensively in software development for "networking systems, artificial intelligence, and machine translation." In fact, today, some Fujitsu customers' routine questions are handled by one of Kikuta's artificial intelligence programs.

Kikuta's interest in new directions with software development is leading her into issues surrounding workplace diversity. Because of the influx of women into the workforce—individuals often with child-care responsibilities—Kikuta is developing a software network that will allow these workers to work primarily at home. For Fujitsu, its decision to take a chance on Kikuta generated a good return on its investment. For Yasuyo, her strong convictions in support of the career decision she made have resulted in a better, more productive work environment for thousands of individuals. ▼

---

this decision. Has the requisition been properly filled out and approved? If not, send the requisition back with a note explaining what is deficient. If the request is complete, the approximate costs are estimated. If the total exceeds $6000, three bids must be obtained. If the total is $6000 or less, only one vendor need be identified and the order placed. The decision-making process is merely the execution of a simple series of sequential steps.

A **rule** is an explicit statement that tells a manager what he or she ought or ought not to do. Rules are frequently used by managers when they confront a well-structured problem because they are simple to follow and ensure consistency. In the illustration above, the $6000 cutoff rule simplifies the purchasing manager's decision about when to use multiple bids.

A third guide for making programmed decisions is a **policy**. It provides guidelines to channel a manager's thinking in a specific direction. In contrast to a rule, a policy establishes parameters for the decision maker rather than specifically stating what should or should not be done. As an analogy, think of the Ten Commandments as rules and the Canadian Constitution as policy. The latter requires judgment and interpretation, the former do not.

rule
An explicit statement that tells managers what they ought or ought not to do.

policy
A guide that establishes parameters for making decisions.

What Do Nonprogrammed Decisions Look Like?

Deciding whether to merge with another organization, how to restructure an organization to improve efficiency, or whether to close an unprofitable division are examples of **nonprogrammed decisions.** Such decisions are unique and nonrecurring. When a manager confronts an ill-structured problem or one that is novel, there is no cut-and-dried solution. It requires a custom-made response.

nonprogrammed decisions
Unique decisions that require a custom-made solution.

The creation of a marketing strategy for a new product represents an example of a nonprogrammed decision. It will be different from previous marketing decisions because the product is new, a different set of competitors exists, and other conditions that may have existed when previous products were introduced years earlier have changed. IBM's introduction of a personal computer in the early 1980s was unlike any other marketing decision the company had previously made. Certainly, IBM had a wealth of experience selling computers. It also had previously sold to small businesses and general consumers through its typewriter division. But it had no substantive experience in mass marketing relatively low-cost personal computers. It faced such aggressive competitors as Osborne, Apple, Hewlett-Packard, and Digital Equipment. The needs and sophistication of personal computer customers differed from those of buyers who purchased multimillion-dollar systems for their corporate headquarters. The hundreds of decisions that went into IBM's marketing strategy for personal computers had never been made before and thus were clearly of the nonprogrammed variety.

Bombardier Inc., of Montreal, is another example of an organization where nonprogrammed decisions are made in a variety of areas. Bombardier had no stake in the aerospace industry in 1985, but between 1986 and 1992 it acquired four firms (all money losers when Bombardier bought them)—Canadair, Learjet, Short Brothers, and de Havilland—and turned them into a highly profitable business. In 1994 the aerospace division made a profit of $136.5 million. Bombardier also built the Channel tunnel shuttle cars for the train that runs between England and France. They started the design from scratch and developed the highly sophisticated cars that are controlled by 524 computers linked to form a network that manages functions like braking, doors, communications and air conditioning.[11] Programmed decisions do not play a dominant part in this type of project.

How Can You Integrate Problems, Types of Decisions, and Level in the Organization?

Exhibit 5-7 describes the relationship between the types of problems, the types of decisions, and level in the organization. Well-structured problems are responded to with programmed decision making. Ill-structured problems require nonprogrammed decision making. Lower-level managers essentially confront familiar and repetitive problems; therefore, they most typically rely on programmed decisions such as standard operating procedures. However, the problems confronting managers are more likely to

Exhibit 5-7 Types of Problems, Types of Decisions, and Level in the Organization

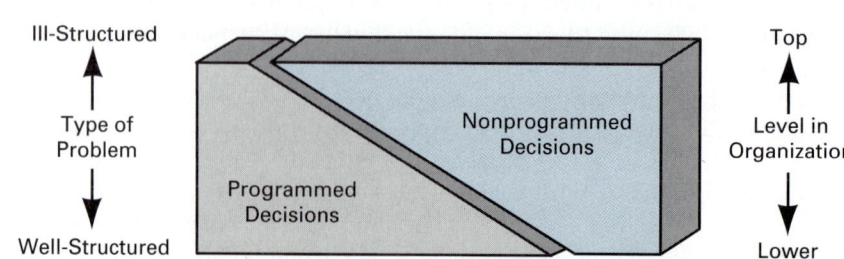

Foundations of Decision Making

become ill-structured as the managers move up the organizational hierarchy. Why? Because lower-level managers handle the routine decisions themselves and pass upward only decisions that they find unique or difficult. Similarly, managers pass down routine decisions to their employees in order to spend their time on more problematic issues.

Few managerial decisions in the real world are either fully programmed or non-programmed. These are extremes, and most decisions fall somewhere in between. Few programmed decisions are designed to eliminate individual judgment completely. At the other extreme, even the most unique situation requiring a nonprogrammed decision can be helped by programmed routines.

A last point on this topic is that organizational efficiency is facilitated by the use of programmed decision making, which may explain its wide popularity. Wherever possible, management decisions are likely to be programmed. Obviously, this is not too realistic at the top of the organization, since most of the problems that top management confronts are of a non-recurring nature. But there are strong economic incentives for top management to create policies, standard operating procedures (SOPs), and rules to guide other managers.

Programmed decisions minimize the need for managers to exercise discretion. This is relevant because discretion costs money. The more nonprogrammed decision making a manager is required to do, the greater the judgment needed. Since sound judgment is an uncommon quality, it costs more to acquire the services of managers who possess this ability.

Decisions reached by this group of Whirlpool employees have helped the company to improve the quality of washing machines made in this plant.

Group Decision Making

Many decisions in organizations, especially important decisions that have a far-reaching impact on organizational activities and personnel, are made in groups. It's a rare organization that doesn't at some time use committees, task forces, review panels, study teams, or similar groups as vehicles for making decisions. Studies tell us that managers spend up to 40 per cent or more of their time in meetings.[12] Undoubtedly, a large portion of that time is involved with defining problems, arriving at solutions to those problems, and determining the means for implementing the solutions. It's possible, in fact, for groups to be assigned any of the eight steps in the decision-making process.

What Are the Advantages to Group Decision Making?

Individual and group decisions each have their own set of strengths. Neither is ideal for all situations. Let's begin by reviewing the advantages that group decisions have over individual decisions. Group decisions provide more complete information. There is often truth to the axiom that two heads are better than one. A group will bring a diversity of experience and perspectives to the decision process that an individual, acting alone, cannot. Groups also generate more alternatives. Because groups have a greater quantity and diversity of information, they can identify more alternatives than can an individual. This is most evident when group members represent different specialties.

Furthermore, group decision making increases acceptance of a solution. Many decisions fail after the final choice has been made because people do not accept the solution. However, if the people who will be affected by a certain solution and who will help implement it get to participate in the decision making itself, they will be more likely to accept the decision and to encourage others to accept it. And last, this process increases legitimacy. The group decision-making process is consistent with democratic ideals; therefore, decisions made by groups may be perceived as more legitimate than decisions made by a single person. The fact that the individual decision maker has complete power and has not consulted others can create a perception that a decision was made autocratically and arbitrarily.

What Are the Disadvantages to Group Decision Making?

If groups are so good, how did the phrase "a camel is a racehorse put together by a committee" become so popular? The answer, of course, is that group decisions are not without their drawbacks. There are several major disadvantages of group decision making. First, they're time-consuming. It takes time to assemble a group. Additionally, the interaction that takes place once the group is in place is frequently inefficient. The result is that groups almost always take more time to reach a solution than it would take an individual making the decision alone. There may also be a situation where there is minority domination. Members of a group are never perfectly equal. They may differ in rank in the organization, experience, knowledge about the problem, influence with other members, verbal skills, assertiveness, and the like. This creates the opportunity for one or more members to use their advantages to dominate others in the group. A minority that dominates a group frequently has an undue influence on the final decision.

groupthink
The withholding by group members of different views in order to appear in agreement.

Another problem focuses on the pressures to conform. There are social pressures to conform in groups. They can lead to what has been called **groupthink**.[13] This is a form of conformity in which group members withhold deviant, minority, or unpopular views in order to give the appearance of agreement. Groupthink undermines critical thinking in the group and eventually harms the quality of the final decision (see Details on a Management Classic). And finally, there is ambiguous responsibility. Group members share responsibility, but who is actually responsible for the final outcome? In an individual decision, it is clear who is responsible. In a group decision, the responsibility of any single member is watered down.

When Are Groups Most Effective?

Whether groups are more effective than individuals depends on the criteria you use for defining effectiveness. Group decisions tend to be more accurate. The evidence indicates that, on the average, groups make better decisions than individuals.[14] This doesn't mean, of course, that all groups outperform every individual. Rather, group decisions have been found to be better than those that would have been reached by the average individual in the group. However, they are seldom better than the performance of the best individual.

If decision effectiveness is defined in terms of speed, individuals are superior. Group decisions are characterized by give and take, which consumes time.

Effectiveness may mean the degree to which a solution demonstrates creativity. If creativity is important, groups tend to be more effective than individuals.[15] This requires, however, that the forces that foster groupthink be constrained.

Details on a Management Classic

IRVING L. JANIS AND GROUPTHINK

Have you ever been in a situation where a number of people were sitting around discussing a particular item? And in the course of that discussion, you had something to say that ran contrary to the consensus views that dominated the group. What did you do? Remain silent? Would you be surprised if you later learned that others shared your views and also had remained silent? What you experienced is what Irving Janis termed groupthink.[16]

Groupthink relates to a situation in which a group's ability to appraise alternatives objectively and arrive at a quality decision is jeopardized. Because of pressures applied for conformity, groups often deter individuals from critically appraising unusual, minority, or unpopular views. Consequently, there is a deterioration of an individual's mental efficiency, reality testing, and moral judgment as a result of the group's pressure.

How does groupthink occur? The following are examples where groupthink is evident:

▶ 1. Group members rationalize any resistance to the assumptions they have made.
▶ 2. Members apply direct pressures on those who momentarily express doubts about any of the group's shared views, or who question the validity of arguments favoured by the majority.
▶ 3. Those members who have doubts or hold differing points of view seek to avoid deviating from what appears to be group consensus.
▶ 4. There appears to be an illusion of unanimity. If someone does not speak, it is assumed that he or she is in full accord.

Although we can recognize that the above may affect groups' decisions, just how much of a problem is it? Several research studies have found that groupthink symptoms were associated with poorer quality decision outcomes. None was more noteworthy than the decision of Lyndon Johnson's administration to escalate the Vietnam War by increasing the tonnage of bombs dropped on North Vietnam—despite continual information that bombing them was not bringing the war any closer to conclusion. Conversely, where groupthink symptoms were not found, such as in the case of President Kennedy and his staff's handling of the Cuban Missile Crisis in 1961, these decisions were viewed as being successful.

Research has found that groupthink can be minimized if the following conditions exist in group decision making: The group is cohesive, fosters open discussion, and is led by an impartial leader who seeks input from all members; furthermore, individuals external to the group become aware of who the group is and what decision it is making. ▼

Another criterion for effectiveness is the degree of acceptance that the final decision achieves. As was previously noted, because group decisions have input from more people, they are likely to result in solutions that will be more widely accepted.

The effectiveness of group decision making is also influenced by the size of the group. The larger the group, the greater the opportunity for heterogeneous representation.

Developing Management Skills

CONDUCTING A GROUP MEETING

▶ **1. Prepare and distribute an agenda well in advance of the meeting.** An agenda defines the meeting's purpose for participants and plans boundaries between relevant and irrelevant discussion topics. Also, the agenda can serve as an important vehicle for pre-meeting discussions with participants.

▶ **2. Consult with participants before the meeting to ensure proper participation.** Let participants know that their input is valuable and that you welcome them speaking up at the meeting when they have something to offer.

▶ **3. Establish specific time parameters for the meeting—when it will start and end.** This helps to keep the meeting on time and focused on the important matters.

▶ **4. Maintain focused discussion during the meeting.** Items not on the agenda should not be given substantial time during the meeting. If an issue is important, maybe another meeting, with its own agenda, should be held to address that issue.

▶ **5. Encourage and support participation by all members.** If you have done a good job in the second step, participants should come prepared to talk but still may need some encouragement at the meeting. Sometimes direct questions about what they think will get them to talk.

▶ **6. Encourage the clash of ideas.** Remember, you want as much information about a topic to surface as possible. Disagreements are fine. That indicates that different voices are being heard. Better to work the differences out now than to have them surface later.

▶ **7. Discourage the clash of personalities.** Disagreements can enhance the process, but they should be substantive disputes. Differences due to personal dislikes are disaster in a meeting.

▶ **8. Bring closure by summarizing accomplishments and allocating follow-up assignments.** This lets participants understand what occurred in the meeting and what they may have to do before the next meeting. This is, in essence, planning.

On the other hand, a larger group requires more coordination and more time to allow all members to contribute. What this means is that groups probably should not be too large: a minimum of five to a maximum of about fifteen. Evidence indicates, in fact, that groups of five and, to a lesser extent, seven are the most effective.[17] Because five and seven are odd numbers, strict deadlocks are avoided. Effectiveness should not be considered without also assessing efficiency. Groups almost always stack up a poor second in efficiency to the individual decision maker. With few exceptions, group decision making consumes more work hours than does individual decision making. In deciding whether to use groups, then, primary consideration must be given to assessing whether increases in effectiveness are more than enough to offset the losses in efficiency.

How Can You Improve Group Decision Making?

When members of a group meet face to face and interact with one another, they create the potential for groupthink. They can censor themselves and pressure other group members into agreement. Four ways of making group decision making more creative have been suggested: brainstorming, the nominal group and Delphi techniques, and electronic meetings. We've also provided some thoughts to ponder regarding how to conduct a meeting (see Developing Management Skills).

What Is Brainstorming? Brainstorming is a relatively simple technique for overcoming pressures for conformity that retard the development of creative alternatives.[18]

brainstorming
An idea-generating process that encourages alternatives while withholding criticism.

116

Foundations of Decision Making

It does this by utilizing an idea-generating process that specifically encourages any and all alternatives while withholding any criticism of those alternatives. In a typical brainstorming session, a half-dozen to a dozen people sit around a table. The group leader states the problem in a clear manner that is understood by all participants. Members then "freewheel" as many alternatives as they can in a given time. No criticism is allowed, and all the alternatives are recorded for later discussion and analysis. Brainstorming, however, is merely a process for generating ideas. The next two techniques go further by offering ways to arrive at a preferred solution.[19]

How Do the Nominal Group Technique and the Delphi Technique Function? The **nominal group technique** restricts discussion during the decision-making process, hence the term. Group members must be present, as in a traditional committee meeting, but they are required to operate independently. The chief advantage of this technique is that it permits the group to meet formally but does not restrict independent thinking as so often happens in the traditional interacting group.

A more complex and time-consuming alternative is the **Delphi technique,** which is similar to the nominal group technique except that it does not require the physical presence of the group members. This is because the Delphi technique never allows the group members to meet face to face. Like the nominal group technique, the Delphi technique shields group members from the undue influence of others. It also does not require the physical presence of the participants. So, for instance, Minolta could use the technique to query its sales managers in Tokyo, Hong Kong, Paris, London, New York, Toronto, Mexico City, and Melbourne as to the best worldwide price for one of the company's new cameras. The cost of bringing the executives together at a central location is avoided, yet input from Minolta's major markets is obtained. Of course, the Delphi technique has its drawbacks. The method is extremely time-consuming. It is frequently not applicable when a speedy decision is necessary. Further, the method might not develop the rich array of alternatives that the interacting or nominal groups do. The ideas that might surface from the heat of face-to-face interaction might never arise. Specific steps for conducting either the nominal group or the Delphi techniques are presented in Exhibit 5-8 on page 118.

nominal group technique
A decision-making technique in which group members are physically present but operate independently.

Delphi technique
A group decision-making technique in which members never meet face to face.

How Can Electronic Meetings Enhance Group Decision Making? The most recent approach to group decision making blends the nominal group technique with sophisticated computer technology.[20] It's called the **electronic meeting.**

Once the technology for the meeting is in place, the concept is simple. Up to fifty people sit around a horseshoe-shaped table that is empty except for a series of computer terminals. Issues are presented to participants who type their responses onto their computer screens. Individual comments, as well as aggregate votes, are displayed on a projection screen in the room.

The major advantages to electronic meetings are anonymity, honesty, and speed. Participants can anonymously type any message they want, and it will flash on the screen for all to see at the push of a board key. It also allows people to be brutally honest with no penalty. And it's fast—chitchat is eliminated, discussions don't digress, and many participants can "talk" at once without stepping on others' toes.

electronic meetings
Decision-making groups that interact by way of linked computers.

Companies like Minolta and IBM use electronic meetings to bring people from all parts of the world together.

Exhibit 5-8 Steps in the Nominal Group Technique and the Delphi Technique

The Nominal Group Technique:

▶ 1. Members meet as a group; but before any discussion takes place, each member independently writes down his or her ideas on the problem.
▶ 2. This silent period is followed by each member presenting one idea to the group. Each member takes his or her turn, going around the table, presenting one idea at a time until all ideas have been presented and recorded (typically on a flip chart or chalkboard). No discussion takes place until all ideas have been recorded.
▶ 3. The group now discusses the ideas for clarity and evaluates them.
▶ 4. Each group member silently and independently assigns a rank to the ideas. The final decision is determined by the idea with the highest aggregate ranking.

The Delphi Technique:

▶ 1. The problem is identified, and members are asked to provide potential solutions through a series of carefully designed questionnaires.
▶ 2. Each member anonymously and independently completes the first questionnaire.
▶ 3. Results of the first questionnaire are compiled at a central location, transcribed, and reproduced.
▶ 4. Each member receives a copy of the results.
▶ 5. After viewing the results, members are again asked for their solutions. The results typically trigger new solutions or cause changes in the original position.
▶ 6. Steps 4 and 5 are repeated as often as necessary until consensus is reached.

Experts claim that electronic meetings are as much as 55 per cent faster than traditional face-to-face meetings.[21] Phelps Dodge Mining, for instance, used the approach to cut its annual planning meeting from several days down to twelve hours. However, there are drawbacks. Those who can type quickly can outshine those who may be verbally eloquent but are lousy typists; those with the best ideas don't get credit for them; and the process lacks the informational richness of face-to-face oral communication. But because this technology is currently only in its infancy, the future of group decision making is very likely to include extensive usage of electronic meetings.

The Effect of National Culture on Decision-Making Styles

The way decisions are made—whether by group, participatively, or autocratically by an individual manager—and the degree of risk a decision maker is willing to take are just two examples of decision variables that reflect a country's cultural environment. Decision making in Japan, for instance, is much more group-oriented than in Canada, and characteristics of the Japanese national culture can explain why.[22]

The Japanese value conformity and cooperation. One can see this in their schools as well as in their business organizations. Before making decisions, Japanese CEOs col-

Foundations of Decision Making

lect a large amount of information, which is then used in consensus-forming group decisions. Since employees in Japanese organizations have high job security, managerial decisions take a long-term perspective rather than focusing on short-term profits, as is often the practice in Canada.

Senior managers in other nations—including France, Germany, and Sweden—also adapt their decision styles to their country's culture. In France, for instance, autocratic decision making is widely practised, and managers avoid risks. Managerial styles in Germany reflect the German culture's concern for structure and order. There are extensive rules and regulations in German organizations. Managers have well-defined responsibilities and accept that decisions must go through channels. Decision styles of Swedish managers differ considerably from those of their French and German counterparts. Managers in Sweden are more aggressive; they take the initiative with problems and are not afraid to take risks. Senior managers in Sweden also push decisions down in the ranks. They encourage lower-level managers and employees to take part in decisions that affect them.

These examples are meant to remind you that managers need to modify their decision styles to reflect the national culture of the country in which they live as well as to reflect the organizational culture of the firm in which they work.

Summary

This Summary is organized by the chapter opening learning objectives found on page 101.

1. Decision making is an eight-step process: (1) formulation of a problem, (2) identification of decision criteria, (3) allocation of weights to the criteria, (4) development of alternatives, (5) analysis of alternatives, (6) selection of an alternative, (7) implementation of the alternative, and (8) evaluation of decision effectiveness.

2. The rational decision maker is assumed to have a clear problem, have no goal conflict, know all options, have a clear preference ordering, keep all preferences constant, have no time or cost constraints, and select a final choice that maximizes his or her economic payoff.

3. Rationality assumptions don't apply in many situations because problems aren't simple, goals are not clear, alternatives are many, and there are time and cost constraints; decision makers sometimes increase commitment to a previous choice to confirm its original correctness; prior decision precedents constrain current choices; there is rarely agreement on a single goal; decision makers must face time and cost constraints; and most organizational cultures discourage taking risks and searching for innovative alternatives.

4. In the perfectly rational decision-making process: (1) the problem identified is important and relevant; (2) all criteria are identified; (3) all criteria are evaluated; (4) a comprehensive list of alternatives is generated; (5) all alternatives are assessed against the decision criteria and weights; (6) the decision with the highest economic outcome is chosen; (7) all organizational members embrace the solution chosen; and (8) the decision's outcome is objectively evaluated against the original problem.

5. In the bounded rational decision-making process: managers construct simplified models that extract essential features from the problems they face without capturing all their complexity. They then attempt to act rationally within this simplified model.

6. Managers face well- and ill-structured problems. Well-structured problems are straightforward, familiar, easily defined, and solved using programmed decisions. Ill-structured problems are new or unusual, involve ambiguous or incomplete information, and are solved using nonprogrammed decisions.

7. Groups offer certain advantages: more complete information, more alternatives, increased acceptance of a solution, and greater legitimacy. On the other hand, groups are time-consuming, can be dominated by a minority, create pressures to conform, and cloud responsibility.

8. Four ways of improving group decision making are brainstorming, the nominal group technique, the Delphi technique, and electronic meetings.

Review and Discussion Questions

1. Explain how decision making is related to the planning process.
2. Describe a decision you have made that closely aligns with the assumptions of perfect rationality. Compare this with the process you used to select your college. Is there a deviation? Explain.
3. What are the steps of the rational decision-making model?
4. How is implementation important to the decision-making process?
5. What is a satisficing decision?
6. Why might a manager use a simplified decision model?
7. What's the difference between a rule and a policy?
8. Is the order in which alternatives are considered more critical under assumptions of perfect rationality or bounded rationality? Why?
9. What is groupthink? What are its implications for decision making?
10. Why do you think organizations have increased the use of groups for making decisions during the past twenty years? When would you recommend using groups to make decisions?

Self-Assessment Exercise

What's Your Intuitive Ability?

For each of the following questions, select the response that first appeals to you by circling the letter of that response. Be honest with yourself.

1. When working on a project, do you prefer to:
   a. be told what the problem is, but left free to decide how to solve it?
   b. get very clear instructions about how to go about solving the problem before you start?
2. When working on a project, do you prefer to work with colleagues who are:
   a. realistic?
   b. imaginative?
3. Do you admire people most who are:
   a. creative?
   b. careful?
4. Do the friends you choose tend to be:
   a. serious and hard working?
   b. exciting and often emotional?
5. When you ask a colleague for advice on a problem you have, do you:
   a. seldom or never get upset if he/she questions your basic assumptions?
   b. often get upset if he/she questions your basic assumptions?
6. When you start your day, do you usually:
   a. seldom make or follow a specific plan?
   b. make a plan first to follow?
7. When working with numbers, do you find that you:
   a. seldom or never make factual errors?
   b. often make factual errors?
8. Do you find that you:
   a. seldom daydream during the day and really don't enjoy doing so when you do do it?
   b. frequently daydream during the day and enjoy doing so?
9. When working on a problem do you:
   a. prefer to follow the instructions or rules when they are given to you?
   b. often enjoy circumventing the instructions or rules when they are given to you?
10. When you are trying to put something together, do you prefer to have:
    a. step-by-step written instructions on how to assemble the item?
    b. a picture of how the item is supposed to look once assembled?
11. Do you find that the person who irritates you the most is the one who appears to be:
    a. disorganized?
    b. organized?
12. When an unexpected crisis comes up that you have to deal with, do you:
    a. feel anxious about the situation?
    b. feel excited by the challenge of the situation?

Turn to page 412 for scoring directions and key.

Source: Weston H. Agor, *AIM Survey* (El Paso, Tex.: ENP Enterprises, 1989), Part I. With permission.

Foundations of Decision Making

Class Exercise

OBJECTIVE

To contrast individual and group decision making.

TIME

Fifteen minutes.

PROCEDURE

A. You have five minutes to read the following story* and respond to each of the eleven questions as either *true, false,* or *unknown* (indicated by a question mark). Begin.

THE STORY

A sales clerk had just turned off the lights in the store when a man appeared and demanded money. The owner opened a cash register. The contents of the cash register were scooped up, and the man sped away. A member of the police force was notified promptly.

STATEMENTS ABOUT THE STORY

1. A man appeared after the owner had turned off his store lights.   T   F   ?
2. The robber was a *man*.   T   F   ?
3. The man did not demand money.   T   F   ?
4. The man who opened the cash register was the owner.   T   F   ?
5. The store owner scooped up the contents of the cash register and ran away.   T   F   ?
6. Someone opened a cash register.   T   F   ?
7. After the man who demanded the money scooped up the contents of the cash register, he ran away.   T   F   ?
8. While the cash register contained money, the story does *not* state how much.   T   F   ?
9. The robber demanded money of the owner.   T   F   ?
10. The story concerns a series of events in which only three persons are referred to: the owner of the store, a man who demanded money, and a member of the police force.   T   F   ?
11. The following events in the story are true: Someone demanded money, a cash register was opened, its contents were scooped up, and a man dashed out of the store.   T   F   ?

B. When your five minutes are up, form groups of four to five members each. Group members have ten minutes to discuss their answers and agree on the correct answers to each of the eleven statements.

C. Your instructor will give you the actual correct answers. How many correct answers did you get at the conclusion of Step A? How many did your group achieve at the conclusion of Step B? Did the group outperform the average individual? The best individual? Discuss the implications of these results.

---

*Adapted from W.V. Haney, *Communication and Interpersonal Relations,* 6th ed. (Homewood, Ill.: Richard D. Irwin, Inc., 1992), pp. 232–33. Reprinted by special permission.

Key Terms

Key terms are listed in the order in which they appear in the chapter.

decision-making process	bounded rationality	policy
problem	well-structured problems	nonprogrammed decisions
decision criteria	ill-structured problems	groupthink
implementation	programmed decision	brainstorming
rational	procedure	nominal group technique
	rule	Delphi technique
		electronic meetings

Case Application

Adidas vs. Nike

If you were a serious runner in the 1960s or early 1970s there was only one real shoe choice: Adidas. A German company, Adidas pioneered lightweight running shoes for competitive athletes. In the Montreal Olympics in 1976, Adidas-equipped athletes accounted for more than 82 per cent of all individual medal winners in track and field. Adidas' strength was experimentation. It tried new materials and techniques to develop stronger and lighter shoes. It introduced kangaroo leather to toughen the sides of shoes, four-spiked running shoes, and track shoes with nylon soles and interchangeable spikes. Its high quality, innovation, and variety of products resulted in Adidas dominating international competition through the mid-1970s.

The physical fitness boom in the 1970s, though, caught Adidas by surprise. Suddenly millions of previously unathletic people became interested in exercise. And the fastest-growing segment of the physical fitness market was jogging. It was estimated that by 1980, 25 to 30 million North Americans were jogging and another 10 million wore running shoes for leisure wear. Secure in its market dominance for athletes' footwear, Adidas didn't pursue the jogging market very aggressively.

A host of competitors surfaced in the 1970s, including Puma, Brooks, New Balance, and Tiger. But one was to become more aggressive and innovative than the rest. That was Nike. Nike's big breakthrough came in 1975 with the development of the "waffle sole," whose tiny rubber studs made it more springy than those of other shoes on the market. The popularity of the waffle sole, along with the rapidly expanding market for running shoes, resulted in sales of $14 million in 1976. Today, Nike has sales in the range of $4 billion a year and is the industry leader with more than 25 per cent market share in athletic shoes.

Nike's success could be traced to the decision to place its emphasis on (1) research and technological improvement and (2) a variety of styles and models. Its focus was expanded well beyond running shoes, with, for example, its dominance of the teen and basketball market with its Air Jordan shoes, built on the image of Michael Jordan. By the time the running boom peaked in the early 1980s, Adidas, the once-dominant player, had become an "also ran" in the market, and by the early 1990s, its market share had fallen to a dismal 4 per cent.

Questions

1. How did poor decision making lead to Adidas' significantly reduced market share by the early 1990s? Did uncertainty play any part in its troubles?
2. In the 1970s, decision making at Adidas was not structured around groups. How might a committee structure have resulted in a different outcome at Adidas? What sort of managers/individuals would you have included in a group to make strategic decisions in Adidas?
3. What decisions did Nike's management make that helped lead to its success? Were these any different from its other competitors like Reebok?
4. What, if anything, do you think Adidas' management can do today to correct past mistakes?

Source: This case is based on data included in Robert F. Hartley, *Management Mistakes and Successes* (New York: John Wiley & Sons, 1991), pp. 46–66.

The Realities of Decision Making

What do you do when you've just graduated from a business program and you're looking for something to do that will use the skills you've just learned? If you're an entrepreneur, you start a business. But what kind of business? Don't you have to have experience, an original idea and lots of capital? The answer is no. But you do have to have some things. You have to have an idea that has commercial attraction, and you have to be able to turn that idea into a product or service that people will buy.

The Earth Buddy is that sort of an idea. It's not original; it's been done before. But, fresh out of business school, Anton Rabie and Ronnen Harary thought they could manufacture and market a product that is (a) easy to assemble, and (b) has market potential. And so did their friends Ben Varadi and Michelle and Austin Muscat. The Earth Buddy is a mixture of grass seed and sawdust, moulded in a nylon stocking, and it's something that people want. It's instant grass. And it was an instant success because they were able to get accounts like Canadian Tire, Zellers and Kmart, and make a profit of $400,000 in their first summer. And then came the big challenge.

The company got a call from Kmart in the U.S., expressing interest in placing an order for half a million Earth Buddies. Sounds fantastic, but there are potential problems. First, the company didn't have the actual order in their hands, and second, Kmart was only interested if delivery could be made on time. And that led to the problem of how to get 500,000 units ready. It meant having to triple production *right away* in order to build up the necessary stock. The problem involved a number of risks, the first of which was the cost of building up an inventory of goods, but not getting the order. And the second was not being able to deliver the 500,000 units on time and thereby losing the order. The two were closely intertwined — a sort of chicken-and-egg situation.

Then there were the added problems of getting enough raw materials — grass seed, sawdust and stockings — and getting them as they were needed, plus hiring and training more workers, creating systems to cope with the work and cash flow, and getting funding from the bank to finance the inventory. The company's accountant was horrified when he looked at the state of the books. His view was, "These are two guys that came out of university. They don't know anything. All they know is the theory. They've never run a business before. They didn't know anything about anything."

Questions

1. Use the decision-making process outlined in the chapter to decide what you would do in this situation. Go through all the steps, writing down the relevant information.
2. List the problems you encountered going through the process in question 3.
3. Get together with two or three other people in the class, compare your notes on the process, and reach a decision as a group. Do you feel you have a better decision as a result? Why or why not?

Video Resource: "Earth Buddy," *Venture* 518 (December 11, 1994).

Foundations of Organizing

Learning Objectives

WHAT WILL I BE ABLE TO DO AFTER I FINISH THIS CHAPTER?

1. Define organization structure.
2. Identify the advantages and disadvantages of division of labour.
3. Contrast power with authority.
4. Explain why wider spans of control are related to increased efficiency.
5. Identify the five different ways by which management can departmentalize.
6. Contrast mechanistic and organic organizations.
7. Explain the strategy-determines-structure thesis.
8. Summarize the effect of size on structure.
9. Explain the effect of technology on structure.
10. Describe how environmental uncertainty affects structure.

In the 1920s and 1930s, as organizations built successive layers of hierarchy, there was a need to provide coordination. Management writers of that time, for instance, argued that formal, rigid organizational structures would best serve the company. That may have been true sixty or more years ago—and these bureaucratic structures flourished. But by the 1980s, the environment was changing. Global competition, technological advancements, a changing workforce, and the like were making bureaucracies inefficient for many businesses. Since the late 1980s, most organizations have restructured themselves to be more customer- and market-oriented and to increase productivity.

The best-laid plans often fail because managers don't have the right structure in place. And what's the right structure at one time may be inappropriate a year or two later. Gerry and Lilo Leeds, the husband and wife team that run CMP Publications, recognize these facts.[1]

The Leedses founded CMP in 1971. By 1987, their firm produced ten business newspapers and magazines that were leaders in their respective markets. The organization they had originally created for CMP centralized all key decision making in their hands. While this worked fine in the early years, by 1987 it was no longer effective. The Leedses became harder to meet with. It became harder and harder for employees to get the answers to day-to-day questions. And important decisions that required rapid responses were regularly delayed. CMP had grown too big for its original structure.

The Leedses recognized the problem and reorganized. First, they broke the company into manageable units and put a separate manager in charge of each. Then they gave each of these managers the authority to run and grow his or her own division. Second, the Leedses created a publications committee to oversee the various divisions. Each of the division managers sits on this committee, as do the Leedses. The division managers report to the publications committee, which in turn, ensures that all the divisions operate within CMP's overall strategy.

These structural changes have proved effective. CMP now puts out a total of fourteen publications, sales are well over $200 million a year, and revenue growth continues at a rate of 30 per cent annually.

Structural changes can also be on a smaller scale, but have large consequences, as Multilin, a subsidiary of Derlan Industries of Toronto, demonstrates. Multilin makes electronic motor relays—the "brains" of switchgears in large electric motors used in places like pulp mills and heavy manufacturing. In 1990, Multilin's on-time delivery to customers had dropped to 55 per cent and the time between order and delivery was forty-two days. The factory was inefficient, as was the warehouse. The problem? The structure of the assembly process. Prior to 1990, manufacturing was done on a classic assembly line—one step after another performed by a sequence of people and machines, with the people being specialized in performing their one, or few, steps in the process. The solution? Changing to a structure made up of teams. A simple change on the face of it, but one that led to a reduction in the time between order and delivery from forty-two days to four days, that helped raise revenues by 30 per cent, that reduced inventory carrying costs by $250,000 a year, and that helped exports to the United States, as a percentage of sales, increase from 48 per cent in 1986 to 66 per cent in 1992.[2]

In this chapter, we'll present the foundations of organization structure. We'll define the concept and its key components, introduce basic organization design options, and consider contingency variables that determine when certain design options work better than others.

As their publishing business grew, Gerry and Lilo Leeds began to experience communications problems that prompted a new structure for the company.

What Is Organization Structure?

organization structure
An organization's framework as expressed by its degree of complexity, formalization, and centralization.

Organization structure describes the organization's framework. Just as human beings have skeletons that define their shapes, organizations have structures that define theirs. An organization's structure can be dissected into three parts: complexity, formalization, and centralization.[3] We have briefly described each in Exhibit 6-1.

When managers construct or change an organization's structure, they are engaged in organization design. When we discuss managers making structural decisions—for example, determining the level at which decisions should be made or the number of standardized rules for employees to follow—we are referring to organization design. In the next chapter, we'll show how the three components of an organization—its complexity, formalization, and centralization—can be mixed and matched to create various organization designs.

Basic Organization Design Concepts

The classical concepts of organization design were formulated by management writers in the early years of this century (see Details on a Management Classic). These classical theorists offered a set of principles for managers to follow in organization design. More than six decades have passed since most of these principles were originally proposed. Given the passing of that much time and all the changes that have taken place in our society, you might think that these principles would be fairly worthless today. Surprisingly, they're not—although they may not be in place as strongly as they were in the 1930s. Nonetheless, for the most part, they still provide valuable insights into designing effective and efficient organizations. Of course, we have also gained a great deal of knowledge over the years as to the limitations of these principles.

We'll discuss the five basic classical principles that have guided organization design decisions over the years. We'll also present an updated analysis of how each has had to be modified to reflect the increasing sophistication and changing nature of organizational activities.

Exhibit 6-1 Characteristics of Organizational Structure

Complexity:	The amount of horizontal, vertical, and spatial differentiation that exists in an organization. The degree of complexity is a function of the extent to which activities are divided horizontally into separate departments (like accounting and marketing), the number of vertical layers in an organization (such as president, senior vice-president, vice-president, director, department manager, unit manager, supervisor), or the geographic dispersement of organizational activities (such as one located in Butte, Montana, and another in Norfolk, Virginia).
Formalization:	Formalization refers to the degree to which an organization relies on rules and procedures to direct the behaviour of employees.
Centralization:	Refers to the location where decisions are made. Centralized decisions are made by top management. Decentralized decisions are made by the level of individual closest to the problem.

Details on a Management Classic

MAX WEBER AND THE IDEAL STRUCTURE: BUREAUCRACY

The central theme in Weber's bureaucratic model is standardization.[4] The behaviour of people in bureaucracies is predetermined by the standardized structure and processes. The model itself can be dissected into three groups of characteristics—those that relate to the structure and function of the organization, those that deal with means of rewarding effort, and those that deal with protection for individual members.

Weber's model stipulates a hierarchy of offices, with each office under the direction of a higher one. Each of these offices is differentiated horizontally by division of labour. This division of labour creates units of expertise, defines areas of action consistent with competence of unit members, assigns responsibilities for carrying out these actions, and allocates commensurate authority to fulfil these responsibilities. All the while, written rules govern the performance of members' duties. This imposition of structure and functions provides a high level of specialized expertise, coordination of roles, and control of group members through standardization.

The second group of characteristics in Weber's model relates to rewards. Members receive salaries in relation to their rank in the organization. Promotions are based on objective criteria such as seniority or achievement. Since members are not owners, it is important that there be a clear separation of their private affairs and property from the organization's property and affairs. It is further expected that commitment to the organization is paramount, the position in the organization being the employee's sole occupation.

Finally, Weber's model seeks to protect the rights of individuals. In return for a career commitment, members receive protection from arbitrary actions by employers, clear knowledge of their responsibilities, the amount of authority their boss holds, and the ability to appeal decisions that they see as unfair or outside the parameters of their boss's authority.

Weber believed that organizations that were structured around these three sets of characteristics would be more rational and efficient. Career advancement would be based on individual qualifications as opposed to favouritism. Employee commitment would be maximized and conflicts of interest would be eliminated by providing lifetime employment and separating employees' off-the-job roles from those required to fulfil organizational goals. ▼

What Is Division of Labour?

As envisioned by classical management writers, **division of labour** means that, rather than an entire job being done by one individual, it is broken down into a number of steps, each step being completed by a separate individual. In essence, individuals specialize in doing part of an activity rather than the entire activity. Assembly line production, in which each worker does the same standardized task over and over again, is an example of division of labour.

Division of labour makes efficient use of the diversity of skills that workers hold. In most organizations, some tasks require highly developed skills; others can be performed by the untrained. If all workers were engaged in each step of, say, an organization's manufacturing process, all would have to have the skills necessary to perform both

division of labour
The breakdown of jobs into narrow, repetitive tasks.

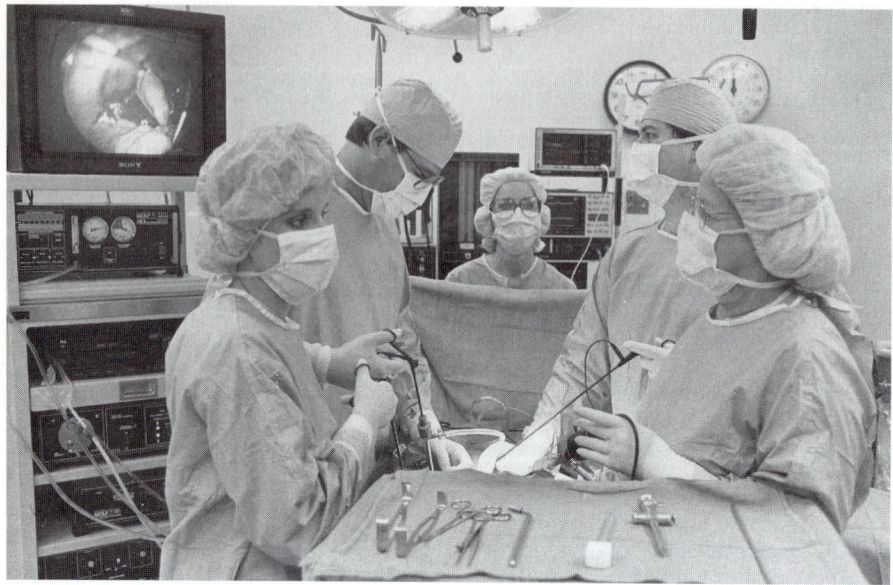

We see the results of division of labour in operating rooms. In this environment, doctors, nurses, and other medical professionals each perform a precise and repetitive set of tasks.

the most demanding and the least demanding jobs. The result would be that, except when performing the most highly skilled or highly sophisticated tasks, employees would be working below their skill level. Because skilled workers are paid more than unskilled workers and their wages tend to reflect their highest level of skill, it represents an inefficient usage of resources to pay highly skilled workers to do easy tasks.

The classical writers viewed division of labour as an unending source of increased productivity. At the turn of the twentieth century and earlier, this generalization was undoubtedly accurate. Because specialization was not widely practised, its introduction almost always generated higher productivity. But a good thing can be carried too far. There is a point at which the human diseconomies from division of labour—which surface as boredom, fatigue, stress, low productivity, poor quality, increased absenteeism, and high turnover—exceed the economic advantages (see Exhibit 6-2).

By the 1960s, that point had been reached in a number of jobs. In such cases, productivity could be increased by enlarging, rather than narrowing, the scope of job activities.[5] For instance, in the next chapter, we'll discuss successful efforts to increase productivity by giving employees a variety of activities to do, allowing them to do a

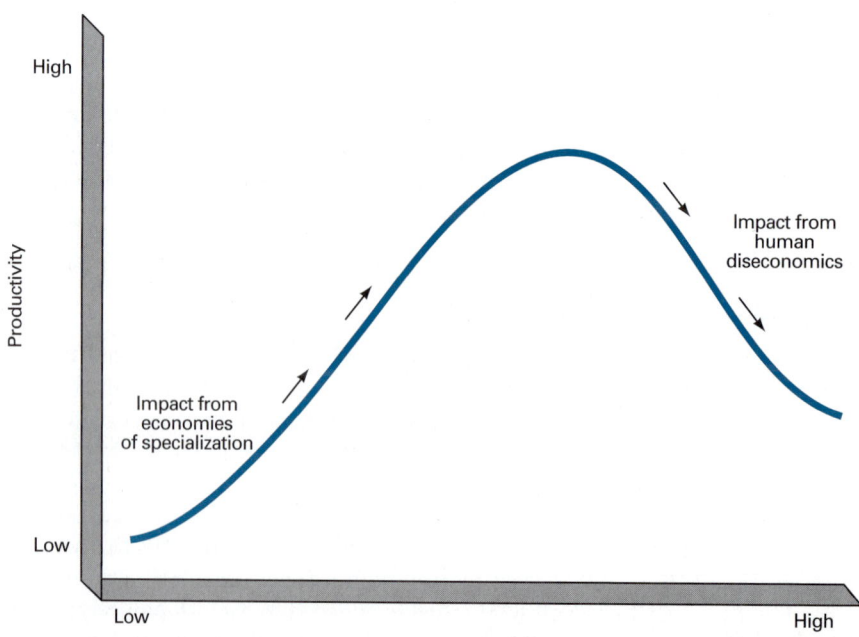

Exhibit 6-2 Economies and Diseconomies of Division of Labour

Foundations of Organizing

whole and complete piece of work, and putting them together into teams. Each of these ideas, of course, runs counter to the division of labour concept. Yet, overall, the division of labour concept is alive and well in most organizations today. We have to recognize the economies it provides in certain types of jobs, but we also have to recognize its limitations.

What Is the Unity of Command?

The classical writers professing the **unity of command** principle argued that a subordinate should have one and only one superior to whom he or she is directly responsible. No person should report to two or more bosses. Otherwise, an employee might have to cope with conflicting demands or priorities from several superiors. In those rare instances when the unity of command principle had to be violated, the classical viewpoint always explicitly designated that there be a clear separation of activities and a supervisor responsible for each.

The unity of command concept was logical when organizations were comparatively simple. Under most circumstances it is still sound advice, and most contemporary organizations closely adhere to this principle. Yet there are instances, which we'll introduce in the next chapter, when strict adherence to the unity of command creates a degree of inflexibility that hinders an organization's performance.[6]

unity of command
The principle that a subordinate should have one and only one superior to whom he or she is directly responsible.

What Is Authority and Responsibility?

Authority refers to the rights inherent in a managerial position to give orders and expect the orders to be obeyed. Authority was a major tenet of the classical writers; it was viewed as the glue that held the organization together. It was to be delegated downward to subordinate managers, giving them certain rights while providing certain prescribed limits within which to operate (see Details on a Management Classic). Each management position has specific inherent rights that incumbents acquire from the position's rank or title. Authority, therefore, relates to one's position within an organization and ignores the personal characteristics of the individual manager. It has nothing directly to do with the individual. The expression, "The king is dead; long live the king," illustrates the concept. Whoever is king acquires the rights inherent in the king's position. When a position of authority is vacated, the person who has left the position no longer has any authority. The authority remains with the position and its new incumbent.

authority
The rights inherent in a managerial position to give orders and expect them to be obeyed.

Army drill instructors exemplify individuals who give orders and expect the orders to be obeyed. This drill sergeant's emphasis is on accomplishing tasks. The recruits' emphasis is on accepting authority figures.

Details on a Management Classic

STANLEY MILGRAM AND FOLLOWING ORDERS

Stanley Milgram, a social psychologist at Yale University, wondered how far individuals would go in following orders.[7] If subjects were placed in the role of a teacher in a learning experiment and told by the experimenter to administer a shock to a learner each time that learner made a mistake, would the subjects follow the commands of the experimenter? Would their willingness to comply decrease as the intensity of the shock was increased?

To test these hypotheses, Milgram hired a set of subjects. Each was led to believe that the experiment was to investigate the effect of punishment on memory. Their job was to act as teachers and administer punishment whenever the learner made a mistake on a learning test. Punishment in this case was administered by electric shock. The subject sat in front of a shock generator with thirty levels of shock; beginning at zero and progressing in 15-volt increments to a high of 450 volts. The demarcations of these positions ranged from "slight shock" at 15 volts to "danger: severe shock" at 450 volts. And to add realism to the experiment, the subjects received a sample shock of 45 volts and saw the learner strapped in an electric chair in an adjacent room. Of course, the learner was an actor, and the electric shocks were phony—but the subjects didn't know this.

The subjects were instructed to shock the learner each time he made a mistake. And subsequent mistakes would result in an increase in shock intensity. Throughout the experiment, the subject got verbal feedback from the learner. At 75 volts, the learner began to grunt and moan; at 150 volts, he demanded to be released from the experiment; at 180 volts he cried out that he could no longer stand the pain; and at 300 volts, he insisted he be let out because of a heart condition. After 300 volts, the learner did not respond to further questions.

Most subjects protested and, fearful they might kill the learner if the increased shocks were to bring on a heart attack, insisted they could not go on. But the experimenter responded by saying that they had to, that was their job. The majority of the subjects dissented. But dissension isn't synonymous with disobedience. Sixty-two per cent of the subjects increased the shock level to the maximum of 450 volts. The average level of shock administered by the remaining 38 per cent was nearly 370 volts—more than enough to kill even the strongest human.

What can we conclude from Milgram's results? Well, one obvious conclusion is that authority is a potent source of getting people to do things. Subjects in Milgram's experiment administered levels of shock far above that which they wanted—but they did it because they were told they had to. That, in spite of the fact, that they could have voluntarily walked out of the room anytime they wanted. ▼

responsibility
An obligation to perform assigned activities.

When we delegate authority, we must allocate commensurate **responsibility**. That is, when one is given "rights," one also assumes a corresponding "obligation" to perform. Allocating authority without responsibility creates opportunities for abuse, and no one should be held responsible for something over which he or she has no authority.

Foundations of Organizing

Are There Different Types of Authority Relationships? The classical writers distinguished between two forms of authority relations: line authority and staff authority. **Line authority** is the authority that entitles a manager to direct the work of an employee. It is the employer-employee authority relationship that extends from the top of the organization to the lowest echelon, following what is called the **chain of command.** This is shown in Exhibit 6-3. As a link in the chain of command, a manager with line authority has the right to direct the work of employees and to make certain decisions without consulting others. Of course, in the chain of command, every manager is also subject to the direction of his or her supervisor.

Sometimes the term line is used to differentiate line managers from staff managers. In this context, line emphasizes managers whose organizational function contributes directly to the achievement of organizational objectives. In a manufacturing firm, line managers are typically in the production and sales functions, whereas managers in human resources management and accounting are considered staff managers. But whether a manager's function is classified as line or staff depends on the organization's objectives. For example, at Drake Personnel Services, a supplier of temporary employees, interviewers have a line function. Similarly, at the accounting firm of Price Waterhouse, accounting is a line function.

As organizations get larger and more complex, line managers find that they do not have the time, expertise, or resources to get their jobs done effectively. In response, they create **staff authority** functions to support, assist, advise, and generally reduce some of the informational burdens they have. The hospital administrator can't effectively handle all the purchasing of supplies that the hospital needs, so she creates a purchasing

line authority
The authority that entitles a manager to direct the work of an employee.

chain of command
The flow of authority from the top to the bottom of an organization.

staff authority
Authority that supports, assists, and advises holders of line authority.

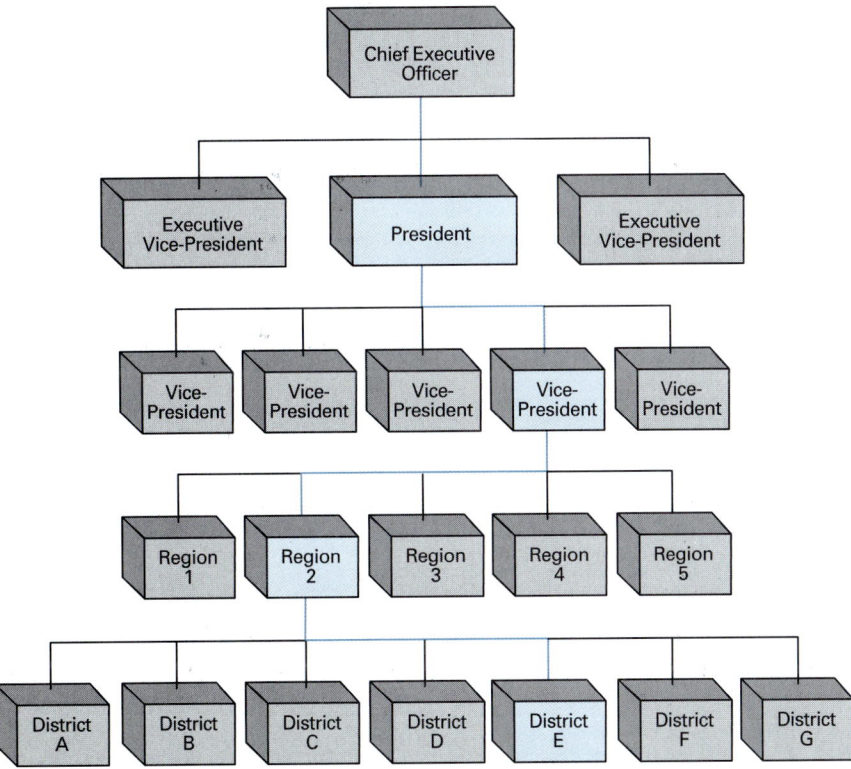

Exhibit 6-3 The Chain of Command

department. The purchasing department is a staff department. Of course, the head of the purchasing department has line authority over her subordinate purchasing agents. The hospital administrator might also find that she is overburdened and needs an assistant. In creating the position of assistant to the hospital administrator, she has created a staff position. Exhibit 6-4 illustrates line and staff authority.

How Is The Contemporary View of Authority and Responsibility Different from the Classical View? The classical writers were enamored with authority. They actively assumed that the rights inherent in one's formal position in an organization were the sole source of influence. They believed that managers were all-powerful. This might have been true sixty or more years ago. Organizations were simpler. Staff was less important. Managers were only minimally dependent on technical specialists. Under such conditions, influence is the same as authority; and the higher a manager's position in the organization, the more influence he or she had. However, those conditions no longer hold. Researchers and practitioners of management now recognize that you don't have to be a manager to have power, nor is power perfectly correlated to one's level in the organization. Authority is an important concept in organizations, but an exclusive focus on authority produces a narrow, unrealistic view of influence in organizations. Today, we recognize that authority is but one element in the larger concept of power.[8]

How Do Authority and Power Differ? The terms authority and power are frequently confused. Authority is a right, the legitimacy of which is based on the authority figure's position in the organization. Authority goes with the job. **Power,** on the other hand, refers to an individual's capacity to influence decisions. Authority is part of the larger concept of power. That is, the formal rights that come with an individual's position in the organization are just one means by which an individual can affect the decision process.

power
The capacity to influence decisions.

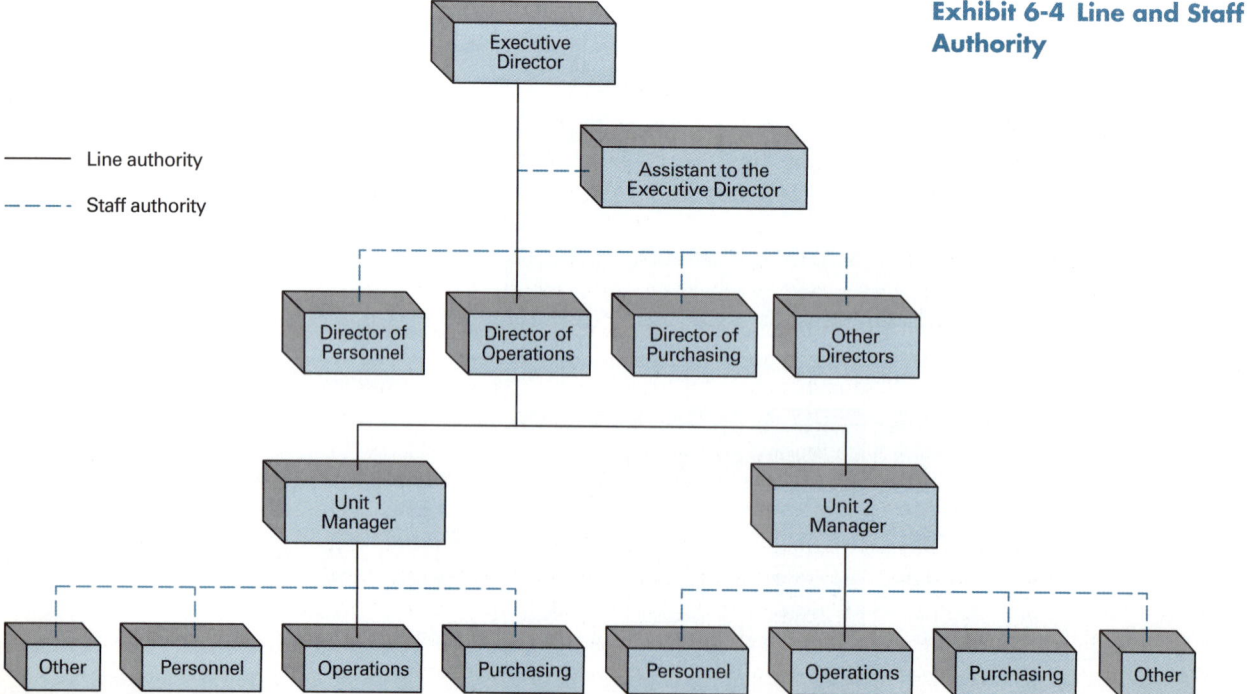

Exhibit 6-4 Line and Staff Authority

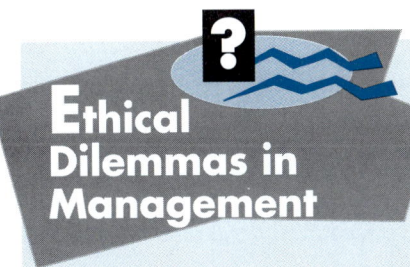

Ethical Dilemmas in Management

▼ SHOULD YOU FOLLOW ORDERS WITH WHICH YOU DON'T AGREE? ▲

A few years back, a study of business executives revealed that most had obeyed orders that they had found personally objectionable or unethical.[9] Far more thought-provoking was a survey taken among the general public near the end of the Vietnam War. In spite of public dismay over the actions of some military personnel during that war, about half the respondents said that they would have shot civilian men, women, and children in cold blood if they had been ordered to do so by their commanding officer.[10]

If you were asked to follow orders that you believed were unconscionable, would you comply? For example, what if your boss asked you to destroy evidence that he or she had been stealing a great deal of money from the organization?

What if you merely disagreed with the orders? For instance, what if your boss asked you to bring him or her coffee each morning even though no such task is included in your job description? What would you do?

Exhibit 6-5 visually depicts the difference between authority and power (p. 134). The two-dimensional arrangement of boxes in Part A portrays authority. The area in which the authority applies is defined by the horizontal dimension. Each horizontal grouping represents a functional area. The influence one holds in the organization is defined by the vertical dimension in the structure. The higher one is in the organization, the greater one's authority.

Power, on the other hand, is a three-dimensional concept (see the cone in Part B of Exhibit 6-5). It includes not only the functional and hierarchical dimensions, but also a third dimension called centrality. While authority is defined by one's vertical position in the hierarchy, power is made up of both one's vertical position and one's distance from the organization's power core, or centre.

Think of the cone in Exhibit 6-5 as being an organization. The centre of the cone is the power core. The closer you are to the power core, the more influence you have on decisions. The existence of a power core is, in fact, the only difference between A and B in Exhibit 6-5. The vertical hierarchy dimension in A is merely one's level on the outer edge of the cone. The top of the cone corresponds to the top of the hierarchy, the middle of the cone to the middle of the hierarchy, and so on. Similarly, the functional groups in A become wedges in the cone. Each wedge represents a functional area.

The cone analogy explicitly acknowledges two facts: (1) the higher one moves in an organization (an increase in authority), the closer one moves to the power core; and (2) it is not necessary to have authority in order to wield power because one can move horizontally inward toward the power core without moving up.

Have you ever noticed that company secretaries usually have a great deal of power, even though they have little authority? As gatekeepers for their bosses, secretaries have considerable say over whom their bosses see and when. Furthermore, because they are regularly relied upon to pass information on to their bosses, they have some control over what their bosses hear. It's not unusual for $75,000-a-year middle managers to tread very carefully in order not to upset their boss's $25,000-a-year secretary. Why? Because the secretary has power! The secretary may be low in the authority hierarchy but close to the power core. Low-ranking employees who have relatives, friends, or associates in high places might also be close to the power core. So, too, are employees with scarce and important skills. The lowly production-engineer with twenty years of experience in a company might be

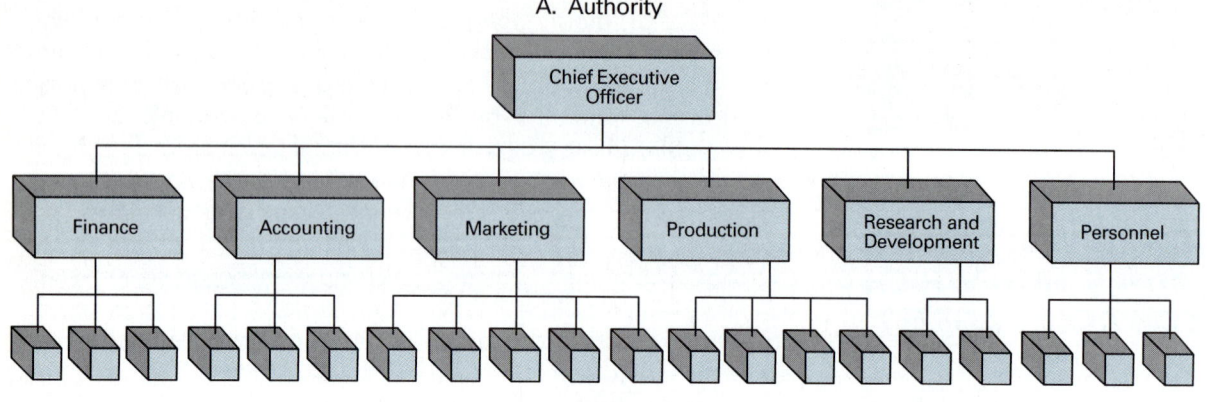

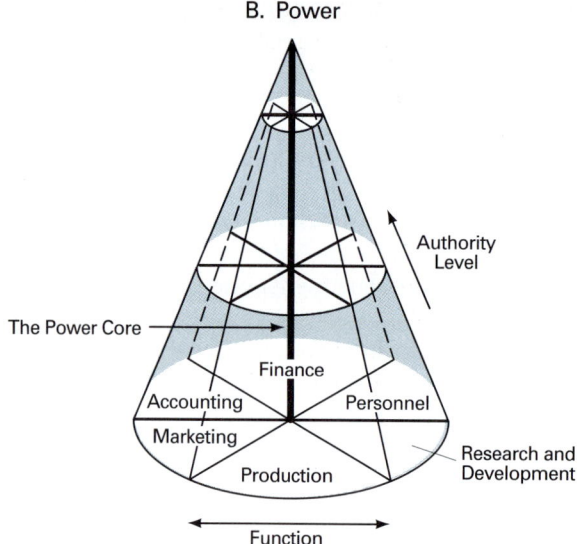

Exhibit 6-5 Authority versus Power

the only one in the firm who knows the inner workings of all the old production machinery. When pieces of this old equipment break down, no one but this engineer understands how to fix them. Suddenly, the engineer's influence is much greater than it would appear from his or her level in the vertical hierarchy. So what does this tell us about power? It states that power can come from different areas (see Developing Management Skills). John French and Bertram Raven have identified five sources or bases of power: coercive, reward, legitimate, expert, and referent.[11] We have summarized them in Exhibit 6-6.

What Is the Span of Control?

span of control
The number of subordinates a manager can direct efficiently and effectively.

How many employees can a manager efficiently and effectively direct? This question of **span of control** received a great deal of attention from early writers. While there was no consensus on a specific number, the classical writers favoured small spans—typically no more than six—in order to maintain close control.[12] However, several writers did acknowledge level in the organization as a contingency variable. They argued that as a manager rises in an organization, he or she has to deal with a greater number of ill-structured problems, so top managers need a smaller span than do middle managers, and middle managers require a smaller span than do supervisors.

Foundations of Organizing

Why Is the Span of Control Concept Important? The span of control concept is important because, to a large degree, it determines the number of levels and managers an organization has. All things being equal, the wider or larger the span, the more efficient the organization design.

Coercive Power:	Power that is dependent on fear.
Reward Power:	Power based on the ability to distribute anything that others may value.
Legitimate Power:	Power based on one's position in the formal hierarchy.
Expert Power:	Power based on one's expertise, special skill, or knowledge.
Referent Power:	Power based on identification with a person who has desirable resources or personal traits.

Exhibit 6-6 Types of Power

How Does the Contemporary View of Span of Control Differ from the Classical View? In 1992, Wal-Mart surpassed Sears as the number-one retailer in the United States. Management writer Tom Peters predicted this result a few years earlier: "Sears doesn't have a chance," he said. "A twelve-layer company can't compete with a three-layer company."[13] Peters might have exaggerated the point a bit, but it clearly reflects the fact that in recent years the pendulum has swung toward designing flat structures with wide spans of control. The Canadian telephone companies are experiencing really strong competitive pressure and many are having trouble adjusting rapidly because of the inflexibility of their multi-level structures.

More organizations are increasing their spans of control. The span for managers at such companies as General Electric and Reynolds Metals has expanded to ten or twelve subordinates—twice the number of fifteen years ago.[14] The span of control is increasingly being determined by looking at contingency variables. It's obvious that the more training and experience employees have, the less direct supervision they need. Managers who have well-trained and experienced employees can function with a wider span. Other contingency variables that will determine the appropriate span include similarity of subordinate tasks, the complexity of those tasks, the physical proximity of subordinates, the

Developing Management Skills

▼ BUILDING A POWER BASE ▲

▶ **1. Gain control over organizational resources that are scarce and important.** In doing so, you generate expert and referent power.

▶ **2. Make yourself appear indispensable.** It's difficult to remove someone who is seen as critical to an operation's success.

▶ **3. Be visible.** By maintaining a high profile and being available, you aid in developing an appearance of being indispensable.

▶ **4. Develop powerful allies.** Powerful allies in the organization can provide you with important information and also help protect you from attacks by others.

▶ **5. Avoid tainted members.** Carefully keep your distance from organizational members whose status is questionable. Don't be judged by the company you keep. Given the reality that effectiveness has a large subjective component, your own effectiveness might be called into question if you are perceived as being too closely associated with tainted people.

▶ **6. Support your boss.** Your immediate future is in the hands of your current boss. Since he or she evaluates your performance, you will typically want to do whatever is necessary to have your boss on your side. Make every effort to help your boss succeed.

Jack Welch, CEO of GE, talks about the Draconian changes occurring at GE, like his 360-degree employee performance review system (where employees appraise bosses as well as the reverse), that have helped the company increase its market value to $68 billion.

degree to which standardized procedures are in place, the sophistication of the organization's management information system, the strength of the organization's culture, and the preferred style of the manager.[15]

Can You Identify the Five Ways to Departmentalize?

The classical writers argued that activities in the organization should be specialized and grouped into departments. Division of labour creates specialists who need coordination. This coordination is facilitated by putting specialists together in departments under the direction of a manager. Creation of these departments is typically based on the work functions being performed, the product or service being offered, the target customer or client, the geographic territory being covered, or the process being used to turn inputs into outputs. No single method of departmentalization was advocated by the classical writers. The method or methods used should reflect the grouping that would best contribute to the attainment of the organization's objectives and the goals of individual units.

functional departmentalization
Grouping activities by functions performed.

What Do the Five Departmentalizations Look Like? One of the most popular ways to group activities is by functions performed, or **functional departmentalization**. A manufacturing manager might organize his or her plant by separating engineering, accounting, manufacturing, personnel, and purchasing specialists into common departments (see Exhibit 6-7). Functional departmentalization can be used in all types of organizations. Only the functions change to reflect the organization's objectives and activities. A hospital might have departments devoted to research, patient care, accounting, and so forth. A professional baseball franchise might have departments labelled player personnel, ticket sales, and travel and accommodations.

Exhibit 6-7 Functional Departmentalization

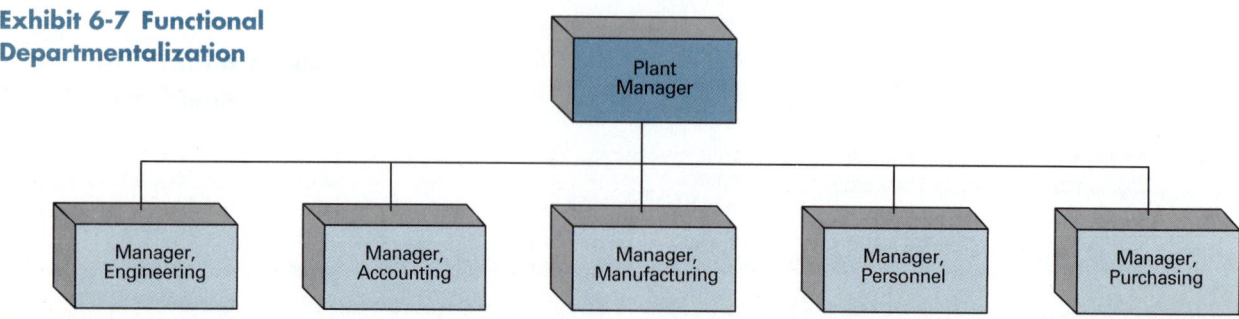

Foundations of Organizing

Exhibit 6-8 illustrates the **product departmentalization** method used at Sun Petroleum Products. Each major product area in the corporation is placed under the authority of a vice-president who is a specialist in, and is responsible for, everything having to do with his or her product line. Notice, for example, in contrast to functional departmentalization, that manufacturing and other major activities have been divided up to give the product managers (vice-presidents, in this case) considerable autonomy and control. If an organization's activities are service-related rather than product-related, each service would be autonomously grouped. For instance, an accounting firm would have departments for tax, management consulting, auditing, and the like. Each offers a common array of services under the direction of a product or service manager.

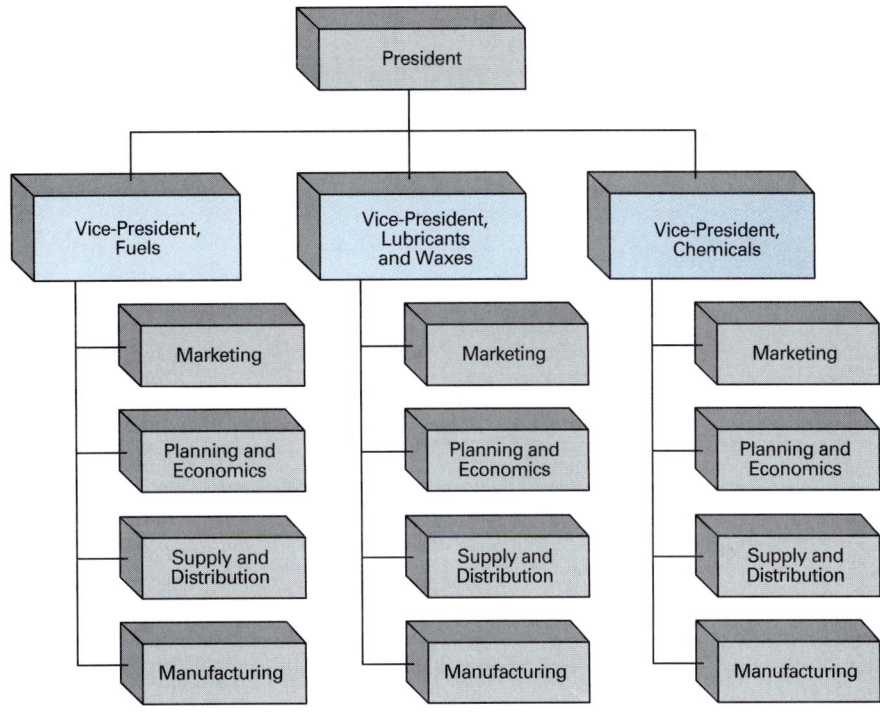

Exhibit 6-8 Product Departmentalization

The particular type of customer the organization seeks to reach can also be used to group employees. The sales activities in an office supply firm, for instance, can be broken down into three departments to serve retail, wholesale, and government customers (see Exhibit 6-9). A large law office can segment its staff on the basis of whether it serves corporate or individual clients. The assumption underlying **customer departmentalization** is that customers in each department have a common set of problems and needs that can best be met by having specialists for each.

Another way to departmentalize is on the basis of geography or territory—**geographic departmentalization.** The sales function might have western, southern, midwestern, and eastern regions (see Exhibit 6-10). A large school district might have six high schools to provide for each of the major geographic territories within the district. If an organization's customers are scattered over a large geographic area, this form of departmentalization can be valuable.

product departmentalization
Grouping activities by product line.

customer departmentalization
Grouping activities on the basis of common customers.

geographic departmentalization
Grouping activities on the basis of territory.

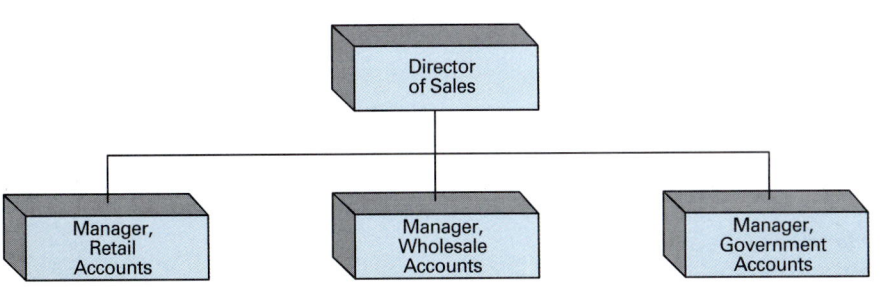

Exhibit 6-9 Customer Departmentalization

Exhibit 6-10 Geographic Departmentalization

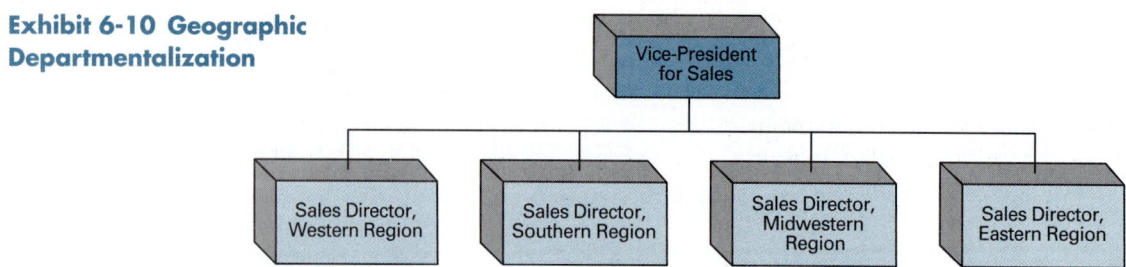

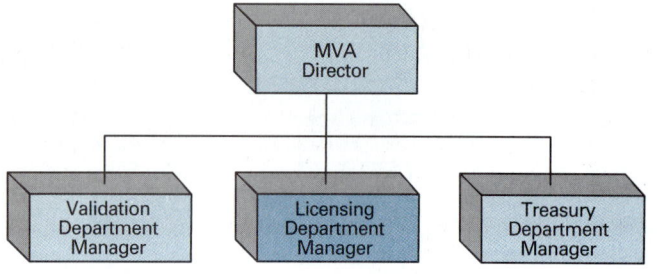

Exhibit 6-11 Process Departmentalization

Exhibit 6-11 represents an example of **process departmentalization** by depicting the various departments in a motor vehicle department. If you have ever been to a motor vehicle office to get a driver's licence, you probably went through several departments before receiving your licence. In some areas, applicants must go through three steps, each handled by a separate department: (1) validation, by the motor vehicles division; (2) processing, by the licensing department; and (3) payment collection, by the treasury department.

How Does the Contemporary View of Departmentalization Differ from the Classical View? Most large organizations continue to use most or all of the departmental groups suggested by the classical writers. Black & Decker, for instance, organizes each of its divisions along functional lines, organizes its manufacturing units around processes, departmentalizes sales around geographic regions, and divides each sales region into customer groupings. But a recent trend needs to be mentioned. That is, rigid departmentalization is being complemented by the use of teams that cross over traditional departmental lines.

Today's competitive environment has refocused the attention of management to its customers. To better monitor the needs of customers and to be able to respond to changes in those needs, many organizations have given greater emphasis to customer departmentalization. Xerox, for example, has eliminated its corporate marketing staff and placed marketing specialists out in the field.[16] This allows the company to better identify its customers and to respond faster to their requirements.

We are also seeing a great deal more use of teams today as a device for accomplishing organizational objectives. A list of some of the companies using cross-departmental teams includes Ford, Imperial Oil, Rubbermaid, most large Canadian hospitals, and a number of government departments. As tasks have become more complex and diverse skills are needed to accomplish these tasks, management has increasingly introduced the use of teams and task forces.

process departmentalization
Grouping activities on the basis of product or customer flow.

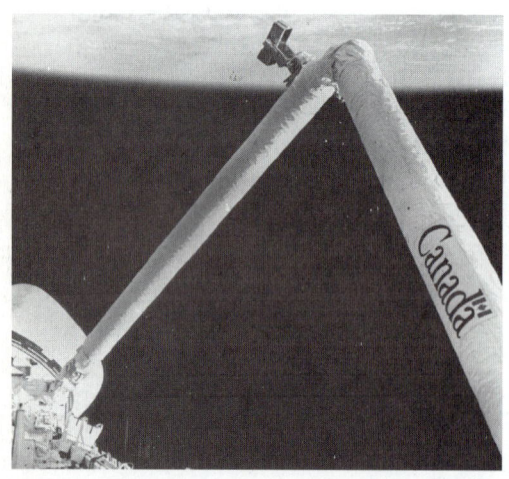

The Canadarm has been Canada's major contribution to the NASA space program. It is an extending arm that allows astronauts to manipulate objects outside the shuttle.

The Contingency Approach to Organization Design

If we combine the classical principles, we arrive at what most of the early writers believed to be the ideal structural design: the mechanistic or bureaucratic organization. Today we recognize that there

Foundations of Organizing

is no single "ideal" organization design for all situations. Rather, the ideal organization design depends on contingency factors. In this section, we'll look at two generic models of organization design and then look at the contingency factors that favour each.

How Is a Mechanistic Organization Different from an Organic Organization?

Exhibit 6-12 describes two diverse organizational forms.[17] The **mechanistic organization** (or **bureaucracy**) was the natural result of combining the classical principles. Adherence to the unity of command principle ensured the existence of a formal hierarchy of authority, with each person controlled and supervised by one superior. Keeping the span of control small at increasingly higher levels in the organization created tall, impersonal structures. As the distance between the top and the bottom of the organization expanded, top management would increasingly impose rules and regulations. Because top managers couldn't control lower-level activities through direct observation and ensure the use of standard practices, they substituted rules and regulations. The classical writers' belief in a high degree of division of labour created jobs that were simple, routine, and standardized. Further specialization through the use of departmentalization increased impersonality and the need for multiple layers of management to coordinate the specialized departments.

The **organic organization** (also referred to as an **adhocracy**) is a direct contrast to the mechanistic form. It is low in complexity, low in formalization, and decentralized. The organic organization is a highly adaptive form that is as loose and flexible as the mechanistic organization is rigid and stable. Rather than having standardized jobs and regulations, the adhocracy's loose structure allows it to change rapidly as needs require. Adhocracies

What can happen to a company that offers early retirement to reduce the number of employees, and twice as many people as expected opt to retire? Texas Instruments created work teams among the remaining employees. These teams have helped the company increase sales per employee from $88,300 in 1989 to $122,820 in 1992.

mechanistic organization
A structure that is high in complexity, formalization, and centralization (bureaucracy).

bureaucracy
A form of organization marked by division of labour, hierarchy, rules and regulations, and impersonal relationships (mechanistic).

organic organization
A structure that is low in complexity, formalization, and centralization (adhocracy).

adhocracy
A structure that is low in complexity, formalization, and centralization (organic).

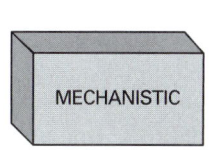
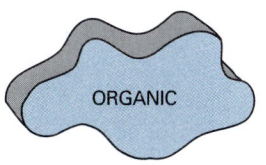

- ☐ Rigid hierarchical relationships
- ☐ Fixed duties
- ☐ High formalization
- ☐ Formalized communication channels
- ☐ Centralized decision authority

- ☐ Collaboration (both vertical and horizontal)
- ☐ Adaptable duties
- ☐ Low formalization
- ☐ Informal communication
- ☐ Decentralized decision authority

Exhibit 6-12 Mechanistic versus Organic Organizations

have division of labour, but the jobs people do are not standardized. Employees tend to be professionals who are technically proficient and trained to handle diverse problems. They need very few formal rules and little direct supervision because their training has instilled in them standards of professional conduct. For instance, a computer engineer who is given an assignment doesn't need to be given procedures on how to do it. The engineer can solve most problems alone or after conferring with colleagues. Professional standards guide his or her behaviour. The organic organization is low in centralization in order for the professional to respond quickly to problems and because top management cannot be expected to possess the expertise to make necessary decisions.

What Contingency Variables Affect Organization Design Options?

When you think of GM, what comes to mind? Pontiacs, Chevrolets, and the like? Probably so, but GM is more than an auto and truck manufacturer. They also make air conditioners, electrical equipment, and turbine engines, as shown here.

Several variables have been found to affect an organization's structure. The more popular of these are strategy, size, technology, and environment. Let's briefly look at each of these.

How Does Strategy Affect Structure? An organization's structure is a means to help management achieve its objectives. Since objectives are derived from the organization's overall strategy, it is only logical that strategy and structure should be closely linked. More specifically, structure should follow strategy. If management makes a significant change in its organization's strategy, it will need to modify structure to accommodate and support this change.

The first important research on the strategy-structure relationship was a study of close to 100 large U.S. companies conducted by Alfred Chandler.[18] After tracing the development of these organizations over a fifty-year period and compiling extensive case histories of companies such as du Pont, General Motors, Standard Oil of New Jersey, and Sears, Chandler concluded that changes in corporate strategy precede and lead to changes in an organization's structure. Specifically, he found that organizations usually begin with a single product or line. The simplicity of the strategy requires only a simple or loose form of structure to execute it. Decisions can be centralized in the hands of a single senior manager, while complexity and formalization will be low. As organizations grow, their strategies become more ambitious and elaborate.

From the single product line, companies often expand their activities within their industry by acquiring suppliers or selling their products directly to customers. For example, General Motors not only assembles automobiles but also owns companies that make air conditioners, electrical equipment, turbine engines, and other car components. This vertical integration strategy leads to increased interdependence between organizational units and creates the need for a more complex coordination device. This is achieved by redesigning the structure to form specialized units based on functions performed. Finally, if growth proceeds further into product diversification, structure needs to be adjusted again to gain efficiency. A product diversification strategy demands a structural form that allows for the efficient allocation of resources, accountability for performance, and coordination between units. This can be achieved best by creating many independent divisions, each responsible for a specified product line.

Recent research has generally confirmed the strategy-structure relationship but has used the strategy terminology presented in Chapter 3.[19] For instance, organizations pursuing a differentiation strategy must innovate to survive. Unless they can maintain their uniqueness, they may lose their competitive advantage. An organic organization matches best with this strategy because it is flexible and maximizes adaptability. In contrast, a cost leadership strategy seeks stability and efficiency. Stability and efficiency help to produce low-cost goods and services. This, then, can best be achieved with a mechanistic organization.

How Does Organizational Size Affect Structure? There is considerable historical evidence that an organization's size significantly affects its structure.[20] For instance, large organizations—those typically employing 2,000 or more employees—tend to have more division of labour, horizontal and vertical differentiation, and rules and regulations than do small organizations. However, the relationship isn't linear. Rather, size affects structure at a decreasing rate. The impact of size becomes less important as an organization expands. Why is this? Essentially, once an organization has around 2,000 employees, it is already fairly mechanistic. An additional 500 employees will not have much impact. On the other hand, adding 500 employees to an organization that has only 300 members is likely to result in a shift toward a more mechanistic structure.

How Does Technology Affect Structure? Every organization uses some form of technology to convert its inputs into outputs. To attain its objectives, the organization uses equipment, materials, knowledge, and/or experienced individuals and puts them together into certain types and patterns of activities. For instance, college instructors teach students by a variety of methods: formal lectures, group discussions, case analyses, programmed learning, and so forth. Each of these methods is a type of technology. Over the years, several studies regarding the effect of technology have been conducted.[21] For instance, in one study Joan Woodward found that distinct relationships exist between size of production runs and the structure of the firm. Additionally, she found that the effectiveness of the organizations was related to "fit" between technology and structure.[22] Most of these studies, like Woodward's, have focused on the processes or methods that transform inputs into outputs and how they differ by their degree of routineness. For example, mass production of steel and automobiles or refining petroleum is characteristic of routine technology. As such, with a more routine technology, the more standardized the structure can be. Conversely, Spar Aerospace's development of the Canadarm, the extending arm used by the NASA space shuttles, would be indicative of a nonroutine technology. Since the technology is more nonroutine, the structure is more organic.[23]

How Does Environment Affect Structure? In Chapter 2, we introduced the organization's environment as a constraint on managerial discretion. Research has demonstrated that environment is also a major influence on structure.[24] Essentially, mechanistic organizations are most effective in stable environments. Organic organizations are best matched with dynamic and uncertain environments.

The evidence on the environment-structure relationship helps to explain why so many managers have restructured their organizations to be lean, fast, and flexible (see Managers Who Made a Difference). Global competition, accelerated product innovation by all competitors, and increased demands from customers for higher quality and faster deliveries are examples of dynamic environmental forces. Mechanistic organizations tend to be ill-equipped to respond to rapid environmental change. As a result, we're seeing managers redesigning their organizations in order to make them more organic.

Chapter 6

Managers Who Made a Difference

MONTE PETERSON AT THERMOS

Successfully reducing the level of bureaucracy in a company is frequently compared, in difficulty, to teaching an elephant to dance. Yet Monte Peterson, the chief executive at Thermos, can take credit for pulling off the trick.[25]

In early 1990, Peterson became aware of how Thermos' bureaucracy was slowing up decision making, especially in creating new products. The environment facing Thermos, as Peterson saw it, required constant innovation, and Thermos' functional structure just wouldn't support that. Consequently, Thermos, the bottle and lunch box company, was not moving forward. Although company sales in 1992 neared $225 million, Peterson saw little growth for the company. With Thermos bottles and lunch boxes as mature products, significant growth in those areas was unlikely. Even the barbecue grill Thermos sold could never build more than a 2 per cent market share in the $1-billion-a-year barbecue grill industry.

Peterson immediately attacked the problem by revamping Thermos' corporate structure. He eliminated the restraining bureaucratic structure and flattened the organization. He developed interdisciplinary teams—project teams composed of employees from such areas as engineering, marketing, manufacturing, and finance. And if that weren't change enough, each team was required to have individuals external to the company—like suppliers or customers—become part of the team. The job of each team was to create new products that would satisfy customer needs. Furthermore, Peterson wanted these products to use the company's core competency—its vacuum technology. This was the result of Peterson's reading of the literature that when a company uses its core competency in new products, it typically gets a greater market share, and thus a larger profit margin.

Has Monte Peterson's plan been successful? One of his first teams, calling themselves the Lifestyle Project Team, spent three years developing a new electric barbecue grill. This grill was in response to environmentally conscious consumers who desired to grill without polluting the air. Over the months, working together, the team was able to achieve its goal. Launched in 1992, Thermos's electric grill has led to a 13 per cent increase in sales for the company. The numbers are supporting Peterson's reorganization. In fact, projections indicate that Thermos may boost its market share in the barbecue grill market from 2 to 20 per cent by 1996. Numbers like that, according to Peterson, just wouldn't happen in a bureaucracy. ▼

Organization Structures Reflect Cultural Values

An organization's structure must adapt to its environment. Included in that environment is the national culture of the country in which the organization is located. Research confirms that organizations mirror, to a considerable degree, the cultural values of their host country.[26]

In a country with a high power distance rating, people prefer that decisions be centralized. Similarly, uncertainty avoidance relates to formalization. High uncertainty avoidance relates to high formalization. Based on these relationships, we find certain patterns. French and Italian managers tend to create rigid bureaucracies that are high in both centralization and formalization. Managers in India prefer centralization and low formalization. Germans prefer formalization with decentralization.

The extensive use of work teams in a country like Japan can also be explained in terms of national culture. Japan scores high on collectivism. In such a culture, employees prefer more organic organizations built around work teams. In contrast, employees in India—where power distance values are high—are likely to perform poorly in teams. They feel more comfortable working in mechanistic, authority-dominated structures.

A recent study of managers' perceptions of the "ideal" organization in the People's Republic of China (PRC) found preferences for structures that fit with their culture.[27] Executives in the PRC favoured high participation in their organizations. The researchers noted that this reflected the cultural value placed on allowing workers formal participation in the planning process as well as retaining some worker authority over the appointment and retention of managers. Managers in the PRC also have an aversion to conflict and a need to "save face," which fosters a mechanistic structure with clear lines of authority and unambiguous standard operating procedures. In addition, managers in the PRC were found to shun internal competition and individual risk-taking initiatives. This is consistent with traditional Chinese values of collective responsibility.

Summary

This Summary is organized by the chapter opening learning objectives found on page 124.

1. An organization's structure is a measure of its degree of complexity, formalization, and centralization.
2. The advantages of division of labour relate to economic efficiencies. It makes efficient use of the diversity of skills that workers hold. Skills are developed through repetition. Less time is wasted. Training is also easier and less costly. The disadvantage of division of labour is that it can result in human diseconomies. Excessive division of labour can cause boredom, fatigue, stress, low productivity, poor quality, increased absence, and high turnover.
3. Authority relates to rights inherent in a position. Power describes all means by which an individual can influence decisions, including formal authority. Authority is synonymous with legitimate power. However, a person can have coercive, reward, expert, or referent power without holding a position of authority. Thus, authority is actually a subset of power.

4. Wider spans of control mean that a manager has more subordinates reporting to him or her. The more subordinates that a manager can effectively supervise, the lower the cost of administrative overhead, and the more efficient the manager becomes.
5. Managers can departmentalize on the basis of function, product, customer, geography, or process. In practice, most large organizations use all five.
6. The mechanistic organization or bureaucracy rates high in complexity, formalization, and centralization. The organic organization or adhocracy scores low on these same three structural dimensions.
7. The strategy-determines-structure thesis argues that structure should follow strategy. As strategies move from single product, to vertical integration, to product diversification, structure must move from organic to mechanistic.
8. Size affects structure at a decreasing rate. As size increases, so too do specialization, formalization, vertical differentiation, and decentralization. But size has less of an impact on large organizations than on small ones because once an organization has around 2,000 employees it tends to be fairly mechanistic.
9. All other things equal, the more routine the technology, the more mechanistic the organization should be. The more nonroutine the technology, the more organic the structure should be.
10. All other things equal, stable environments are better matched with mechanistic organizations, while dynamic environments fit better with organic organizations.

Review and Discussion Questions

1. Can you reconcile the following two statements: (a) An organization should have as few levels as possible to foster coordination; and (b) An organization should have narrow spans of control to facilitate control.
2. Which is more efficient—a wide or a narrow span of control? Why?
3. Why did the classical writers argue that authority should equal responsibility?
4. Can the manager of a staff department have line authority? Explain.
5. How are authority and organization structure related?
6. What are the five sources of power?
7. Why is an understanding of power important?
8. In what ways can management departmentalize?
9. Is your college organized as a mechanistic or an organic organization? Is this the type of structure you would ideally choose for it? Explain.
10. Under what conditions is the mechanistic organization most effective? When is the organic organization most effective?

Foundations of Organizing

Self-Assessment Exercise

How Power Oriented Are You?

Answer the following ten questions based on a scale of 1 (disagree a lot); 2 (disagree a little); 3 (neutral); 4 (agree a little); or 5 (agree a lot).

Statement	DISAGREE			AGREE	
	A Lot	A Little	Neutral	A Little	A Lot
1. The best way to handle people is to tell them what they want to hear.	1	2	3	4	5
2. When you ask someone to do something for you, it is best to give the real reason for wanting it rather than giving reasons that might carry more weight.	1	2	3	4	5
3. Anyone who completely trusts anyone else is asking for trouble.	1	2	3	4	5
4. It is hard to get ahead without cutting corners here and there.	1	2	3	4	5
5. It is safest to assume that all people have a vicious streak, and it will come out when they are given a chance.	1	2	3	4	5
6. One should take action only when it is morally right.	1	2	3	4	5
7. Most people are basically good and kind.	1	2	3	4	5
8. There is no excuse for lying to someone else.	1	2	3	4	5
9. Most people forget the death of their father more easily than the loss of their property.	1	2	3	4	5
10. Generally speaking, people won't work hard unless they're forced to do so.	1	2	3	4	5

Turn to page 412 for scoring directions and key.

Source: R. Christie and F.L. Geis, *Studies in Machiavellianism* (London, England: Academic Press, 1970). Reprinted by permission.

Class Exercise

How Is Your School Organized?

Every university or college displays a specific type of organizational structure. That is, if you are a business major, your classes are often "housed" in a department, school, or college of business. But have you ever asked why? Or is it something you just take for granted?

In Chapter 3 you had an opportunity to assess your college's strengths, weaknesses, and comparative advantage and see how this fits into its strategy. Now, in this chapter we have built a case that structure follows strategy. Given your analysis in Chapter 3 (if you have not done so, you may want to turn to page 76 for the strategy part of this exercise), analyse your college's overall structure in terms of formalization, centralization, and complexity. Furthermore, look at the departmentalization that exists. Is your college more organic or mechanistic? Now analyse how well your college's structure fits with its strategy. Do the same thing for your college's size, technology, and environment. That is, assess its size, degree of technological routineness, and environmental uncertainty. Based on these assessments, what kind of structure would you predict your college to have? Does it have this structure now? Compare your findings with other classmates. Are there similarities in how each viewed the college? Differences? What do you believe has attributed to these findings?

Key Terms

Key terms are listed in the order in which they appear in the chapter.

organization structure
division of labour
unity of command
authority
responsibility
line authority
chain of command

staff authority
power
span of control
functional departmentalization
product departmentalization
customer departmentalization
geographic departmentalization

process departmentalization
mechanistic organization
bureaucracy
organic organization
adhocracy

Case Application

The General Hospital

Diane Wetherby called the hospital's executive director, Dr. Joanne Davis, and asked for a meeting right away. Dr. Davis could tell by the anxiousness of Diane's voice that something was wrong, and told her to come right down to her office. About ten minutes later, Diane Wetherby walked into Dr. Davis's office and handed her a letter of resignation.

"I can't take it here any longer, Dr. Davis," she began. "I've been a nursing supervisor in the maternity wing for four months, but I can't get the job done. How can I do a job when I've got two or three bosses, each one with different demands and priorities? Listen, I'm only human. I've tried my darnedest to adapt to this job but I don't think it's possible. Let me give you an example, but believe me, this is not an unusual case. Things like this are happening every day.

"When I came into my office yesterday morning at about 7.45, I found a message on my desk from Dana Jackson (the hospital's director of nursing). She said that she needed the bed utilization report by 10.00 a.m. so that she could have the information for her presentation to the hospital's board in the afternoon. I knew the report would take at least an hour and a half to prepare. Thirty minutes later Joyce (the nursing floor supervisor and Diane's immediate boss) came in and asked me why two of the nurses weren't on duty. I told her that Dr. Reynolds (head of surgery) had taken them off the floor and was using them to handle an overload in surgery. I told her I had objected, but Reynolds said there were no other options because surgery was short-staffed due to illness and the O.R. schedule was completely full and couldn't be changed. So what did Joyce say? She told me to get those nurses back to maternity immediately. What's more, she would check back in an hour to ensure that I had got things straightened out. I'm telling you, Dr. Davis, things like this happen more than once a day. Is this any way to run a hospital?"

Questions

1. What is the formal chain of command?
2. Has anyone acted outside his or her authority?
3. What can Dr. Davis do to improve things and make the hospital more effective?
4. "There's nothing wrong with the structure of the hospital—hospitals have to be able to respond to emergencies and rapid changes in plans. The problem is that Diane Wetherby is an ineffective supervisor." Do you agree or disagree? Support your position
5. Could Diane have developed any power bases that might have allowed her to deal better with the competing demands on her?

How Real Is Bureaucracy?

Joe Kane and Lee Heitman have a company called Zlin Aerospace. It sells airplanes imported from the Czech Republic — or it tries to sell them. The customers are ready to buy. They love the airplane, which Joe compares to a Porsche in terms of the way it handles. (Its Czech makers know what they're doing — they used to be principal manufacturers of championship aerobatic planes for the Russian military.) The problem is getting the planes to the customers. It's fine in Canada. The eight or more planes ordered here have all been delivered and paid for. But the U.S. is a different matter.

Joe and Lee raised $1.2 million to enter into a joint venture with the Czech manufacturers. The Czechs have been highly supportive partners and are willing to ship planes without advance payment, which is fortunate for Zlin Aerospace because the holdups to making delivery would otherwise have swamped them. With 33 committed orders in the United States, the principal issue facing Zlin in early 1994 was how to get certification from the U.S. authorities to deliver planes to waiting customers.

After two and a half years, Zlin thought they had achieved the breakthrough. On April 9, 1994, they received U.S. type certification — with a few modifications to be made. On April 22, the company found out what those modifications entailed. Master drawings had to *exactly* match the airplane itself. To get a sense of what "exactly" means, one of the things holding up final certification to sell in the U.S. was the fact that the labels that had been attached to the plane were *just over two centimetres* off where the master drawings said they should be.

Not a big problem, you say. Simply move the labels. But that's not what the bureaucracy said. The rules say you can't modify the airplane in any way; you have to change the drawings. That meant another three to four months to redo the master drawings. In the meantime, Joe Kane was sitting on $2-million worth of planes.

Questions

1. This is an example of bureaucracy being obstructive. Should the rules be this tight? Where do you start to bend them? If you were to try to design a more flexible bureaucracy, what are the principles you might recommend?
2. As Joe Kane, how could you have avoided this problem? Are there "rules" that people who have to deal with the bureaucracy's rules should apply to themselves? Give some examples.

Video Resource: "Zlin Aerospace," *Venture* 493 (June 19, 1994).

7

Organization Design for the Twenty-first Century

Learning Objectives

WHAT WILL I BE ABLE TO DO AFTER I FINISH THIS CHAPTER?

1. Define the simple structure.
2. Describe the strengths of the functional structure.
3. Contrast the divisional and functional structures.
4. Explain the strengths of the matrix structure.
5. Describe the recent popularity of the network structure.
6. Define a strategic alliance.
7. Identify the advantages of using organic appendages.
8. Explain what is meant by the term horizontal organization.
9. Explain the preferred structural design for TQM programs.
10. Describe what is meant by the term organization culture.
11. Contrast job specialization, job enlargement, and job enrichment.

As the world of business becomes more and more complex, innovative ideas on how to structure organizations are beginning to spring up. Two small businesses in Toronto have taken the idea of divisional structure, combined it with entrepreneurial ownership and drive, added the element of partnership and collaboration, and come up with something that makes a lot of sense—and works. The two companies are Nuroc Plumbing and Heating Supplies Ltd., and Independent Electric Supply Inc.[1]

The idea for the alliance is the brainchild of Paul Mashinter, a partner at Ernst & Young. He put the two firms together because Bob Branscome at Independent Electric was looking for an investor to buy out his partner, and Gary Tester, Paul Rocamora, and John Hudson of Nuroc were looking for ways to expand their business. By putting the two firms together, Branscombe could arrange the buyout of his partner and Nuroc could expand its customer base without opening another outlet or acquiring another company. The two companies now share information, customers, and support infrastructure. For instance, they jointly invested in a new IBM computer, saving them $30,000. The computer is set up at Nuroc, uses Independent's software, and has a direct access linking the two companies located on opposite sides of Toronto. They are exploring collaborating on inventory systems and trying to develop a common invoice for customers. As a result of the partnership, Independent's customer base doubled in the first year, and sales increased 17 per cent. It also gave Independent a larger line of credit at the bank. The companies are still run by their owners but they consult with one another weekly. Nuroc's financial controller visits Independent once or twice a week. When Bob Branscome wanted to buy a new truck, he and Gary Tester researched the purchase together. Branscome says, "I use Nuroc as a sounding board on a regular basis."

Bob Branscome (left), Gary Tester (right) and Paul Rocamora (middle), have created a new form of small business venture that may become a model for the next decade.

Given that small businesses are driving the growth in the Canadian economy, the model that Nuroc and Independent have created may turn out not only to answer the needs of entrepreneurs to maintain control over their own businesses, but also to be able to grow without having to raise large amounts of capital and become burdened by heavy debt and overhead costs.

In this chapter, we'll show that there are a number of structural options at management's disposal. There are traditional structures, like the functional bureaucracy, which have been dominant organizational structures since the 1930s. Although these structures worked well in the past, today's managers are looking at new and unique ways of reorganizing. Accordingly, we'll explore some of the new organization design options, taking a look at matrix, network, and horizontal structures.

Keep in mind that organizational design decisions are typically made by senior executives, possibly with input from mid-level managers. This realization, however, should not diminish our desire to understand how these structures work. Why? Because each of us works in some type of structure, and we need to know why we are "arranged" like we are. Additionally, given the changing environment and the needs for organizations to rapidly adapt, we should understand what the organizations we'll be working in "tomorrow" are going to look like.

Even though structures may dictate specific work activities, every organization has a personality that influences how its members behave. This personality is the organization's culture. We'll explore the concept of organizational culture in this chapter and discuss what goes into its development.

Finally, we'll close this chapter with a discussion of how jobs can be designed to better facilitate employee productivity. We'll show that understanding job design is important for managers at all levels.

Traditional Organization Designs

Traditional organization designs typically come in one of three varieties—the simple structure, the functional structure, and the divisional structure. Most organizations in North America are small. In Canada, the vast majority of new jobs in the economy for the last fifteen years have been created by small business—more than 85 per cent of new jobs created from 1980 to 1990 were from small business, with roughly half of these being created by firms with fewer than five employees, and about a quarter by firms with between five and twenty employees. The same scenario exists in the United States. Between 1980 and 1990, Fortune 500 companies *cut* 3.4 million jobs,[2] but companies with fewer than 500 employees *created* more than 13 million jobs.[3] Small organizations don't require a highly complex, formal structural design. What they need is a simple structure—one that minimizes structural complexity.

Small organizations like Classic Casuals represent the majority of businesses in Canada.

When contingencies like strategy, size, or technology favour a highly complex, formalized, and centralized (mechanistic) organization design, one of two options is traditionally considered—a functional or divisional structure. The functional structure's primary focus is on achieving the efficiencies of division of labour by grouping like specialists together. The divisional structure creates self-contained, autonomous units that are usually organized along mechanistic lines. Let's explore these three—simple, functional, and divisional—traditional structures.

What Is the Simple Structure?

simple structure
An organization that is low in complexity and formalization but high in centralization.

If bureaucracy is the term that best describes most large organizations, simple structure is the one that best characterizes most small ones. A **simple structure** is defined more by what it is not than by what it is. It is not an elaborate structure.[4] If you see an organization that appears to have almost no structure, it is probably of the simple variety. By that we mean that it is low in complexity, has little formalization, and has its

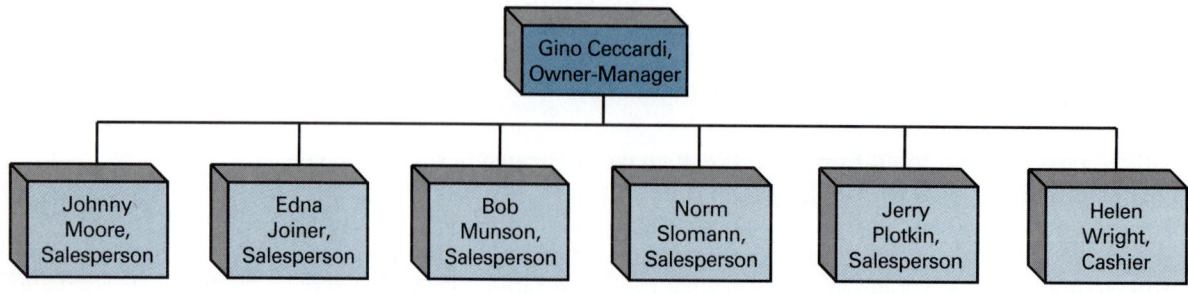

Exhibit 7-1 Organization Chart for a Simple Structure (Gino Ceccardi's Men's Store)

Developing Management Skills

EMPOWERING EMPLOYEES

▶ **1. Be sure employees have the abilities and motivation to perform empowered tasks.** Unless employees have the ability and desire to perform the empowered tasks, no amount of "empowerment" will work. Thus, when filling empowered jobs, employees should be screened for their ability to perform in an empowered setting or be appropriately trained to do so.

▶ **2. Clarify the assignment and decisions to be empowered.** Empowerment may mean many things to different employees—especially if left up to them to decide. Be specific what employees can and cannot do.

▶ **3. Specify employees' range of discretion.** Similar to step two, you must let employees know how much freedom they can exercise. By knowing, they can then act freely within that range. Outside of the range, they should consult you.

▶ **4. Inform others that empowerment has occurred.** Why? Because others in the organization may think your employees are acting on their own or without your "approval." Letting others know what you've "given" your employees will help all parties involved to be effective in their jobs.

▶ **5. Establish feedback controls.** Remember, empowerment does not mean abdication. You still have ultimate responsibility for whatever you have pushed downward. As such, getting feedback on what is happening in your unit is necessary.

---

authority centralized in a single person. The simple structure is a "flat" organization; it usually has only two or three vertical levels, a loose body of empowered employees (see Developing Management Skills), and one individual in whom the decision-making authority is centralized.

The simple structure is most widely practised in small businesses in which the manager and the owner are one and the same. This, for example, is illustrated in Exhibit 7-1—an organization chart for a men's retail store. Gino Ceccardi owns and manages this store. Although Gino employs five full-time salespeople, a cashier, and extra personnel for weekends and holidays, he "runs the show."

The strengths of the simple structure should be obvious. It is fast, flexible, and inexpensive to maintain, and accountability is clear. One major weakness is that it is effective only in small organizations. It becomes increasingly inadequate as an organization grows because its low formalization and high centralization result in information overload at the top. As size increases, decision making becomes slower and can eventually come to a standstill as the single executive tries to continue making all the decisions. This often proves to be the undoing of many small businesses. When a company's sales begin to exceed about $5 million a year, it's very difficult for the owner-manager to make all the choices. If the structure isn't changed and made more elaborate, the firm is likely to lose momentum and eventually fail. The simple structure's other weakness is that it is risky: everything depends on one person. One heart attack or a fatal auto accident on the way to work can literally destroy the organization's information and decision-making centre.

What Is the Functional Structure?

We introduced functional departmentalization in the previous chapter, so the idea of organizing around functions is already familiar to you. The **functional structure** merely expands the functional orientation to make it the dominant form for the entire

functional structure
A design that groups similar or related occupational specialties together.

Exhibit 7-2 Functional Structure in a Manufacturing Organization

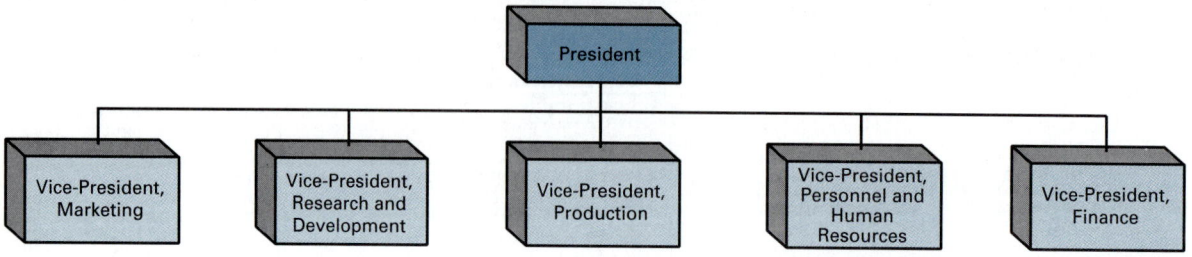

organization. As depicted in Exhibit 7-2, management can choose to organize its structure by grouping similar and related occupational specialties together. When it does this, management has chosen a functional structure.

Can You Identify the Major Strength of the Functional Structure? The strength of the functional structure lies in the advantages that accrue from specialization. Putting like specialties together results in economies of scale, minimizes duplication of personnel and equipment, and makes employees comfortable and satisfied because it gives them the opportunity to "talk the same language" as their peers.

What Are the Weaknesses of the Functional Structure? The most obvious weakness of the functional structure is that the organization frequently loses sight of its best interests in the pursuit of functional goals. No one function is totally responsible for end results, so members within individual functions become insulated and have little understanding of what people in other functions are doing. Because only top management can see the whole picture, it must assume the coordination role. The diversity of interests and perspectives that exists between functions can result in continual conflict between functions as each tries to assert its importance. An additional weakness of the functional structure is that it provides little or no training for future senior managers. Functional managers only see one narrow segment of the organization—the one dealing with their function. Exposure to other functions is limited. As a result, the structure does not give these managers a broad perspective on the organization's activities.

What Is the Divisional Structure?

The CBC, General Motors and Bombardier are examples of organizations that have adopted the divisional structure. An illustration of what this structural form looks like at Hershey Foods Corporation can be seen from the organization chart in Exhibit 7-3.

The **divisional structure,** which was pioneered in the 1920s by General Motors and du Pont, is designed to foster self-contained units. Each unit or division is generally autonomous, with a division manager responsible for performance and holding complete strategic and operational decision-making authority. At Hershey Foods, each of the groups is a separate division headed by a group president who is totally responsible for results. As in most divisional structures, a central headquarters provides support services to the divisions. This typically includes financial and legal services. Of course, the headquarters also acts as an external overseer to coordinate and control the various divisions. Divisions are, therefore, autonomous within given parameters. Division managers are usually free to direct their division as they see fit, as long as it is within

Organization Design for the Twenty-first Century

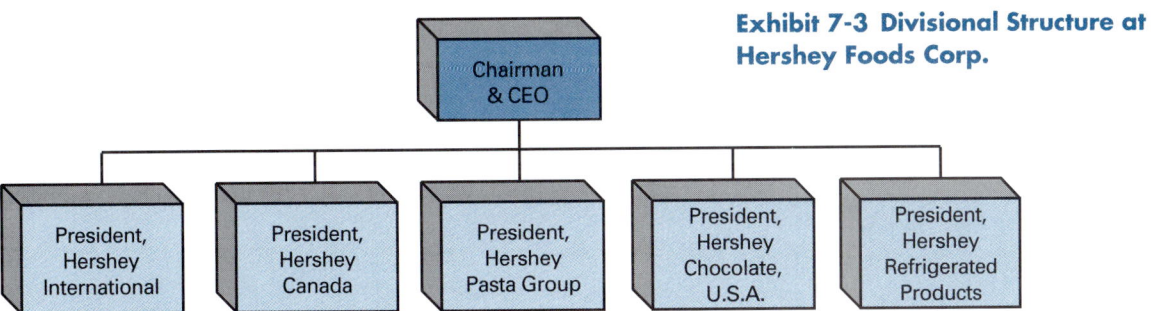

Exhibit 7-3 Divisional Structure at Hershey Foods Corp.

the overall guidelines set down by headquarters.

A closer look at divisional structures reveals that their "innards" contain functional structures. The divisional framework creates a set of autonomous "little companies." Within each of these companies lies another organizational form, and it is almost always of the functional variety.

divisional structure
An organization structure made up of autonomous, self-contained units.

Can You Identify the Strengths of the Divisional Structure? What advantages does the divisional structure offer? It focuses on results. Division managers have full responsibility for a product or service. The divisional structure also frees the headquarters staff from being concerned with day-to-day operating details so that they can pay attention to long-term and strategic planning.

In contrast to functional structures, the divisional form is also an excellent vehicle for developing senior executives. Division managers gain a broad range of experience in running their autonomous units. The individual responsibility and independence give them an opportunity to run an entire company with its frustrations and satisfactions. So a large organization with fifteen divisions has fifteen division managers who are developing the kind of generalist perspective that is needed in the organization's top spots.

Some large companies, like General Motors, structure themselves around self-contained units— like that of GM's Buick Division.

What Is the Primary Weakness of the Divisional Structure? The major disadvantage of the divisional structure is duplication of activities and resources. Each division, for instance, may have a marketing research department. In the absence of autonomous divisions, all of the organization's marketing research might be centralized and done for a fraction of the cost that divisionalization requires. Thus the divisional form's duplication of functions increases the organization's costs and reduces efficiency.

Designs for a Changing World

In this section, we present a selection of more organic design options. These include the matrix, network, task force, and committee structures (see Managers Who Made a Difference). We'll also introduce you to an increasingly popular design that is moving us toward the boundary-free organization—the horizontal structure.

What Is the Matrix Structure?

matrix structure
A structural design that assigns specialists from functional departments to work on one or more projects that are led by a project manager.

The functional structure offers the advantages that accrue from specialization. The divisional structure has a greater focus on results but suffers from duplication of activities and resources. Does any structure combine the advantages of functional specialization with the focus and accountability that product departmentalization provides? The answer is yes, and it's called the **matrix structure**.[5]

Managers Who Made a Difference

PERCY BARNEVIK, CEO OF ABB

Percy Barnevik is the CEO of ABB, a global equipment giant that has sales of $29 billion a year and is larger than Westinghouse.[6] It is, for instance, the world leader in high-speed trains, robotics, and environmental control. ABB was created in 1988 through the merger of ASEA, a Swedish engineering group, with Brown Boveri, a Swiss competitor. Management then added seventy more companies to create the current ABB giant. In doing so, an interesting challenge arose for Barnevik. That was, how do you organize a corporation that has 210,000 employees in locations around the world, that frequently shifts whole businesses from one country to another, and that tries to get its various businesses to share technology and products? Percy believed that he had the answer. He drastically cut the staff at the corporation's headquarters and introduced a dual chain of command structure that gives all employees a country manager and a business segment manager.

ABB has about 100 country managers who run traditional, national companies with local boards of directors. Most of these managers are citizens of the country in which they work. In addition, there are sixty-five global managers who are organized into eight segments: transportation; process automation and engineering; environmental devices; financial services; electrical equipment; and three electric power businesses, generation, transmission, and distribution. This structure, according to Barnevik, makes it easier for managers such as Gerhard Schulmeyer, a German who heads ABB's U.S. businesses as well as the automation segment, to use technology from other countries. For instance, Schulmeyer used techniques developed by ABB in Switzerland to service U.S. steam turbines and ABB's European technology to convert a nuclear reactor into a natural-gas-fired plant. ▼

Organization Design for the Twenty-first Century

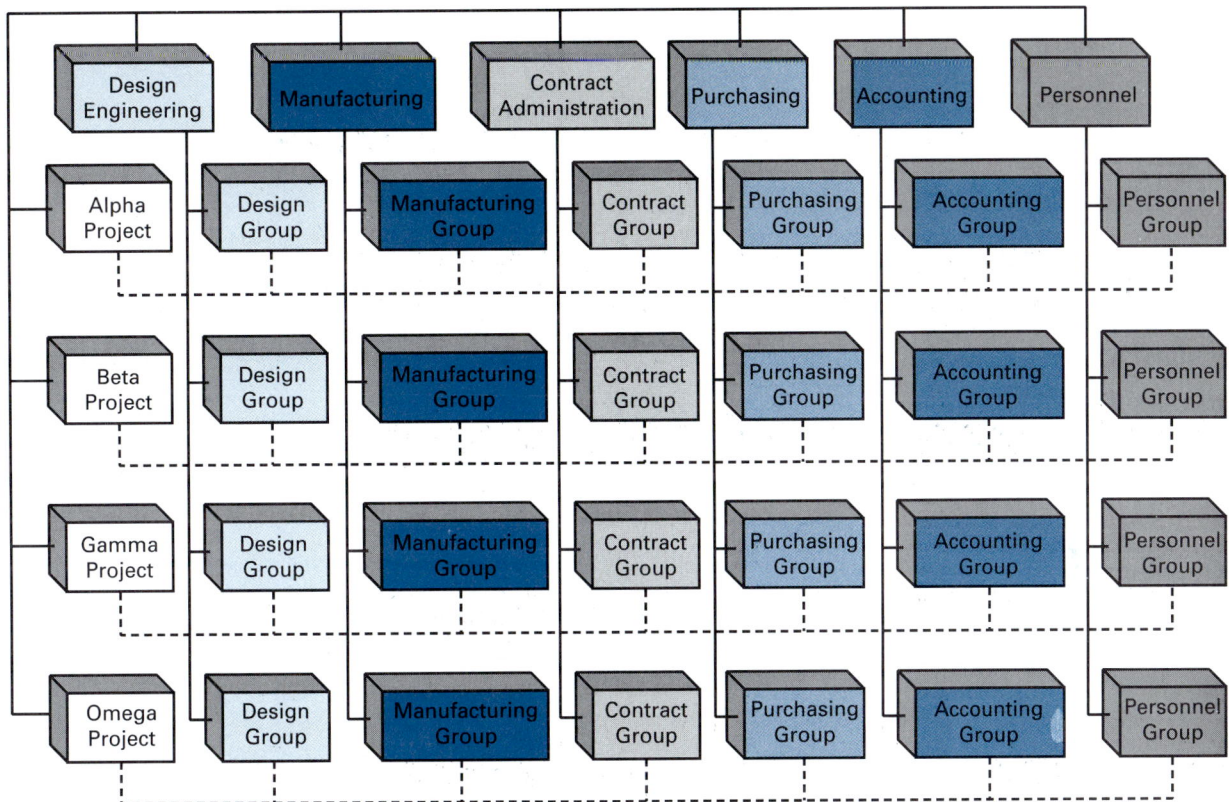

Exhibit 7-4 Matrix Structure of an Aerospace Firm

Remember earlier we stated that functional departmentalization is used to gain the economies from specialization. The matrix overlaps the functional departments with a set of managers who are responsible for specific products, projects, or programs within the organization. (We will use these terms—products, projects, programs—interchangeably, since matrix structures can use any of the three.) Exhibit 7-4 illustrates the matrix structure of an aerospace firm. Notice that along the top of the figure are the familiar functions of engineering, accounting, human resources management, and so forth. Along the vertical dimension, however, the various projects that the aerospace firm is currently working on have been added. Each project is directed by a manager who staffs his or her project with people from the functional departments. The addition of this vertical dimension to the traditional horizontal functional departments, in effect, weaves together elements of functional and product departmentalization—hence the term matrix.

What Is Unique About the Matrix? In Chapter 4, we introduced the concept of PERT and project management. In part, much of that discussion related directly to a matrix structure. How? Project management looks at employing specific resources (functional) on specific work activities (projects). Accordingly, when you work in a project management setting, you are actually working in a form of a matrix.

The most unique characteristic of the matrix is that employees in this structure have at least two bosses: their functional departmental manager and their product or project managers—just like those working for ABB, a global equipment corporation. The project managers have authority over the functional members who are part of that

Companies like the Jet Propulsion Lab in Pasadena, California, use a matrix structure to facilitate coordination of multiple complex projects.

network structure
A small centralized organization that relies on other organizations to perform its basic business functions on a contract basis.

manager's project team. The purchasing specialists, for instance, who are responsible for procurement activities on the Gamma project are responsible to both the manager of purchasing and the Gamma project manager. Authority is shared between the two managers. Typically, this is done by giving the project manager authority over project employees relative to the project's goals. However, decisions such as promotions, salary recommendations, and annual reviews remain the functional manager's responsibility. To work effectively, project and functional managers must communicate regularly and coordinate the demands upon their common employees.

What Are the Strengths and Weaknesses of a Matrix Structure? The primary strength of the matrix is that it can facilitate coordination of a multiple set of complex and interdependent projects while still retaining the economies that result from keeping functional specialists grouped together. The major disadvantages of the matrix lie in the confusion it creates and its propensity to foster power struggles. When you dispense with the unity of command principle, you significantly increase ambiguity. Confusion can exist over who reports to whom. This confusion and ambiguity, in turn, plant the seeds for power struggles. Because the relationships between functional and project managers typically are not specified by rules and procedures, they need to be negotiated, and this gives rise to power struggles. Deciding whether to implement the matrix requires managers to weigh these disadvantages against the advantages.

How Does the Network Structure Work?

A new form of organization design is currently gaining popularity. It allows management great flexibility in responding to new technology, fashion, or low-cost foreign competition. It is the **network structure**—a small central organization that relies on other organizations to perform manufacturing, distribution, marketing, or other crucial business functions on a contract basis.[7]

The network structure is a viable option for the small organization. Behavioural Science Systems Ltd., a management consultancy that operates in Canada, Britain, and Southeast Asia links its consultants on a computer network. It maintains a head office in London, England—which none of the consultants ever visits! Their business is done at the client's place of business, and the office is only used to provide the supporting infrastructure of financial controls, coordination of materials production, etc. James Naisbitt, the futurist and author of *Megatrends*, likewise has an office in Washington, DC, that he never visits; he lives and works out of a small town in Colorado, with faxes, phones, computers, and Federal Express to link him with his clients.

Nike uses the network structure to create great flexibility in responding to new athletic shoes.

Organization Design for the Twenty-first Century

The network structure is also applicable to large organizations like Nike, Esprit and Liz Claiborne, which have found that they can sell hundreds of millions of dollars of products every year and earn a very competitive return with few or no manufacturing facilities of their own and only a few hundred employees. What these firms have done is to create an organization of relationships. They contract with independent designers, manufacturers, commissioned sales representatives, or the like to perform the functions they need on a set fee.

Other large companies have developed variants of the network structure by farming out just a limited set of functions. Hudson Bay creates the design specifications for their clothing requirements and contracts out their manufacture largely to Asian suppliers. Maritime Telegraph & Telephone contracts out its computer and information systems operations. And most book publishing companies—the large ones as well as the small ones—rely on outside contractors for editing, designing, printing, and binding.

The network stands in sharp contrast to those divisional structures that have many vertical levels of management and those in which organizations seek to control their destiny through ownership. In such organizations, research and development are done in-house, production occurs in company-owned manufacturing plants, and sales and marketing are performed by their own employees. To support all this, management has to employ extra personnel including accountants, human resource specialists, and lawyers. In the network structure, most of these functions are bought outside the organization. This gives management a high degree of flexibility and allows the organization to concentrate on what it does best. For most U.S. firms, that means focusing on design or marketing.

Example 7-5 shows a network structure in which management contracts out all of the primary functions of the business. The core of the network organization is a small group of managers. Their job is to oversee directly any activities that are done in-house and to coordinate relationships with the other organizations that manufacture, distribute, and perform other crucial functions for the network organization. The dotted lines in Exhibit 7-5 represent those contractual relationships. In essence, managers in network structures spend most of their time coordinating and controlling external relations.

Where Would a Network Structure Best Fit? The network organization is not appropriate for all endeavours. It fits industrial companies such as toy and apparel firms, which require very high flexibility in order to respond quickly to market changes. It also fits firms whose manufacturing operations require low-cost labour and can best be utilized by contracting with foreign suppliers. On the negative side, management in network structures lacks the close control of manufacturing operations that exists in more traditional organizations. Reliability of supply is also less predictable.

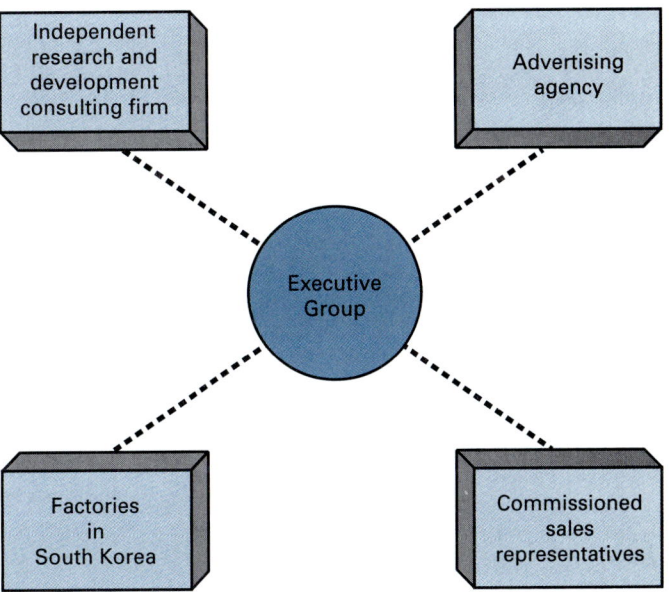

Exhibit 7-5 Network Structure

Finally, any innovation in design that a network organization acquires is susceptible to being "ripped off." It is very difficult, if not impossible, to guard closely innovations that are under the direction of management in another organization. Yet with computers in one organization now interfacing and communicating directly with computers in other organizations, the network structure is becoming an increasingly viable alternative.

What Is a Strategic Alliance? Before we leave networks, we'd like to introduce another element that is gaining momentum in a number of large companies like IBM, and small ones like the two mentioned at the start of the chapter—Nuroc Plumbing and Heating and Independent Electric Supply. This new "structure" revolves around building a **strategic alliance**.[8] Just as there were dotted line relationships with a headquarters staff and its suppliers in a network, a strategic alliance allows organizations to cooperate with one another, sharing resources, and spreading development costs and risks.

A strategic alliance, then, exists when two separate companies come together to develop a joint product or share marketing capabilities. This usually happens when one company needs specific resources or skills that another company has. For example, Apple Computer developed an alliance with Sony. Why? Apple didn't have enough engineers to handle the large number of new products it wanted to bring to market, so it turned to Sony for help. Sony's design team, with its expertise in miniaturization, helped Apple to develop the notebook-sized Macintosh computer called the Powerbook.

Can Mechanistic and Organic Structures Be Combined?

The design options previously described are intended for organizationwide application. Sometimes, however, management might want to maintain an overall mechanistic structure but gain the flexibility of an organic structure. An alternative is to append an organic structural unit to a mechanistic organization. Two examples of such appendages are the task force and the committee structure.

What Is a Task Force? The **task force structure** is a temporary structure created to accomplish a specific, well-defined, and complex task that requires the involvement of personnel from a number of organizational subunits. It can be thought of as a scaled-down version of the temporary matrix. Members serve on the task force until its goal is achieved. Then the task force is disbanded, and its members move on to a new task force, return to their permanent functional department, or leave the organization.[9]

The task force is a common tool of consumer product firms. For instance, when the Kellogg Company decides to create a new breakfast cereal, it brings together people with expertise in product design, food research, marketing, manufacturing, finance, and other relevant functions to formulate the product, design its package, determine its market, compute its manufacturing costs, and project its profits. Once the problems have been worked out and the product is ready to be mass produced, the task force disbands, and the cereal is integrated into the permanent structure. At Kellogg, the new cereal is then assigned its own product manager and becomes a part of Kellogg's matrix structure.

What Is a Committee Structure? Another option that combines a range of individual experiences and backgrounds for dealing with problems and cuts across functional lines is the **committee structure.** Committees may be temporary or permanent in nature. A temporary committee is typically the same as the task force. Permanent

---

strategic alliance
Joint partnerships between two or more firms that are created to gain a competitive advantage in a market.

task force structure
A temporary structure created to accomplish a specific, well-defined, complex task that requires the involvement of personnel from a number of organizational subunits.

committee structure
A structure that brings together a range of individuals from across functional lines to deal with problems.

Organization Design for the Twenty-first Century

committees facilitate the unity of diverse inputs as does the task force, but they offer the stability and consistency of the matrix. However, committees are appendages. Members of the committee are permanently attached to a functional department. They can meet at regular or irregular intervals to analyse problems, make recommendations or final decisions, coordinate activities, or oversee projects. As a result, they are mechanisms for bringing together the input of diverse departments. Colleges frequently use permanent committees for everything from student admissions to faculty promotions and alumni relations. Large business firms use committees as coordinating and control mechanisms. For instance, many firms have a compensation committee to review salary and bonuses provided to management personnel and an audit committee to objectively evaluate the organization's operations. A few firms even use the committee as the central coordinating device in their structure. Many companies have a management committee that consists of the firm's top managers. They debate and pass on decisions to such disparate areas as strategic planning, public affairs, personnel, and merchandising. Permanent subcommittees are used to focus on key parts of the business, while temporary committees are formed for specific issues.

Why Is There Movement Toward a Boundary-free Organization?

Recall our discussion in Chapter 2 regarding the challenges that managers face. Two of these—downsizing and reengineering—are particularly relevant to today's organization structural changes.[10] How? To answer, let's briefly review some facts regarding traditional structures. These bureaucratic designs were highly complex and formalized, and decisions were made in a centralized fashion—resulting in rigid, often massive, vertical structures. Although they were designed to promote efficiency, they did not lend themselves well to helping management adapt quickly to a changing environment.[11]

Network organizations and strategic alliances are structural responses to a rapidly changing environment. Both blur the historic boundaries surrounding an organization by increasing the interdependence with which it interacts. In terms of quantum change, managers are increasingly turning to still another structural option that downplays rigid boundaries. This can involve horizontal changes in the organization (like using task forces), vertical integration (multilevel teams), or interorganizational blends (for example, strategic alliances) (see Exhibit 7-6). Only this time the focus is on the inside of the organization (intraorganizational) rather than between organizations (interorganizational). We're talking about the horizontal structure.

What Is a Horizontal Structure? A horizontal structure is really nothing new. **Horizontal structures** are organization design options that reflect very flat structures. If you're making the connection to a few pages back when we discussed simple structures, you're on the right track. What's new about these structures, however, is that they are being used not only in small businesses but in giant companies like du Pont, General Electric, and Motorola.[12]

Horizontal organizations, as the term implies, cut across all aspects of the organization. Rather than having functional specialties located in departments working on distinctive tasks, these internally boundary-free organizations group employees to accomplish some core processes.[13] A **core process** is a basic focus of the business, like Bell Northern Research's product development. Core processes, then, encompass the entire work to be accomplished, from beginning to end, rather than focus on individualized job tasks. Let's look at an example to help clarify what we mean by core processes.

horizontal structure
An organization design option characterized by very flat structures.

core process
A basic focus of the business.

Exhibit 7-6 Methods Used in the Boundary-free Organization to Break Down Horizontal, Vertical, and Interorganizational Barriers

Horizontal:	Crossfunctional teams and task forces can be used to break down the traditional horizontal differentiation derived from division of labour.
Vertical:	Multilevel teams, empowerment, and 360-degree performance evaluations can be used to break down vertical barriers derived from authoritative hierarchies.
Interorganizational:	Strategic alliances, interorganizational computer networks, and using customers' input in the evaluation of employees can be used to break down the barriers derived from the classical organization design principles of bureaucracies.

Ryder Systems, the company that rents and leases trucks, recently reorganized to focus on its mainstay business.[14] Previously, it took almost an entire year from the time managers decided to purchase a vehicle until the truck was ready for customer use. There were upwards of seventeen functional departments that were required to get involved, even if it was only to sign some papers. Ryder managers knew they couldn't remain competitive in this self-moving market unless they made drastic changes. Competition from companies such as U-Haul mandated that something be done.

Ryder's management wanted to eliminate the unnecessary activities involved in this drawn-out process. They realized they had a single core process—purchase a vehicle and prepare it for customer rental.[15] Ryder was able to eliminate the involvement of fifteen functional areas by creating a single "team" that did all the activities from start to finish. The result? Ryder reduced their cycle time to four months.

Horizontal organizations are not just "flatter" organizations. To achieve what Ryder did required an internal revolution.[16] This means that managers must break down the traditional hierarchies that have existed for so many decades. In doing so, horizontal organizations will require work teams—groups of employees who come from all specialties working together on a common objective. These multidisciplinary teams will be given the authority to make the necessary decisions to do the work and be held accountable for measurable outcomes.[17]

As these changes are made, employees in horizontal organizations will also see new ways of being evaluated. Rather than being measured on individual performance, employee rewards will be based on how the team performs. Additionally, team members will be rewarded for mastering multiple skills, rather than just a select few. But probably the biggest difference will come in who evaluates. In traditional structures, one's supervisor conducts the performance evaluation. In a horizontal organization, supervisory evaluations will no longer be the only ones. For instance, at General Electric, CEO Jack Welch has implemented what he calls a 360-degree appraisal process.[18] At GE, team members are evaluated by team leaders, peer members, and other employees with whom they work.[19]

Ryder eliminated 15 functional departments, flattened the organization by creating teams, and reduced its cycle time by 66 per cent in delivering new trucks to customers.

Is There a Typical Form of Horizontal Organization? Horizontal organizations can almost be described in much the same way that we described simple structures. They are more representative of what they don't have as what they do. However, all horizontal organizations share one common element. That is, they're flat. Beyond that, each is specifically tailored to the organization's core process. Although designs will vary, there is some indication that horizontal organizations may share the following characteristics.[20] They will have few senior executives. Those that are present will more than likely be from two critical areas that permeate all core processes. That would be finance and human resources. Beyond these, the remaining employees will form multidisciplinary teams. Although there will be team or process leaders, it is estimated that horizontal organizations will have no more than three or four layers of management. That means from the CEO to employee, there will be two management groups. So what might this structure look like?

The network structure probably gives us the foundation for a horizontal framework. Unlike the network, however, the outlying areas will represent organizational teams, not contractual relationships. One design that typifies horizontal organizations is that of Eastman Chemical Company.[21] Eastman's organization chart can best be conceptualized as a pepperoni pizza (see Exhibit 7-7). At the centre of the pizza is the small staff of executives who set the strategic direction. Around the circle are many pepperoni, each representing a multidisciplinary team "responsible for managing a business, a geographic area, or a core competency."[22] And what does the cheese that covers the pizza signify? In a true horizontal fashion, even teams must cross over to assist one another. The cheese, then, on Eastman's pizza shows how all team members are strung together.

Organizational charts, such as Eastman's, tell employees they are all important to the organization's success. Being part of a pie, or whatever analogy is used, indicates that all employees are "equal" and are working toward a common goal. In fact, this addresses one of the problem areas that is inherent in traditional structures. On typical organizational charts, employees are often shown at the very bottom of a pyramid—reinforcing to organizational members who is in power and who has authority over them. Employees do not need to be told that they are perceived as the lowest element in the organizational cog. In fact, Pepsico has inverted its organization chart to show that its field representatives are the number one reason for company success. Having management at the bottom of the pyramid shows Pepsi employees what management is supposed to be—a team that exists to support worker efforts.[23]

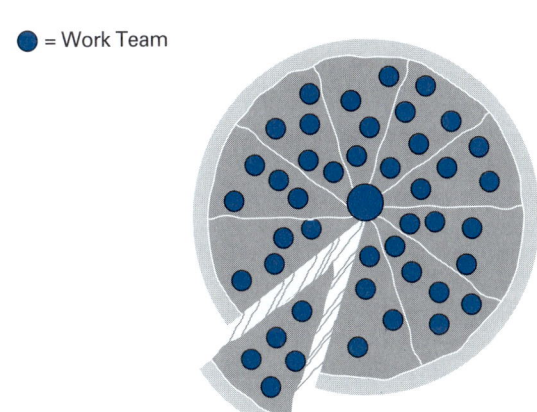

Exhibit 7-7 Horizontal Structure at Eastman Chemical Company

● = Work Team

Whether or not a specific "picture" is used to represent horizontal organizations, these structures will follow a common format. That is, no matter what they look like, horizontal organizations will focus and organize around core processes that meet strategic goals and will have empowered multidisciplinary teams working to achieve these objectives. But keep one thing in mind. Horizontal organizations must be used where appropriate. In some industries where efficiency of mass production is warranted, a traditional structure may better serve the organization. The question raised then is, When do the different structures work best? The answer will depend on the environment in which a company operates.

So What's the Key to Organization Design?

The right organization design, like many activities in management, is dependent on the situation. As such, conditions making one organization design preferable eliminate others. In Exhibit 7-8, we have summarized the options we have discussed and note the conditions that favour the use of each.

TQM and Structural Design

Several concepts introduced in this and the prior chapter have direct relevance to the Total Quality Management movement. These include vertical differentiation, division of labour, and centralization.

One common characteristic of TQM programs is an effort to reduce vertical differentiation. By widening spans of control and flattening organizations, management cuts overhead and improves vertical communication. A second common TQM charac-

STRUCTURE	ADVANTAGES	BEST USED
Simple	Speed, flexibility, economy	In small organizations; during formative years of development; in simple and dynamic environments
Functional	Economies through specialization	In single-product or single-service organizations
Divisional	High accountability for results	In large organizations, in multiple-product or multiple-market organizations
Matrix	Economies through specialization and accountability for product results	In organizations with multiple products or programs that rely on functional expertise
Network	Speed, flexibility, economy	In industrial firms; during formative years of development; when many reliable suppliers are available; when low-cost foreign labour is available
Task Force	Flexibility	In organizations with important tasks that are unique and unfamiliar, that require expertise that crosses functional lines
Committee	Flexibility	In organizations with tasks that require expertise that crosses functional lines
Horizontal	Speed, flexibility, customer focus	In large organizations facing complex and dynamic environments; when tasks require expertise that crosses functional lines; when ability to deal with rapid change is paramount

Exhibit 7-8 Organization Design Options

Ethical Dilemmas in Management

▼ DO MATRIX STRUCTURES CREATE SCHIZOPHRENIC EMPLOYEES? ▲

Workers who work on multiple projects often face a difficult issue that never arose in traditional bureaucracies. That is, many of these employees have at least two bosses. They are responsible to their functional managers, who, in many cases, are the individuals who have the responsibility to evaluate the employees' performance and make salary increase determinations. But concurrent with that reporting relationship is the fact that these employees are responsible to their project managers for specific project tasks.

So who is the more important person? Do employees give their functional manager's requests priority, because, after all, this individual handles the administrative and personnel-related paperwork? Or is it the project manager—who is involved with the employees on a day-to-day basis—who gets the "top billing"? Failure to complete the required tasks on the project could result in being removed from the project team—a decision that may result in an employee being severed from the organization. Or are both given equal priorities, and employees simply accept that they have to serve "two masters"? What do you think?

teristic is reduced division of labour. High division of labour emphasizes specialization, promotes an "us versus them" mentality, and retards collaboration and horizontal communication. In contrast, TQM encourages the use of teams that cut across functional specializations (see Ethical Dilemmas in Management).

Finally, TQM emphasizes decentralized decision making. Authority and responsibility are pushed as far down, and as close to the customer, as possible. The reason, of course, is that TQM's success depends on quickly and continually responding to the changing needs of customers.

Amoco Production Company illustrates the effectiveness of these structural changes.[24] The company, a subsidiary of the Chicago oil giant, realized that its matrix structure—six tiers of management cross-laden with a multitude of functional units—had become too cumbersome. Geologists, for instance, were spending nearly 40 per cent of their time in committee meetings trying to get approvals to search for oil when they actually could have been searching for oil. So Amoco's management reorganized. They eliminated three layers of management and dismantled the functional hierarchies. Workers were grouped into units of approximately 500, organized around multidisciplinary teams, and given considerable authority to make decisions. Noted one unit leader, "We're finding more oil and getting better financial results with the same number of professionals and fewer managers."[25]

Organization Culture and Structural Design

We know that every individual has something that psychologists have termed "personality." An individual's personality is made up of a set of relatively permanent and stable traits. When we describe someone as warm, innovative, relaxed, or conservative, we are describing personality traits. An organization, too, has a personality, which we call the organization's culture.

organization culture
A system of shared meaning within an organization that determines, in a large degree, how employees act.

What Is Organization Culture?

What do we specifically mean by the term **organization culture**? We use the term to refer to a system of shared meaning. Just as tribal cultures have totems and taboos that dictate how each member will act toward fellow members and outsiders, organizations have cultures that govern how their members should behave. In every organization, there are systems or patterns of values, symbols, rituals, myths, and practices that have evolved over time.[26] These shared values determine, in large degree, what employees see and how they respond to their world.[27]

How Can Cultures Be Assessed?

Though we currently have no definitive method for measuring an organization's culture, preliminary research suggests that cultures can be analysed by assessing how an organization rates on ten characteristics.[28] We have listed these characteristics in Exhibit 7-9.

These ten characteristics are relatively stable and permanent over time. Just as an individual's personality is stable and permanent—if you were outgoing last month, you're likely to be outgoing next month—so, too, is an organization's culture.

General Motors has been almost universally described as a cold, formal, risk-aversive firm. It was that way in the 1930s, and it is basically the same today. In contrast, Hewlett-Packard is an informal, loosely structured, highly humanistic organization.

Exhibit 7-9 Cultural Characteristics

▶ 1. Member identity: the degree to which employees identify with the organization as a whole rather than with their type of job or field of professional expertise.
▶ 2. Group emphasis: the degree to which work activities are organized around groups rather than individuals.
▶ 3. People focus: the degree to which management decisions take into consideration the effect of outcomes on people within the organization.
▶ 4. Unit integration: the degree to which units within the organization are encouraged to operate in a coordinated or interdependent manner.
▶ 5. Control: the degree to which rules, regulations, and direct supervision are used to oversee and control employee behaviour.
▶ 6. Risk tolerance: the degree to which employees are encouraged to be aggressive, innovative, and risk-seeking.
▶ 7. Reward criteria: the degree to which rewards such as salary increases and promotions are allocated on employee performance criteria in contrast to seniority, favouritism, or other nonperformance factors.
▶ 8. Conflict tolerance: the degree to which employees are encouraged to air conflicts and criticisms openly.
▶ 9. Means-end orientation: the degree to which management focuses on results or outcomes rather than the techniques and processes used to achieve those outcomes.
▶ 10. Open-systems focus: the degree to which the organization monitors and responds to changes in the external environment.

Organization Design for the Twenty-first Century

Both General Motors and Hewlett-Packard have been essentially successful over the decades despite having completely different cultures.

Where Does an Organization's Culture Come From?

An organization's culture usually reflects the vision or mission of the organization's founders. Because the founders have the original idea, they also have biases on how to carry out the idea. They are unconstrained by previous customs or ideologies. The founders establish the early culture by projecting an image of what the organization should be. The small size of most new organizations also helps the founders impose their vision on all organizational members. An organization's culture, then, results from the interaction between (1) the founders' biases and assumptions, and (2) what the first employees learn subsequently from their own experiences.[29]

Thomas Watson at IBM and Frank Stronach at Magna are just two examples of individuals who have had an immeasurable influence on shaping their organizations' cultures. For instance, Watson's views on research and development, product quality, employee attire, and compensation policies are still evident at IBM, although he died in 1956. Frank Stronach's belief that business units must remain small to be effective, and that Magna's design and development functions must be a part of their customer's design and development functions are two of the major differentiating factors that make Magna stand out in the automobile industry.

Mary Kay Cosmetics is known for its strong culture established by its founder, Mary Kay.

Does Culture Influence Structure?

An organization's culture may have an effect on an organization's structure depending on how strong, or weak, the culture may be. For instance, in organizations where there is a **strong culture**—one in which the dominant values of organizational members are accepted, intensely held, and widely shared—behavioural consistency of employees increases. In a sense, culture can act as a substitute for formalization.

In our last chapter, we discussed how formalization's rules and regulations act to regulate employee behaviour. High degrees of formalization in an organization create predictability, orderliness, and consistency. Strong cultures achieve the same end without the need for written documentation. Therefore, we can view formalization and culture as two different roads to a common destination. The stronger an organization's culture, the less managers need to be concerned with developing formal rules and regulations to guide employee behaviour. Instead, those guides will be internalized in employees when they accept the organization's culture. If an organization's culture is weak—where there are no dominant shared values—its effect on structure is less clear.

strong culture
Organizations in which the key values are accepted, intensely held, and widely shared.

Job Design Options

If you put an organization under a microscope, you would find that it is composed of thousands, maybe even millions, of tasks. These tasks, in turn, are aggregated into jobs.[30] The jobs that people do in any organization should not evolve by chance. Managers should design jobs thoughtfully to reflect the organization's technology, as well as

job design
The way in which tasks are combined to form complete jobs.

the skills, abilities, and preferences of its employees. When this is done, employees can reach their full productive capabilities.

We use the term **job design** to refer to the way in which tasks are combined to form complete jobs. Some jobs are routine because the tasks are standardized and repetitive; others are nonroutine. Some require a large number of varied and diverse skills; others are narrow in scope. Some jobs constrain employees by requiring them to follow very precise procedures; others allow employees substantial freedom in how they do their work. Some jobs are most effectively accomplished by groups of employees working as a team, whereas other jobs are best done by individuals acting independently. Our point is that jobs differ in the way their tasks are combined, and these different combinations create a variety of job designs. Exhibit 7-10 describes some popular job design options.

job characteristics model (JCM)
A framework for analysing and designing jobs; identifies five primary job characteristics, their interrelationships, and impact on outcome variables.

What Is the Job Characteristics Model?

None of the approaches listed in Exhibit 7-10 provide a conceptual framework for analysing jobs or for guiding managers in designing jobs. The **job characteristics model (JCM),** however, offers such a framework.[31] It identifies five primary job characteristics, their interrelationships, and their impact on employee productivity, motivation, and satisfaction.

According to the JCM, any job can be described in terms of five core dimensions,

Job Specialization:	Under job specialization, jobs are divided into minute, specialized tasks. Job specialization is synonymous with the early management writers.
Job Rotation:	Job rotation is designed to allow workers to diversify their activities and avoid boredom. There are actually two types of rotation: vertical and horizontal. Vertical rotation refers to promotions and demotions. However, traditional job rotation involves lateral transfers of workers among jobs involving different tasks.
Job Enlargement:	Job enlargement increases the number of different tasks required in a job and decreases the frequency with which the job cycle is repeated. By increasing the number of tasks an individual performs, job enlargement increases job diversity.
Job Enrichment:	Job enrichment increases job depth. This option allows employees greater control over their work. They're allowed to assume some of the tasks typically done by their supervisors—particularly planning and evaluating their own work.
Integrated Work Teams:	In integrated work teams, a large number of tasks are assigned to a group. The group then decides the specific assignments of members and is responsible for rotating jobs among the members as the tasks require. The team still has a supervisor who oversees the group's activities.
Self-Managed Work Teams:	Self-managed work teams are more vertically integrated and have a wider range of discretion than their integrated counterparts. The self-managed work team is given a goal to achieve and then is free to determine work assignments, rest breaks, inspection procedures, and so forth. These teams often even select their own members and have the members evaluate one another's performances. As a result, supervisory positions become less important and may sometimes be eliminated.

Exhibit 7-10 Some Examples of Job Design Options

Details on a Management Classic

J. RICHARD HACKMAN AND GREG R. OLDHAM: THE JOB CHARACTERISTICS MODEL

The dominant framework today for defining task characteristics and understanding their relationships to employee motivation is Hackman and Oldham's job characteristics model (JCM).[32] Research on the JCM has found that the first three dimensions—skill variety, task identity, and task significance—combine to create meaningful work. That is, if these three characteristics exist in a job, we can predict that the person will view his or her job as being important, valuable, and worthwhile. Jobs that possess autonomy give the job incumbent a feeling of personal responsibility for the results, and jobs that provide feedback let the employee know how effectively he or she is performing.

From a motivational standpoint, the JCM says that internal rewards are obtained when one *learns* (knowledge of results) that one *personally* (experienced responsibility) has performed well on a task that one *cares about* (experienced meaningfulness).[33] The more these three conditions are present, the greater will be the employee's motivation, performance, and satisfaction.[34]

The core dimensions can be combined into a single index called the Motivating Potential Score (MPS). The MPS is calculated as follows:

$$\text{Motivating Potential Score (MPS)} = \left[\frac{\text{Skill Variety} + \text{Task Identity} + \text{Task Significance}}{3} \right] \times \text{Autonomy} \times \text{Feedback}$$

What does the JCM tell us? To score high on motivating potential, managers must design jobs so that they are high on at least one of the three factors that lead to experiencing meaningfulness (skill variety, task identity, or task significance). Furthermore, jobs must also be high on both autonomy and feedback. Creating jobs that meet these requirements will result in a high motivating potential score. In doing so, motivation, performance, and satisfaction will be positively affected, while the likelihood of absenteeism and turnover will be lessened.[35] ▼

defined as follows: **skill variety,** the degree to which a job requires a variety of activities so that an employee can use a number of different skills and talents; **task identity,** the degree to which a job requires completion of a whole and identifiable piece of work; **task significance,** the degree to which a job has a substantial impact on the lives or work of other people; **autonomy,** the degree to which a job provides substantial freedom, independence, and discretion to the individual in scheduling the work and determining the procedures to be used in carrying it out; and **feedback,** the degree to which carrying out the work activities required by a job results in the individual's obtaining direct and clear information about the effectiveness of his or her performance (see Details on a Management Classic).

What Guidance Can the JCM Offer Managers in Designing Jobs?

The JCM provides specific guidance to managers in the designing of jobs. The following suggestions, which derive from the JCM, specify the types of changes in jobs that are most likely to lead to improvements in each of the five core dimensions:

skill variety
The degree to which a job includes a variety of activities that call for a number of different skills and talents.

task identity
The degree to which a job requires completion of a whole and identifiable piece of work.

task significance
The degree to which a job has a substantial impact on the lives or work of other people.

autonomy
The degree to which a job provides substantial freedom, independence, and discretion to an individual in scheduling and carrying out his or her work.

feedback
The degree to which carrying out the work activities required by a job results in an individual's obtaining direct and clear information about the effectiveness of his or her performance.

▶ 1. Combine tasks. Managers should put existing fractionalized tasks back together to form a new, larger module of work. This increases employees' skills and allows them to complete the whole job.
▶ 2. Create natural work units. Managers should design tasks that form an identifiable and meaningful whole. This increases employee "ownership" of the work and encourages employees to view their work as meaningful and important rather than as irrelevant and boring.
▶ 3. Establish client relationships. The client is the user of the product or service that the employee works on. Wherever possible, managers should establish direct relationships between workers and their clients. This increases employees' skills and provides them with feedback.
▶ 4. Expand jobs vertically. Vertical expansion gives employees responsibilities and controls that were formerly reserved for management. It partially closes the gap between the "doing" and "controlling" aspects of the job, and it increases employee autonomy.
▶ 5. Open feedback channels. By increasing feedback, employees learn not only how well they are performing their jobs but also whether their performances are improving, deteriorating, or remaining at a constant level. Ideally, employees should receive performance feedback directly as they do their jobs rather than from management on an occasional basis.[36]

Summary

This Summary is organized by the chapter opening learning objectives found on page 148.

1. The simple structure is low in complexity, has little formalization, and has authority centralized in a single person. It is widely used in small businesses.
2. The functional structure groups similar or related occupational specialties together. It takes advantage of specialization and provides economies of scale by allowing people with common skills to work together.
3. The divisional structure is composed of autonomous units, with managers having full responsibility for a product or service. However, these units are frequently organized as functional structures inside their divisional framework. So divisional structures typically contain functional structures within them.
4. By assigning specialists from functional departments to work on one or more projects led by project managers, the matrix structure combines functional and product departmentalization. It thus has the advantage of both specialization and high accountability.
5. The recent popularity of the network structure is due to its high flexibility. It allows management to perform manufacturing, distribution, marketing, or other crucial business functions with a minimal commitment of resources.
6. A strategic alliance allows for different organizations to combine resources, skills, and share costs and risks in an effort to produce a joint product.
7. Organic appendages allow organizations to be responsive and flexible while, at the same time, maintaining an overall mechanistic structure.
8. The term horizontal organization refers to a structural design characterized by multidisciplinary teams who perform core processes.
9. TQM encourages low vertical differentiation, minimal division of labour, and decentralized decision making.
10. Organization culture is a system of shared meaning within an organization that determines, in large degree, how employees act.
11. Job specialization is concerned with breaking down jobs into ever-smaller tasks. Job enlargement is the reverse. It expands jobs horizontally by increasing their scope. Like enlargement, job enrichment expands jobs, but vertically rather than horizontally. Enriched jobs increase depth by allowing employees greater control over their work.

Review and Discussion Questions

1. Show how both the functional and matrix structures might create conflict within an organization.
2. What are the strengths and weaknesses of
   a. the functional structure
   b. the divisional structure
3. Why is the simple structure inadequate in large organizations?
4. Can an organization have no structure?
5. When should management use
   a. the matrix structure
   b. the network structure
   c. a committee
6. Of the following structural designs—functional, divisional, simple, network, or matrix—which one would you most prefer to work in? Least prefer? Why?
7. "What a manager does in terms of the organizing function depends on what level he or she occupies in the organizational hierarchy." Discuss.
8. Describe the characteristics of a horizontal organizational structure. How do you think "tomorrow's" employees will accept these characteristics?
9. Contrast job enlargement and job enrichment in terms of the job characteristics model.
10. Define organizational culture.
11. Contrast organizational culture with formalization.
12. Classrooms have cultures. Describe your class culture. How does it affect your instructor?

Self-Assessment Exercise

Is an Enriched Job for You?

Instructions: People differ in what they like and dislike in their jobs. Listed below are twelve pairs of jobs. For each pair, indicate which job you would prefer. Assume that everything else about the jobs is the same—pay attention only to the characteristics actually listed for each pair of jobs. If you would prefer the job in the left-hand column (Column A), indicate how much you prefer it by putting a check mark in a blank to the left of the Neutral point. If you prefer the job in the right-hand column (Column B), check one of the blanks to the right of Neutral. Check the Neutral blank only if you find the two jobs equally attractive or unattractive. Try to use the Neutral blank rarely.

COLUMN A		COLUMN B
1. A job that offers little or no challenge.	Strongly prefer A — Neutral — Strongly prefer B	A job that requires you to be completely isolated from co-workers.
2. A job that pays very well.	Strongly prefer A — Neutral — Strongly prefer B	A job that allows considerable opportunity to be creative and innovative.
3. A job that often requires you to make important decisions.	Strongly prefer A — Neutral — Strongly prefer B	A job in which there are many pleasant people to work with.
4. A job with little security in a somewhat unstable organization.	Strongly prefer A — Neutral — Strongly prefer B	A job in which you have little or no opportunity to participate in decisions that affect your work.
5. A job in which greater responsibility is given to those who do the best work.	Strongly prefer A — Neutral — Strongly prefer B	A job in which greater responsibility is given to loyal employees who have the most seniority.
6. A job with a supervisor who sometimes is highly critical.	Strongly prefer A — Neutral — Strongly prefer B	A job that does not require you to use much of your talent.
7. A very routine job.	Strongly prefer A — Neutral — Strongly prefer B	A job in which your co-workers are not very friendly.
8. A job with a supervisor who respects you and treats you fairly.	Strongly prefer A — Neutral — Strongly prefer B	A job that provides constant opportunities for you to learn new and interesting things.

COLUMN A		COLUMN B
9. A job that gives you a real chance to develop yourself personally.	Strongly prefer A | | Neutral | | Strongly prefer B	A job with excellent vacations and fringe benefits.
10. A job in which there is a real chance you could be laid off.	Strongly prefer A | | Neutral | | Strongly prefer B	A job with very little chance to do challenging work.
11. A job with little freedom and independence to do your work in the way you think best.	Strongly prefer A | | Neutral | | Strongly prefer B	A job with poor working conditions.
12. A job with very satisfying teamwork.	Strongly prefer A | | Neutral | | Strongly prefer B	A job that allows you to use your skills and abilities to the fullest extent.

Turn to page 413 for scoring directions and key.

Source: J.R. Hackman and G.R. Oldham, *The Job Diagnostic Survey: An Instrument for the Diagnosis of Jobs and the Evaluation of Job Redesign Projects,* Technical Report No. 4 (New Haven, Conn.: Yale University, Department of Administrative Sciences, 1974). With permission.

Class Exercise

What Kind of Organization Design Do You Want to Work For?

Do you have an idea of what type of organization you'd like to work for? Most likely you have given it some thought, but that focus has probably been on the type of job or maybe its location. But what about the personality of the organization? How much consideration have you given to the culture you'd work best in?

For this exercise, first complete the questions below and score them. Then, in your group, compare responses. Are there group members who prefer to work in more bureaucratic organizations? Those who prefer to work in smaller companies? Discuss with your group members why you feel that type of organization will best suit you. Also, imagine that you work in an organization whose culture is opposite of your preference. How might that affect your work? Discuss with your class members.

For each of the following statements, circle the level of agreement or disagreement that you personally feel:

SA = Strongly Agree
A = Agree
U = Uncertain
D = Disagree
SD = Strongly Disagree

1. I like being part of a team and having my performance assessed in terms of my contribution to the team.   SA A U D SD
2. No person's needs should be compromised in order for a department to achieve its goals.   SA A U D SD
3. I prefer a job where my boss leaves me alone.   SA A U D SD
4. I like the thrill and excitement from taking risks.   SA A U D SD
5. People shouldn't break rules.   SA A U D SD
6. Seniority in an organization should be highly rewarded.   SA A U D SD
7. I respect authority.   SA A U D SD
8. If a person's job performance is inadequate, it's irrelevant how much effort he or she made.   SA A U D SD
9. I like things to be predictable.   SA A U D SD
10. I'd prefer my identity and status to come from my professional expertise than from the organization that employs me.   SA A U D SD

For items 5, 6, 7, and 9, give yourself +2 for each strongly agree, +1 for agree, 0 for uncertain, −1 for disagree, and −2 for strongly disagree. For items 1, 2, 3, 4, 8, and 10, reverse the scoring (strongly agree = −2, and so forth). Add up your total. Your score will fall somewhere between +20 and −20. The higher your score (positive) the more comfortable you'll be in a stable, rule-oriented culture. This is synonymous with large companies and government agencies. Negative scores indicate a preference for small, innovative, flexible, team-oriented cultures that are more likely to be found in research units or small businesses.

Key Terms

Key terms are listed in the order in which they appear in the chapter.

simple structure	committee structure	skill variety
functional structure	horizontal structure	task identity
divisional structure	core process	task significance
matrix structure	organization culture	autonomy
network structure	strong culture	feedback
strategic alliance	job design	
task force structure	job characteristics model (JCM)	

Case Application

Magna International

Magna International is one of the top ten auto-parts makers in North America. This Canadian firm produces 4,000 components—from flywheels to fenders—for nearly every major auto manufacturer with a U.S. factory. For instance, it is Chrysler's biggest component supplier.

Magna's top management has long been committed to keeping the company's structure loose and giving a great deal of freedom to its unit managers. In the mid-1980s, the company had more than 10,000 employees and almost $1 billion in annual sales. These employees were organized into 120 separate enterprises. Each enterprise operated under its own name and had one factory. Magna's philosophy was to keep units small—no more than 200 people—to encourage entrepreneurship and focus responsibility squarely with the plant manager. When a plant got more work than it could handle, rather than add to the plant's size, Magna would "clone" the facility and start a new company.

The structure worked fine during the 1980s. Overall sales grew thirteen-fold during that decade. Plant managers, acting with almost complete autonomy, aggressively expanded their businesses. Their motivation? They shared not only in their plant's profits, but all spin-offs that their business created. Thus, free from corporate interference, plant managers built factories, took on debt, and signed supply contracts with Detroit auto makers.

The bubble burst in 1990. Auto sales had slowed and the expansion-driven managers had burdened the company with US$1 billion in new debt. In 1990, Magna lost $191 million on sales of $1.6 billion and seemed headed for bankruptcy. In January 1991, Magna stock fell to $2 a share.

But Magna didn't go bankrupt. Top management interceded and has turned the company's fortunes around. The company sold or shut nearly half of its factories and used the proceeds to pay off its debt. The remaining plants are small, new, efficient, and flexible. And management succeeded in getting Magna parts used in popular cars such as the Ford Taurus and Toyota Camry. By 1992, Magna's sales had risen to $2 billion, earnings were $81 million, and the company's stock had rebounded to $26 a share.

Questions

1. Using structural concepts developed in this chapter, describe Magna International's structure in 1985, and in 1992.
2. Magna isn't alone in changing its structure. Many companies, even large ones like IBM, are scorning bureaucracy and creating loosely structured, independent businesses. Why?
3. What does the Magna case imply about creating a structure made up of a federation of independent businesses? What are the good and the bad aspects of this type of structure?

Process Engineering Restructures Organizations

As organizations redesign and restucture themselves for the 21st century, they often start by downsizing — removing layers of management and laying off workers. But sometimes it's the wrong managers and people. James Champy used a medical analogy when he argued, "We are amputating before we do a diagnosis — downsizing without looking at process and structure." There is little doubt that the structure of most organizations of more than a decade ago had lots of managers and lots of layers. It took a great deal of time for information to get from the bottom to the top and for decisions to get from the top to the bottom. The highly competitive demands of business in the 1990s no longer afford the luxury of time, and so organizations are having to streamline their processes and structure. It's called process reengineering.

When James Champy and his colleagues studied an insurance company, for instance, they found it took 24 days to receive a policy after buying it. But, what was most interesting was that when they tracked the policies, they found that only 10 minutes of actual work was done over the period. The rest was taken up by transferring it from office to office. In fact, a policy went through 14 different departments. Much of the work in organizations is based on tradition — "we've always done it that way" — and there has not been an objective analysis of why.

Process reengineering critically examines the traditional method of structuring work, which is to fragment it and specialize it. For instance, Henry Ford built his Model Ts on an assembly line where the average job took less that 90 seconds to complete before repeating it. Fifty years later, General Motors was still doing it the same way. As Champy says, "For fifty years we thought of companies as machines; the problem is they ran the machine that way for too long." So, we see the struggle to redesign structures and the way the work is actually done.

By looking at work first from the perspective of the customer — what does the customer want — processes can be restructured to achieve things like shortening the time for the introduction of new products and services. A decade ago, the telephone company took weeks to provide new products or services ordered by their customers. Now they take a day. Pharmaceutical companies that used to take eight years to bring a new drug to market have halved the time. The savings are enormous. Process reengineering may be a current buzzword, but it appears to be here to stay.

Questions

1. What are the differences in the way work is done in network structured vs. horizontally structured organizations?
2. Does changing to a matrix structure from a traditional functional structure require reengineering of the way work is done in an organization? How? What has to be changed?
3. Can an organization with a very strong culture, like Microsoft, be reengineered and changed significantly? What sorts of problems are likely to arise?

Video Resource: "James Champy Interview," *Venture* 487 (May 8, 1994).

8

Human Resource Management

Learning Objectives

WHAT WILL I BE ABLE TO DO AFTER I FINISH THIS CHAPTER?

1. Describe the strategic human resource management process.
2. Discuss the influence of government regulations on human resource decisions.
3. Differentiate between job descriptions and job specifications.
4. Contrast recruitment and decruitment options.
5. Explain the importance of validity and reliability in selection.
6. Describe the selection devices that work best with various kinds of jobs.
7. Identify various training methods.
8. Outline the five stages in a career.
9. Explain the collective bargaining process.
10. Describe how HRM practices can facilitate workforce diversity.

Honeywell Limited's Scarborough, Ontario, plant is both an assembly line operation and a school. The plant manufactures control devices for heating, cooling and ventilation, employing 470 production workers. It used to produce 15 types of controls, most of them sold in Canada, but in 1988 the company reduced its production to five key products in which it could compete on a global basis. John MacMillan, director of manufacturing, set about transforming the factory, implementing just-in-time inventory systems, Total Quality Management, and self-directed work teams.

To help employees adjust to the new working methods, Honeywell provided mandatory training on company time. Courses included Total Quality Management, just-in-time techniques and team skills.

Most of the employees had less than a grade 12 education and half did not speak English as their first language. Although that had been fine when workers did one job and didn't have to work in teams and communicate with one another, the new structure placed quite different demands on them. Honeywell determined that more fundamental training was needed. The company set up an education program called Learning for Life—its goal: to enrich people and to help make them more productive.

Courses teach English, mathematics, computers, communications, and team skills, and a variety of other things. This training was paid for by the company, but taken on the employees' own time.

It soon became apparent that the employees were hungry for education and when the company offered 30 spaces for a course in English, there were

Honeywell believes in educating its workforce to improve communications.

130 applicants, while a computer course had 200 applicants.

The effects of these new manufacturing techniques and training programs have been dramatic. There has been more than a 40 per cent productivity increase since 1990. And workers feel a stronger sense of identity with the company and are heavily involved in changes being made on the shop floor.[1]

As Honeywell illustrates, the quality of an organization is, to a large degree, merely the summation of the quality of its people. Getting, training, and keeping competent employees is critical to the success of every organization, whether the organization is just starting or well established. Therefore, part of every manager's job in the organizing function is putting the right person into the right job.

Managers and Human Resource Management

Some readers may be thinking, "Sure, personnel decisions are important, but aren't they made by people in human resource departments? These aren't decisions that all managers are involved in."

It's true that, in large organizations, a number of the activities grouped under the label **human resource management (HRM)** often are done by specialists in human resources. However, not all managers work in organizations that have formal HRM functions; and even those who do still have to be engaged in some human resource activities. Small business managers are an obvious example of individuals who frequently must do their hiring without the assistance of HRM. But even managers in billion-dollar corporations are involved in recruiting candidates, reviewing application forms, interviewing applicants, inducting new employees, making decisions about employee training, and providing career advice to employees. Whether or not an organization has an HRM department, every manager is involved with human resource decisions in his or her unit.

human resource management
Function in management concerned with getting, training, motivating, and keeping employees.

The Human Resource Management Process

Exhibit 8-1 introduces the key components of an organization's human resource management process. It represents nine activities, or steps (the yellow-shaded boxes), that, if properly executed, will staff an organization with competent, high-performing employees who are capable of sustaining their performance level over the long term.

The first four steps represent strategic human resource planning, the adding of staff through recruitment, the reduction in staff through decruitment, and selection, resulting in the identification and selection of competent employees. Once you've got competent people, you need to help them adapt to the organization and ensure that their job skills and knowledge are kept current. You do this through orientation and training. The last steps in the HRM process are designed to identify performance problems, correct them, and help employees to sustain a high level of performance over their entire career. The activities involved here include performance appraisal, career development, and, where employees are unionized, labour-management relations. Because performance appraisals focus on behavioural control, we'll delay this discussion until Chapter 16.

Notice in Exhibit 8-1 that the entire HRM process is influenced by the external environment. In Chapter 2 we introduced constraints that the environment (both specific and general) places on management. Those constraints are probably most severe in the management of human resources. Before we review the nine steps in the process, therefore, we will briefly examine how environmental forces influence the process.

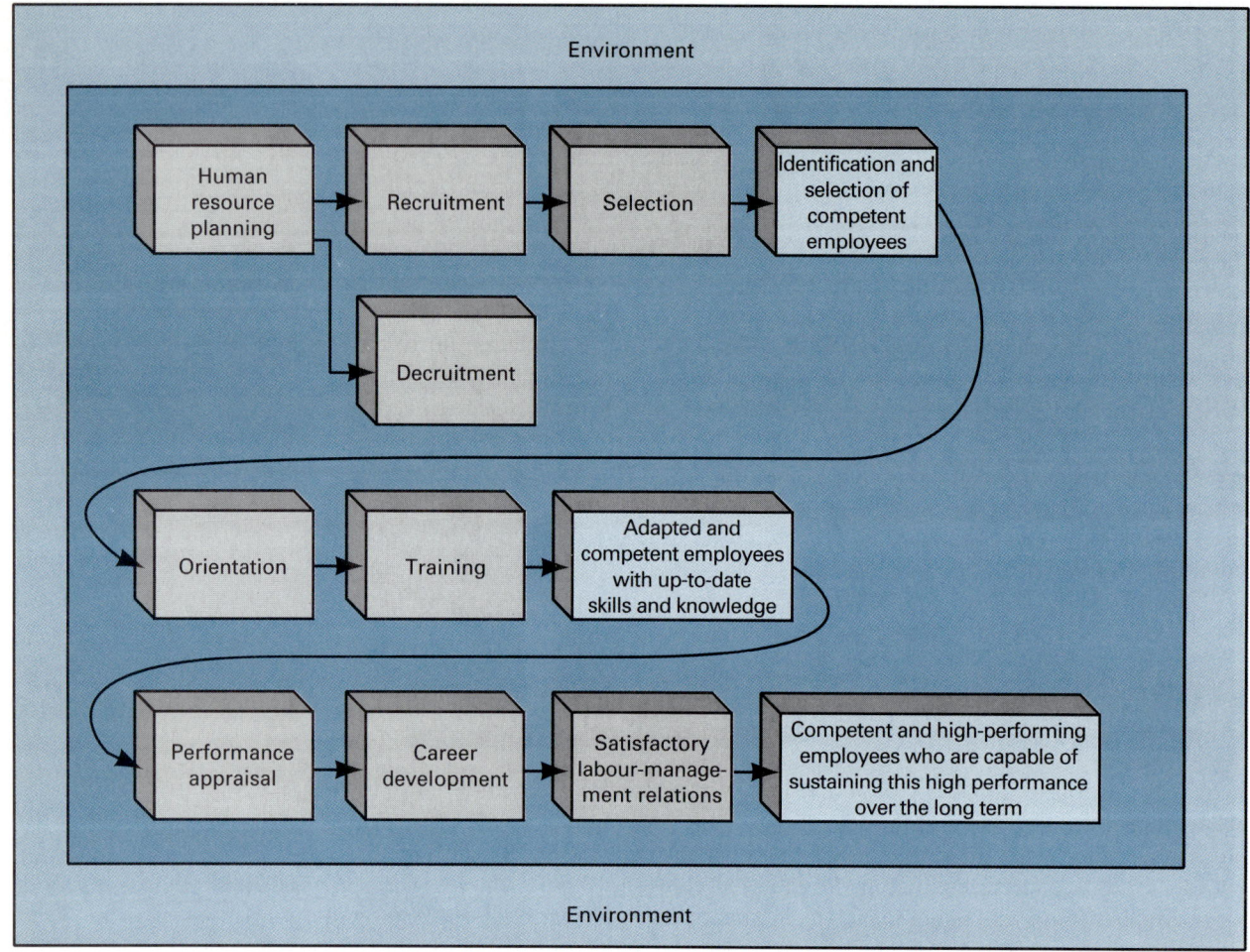

Exhibit 8-1 The Strategic Human Resources Management Process

Important Environmental Factors Affecting HRM

Numerous environmental forces impinge on human resource management activities. In unionized organizations, many key personnel decisions are regulated by the terms of collective bargaining agreements. These agreements usually define such things as wages, work hours, criteria for promotions, and layoffs; training eligibility; and disciplinary practices. But no environmental constraint can match the influence of government laws and regulations.

Since the mid-1960s, the federal government has greatly expanded its influence over HRM decisions by enacting a wealth of laws and regulations (see Exhibit 8-2 for examples). As a result of this legislation, employers today must ensure that equal employment opportunities exist for job applicants and current employees. Decisions regarding who will be hired, for example, or which employees will be chosen for a management training program must be made without regard to race, sex, religion, age,

Human Resource Management

colour, national origin, or disability. Exceptions can occur only for requirements that are **bona fide occupational qualifications (BFOQ).** This explains why, for instance, airlines today have flight attendants of both sexes and of varying ages. In the early 1960s, airlines hired almost exclusively flight attendants who were young, attractive females. But age, beauty, and gender are not BFOQs for this job; and so such criteria had to be dropped.

Many organizations have **affirmative action programs** to ensure that decisions and practices enhance the employment, upgrading, and retention of members from protected groups, such as minorities and females. That is, not only will the organization refrain from discrimination, but it will also actively seek to enhance the status of members from protected groups. Our conclusion is that managers are not completely free to choose whom they hire, promote, or fire. While these regulations have significantly helped to reduce discrimination and unfair employment practices in organizations, they have, at the same time, also reduced management's discretion over human resource decisions. The case of *Central Okanagan School District No 73 vs. Renaud, 1992*, where Mr. Renaud's request not to have to work on Saturdays because of religion was not granted, went all the way to the Supreme Court of Canada, which determined that the employee had been discriminated against. Interestingly, the court found both the employer and the union equally responsible.

bona fide occupational qualifications (BFOQ)
A criterion such as sex, age, or national origin may be used as a basis for hiring if it can be clearly demonstrated to be job related.

affirmative action programs
Programs that enhance the organizational status of members of protected groups.

Strategic Human Resource Planning

Strategic human resource planning (SHRP) is the process by which management ensures that it has the right number and kinds of people in the right places, and at the right times, who are capable of effectively and efficiently completing those tasks that will help the organization achieve its overall objectives. Strategic human resource planning, then, translates the organization's objectives (assuming, of course, that they have been established) in terms of the workers needed to meet those objectives.[2]

SHRP can be condensed into two steps: (1) assessing current human resources, and (2) assessing future human resource needs and developing a program to meet future human resource needs.

How Does an Organization Conduct an Employee Assessment?

Management begins by reviewing its current human resource status. This is typically done by generating a **human resource inventory.** In an era of sophisticated computer systems, it is not too difficult for most organizations to generate a human resource inventory report. The input for this report is derived from forms completed by employees. Such reports might list the name, education, training, prior employment, languages spoken, capabilities, and specialized skills of each employee in the organization. This inventory allows management to assess which talents and skills are available.

Another part of the current assessment is the **job analysis.** While the human resource inventory is concerned with telling management what individual employees can do, job analysis is more fundamental. It defines the jobs within the organization and the

strategic human resource planning
The process by which management ensures that it has the right personnel, who are capable of completing those tasks that help the organization reach its objectives.

human resource inventory
A database containing information on employees' skills and competencies

job analysis
An assessment that defines jobs and the behaviours necessary to perform them.

LAW OR REGULATION

Canadian Human Rights Act
Canada Labour Code
Official Languages Act
Privacy Act
Access to Information Act

Exhibit 8-2 Major Canadian Federal Laws and Regulations Related to HRM

behaviours that are necessary to perform those jobs. For instance, what are the duties of a purchasing specialist, grade 3, who works for Ford of Canada? What minimal knowledge, skills, and abilities are necessary for the adequate performance of this particular job? How do the requirements for a purchasing specialist, grade 3, compare with those for a purchasing specialist, grade 2, or for a purchasing analyst? These are questions that job analysis can answer. It seeks to determine the kind of people needed to fill each job and culminates in job descriptions and job specifications.

There are several methods for analysing jobs. There is the observation method, in which employees are either watched directly or filmed on the job. Employees can also be interviewed individually or in a group. A third method is the use of structured questionnaires on which employees check or rate the items they perform in their jobs from a long list of possible task items. A fourth method is the use of a technical conference, at which "experts"—usually supervisors with extensive knowledge of a job—identify its specific characteristics. A fifth method is to have employees record their daily activities in a diary or notebook, which can then be reviewed and structured into job activities. In practice, usually some combination of the above are used.[3]

Information gathered by using one or more of these methods allows management to draw up a **job description** and **job specification.** The former is a written statement of what a jobholder does, how it is done, and why it is done. It typically portrays job content, environment, and conditions of employment. The job specification states the minimum acceptable qualifications that an incumbent must possess to perform a given job successfully. It identifies the knowledge, skills, and abilities needed to do the job effectively.

job description
A written statement of what a jobholder does, how it is done, and why it is done.

job specification
A statement of the minimum acceptable qualifications that an incumbent must possess to perform a given job successfully.

The job description and specification are important documents when managers begin recruiting and selecting. The job description can be used to describe the job to potential candidates. The job specification keeps the manager's attention on the list of qualifications necessary for an incumbent to perform a job and assists in determining whether candidates are qualified. Consequently, hiring individuals based on the information contained in these two documents helps to ensure that the hiring process is not discriminatory.

How Are Future Employee Needs Determined?

Future human resource needs are determined by the organization's objectives and strategies. Demand for human resources is a result of demand for the organization's products or services. On the basis of its estimate of total revenue, management can attempt to establish the number and mix of human resources needed to reach these revenues. In some cases, the situation may be reversed. Where particular skills are

This individual analyses jobs. Through this process, each job will be explained in terms of the skills, knowledge, and abilities needed by a job holder to be a successful performer.

necessary and in scarce supply, the availability of satisfactory human resources determines revenues. This might be the case, for example, in a tax-consulting firm that finds it has more business opportunities than it can handle. Its only limiting factor in building revenues might be its ability to locate and hire staff with the qualifications necessary to satisfy the consulting firm's clients. In most cases, however, the overall organizational goals and the resulting revenue forecast provide the major input determining the organization's human resource demand requirements.

After it has assessed both current capabilities and future needs, management is able to estimate shortages—both in number and in kind—and to highlight areas in which the organization is overstaffed. A program can then be developed that matches these estimates with forecasts of future labour supply. So strategic human resource planning provides not only information to guide current staffing needs but also projections of future employee needs and availability.

Recruitment and Selection

Once managers know their current SHRP status (whether they are understaffed or overstaffed), they can begin to do something about it. If one or more vacancies exist, they can use the information gathered through job analysis to guide them in **recruitment**—that is, the process of locating, identifying, and attracting capable applicants.[4] On the other hand, if strategic human resource planning indicates a surplus, management will want to reduce the labour supply within the organization. This activity is called **decruitment**.[5]

Where Does a Manager Look to Recruit Potential Candidates? Candidates can be found by using several sources. Exhibit 8-3 offers some guidance. The source that is used should reflect the local labour market, the type or level of position, and the size of the organization.

Are Certain Recruiting Sources Superior to Others? Do certain recruiting sources produce superior candidates? The answer is yes. The majority of studies find that employee referrals prove to be superior.[6] The explanation for this finding is intuitively logical. First, applicants referred by current employees are prescreened by these employees. Because the recommenders know both the job and the person being recommended, they tend to refer applicants who are better qualified for the job. Second, because current employees often feel their reputation in the organization is at stake with a referral, they tend to refer others only when they are reasonably confident that the referral won't make them look bad.

How Does a Manager Handle Decruitment? In the past decade, most large Canadian corporations, as well as many government agencies, small businesses, and foreign companies, have been forced to engage in some decruitment activities.[7] The decline in many manufacturing industries, market changes, foreign competition, and mergers have been the primary causes of personnel cutbacks. Decruitment is not a pleasant task for any manager to perform. But as many organizations are forced to shrink the size of their workforce or restructure their skill composition, decruitment is becoming an increasingly relevant activity in human resource management (see Managers Who Made a Difference).

recruitment
The process of locating, identifying, and attracting capable applicants.

decruitment
Techniques for reducing the labour supply within an organization.

Exhibit 8-3 Major Sources of Potential Job Candidates

SOURCE	ADVANTAGES	DISADVANTAGES
Internal Searches	Low cost; build employee morale; candidates are familiar with organization	Limited supply; may not increase proportion of protected group employees
Advertisements	Wide distribution can be targeted to specific groups	Generate many unqualified candidates
Employee Referrals	Knowledge about the organization provided by current employees; can generate strong candidates because a good referral reflects on the recommender	May not increase the diversity and mix of employees
Public Employment Agencies	Free or nominal cost	Candidates tend to be lower skilled, although some skilled employees available
Private Employment Agencies	Wide contacts; careful screening; short-term guarantees often given	High cost
School Placement	Large, centralized body of candidates	Limited to entry-level positions
Temporary Help Services	Fill temporary needs	Expensive
Employee Leasing and Independent Contractors	Fill temporary needs, but usually for more specific, longer-term projects	Little commitment to organization other than current project

What are a manager's decruitment options? Obviously, people can be fired. But other choices may be more beneficial to the organization and/or the employee.[8] Exhibit 8-4 summarizes a manager's major options.

Is There a Basic Premise to Selecting Job Candidates?

selection process
The process of screening job applicants to ensure that the most appropriate candidates are hired.

The **selection process** is a prediction exercise. It seeks to predict which applicants will be successful if hired. "Successful" in this case means performing well on the criteria the organization uses to evaluate its employees. In filling a sales position, for example,

Exhibit 8-4 Decruitment Options

OPTION	DESCRIPTION
Firing	Permanent involuntary termination
Layoffs	Temporary involuntary termination; may last only a few days or extend to years
Attrition	Not filling openings created by voluntary resignations or normal retirements
Transfers	Moving employees either laterally or downward; usually does not reduce costs but can reduce intraorganizational supply-demand imbalances
Reduced Workweeks	Having employees work fewer hours per week, share jobs, or perform their jobs on a part-time basis
Early Retirements	Providing incentives to older and more senior employees for retiring before their normal retirement date
Job Sharing	Having employees, typically two part-timers, share one full-time position

Managers Who Made a Difference

MIKE HANER AT SASKATOON CHEMICALS

Mike Haner is the general manager of Saskatoon Chemicals Ltd., a wholly owned subsidiary of Weyerhaeuser Canada Ltd. Saskatoon Chemicals produces chlorine-based chemicals for the pulp and paper industry, water treatment plants, and swimming pools. It employs 157 people and has revenues of about $60 million a year. But what makes it different from most other companies, and what makes Mike's job different, is how work gets done by 16 union-management committees. Essentially, the union and managers co-manage the company. Mike Haner describes it this way: "In the traditional system, management decides and the union objects. In this system, management and union decide, implement, and correct." Mike Haner has had to break the traditional perception and role of a manager.

But things didn't always work smoothly at Saskatoon Chemicals. In the 1980s, there was a running battle between the union and management, with neither side trusting the other. In 1989, there was a backlog of 100 grievances and just after Christmas, the workers went out on strike, not about wages (the average wage is about $22 an hour), but about work scheduling. Both sides finally realized that they had had enough, and they started to try to work together with the help of a consultant. Both sides had to make compromises. For instance, management began to share confidential information with the union and allowed employees' input into decisions about their work and jobs.

One committee of managers and workers is looking at a major overhaul of the plant's work flow. A possible scenario is to create three separate businesses, each concentrating on a group of chemicals. The goal is to improve business performance and expand product lines to ensure the viability of the business and employment on the site. To date, productivity has been increased, costs cut, and the plant made safer. There are no grievances on file, and it only took five days to negotiate the 1994 collective agreement. Something is working![9] ▼

---

the selection process should be able to predict which applicants will generate a high volume of sales; for a position as a high school teacher, it should predict which applicants will be effective educators. Consider, for a moment, that any selection decision can result in four possible outcomes. As shown in Exhibit 8-5, two of these outcomes would indicate correct decisions, but two would indicate errors.

Exhibit 8-5
Selection Decision Outcomes

		Selection Decision	
Later Job Performance	Successful	Reject error	Correct decision
	Unsuccessful	Correct decision	Accept error

A decision is correct when the applicant was predicted to be successful and later proved to be successful on the job; or when the applicant was predicted to be unsuccessful and would perform accordingly if hired. In the former case, we have successfully accepted; in the latter case, we have successfully rejected.

Problems occur when we make errors by rejecting candidates who would later perform successfully on the job (reject errors) or accepting those who subsequently perform poorly (accept errors). These problems are, unfortunately, far from insignificant. A generation ago, reject errors meant only that the costs of selection would be increased because more candidates would have to be screened. Today, selection techniques that result in reject errors can open the organization to charges of employment discrimination, especially if applicants from protected groups are disproportionately rejected. Accept errors, on the other hand, have very obvious costs to the organization, including the cost of training the employee, the costs generated or profits foregone because of the employee's incompetence, and the cost of severance and the subsequent costs of further recruiting and selection screening. The major thrust of any selection activity is therefore to reduce the probability of making reject errors or accept errors, while increasing the probability of making correct decisions. We do this by using selection activities that are both reliable and valid.

reliability
The ability of a selection device to measure the same thing consistently.

What Is Reliability? Reliability addresses whether a selection device measures the same thing consistently. For example, if a test is reliable, any single individual's score should remain fairly stable over time, assuming that the characteristics it is measuring are also stable.

The importance of reliability should be evident. No selection device can be effective if it is low in reliability. That is equivalent to weighing yourself every day on an erratic scale. If the scale is unreliable—randomly fluctuating, say, ten to fifteen pounds every time you step on it—the results will not mean much. To be effective predictors, selection devices must possess an acceptable level of consistency.

validity
The proven relationship that exists between a selection device and some relevant criterion.

What Is Validity? Any selection device that a manager uses—such as application forms, tests, interviews, or physical examinations—must also demonstrate **validity.** That is, there must be a proven relationship between the selection device and some relevant criterion. For example, the law prohibits management from using a test score as a selection device unless there is clear evidence that, once on the job, individuals with high scores on this test outperform individuals with low test scores.

The burden is on management to support that any selection device it uses to differentiate applicants is related to job performance. While management can give applicants an intelligence test and use the results to help make selection decisions, it must be prepared to demonstrate, if challenged, that this intelligence test is a valid measure—that is, that scores on the test are positively related to later job performance.

Are There Selection Devices That Every Manager Should Use?

Managers can use a number of selection devices to reduce accept and reject errors. The best-known devices include an analysis of the prospect's completed application form, written and performance-simulation tests, interviews, background investigations, and in some cases a physical examination. Let's briefly review each of these devices, giving particular attention to the validity of each in predicting job performance. After we review the devices, we will discuss when each should be used.

What Is the Application Form? Almost all organizations require candidates to complete an application. It may be only a form on which a prospect gives his or her name, address, and telephone number. At the other extreme, it might be a comprehensive personal history profile, detailing the applicant's activities, skills, and accomplishments (see Ethical Dilemmas in Management).

Hard and relevant biographical data that can be verified—for example, rank in high school graduating class—have shown to be valid measures of performance for some jobs.[10] Additionally, when application form items have been appropriately weighted to reflect job relatedness, the device has proven a valid predictor for such diverse groups as salesclerks, engineers, factory workers, district managers, clerical employees, and technicians.[11] But, typically, only a couple of items on the application prove to be valid predictors, and then only for a specific job. Use of weighted applications for selection purposes is difficult and expensive because the weights have to be validated for each specific job and must be continually reviewed and updated to reflect changes in weights over time.

Do Written Tests Serve a Useful Purpose? Typical written tests include tests of intelligence, aptitude, ability, and interest. Such tests have long been used as selection devices, although their popularity has run in cycles. Written tests were widely used for twenty years following World War II. Beginning in the late 1960s, however, they fell into disfavour. Written tests were frequently characterized as discriminatory, and many organizations couldn't validate that their written tests were job-related.[12] But since the late 1980s, written tests have made a comeback.[13] Managers have become increasingly aware that poor hiring decisions are costly and that properly designed tests could reduce the likelihood of these decisions occurring. In addition, the cost of developing and validating a set of written tests for a specific job has come down markedly. "Ten years ago," says an executive at Personnel Decisions Inc., "if an employer called us and wanted to put together a test battery for salespeople or copywriters, we told him [or her] it would take $100,000 and six months. Now we're talking about $6,000 and a couple of weeks."[14]

A review of the evidence finds that tests of intellectual ability, spatial and mechanical ability, perceptual accuracy, and motor ability are moderately valid predictors for many semiskilled and unskilled operative jobs in industrial organizations.[15] And intelligence tests are reasonably good predictors for supervisory positions.[16] However, an enduring criticism of written tests is that intelligence, and other tested characteristics, can be somewhat removed from the actual performance of the job itself. For example, a high score on an intelligence test is not necessarily a good indicator that the applicant will perform well as a computer programmer. This criticism has led to an increased use of performance-simulation tests.

Ethical Dilemmas in Management

IS IT WRONG TO WRITE A "CREATIVE" RESUMÉ?

Almost all of us have written, or will write, a resumé to give to prospective employers. It summarizes our background, experiences, and accomplishments. Should it be 100 per cent truthful? Let's take a few examples.

Person A leaves a job where his title was "credit clerk." When looking for a new job, he describes his previous title as "credit analyst." He thinks it sounds more impressive. Is this retitling of a former job wrong?

Person B made $2700 a month when she left her previous job. On her resumé, she says that she was making $2900. Is that wrong?

Person C, about eight years ago, took nine months off between jobs to travel overseas. Afraid that people might consider her unstable or lacking in career motivation, on her resumé she states that she was engaged in "independent consulting activities" during the period. Was she wrong?

Person D is fifty years old with an impressive career record. He spent five years in college thirty years ago, but he never got a degree. He is being considered for a $150,000-a-year vice-presidency at another firm. He knows that he has the ability and track record to do the job, but he won't get the interview if he admits to not having a college degree. He knows that the probability that anyone would check his college records is very low. Should he put on his resumé that he completed his degree?

Falsehoods on resumés are widespread. A recent survey of 200 applicants found that 30 per cent reported incorrect dates of employment. Eleven per cent misrepresented reasons for leaving a previous job to cover up the fact that they were fired. Some falsely claimed college degrees or totally fabricated work histories. In a larger study of 11,000 applicants, 488 failed to disclose criminal records; most of these were drug or alcohol offences, but some were as serious as rape or attempted murder.[17]

Is it wrong to write a "creative" resumé? What deviations from the truth, if any, would you make?

work sampling
A personnel selection device in which job applicants are presented with a miniature replica of a job and are asked to perform tasks central to that job.

assessment centres
Places in which job candidates undergo performance simulation tests that evaluate managerial potential.

What Are Performance-Simulation Tests? What better way to find out whether an applicant for a technical writing position at Spar Aerospace can write technical manuals than by having him or her do it? The logic of this question has led to the expanding interest in performance-simulation tests. Undoubtedly, the enthusiasm for these tests lies in the fact that they are based on job analysis data and therefore should more easily meet the requirement of job relatedness than do written tests. Performance-simulation tests are made up of actual job behaviours rather than surrogates. The best-known performance-simulation tests are **work sampling** (a miniature replica of the job) and **assessment centres** (simulating real problems that one may face on the job). The former is suited to routine jobs, the latter to selecting managerial personnel. We've identified characteristics about these two in Exhibit 8-6.

Is the Interview Effective? The interview, along with the application form, is an almost universal selection device.[18] Few of us have ever gotten a job without one or more interviews. The irony of this is that the value of the interview as a selection device has been the subject of considerable debate.[19]

Interviews can be reliable and valid selection tools, but too often they're not. When interviews are structured and well organized, and when interviewers are held to common questioning, interviews are effective predictors.[20] But those conditions don't

METHOD	ACTIVITIES	BEST USED FOR
Work Sampling	Presents applicants with a miniature replica of the job	Matching the knowledge, skills, and abilities needed for successful performance on each job and an applicant's ability to demonstrate proficiency on these elements
Assessment Centres	An elaborate set of performance-simulation tests that simulate real problems individuals may confront on the job. Usually includes interviews, in-basket problem-solving exercises, group discussions, and business decision games	Evaluating a candidate's managerial potential

Exhibit 8-6 Characteristics of Work Sampling and Assessment Centers

characterize most interviews. The typical interview—in which applicants are asked a varying set of essentially random questions in an informal setting—usually provides little in the way of valuable information.

There are all kinds of potential biases that can creep into interviews if they are not well structured and standardized. To illustrate, a review of the research leads us to the following conclusions:

▶ 1. Prior knowledge about the applicant will bias the interviewer's evaluation.
▶ 2. The interviewer tends to hold a stereotype of what represents a "good" applicant.
▶ 3. The interviewer tends to favour applicants who share his or her own attitudes.
▶ 4. The order in which applicants are interviewed will influence evaluations.
▶ 5. The order in which information is elicited during the interview will influence evaluations.
▶ 6. Negative information is given unduly high weight.
▶ 7. The interviewer may make a decision concerning the applicant's suitability within the first four or five minutes of the interview.
▶ 8. The interviewer may forget much of the interview's content within minutes after its conclusion.
▶ 9. The interview is most valid in determining an applicant's intelligence, level of motivation, and interpersonal skills.[21]

What can managers do to make interviews more valid and reliable? Specifically, we suggest (1) structuring a fixed set of questions for all applicants; (2) having detailed information about the job for which applicants are interviewing; (3) minimizing any foreknowledge of applicants' background, experience, interests, test scores, or other characteristics; (4) asking behavioural questions that require applicants to give detailed accounts of actual job behaviours (for example, Give me a specific example of a time you had to reprimand an employee, tell me what action you took, and describe the result); (5) using a standardized evaluation form; (6) taking notes during the interview; and (7) avoiding short interviews that encourage premature decision making (see Developing Management Skills).[22]

What Is a Background Investigation? Background investigations are of two types: verifications of application data and reference checks. The first type has proven to be a valuable source of selection information, whereas the latter is essentially worthless. Let's briefly review each.

Several studies indicate that verifying "facts" given on the application form pays dividends. A significant percentage of job applicants—upward of 15 per cent—exaggerate or misrepresent dates of employment, job titles, past salaries, or reasons for leaving a prior position.[23] Confirmation of hard data on the application with prior employers is therefore a worthwhile endeavour.

The reference check is used by many organizations but is extremely difficult to justify. Whether they are work related or personal, references provide little valid information for the selection decision.[24] Why? Employers are frequently reluctant to give candid evaluations of a former employee's job performance for fear of legal repercussions. In fact, a survey found that only 55 per cent of human resource executives would "always" provide accurate references to a prospective employer. Moreover, 7 per cent said they would never give an accurate reference.[25] Personal likes and dislikes also heavily influence the type of recommendation given. Personal references are likely to provide biased information. Who among us doesn't have three or four friends who will speak in glowing terms about our integrity, work habits, positive attitudes, knowledge, and skills?

Is a Physical Examination Necessary? For jobs with certain physical requirements, the physical examination has some validity. However, this includes a very small number of jobs today. In many cases, the physical examination primarily is done for insurance purposes—especially if a company has an insurance policy that does not provide medical coverage for pre-existing conditions.

Great care must be taken to ensure that physical requirements are job-related and do not discriminate. Some physical requirements may exclude certain disabled persons, when, in fact, such requirements do not affect job performance.

All applicants will eventually go through some type of interview. But do the interviewers give all candidates a fair shake? Research has shown that they may have not. However, following some basic steps, like structuring the interview, can help immensely.

What Selection Device Works Best and When? Many selection devices are of limited value to managers in making selection decisions. An understanding of strengths and weaknesses of each will help you to determine when each should be used. We offer the following advice to guide your choices.

Since the validity of selection devices varies for different types of jobs, you should use only those devices that predict for a given job (see Exhibit 8-7 on page 188). The application form offers limited information. Traditional written tests are reasonably effective devices for routine jobs. Work samples, however, are clearly preferable to written tests. For supervisory and managerial selection, the assessment centre is strongly recommended. If the interview has a place in the selection decision, it is most likely among less-routine jobs, particularly managerial positions. The interview is a reasonably good device for discerning intelligence and interpersonal skills.[26] These are more likely to be related to job performance in nonroutine activities. Verification of application data is valuable for all jobs. Finally, physical examinations only provide valid selection information in rare instances.

Developing Management Skills

▼ INTERVIEWING SKILLS ▲

▶ **1. Review job description and job specification.** Reviewing pertinent information about the job provides valuable information about what you'll assess the candidate on. Furthermore, relevant job requirements help to eliminate bias.

▶ **2. Prepare a structured set of questions you want to ask all applicants for the job.** By having a set of prepared questions, you ensure that the information you wish to elicit is attainable. Furthermore, by asking similar questions, you are able to better compare all candidates' answers.

▶ **3. Prior to meeting a candidate, review his or her application form and resumé.** Doing so helps you to create a complete picture of the candidate in terms of what is represented on the resumé/application, and what the job requires. You will also begin to identify areas to explore in the interview. That is, areas not clearly defined on the resumé/application that are essential for your job become a focal point in your discussion with the candidate.

▶ **4. Open the interview by putting the applicant at ease and by providing a brief preview of the topics to be discussed.** Interviews are stressful for job candidates. By opening with small talk—e.g., the weather, etc.—you give the candidate time to adjust to the interview setting. By providing a preview of topics to come, you are giving the candidate an "agenda." This helps the candidate to begin framing what he or she will say in response to your questions.

▶ **5. Ask your questions and listen carefully to the applicant's answers.** Select follow-up questions that naturally flow from the answers given. Focus on the responses as they relate to information you need to ensure that the candidate meets your job requirements. Any uncertainty you may still have requires a follow-up question to further probe for the information.

▶ **6. Close the interview by telling the applicant what's going to happen next.** Applicants are anxious about the status of your hiring decision. Be upfront with the candidate regarding others who will be interviewed and the remaining steps in the hiring process. If you plan to make a decision in two weeks or so, let the candidate know what you intend to do. Additionally, tell the applicant how you will respond to him or her about your decision.

▶ **7. Write your evaluation of the applicant while the interview is still fresh in your mind.** Don't wait until the end of your day, after interviewing several candidates, to write your analysis of a candidate. Memory can fail you! The sooner you complete your write-up after an interview, the better chance you have for accurately recording what occurred in the interview.

What Should One Look for in Selecting Managers for Global Assignments?
Transferring managers into new and different national cultures, without careful thought and proper selection, sets those managers up to fail. Most research on the transfer of managers between diverse countries—particularly the moving of Canadian executives overseas—indicates a fairly high failure rate.

Why don't more managers succeed when they are placed in foreign countries? One possible reason is that most organizations still select transfer candidates on the basis of technical competence alone, ignoring other predictors of success such as language skills, flexibility, and family adaptability.[27]

SELECTION DEVICE	POSITION[a]			
	SENIOR MANAGEMENT	MIDDLE AND LOWER MANAGEMENT	COMPLEX NONMAN-AGERIAL	ROUTINE OPERATIVE
Application form	2	2	2	2
Written tests	1	1	2	3
Work samples	—	—	4	4
Assessment centre	5	5	—	—
Interviews	4	3	2	2
Verification of application data	3	3	3	3
Reference checks	1	1	1	1
Physical exam	1	1	1	2

[a] Validity is measured on a scale from 5 (highest) to 1 (lowest).

Exhibit 8-7 Quality of Selection Devices as Predictors

Orientation and Training

If we have done our recruiting and selecting properly, we should have hired competent individuals who can perform successfully. But successful performance requires more than possession of certain skills. New hires must be acclimated to the organization's culture and be trained to do the job in a manner consistent with the organization's objectives. To achieve these ends, HRM embarks on two processes—orientation and training.

How Do We Introduce New Hires to the Organization?

orientation
The introduction of a new employee to his or her job and the organization.

Once a job candidate has been selected, he or she needs to be introduced to the job and organization. This introduction is called **orientation.** The major objectives of orientation are to reduce the initial anxiety all new employees feel as they begin a new job; to familiarize new employees with the job, the work unit, and the organization as a whole; and to facilitate the outsider-insider transition. Job orientation expands on the information the employee obtained during the recruitment and selection stages. The new employee's specific duties and responsibilities are clarified, as well as how his or her performance will be evaluated. This is also the time to rectify any unrealistic expectations new employees might hold about the job. Work-unit orientation familiarizes the employee with the goals of the work unit, makes clear how his or her job contributes to the unit's goals, and includes introduction to his or her coworkers. Organization orientation informs the new employee about the organization's objectives, history, philosophy, procedures, and rules. This should include relevant personnel policies and benefits such as work hours, pay procedures, overtime requirements, and benefits. A tour of the organization's physical facilities is often part of the organization orientation.

Human Resource Management

Management has an obligation to make the integration of the new employee into the organization as smooth and as free of anxiety as possible. Successful orientation, whether formal or informal, results in an outsider-insider transition that makes the new member feel comfortable and fairly well adjusted, lowers the likelihood of poor work performance, and reduces the probability of a surprise resignation by the new employee only a week or two into the job.

What Is Employee Training?

On the whole, planes don't cause airline accidents, people do. Most collisions, crashes, and other mishaps—about 74 per cent to be exact—result from errors by the pilot or air traffic controller or inadequate maintenance. Weather and structural failures cause only 15 per cent of accidents.[28] We cite these statistics to illustrate the importance of training in the airline industry. These maintenance and human errors could be prevented or significantly reduced by better employee training.

The Conference Board of Canada estimated that Canadian organizations spent an average of $659 per capita on training and development in 1992. Spending on training and development varies by sector, with oil and gas companies spending more than $1200 per capita on average, and the accommodation and food services industry coming in at the low end with an average of roughly $130 per capita. Interestingly enough, the recession did not affect training budgets as much as might be expected. While about 85 per cent of companies surveyed by the Conference Board indicated they had been adversely affected by the recession, only 56 per cent said they had cut their training budgets.

All new Disney World employees go through an eight-hour orientation followed by forty hours of apprenticeship training on park grounds. The purpose is to familiarize new employees with Disney's history, tradition, policies, expectations, and ways of doing things.

How Are Employees Trained? Most training takes place on the job. This can be attributed to the simplicity of such methods and their usually lower cost. However, on-the-job training can disrupt the workplace and result in an increase in errors while learning takes place. Also, some skill training is too complex to learn on the job. In such cases, it should take place outside the work setting.

Individuals being trained as pilots are often trained on flight simulators. Why? In a simulator all aspects of flying a plane can be experienced. And if they react improperly, the simulator can be reset, and the individuals can try again. A mistake while actually flying could be too tragic and costly.

career
The sequence of positions occupied by a person during the course of a lifetime.

What Are Some of the Typical Methods Used? There are many different types of training methods that are available for organizations to use. For the most part, however, we can classify them in two ways. That is, training programs can be viewed as on-the-job or off-the-job training methods. We have summarized the more popular of these training methods in Exhibit 8-8.

Career Development

The term career has a number of meanings. In popular usage, it can mean advancement ("his career is progressing nicely"), a profession ("she has chosen a career in medicine"), or a lifelong sequence of jobs ("his career has included fifteen jobs in six different organizations"). For our purposes, we define a **career** as the sequence of positions occupied by a person during the course of a lifetime.[29] By this definition, it is apparent that we all have, or will have, careers. Moreover, the concept is as relevant to transient, unskilled labourers as to engineers or physicians.

Why should an organization be concerned with careers? More specifically, why should management spend time on career development? Focusing on careers forces management to adopt a long-term perspective on its human resources. An effective career-development program ensures that needed talent will be available and that women and minorities get opportunities for growth and development. It also improves the organization's ability to attract and retain highly talented personnel.

Sample On-the-Job Training Methods	
Job Rotation:	Lateral transfers allowing employees to work at different jobs. Provides good exposure to a variety of tasks.
Understudy Assignments:	Working with a seasoned veteran, coach, or mentor. Provides support and encouragement from an experienced worker. In the trades industry, this may also be an apprenticeship.
Sample Off-the-Job Training Methods	
Classroom Lectures:	Lectures designed to convey specific technical, interpersonal, or problem-solving skills.
Films and Videos:	Using the media to explicitly demonstrate technical skills that are not easily presented by other training methods.
Simulation Exercises:	Learning a job by actually performing the work (or its simulation). May include case analyses, experiential exercises, role playing, and group interaction.
Vestibule Training:	Learning tasks on the same equipment that one actually will use on the job, but in a simulated work environment.

Exhibit 8-8 Typical Training Methods

Do All Employees Progress Through Career Stages?

The most popular way of analysing and discussing careers is to view them as a series of stages.[30] We'll look at a five-stage model that applies to most people during their adult years, regardless of the type of work they do.

Most individuals begin to form ideas about their careers during their elementary and secondary school years. Their careers begin to wind down as they reach retirement age. We can identify five career stages that most people will go through during these years: **exploration, establishment, mid-career, late career,** and **decline.** These stages and the challenges for individuals are depicted in Exhibit 8-9.

After more than forty years of work, these individuals are now relaxing and enjoying the remaining years of life in retirement.

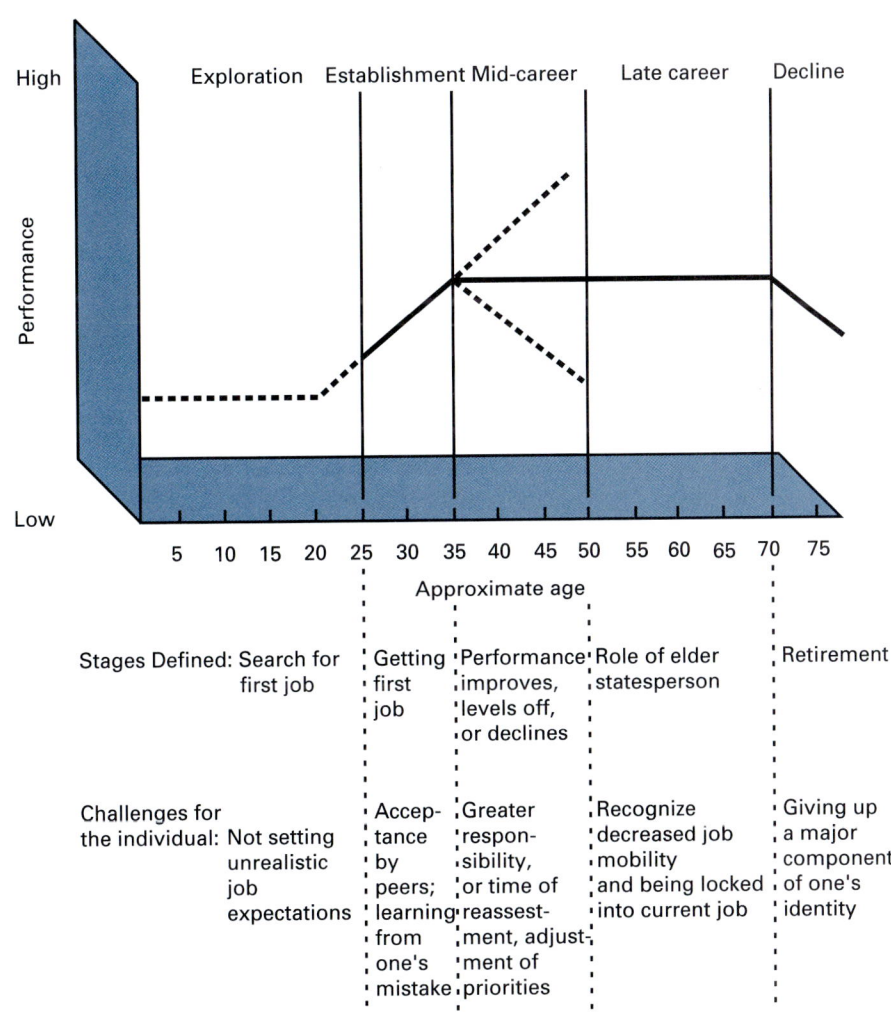

Exhibit 8-9 Stages in Career Development

Source: D.T. Hall, *Careers in Organizations* (Glenview, IL: Scott Foresman and Company, 1976), p. 57. Reprinted with permission of the author.

exploration career stage
A career stage that usually ends in one's mid-20's as one makes the transition from school to work.

establishment career stage
A period in which one begins to search for work. It includes getting one's first job.

mid-career stage
A period marked by continuous improvement in performance, levelling off in performance, or beginning to deteriorate in performance.

late career stage
A period in which one is no longer learning about his or her job, nor is it expected that he or she should be trying to outdo his or her levels of performance from previous years.

decline career stage
The final phase in one's career, usually marked by retirement.

How Can You Apply the Career-Stage Model?

The concept of career stages can be of great benefit to managers. The following are some possible insights. New employees often hold unrealistic expectations about their work. A **realistic job preview (RJP)**—in which job candidates are exposed to negative as well as positive information about the job and organization—can reduce the number of surprise resignations[31] (see Details on a Management Classic). Employees in the establishment stage need training and mentoring to ensure that they have the abilities to perform their jobs well and to provide them with guidance and encouragement.

Managers should keep an eye out for employees who, in mid-career, fail to understand that they are no longer apprentices and that mistakes now carry penalties. Disciplinary action is more likely to be necessary at this stage, when employees first start to show signs of insecurity. Younger employees may be threats. Mid-career failures will occur, but so too will frustration, boredom, and burnout. Managers should be prepared to help employees with their insecurities and consider ways of making jobs more interesting or varied.

Individuals in their late careers make excellent mentors. Managers should exploit this resource. Managers also need to recognize that people in the late career stage frequently undergo significant changes in personal priorities. They may become less interested in work or prefer more free time or a less stressful position instead of more money. Finally, managers should recognize that the decline stage is difficult for every employee to confront. Periods of depression are not uncommon. Employees may also become more hostile and aggressive.

realistic job preview (RJP)
Exposing job candidates to both negative and positive information about a job and an organization.

Labour-Management Relations

Why Are Good Labour-Management Relations Important?

For many managers in unionized organizations, the management of human resources is largely composed of procedures and policies laid out in the labour contract. Decisions about wages, hours, and terms and conditions of employment are no longer unilateral prerogatives of management for jobs within the union's province. Such decisions are substantially made at the time the labour contract is negotiated. However, the development of good **labour-management relations**, the formal interaction between labour unions and an organization's management, can produce a number of positive outcomes for management during these negotiations: for instance, work rules that don't place unreasonable constraints on managerial decision options, employment stability, and reduced threats of costly strikes and work stoppages.[32]

Chrysler Canada is a good example of how management and unions can cooperate to make an organization stronger and better. The recession and the threat of the Japanese car makers have brought the goal of both groups together—to make a better and more competitive car. Workers at Chrysler were given a say both in designing the new plant layout in Bramalea, Ontario, and a voice in the design of the cars. They also have much greater authority than before; a worker can shut down the assembly line if he or she notices a problem. The absenteeism rate at the Bramalea plant is 1.9 per cent, the lowest of any Chrysler assembly plant, the average rate being between 4.5 and 5 per cent.

labour-management relations
The formal interactions between unions and an organization's management.

Details on a Management Classic

JOHN P. WANOUS AND THE REALISTIC JOB PREVIEW

Managers who treat the recruiting and hiring of employees as if the applicants must be sold on the job and exposed only to an organization's positive characteristics set themselves up to have a workforce that is dissatisfied and prone to high turnover. That is the conclusion of John P. Wanous.[33]

Every job applicant acquires, during the hiring process, a set of expectations about the company and about the job for which he or she is interviewing. When the information an applicant receives is excessively inflated, a number of things happen that have potentially negative effects on the company. First, Wanous found that mismatched applicants who would probably become dissatisfied with the job and quit soon would be less likely to withdraw from the search process. Second, he found the absence of accurate information builds unrealistic expectations. Consequently, if hired, the new employees are likely to become quickly dissatisfied—leading to premature resignations. Third, new hires are prone to become disillusioned and less committed to the organization when they face the "harsh" realities of the job. In many cases, Wanous revealed that these individuals feel that they were duped or misled during the hiring process and, therefore, may become problem employees.

To increase job satisfaction among employees and reduce turnover, Wanous advocated providing applicants with a realistic job preview (RJP). An RJP includes both the positive and negative information about the job and the company. For example, in addition to the positive comments typically expressed in the interview, the candidate would be told of the downside of joining the company. For instance, he or she might be told that there are limited opportunities to talk to co-workers during work hours, that promotional advancement is slim, or that work hours fluctuate so erratically that employees may be required to work during typically off hours (nights and weekends). Wanous' research, supported by others, indicates that applicants who have been given a more realistic job preview hold lower and more realistic job expectations for the jobs they'll be performing and are better able to cope with the job and its frustrating elements. The result is fewer unexpected resignations by new employees.

For managers, realistic job previews offer a major insight into the HRM process. That is, retaining good people is as important as hiring them in the first place. Presenting only the positive aspects of a job to a job applicant may initially entice him or her to join the organization, but it may be an affiliation that both parties quickly regret. ▼

What Is the Collective Bargaining Process?

collective bargaining
A process for negotiating a union contract and for administrating the contract after it has been negotiated.

When we talk about the **collective bargaining** process, we are referring to the negotiation, administration, and interpretation of a labour contract. The following discussion summarizes how the process typically flows. See also Exhibit 8-10.

Efforts to organize a group of employees may begin when employee representatives ask union officials to visit the employees' organization and solicit members, or when the union itself initiates a membership drive. Federal legislation requires a union to secure signed authorization cards from 50 per cent of the employees, after which the union is automatically certified. Provincial legislation varies, but generally if 50 to 55 per cent of employees sign authorization cards, a vote on unionization is ordered. Occasionally, employees become dissatisfied with a certified union. In such instances, employees may request a decertification election. If a majority of the members vote for decertification, the union is out.

Once a union has been certified, management will begin preparing for negotiations. It will gather information on the economy, copies of recently negotiated contracts between other unions and employers, cost-of-living data, labour market statistics, and similar environmental concerns. It will also gather internal information on grievance and accident records, employee performance reports, and overtime figures.

This information will tell management the organization's current labour-performance status, what similar organizations are doing, and what it can anticipate from the economy in the near future. Management then uses these data to determine what it can expect to achieve in the negotiation. What can it expect the union to ask for? What is management prepared to acquiesce on?

Negotiation customarily begins when the union delivers a list of demands to management. These are typically ambitious in order to create room for trading in the later

Exhibit 8-10 Stages of the Collective Bargaining Process

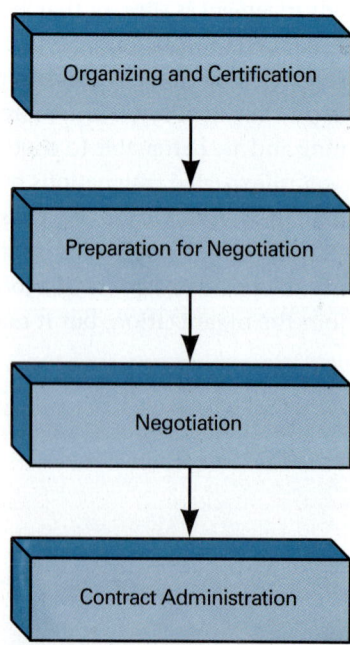

stages of negotiation. Not surprisingly, management's initial response is typically to counter by offering little more than the terms of the previous contract. In recent years, some managements have even begun by proposing a reduction in wages and benefits and demanding that the union take a lesser role in the organization's decision-making process. These introductory proposals usually initiate a period of long and intense bargaining. Compromises are made, and after an oral agreement is achieved, it is converted into a written contract. Finally, negotiation concludes with the union's representatives submitting the contract to its members for ratification.

Once a contract is agreed upon and ratified, it must be administered. The way in which it will be administered is included in the contract itself. Probably the most important element of contract administration has to do with the spelling out of a procedure for handling contractual disputes. Almost all collective bargaining agreements contain formal procedures for resolving grievances over the interpretation and application of the contract.

HRM and Workforce Diversity

We've previously discussed the changing makeup of the workforce in several places in this book. Let's now consider how workforce diversity will affect such basic HRM concerns as recruitment and selection.

Improving workforce diversity requires managers to widen their recruiting net. For example, the popular practice of relying on current employee referrals as a source of new job applicants tends to result in candidates who have similar characteristics to present employees. So managers have to look for applicants in places where they haven't typically looked before. To increase diversity, managers are increasingly turning to nontraditional recruitment sources. This includes women's job networks, over-fifty clubs, urban job banks, disabled people's training centres, ethnic newspapers, and gay-rights organizations.

Once a diverse set of applicants exists, efforts must be made to ensure that the selection process doesn't discriminate. Moreover, applicants need to be made comfortable with the organization's culture and be made aware of management's desire to accommodate their needs.

The insider-outsider transition (orientation) is often more difficult for women and minorities. Many organizations today provide special workshops to raise diversity consciousness among current employees, as well as programs for new employees that focus on diversity issues. The thrust of these efforts is to increase individual understanding of the differences that each of us brings to the workplace.

Syncrude Canada Ltd. is Canada's largest mine—an oil mine. It sits on the Alberta oil sands, which contain more energy than all the crude oil reserves of the Middle East. It has changed Fort McMurray from a small river town into a bustling centre of 30,000 people. Capital investment in the project is about $4.3 billion. Syncrude spends $25 million on R&D annually. In 1995 it produced $1.5 billion worth of crude oil. But all this notwithstanding, it is also a sparkling example of effective human resource management.

Gender equality is an area in which it excels: about 700 of Syncrude's employees are women, of whom 450 are in "non traditional" jobs, a result of the company's "Bridges" program that helps women move away from clerical tasks and other "traditional" jobs.

Diversity of the workforce is something that all employees must understand and accept. At this training seminar, these employees are learning to better appreciate one another.

For instance, one-quarter of the heavy-equipment operators are women. Syncrude is also Canada's largest industrial employer of First Nations people, with about 300 on the payroll. In addition, it operates programs for natives among its suppliers that encourage and support entrepreneurship and job opportunities. Everyone with supervisory responsibilities (about 1,000 people) undergoes training that facilitates teamwork and the ability to manage diversity. The training centres on leadership, communications, and cultural sensitivity. The company spends between five and seven per cent of annual payroll costs on training. Employees work within a team concept that allows them to participate in decisions and even customize their job descriptions.

In 1989, Syncrude began to focus on continuous improvement. Part of that initiative was to develop a vision statement that tried to get people energized, and over the next four or five years the company has increased production by 30 per cent and reduced cost per barrel by two to three dollars. Output per worker has increased by more than 50 per cent, and all the staff reduction that has taken place has been achieved without layoffs. Furthermore, Syncrude has generated an operating profit every year since 1980. It seems that there is a real payoff in managing human resources well![34]

Summary

This Summary is organized by the chapter opening learning objectives found on page 173.

1. The human resource management process seeks to staff the organization and sustain high employee performance through human resource planning, recruitment or decruitment, selection, orientation, training, performance appraisal, career development, and labour-management relations.

2. Since the mid-1960s, the U.S. government has greatly expanded its influence over HRM decisions by enacting new laws and regulations. Because of the government's effort to provide equal employment opportunities, management must ensure that key HRM decisions—such as recruitment, selection, training, promotions, and terminations—are made without regard to race, sex, religion, age, colour, or national origin. Extensive financial penalties can be imposed on organizations that fail to follow these laws and regulations.

3. A job description is a written statement of what a jobholder does, how it's done, and why it's done. A job specification states the minimum acceptable qualifications that an incumbent must possess to perform a given job successfully.

4. Recruitment seeks to develop a pool of potential job candidates. Typical sources include an internal search, advertisements, employee referrals, employment agencies, school placement centres, and temporary help services. Decruitment reduces the labour supply within an organization through options such as firing, layoffs, attrition, transfers, reduced workweeks, early retirements, and job sharing.

5. The quality of a selection device is determined by its validity and reliability. If a device is not valid, then no proven relationship exists between it and relevant job criteria. If a selection device isn't reliable, then it cannot be assumed to be a consistent measure.

6. Selection devices must match the job in question. Work sampling works best with low-level jobs. Assessment centres work best for managerial positions. The validity of the interview as a selection device increases at progressively higher levels of management.

7. Employee training can be on-the-job or off-the-job. Popular on-the-job methods include job rotation, understudying, and apprenticeships. The more popular off-the-job methods are classroom lectures, films, and simulation exercises.

8. The five career stages are exploration, establishment, mid-career, late career, and decline.

9. The collective bargaining process begins with a union organizing effort and attainment of certification. Once a union has been certified, management begins preparation for negotiations by reviewing internal documents and environmental data. Negotiations then proceed, which often involve long and intense bargaining, leading to a written contract. Once a contract is agreed upon and ratified, it must be administered, and a procedure must be spelled out for handling contract disputes.

10. HRM practices can facilitate workforce diversity by widening the recruitment net, eliminating any discriminatory practices in the selection process, making applicants aware of the willingness to accommodate their needs, and providing programs that focus on diversity issues.

Review and Discussion Questions

1. How does HRM affect all managers?
2. What are the possible sources for finding new employees?
3. Contrast reject errors and accept errors. Which one is most likely to open an employer to charges of discrimination? Why?
4. Why is decruitment now a major concern for managers?
5. What are the major problems of the interview as a selection device?
6. What is the relationship between selection, recruitment, and job analysis?
7. Do you think there are moral limits on how far a prospective employer should delve into an applicant's life by means of interviews and tests? Explain your position.

8. Identify three skill categories for which organizations do employee training.
9. What is the goal of orientation?
10. Do you believe that the government should be able to influence the HRM process of organizations through legislation and regulations? Support your position.
11. Assuming that management is already responsive to employee needs, do you think that labour unions benefit employees? Support your position.

Self-Assessment Exercise

How Do You Define Life Success?

People have different ideas about what it means to be successful. Rate each of the following ideas on life success by circling the number that best represents its importance to you.

	ALWAYS IMPORTANT	VERY OFTEN IMPORTANT	FAIRLY OFTEN IMPORTANT	OCCASIONALLY IMPORTANT	NEVER IMPORTANT
1. Getting others to do what I want	5	4	3	2	1
2. Having inner peace and contentment	5	4	3	2	1
3. Having a happy marriage	5	4	3	2	1
4. Having economic security	5	4	3	2	1
5. Being committed to my organization	5	4	3	2	1
6. Being able to give help, assistance, advice, and support to others	5	4	3	2	1
7. Having a job that pays more than peers earn	5	4	3	2	1
8. Being a good parent	5	4	3	2	1
9. Having good job benefits	5	4	3	2	1
10. Having a rewarding family life	5	4	3	2	1
11. Raising children to be independent adults	5	4	3	2	1
12. Having people work for me	5	4	3	2	1
13. Being accepted at work	5	4	3	2	1
14. Enjoying my nonwork activities	5	4	3	2	1
15. Making or doing things that are useful to society	5	4	3	2	1
16. Having high income and the resulting benefits	5	4	3	2	1
17. Having a sense of personal worth	5	4	3	2	1
18. Contributing to society	5	4	3	2	1
19. Having long-term job security	5	4	3	2	1
20. Having children	5	4	3	2	1
21. Getting good performance evaluations	5	4	3	2	1

	ALWAYS IMPORTANT	VERY OFTEN IMPORTANT	FAIRLY OFTEN IMPORTANT	OCCASIONALLY IMPORTANT	NEVER IMPORTANT
22. Having opportunities for personal creativity	5	4	3	2	1
23. Being competent	5	4	3	2	1
24. Having public recognition	5	4	3	2	1
25. Having children who are successful emotionally and professionally	5	4	3	2	1
26. Having influence over others	5	4	3	2	1
27. Being happy with my private life	5	4	3	2	1
28. Earning regular salary increases	5	4	3	2	1
29. Having personal satisfaction	5	4	3	2	1
30. Improving the well-being of the workforce	5	4	3	2	1
31. Having a stable marriage	5	4	3	2	1
32. Having the confidence of my bosses	5	4	3	2	1
33. Having the resources to help others	5	4	3	2	1
34. Being in a high-status occupation	5	4	3	2	1
35. Being able to make a difference in something	5	4	3	2	1
36. Having money to buy or do anything	5	4	3	2	1
37. Being satisfied with my job	5	4	3	2	1
38. Having self-respect	5	4	3	2	1
39. Helping others to achieve	5	4	3	2	1
40. Having personal happiness	5	4	3	2	1
41. Being able to provide quality education for my children	5	4	3	2	1
42. Making a contribution to society	5	4	3	2	1

Turn to page 413 for scoring directions and key.

Source: Barbara Parker and Leonard H. Chusmir, *Development and Validation of the Life Success Measures Scale* (Miami, Fla.: Florida International University, 1991). Used with permission.

Class Exercise

Decruitment

Every manager, at some point in his or her career, will be faced with one of the more difficult tasks of managing—laying off employees. No matter how unpleasant this may be to some, when it is necessary, it must be done. Assume you are the manager in the information-processing department of a large corporation, and you have been notified that you must permanently reduce your staff by two individuals.[35] Below are some data about your employees.

Cara Burns. Inuit female, age 34. Cara has been employed with your company for five years, all in your department. Her evaluations over the past three years have been outstanding, above average, and outstanding. Cara has a master's degree in computer science. She has been on short-term disability the past few weeks due to the birth of her second child and is expected to return to work in twenty weeks.

Bill Volkme. White male, age 30. Bill has been with you for four months and has eleven years of experience in the company in computer operations. He has an associate's degree in data processing and bachelor's and master's degrees in business. Last month Bill got married, and he and his new wife just bought an expensive home. Additionally, Bill's evaluations over the past three years have been average, but he did save the company $550,000 on a suggestion he made regarding computer software vendors.

Louis-Claude Vachon. French Canadian male, age 59. Louis-Claude has been with the company almost forty years. He started as a janitor and worked up to data processor by attending technical school at night. Louis-Claude's evaluations over the past three years in your department have been outstanding. He is committed to getting the job done and devoting whatever it takes. He has three grown children, all college educated. Furthermore, when you took over the job as manager in this department, he made every effort to help you succeed by providing all the historical information you needed.

Leslie Anderson. White female, age 35. Leslie has been with your company fourteen months. Five years ago, Leslie was in an automobile accident that left her wheelchair bound. Rumours have it that she is about to receive several million dollars from the insurance company of the driver that hit her. Her performance last year was above average. She has a bachelor's degree in computer programming.

Robert Oboke. Nigerian-born male, age 41. Bob just completed his master's degree in computer science. Bob has been with your department the past three years. His evaluations have been good to above average. Five years ago, Bob won a lawsuit against your company for discriminating against him in a promotion to a supervisory position. Rumours have it that now with his new degree, Bob is actively pursuing another job outside the company.

Given these five brief descriptions, make a decision on which two employees will be laid off. Then, in your group, seek consensus on which two the group would let go. In both cases, be prepared to defend your action, especially assuming that it may be challenged in court.

Key Terms

Key terms are listed in the order in which they appear in the chapter.

- human resource management (HRM)
- bona fide occupational qualifications (BFOQ)
- affirmative action programs
- strategic human resource planning (SHRP)
- human resource inventory
- job analysis
- job description
- job specification
- recruitment
- decruitment
- selection process
- reliability
- validity
- work sampling
- assessment centres
- orientation
- career
- exploration career stage
- establishment career stage
- mid-career stage
- late career stage
- decline career stage
- realistic job preview (RJP)
- labour-management relations
- collective bargaining

Case Application

Edgar's Supermarkets

Susan Chapman is a regional manager for Edgar's Supermarkets. Five district supervisors report to her. Each of the district supervisors oversees the activities of eight to twelve stores.

One spring morning, as Susan was reviewing her morning reports, her secretary phoned her. "Ms. Chapman, did you see the business section of this morning's paper?" "No, why?" Susan replied. "Well, it says here that Chuck Bailey has accepted the position of regional manager for Loblaws." Leaping to her feet, Susan went to look at the article herself.

Chuck Bailey was one of her senior district supervisors, having been in the job for four years. Edgar's had hired him away from a competitor where he had been a store manager. Susan felt hurt to have learned about Chuck's departure through the newspaper and that he'd not told her of his decision. But she knew she'd get over that. The big question now was where to find a replacement. Chuck was a very effective district supervisor and his group of stores had consistently outperformed the others.

Several days passed. She talked to Chuck and sincerely wished him well in his new job. She also discussed with him the problem of finding a replacement. Her final decision was to transfer one of the other supervisors into Chuck's position and immediately begin the search to fill the vacancy created. She went to the files and pulled out the job description for a district supervisor's position (no job specification was available). The job's duties included ensuring the maintenance of corporate standards of cleanliness, service, and product quality; supervising store managers and evaluating their performance; preparing monthly, quarterly, and annual revenue and expense forecasts for the district; making cost-saving suggestions to head office and/or store managers; coordinating buying; negotiating cooperative advertising programs with suppliers; and participating in union negotiations.

Questions

1. What recruitment sources would you recommend that Susan use? Why?
2. Define the factors that should predict success in this job.
3. Which selection devices would you recommend that Susan use to screen applicants? Why?
4. In terms of career development, what might Susan have done to ensure Chuck's continued employment with Edgar's?

Retraining Canada's Workers

How do you get the right training for a job? Governments across Canada spend $8 billion a year on retraining in an effort to overcome the double-digit unemployment that grips the country. Free trade and global competition have forced large restructurings of organizations, modernization of manufacturing, and computerization and automation that have driven the skill requirements for many jobs significantly higher. Occupations like typesetters have disappeared as print composition is done by computers. Travel agents must master complicated reservation and ticketing systems and be able to work their way through the vast complexities of airline fare structures in order to provide a high level of service to their clients, not just look through books of travel schedules. The overall skill and knowledge levels of jobs in the 1990s are probably triple what they were in the 1970s, which puts severe demands on the training and education system in Canada.

A recent federal governmemt report questioned the effectiveness of the retraining initiative in Canada. CBC *Venture* interprets the report as saying that "people who participate in some retraining programs are no more likely to get a job than those who simply collect unemployment insurance." Even worse, *Venture* notes that the report goes on to say that "some Canadians were significantly less likely to get a job if they had been retrained." How can this be?

An examination of want ads across the country reveals a demand for a number of jobs, but they tend to require higher levels of specific skills — engineers, graphic designers, physiotherapists, accountants, etc. There is no doubt that there are lots of jobs available, with few people to work in them. The question, of course, is "What are the jobs?" The government retraining programs tend to focus on two main areas: construction and the service industries. But if, at the end of a retraining program, an individual's chances of finding a job are no better, there's a problem. Lloyd Axworthy feels that there hasn't been enough creative thought and research into what retraining really is. He argues, "We really have to, I think, get away from traditional notions of education and training and start doing some really serious experimentation." But how, and what?

Questions

1. Chapter Eight looks at the issue of human resource planning. If companies can have a system of human resource planning (and presumably government departments plan the same way), why can't governments use the techniques for retraining programs? If you were placed in charge of retraining for Canada, what steps would you take to make the system more effective?
2. As you review the contents of Chapter Eight, are there ideas that come to mind about how we might be able to match organizations' demand for people and the supply of people with suitable skills and knowledge?
3. Does the career stage model explain some of the difficulties that retraining programs are experiencing in Canada? How might it help?

Video Resource: "Retraining Bust," *Venture* 474 (February 6, 1994).

Managing Change and Innovation

Learning Objectives

WHAT WILL I BE ABLE TO DO AFTER I FINISH THIS CHAPTER?

1. Describe what managers can change in organizations.
2. Identify the external and internal forces for change.
3. Explain how managers can serve as change agents.
4. Contrast the "calm waters" and "white water rapids" metaphors of change.
5. Explain why people are likely to resist change.
6. Explain how TQM is a change effort.
7. Differentiate between creativity and innovation.
8. Explain how organizations can stimulate innovation.

Algoma Steel has undergone immense change and in 1994 was the most profitable steel company in North America.

Change requires a movement away from the familiar, if not necessarily the comfortable. Sometimes it takes quite a lot of discomfort to get people to change. In January 1991, Dofasco decided it could no longer sustain the losses at Algoma Steel, its subsidiary, and announced it was writing off its $800-million debt at Algoma. Dofasco offered to keep part of the Algoma plant at Sault Ste. Marie open if the steelworkers agreed to major wage concessions. The union rejected the proposal. But it countered with another proposal: the workers would take a $10-million wage cutback in return for 60 per cent ownership in Algoma and a restructuring of the company's debt. The Ontario government backed the plan and the union ended up with a 15 per cent wage cut ($2.89 an hour), and layoffs of 1,600 workers.

Restructuring the debt and taking labour costs out of the company are one thing, but a lot more had to be changed to make Algoma successful. The Steelworkers Union decided that while it would have four directors on the thirteen member board, it did not want to actually manage Algoma. Steve Boniferro, a union leader commented, "Somebody has to be looking after the business, and, quite frankly, we aren't trained, prepared, or interested in looking after the business. We want to balance what's best for the company with what's best for the workers." Management philosophy has changed at Algoma to recognize that its success is based on the balance of a "strong independent union and a strong, independent management."

Among the changes that have taken place in Algoma since 1991: virtually all of the old senior management have left; a new CEO, Al Hopkins, former vice-president of Stelco and a steel man for thirty-five years, has taken the company reins; self-directed work groups that are empowered to deal with everything from vacation schedules to redesigning their workplace have replaced the old command and control structure (so, for instance, at No.1 Ladle Transfer Station, where there were once three foremen there are now none, and where there were twenty workers per shift there are now seven); costs have been reduced by $27 per ton; productivity has increased; the workforce has actu-

Managing Change and Innovation

ally grown by about 700; and the company, which was being written off as bankrupt in 1991, made a profit of $127.3 million in 1994. That's a lot of change! And change is what this chapter is about.[1]

What Is Change?

change
An alteration in structure, technology, or people.

If it weren't for **change,** the manager's job would be relatively easy. Planning would be without problems because tomorrow would be no different from today. The issue of organization design would be solved. Since the environment would be free from uncertainty, there would be no need to adapt. All organizations would be tightly structured. Similarly, decision making would be dramatically simplified because the outcome of each alternative could be predicted with almost certain accuracy. It would, indeed, simplify the manager's job if, for example, competitors didn't introduce new products or services, if customers didn't make new demands, if government regulations were never modified, or if employees' needs didn't change.

However, change is an organizational reality. Handling change is an integral part of every manager's job. But what can a manager change? The manager's options essentially fall into one of three categories: altering structure, technology, or people (see Exhibit 9-1). Changing structure includes any alteration in authority relations, coordination mechanisms, degree of centralization, job redesign, or similar structural variables. Changing technology encompasses modifications in the way work is processed or methods and equipment are used. Changing people refers to changes in employee attitudes, expectations, perceptions, or behaviour. In this chapter, we'll look at the key managerial issues related to managing change.

Forces for Change

In Chapter 2, we pointed out that there are both external and internal forces that constrain managers. These same forces also bring about the need for change. Let's briefly look at the factors that can create the need for change.

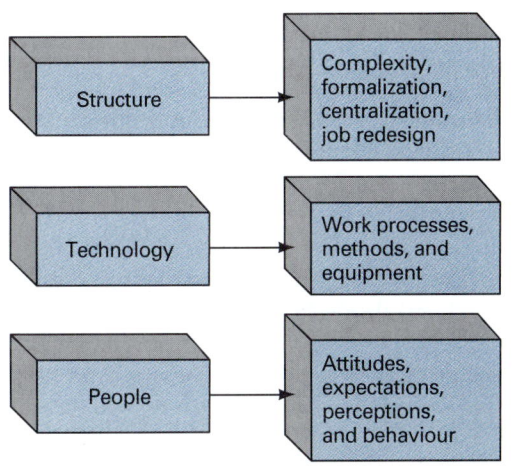

Exhibit 9-1 Three Categories of Change

Fishery Products International, by changing its business focus to processing fish, is adapting to the competition.

What Are the External Forces Creating a Need for Change?

The external forces that create the need for change come from various sources. In recent years, the marketplace has affected firms like BMW and Domino's by introducing new competition. BMW now has upscale Japanese cars produced by Lexus and Infiniti to compete against, and Domino's must now contend with Pizza Hut, which recently moved into the home-delivery market. Government laws and regulations are a frequent impetus for change. The northern cod have been severely depleted on the Grand Banks and Newfoundland's economy has been severely damaged, causing heavy unemployment. Fishery Products International, the giant Newfoundland-based fish processor has been forced to change its business focus to processing of fish, which it acquires from around the world. Chains like The Bay and Sears must adapt to competition from market entrants like Price-Costco and Wal-Mart. The old telephone companies must adapt to competition from Unitel and others.

NAFTA, the North American Free Trade Agreement, has opened up a number of markets for Canadian companies—but also opened up Canadian markets to competitors from the United States and Mexico. Pollution laws have changed the way companies in industries like pulp and paper and mining run their operations. Changes in allowable emissions have forced the automobile industry to redesign their vehicles.

Technology also creates the need for change. Recent developments in sophisticated and extremely expensive diagnostic equipment have created significant economies of scale for hospitals and medical centres. The assembly line in many industries is undergoing dramatic changes as employers replace human labour with technologically advanced mechanical robots. The fluctuation in labour markets also forces managers to initiate change. For instance, the shortage of medical practitioners forced hospitals to redesign jobs and alter their reward and benefit packages.

Economic changes, of course, affect almost all organizations. The recession of 1991 caused a drop in world demand for commercial real estate and, combined with the pressure of high interest rates, brought about the fall of some of the major projects of the Reichmanns, like Canary Wharf in London, England. The effects have been much greater in Japan, which operates on a "land standard." This means that much of its economy is tied to the value of the land it sits on. Land prices soared in the 1980s. In cities like Osaka, they rose by as much as 10 per cent a month. Development was based on these values, and banks lent against them. Now the banks are closing some of their subsidiaries and a number of the major Japanese banks are technically insolvent without government support. The exchange rate of the Canadian dollar also has a major effect on business. The higher the dollar, the more difficult it is for Canadian exporters to sell to the United States, our major trading partner.

What Are the Internal Forces Creating a Need for Change?

In addition to the external forces noted above, internal forces can also stimulate the need for change. These internal forces tend to originate primarily from the internal operations of the organization or from the impact of external changes.

When management redefines or modifies its strategy, it often introduces a host of changes. As noted at the beginning of this chapter, Algoma Steel's need to be competitive has required a major reorganization in how the business operates. The introduction of new equipment represents another internal force for change. Employees may have their jobs redesigned, need to undergo training to operate the new equipment, or be required to establish new interaction patterns within their formal group. An organization's workforce is rarely static. Its composition changes in terms of age, education, sex, nationality, and so forth. In a stable organization where managers have been in their positions for years, there might be a need to restructure jobs in order to retain the more ambitious employees, affording them some upward mobility. The compensation and benefits systems might also need to be reworked to reflect the needs of a diverse workforce. Employee attitudes, such as increased job dissatisfaction, may lead to increased absenteeism, more voluntary resignations, and even strikes. Such events will, in turn, often lead to changes in management policies and practices.

Rockwell International of Canada signed a new agreement with their workers three and a half months before the old agreement ran out in 1993. The reasons for this are several, but principally, being a just-in-time supplier of parts to Chrysler has put added pressure on the need to avoid a strike. It's normal for manufacturers working on a just-in-time system to finish making a batch of parts only sixty to ninety minutes before they are needed at the customer's plant. Inventory levels are kept at a minimum so that when problems arise there are tremendous pressures on everybody to find a solution—a big change from the days when strikes and walkouts were common. As Guido Tonin, chairman of the Canadian Auto Workers plant committee at Rockwell's plant in Milton, Ontario says, "We're the only supplier for Chrysler and we don't want to lose that customer. If we lose Chrysler, we've lost our jobs."[2]

How Can a Manager Serve as a Change Agent?

Changes within an organization need a catalyst. People who act as catalysts and assume the responsibility for managing the change process are called **change agents.**

change agents
People who act as catalysts and manage the change process.

Any manager can be a change agent. As we review the topic of change, we assume that it is initiated and carried out by a manager within the organization. However, the change agent can be a nonmanager—for example, an internal staff specialist or outside consultant whose expertise is in change implementation. For major systemwide changes, internal management will often hire outside consultants to provide advice and assistance. Because they are from the outside, they often can offer an objective perspective usually lacking in insiders. However, outside consultants may be at a disadvantage because they have an inadequate understanding of the organization's history, culture, operating procedures, and personnel. Outside consultants are also prone to initiate more drastic changes than insiders—which can be either a benefit or a disadvantage—because they do not have to live with the repercussions after the change is implemented. In contrast, internal managers who act as change agents may be more thoughtful (and possibly more cautious) because they must live with the consequences of their actions.

Two Different Views on the Change Process

We often use two very different metaphors to clarify the change process.[3] One envisions the organization as a large ship crossing a calm sea. The ship's captain and crew know exactly where they're going because they've made the trip many times before. Change surfaces as the occasional storm, a brief distraction in an otherwise calm and predictable trip. In the other metaphor, the organization is seen as a small raft navigating a raging river with uninterrupted white water rapids. Aboard the raft are half-a-dozen people who've never worked together before, who are totally unfamiliar with the river, who are unsure of their eventual destination, and, as if things weren't bad enough, who are travelling in the pitch-dark of night. In the white water rapids metaphor, change is a natural state, and managing change is a continual process.

These two metaphors present very different approaches to understanding and responding to change. Let's take a closer look at each one.

What Is the "Calm Waters" Metaphor?

Until very recently, the "calm waters" metaphor dominated the thinking of practising managers and academics. It is best illustrated in Kurt Lewin's three-step description of the change process[4] (see Exhibit 9-2).

According to Lewin, successful change requires unfreezing the status quo, changing to a new state, and refreezing the new change to make it permanent. The status quo can be considered an equilibrium state. To move from this equilibrium, unfreezing is necessary. It can be achieved in one of three ways:

▶ 1. The driving forces, which direct behaviour away from the status quo, can be increased.
▶ 2. The restraining forces, which hinder movement from the existing equilibrium, can be decreased.
▶ 3. The two approaches can be combined.

Once unfreezing has been accomplished, the change itself can be implemented. However, the mere introduction of change does not ensure that it will take hold. The new situation, therefore, needs to be refrozen so that it can be sustained over time. Unless this last step is attended to, there is a strong chance that the change will be short-

Exhibit 9-2 The Change Process

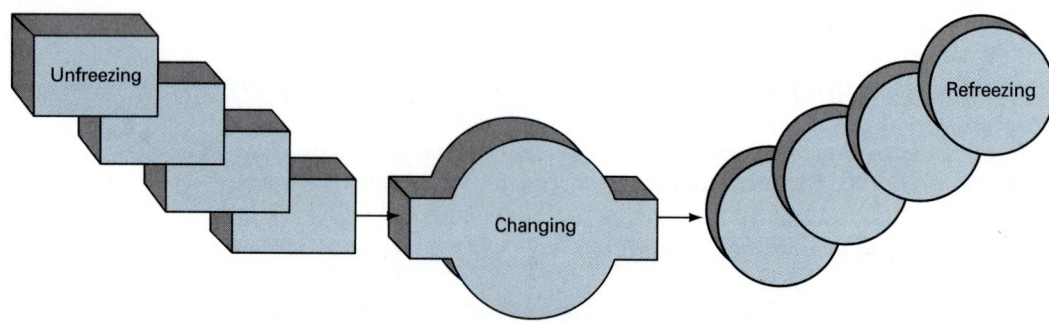

Managing Change and Innovation

lived and employees will revert to the previous equilibrium state. The objective of refreezing, then, is to stabilize the new situation by balancing the driving and restraining forces.

Note how Lewin's three-step process treats change as a break in the organization's equilibrium state. The status quo has been disturbed, and change is necessary to establish a new equilibrium state. This view might have been appropriate to the relatively calm environment that most organizations faced in the 1950s, 1960s, and early 1970s. But the "calm waters" metaphor is increasingly obsolete as a way to describe the kind of seas that current managers have to navigate.

What Is the "White Water Rapids" Metaphor?

The "white water rapids" metaphor takes into consideration that environments are both uncertain and dynamic. To get a feeling for what managing change might be like when you have to continually maneuver in uninterrupted rapids, consider attending a college that had the following curriculum: Courses vary in length. Unfortunately, when you sign up, you don't know how long a course will last. It might go for two weeks or thirty weeks. Furthermore, the instructor can end a course any time he or she wants, with no prior warning. If that isn't bad enough, the length of the class changes each time it meets—sometimes it lasts twenty minutes, while other times it runs for three hours—and determination of the time of the next class meeting is set by the instructor during the previous class. Oh yes, there's one more thing. The exams are all unannounced, so you have to be ready for a test at any time. To succeed in this college, you would have to be incredibly flexible and be able to respond quickly to every changing condition. Students who were too structured or slow on their feet wouldn't survive.

A growing number of managers are coming to accept that their job is much like what a student would face in such a college. The stability and predictability of the "calm water" metaphor don't exist. Disruptions in the status quo are not occasional and temporary, followed by a return to calm waters. Many of today's managers never get out of the rapids. They face constant change, bordering on chaos. These managers are being forced to play a game they've never played before which is governed by rules that are created as the game progresses.[5]

Most change is uncertain and dynamic. Just like the continuous maneuvering through these rapids, a manager must be prepared to deal with the unexpected.

Is the "white water rapids" metaphor merely an overstatement? No! On a large scale, the airline industry has gone through rapid, whitewater changes. A number of very big carriers have gone bankrupt—Pan Am, Eastern, People's. Almost every major player has merged or formed associations with other airlines—Canadian with American Air Lines, and Air Canada with Continental, British Airways with Quantas. Commuter airlines have sprung out of nowhere; hub-and-spoke, where airlines fly their routes

Details on a Management Classic

COCH AND FRENCH: RESISTANCE TO CHANGE

One of the most famous studies on organizational change took place in the late 1940s at a plant of the Harwood Manufacturing Company where pajamas were made.[6] The plant employed about 500 people and had a long history of disruptions every time changes were made in the way work progressed. Although the changes were typically minor—for example, pajama folders who formerly folded tops with prefolded bottoms would be required to fold the bottoms as well—the employees resisted. They would complain bitterly and would openly refuse to make the changes. Production decreased; and grievances, absenteeism, and job turnover increased.

The usual way that Harwood's management made these changes was autocratically. Management made the decision, then would call a group meeting where they would announce the changes to employees. The changes would be implemented immediately. Then, as mentioned, the employees rebelled. So Harwood's executives brought in a consultant as a change agent to help with their problem. As an experiment, the consultant arranged for the next change to be conducted in three groups, using three different methods. In the first group, the change was initiated in the usual manner—autocratically. This was the control group. The second group involved employee participation through selective representatives. These representatives, with management, worked out the details of the change, then tried the new methods and trained others in the new procedures. In the third group, there was full participation. All employees shared in the designing of the new methods with management.

The change agent gathered data over a forty-day period and what he found strongly supported the value of participation. In the control group, resistance occurred as before. Seventeen per cent of the employees quit their jobs during the forty-day period; and grievances and absenteeism increased. However, in the representative and full participation groups, there were no resignations, only one grievance, and no absenteeism. Moreover, participation was positively related to productivity. In the control group, output actually dropped from an average of sixty units per hour to forty-eight during the experimental period. The participation group generated sixty-eight units per hour, and the total participation group averaged seventy-three units per hour.

The conclusion of the Coch and French study back in the late 1940s holds a major key for today's organizational change. That is, for permanent change to occur without extensive resistance, employees must be involved. Without employee involvement in those things that directly affect their work, companies run the risk of negating any possible gain a change can bring about or, worse, make the situation more serious than it originally was. ▼

Managing Change and Innovation

in and out of "hub" airports has changed routings; there have been widespread price wars; and virtually every airline has a frequent flyer program.

Do you remember when you ordered something, having to wait days or weeks for delivery? Not any more. The big wholesale distributors for things like computers and software fight over what they call "differentials"—how quickly and well they service their retail customers.[7] Ingram, a Toronto-based distributor offers same-day delivery for orders placed before 11.30 a.m. Merisel, another distributor, instantly flashes order data on a salesperson's computer screen when the customer calls—for a twenty-second per-call saving! A similar change has happened to home-delivery pizza. Now, in a number of markets, delivery is guaranteed within 15 minutes—because the pizza is made on the delivery van.

Publishing books was once thought of as an industry that experienced little change. Now, faced with high-tech publishing systems, mega-mergers and takeovers among publishing companies, even this industry is facing the world of white water rapids.

Does Every Manager Face a World of Constant and Chaotic Change?

Every manager doesn't face a world of constant and chaotic change. However, the set of managers who don't is dwindling rapidly.

Managers in such businesses as high-fashion apparel and computer software have long confronted a world of white water rapids. These managers used to look with envy at their counterparts in industries such as auto manufacturing, oil exploration, banking, publishing, telecommunications, and air transportation, who historically faced a stable and predictable environment. That might have been true in the 1960s, but it's not true in the 1990s!

Few organizations today can treat change as the occasional disturbance in an otherwise peaceful world. Even these few do so at great risk. Too much is changing too fast for any organization or its managers to be complacent.[8] Most competitive advantages last less than eighteen months. A firm like People Express—a no-frills, no-reservations airline—was described in business periodicals as the model "new look" firm, then went bankrupt a short time later. As management writer Tom Peters has aptly noted, the old saying "If it ain't broke, don't fix it" no longer applies. In its place, he suggests "If it ain't broke, you just haven't looked hard enough. Fix it anyway."[9] Of course, what Peters is saying is consistent with current reengineering trends. Recall from our discussion of reengineering in Chapter 2, management needs to rethink all of the activities and processes in its organization. The quantum change that is required to remain competitive in today's global marketplace cannot be overstated.

Organizational Change

As change agents, managers should be motivated to initiate change because they're concerned with improving their organization's effectiveness. However, change can be a threat to managers. It can also be a threat to nonmanagerial personnel. Organizations, and people within them, can build up inertia that propels them to resist any change, even if that change might be beneficial (see Details on a Management Classic). In this section, we want to review why people in organizations resist change and what can be done to lessen this resistance.

Why Do People Resist Change?

It has been said that most people hate any change that doesn't jingle in their pockets. This awareness of resistance to change is well documented.[10] But why do people resist change? An individual is likely to resist change for three reasons: uncertainty, concern over personal loss, and the belief that the change is not in the organization's best interest[11] (see Exhibit 9-3).

Changes substitute ambiguity and uncertainty for the known. Regardless of how much you may dislike some of the work associated with attending college, at least you know the ropes. You understand what is expected of you. When you leave college and venture out into the world of full-time employment, regardless of how anxious you are to get out of college, you will have to trade the known for the unknown. Employees in organizations hold the same dislike for uncertainty. For example, the introduction in manufacturing plants of quality control methods based on sophisticated statistical models means that many quality control inspectors will have to learn these new methods. Some inspectors may fear that they will be unable to do so. They may, therefore, develop a negative attitude toward statistical control techniques or behave dysfunctionally if required to use them.

The second cause of resistance is the fear of losing something already possessed. Change threatens the investment one has already made in the status quo. The more people have invested in the current system, the more they resist change. Why? They fear the loss of status, money, authority, friendships, personal convenience, or other benefits that they value. This explains why senior employees resist change more than do relatively new employees to an organization. Senior employees have generally invested more in the current system and, therefore, have more to lose by adapting to a change.

Individuals who spent twenty years as mail sorters for the post office were likely to resist automatic letter sorters more actively than recent hires. The latter had less personal investment in the old system and were less threatened by automation.

Exhibit 9-3 Reasons for Resistance to Change

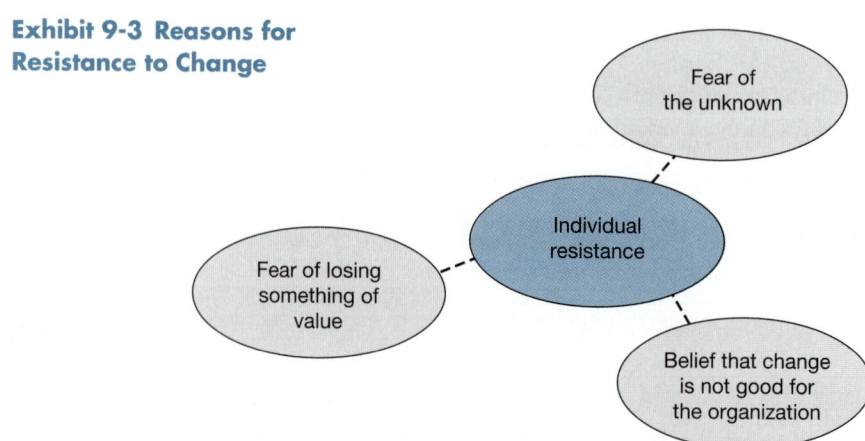

Developing Management Skills

▼ OVERCOMING RESISTANCE TO CHANGE ▲

▶ 1. **Allow the employee to openly talk about his or her fears.** Understanding what concerns employees is the first step in allaying those fears. Giving employees a chance to express their feelings creates a climate in which the manager is seen as truly being interested.

▶ 2. **Learn the true reason(s) why the employee is resistant to change.** Employees may typically perceive the change as threatening something of value to them. Knowing exactly what employees feel they'll "lose" helps you to begin the change process.

▶ 3. **Explain how the change can benefit the employee.** Some change may be difficult for employees to accept. Whenever possible, changes that may generate some benefit for employees should be communicated so that they understand the impact of the change effort.

▶ 4. **Allow the employee to participate in decisions regarding the change.** Change that is pushed down on employees, without their participation, is less likely to succeed. Employee participation also helps to reduce fears and increases the likelihood employees will see the benefit of the change.

▶ 5. **Use group members who accept the change to positively influence resisters.** Change from "within" can be viewed more positively than change from above. Those group members who support the change effort can serve as a catalyst for the change effort and influence their peers to reduce their resistance.

A final cause of resistance is a person's belief that the change is incompatible with the goals and best interests of the organization. If an employee believes that a new job procedure proposed by a change agent will reduce productivity or product quality, that employee can be expected to resist the change. If the employee expresses his or her resistance positively (clearly expressing it to the change agent, along with substantiation), this form of resistance can be beneficial to the organization.

What Are Some Techniques for Reducing Resistance to Organizational Change?

When management sees resistance to change as dysfunctional, what actions can it take? Several tactics have been suggested for use by managers or other change agents in dealing with resistance to change[12] (see Developing Management Skills).

Change and TQM

Total Quality Management is essentially a continuous, incremental change program. It is compatible with the white water metaphor of change that we discussed earlier. In this section, we want to draw on our knowledge of change processes to consider how managers can effectively implement TQM.

First, let's briefly review the key components of TQM. You'll remember that it focuses on customer needs, emphasizes participation and teamwork, and seeks to create a culture in which all employees strive to improve continuously not only the quality of the organization's products or services, but also such factors as work processes and customer response time. It might be helpful if we look at TQM in terms of the three areas toward which management can direct its change efforts: structure, technology, and people (see Exhibit 9-4).

TECHNOLOGY	STRUCTURE	PEOPLE	CHANGE AGENT
Flexible process Education and training of workers	Decentralization Reduced vertical differentiation Reduced division of labour Wider spans of control Cross-functional teams	Education and training Supportive performance evaluation and reward system	Active leadership from the top

Exhibit 9-4 Factors That Facilitate Continuous Incremental Improvement

As first discussed in Chapter 7, the structure of an organization that expects to implement TQM effectively will be decentralized; will have reduced vertical differentiation, wider spans of control, and reduced division of labour; and will support cross-functional teams. These structural components give employees the authority and means to implement process improvements. For instance, the creation of work teams that cut across departmental lines allows those people who understand a problem best to solve that problem. Additionally, cross-functional teams encourage cooperative problem solving rather than "us versus them" blame placing.

The primary focus on technological change in TQM is directed at developing flexible processes to support continuous improvement. Employees committed to TQM are constantly looking for things to fix. Thus, work processes must be adaptable to continual change and fine-tuning. To achieve this, TQM requires an extensive commitment to educating and training workers. The organization must provide employees with skills training in problem solving, decision making, negotiation, statistical analysis, and team building.[13] For example, employees need to be able to analyse and act on data. An organization with a TQM program should provide work teams with quality data such as failure rates, reject rates, and scrap rates. It should provide feedback data on customer satisfaction. It should give the teams the necessary information to create and monitor process control charts. And, of course, the structure should allow the work teams to make continual improvements in the operations based on process control data.

The people dimension of TQM requires a workforce committed to the organization's objectives of quality and continual improvement. Again, this necessitates proper education and training. It also demands a performance evaluation and reward system that supports and encourages TQM objectives. For example, successful programs put quality objectives into bonus plans for executives and incentives for operating employees.[14]

The discussion above is critical for change to be promoted and implemented. But remember, too, that needed change may require more than incremental movements. In these cases, radical or massive changes are in order. When that occurs—a process we described in Chapter 2 when we discussed reengineering—the same principles may hold but on a much larger scale. That is, to be competitive, organizations may need to reengineer or initiate quantum change. Then to remain competitive, managers must seek continuous improvements. For example, consider our wave analogy. Reengineering can be likened to a big, sweeping tidal wave. As it hits, everything in its path is scattered. But the energies behind tidal waves cannot continue forever. Instead, what it began to set adrift is now propelled to its new destination by a number of smaller waves (continuous improvement).

Stimulating Innovation

"Innovate or die!" That has increasingly become the rallying cry of today's contemporary managers. In the dynamic world of global competition, organizations must create new products and services and adopt state-of-the-art technology if they are to compete successfully. The standard of innovation to which many organizations strive is that achieved by the 3M Company.[15] 3M has developed a reputation for being able to stimulate innovation over a long period of time. One of its stated objectives is that 25 per cent of each division's profits are to come from products less than five years old. Toward that end, 3M typically launches more than 200 new products each year. During a recent five-year period, 3M generated better than 30 per cent of its $13 billion in revenues from products introduced during the previous five years.

What's the secret to 3M's success? What, if anything, can other managers do to make their organizations more innovative? In the following pages, we'll try to answer these questions as we discuss the factors behind innovation.

How Do Creativity and Innovation Differ?

In general usage, **creativity** means the ability to combine ideas in a unique way or to make unusual associations between ideas.[16] An organization that stimulates creativity is one that develops novel approaches to things or unique solutions to problems (see Managers Who Made a Difference). **Innovation** is the process of taking a creative idea and turning it into a useful product, service, or method of operation. Thus, the innovative organization is characterized by the ability to channel its creative juices into useful outcomes. When managers talk about changing an organization to make it more creative, they usually mean that they want to stimulate innovation. The 3M Company is aptly described as innovative because it has taken novel ideas and turned them into profitable products such as cellophane tape, Scotchgard protective coatings, Post-it note pads, and diapers with elastic waistbands. So, too, is the highly successful microchip

creativity
The ability to combine ideas in a unique way or to make unusual associations between ideas.

innovation
The process of taking a creative idea and turning it into a useful product, service, or method of operation.

The pentium chip is just one product in a long line of innovative products at Intel. The company has long supported a culture that stimulates innovation.

Chapter 9

Managers Who Made a Difference

COLIN PATEY AT THE WATERFORD HOSPITAL

Hospitals haven't traditionally been held up as examples of change. In fact, until the 1990s change was a word to be avoided in the health care system in Canada. But two factors have changed that: first, severe pressure on funding, and second, consumer demand for better service. Big hospitals are big business; they have budgets in the hundreds of millions of dollars and are managed professionally. But being staffed largely by professionals—doctors, nurses, pharmacists and other specialists—they tend to have reasonably well-defined "territories" that are well guarded. Cooperation is often something that is difficult to attain. Things have changed, however, and the health care system in Newfoundland has led the change in many areas.

A outstanding leader of change in the health care system is Colin Patey, executive director of the Waterford Hospital in St. John's, Newfoundland. Whether or not Patey watched "Star Trek" when he was a boy, he can perhaps best be described as something of a Captain Kirk—daring to boldly go where no one has gone before. In 1990, when he joined the Waterford Hospital as executive director, it was an institution in gridlock. As Peter Dawe, the director of the hospital's foundation, describes it, "This was the epitome of a bureaucratic institution; nothing happened, nothing changed. There were a lot of problems identified—I mean, everybody knew the problems, but nobody did anything about them." Because he came to the Waterford with a reputation for change, as he took on his new post Patey

was greeted with a strike. And, for good measure, after he had successfully dealt with that and begun to gain the trust of the staff, he was told by the government to take $2 million out of his budget.

Large budget cuts most often translate into staff cuts. But Patey knew that if he was ever to get the staff motivated, committed to change, and proud of themselves and their hospital, he would have to avoid the "easy" route of simply cutting jobs. He had to involve staff at all levels in the process of how to operate the hospital more efficiently and effectively. So, rather than go to his executive team for suggestions as to how they would effect the cuts, he went to the entire hospital! Working on the belief that it is the people working on a job who know most about it, he put the problem to them: how to operate with $2 million less, provide the same level of patient care, and not lose any jobs. Within a short period, all the solutions were provided and the budget cut was absorbed without loss of jobs.

It is virtually impossible to gain commitment to change in a climate of low trust. But once Patey had earned the trust of the staff, he set about creating a vision for the hospital to which everyone could subscribe and that would instil pride in individuals and their institution. Change implies risks, and it also requires a high degree of

216

Managing Change and Innovation

openness. As part of his change plan, Patey did things like inviting the CBC into the hospital to produce a documentary; involving all the stakeholders in the hospital—doctors, nurses, staff, patients, the board, and the community—to express their views on its mission; changing the focus of his executive team from "the problems are too large to handle" to "one problem at a time, and one step at a time." And an element of successful change which is often overlooked, communication—of the changes, of the problems, and most importantly of the successes—was tackled head-on by a communications professional.

In 1995, the Waterford hospital came under one board which amalgamated all the hospitals in St. John's. But it wasn't the same hospital that Colin Patey had joined in 1990. Hundreds of patients had been reintroduced into the community with careful and comprehensive support; the new openness of the hospital was clearly symbolized by physical changes to the facilities; locked wards had been unlocked; outpatient services had flourished; the hospital had benchmarked what it considered to be the best providers of psychiatric care in Canada and focused on bringing the Waterford's services to those levels; ownership of the change had been embedded at all levels; and there was real pride of ownership by the staff. Managers of successful change make a very big difference, and Colin Patey is one of them. ▼

manufacturer Intel. It leads all chip manufacturers in miniaturization, and the success of its 386 and 486 chips gives the company a 75 per cent share of the microprocessor market for IBM-compatible PC machines. With $5 billion a year in sales, Intel's commitment to staying ahead of the competition by introducing a stream of new and more powerful products is supported by annual expenditures of $1.2 billion for its plant and equipment and $800 million for research and development.

How Can a Manager Foster Innovation?

There are three sets of variables that have been found to stimulate innovation. They pertain to the organization's structure, culture, and human resource practices (see Figure 9-4, p. 214).

How Do Structural Variables Affect Innovation? Based on extensive research, we can make three statements regarding the effect of structural variables on innovation.[17] First, organic structures positively influence innovation. Because they're lower in vertical differentiation, formalization, and centralization, organic structures facilitate the flexibility, adaptation, and cross-fertilization that make the adoption of innovations easier. Second, the easy availability of plentiful resources provides a key building block for innovation. An abundance of resources allows management to afford to purchase innovations, bear the cost of instituting innovations, and absorb failures. Finally, frequent interunit communication helps to break down possible barriers to innovation.[18] Committees, task forces, and other such mechanisms facilitate interaction across departmental lines and are widely used in successfully innovative organizations. 3M, for instance, is highly decentralized and takes on many of the characteristics of small, organic organizations. The company also has the "deep pockets" needed to support its policy of allowing scientists and engineers to use up to 15 per cent of their time on projects of their own choosing.

How Does an Organization's Culture Affect Innovation? Innovative organizations tend to have similar cultures.[19] They encourage experimentation. They reward both successes and failures. They celebrate mistakes. An innovative culture is likely to have the following seven characteristics:

▶ 1. **Acceptance of ambiguity.** Too much emphasis on objectivity and specificity constrains creativity.
▶ 2. **Tolerance of the impractical.** Individuals who offer impractical, even foolish, answers to "what if" questions are not stifled. What seems impractical at first might lead to innovative solutions.
▶ 3. **Low external controls.** Rules, regulations, policies, and similar controls are kept to a minimum.
▶ 4. **Tolerance of risk.** Employees are encouraged to experiment without fear of consequences should they fail. Mistakes are treated as learning opportunities.
▶ 5. **Tolerance of conflict.** Diversity of opinions is encouraged. Harmony and agreement between individuals and/or units are not assumed to be evidence of high performance.
▶ 6. **Focus on ends rather than means.** Goals are made clear, and individuals are encouraged to consider alternative routes toward their attainment. Focusing on ends suggests that there might be several right answers to any given problem.
▶ 7. **Open systems focus.** The organization closely monitors the environment and responds rapidly to changes as they occur.

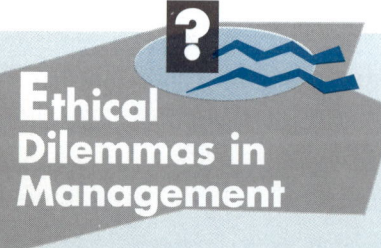

Ethical Dilemmas in Management

▼ WHAT WOULD YOU DO IF YOU HAD DETAILS ON A COMPETITOR'S TRADE SECRET? ▲

A disgruntled employee who works for one of your key competitors mails you samples of a top-secret new product that your competitor is working on. He even offers, for a small fee, to help you unravel its ground-breaking technology. You realize that this new technology will make your competition's new products unbeatable. Should you send the samples back to the employee and turn him in to his employer? Or should you turn the samples over to your research and development team for analysis and encourage them to break the code? Sound far-fetched? Not really. This dilemma was actually faced by managers at Johnson & Johnson.[20]

Philip A. Stegora, a disgruntled employee at 3M Company, got hold of some samples of a new casting tape that 3M developed for doctors to use to set broken bones. He mailed the tape to Johnson & Johnson and offered to help them unravel 3M's technology for a fee of only $20,000. As the manager at J&J who received the package, you'd love to understand the technology that 3M has developed. The new products that might evolve from this technology could be unbeatable in the $200-million market for casting tapes. What would you do?

What Human Resource Variables Affect Innovation? Within the human resources category, we find that innovative organizations actively promote the training and development of their members so that their knowledge remains current, offer their employees high job security to reduce the fear of getting fired for making mistakes, and encourage individuals to become champions of change. Once a new idea is developed, champions of change actively and enthusiastically promote the idea, build support, overcome resistance, and ensure that the innovation is implemented. Recent research finds that champions have common personality characteristics: extremely high self-confidence, persistence, energy, and a tendency to take risks. Champions also display characteristics associated with dynamic leadership. They inspire and energize others with their vision of the potential of an innovation and through their strong personal conviction in their mission. They are also good at gaining the commitment of others to support their mission. Additionally, champions have jobs that provide considerable decision-making discretion (see Ethical Dilemmas in Management). This autonomy helps them introduce and implement innovations in organizations.[21]

Summary

This Summary is organized by the chapter opening learning objectives found on page 203.

1. Managers can change the organization's structure by altering complexity, formalization, or centralization variables or by redesigning jobs; changing the organization's technology by altering work processes, methods, and equipment; or changing people by altering attitudes, expectations, perceptions, or behaviour.

2. External forces for change include the marketplace, government laws and regulations, technology, labour markets, and economic changes. Internal forces of change include organizational strategy, equipment, the workforce, and employee attitudes.

3. Managers can serve as change agents by becoming the catalyst for change in their units and by managing the change process.

4. The "calm waters" metaphor views change as a break in the organization's equilibrium state. Organizations are seen as stable and predictable, disturbed by an occasional crisis. The "white water rapids" metaphor views change as continual and unpredictable. Managers must deal with ongoing and almost chaotic change.

5. Change is often resisted because of the uncertainty it creates, concern for personal loss, and a belief that it might not be in the organization's best interest.

6. TQM is essentially a change effort, as it focuses on continuous, incremental change on some aspect of the organization's operations.

7. Creativity is the ability to combine ideas in a unique way or to make unusual associations between ideas. Innovation is the process of taking creative ideas and turning them into a useful product, service, or method of operation.

8. Organizations that stimulate innovation will have structures that are flexible, easy access to resources, and fluid communication; a culture that is relaxed, supportive of new ideas, and encourages monitoring of the environment; and creative people who are well trained, current in their fields, and secure in their jobs.

Review and Discussion Questions

1. Why is handling change an integral part of every manager's job?
2. What internal and external forces create the need for organizations to change?
3. Who are change agents?
4. Do you think that a low-level employee could act as a change catalyst? Explain.
5. Describe Lewin's three-step change process.
6. Is TQM consistent with the goal of introducing revolutionary change into an organization? Discuss.
7. How do creativity and innovation differ? Give an example of each.
8. How can an innovative culture make an organization more effective? Could such an innovative culture make an organization less effective? Explain.
9. How can management foster innovation?
10. Can changes occur in an organization without a champion to foster innovation? Explain.

Self-Assessment Exercise

How Ready Are You for Managing in a Turbulent World?

Instructions: Listed below are some statements that a 37-year-old manager made about his job at a large, successful corporation. If your job had these characteristics, how would you react to them? After each statement are five letters, A to E. Circle the letter that best describes how you think you would react according to the following scale:

A I would enjoy this very much; it's completely acceptable.
B This would be enjoyable and acceptable most of the time.
C I'd have no reaction to this feature one way or another, or it would be about equally enjoyable and unpleasant.
D This feature would be somewhat unpleasant for me.
E This feature would be very unpleasant for me.

1. I regularly spend 30 to 40 per cent of my time in meetings. A B C D E
2. A year and a half ago, my job did not exist, and I have been essentially inventing it as I go along. A B C D E
3. The responsibilities I either assume or am assigned consistently exceed the authority I have for discharging them. A B C D E
4. At any given moment in my job, I have on the average about a dozen phone calls to be returned. A B C D E
5. There seems to be very little relation in my job between the quality of my performance and my actual pay and fringe benefits. A B C D E
6. About two weeks a year of formal management training is needed in my job just to stay current. A B C D E
7. Because we have very effective equal employment opportunity (EEO) in my company and because it is thoroughly multinational, my job consistently brings me into close working contact at a professional level with people of many races, ethnic groups, and nationalities and of both sexes. A B C D E
8. There is no objective way to measure my effectiveness. A B C D E
9. I report to three different bosses for different aspects of my job, and each has an equal say in my performance appraisal. A B C D E
10. On average, about a third of my time is spent dealing with unexpected emergencies that force all scheduled work to be postponed. A B C D E
11. When I have to have a meeting of the people who report to me, it takes my secretary most of a day to find a time when we are all available, and even then, I have yet to have a meeting where everyone is present for the entire meeting. A B C D E
12. The college degree I earned in preparation for this this type of work is now obsolete, and I probably should go back for another degree. A B C D E
13. My job requires that I absorb 100-200 pages per week of technical materials. A B C D E
14. I am out of town overnight at least one night per week. A B C D E
15. My department is so interdependent with several other departments in the company that all distinctions about which departments are responsible for which tasks are quite arbitrary. A B C D E

Managing Change and Innovation

16. I will probably get a promotion in about a year to a job in another division that has most of these same characteristics.   A B C D E
17. During the period of my employment here, either the entire company or the division I worked in has been reorganized every year or so.   A B C D E
18. While there are several possible promotions I can see ahead of me, I have no real career path in an objective sense.   A B C D E
19. While there are several possible promotions I can see ahead of me, I think I have no realistic chance of getting to the top levels of the company.   A B C D E
20. While I have many ideas about how to make things work better, I have no direct influence on either the business policies or the personnel policies that govern my division.   A B C D E
21. My company has recently put in an "assessment centre" where I and all other managers will be required to go through an extensive battery of psychological tests to assess our potential.   A B C D E
22. My company is a defendant in an antitrust suit, and if the case comes to trial, I will probably have to testify about some decisions that were made a few years ago.   A B C D E
23. Advanced computer and other electronic office technology is continually being introduced into my division, necessitating constant learning on my part.   A B C D E
24. The computer terminal and screen I have in my office can be monitored in my bosses' offices without my knowledge.   A B C D E

Turn to page 414 for scoring directions and key.

Source: From Peter B. Vaill, *Managing as a Performing Art: New Ideas for a World of Chaotic Change* (San Francisco: Jossey-Bass, 1989), pp. 8–9. With permission.

Class Exercise

The Celestial Aerospace Company

Objectives:
1. To illustrate how forces for change and stability must be managed in organizations.
2. To illustrate the effects of alternative change techniques on the relative strength of forces for change and forces for stability.

The Situation: The marketing division of the Celestial Aerospace Company (CAP) has gone through two major reorganizations in the past three years. Initially, its structure changed from a functional to a matrix form. But the matrix form did not satisfy some functional managers. They complained that the structure confused the authority and responsibility relationships. In reaction to these complaints, the marketing department revised the structure back to the functional form. This new structure maintained market and project teams, which were managed by project managers with a few general staff personnel. But no functional specialists were assigned to these groups. After the change, some problems began to surface. Project managers complained that they could not obtain necessary assistance from functional staffs. It not only took more time to obtain necessary assistance but also created problems in establishing stable relationships with functional staff members. Since these problems affected their services to customers, project managers demanded a change in the organizational structure—probably again toward a matrix structure. Faced with these complaints and demands from project managers, the vice-president is pondering another reorganization. He has requested an outside consultant (you) to help him in the reorganization plan.

1. Divide yourselves into groups of five to seven and take the role of consultants.
2. Each group should identify the forces necessitating the change and the resistance to that change found in the company.
3. Each group should develop a set of strategies for dealing with the resistance to change and how they would implement these strategies.
4. Reassemble the class and hear each group's recommendations and explanations.

Source: Adapted from K.H. Chung and L.C. Megginson, *Organizational Behavior* (New York: Harper & Row, 1981), pp. 498–99. With permission.

Key Terms

Key terms are listed in the order in which they appear in the chapter.

change   change agents   creativity   innovation

Case Application

Change in the Big Accounting Firms

The accounting industry has undergone a series of changes, both structural and technical. What were once the Big Ten firms became the Big Eight and are now the Big Six. Are they soon to become the Big Five? Several factors have sparked the move to consolidate the large firms and make them larger still. Foremost has been the need to service the worldwide divisions and subsidiaries of multinational companies. This means that a firm must have offices where the clients are, and they must be able to offer the same level of service in the same way. A number of large accounting firms have grown by acquiring existing partnerships and merging them with the firm. And this has created a change problem because each of the acquired firms must adapt to the acquiring firm's culture.

And this brings a second change problem into play. Professionals—doctors, lawyers, architects, accountants, and so on—are, by their nature, technically expert in their fields, but not managerially expert. Their education and training is focused on professional skills, but not the management of people. So the changes that the large accounting firms are facing: creating a uniform culture, moving decision making down the hierarchy, increasing employee involvement, improving productivity, delivering real customer service, adding value, etc., are doubly difficult for them. Generally speaking, the partners in the firms went into the profession because they wanted to be accountants, not managers. Those who opt for the latter career leave and join industry.

One of the big problems facing accounting firms is severe pressure on fees. Clients are resisting paying what they believe to be overly high fees and are putting work out to tender—i.e., asking competing firms to quote on the price for doing a job. The result of this, in some major markets, has been an average decrease in fees of 35 to 40 per cent. The effect on profits is significant.

Questions

1. Identify (a) the internal forces for change and (b) the external forces for change. What are the factors that are resistant to change?
2. If you were called in as a consultant to a large accounting firm, describe what you would do to overcome resistance to change.
3. The standards of most professions are very high. It's difficult to pass the bar exams or the chartered accounting exams. So people in the professions must, by and large, be relatively clever. Why couldn't you just explain the logical need for them to change and get them to change on the basis of the logical argument you put forward?

Pressures to Change

The pulp and paper industry has traditionally been run on the basis of agreements between management, unions, and the government. But these agreements are breaking down and generating huge pressures for change. MacMillan Bloedel's Port Alberni mill on Vancouver Island is a good example of how difficult change can be and how severe the pressures on people can become. Port Alberni has always been a union town. The mill paid very good wages and the standard of living was among the highest in Canada. Port Alberni was a home of traditional unionism. The company operated with a "closed shop" system — i.e., everyone had to belong to a traditional union.

But MacMillan Bloedel maintains that the costs of operating under the old union structures are too high and it now wishes to operate with an "open shop" environment. That translates into giving jobs to people who do not belong to traditional unions. And the union members see it as giving *their* jobs to nonunion members. MacMillan Bloedel engaged a construction company to work on its $200-million mill expansion, and while the construction company has a union, it is what the traditional union movement describes as a management-oriented and controlled union — colloquially known as a "rat" union. There are a lot of jobs at stake; union jobs that are going to so-called "rat" union employees because of wage rates and union regulations. Management claims that they need different rules of work from the old union system — rules that open the criteria for hiring, promotion, reward, and union relations. They maintain that the old rules are too inflexible and protect jobs for numbers of workers who are not needed. This fight is over control of the workplace. The traditional unions are not faring well in this battle, having gone in the last decade from having 80 per cent of the industry's workforce unionized, to 20 per cent of the workforce.

The changes being driven by the company affect the lives of a large number of people in Port Alberni. The union is resisting them because they maintain that they will lead to loss of jobs, and the union's duty is to its members. And they say that management is simply passing the blame for its own poor performance. Who is right?

Questions

1. Describe the forces that are creating the pressure for change in this situation.
2. Is this a "calm waters" situation or a "white water rapids" situation? Explain your answer.
3. What are the underlying reasons behind the resistance to change? What could you, as a change agent, do about managing them?

Video Resource: "Port Alberni," *Prime Time Magazine* (December 12, 1994).

10

Foundations of Behaviour

Learning Objectives

WHAT WILL I BE ABLE TO DO AFTER I FINISH THIS CHAPTER?

1. Define the focus and goals of organizational behaviour.
2. Identify and describe the three components of attitudes.
3. Explain the role consistency plays in attitudes.
4. Define cognitive dissonance.
5. Explain why companies use attitude surveys.
6. Identify the six personality traits linked to organizational behaviour.
7. Describe Holland's personality-job fit theory.
8. Define perception and describe the factors that can shape or distort perception.
9. Describe attribution theory.
10. Explain how managers can shape employee behaviour.

Doesn't it seem reasonable that senior managers who spend time in the trenches—performing the day-to-day activities of operating employees—will have a better understanding of their employees and the problems those employees face than managers who rarely venture out of their headquarters offices? It does, but very few organizations do anything about it. One exception is Hyatt Hotels.[1]

Hyatt's president, Darryl Hartley Leonard, came up with the idea of "in-touch day" in 1989. On this day, once a year, the company closes its headquarters office and the firm's senior management staff spreads out to 100 Hyatt hotels in the United States and Canada. There, they take jobs as bellhops, chambermaids, cooks, carpenters, and similar front-line positions. Even though most Hyatt executives visit company hotels about thirty-five times a year, there's a big difference between seeing hotel operations from the vantage point of a guest and seeing them from the point of view of a desk clerk or a waiter. Actually performing such jobs allows managers to learn firsthand the problems that employees confront. For instance, a member of the purchasing department spent the day as a housekeeper. During the course of her rounds, she didn't have enough linens to make all the beds. As a result, she had to go to the laundry room, launder the sheets, and return to the rooms—wasting valuable time. The irony was that she was the individual responsible for "sitting" on the purchase requisition to buy more sheets. Needless to say, her time spent "working" that day led her to vow never to delay requisitions again.

Hyatt's Darryl Hartley Leonard learns firsthand that carrying baggage is one of the hotel's first points of contact with customers.

In addition to creating a better understanding of what employees face, in-touch day provides tangible evidence to employees that management cares about them and their job problems. It's one thing to talk about improving employee jobs, but another to put yourself in the shoes of your employees and work right alongside them.

Hyatt's in-touch day illustrates one way for managers to better understand their employees. This chapter looks at a number of factors that influence employee behaviour and their implications for management practice.

Toward Explaining and Predicting Behaviour

The material in this and the following four chapters draws heavily on the field of study that has come to be known as organizational behaviour (OB). While it is concerned with the subject of **behaviour**—that is, the actions of people—**organizational behaviour** is concerned more specifically with the actions of people at work.

One of the challenges to understanding organizational behaviour is that it addresses a number of issues that are not obvious. Like an iceberg, a lot of organizational behaviour is not visible to the naked eye (see Exhibit 10-1). What we tend to see when we look at organizations are their formal aspects—strategies, objectives, policies and procedures, structure, technology, formal authority, and chains of command. But just under

behaviour
The actions of people.

organizational behaviour
The study of the actions of people at work.

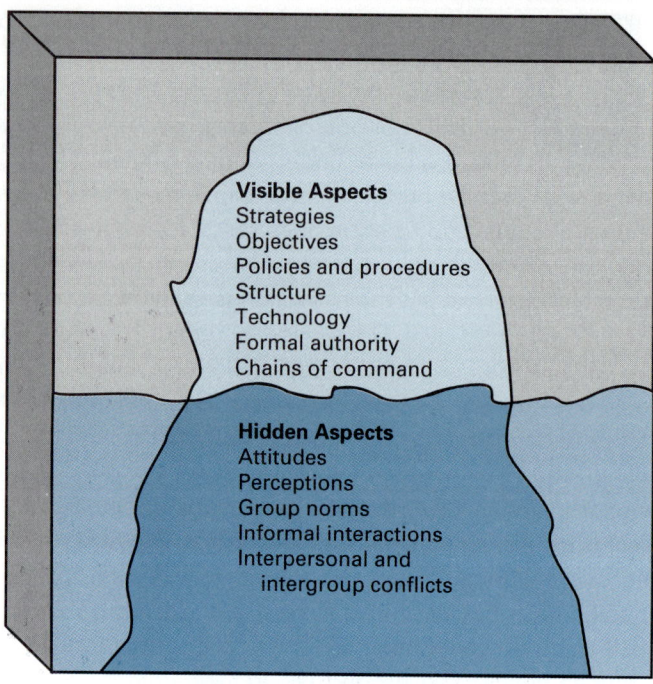

**Exhibit 10-1
The "Organization as an Iceberg" Metaphor**

the surface lies a number of informal elements that managers need to understand. As we'll show, OB provides managers with considerable insight into these important, but hidden, aspects of the organization.

What Is the Focus of Organizational Behaviour?

Organizational behaviour focuses primarily on two major areas. First, OB looks at individual behaviour. Based predominantly on contributions from psychologists, this area includes such topics as attitudes, personality, perception, learning, and motivation. Second, OB is concerned with group behaviour, which includes norms, roles, team building, and conflict. Our knowledge about groups comes basically from the work of sociologists and social psychologists. Unfortunately, the behaviour of a group of employees cannot be understood by merely summing up the actions of each individual, because individuals in groups behave differently from individuals acting alone. You see this characteristic when a street gang in a large city harasses innocent citizens. The gang members, acting individually, might never engage in such behaviour. Put them together, and they act differently. Therefore, because employees in an organization are both individuals and members of groups, we need to study them at two levels. In this chapter, we'll provide the foundation for understanding individual behaviour. In the next chapter, we'll introduce basic concepts related to understanding group behaviour.

What Are the Goals of Organizational Behaviour?

The goals of OB are to explain and to predict behaviour. Why do managers need this skill? Simply, in order to manage their employees' behaviour. We know that a manager's success depends on getting things done through other people. Toward this goal, the manager needs to be able to explain why employees engage in some behaviours rather than others and to predict how employees will respond to various actions the manager might take.

Foundations of Behaviour

What employee behaviours are we specifically concerned about explaining and predicting? The emphasis will be on employee productivity, absenteeism, and turnover. In addition, we'll also look at job satisfaction. While job satisfaction is an attitude rather than a behaviour, it is an outcome about which many managers are concerned.

In the following pages, we'll address how an understanding of employee attitudes, personality, perception, and learning can help us to predict and explain employee productivity, absence and turnover rates, and job satisfaction.

Attitudes

Attitudes are evaluative statements—either favourable or unfavourable—concerning objects, people, or events. They reflect how an individual feels about something. When a person says, "I like my job," he or she is expressing an attitude about work.

To better understand the concept of attitudes, we should look at an attitude as being made up of three components: cognition, affect, and behaviour.[2] The **cognitive component of an attitude** makes up the beliefs, opinions, knowledge, or information held by a person. The belief that "discrimination is wrong" illustrates a cognition. The **affective component of an attitude** is the emotional or feeling segment of an attitude. Using our example, this component would be reflected in the statement, "I don't like Jon because he discriminates against minorities." Finally, affect can lead to behavioural outcomes. The **behavioural component of an attitude** refers to an intention to behave in a certain way toward someone or something. So, to continue our example, I might choose to avoid Jon because of my feelings about him. Looking at attitudes as being made up of three components—cognition, affect, and behaviour—helps to show the complexity of attitudes. But for the sake of clarity, keep in mind that the term attitude usually refers only to the affective component.

Naturally, managers aren't interested in every attitude an employee might hold. They're specifically interested in job-related attitudes. The three most popular of these are job satisfaction, job involvement, and organizational commitment.[3] **Job satisfaction** is an employee's general attitude toward his or her job. When people speak of employee attitudes, more often than not they mean job satisfaction. **Job involvement** is the degree to which an employee identifies with his or her job, actively participates in it, and considers his or her job performance important to his or her self-worth. Finally, **organizational commitment** represents an employee's orientation toward the organization in terms of his or her loyalty to, identification with, and involvement in the organization.

Does an Individual's Attitude and Behaviour Need to Be Consistent?

Did you ever notice how people change what they say so it doesn't contradict what they do? Perhaps a friend of yours has consistently argued that American cars were poorly built and that he'd never own anything but a foreign import. But his dad gives him a late-model American-made car, and suddenly they're not so bad. Or, when going through sorority rush, a new freshman believes that sororities are good and that pledging a sorority is important. If she fails to make a sorority, however, she may say, "I recognized that sorority life isn't all it's cracked up to be, anyway!"

Research has generally concluded that people seek consistency among their attitudes and between their attitudes and their behaviour.[4] This means that individuals try

---

attitudes
Evaluative statements concerning objects, people, or events.

cognitive component of an attitude
The beliefs, opinions, knowledge, or information held by a person.

affective component of an attitude
The emotional or feeling segment of an attitude.

behavioural component of an attitude
An intention to behave in a certain way toward someone or something.

job satisfaction
A person's general attitude toward his or her job.

job involvement
The degree to which an employee identifies with his or her job, actively participates in it, and considers his or her job performance important to his or her self-worth.

organizational commitment
An employee's orientation toward the organization in terms of his or her loyalty to, identification with, and involvement in the organization.

to reconcile differing attitudes and align their attitudes and behaviour so they appear rational and consistent. When there is an inconsistency, individuals will take steps to correct it. This can be done by altering either the attitudes or the behaviour or by developing a rationalization for the discrepancy.

For example, a recruiter for Ontario Electronics Ltd. (OEL), whose job it is to visit college campuses, identify qualified job candidates, and sell them on the advantages of OEL as a place to work, would be in conflict if he personally believed OEL had poor working conditions and few opportunities for new college graduates. This recruiter could, over time, find his attitudes toward OEL becoming more positive. He may, in effect, convince himself by continually articulating the merits of working for OEL. Another alternative would be for the recruiter to remain negative about OEL and the opportunities within the firm for prospective candidates. However, the recruiter might acknowledge that although OEL is an undesirable place to work, his obligation as a professional recruiter is to present the positive side of working for the company. He might, therefore, rationalize that no workplace is perfect and that his job is not to present both sides of the issue but rather to present a rosy picture of the company.

What Is Cognitive Dissonance Theory?

Can we additionally assume from this consistency principle that an individual's behaviour can always be predicted if we know his or her attitude on a subject? The answer to this question is, unfortunately, more complex than merely a yes or a no.

cognitive dissonance
Any incompatibility between two or more attitudes or between behaviour and attitudes.

Leon Festinger, in the late 1950s, proposed the theory of **cognitive dissonance.**[5] This theory sought to explain the relationship between attitudes and behaviour. Dissonance in this case means inconsistency. Cognitive dissonance refers to any incompatibility that an individual might perceive between two or more of his or her attitudes, or between his or her behaviour and attitudes. Festinger argued that any form of inconsistency is uncomfortable and that individuals will attempt to reduce the dissonance and, hence, the discomfort. Therefore, individuals will seek a stable state where there is a minimum of dissonance.

Of course, no individual can completely avoid dissonance. You know that cheating on your income tax is wrong, but you may "fudge" the numbers a bit every year, and hope you're not audited. Or you tell your children to brush after every meal, but you might not. So how do people cope? Festinger proposed that the desire to reduce dissonance is determined by the importance of the elements creating the dissonance, the degree of influence the individual believes he or she has over the elements, and the rewards that may be involved in dissonance (see Details on a Management Classic).

Details on a Management Classic

LEON FESTINGER AND COGNITIVE DISSONANCE THEORY

Cognitive dissonance theory argues that individuals' motivation to change their attitudes is based on their desire to appear consistent. In other words, individuals strive to appear rational. According to Leon Festinger, how this level of rationality is achieved is contingent on individuals' perception of the importance of and control over what is

Foundations of Behaviour

affecting them, as well as the reward structures that are in place to make the inconsistencies more palatable.[6]

If the elements creating the dissonance are relatively unimportant, the pressure to correct this imbalance will be low. For example, a required class that you must take next semester is offered only at 11:00 A.M., at the same time when you wanted to take an elective class from a popular professor. You know, however, that this professor offers the class frequently, and it can easily be taken another time. But consider a case where the issues are important. For example, a manager—Mrs. Ryan—believes strongly that no company should lay off employees. Unfortunately, Mrs. Ryan, because of the requirements of her job, is placed in the position of having to make decisions that would trade off her company's strategic direction against her attitudes on layoffs. She knows that restructuring in the company may result in some jobs no longer being needed; and this is in the best economic interest of her firm. What will she do? Undoubtedly, Mrs. Ryan is experiencing a high degree of cognitive dissonance. Because of the importance of the elements in this example, we cannot expect Mrs. Ryan to ignore the inconsistency. As such, there are several paths that she can follow to deal with her dilemma. She can change her behaviour (lay off employees). Or she can reduce dissonance by concluding that the dissonant behaviour is not so important after all ("I've got to make a living, and in my role as a decision maker, I often have to place the good of my company above that of individual organizational members"). A third alternative would be for Mrs. Ryan to change her attitude ("There is nothing wrong in laying off employees"). Still another choice would be to seek out more consonant elements to outweigh the dissonant ones ("The long-term benefits to the surviving employees from our restructuring more than offset the cost associated with the retrenchment effort").

The degree of influence that individuals believe they have over the elements also will have an impact on how they will react to the dissonance. If they perceive the dissonance to be an uncontrollable result—something over which they have no choice—they are less likely to be receptive to attitude change. If, for example, the dissonance-producing behaviour was required as a result of the boss's directive, the pressure to reduce dissonance would be less than if the behaviour was performed voluntarily. While dissonance exists, it can be rationalized and justified.

Finally, rewards influence the degree to which individuals are motivated to reduce dissonance. High dissonance, when accompanied by high rewards, tends to reduce the tension inherent in the dissonance. The reward acts to reduce dissonance by increasing the consistency side of the individual's balance sheet.

These moderating factors suggest that just because individuals experience dissonance they will not necessarily move directly toward consistency, that is, toward reduction of this dissonance. If the issues underlying the dissonance are of minimal importance, if an individual perceives that the dissonance is externally imposed and is substantially uncontrollable by him or her, or if rewards are significant enough to offset the dissonance, the individual will not be under great tension to reduce the dissonance. ▼

What conclusions about organizational behaviour can we draw from Festinger's work? Cognitive dissonance can help us to predict the willingness of employees to engage in attitude or behavioural change. If employees are required, for example, by the demands of their job to say or do things that contradict their personal opinions, they will tend to modify their beliefs to make them more compatible with what they have said or done. Additionally, the greater the inconsistency, the more likely one is to reduce it.

How Can Managers Be Kept Informed About Employee Attitudes?

attitude surveys
Eliciting responses from employees through questionnaires about how they feel about their jobs, work groups, supervisors, and/or the organization.

In order to keep informed of their workers' attitudes, an increasing number of organizations are regularly surveying their employees. Exhibit 10-2 illustrates what an attitude survey might look like. Typically, **attitude surveys** present the employee with a set of statements or questions. Ideally, the items will be tailor-made to obtain the specific information that management desires. An attitude score is achieved by summing up responses to individual questionnaire items. These scores can then be averaged for job groups, departments, divisions, or the organization as a whole. General Electric, for example, in surveying more than 20,000 of its employees, found that over half of the respondents were dissatisfied with the information and the recognition they received from the company and with their opportunities for advancement.[7] As a result, management instituted regular monthly information meetings, brought in experts to answer questions, and began printing a newsletter. One year later, a follow-up survey found that the number of employees dissatisfied with the information they received had dropped to zero, while the number dissatisfied with promotional opportunities fell from 50 to 20 per cent.

How Can an Understanding of Attitudes Help Managers Be More Effective?

We know that employees can be expected to try to reduce dissonance. Therefore, not surprisingly, there is relatively strong evidence that committed and satisfied employees

---

Please answer each of the following statements using the following rating scale:

   5 = Strongly agree
   4 = Agree
   3 = Undecided
   2 = Disagree
   1 = Strongly disagree

Statement   **Rating**

1. This company is a pretty good place to work. _____
2. I can get ahead in this company if I make the effort. _____
3. This company's wage rates are competitive with those of other companies. _____
4. Employee promotion decisions are handled fairly. _____
5. I understand the various fringe benefits the company offers. _____
6. My job makes the best use of my abilities. _____
7. My workload is challenging but not burdensome. _____
8. I have trust and confidence in my boss. _____
9. I feel free to tell my boss what I think. _____
10. I know what my boss expects of me. _____

Exhibit 10-2 Sample Attitude Survey

Foundations of Behaviour

have lower rates of turnover and absenteeism.[8] Because most managers want to minimize the number of resignations and absences—especially among their more productive employees—they should do those things that will generate positive job attitudes. Dissonance, however, can be managed. If employees are required to engage in activities that appear inconsistent to them or that are at odds with their attitudes, managers should remember that pressure to reduce the dissonance is lessened when the employee perceives that the dissonance is externally imposed and uncontrollable. The pressure is also lessened if rewards are significant enough to offset the dissonance.

But let's not confuse satisfied workers with happy workers. We need to be aware of a debate that has lasted for over five decades. That is, are happy workers more productive? Several research studies in the past have provided important implications for managers.[9] They suggest that the goal of making employees happy on the assumption that this will lead to high productivity is probably misdirected. Managers who follow this strategy could end up with a very happy but poorly performing group of employees. Managers would get better results by directing their attention primarily to what will help employees to become more productive. Successful job performance should then lead to feelings of accomplishment, increased pay, promotions, and other rewards—all desirable outcomes—which then lead to satisfaction with the job.

Personality

Some people are quiet and passive while others are loud and aggressive. When we describe people using terms such as quiet, passive, loud, aggressive, ambitious, extroverted, loyal, tense, or sociable, we are categorizing them in terms of personality traits. An individual's **personality** is the combination of the psychological traits we use to classify that person.

personality
A combination of psychological traits that classifies a person.

Can Behaviour Be Predicted from Personality Traits?

There are literally dozens of personality traits. However, six have received the bulk of attention in the search to link personality traits to behaviour in organizations. They include locus of control, authoritarianism, Machiavellianism, self-esteem, self-monitoring, and risk propensity.

Who has control over people's behaviour? Some people believe that they control their own fate. Others see themselves as pawns of fate, believing that what happens to them in their lives is due to luck or chance. The **locus of control** in the first case is internal; these people believe that they control their destiny (see Managers Who Made a Difference). In the second case it is external; these people believe that their lives are controlled by outside forces.[10] The evidence indicates that employees who rate high in externality are less satisfied with their jobs, more alienated from the work setting, and less involved in their jobs than those who rate high in internality.[11] A manager might also expect to find that externals blame a poor performance evaluation on their boss's prejudice, their coworkers, or other events outside their control, whereas internals explain the same evaluation in terms of their own actions.

locus of control
A personality attribute that measures the degree to which people believe they are masters of their own fate.

Authoritarianism refers to a belief that there should be status and power differences among people in organizations.[12] The extremely high authoritarian personality is intellectually rigid, judgmental of others, deferential to those above, exploitative of those below, distrustful, and resistant to change. Because few people are extreme

authoritarianism
A measure of a person's belief that there should be status and power differences among people in organizations.

authoritarians, our conclusions must be guarded. It seems reasonable to postulate, however, that possessing a high authoritarian personality would be negatively related to the performance of a job that demands sensitivity to the feelings of others, tact, and the ability to adapt to complex and changing situations.[13] On the other hand, in a job that is highly structured and in which success depends on close conformance to rules and regulations, the highly authoritarian employee should perform quite well.

Closely related to authoritarianism is the characteristic of **Machiavellianism** ("Mach"), named after Niccolo Machiavelli, who wrote in the sixteenth century on how to gain and manipulate power. An individual who is high in Machiavellianism—in contrast to someone who is low—is pragmatic, maintains emotional distance, and believes that ends can justify means.[14] "If it works, use it" is consistent with a high Mach perspective. Do high Machs make good employees? That answer depends on the type of job and whether you consider ethical implications in evaluating performance. In jobs that require bargaining skills (such as labour negotiator) or that have substantial rewards for winning (such as a commissioned salesperson), high Machs are productive. In jobs in which ends do not justify the means or that lack absolute standards of performance, it is difficult to predict the performance of high Machs.

People differ in the degree to which they like or dislike themselves. This trait is called **self-esteem**.[15] The research on self-esteem (SE) offers some interesting insights into organizational behaviour. For example, self-esteem is directly related to expectations for success. High SEs believe that they possess more of the ability they need in order to succeed at work. Individuals with high SE will take more risks in job selection and are more likely to choose unconventional jobs than people with low SE.

The most common finding on self-esteem is that low SEs are more susceptible to external influence than are high SEs. Low SEs depend on the receipt of positive evaluations from others. As a result, they are more likely to seek approval from others and more prone to conform to the beliefs and behaviours of those they respect than are high SEs. In managerial positions, low SEs will tend to be concerned with pleasing others and, therefore, less likely to take unpopular stands than are high SEs.

Not surprisingly, self-esteem has also been found to be related to job satisfaction. A number of studies confirm that high SEs are more satisfied with their jobs than low SEs.

Machiavellianism
A measure of the degree to which people are pragmatic, maintain emotional distance, and believe that ends can justify means.

self-esteem
An individual's degree of like or dislike for him or herself.

Managers Who Made a Difference
JOHN FORZANI

John Forzani won a football scholarship to Utah State University and came back to Canada to play as an offensive lineman for his hometown team, the Calgary Stampeders in the early 1970s. He noticed that there weren't any good suppliers of athletic shoes in town, and so he and his brothers, Joe and Tom, and a fellow Calgary Stampeder, Basil Bark, started a business that made a profit of $10,000 in its first year. When they opened a second store, profits shot to $80,000 and Forzani was hooked on business. He quit the Stampeders in 1977 and went into business full time when, as he says, "You're in the huddle, and you're thinking about the order of Adidas that is two weeks late rather than the next play."

Foundations of Behaviour

His stores, Forzani's Locker Room, which focused on athletic shoes, formed the start, and led to expansion into Sun Sports, a chain selling high-end ski-, swim-, and beachwear, then into Jersey City, which sells licensed apparel such as caps and shirts. Another outlet in Forzani's group is RnR The Walking Store, which sells walking and hiking shoes and the clothing and accessories for walking. And in April 1994, he acquired Sports Experts.

The market for sports goods is growing exponentially in Canada. Sales of licensed goods—i.e., with team names and logos—in North America went from $2 billion in 1992 to $8.7 billion in 1993, and forecasts for Canada indicate that there will be growth of more than 10 per cent in the sale of all types of sporting goods for the next few years. The market is estimated to be $3.5 billion in 1996.

But there's a challenge for Forzani, and, being a competitor, he's up for it. The Big Box concept of marketing that Price-Costco and others have applied to groceries and home goods has come to sports goods. Two American companies, Sports Authority and Sportsmart Inc., are crashing the Canadian market with stores that are 40,000 square feet or larger. They sell a vast range of goods. Sports Authority sells more than 500 styles of athletic shoes, 164 types of baseball hats, and 20,000 pieces of sports apparel.

Forzani's answer is Sport Check, a Big-Box equivalent, but with slightly smaller size per store and a much stronger emphasis on the customer. The strengths of the American competitors are their product diversity, size, and low price. But their weakness is lack of personal service. Sport Check has a more inviting and upscale look, away from the barnlike appearance of the Big Box stores. And some of its stores have features like a golf driving range, a batting cage, or a mini-basketball court. They also have a more flexible store size and therefore can locate in traditional shopping centres rather than on the outskirts of town where the other Big Box stores are. Sport Check also emphasizes knowledgable staff and helpful service.

So the contest is on. What will appeal most to consumers? Will the behavioural elements of service, atmosphere, and human interaction outweigh the pure economic elements? Consumer behaviour is a central issue here and Forzani plans to compete largely on the basis of how people will react to the human and emotional elements of business.[16] ▼

Another personality trait that has recently received increased attention is called **self-monitoring**.[17] It refers to an individual's ability to adjust his or her behaviour to external, situational factors. Individuals high in self-monitoring can show considerable adaptability in adjusting their behaviour to external, situational factors. They are highly sensitive to external cues and can behave differently in different situations. High self-monitors are capable of presenting striking contradictions between their public persona and their private selves. Low self-monitors can't alter their behaviour. They tend to display their true dispositions and attitudes in every situation; hence, there is high behavioural consistency between who they are and what they do.

The research on self-monitoring is in its infancy; thus, predictions are hard to make. However, preliminary evidence suggests that high self-monitors tend to pay closer attention to the behaviour of others and are more capable of conforming than are low self-monitors.[18] We might also hypothesize that high self-monitors will be more successful in managerial positions where individuals are required to play multiple, and even contradicting, roles. The high self-monitor is capable of putting on different "faces" for different audiences.

self-monitoring
A personality trait that measures an individual's ability to adjust his or her behaviour to external, situational factors.

risk taking
The willingness to take chances.

People differ in their willingness to take chances—their propensity for **risk taking.** This preference to assume or avoid risk has been shown to have an impact on how long it takes individuals to make a decision and how much information they require before making their choice. For instance, in a recent study, a group of individuals worked on simulated HRM exercises that required them to make hiring decisions.[19] High-risk-taking individuals made more rapid decisions and used less information in making their choices than did the low-risk-taking individuals. Interestingly, the decision accuracy was the same for both groups.

While it is generally correct to conclude that managers in organizations are risk aversive,[20] there are still individual differences on this dimension.[21] As a result, it makes sense to recognize these differences and even to consider aligning risk-taking propensity with specific job demands. For instance, a high-risk-taking propensity may lead to effective performance for a stock trader in a brokerage firm. This type of job demands rapid decision making. On the other hand, this personality characteristic might prove a major obstacle to accountants performing auditing activities. This latter job might be better filled by someone with a low-risk-taking propensity.

How Do We Match Personalities and Jobs?

Obviously, individual personalities differ. So, too, do jobs. Following this logic, efforts have been made to match the proper personalities with the proper jobs. The best documented personality-job fit theory has been developed by psychologist John Holland.[22] His theory states that an employee's satisfaction with his or her job, as well as his or her propensity to leave that job, depends on the degree to which the individual's personality matches his or her occupational environment. Holland has identified six basic personality types an organization's employees might possess. Exhibit 10-3 describes each of

TYPE	PERSONALITY CHARACTERISTICS	SAMPLE OCCUPATIONS
Realistic - Prefers physical activities that require skill, strength, and coordination	Shy, genuine, persistent, stable, conforming, practical	Mechanic, drill press operator, assembly line worker, farmer
Investigative - Prefers activities involving thinking, organizing, and understanding	Analytical, original, curious, independent	Biologist, economist, mathematician, news reporter
Social - Prefers activities that involve helping and developing others	Sociable, friendly, cooperative, understanding	Social worker, teacher, counselor, clinical psychologist
Conventional - Prefers rule-regulated, orderly, and unambiguous activities	Conforming, efficient, practical, unimaginative, inflexible	Accountant, corporate manager, bank teller, file clerk
Enterprising - Prefers verbal activities where there are opportunities to influence others and attain power	Self-confident, ambitious, energetic, domineering	Lawyer, real estate agent, public relations specialist, small business manager
Artistic - Prefers ambiguous and unsystematic activities which allow creative expression	Imaginative, disorderly, idealistic, emotional, impractical	Painter, musician, writer, interior decorator

Exhibit 10-3 Holland's Typology of Personality and Sample Occupations

Source: Reproduced by special permission of the publisher, Psychological Assessment Resources, Inc., *Making Vocational Choices,* copyright 1973, 1985 by Psychological Assessment Resources, Inc. All rights reserved.

Foundations of Behaviour

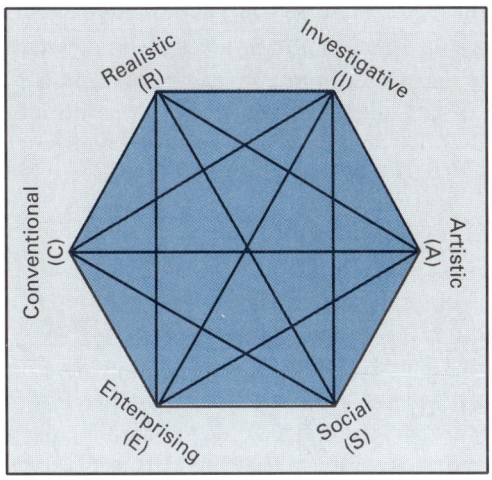

Exhibit 10-4 Relationship among Occupational Personality Types

Source: Reproduced by special permission of the publisher, Psychological Assessment Resources, Inc., *Making Vocational Choices*, copyright 1973, 1985 by Psychological Assessment Resources, Inc. All rights reserved.

the six types, their personality characteristics, and examples of congruent occupations.

Holland's research strongly supports the hexagonal diagram in Exhibit 10-4.[23] This exhibit shows that the closer two fields or orientations are in the hexagon, the more compatible they are. Adjacent categories are quite similar, while those diagonally opposite are highly dissimilar.

What does all this mean? The theory argues that satisfaction is highest and turnover lowest where personality and occupation are in agreement. Social individuals should be in social jobs, conventional people in conventional jobs, and so forth. A realistic person in a realistic job is in a more congruent situation than is a realistic person in an investigative job. A realistic person in a social job is in the most incongruent situation possible. The key points of this model are that (1) there do appear to be intrinsic differences in personality among individuals, (2) there are different types of jobs, and (3) people in job environments congruent with their personality types should be more satisfied and less likely to resign voluntarily than should people in incongruent jobs.

How Can an Understanding of Personality Help Managers Be More Effective?

The major value of a manager's understanding personality differences probably lies in selection. Managers are likely to have higher-performing and more satisfied employees if consideration is given to matching personality types with compatible jobs. In addition, there may be other benefits. For instance, managers can expect that individuals with an external locus of control may be less satisfied with their jobs than internals and also that they may be less willing to accept responsibility for their actions.

Do Personality Attributes Differ Across National Cultures?

There are certainly no common personality types for a given country. You can, for instance, find high risk takers and low risk takers in almost any culture. Yet a country's culture should influence the dominant personality characteristics of its population. We can see this by looking at two personality traits—locus of control and authoritarianism.

National cultures differ in terms of the degree to which people believe they control their environment. North Americans, for example, believe that they can dominate their environment while other societies, such as Middle Eastern countries, believe that life is essentially preordained. Notice the close parallel to internal and external locus of control. We should expect a larger proportion of internals in the Canadian and U.S. workforces than in the workforces of Saudi Arabia or Iran.

Authoritarianism is closely related to the concept of power distance. In high power-distance societies, such as Mexico or Venezuela, there should be a large proportion of individuals with authoritarian personalities, especially among the ruling class. In contrast, because Canada rates below average on this dimension, we'd expect authoritarian personalities to be less prevalent here than in the high power-distance countries.

Perception

Perception is a process by which individuals organize and interpret their sensory impressions in order to give meaning to their environment. Research on perception consistently demonstrates that individuals may look at the same thing yet perceive it differently. One manager, for instance, can interpret the fact that her assistant regularly takes several days to make important decisions as evidence that the assistant is slow, disorganized, and afraid to make decisions. Another manager, with the same assistant, might interpret the same action as evidence that the assistant is thoughtful, thorough, and deliberate. The first manager would probably evaluate her assistant negatively, while the second manager would probably evaluate the person positively. The point is that none of us actually sees reality. We interpret what we see and call it reality. And, of course, as the above example illustrates, we act according to our perceptions.

perception
The process of organizing and interpreting sensory impressions in order to give meaning to the environment.

What Influences Perception?

How do we explain the fact that people can perceive the same thing differently? A number of factors operate to shape and sometimes distort perception. These factors can reside in the perceiver; in the object, or target, being perceived; or in the context of the situation in which the perception is made.

When an individual looks at a target and attempts to interpret what he or she sees, the individual's personal characteristics are going to influence heavily the interpretation. These personal characteristics include attitudes, personality, motives, interests, past experiences, and expectations.

The characteristics of the target being observed can also affect what is perceived. Loud people are more likely than quiet people to be noticed in a group. So, too, are extremely attractive or unattractive individuals. Because targets are not looked at in isolation, the relationship of a target to its background also influences perception (see Exhibit 10-5), as does our tendency to group close things and similar things together.

The context in which we see objects or events is also important. The time at which an object or event is seen can influence attention, as can location, light, heat, and any number of other situational factors.

How Do Managers Judge Employees?

Much of the research on perception is directed at inanimate objects. Managers, though, are more concerned with human beings. So our discussion of perception should focus on person perception. Our perceptions of people differ from our perceptions of such inanimate objects as desks, machines, or buildings because we make inferences about the actions of people that we don't make about inanimate objects. Nonliving objects have no beliefs, motives, or intentions; people do. The result is that when we observe people, we attempt to develop explanations of why they behave in certain ways. Our

Foundations of Behaviour

Do you see a young woman with locks of flowing hair, or an old woman?

Exhibit 10-5 Perception Challenges

perception and judgment of a person's actions, therefore, will be significantly influenced by the assumptions we make about the person's internal state. Many of these assumptions have led researchers to the development of attribution theory.

What Is Attribution Theory?

Attribution theory has been proposed to develop explanations of how we judge people differently depending on what meaning we attribute to a given behaviour.[24] Basically, the theory suggests that when we observe an individual's behaviour, we attempt to determine whether it was internally or externally caused. Internally caused behaviours are those that are believed to be under the personal control of the individual. Externally caused behaviour results from outside causes; that is, the person is seen as forced into the behaviour by the situation. That determination, however, depends on three factors: (1) distinctiveness, (2) consensus, and (3) consistency.

Distinctiveness refers to whether an individual displays a behaviour in many situations or whether it is particular to one situation. Is the employee who arrives late today also the source of complaints by coworkers for being a "goof-off"? What we want to know is whether this behaviour is unusual. If it is, the observer is likely to give the behaviour an external attribution. If this action is not unique, it will probably be judged as internal.

If everyone who is faced with a similar situation responds in the same way, we can say the behaviour shows consensus. Our tardy employee's behaviour would meet this criterion if all employees who took the same route to work were also late. From an attribution perspective, if consensus is high you would be expected to give an external attribution to the employee's tardiness; whereas if other employees who took the

attribution theory
A theory used to develop explanations of how we judge people differently depending on the meaning we attribute to a given behaviour.

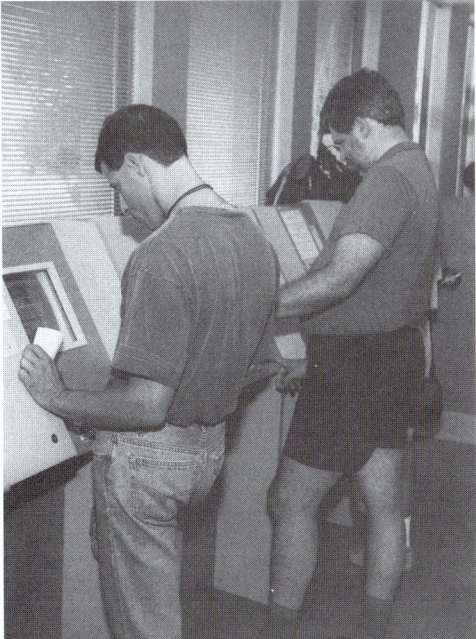

Why are these individuals unemployed? Is it because they are lazy and can't keep a job? Or was it the economic downturn and just bad luck? Your response will depend on what you believe caused the unemployment. That's precisely what attribution theory tells us.

Exhibit 10-6
The Process of Attribution Theory

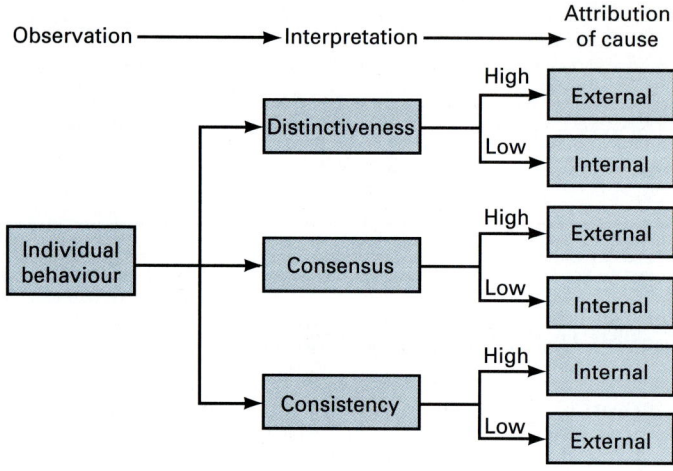

same route made it to work on time, your conclusion for causation would be internal.

Finally, an observer looks for consistency in a person's actions. Does the person engage in the behaviours regularly and consistently? Does the person respond the same way over time? Coming in ten minutes late for work is not perceived in the same way if for one employee it represents an unusual case (she hasn't been late for several months), while for another it is part of a routine pattern (she is regularly late two or three times a week). The more consistent the behaviour, the more the observer is inclined to attribute it to internal causes.

Exhibit 10-6 summarizes the key elements in attribution theory. It would tell us, for instance, that if an employee—let's call her Ms. Parker—generally performs at about the same level on other related tasks as she does on her current task (low distinctiveness), if other employees frequently perform differently—better or worse—than Ms. Parker does on that current task (low consensus), and if Ms. Parker's performance on this current task is consistent over time (high consistency), her manager or anyone else who is judging Ms. Parker's work is likely to hold her primarily responsible for her task performance (internal attribution).

Can Attributions Be Distorted?

fundamental attribution error
The tendency to underestimate the influence of external factors and overestimate the influence of internal factors when making judgments about the behaviour of others.

self-serving bias
The tendency for individuals to attribute their own successes to internal factors while putting the blame for failures on external factors.

One of the more interesting findings drawn from attribution theory is that there are errors or biases that distort attributions. For instance, there is substantial evidence to support that when we make judgments about the behaviour of other people, we have a tendency to underestimate the influence of external factors and overestimate the influence of internal or personal factors.[25] This is called the **fundamental attribution error** and can explain why a sales manager may be prone to attribute the poor performance of her sales agents to laziness rather than the innovative product line introduced by a competitor. There is also a tendency for individuals to attribute their own successes to internal factors like ability or effort while putting the blame for failure on external factors like luck. This is called the **self-serving bias** and suggests that feedback provided to employees in performance reviews will be predictably distorted by recipients depending on whether it is positive or negative.

What Shortcuts Do Managers Use in Judging Others?

Managers use a number of shortcuts to judge others. Perceiving and interpreting what others do is burdensome. As a result, individuals develop techniques for making the task more manageable. These techniques are frequently valuable; they allow us to make accurate perceptions rapidly and provide valid data for making predictions. However, they are not foolproof. They can and do get us into trouble. An understanding of these shortcuts can be helpful toward recognizing when they can result in significant distortions (see Exhibit 10-7).

Individuals cannot assimilate all they observe, so they engage in **selectivity.** They take in bits and pieces. These bits and pieces are not chosen randomly; rather, they are selectively chosen depending on the interests, background, experience, and attitudes of the observer. Selective perception allows us to "speed read" others but not without the risk of drawing an inaccurate picture.

It is easy to judge others if we assume that they are similar to us. In **assumed similarity,** or the "like me" effect, the observer's perception of others is influenced more by the observer's own characteristics than by those of the person observed. For example, if you want challenge and responsibility in your job, you will assume that others want the same. People who assume that others are like them can, of course, be right, but most of the time they're wrong.

When we judge someone on the basis of our perception of a group to which he or she belongs, we are using the shortcut called **stereotyping.** "Married people are more stable employees than singles" and "union people expect something for nothing" are examples of stereotyping. To the degree that a stereotype is based on fact, it may produce accurate judgments. However, many stereotypes have no foundation in fact. In such cases, stereotypes distort judgments.

When we form a general impression about an individual based on a single characteristic such as intelligence, sociability, or appearance, we are being influenced by the **halo effect.** This effect frequently occurs when students evaluate their classroom

selectivity
The process by which people assimilate certain bits and pieces of what they observe, depending on their interests, background, experience, and attitudes.

assumed similarity
The belief that others are like yourself.

stereotyping
Judging a person on the basis of one's perception of a group to which he or she belongs.

halo effect
A general impression of an individual based on a single characteristic.

SHORTCUT	WHAT IT IS	DISTORTION
Selectivity	People assimilate certain bits and pieces of what they observe depending on their interests, background, experience, and attitudes	By "speed reading" others, may draw an inaccurate picture of others
Assumed Similarity	People assume others are like themselves	May fail to take into account individual differences resulting in incorrect similarities
Stereotyping	People judge others based on their perception of a group to which others belong	May result in distorted judgments because many stereotypes have no factual foundation
Halo Effect	People form an impression of others based on a single trait	Fails to take into account the "total" picture of what an employee has done

Exhibit 10-7 Distortions in Shortcut Methods in Judging Others

Learning never stops. These employees are continuing their education by attending seminars designed to address new methods and techniques for sales presentation graphics.

instructor. Students may isolate a single trait such as enthusiasm and allow their entire evaluation to be tainted by their perception of this one trait. An instructor might be quiet, assured, knowledgable, and highly qualified, but if his or her style lacks zeal, the instructor will be rated lower on a number of other characteristics.

How Can an Understanding of Perceptions Help Managers Be More Effective?

Managers need to recognize that their employees react to perceptions, not reality. So whether a manager's appraisal of an employee is actually objective and unbiased or whether the organization's wage levels are actually among the highest in the industry is less relevant than what employees perceive them to be. If individuals perceive appraisals to be biased or wage levels as low, they will behave as if these conditions actually exist. Employees organize and interpret what they see; this creates the potential for perceptual distortion.

The message to managers should be clear: Close attention needs to be paid to how employees perceive both their jobs and management practices. Remember, the valuable employee who quits because of an incorrect perception is just as great a loss to an organization as the valuable employee who quits for a valid reason.

Learning

The last individual-behaviour concept we want to introduce in this chapter is learning. It is included for the obvious reason that almost all complex behaviour is learned. If we want to explain and predict behaviour, we need to understand how people learn. What is **learning**? A psychologist's definition is considerably broader than the layperson's view that "it's what we did when we went to school." In actuality, each of us is continuously "going to school." Learning occurs all the time. We continually learn from our experiences. A workable definition of learning is, therefore, any relatively permanent change in behaviour that occurs as a result of experience.

learning
Any relatively permanent change in behaviour that occurs as a result of experience.

What Is Operant Conditioning?

operant conditioning
A type of conditioning in which desired voluntary behaviour leads to a reward or prevents a punishment.

Operant conditioning argues that behaviour is a function of its consequences. People learn to behave to get something they want or to avoid something they don't want. Operant behaviour means voluntary or learned behaviour in contrast to reflexive or unlearned behaviour. The tendency to repeat such behaviour is influenced as a result of the reinforcement or lack of reinforcement brought about by the consequences of the behaviour. Reinforcement, therefore, strengthens a behaviour and increases the likelihood that it will be repeated.

Building on earlier work in the field, the late Harvard psychologist B.F. Skinner's research has extensively expanded our knowledge of operant conditioning.[26] Even his staunchest critics, who represent a sizeable group, admit that his operant concepts work.

Foundations of Behaviour

Behaviour is assumed to be determined from without—that is, learned—rather than from within—reflexive or unlearned. Skinner argued that by creating pleasing consequences to follow specific forms of behaviour, the frequency of that behaviour will increase. People will most likely engage in desired behaviours if they are positively reinforced for doing so. Rewards, for example, are most effective if they immediately follow the desired response. Additionally, behaviour that is not rewarded, or is punished, is less likely to be repeated.

You see illustrations of operant conditioning everywhere. For example, any situation in which it is either explicitly stated or implicitly suggested that reinforcements are contingent on some action on your part involves the use of operant learning. Your instructor says that if you want a high grade in the course you must supply correct answers on the test. A commissioned salesperson wanting to earn a sizeable income finds that this is contingent on generating high sales in his or her territory. Of course, the linkage can also work to teach the individual to engage in behaviours that work against the best interests of the organization. Assume that your boss tells you that if you will work overtime during the next three-week busy season, you will be compensated for it at the next performance appraisal. However, when performance appraisal time comes, you find that you are given no positive reinforcement for your overtime work. The next time your boss asks you to work overtime, what will you do? You will probably decline! Your behaviour can be explained by operant conditioning: If a behaviour fails to be positively reinforced, the probability that the behaviour will be repeated declines.

social learning theory People can learn through observation and direct experience.

What Is Social Learning Theory?

Individuals can also learn by observing what happens to other people and just by being told about something, as well as by direct experiences. So, for example, much of what we have learned comes from watching models—parents, teachers, peers, television and movie performers, bosses, and so forth. This view that we can learn both through observation and direct experience has been called **social learning theory**.[27]

While social learning theory is an extension of operant conditioning—that is, it assumes that behaviour is a function of consequences—it also acknowledges the existence of observational learning and the importance of perception in learning. People respond to how they perceive and define consequences, not to the objective consequences themselves.

The influence of models is central to the social learning viewpoint. Four processes have been found to determine the influence that a model will have on an individual:

▶ 1. **Attentional processes.** People learn from a model only when they recognize and pay attention to its critical features. We tend to be most influenced by repeatedly available models that we think are attractive, important, or similar to us.

▶ 2. **Retention processes.** A model's influence will depend on how well the individual remembers the model's action, even after the model is no longer readily available.

▶ 3. **Motor reproduction processes.** After a person has seen a new behaviour by observing the

Social learning theory tells us that we learn, in part, by being told about something. In the movie *Schindler's List,* director Stephen Spielberg teaches us about the heroic efforts of one special individual.

model, the watching must be converted to doing. This process then demonstrates that the individual can perform the modelled activities.

▶ 4. **Reinforcement processes.** Individuals will be motivated to exhibit the modelled behaviour if positive incentives or rewards are provided. Behaviours that are reinforced will be given more attention, learned better, and performed more often.

How Can Managers Shape Behaviour?

Because learning takes place on the job as well as prior to it, managers will be concerned with how they can teach employees to behave in ways that most benefit the organization. Thus, managers will often attempt to mould individuals by guiding their learning in graduated steps. This process is called **shaping behaviour** (see Developing Management Skills).

shaping behaviour
Systematically reinforcing each successive step that moves an individual closer to the desired response.

Consider the situation in which an employee's behaviour is significantly different from that sought by management. If management only reinforced the individual when he or she showed desirable responses, there might be very little reinforcement taking place. In such a case, shaping offers a logical approach toward achieving the desired behaviour.

We shape behaviour by systematically reinforcing each successive step that moves the individual closer to the desired response. If an employee who has chronically been thirty minutes late for work comes in only twenty minutes late, we can reinforce this improvement. Reinforcement would increase as responses more closely approximate the desired behaviour.

Developing Management Skills

▼ SHAPING BEHAVIOUR SKILLS ▲

▶ 1. **Identify the critical behaviours that have a significant impact on an employee's performance.** Not everything employees do on the job is equally important in terms of performance outcomes. A few critical behaviours may, in fact, account for the majority of one's performance. It is these high-impact behaviours that need identifying.

▶ 2. **Establish a base line of performance.** This is obtained by determining the number of times the identified behaviours occur under the employee's present job conditions.

▶ 3. **Analyse contributing factors to performance and their consequences.** A number of factors, like the norms of a group, may be contributing to the base line performance. Identify these factors and their effect on performance.

▶ 4. **Develop a "shaping" strategy.** The change that may occur will entail changing some element of performance—structure, processes, technology, groups, or the task. The purpose of the strategy is to strengthen the desirable behaviours and weaken the undesirable ones.

▶ 5. **Apply the appropriate strategy.** Once the strategy has been developed, it needs to be implemented. In this step, the intervention occurs.

▶ 6. **Measure the change that has occurred.** The intervention should produce desired results in performance behaviours. Evaluate the number of times the identified behaviours now occur. Compare these with the base line evaluation in step 2.

▶ 7. **Reinforce desired behaviours.** If the intervention has been successful and the new behaviours are producing the desired results, maintain these behaviours through reinforcement mechanisms.

Ethical Dilemmas in Management

IS SHAPING BEHAVIOUR A FORM OF MANIPULATIVE CONTROL?

Animal trainers use rewards — typically food — to get dogs, porpoises, and whales to perform extraordinary stunts. Behavioural psychologists have put rats through thousands of experiments by manipulating their food supply. These trainers and researchers have shaped the behaviour of these animals by controlling consequences. Such learning techniques may be appropriate for animals performing in zoos, circuses, or laboratories, but are they appropriate for managing the behaviour of people at work?

Critics argue that human beings are not rats in an experiment. Human beings should be treated with respect and dignity. To explicitly use rewards as a learning device — to encourage the repetition of desired behaviours — is manipulative. Human beings in organizations should act of free will and not be subjected to manipulative control techniques by their bosses.

No well-schooled behavioural scientist would argue that shaping isn't a powerful tool for controlling behaviour. But when used by managers, is it a form of manipulation? If an employee engages in behaviours that the organization later judges wrong but that were motivated by a manager's control of rewards, is that employee any less responsible for his or her actions than if such rewards were not involved? What do you think?

There are four ways in which to shape behaviour: through positive reinforcement, negative reinforcement, punishment, or extinction. When a response is followed with something pleasant, such as when a manager praises an employee for a job well done, it is called positive reinforcement. Rewarding a response with the termination or withdrawal of something unpleasant is called negative reinforcement. Managers who habitually criticize their employees for taking extended coffee breaks are using negative reinforcement. The only way these employees can stop the criticism is to shorten their breaks. Punishment penalizes undesirable behaviour. Suspending an employee for two days without pay for showing up drunk is an example of punishment. Eliminating any reinforcement that is maintaining a behaviour is called extinction. When the behaviour is not reinforced, gradually it tends to be extinguished. In meetings, managers who wish to discourage employees from continually asking distracting or irrelevant questions can eliminate this behaviour by ignoring these employees when they raise their hands to speak. Hand raising will become extinct when it is invariably met with an absence of reinforcement.

Both positive and negative reinforcement result in learning. They strengthen a desired response and increase the probability of repetition. Both punishment and extinction also result in learning; however, they weaken behaviour and tend to decrease its subsequent frequency (see Ethical Dilemmas in Management).

How Can an Understanding of Learning Help Managers Be More Effective?

Managers can undoubtedly benefit from understanding the learning process. Because employees continually learn on the job, the only issue is whether managers are going to let employee learning occur randomly or whether they are going to manage learning through the rewards they allocate and the examples they set. If marginal employees are rewarded with pay raises and promotions, they will have little reason to change their behaviour. If managers want a certain type of behaviour but reward a different type of behaviour, it shouldn't surprise them to find employees learning to engage in the other type of behaviour. Similarly, managers should expect that employees will look to them as models. Managers who are constantly late to work, or take two hours for lunch, or help themselves to company office supplies for personal use should expect employees to read the message they're sending and model their behaviour accordingly.

Summary

This Summary is organized by the chapter opening learning objectives found on page 224.

1. The field of organizational behaviour is concerned with the actions of people—managers and operatives alike—in organizations. By focusing on individual- and group-level concepts, OB seeks to explain and predict behaviour. Because they get things done through other people, managers will be more effective leaders if they have an understanding of behaviour.

2. Attitudes are made up of three components. The cognitive component are the beliefs, opinions, knowledge, or information held by the person. The affective component is the emotional or feeling segment of the individual, and the behavioural component of an attitude is one's intention to behave in a certain manner toward someone or something.

3. People seek consistency among their attitudes and between their attitudes and their behaviour. They seek to reconcile divergent attitudes and align their attitudes and behaviour so they appear rational and consistent.

4. Cognitive dissonance, proposed by Leon Festinger in the late 1950s, explains the relationship between attitudes and behaviour. Cognitive dissonance refers to any incompatibility that an individual might perceive between two or more attitudes or between behaviour and attitudes.

5. Companies use attitude surveys to elicit responses from employees about how they feel about their jobs, work groups, supervisors, and/or the organization.

6. Six personality traits have been linked to organizational behaviour. These are locus of control, authoritarianism, Machiavellianism, self-esteem, self-monitoring, and risk propensity.

7. Holland identified six basic personality types and six sets of congruent occupations. He found that when individuals were properly matched with occupations that were congruent with their personality types, they experienced high satisfaction with their job and lower turnover rates.

8. Perception is the process of organizing and interpreting sensory impressions in order to give meaning to the environment. Several factors operate to shape and sometimes distort perceptions. These factors can reside in the perceiver, in the target being perceived, or in the context of the situation in which the perception is being made.

9. Attribution theory proposes that we judge people differently depending on whether we attribute their behaviour to internal or external causation. This determination, in turn, depends on three factors: distinctiveness, consensus, and consistency.

10. Managers can shape or mould employee behaviour by systematically reinforcing each successive step that moves the employee closer to the response desired by the manager.

Review and Discussion Questions

1. How is an organization like an iceberg? Use the "iceberg metaphor" to describe the field of organizational behaviour.
2. What are the three components of an attitude?
3. Clarify how individuals reconcile inconsistencies between attitudes and behaviours.
4. What are attitude surveys and how do they help managers?
5. What behavioural predictions might you make if you knew that an employee had (a) an external locus of control? (b) a low Mach score? (c) low self-esteem? (d) high self-monitoring tendencies?
6. How could you use personality traits to improve employee selection?
7. What factors do you think might create the fundamental attribution error?

Foundations of Behaviour

8. Name four different shortcuts used in judging others. What effect does each of these have on perception?
9. What is the self-serving bias?
10. What is social learning theory? What are its implications for managing people at work?

Self-Assessment Exercise

Who Controls Your Life?

Instructions: Read the following statement and indicate whether you agree more with choice A or choice B.

A	B	
1. Making a lot of money is largely a matter of getting the right breaks.	1. Promotions are earned through hard work and persistence.	_____
2. I have noticed that there is usually a direct connection between how hard I study and the grades I get.	2. Many times the reactions of teachers seem haphazard to me.	_____
3. The number of divorces indicates that more and more people are not trying to make their marriages work.	3. Marriage is largely a gamble.	_____
4. It is silly to think that one can really change another person's basic attitudes.	4. When I am right I can convince others.	_____
5. Getting promoted is really a matter of being a little luckier than the next person.	5. In our society a person's future earning power depends upon his or her ability.	_____
6. If one knows how to deal with people, they are really quite easily led.	6. I have little influence over the way other people behave.	_____
7. The grades I make are the result of my own efforts; luck has little or nothing to do with it.	7. Sometimes I feel that I have little to do with the grades I get.	_____
8. People like me can change the course of world affairs if we make ourselves heard.	8. It is only wishful thinking to believe that one can really influence what happens in our society at large.	_____
9. A great deal that happens to me is probably a matter of chance.	9. I am the master of my fate.	_____
10. Getting along with people is a skill that must be practised.	10. It is almost impossible to figure out how to please some people.	_____

Turn to page 414 for scoring directions and key.

Source: Adapted from Julian B. Rotter, "External Control and Internal Control," *Psychology Today,* June 1971, p. 42. Copyright 1971 by the American Psychological Association. Adapted with permission.

Class Exercise

Salary Increase Request[28]

Objectives:
1. To illustrate how perceptions can influence decisions.
2. To illustrate the effects of shortcuts used in evaluating others.

The Situation: You will be given a composite of an employee who is submitting a salary increase request for consideration. Your instructor will hand these out. You are to read this scenario and make a recommendation to HRM (either favourably or unfavourably) about the raise.

1. Divide yourselves into groups of five to seven and take the role of manager making the salary increase decision.
2. Each group should identify their perceptions about the employee, work habits, etc., in support of its decision.
3. Reassemble the class and hear each group's recommendations and explanations.

Key Terms

Key terms are listed in the order in which they appear in the chapter.

behaviour	attitude surveys	fundamental attribution error
organizational behaviour	personality	self-serving bias
attitudes	locus of control	selectivity
cognitive component of an attitude	authoritarianism	assumed similarity
affective component of an attitude	Machiavellianism	stereotyping
behavioural component of an attitude	self-esteem	halo effect
job satisfaction	self-monitoring	learning
job involvement	risk taking	operant conditioning
organizational commitment	perception	social learning theory
cognitive dissonance	attribution theory	shaping behaviour

Case Application

Binney & Smith (Canada)

Binney & Smith (Canada) operates a plant in Lindsay, Ontario, to produce crayons. Their brand name is Crayola, familiar to every pre-schooler and young grade-schooler in Canada. In 1992, the production goals for the Lindsay plant were doubled, to four million 16-stick boxes of assorted colour crayons. Little more than a year previously, the plant produced about a quarter of that volume. However, they are now working at new peaks, additional people have been hired, and the employees, most of whom have been with the company for at least ten years, are more excited about their jobs and more satisfied with their working lives than ever before.

Workers at Binney & Smith traditionally knew their own jobs well, and many of these jobs were repetitive and unchallenging. For instance, one job is to run the machine that glues labels to crayon sticks—172 labels per minute. Employees, like the label-gluing machine operator, were expert at their own jobs but knew little about the other jobs in the plant. Now they work in teams and are encouraged to learn the functions of the other workers in the team. Job rotation is common. Cross-training means that there is more flexibility in planning things like vacations. And teams are now responsible for solving problems. Involvement has spread to other areas and employees have devised charts for tracking production, made changes in the production layout that have solved quality problems, and developed recycling processes that are more cost-effective.

There are no monetary rewards or prizes for these changes, just recognition. And that's increased job satisfaction and self-esteem. Also, the plant more than doubled its profit in the first year of the new approach. It is now competitive in the North American environment, rather than labouring under a 15 to 25 per cent cost disadvantage to its U.S. sister plants.[29]

Questions

1. How does the Binney & Smith experience in its Lindsay plant compare with the satisfaction-productivity relationship research evidence presented in this chapter? Explain the differences and similarities.

2. Binney & Smith's turnover rate for staff is very low. Why? Shouldn't a plant with jobs as boring as gluing 172 labels a minute on crayon sticks have high absenteeism and turnover? What implications might your explanation have for managers in other businesses?

3. Why does the Binney & Smith formula for managing employees work?

Men and Women Working Together

Research into the differences between men and women shows that women are socialized to value affiliation and attachment, men to value power and competition. This difference has major consequences when they work together and try to understand one another. Deborah Tannen, who has studied the way men and women communicate (or don't communicate), says that men use talk to emphasize status and women use it to create communication. This discrepancy creates distinct cultures in the workplace.

The CIBC is trying to deal with the differences and difficulties and make the bank a place that both men and women find attractive to work in. Women occupy only 14 per cent of senior management positions in the bank, but hold more than 50 per cent of middle management jobs. Women managers interviewed at the bank state that they tend to find the environment blocks their ability to grow and to contribute at the level they feel they are capable of. They get turned off by the traditional male culture.

At a two-day seminar for 15 CIBC middle managers from across Ontario, the differences were highlighted in comments from the group. "Men don't listen." "Women take everything personally." When men say yes they mean "I agree with you"; when women say yes they mean "I'm following what you're saying." "Women use talking to focus thoughts; men get straight to the issues." Barbara Annis, a consultant working with the CIBC, notes that both men and women get angry and defensive about their positions, and it is this defensiveness that gets in the way of real communication. The truth is, she says, that both sides are right, but unless they can get beyond the aggression and defensiveness, they can't make any progress.

Deborah Tannen points out that women speak and hear a language of connection and intimacy; men speak and hear one of status and independence. For many men, conversations are primarily a means to preserve independence and maintain status in a hierarchical social order. For many women, conversations are negotiations for closeness in which people try to seek and give confirmation and support. For example, men frequently criticize women for talking about their problems; what's happening is that when men hear problems, they frequently assert their need for independence and control by providing solutions. Many women, however, view talking about a problem as a means to promote closeness. They present the problem to gain support and connection, not to get a man's advice.

Questions

1. "The fact that women have better honed senses, are less aggressive, and use communication to facilitate connection rather than competition tends to suggest they have superior qualities than men for managing in the 1990s." Agree or disagree? Support your position.
2. If managers can shape behaviour, how can organizations shape male and female behaviour so that men and women work more effectively together?
3. How can an understanding of perception improve the way women and men judge one another and react to one another?

Source: Deborah Tannen, *You Just Don't Understand: Women and Men in Conversation* (New York: Ballantine Books, 1991).

Video Resource: "Men/Women," *Venture* 480 (March 20, 1994).

11

Understanding Groups and Teams

Learning Objectives

WHAT WILL I BE ABLE TO DO AFTER I FINISH THIS CHAPTER?

1. Contrast formal and informal groups.
2. Explain why people join groups.
3. State how roles and norms influence an employee's behaviour.
4. Explain how norms affect group performance.
5. Describe how group size affects group behaviour.
6. Explain the increased popularity of work teams in organizations.
7. Describe the characteristics of effective teams.
8. Identify the obstacles that exist for creating effective teams.
9. Describe the role of teams in TQM.

Self-directed teams are one of the most powerful techniques for increasing productivity currently in use in Canada. Results show productivity increases of up to 30 percent in a variety of industries and organizations. But while the concept is being trumpeted as something brand new and innovative — a new 1990s approach — 3M was empowering people and teams in the 1920s!

In 3M they love to tell the story of Richard Drew and William McKnight. Drew, as a laboratory assistant in the early 1920s, came up with a type of adhesive tape which could be easily applied and removed, making it simpler for automobile manufacturers to paint cars without the paint running onto areas such as headlights, windshields, or other areas. 3M in the 1920s was principally a sandpaper manufacturer and William McKnight, Drew's boss, was unimpressed by the new idea. But Drew persisted and masking tape was born, the first in the family of Scotch brand tape products. When McKnight became president of 3M, he laid down the basic principle of self-directed teams and employee empowerment — employees were allowed to perform jobs their own way. A second basic principle of self-direction is that mistakes are acceptable, and as McKnight proclaimed, these mistakes will always tend to be less serious than those made by a management that undertakes to "tell those under its authority exactly how they must do their job."[1]

A clear application of the principle of self-direction is quality control. Most manufacturers in Canada used to have groups of people who fixed defective products which came off the production line. But that, of course, is the equivalent of doing the work twice, once to make it and once to fix it. It's a costly way to make things. Self-directed teams have responsibility over things like daily work routines, work assignments, ordering materials, training team members, checking quality, and maintaining equipment. They fix problems before they occur. And because they take responsibility for their output they don't need managers to tell them what to do.

In 3M, the philosophy of self-directed, empowered individuals and teams has made the company into one of the world's most innovative companies, manufacturing 60,000 products. One of these products is familiar to almost everyone: Post-It Notes, developed by a 3M researcher.

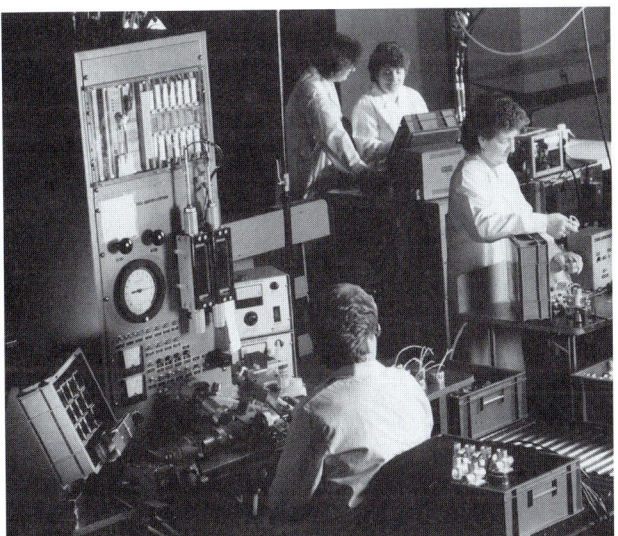

Workers at 3M have demonstrated the power of groups.

3M's organization is no longer unique. Thousands of organizations have recently made the move to restructure work around groups and teams and empowered individuals. Why has this occurred? What do these teams look like? How can interested managers build effective teams? We'll answer these questions in this chapter. First, however, let's begin by developing our understanding of group behaviour.

Understanding Group Behaviour

The behaviour of individuals in groups is not the same as the sum total of each individual's behaviour. This is because individuals act differently in groups than they do when they are alone. Therefore, if we want to understand organizational behaviour more fully, we need to study groups.

What Is a Group?

group
Two or more interacting and interdependent individuals who come together to achieve particular objectives.

A **group** is defined as two or more interacting and interdependent individuals who come together to achieve particular objectives. Groups can be either formal or informal. Formal groups are work groups established by the organization and have designated work assignments and established tasks. In formal groups, the behaviours in which one should engage are stipulated by and directed toward organizational goals. Exhibit 11-1 provides some examples of different types of formal groups used in organizations today.

In contrast, informal groups are of a social nature. These groups are natural formations that appear in the work environment in response to the need for social contact. Informal groups tend to form around friendships and common interests.

Why Do People Join Groups?

There is no single reason why individuals join groups. Because most people belong to a number of groups, it's obvious that different groups provide different benefits to their members. Most people, then, join a group out of needs for security, status, self-esteem, affiliation, power, or goal achievement.

Security reflects a strength in numbers. By joining a group, individuals can reduce the insecurity of "standing alone," which results in feeling stronger, having fewer self-doubts, and being more resistant to threats. Status indicates a prestige that comes from belonging to a particular group. Inclusion in a group that others view as important provides recognition and status for its members. Self-esteem conveys people's feelings of self-worth. That is, in addition to conveying status to those outside the group, membership can also raise feelings of self-esteem—being accepted into a highly valued group.

Affiliation with groups can fulfil one's social needs. People enjoy the regular inter-

Command Groups	These are the basic, traditional work groups determined by formal authority relationships and depicted on the organizational chart. They typically include a manager and those subordinates who report directly to him or her.
Cross-functional Teams	These bring together the knowledge and skills of individuals from various work areas in order to come up with solutions to operational problems. Cross-functional teams also include groups whose members have been trained to do each other's jobs.
Self-managed Teams	These are essentially independent groups that, in addition to doing their operating jobs, take on traditional management responsibilities such as hiring, planning and scheduling, and performance evaluations.
Task Forces	These are temporary groups created to accomplish a specific task. Once the task is complete, the group is disbanded.

Exhibit 11-1 Examples of Formal Groups

Understanding Groups and Teams

action that comes with group membership. For many people, these on-the-job interactions are their primary means of fulfilling their need for affiliation. For almost all people, work groups significantly contribute to fulfilling their need for friendships and social relations. One of the appealing aspects of groups is that they represent power. What often cannot be achieved individually becomes possible through group action. Of course, this power might not be sought only to make demands on others. It might be desired merely as a countermeasure. To protect themselves from unreasonable demands by management, individuals may align with others. Informal groups additionally provide opportunities for individuals to exercise power over others. For individuals who desire to influence others, groups can offer power without a formal position of authority in the organization. As a group leader, you might be able to make requests of group members and obtain compliance without any of the responsibilities that traditionally go with formal managerial positions. For people with a high power need, groups can be a vehicle for fulfilment. Finally, people may join a group for goal achievement. There are times when it takes more than one person to accomplish a particular task; there is a need to pool talents, knowledge, or power in order to get a job completed. In such instances, management will rely on the use of a formal group.

Employees participate on the company's softball team. This group helps meet members' needs for affiliation. When the team wins, it also enhances members' status and self-esteem.

What Are the Basic Concepts for Understanding Group Behaviours?

The basic foundation for understanding group behaviour includes roles, norms and conformity, status systems, and group cohesiveness. Let's take a closer look at each of these concepts.

What Are Roles? We introduced the concept of roles in Chapter 1 when we discussed what managers do. Of course, managers are not the only individuals in an organization who have roles. The concept of roles applies to all employees in organizations and to their life outside the organization as well.

A **role** refers to a set of expected behaviour patterns attributed to someone who occupies a given position in a social unit. Individuals play multiple roles, adjusting their roles to the group to which they belong at the time. In an organization, employees attempt to determine what behaviours are expected of them. They'll read their job descriptions, get suggestions from their boss, and watch what their coworkers do. An individual who is confronted by divergent role expectations experiences role conflict. Employees in organizations often face such role conflicts. The credit manager expects

role
A set of behaviour patterns expected of someone occupying a given position in a social unit.

her credit analysts to process a minimum of thirty applications a week, but the work group pressures members to restrict output to twenty applications a week so that everyone has work to do and no one gets laid off. A young college instructor's colleagues want him to give out very few high grades in order to maintain the department's "tough standards" reputation, whereas students want him to give out lots of high grades to enhance their grade point averages. To the degree that the instructor sincerely seeks to satisfy the expectations of both his colleagues and his students, he faces role conflict.

How Do Norms and Conformity Affect Group Behaviour? All groups have established **norms,** or acceptable standards that are shared by the group's members. Norms dictate things like output levels, absenteeism rates, promptness or tardiness, and the amount of socializing allowed on the job.

norms
Acceptable standards shared by a group's members.

Norms, for example, dictate the "dress code" among customer service representatives at one national health insurance company. Most workers who have little face-to-face customer contact come to work dressed very casually. However, on occasion, a newly hired employee will come to work the first few days dressed up in a suit. Those who do are often teased and pressured until their dress conforms to the group's standard.

Although each group will have its own unique set of norms, there are common classes of norms that appear in most organizations. These focus on effort and performance, dress, and loyalty.

Students behave differently in class on Monday than they do when they attend a sporting event on Saturday afternoon. They understand that role expectations in college classes differ from those at sporting events.

Probably the most widespread norms relate to levels of effort and performance. Work groups typically provide their members with very explicit cues on how hard to work, what level of output to have, when to look busy, when it's acceptable to goof off, and the like. These norms are extremely powerful in affecting an individual employee's performance. They are so powerful that performance predictions that are based solely on an employee's ability and level of personal motivation often prove to be wrong.

Some organizations have formal dress codes. However, even in their absence, norms frequently develop to dictate the kind of clothing that should be worn to work. College seniors, interviewing for their first postgraduate job, pick up this norm quickly. Every spring on college campuses throughout the country, those interviewing for jobs can usually be spotted—they're the ones walking around in the dark gray or blue pinstriped suits. They are enacting the dress norms they have learned are expected in professional positions. Of course, what connotes acceptable dress in one organization may be very different from another.

Few managers appreciate employees who ridicule the organization. Similarly, professional employees and those in the executive ranks recognize that most employers view those who actively look for another job unfavourably. If such people are unhappy, they know to keep their job searches secret. These examples demonstrate that loyalty norms are widespread in organizations. This concern for demonstrating loyalty, by the way, often explains why ambitious aspirants to top management positions in an organization willingly take work home at night, come in on weekends, and accept transfers to cities where they would otherwise not prefer to live.

Because individuals desire acceptance by the groups to which they belong, they are susceptible to conformity pressures. The impact that group pressures for conformity can have on an individual member's judgment and attitudes was demonstrated in the now-classic studies by Solomon Asch[2] (see Details on a Management Classic). Asch's results suggest that there are group norms that press us toward conformity. We desire

Understanding Groups and Teams

to be one of the group and avoid being visibly different. We can generalize this finding further to say that when an individual's opinion of objective data differs significantly from that of others in the group, he or she feels extensive pressure to align his or her opinion to conform with those of the others.

Details on a Management Classic

SOLOMON ASCH AND GROUP CONFORMITY

Does one's desire to be accepted as part of a group leave him or her susceptible to conforming to the groups's norms? Will the group place strong enough pressure to change a member's attitude and behaviour? In the research by Solomon Asch, the answer appears to be yes.

Asch's study involved groups of seven or eight people who sat in a classroom and were asked to compare two cards held by an investigator. One card had one line, the other had three lines of varying length. As shown in Exhibit MC11-1, one of the lines on the three-line card was identical to the line on the one-line card. Also, as shown in MC11-1, the difference in line length was quite obvious; under ordinary conditions, subjects made less than 1 per cent errors. The object was to announce aloud which of the three lines matched the single line. But, what happens if all the members in the group begin to give incorrect answers? Will the pressures to conform result in the unsuspecting subject (USS) altering his or her answers to align with the others? That was what Asch wanted to know. So he arranged the group so only the USS was unaware that the experiment was "fixed." The seating was prearranged so that the USS was the last to announce his or her decision.

The experiment began with two sets of matching exercises. All the subjects gave the right answers. On the third set, however, the first subject gave an obviously wrong answer—for example, saying "C" in Exhibit MC11-1. The next subject gave the same wrong answer, and so did the others until it got to the unsuspecting subject. He knew "B" was the same as "X," yet everyone had said "C." The decision confronting the USS was this: Do you state a perception publicly that differs from the preannounced position of the others? Or do you give an answer that you strongly believe is incorrect in order to have your response agree with the other group members? The results obtained by Asch demonstrated that over many experiments and many trials, subjects conformed in about 35 per cent of the trials. That is, the subjects gave answers that they knew were wrong but that were consistent with the replies of other group members.

For managers, the Asch study provides considerable insight into group behaviours. The tendency, as Asch has shown, is for individual members to go along with the "pack." To diminish the negative aspects of conformity, however, it becomes necessary for managers to create a climate of openness where employees are free to discuss problems without fear of retaliation. ▼

 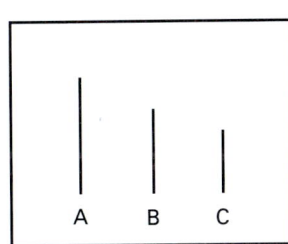

Exhibit MC11-1 Examples of Cards Used in the Asch Study

status
A prestige grading, position, or rank within a group.

What Is Status and Why Is It Important? **Status** is a prestige grading, position, or rank within a group. As far back as scientists have been able to trace human groupings, they have found status hierarchies: tribal chiefs and their followers, nobles and peasants, the haves and the have-nots. Status systems are an important factor in understanding behaviour. Status is a significant motivator and has behavioural consequences when individuals see a disparity between what they perceive their status to be and what others perceive it to be.

Status may be informally conferred by characteristics such as education, age, skill, or experience. Anything can have status value if others in the group evaluate it as such. Of course, just because status is informal does not mean that it is less important or that there is less agreement on who has it or who does not. Members of groups have no problem placing people into status categories, and they usually agree closely about who is high, low, and in the middle.

It is important for employees to believe that the organization's formal status system is congruent. That is, there should be equity between the perceived ranking of an individual and the status "symbols" he or she is given by the organization. For instance, incongruence may occur when a supervisor is earning less than his or her employees or when a desirable office is occupied by a lower-ranking individual. In such cases, employees may view this as a disruption to the general pattern of order and consistency in the organization.

Does Group Size Affect Group Behaviour? The size of a group has an effect on the group's behaviour. However, that effect depends on what criteria you are looking at.[3]

The evidence indicates, for instance, that small groups are faster at completing tasks than are larger ones. However, if the group is engaged in problem solving, large groups consistently get better marks than their smaller counterparts. Translating these results into specific numbers is a bit more hazardous, but we can offer some parameters. Large groups—with a dozen or more members—are good for gaining diverse input. Thus, if the goal of the group is finding facts, larger groups should be more effective. On the other

A senior manager's office conveys the high status of the position. That is, this office tells whoever visits that this individual has power in the organization.

Understanding Groups and Teams

hand, smaller groups are better at doing something productive with those facts. Groups of approximately five to seven members tend to be more effective for taking action.

One of the more disturbing findings related to group size is that, as groups get incrementally larger, the contribution of individual members often tends to lessen.[4] That is, while the total productivity of a group of four is generally greater than that of a group of three, the individual productivity of each group member declines as the group expands. Thus, a group of four will tend to produce at a level less than four times the average individual performance. The best explanation for this reduction of effort in groups is that dispersion of responsibility encourages individuals to slack off. When the results of the group cannot be attributed to any single person, the relationship between an individual's input and the group's output is clouded. In such situations, individuals may be tempted to become "free riders" and coast on the group's efforts. In other words, there will be a reduction in efficiency where individuals think that their contributions cannot be measured. The obvious conclusion from this finding is that when managers use work teams they should also provide means by which individual efforts can be identified.

When a group's attitude aligns with its formal goals, the more cohesive and productive the group will be.

Are Cohesive Groups More Effective? Intuitively, it makes sense that groups in which there is a lot of internal disagreement and lack of cooperation are less effective in completing their tasks than groups in which individuals generally agree, cooperate, and like each other. Research on this position has focused on group cohesiveness, or the degree to which members are attracted to one another and share the group's goals. The more the members are attracted to one another and the more the group's goals align with their individual goals, the greater the group's cohesiveness.

Research has generally shown that highly cohesive groups are more effective than those with less cohesiveness,[5] but the relationship between cohesiveness and effectiveness is more complex. A key moderating variable is the degree to which the group's attitude aligns with its formal goals or those of the larger organization of which it is a part.[6] The more cohesive a group is, the more its members will follow its goals. If these goals are favorable (for instance, high output, quality work, cooperation with individuals outside the group), a cohesive group is more productive than a less cohesive group. But if cohesiveness is high and attitudes are unfavorable, productivity decreases. If cohesiveness is low and goals are supported, productivity increases but not as much as when both cohesiveness and support are high. When cohesiveness is low and goals are not supported, cohesiveness has no significant effect upon productivity. These conclusions are summarized in Exhibit 11-2.

Building Real Teams

Teams are increasingly becoming the leading means around which work is being designed. Why? Because teams typically outperform individuals when the tasks being done require multiple skills, judgment, and experience. As organizations restructure

Exhibit 11-2 The Relationship Between Cohesiveness and Productivity

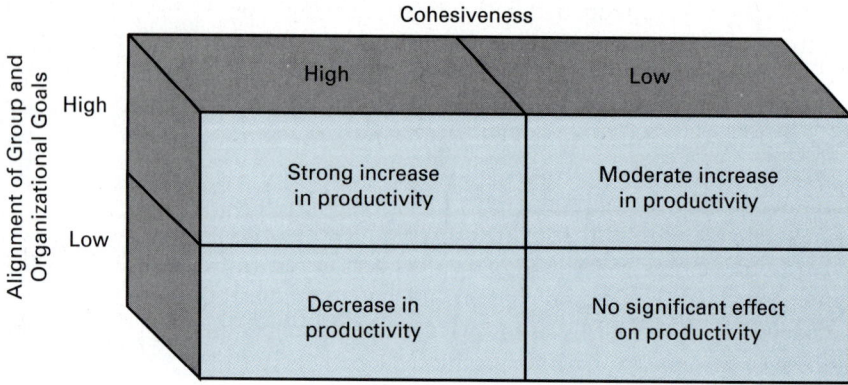

themselves to compete more effectively and efficiently, they are turning to teams as a way to better utilize employee talents. Teams are more flexible and thus more responsive to a changing environment than bureaucratic groupings of employees. They also can be quickly assembled, deployed, refocused, and disbanded.

What Are Work Teams?

work teams
Formal groups made up of interdependent individuals, responsible for the attainment of a goal.

Work teams are formal groups, made up of interdependent individuals, responsible for the attainment of a goal.[7] Teams tend to fall into one of three categories based on their objectives. Some organizations use teams to provide advice. For instance, a team may be assembled to recommend ways to cut costs, improve quality, or select a new piece of machinery (see Managers Who Made a Difference). Some teams manage. They exist at various levels to run things. For example, Thermos created a team to manage the development of a "customer-oriented, environmentally friendly" electric grill.[8] And finally, teams are created to make or do things. These would include production teams, design teams, and office teams that handle administrative work.

In this section, we'll discuss why organizations are increasingly designing work around teams rather than individuals and consider the various characteristics that are associated with effective work teams.

Managers Who Made a Difference

KEN BALL AT IMPERIAL OIL

Imperial Oil's refinery in Dartmouth, Nova Scotia is small by North American standards, but medium-sized by Canadian standards, with a capacity of 86,000 barrels a day. In terms of performance, in 1991 it ranked among the lowest 25 per cent of the 116 refineries in North America. Its energy, maintenance, and people costs were well

Understanding Groups and Teams

out of line with industry standards. Imperial Oil considered closing down the refinery, but Ken Ball, the refinery manager, had other ideas. He presented a plan to head office in January 1992 that was accepted with the understanding that he had until the end of the year to make it work or the shutdown would proceed.

Ball's analysis of the situation showed that the main problems rested with the people rather than the technology or equipment. Over time the refinery had spawned little empires that insulated themselves from one another. Job descriptions were important—people tended to do what their job descriptions said and little outside them. There was almost no crossing of functional boundaries. For instance, it was difficult to get a pipefitter to help a mechanic without the approval of up to four levels of supervision. The boundaries between units made cooperative effort both very costly and very time- and energy-consuming.

Ken Ball created four main business teams to tackle the problem—first-stage conversion, upgrading, oil movement and storage, and maintenance support. Each business team was responsible for a large segment of the refinery's operation, whereas before, each of these main operations was managed by a wide cross-section of workers from a variety of skills and trades, all reporting to their own supervisors and managers in different departments. Now, everyone in a business team, composed of about forty to fifty people, worked under the overall management of the team leader.

Ball disbanded the refinery's joint industrial council, which had managed the relations between management and workers, and substituted a system where worker concerns were handled one-to-one with business team leaders. Where once seniority was the major criterion for promotion or protection from layoff, an individual's performance record now became the criterion. The workforce was cut back from 330 employees to 235 with cuts to both contract work and overtime. The employees' reactions to the changes were seen in two attempts at union certification, one before the joint industrial council was disbanded and the other afterwards. In both cases, employees voted down the certification by a majority of 60 per cent.

The refinery managed to cut its costs by 30 per cent and rose to the top 20 to 25 per cent of North American refineries in terms of performance. Communication is much better; employees receive a monthly bulletin that breaks down costs and performance. They have developed innovative ways to solve problems. For instance, a brain storming session developed a better way to use the on-line quality monitoring system. And where once there were thirty workers on the docks, now there are twelve. And when a tanker docks, other workers and supervisors who have been trained are summoned from the plant to help.[9] ▼

Why Use Teams?

There's no single explanation for the recent increased popularity of teams. We propose, however, that there are a number of reasons: worker morale, strategic flow, quicker decisions, workforce diversity, and better performance.

Team members expect and demand a lot from each other. In so doing, they facilitate cooperation and improve employee morale. So we find that team norms tend to encourage members to excel and, at the same time, create a climate that increases job satisfaction. The use of teams, especially self-managed ones, frees up managers to do more strategic planning. When jobs are designed around individuals, managers often spend an inordinate amount of their time supervising their people and "putting out fires." They're too busy to do much strategic thinking. Implementing work teams allows managers to redirect their energy toward bigger issues such as long-term plans. Moving decision making vertically down to teams allows the organization greater flexibility for faster decisions. Team members frequently know more about work-related problems than do managers. Moreover, team members are closer to those problems. As a result, decisions are often made more quickly when teams exist than when jobs are designed around individuals. Groups made up of individuals from different backgrounds and with different experiences often see things that homogeneous groups don't. Therefore, the use of diverse teams may result in more innovative ideas and better decisions than might arise if individuals alone made the decisions. Finally, all of the above factors can combine to make team performance higher than might be achieved by the same individuals working alone.

What Common Characteristics Exist in Effective Teams?

Teams are not automatic productivity enhancers. They can also be disappointments for management. Fortunately, recent research provides insight into the primary characteristics related to effective teams.[10] Let's take a look at these characteristics as summarized in Exhibit 11-3.

High-performance teams have both a clear understanding of the goal to be achieved and a belief that the goal embodies a worthwhile or important result. Moreover, the importance of these goals encourages individuals to sublimate personal concerns to

**Exhibit 11-3
Characteristics of
Effective Teams**

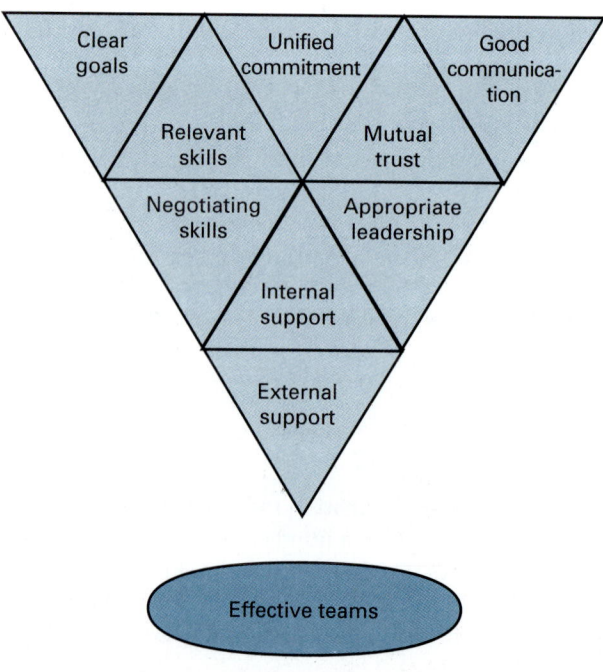

Developing Management Skills

BUILDING TRUST AMONG TEAM MEMBERS[11]

▶ **1. Communicate with team members.** Keep team members and others informed by explaining decisions and policies and providing accurate feedback. Be candid about your own problems and limitations.

▶ **2. Be supportive of team members and their efforts.** Be available and approachable. Encourage and support team members' ideas.

▶ **3. Be respectful of team members' capabilities.** Delegate real authority to team members and listen to their ideas.

▶ **4. Be fair, equitable, and consistent.** Give credit where it's due, be objective and impartial in performance evaluations, and be generous with your praise.

▶ **5. Be predictable.** Be consistent in your daily affairs. Make good on your explicit and implied promises.

▶ **6. Demonstrate competence.** Develop the admiration and respect of team members by demonstrating technical and professional ability and good business sense.

---

these team goals. In effective teams, members are committed to the team's goals, know what they are expected to accomplish, and understand how they will work together to achieve these goals. Effective teams are composed of competent individuals. They have the necessary technical skills and abilities to achieve the desired goals and the personal characteristics required to achieve excellence while working well with others. This second point is important and often overlooked. Not everyone who is technically competent has the skills to work well as a team member. High-performing teams have members who possess both technical and interpersonal skills.

Effective teams are characterized by high mutual trust among members. That is, members believe in the integrity, character, and ability of one another. But as you probably know from personal relationships, trust is fragile. It takes a long time to build and can be easily destroyed. The climate of trust within a group tends to be strongly influenced by the organization's culture and the actions of management. Organizations that value openness, honesty, and collaborative processes and that additionally encourage employee involvement and autonomy are likely to create trusting cultures (see Developing Management Skills).

Members of an effective team exhibit intense loyalty and dedication to the team. They're willing to do anything that has to be done to help their team succeed. We call this loyalty and dedication unified commitment. Studies of successful teams have found that members identify with their teams.[12] Members redefine themselves to include membership in the team as an important aspect of the self. Unified commitment, then, is characterized by dedication to the team's goals and a willingness to expend extraordinary amounts of energy to achieve it.

Not surprisingly, effective teams are characterized by good communication. Members can convey messages between each other in a form that is readily and clearly understood. This includes nonverbal as well as spoken messages. Good communication is also characterized by a healthy dose of feedback from team members and management. This helps to guide team members and to correct misunderstandings. Like a couple who have been together for many years, members on high-performing teams are able to quickly and efficiently share ideas and feelings.

When jobs are designed around individuals, job descriptions, rules and procedures,

Supervisors of these Saturn employees give their workers the responsibility to share in decision making—deciding on everything from hiring coworkers to buying equipment. Supervisors intervene only when needed and when asked by the group.

and other types of formalized documentation clarify employee roles. Effective teams, on the other hand, tend to be flexible and continually making adjustments. This requires team members to possess adequate negotiating skills. Problems and relationships are regularly changing in teams, requiring members to confront and reconcile differences.

Effective leaders can motivate a team to follow them through the most difficult situations. How? Leaders help clarify goals. They demonstrate that change is possible by overcoming inertia. And they increase the self-confidence of team members, helping members to realize their potential more fully. Importantly, the best leaders are not necessarily directive or controlling. Increasingly, effective team leaders are taking the role of coach and facilitator. They help guide and support the team, but they don't control it. This obviously applies to self-managed teams but also increasingly applies to task forces and cross-functional teams in which the members themselves are empowered. For some traditional managers, changing their role from boss to facilitator—from giving orders to working for the team—is a difficult transition. While most managers relish the new-found shared authority or come to understand its advantages through leadership training, some hard-nosed dictatorial managers are just ill-suited to the team concept and must be transferred or replaced.

The final condition necessary to making an effective team is a supportive climate. Internally, the team should be provided with a sound infrastructure. This includes proper training, an understandable measurement system with which team members can evaluate their overall performance, an incentive program that recognizes and rewards team activities, and a supportive human resource system. The right infrastructure should support members and reinforce behaviours that lead to high levels of performance. Externally, management should provide the team with the resources needed to get the job done.

What Challenges Do Teams Present for Managers?

The idea of using teams to enhance productivity is nothing new for management. Teams have long been popular in Japan. When Canadian managers began to broadly introduce them in the late 1980s, critics warned that they were destined to fail. Why? Recall our discussion of culture in Chapter 2. Specifically, Japan could be classified as a collective society—where the "good of the whole" is dominant. Canadian culture, on the other hand, is based on individualism—taking care of oneself and one's immediate family. This led many observers to believe that Canadian workers would not diminish their needs for individual responsibility and recognition in order to be an anonymous part of a team. While the introduction of work teams in some organizations has met with resistance and disappointments, the overall picture has been encouraging. When teams are properly used in organizations and when the organization's culture is consistent with a team approach, results have been positive.

Let's look at these obstacles that may exist and review some suggestions for overcoming them.

What Can Block Team Effectiveness? Any time two or more people are brought together, there is a tendency for problems to arise. Teams are no exceptions (see Ethical Dilemmas in Management)! As managers, we must understand what may cause team effectiveness to decrease—blocking our team from becoming a high performer. These barriers can be found in a weak sense of direction, lack of organizational support, infighting, and lack of trust.

Teams perform poorly when they have a weak sense of direction. Nothing will undermine the enthusiasm for the team concept as quickly as the frustration of being on a team where the purpose, goals, or approach are unclear. Teams exist within the larger organization. They rely on that organization for a variety of resources—people, money, and equipment. If those resources are lacking or insufficient, it will be difficult for teams to reach their objectives.

Team effectiveness will also decrease when there is an inordinate amount of infighting. For teams to be effective, all members do not have to like each other. Rather, team members must be willing to put aside petty differences in order to reach their goals. Closely aligned with infighting is lack of trust. Where there is trust, team members believe in the integrity, character, and ability of one another. When trust is lacking, members are unable to depend on each other. Consequently, such teams are typically short-lived.

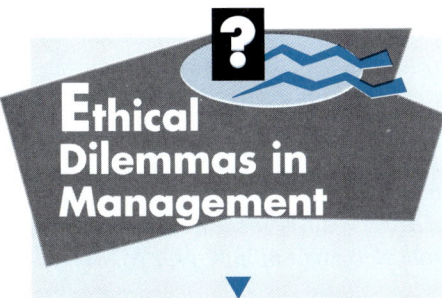

Ethical Dilemmas in Management

▼ SHOULD MANAGERS AGREE WITH THEIR BOSS WHEN THEY DON'T? ▲

Asch's studies looked at how group norms press individuals toward conformity. This suggests an ethical dilemma that many managers face: whether it is ethical to outwardly agree with their boss when, in actuality, they think he or she is wrong.

Are managers who disagree with their boss acting unethically by claiming to agree? Are they compromising personal standards of integrity? Would it be unethical merely to suppress their disagreement? Open agreement may be the politically astute thing to do, but does it display a lack of moral character?

The norms of conformity can be very strong in an organization. Individuals who openly challenge long-condoned but questionable practices may be labelled as disloyal or lacking in commitment. Another perspective is that conformance with group and organizational norms acts to bond people together. Conformity facilitates cooperation and cohesiveness. It also contributes toward standardizing behaviour. These are qualities that can enhance organizational effectiveness. Still another argument might be that suppression of dissent and the appearance of conformity doesn't improve organizational effectiveness; it merely plants the seeds for later hostilities and conflicts.

What should a manager do when he or she disagrees with the boss? What can organizations do to avoid encouraging individuals from unethically conforming while, at the same time, maintaining cohesiveness and commitment?

TO OVERCOME OBSTACLES	HOW IT AFFECTS TEAMS
Create a clear purpose and goals	High-performance teams have both a clear understanding of the goals to be achieved and a belief that each goal embodies a worthwhile or important result.
Provide the necessary resources	Without necessary resources, achieving team goals is, at best, a hit-or-miss proposition. Skilful team managers will influence decision makers to provide the necessary resources.
Build mutual trust	Mutual trust creates an environment that is conducive to high-performing teams. This includes open communications, respect for team members, fair and equitable treatment, consistency in actions, follow through on promises made, and training team members in problem-solving, communication, negotiation, conflict resolution, and group-processing skills.
Change the team's membership	Rotating team members, when team problems arise, may result in the meshing of different personalities, and better complements of skills.

Exhibit 11-4 Overcoming Obstacles to Effective Teams

How Can a Manager Overcome the Obstacles to Team Effectiveness? There are a number of things managers can do to overcome the obstacles mentioned and help their teams to reach their full potential (see Exhibit 11-4).

High-performance teams have both a clear understanding of their purpose and goals and a belief that each goal embodies a worthwhile or important result. The team must understand and believe in its mission. This mission must then be translated into specific, measurable, and realistic performance goals. In effective teams, members are committed to the team's goals, know what they are expected to accomplish, and understand how they will work together to achieve these goals.

Managers of teams need to accept the responsibility of ensuring their teams are provided with the necessary organizational resources. They must prepare their case and present it to key decision makers in the organization for tools, equipment, training, personnel, physical space, or other resources that the team needs.

Managers must also recognize that team trust is fragile. As such, they must create an environment that builds and supports mutual trust. This is accomplished by providing continuous feedback, respecting team members, being fair and objective in the

These Ford Motor employees work together toward enhancing quality at this Oakville, Ontario, plant. Through their involvement and teamwork, they are dramatically improving the productive quality of the company.

treatment of the team, and holding team members accountable at both the individual and group level. Furthermore, these managers recognize that team trust and cohesiveness is not formulated overnight. Rather it is a function of time together. Consequently, effective team managers ensure that members experience team-building training.

Finally, one must recognize that at times, teams do get bogged down and some individuals just cannot work with others. In some cases, this may be the result of an incorrect mix of the technical, problem solving, or interpersonal skills that group members bring to the team. In these cases, change the team's membership. Rotating some team members may result in a "reformed" team that has a better complement of skills.

Teams and TQM

One of the central characteristics of total quality management is the use of teams. But why teams? The essence of TQM is process improvement, and employee participation is the linchpin of process improvement. In other words, TQM requires management to give employees the encouragement to share ideas and act on what they suggest. Problem-solving teams provide the natural vehicle for employees to share ideas and to implement improvements. As stated by Gil Mosard, a TQM specialist at McDonnell Douglas: "When your measurement system tells you your process is out of control, you need teamwork for structured problem-solving. Not everyone needs to know how to do all kinds of fancy control charts for performance tracking, but everybody does need to know where their process stands so they can judge if it is improving."[13]

Ford began its TQM efforts in the early 1980s with teams as the primary organizing mechanism. "Because this business is so complex, you can't make an impact on it without using a team approach," noted one Ford manager. In designing their quality problem-solving teams, Ford's management identified five goals. The teams should (1) be small enough to be efficient and effective; (2) be properly trained in the skills their members will need; (3) be allocated enough time to work on the problems they plan to address; (4) be given the authority to resolve the problems and implement corrective action; and (5) each have a designated "champion" whose job it is to help the team get around roadblocks that arise.

Consumers Packaging's glass container plant in Bramalea was a chronic underperformer in the late 1980s. Nearly all of its operations needed improvement so the company set up twelve teams called "communication teams" to solve problems. Each of the teams is free to set its own agenda, but it must find ways to improve the plant's performance in relation to eight performance indicators set down by management. These indicators include, among other things, measures of productivity, profitability, and even absenteeism.

Another team application to TQM is **quality circles.** These are work groups of eight to ten employees and supervisors who share an area of responsibility. They meet regularly (typically once a week on company time and on company premises) to discuss their quality problems, investigate causes of the problems, recommend solutions, and take corrective actions. They assume responsibility for solving quality problems, and they generate and evaluate their own feedback. However, management usually makes the final decision about the implementation of recommended solutions. Exhibit 11-5 describes a typical quality circle process.

quality circles
Work groups that meet regularly to discuss, investigate, and correct quality problems.

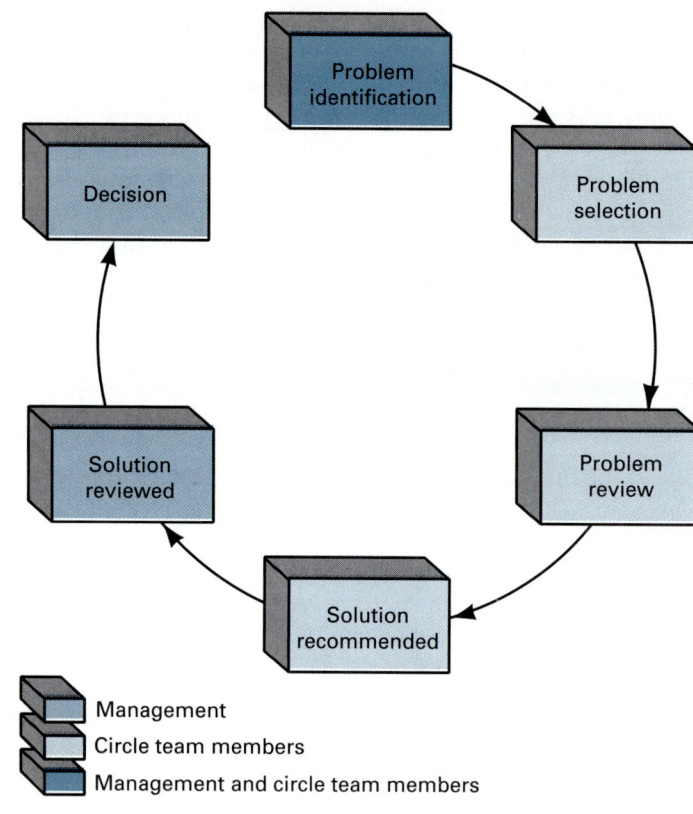

Exhibit 11-5 How a Typical Quality Circle Operates

Summary

This Summary is organized by the chapter opening learning objectives found on page 248.

1. Formal groups are defined by the organization's structure, with designated work assignments establishing tasks. Informal groups are social alliances that are neither structured nor organizationally determined.
2. People join groups because of their needs for security, status, self-esteem, affiliation, power, or goal achievement.
3. A role refers to a set of behaviour patterns expected of someone occupying a given position in a social unit. At any given time, employees adjust their role behaviours to the group of which they are a part. Norms are standards shared by group members. They informally convey to employees which behaviours are acceptable and which are unacceptable.
4. Norms relate to levels of effort and performance in several ways. Work groups typically provide their members with very explicit cues on how hard to work, what level of output to have, when to look busy, when it's acceptable to goof off, and the like.
5. Group size affects group behaviour in various ways. Smaller groups are faster at completing tasks than larger ones. However, larger groups are better for fact finding.
6. Teams have become increasingly popular in organizations because they build esprit de corps, free up

management to think more strategically, permit faster decision making, facilitate workforce diversity, and usually increase performance.
7. Effective work teams are characterized by clear goals, members with relevant skills, mutual trust among members, unified commitment, good communication, adequate negotiating skills, and appropriate leadership.
8. Obstacles for creating effective work teams can be viewed from several perspectives. These can be a weak sense of direction, a lack of resources, infighting among team members, and a lack of members' trust.
9. Problem-solving teams provide a natural vehicle for employees to share ideas and to implement improvements as part of the TQM process. Teams are particularly effective for resolving complex problems.

Review and Discussion Questions

1. How can joining a group increase an individual's sense of power?
2. How might organizations create role conflicts for an employee?
3. Identify five roles you play. What behaviours do they require? Are any of these roles in conflict? If so, in what way? How do you resolve these conflicts?
4. What is the relationship between a work group and the organization of which it is a part?
5. What is the most effective size for a group?
6. What is the relationship between group cohesiveness and effectiveness?
7. Why are some groups more successful than others?
8. When might individuals, acting independently, outperform teams in an organization?
9. How do you explain the rapidly increasing popularity of work teams in Canada when our culture places such high value on individualism?
10. In what ways can the obstacles to effective teams be overcome?
11. How do you think scientific management theorists would react to the increased reliance on teams in organizations? How about the behavioural science theorists?

Self-Assessment Exercise

How Trustworthy Are You?

Answer these eight questions using the following scale:

Strongly Disagree									Strongly Agree
1	2	3	4	5	6	7	8	9	10

1. People can expect me to play fair. ____
2. People can confide in me and know that I will listen. ____
3. People can expect me to tell the truth. ____
4. People know that I would never intentionally misrepresent their points of view to others. ____
5. People can confide in me and know that I will not discuss it with others. ____
6. People know that if I promised to do them a favour, I would carry out that promise. ____
7. If I had an appointment with someone, he or she could count on me showing up. ____
8. If I borrowed money from someone, he or she could count on getting it back as soon as possible. ____

Total score = ____

Turn to page 415 for scoring directions and key.

Source: Based on Cynthia Johnson-George and Walter C. Swap, "Measurement of Specific Interpersonal Trust: Construction and Validation of a Scale to Assess Trust in a Specific Other," *Journal of Personality and Social Psychology,* December 1982, pp. 1306–17.

Class Exercise

Building an Airplane

Step 1: Get into groups of five to seven people.

Step 2: Each group will be given a piece of poster paper, a pair of scissors, a box of paper clips, a roll of tape, and a magic marker.

Step 3: You have thirty minutes to design, manufacture, and assemble your airplane.

Step 4: At the end of the assembly process, your instructor will take you to a safe place to fly the planes. You have one throw. The winner will be determined from which group's plane flies the farthest; second place, the second farthest; and so on.

Step 5: After rankings have been determined, return to your classroom, and in your group, discuss the following:

   a. How much did each group member contribute to the design, manufacture, and assembly of the plane?

   b. Was there a group leader? If so, how did that person become the leader?

   c. Were you able to express yourself freely, especially if you disagreed with the majority of the group?

   d. Using the information from the text on pages 261-62, describe what barriers your group encountered. How did the group attempt to overcome these?

Step 6: Assembling as a large group, discuss your responses to Step 5 above.

Source: This exercise was directly influenced by P.L. Hunsaker's and J.S. Hunsaker's "The Paper Towel Exercise: Experiencing Leadership and Group Dynamics," published in Stephen P. Robbins, *Organizational Behavior: Concepts, Controversies, and Applications* (Englewood Cliffs, N.J.: Prentice-Hall, Inc., 1993), p. 318.

Key Terms

Key terms are listed in the order in which they appear in the chapter.

group   role   norms   status   work teams   quality circles

Case Application

Ford Electronics Manufacturing

Ford Electronics Manufacturing has taken a team approach to management. It makes electronic parts for vehicles—for instance, the units that control dashboard displays, temperature systems, monitoring systems, and safety systems such as air bags. Teams of seven to twenty employees are responsible for a specific product line. Every worker belongs to at least one team.

Workers plan everything from work schedules and production schedules to the introduction of innovations. Most of the work is done by computer-controlled machines and robots. Each day, the plant assembles some four million components and solders nine million joints to make 35,000 circuit boards. The work is exacting and the increasing speed with which it has been accomplished has been attributed to the work of teams. The time it takes to make a typical control unit has dropped from twelve days in 1988 to half a day in 1992. Inventory has been cut by 50 per cent. And production costs have fallen by between 5 and 8 per cent per year since 1988.

The union, the International Machinists and Aerospace Workers Union, representing 1,000 workers, mainly women, has supported the move toward teams because workers have felt good about sharing control over their work and about their accomplishments.[14]

Questions

1. If you were on one of these teams, do you think it would increase or decrease your job satisfaction? Why? Do you think you'd be more productive as a team member than as part of a functional department? Explain.

2. "Here's a classic example of management responding to the latest fad. Assembly operations have always worked well when organized by functional departments. The kind of work they do doesn't require, nor is it likely to benefit by, the use of teams." Do you agree or disagree with this criticism? Explain your point of view.

Saskatchewan Oil

If you wanted to build an oil company, would you put your head office in Arcola (population 525), Saskatchewan? Perhaps you wouldn't, but that's what Mary Tidlund, president of Williston Wildcatters Oil Corp., and her partner Mark Langfeld did, and they built a successful company with 115 producing wells and more than 200 employees.

Williston sees itself as a rebel in the oil business. It felt sure there was oil in a field in Saskatchewan that conventional techniques had been unable to find. And by developing a new drilling technique, it found the oil. But when it went to Calgary to get financing, it came up against a brick wall. As is often the case, it is difficult to get established companies to do something different. As Mark Langfeld put it, "You have to be like General Patton. Cross the river and say 'I'm over here guys.'" That way, you can perhaps get them to follow, but you have to take the lead and show it can be done. Finally, two Calgary companies bought in.

Williston does things differently. For instance, by locating in Arcola and hiring local people, it has been able to reduce its costs. It has also bought its own drilling rigs, something that nobody in the industry does. Everyone leases them so they don't have to carry the cost when they're idle. But Williston took a gamble that it would be able to keep the rigs busy, and because it would therefore be able to drill at lower cost, it would be able to afford more exploration. The gamble paid off. Williston did a similar thing when its trucking contractor failed to meet its needs — it bought its own trucks.

Mary Tidlund's management style is very much centred on building a strong team. She constantly works for agreement, getting people to contribute their thoughts to a decision, and that's one of the things that's helped Williston be innovative and different. Everyone, from the top to the bottom, has ideas and suggestions, and Mary works hard at keeping people involved. For instance, faced with the problem of a shortage of skilled workers for a new job, rather than make the decision of who to take from existing jobs, she got the job managers to decide. And it's all done in an atmosphere of fun. Mary Tidlund believes that fun is important, and that's a message that goes through the company. It seems to be working.

Questions

1. What makes group and team concepts so important in an organzation like Williston Wildcatters?
2. Does the size of the company make any difference to Mary Tidlund's ability to stress involvement, agreement, and consensus? Explain why or why not.
3. If Mary Tidlund hired you to work for Williston Wildcatters and gave you the job of creating effective teams in the organization, what would you do?

Video Resource: "Oil Lady," *Venture* 473 (January 30, 1994).

12

Motivating Employees

Learning Objectives

WHAT WILL I BE ABLE TO DO AFTER I FINISH THIS CHAPTER?

1. Describe the motivation process.
2. Define needs.
3. Explain the hierarchy of needs theory.
4. Differentiate Theory X from Theory Y.
5. Explain the motivational implications of the motivation-hygiene theory.
6. Identify the characteristics that high achievers seek in a job.
7. Describe the motivational implications of equity theory.
8. Explain the key relationships in expectancy theory.

What would you think about giving production workers substantial freedom to work as they wished—so long as they met their goals? In essence, you'd be treating operatives as "managerial" employees, giving them the flexibility in their schedules to do their work, eliminating the traditional "clock punching" practice. Do you think workers would take advantage of the situation? Would management lose control? Well, don't ask Don Miller to support those views.[1]

Don Miller is the CEO of Roppe Corporation. This producer of rubber products (baseboards, stair treads, floor tiles, etc.) is revolutionizing the production process. How? Through technological innovation, TQM, or reengineering efforts? No! Very simply, Don Miller has given his employees new freedom: When they've met their daily goals, they can go home.

Prior to Miller's intervention, Roppe Corporation generated annual sales in the $50-million range. Although this was "adequate" in Miller's view (especially during a period of declining construction projects), he knew that the company could do better. In fact, although sales growth appeared imminent with the upswing in the economy in the mid-1990s, production employees were only producing at 75 per cent of standard. And Miller knew why. His employees felt that by producing more to meet the quota, management would merely increase the standard. As a result, the employees, after hitting the 75 per cent range, just stopped working. So Don tried an experiment. He offered his employees the following proposition: he would increase the current quota rate by 10 per cent, and when employees met the new standard, he would increase their hourly pay by 10 per cent. Furthermore, although the standard would be set according to what time studies showed could be produced in eight hours of work, if the employees met the daily goals more quickly, they could go home—and still get eight hours of pay at the 10 per cent increased level.

In less than one week, Miller noticed a dramatic change. Employees increased their productivity (and the quality of the products) to meet the new standard. For example, the old standard for rubber baseboards

By giving his employees more freedom on the job, Don Miller has witnessed a significant increase in productivity brought about by motivated employees.

was about 8,666 metres per day per line. Typically workers made approximately 7,166 metres. Yet under this new plan, the goal was increased to 9,666 metres per day per line. And the workers produced every inch of it! That's a 35 per cent increase over what they had been producing the week before! What's more, they did it in under seven hours and left for the day.

It is also interesting to note that over the past few years since this new practice was implemented, in addition to a production increase, the company has witnessed some other "benefits." The workers now police themselves. Sabotage of machinery has disappeared. The machines don't suddenly break down after reaching 75 per cent of standard. Supervisors don't have to monitor the length of workers' breaks or lunch periods. And, overtime for maintenance workers has significantly decreased. In fact, routine, preventive maintenance can often be performed between shifts now—especially when the employees leave early.

As a result of Don Miller's idea, Roppe Corporation is maintaining its 35 per cent increase in productivity—with only a 10 per cent increase in costs. Needless to say, both Miller and his employees are much more satisfied!

Motivation and Individual Needs

To understand what motivation is, let us begin by pointing out what motivation isn't. Why? Because many people incorrectly view motivation as a personal trait—that is, some have it and others don't. In practice, this would characterize the manager who labels a certain employee as unmotivated. Our knowledge of motivation, though, tells us that this just isn't true. What we know is that motivation is the result of the interaction between the individual and the situation. Certainly, individuals differ in motivational drive, but overall motivation varies from situation to situation. As we analyse the concept of motivation, keep in mind that level of motivation varies both between individuals and within individuals at different times.

We'll define **motivation** as the willingness to exert high levels of effort to reach organizational goals, conditioned by the effort's ability to satisfy some individual need. While general motivation refers to effort toward any goal, here it will refer to organizational goals because our focus is on work-related behaviour. The three key elements in our definition are effort, organizational goals, and needs.

The effort element is a measure of intensity. When someone is motivated, he or she tries hard. But high levels of effort are unlikely to lead to favourable job performance outcomes unless the effort is channelled in a direction that benefits the organization.[2] Therefore, we must consider the quality of the effort as well as its intensity. Effort that is directed toward, and consistent with, the organization's goals is the kind of effort that we should be seeking. Finally, we will treat motivation as a need-satisfying process. This is depicted in Exhibit 12-1.

motivation
The willingness to exert high levels of effort to reach organizational goals, conditioned by the effort's ability to satisfy some individual need.

Despite a serious accident and predictions that her rowing career was over, Silken Laumann came back to win a medal at the Olympics.

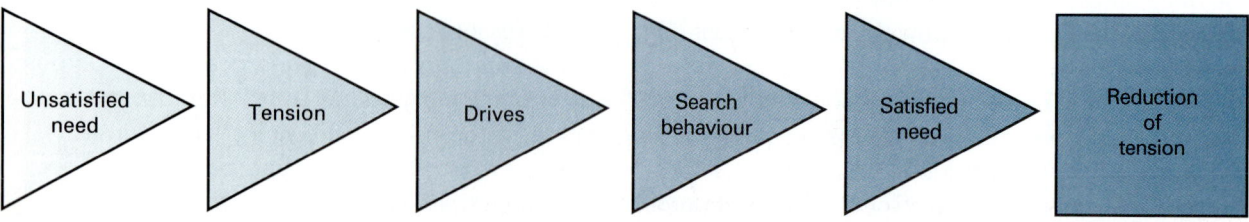

Exhibit 12-1 The Motivation Process

Unsatisfied need → Tension → Drives → Search behaviour → Satisfied need → Reduction of tension

Motivating Employees

A **need**, in our terminology, means some internal state that makes certain outcomes appear attractive. An unsatisfied need creates tension that stimulates drives within an individual. These drives generate a search behaviour to find particular goals that, if attained, will satisfy the need and reduce the tension.

We can say that motivated employees are in a state of tension. To relieve this tension, they exert effort. The greater the tension, the higher the effort level. If this effort successfully leads to the satisfaction of the need, it reduces tension. Since we are interested in work behaviour, this tension-reduction effort must also be directed toward organizational goals. Therefore, inherent in our definition of motivation is the requirement that the individual's needs be compatible and consistent with the organization's goals. When this does not occur, individuals may exert high levels of effort that run counter to the interests of the organization. Incidentally, this is not so unusual. Some employees regularly spend a lot of time talking with friends at work in order to satisfy their social needs. There is a high level of effort, but it's being unproductively directed.

need
An internal state that makes certain outcomes appear attractive.

Early Theories of Motivation

The 1950s were a fruitful time for the development of motivation concepts. Three specific theories were formulated during this period that, although heavily attacked and now considered questionably valid, are probably still the best-known explanations for employee motivation. These are the hierarchy of needs theory, Theories X and Y, and the motivation-hygiene theory. While more valid explanations of motivation have been developed, you should know these theories for at least two reasons: (1) They represent the foundation from which contemporary theories grew; and (2) practising managers regularly use these theories and their terminology in explaining employee motivation.

What Is Maslow's Hierarchy of Needs Theory?

The best-known theory of motivation is probably Abraham Maslow's **hierarchy of needs theory**.³ He imagined that within every human being there exists a hierarchy of five needs:

▶ 1. **Physiological needs:** food, drink, shelter, sexual satisfaction, and other bodily requirements
▶ 2. **Safety needs:** security and protection from physical and emotional harm

hierarchy of needs theory
Maslow's theory is that there is a hierarchy of five human needs: physiological, safety, social, esteem, and self-actualization. As each need is substantially satisfied, the next becomes dominant.

physiological needs
Basic food, drink, shelter, and sexual needs.

safety needs
A person's needs for security and protection from physical and emotional harm.

Abraham Maslow believed that motivation stemmed from fulfilling successively higher level needs, such as physiological, safety, social, esteem, and self-actualization needs.

Exhibit 12-2 Maslow's Hierarchy of Needs

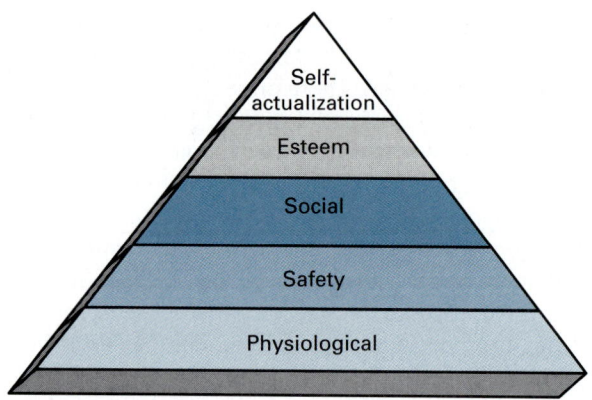

social needs
A person's needs for affection, belongingness, acceptance, and friendship.

esteem needs
Internal factors such as self-respect, autonomy, and achievement; and external factors such as status, recognition, and attention.

self-actualization needs
A person's drive to become what he or she is capable of becoming.

▶ 3. **Social needs:** affection, belongingness, acceptance, and friendship
▶ 4. **Esteem needs:** internal esteem factors such as self-respect, autonomy, and achievement; and external esteem factors such as status, recognition, and attention
▶ 5. **Self-actualization needs:** growth, achieving one's potential, and self-fulfilment; the drive to become what one is capable of becoming

As each need is substantially satisfied, the next need becomes dominant. In terms of Exhibit 12-2, the individual moves up the hierarchy. From a motivation viewpoint, the theory says that although no need is ever fully gratified, a substantially satisfied need no longer motivates. If you want to motivate someone, according to Maslow, you need to understand where that person is in the hierarchy and focus on satisfying needs at or above that level.

Maslow's need theory has received wide recognition, particularly among practising managers. This can be attributed to the theory's intuitive logic and ease of understanding. Unfortunately, however, research does not generally validate the theory. Maslow provided no empirical substantiation for his theory, and several studies that sought to validate it found no support.[4]

What Is McGregor's Theory X and Theory Y?

Douglas McGregor proposed two distinct views of the nature of human beings: a basically negative view, labelled **Theory X,** and a basically positive view, labelled **Theory Y.**[5] After viewing the way managers dealt with employees, McGregor concluded that a manager's view of human nature is based on a group of assumptions, either positive or negative (see Exhibit 12-3), and that the manager moulds his or her behaviour toward employees according to these suppositions.

Theory X
The assumption that employees dislike work, are lazy, seek to avoid responsibility, and must be coerced to perform.

Theory Y
The assumption that employees are creative, seek responsibility, and can exercise self-direction.

What does McGregor's analysis imply about motivation? The answer is best expressed in the framework presented by Maslow. Theory X assumes that physiological and safety needs dominate the individual. Theory Y assumes needs like social and esteem are dominant. McGregor himself believed that the assumptions of Theory Y were more valid than those of Theory X. Therefore, he proposed that participation in decision making, responsible and challenging jobs, and good group relations would maximize work effort.

Unfortunately, there is no evidence to confirm that either set of assumptions is valid or that accepting Theory Y assumptions and altering one's actions accordingly will

> **Theory X: A manager who views employees from a Theory X (negative) perspective, believes:**
> ▶ 1. Employees inherently dislike work and, whenever possible, will attempt to avoid it
> ▶ 2. Because employees dislike work, they must be coerced, controlled, or threatened with punishment to achieve desired goals
> ▶ 3. Employees will shirk responsibilities and seek formal direction whenever possible
> ▶ 4. Most workers place security above all other factors associated with work and will display little ambition
>
> **Theory Y: A manager who views employees from a Theory Y (positive) perspective believes:**
> ▶ 1. Employees can view work as being as natural as rest or play
> ▶ 2. Men and women will exercise self-direction and self-control if they are committed to the objectives
> ▶ 3. The average person can learn to accept, even seek, responsibility
> ▶ 4. The ability to make good decisions is widely dispersed throughout the population and is not necessarily the sole province of managers

Exhibit 12-3 Theory X and Theory Y Premises

make one's employees more motivated. In the real world, there are examples of effective managers who make Theory X assumptions. For instance, Bob McCurry, vice-president of Toyota's U.S. marketing operations, essentially follows Theory X. He drives his staff hard and uses a "crack-the-whip" style. Yet he has been extremely successful at increasing Toyota's market share in a highly competitive environment.

What Is Herzberg's Motivation-Hygiene Theory?

The **motivation-hygiene theory** was proposed by psychologist Frederick Herzberg.[6] Believing that an individual's relation to his or her work is a basic one and that his or her attitude toward work can very well determine success or failure, Herzberg investigated the question, "What do people want from their jobs?" He asked people to describe in detail situations in which they felt exceptionally good or bad about their jobs. These responses were then tabulated and categorized. Exhibit 12-4 represents Herzberg's findings.

From analysing the responses, Herzberg concluded that the replies people gave when they felt good about their jobs were significantly different from the replies given when they felt bad. As seen in Exhibit 12-4, certain characteristics were consistently related to job satisfaction (factors on the left side of the figure) and others to job dissatisfaction (the right side of the figure). Intrinsic factors such as achievement, recognition, and responsibility were related to job satisfaction. When those questioned felt good about their work, they tended to attribute these characteristics to themselves. On the other hand, when they were dissatisfied, they tended to cite extrinsic factors such

motivation-hygiene theory
The theory that intrinsic factors are related to job satisfaction, while extrinsic factors are associated with dissatisfaction.

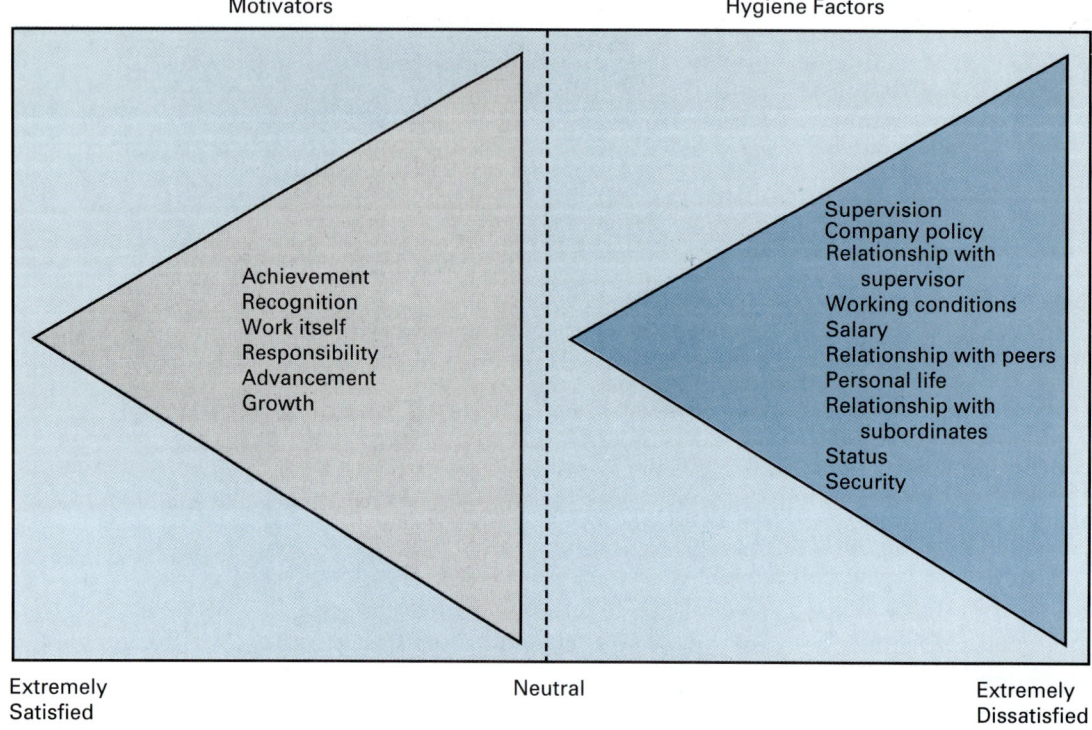

Exhibit 12-4 Herzberg's Motivation-Hygiene Theory

as company policy and administration, supervision, interpersonal relationships, and working conditions.

The data suggest, said Herzberg, that the opposite of satisfaction is not dissatisfaction, as was traditionally believed. Removing dissatisfying characteristics from a job does not necessarily make the job satisfying. As illustrated in Exhibit 12-5, Herzberg proposed that his findings indicate the existence of a dual continuum: The opposite of "satisfaction" is "no satisfaction," and the opposite of "dissatisfaction" is "no dissatisfaction."

According to Herzberg, the factors leading to job satisfaction are separate and distinct from those that lead to job dissatisfaction. Therefore, managers who seek to

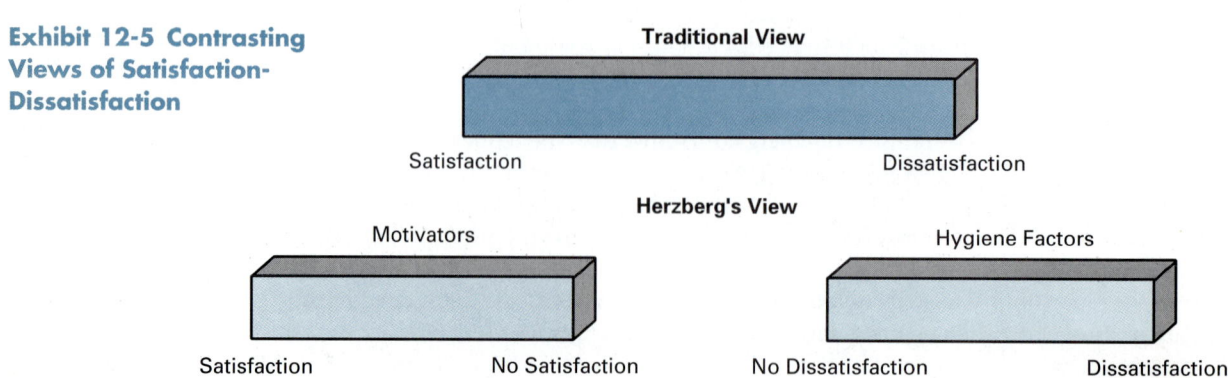

Exhibit 12-5 Contrasting Views of Satisfaction-Dissatisfaction

Motivating Employees

eliminate factors that create job dissatisfaction can bring about peace but not necessarily motivation. They are placating their workforce rather than motivating it. Because they don't motivate employees, the factors that eliminate job dissatisfaction were characterized by Herzberg as **hygiene factors**. When these factors are adequate, people will not be dissatisfied; however, neither will they be satisfied. To motivate people on their jobs, Herzberg suggested emphasizing **motivators,** the factors that increase job satisfaction.

The motivation-hygiene theory is not without its detractors. The criticisms of the theory include the methodology Herzberg used to collect data and his failure to account for situational variables.[7] Regardless of any criticism, Herzberg's theory has been widely popularized and few managers are unfamiliar with his recommendations. Much of the enthusiasm for job enrichment, cited in Chapter 7, can be attributed to Herzberg's findings and recommendations.

hygiene factors
Factors that eliminate dissatisfaction.

motivators
Factors that increase job satisfaction.

Contemporary Theories of Motivation

While the previous theories are well known, they unfortunately have not held up well under close examination. However, all is not lost. Some contemporary theories have one thing in common: each has a reasonable degree of valid supporting documentation. The following theories represent the current "state-of-the-art" explanations of employee motivation.

What Is McClelland's Three-Needs Theory?

David McClelland and others have proposed the **three-needs theory**, which maintains that there are three major relevant motives or needs in work situations:

▶ 1. **Need for achievement (*nAch*):** the drive to excel, to achieve in relation to a set of standards, to strive to succeed

three-needs theory
The needs for achievement, power, and affiliation are major motives in work.

need for achievement
The drive to excel, to achieve in relation to a set of standards, to strive to succeed.

This is a sample of the test McClelland used to measure achievement. Individuals looked at ambiguous pictures and created stories based on what they saw. McClelland and his associates then analysed the story to assess the degree of achievement the individuals projected.

Details on a Management Classic

DAVID MCCLELLAND AND THE THREE-NEEDS THEORY

David McClelland's work in helping to understand motivation in organizational settings focused on aspects of personality characteristics. Much of his research centred on achievement, power, and affiliation orientations. Of the three needs, McClelland found that some people have a compelling drive to succeed for personal achievement rather than rewards of success per se. The question then is how do you find out if someone is, for instance, a high achiever, and what effect can that have on an organization?

In his research, McClelland would give individuals a projective test in which subjects responded to a set of pictures. Each picture was briefly shown to a subject who then wrote a story based on the picture. Those responses generated were then classified by McClelland as focusing on a need for achievement, power, or affiliation. Those who had a high need for achievement, however, shared some similar attributes.

High achievers perform best when they perceive their probability of success as being 0.5—that is, when they estimate they have a fifty-fifty chance of success. They dislike gambling when the odds are high because they get no achievement satisfaction from happenstance success. Similarly, they dislike low odds (high probability of success) because then there is no challenge to their skills. They like to set goals that require stretching themselves a little. When there is an approximately equal chance of success or failure, there is optimum opportunity to experience feelings of successful accomplishment and satisfaction in their efforts.

Based on an extensive amount of research, some reasonably well-supported predictions can be made between the relationship of the achievement need and job performance. Though less research has been done on power and affiliation needs, there are consistent findings here too. First, individuals with a high need to achieve prefer job situations with personal responsibility, feedback, and an intermediate degree of risk. When these characteristics are prevalent, high achievers are strongly motivated. The evidence consistently demonstrates, for instance, that high achievers are successful in entrepreneurial activities like running their own business, managing a self-contained unit within a large organization, and many sales positions.[8] Second, a high need to achieve does not necessarily lead to being a good manager, especially in large organizations. A high nAch salesperson at Pfizer does not necessarily make a good sales manager, and good managers in large organizations like Exxon, AT&T, or Sears do not necessarily have a high need to achieve.[9] Third, the needs for affiliation and power are closely related to managerial success.[10] The best managers are high in the need for power and low in the need for affiliation. Last, employees can be trained successfully to stimulate their achievement need.[11] If a job calls for a high achiever, management can select a person with a high nAch or develop its own candidate through achievement training. ▼

Motivating Employees

> 2. **Need for power (*nPow*):** the need to make others behave in a way that they would not have behaved otherwise
> 3. **Need for affiliation (*nAff*):** the desire for friendly and close interpersonal relationships[12]

Some people have a compelling drive to succeed, but they are striving for personal achievement rather than for the rewards of success per se (*nAch*). They have a desire to do something better or more efficiently than it has been done before. This drive is the need for achievement. From research concerning the achievement need, McClelland found that high achievers differentiate themselves from others by their desire to do things better.[13] They seek situations in which they can attain personal responsibility for finding solutions to problems, in which they can receive rapid and unambiguous feedback on their performance in order to tell whether they are improving, and in which they can set moderately challenging goals (see Details on a Management Classic). High achievers are not gamblers; they dislike succeeding by chance. They prefer the challenge of working at a problem and accepting the personal responsibility for success or failure, rather than leaving the outcome to chance or the actions of others. An important point is that they avoid what they perceive to be very easy or very difficult tasks.

The need for power (*nPow*) is the desire to have impact and to be influential. Individuals high in nPow enjoy being "in charge," strive for influence over others, and prefer to be in competitive and status-oriented situations. The third need isolated by McClelland is affiliation (*nAff*), which is the desire to be liked and accepted by others. This need has received the least attention by researchers. Individuals with high nAff strive for friendships, prefer cooperative situations rather than competitive ones, and desire relationships involving a high degree of mutual understanding.

How Does Adams' Equity Theory Help Explain Employee Motivation?

Employees don't work in a vacuum. They make comparisons. If someone offered you $60,000 a year on your first job upon graduation from college, you'd probably grab the offer and report to work enthusiastic and certainly satisfied with your pay. How would you react if you found out a month or so into the job that a coworker—another recent graduate, your age, with comparable grades from a comparable college—was getting $70,000 a year? You would probably be upset! Even though, in absolute terms, $60,000 is a lot of money for a new graduate to make (and you know it!), that suddenly would not be the issue. The issue would now centre on relative rewards and what you believe is fair. There is considerable evidence that employees make comparisons of their job inputs and outcomes relative to others and that inequities influence the degree of effort that employees exert.[14]

Developed by J. Stacey Adams, **equity theory** says that employees perceive what they get from a job situation (outcomes) in relation to what they put into it (inputs) and then compare their inputs-outcomes ratio with the inputs-outcomes ratio of relevant others. This is shown in Exhibit 12-6 on page 279. If they perceive their ratio to be equal to those of the relevant others with whom they compare themselves, a state of equity exists. They perceive that their situation is fair—that justice prevails. If the ratios are unequal, inequity exists; that is, they view themselves as underrewarded or overrewarded. When inequities occur, employees attempt to correct them.

The **referent** with whom employees choose to compare themselves is an important variable in equity theory.[15] The three referent categories have been classified as

need for power
The need to make others behave in a way that they would not have behaved otherwise.

need for affiliation
The desire for friendly and close interpersonal relationships.

equity theory
The theory that an employee compares his or her job's inputs-outcomes ratio to that of relevant others and then corrects any inequity.

referents
The persons, systems, or selves against which individuals compare themselves to assess equity.

Ethical Dilemmas in Management

▼ THE ETHICS OF CEO COMPENSATION ▲

The chief executive officers of some of Canada's largest companies earn multimillion-dollar compensation packages a year, hundreds of times as much as the typical blue-collar worker. Ted Newall, Nova Corp's CEO received compensation in 1994 (salary plus bonus) of $1.64 million. Jean Monty, CEO of Northern Telecom received just under $2 million in 1994, while Alan Taylor, chairman of the Royal Bank received $2.65 million, Matthew Barrett, chairman of the Bank of Montreal received $1.9 million, as did Peter Godsoe, chairman of the Bank of Nova Scotia (a $1.08 million increase over his earnings in 1993). The *Globe & Mail* calculated the hourly pay of senior Canadian bankers. Royal Bank: Alan Taylor, $1,020 per hour, John Cleghorn, president, $638 per hour. Toronto-Dominion Bank: Richard Thompson, chairman, $1,011 per hour, Robert Korthals, president, $716 per hour. Bank of Montreal: Matthew Barrett , chairman, $737, Tony Comper, president, $464 per hour. Bank of Nova Scotia: Peter Godsoe, chairman, $731 per hour, Bruce Birmingham, vice-chairman, $375 per hour. CIBC: Al Flood, chairman, $733 per hour, Holger Kluge, president, $487 per hour. National Bank: André Berard, chairman, $421 per hour, Leon Courville, president, $236 per hour.[16]

Some say this represents a classic economic response to a situation in which the demand is great for high-quality top-executive talent and the supply is low. Other arguments in favour of paying CEOs $1 million a year or more include the need to compensate people for the tremendous responsibilities and stress that go with such jobs, the motivating potential that seven- and eight-figure annual incomes provide to both the CEOs and those who might aspire to the position, and the CEO's influence on their companies' bottom lines.

Critics describe the astronomical pay packages given to American CEOs as indicative of "rampant greed." They note, for instance, that during the 1980s, CEO compensation jumped by 212 per cent, while factory workers saw their pay increase by just 53 per cent. During the same decade, the average earnings per share of the Standard & Poor's 500 companies grew by only 78 per cent. In 1993, the average chief executive's salary and bonus rose by 15 per cent to $1,274,893. Moreover, in the year 1993, all twenty of the highest-paid U.S. CEOs earned in excess of $11.2 million.

Executive pay is considerably higher in the United States than in most other countries. American CEOs typically make two or three times as much as their counterparts in Canada and Europe. In Japan, CEOs earn only seventeen times the pay of an ordinary worker. For example, in 1992, the top three U.S. auto company chiefs were paid a total of $20.2 million. By contrast, the combined income for the heads of Japan's top three automakers in that same year was $5.3 million. Critics of executive pay practices argue that CEOs choose board members who can be counted on to support ever-increasing pay for top management. If board members fail to "play along," they risk losing their positions, their fees, and the prestige and power inherent in board membership.

Does the blame for the problem lie with CEOs or with the shareholders and boards that knowingly allow the practice? Should we fault Michael Eisner, chairman of Walt Disney Company, for collecting $203,010,590 in salary, bonuses, and stock-based incentive plans in 1993 while, during that same year, his company's profits dropped 40 per cent?

Are CEOs greedy? Are these CEOs acting unethically? What do you think?

Exhibit 12-6 Equity Theory Relationships

*Person A is the employee, and Person B is a relevant other or referrent.

PERCEIVED RATIO COMPARISON*		EMPLOYEE'S ASSESSMENT
$\frac{\text{Outcomes A}}{\text{Inputs A}}$ < $\frac{\text{Outcomes B}}{\text{Inputs B}}$		Inequity (underrewarded)
$\frac{\text{Outcomes A}}{\text{Inputs A}}$ = $\frac{\text{Outcomes B}}{\text{Inputs B}}$		Equity
$\frac{\text{Outcomes A}}{\text{Inputs A}}$ > $\frac{\text{Outcomes B}}{\text{Inputs B}}$		Inequity (overrewarded)

"other," "system," and "self." The "other" category includes other individuals with similar jobs in the same organization and also includes friends, neighbours, or professional associates. On the basis of information they receive through word of mouth, newspapers, and magazine articles on issues such as executive salaries or a recent union contract, employees compare their pay with that of others (see Ethical Dilemmas in Management).

The "system" category considers organizational pay policies and procedures and the administration of this system. It considers organizationwide pay policies, both implied and explicit. Patterns by the organization in terms of allocation of pay are major determinants in this category.

The "self" category refers to inputs-outcomes ratios that are unique to the individual. It reflects past personal experiences and contacts. This category is influenced by criteria such as past jobs or family commitments.

The choice of a particular set of referents is related to the information available about referents as well as to their perceived relevance. On the basis of equity theory, when employees perceive an inequity, they might (1) distort either their own or others' inputs or outcomes; (2) behave in some way to induce others to change their inputs or outcomes; (3) behave in some way to change their own inputs or outcomes; (4) choose a different comparison referent; and/or (5) quit their jobs.

Equity theory recognizes that individuals are concerned not only with the absolute rewards they receive for their efforts but also with the relationship of these rewards to what others receive. They make judgments concerning the relationship between their inputs and outcomes and the inputs and outcomes of others. On the basis of one's inputs, such as effort, experience, education, and competence, one compares outcomes such as salary levels, raises, recognition, and other factors. When people perceive an imbalance in their inputs-outcomes ratio relative to those of others, they experience tension. This tension provides the basis for motivation as people strive for what they perceive as equity and fairness.

The theory establishes the four propositions relating to inequitable pay. These propositions listed in Exhibit 12-7 have generally proven to be correct.[17] A review of the research consistently confirms the equity thesis: employee motivation is influenced significantly by relative rewards as well as by absolute rewards. Whenever employees perceive inequity, they will act to correct the situation.[18] The result might be lower or higher productivity, improved or reduced quality of output, increased absenteeism, or voluntary resignation.

From the discussion above, however, we should not conclude that equity theory is without problems. The theory leaves some key issues still unclear.[19] For instance, how do employees define inputs and outcomes? How do they combine and weigh their

Exhibit 12-7 Equity Theory Propositions

> 1. **Given payment by time, overrewarded employees will produce more than equitably paid employees.** Hourly and salaried employees will generate a high quantity or quality of production in order to increase the input side of the ratio and bring about equity.
> 2. **Given payment by quantity of production, overrewarded employees will produce fewer but higher-quality units than equitably paid employees.** Individuals paid on a piece-rate basis will increase their effort to achieve equity, which can result in greater quality or quantity. However, increases in quantity will only increase inequity, since every unit produced results in further overpayment. Therefore, effort is directed toward increasing quality rather than quantity.
> 3. **Given payment by time, underrewarded employees will produce less or poorer-quality output.** Effort will be decreased, which will bring about lower productivity or poorer-quality output than equitably paid subjects.
> 4. **Given payment by quantity of production, underrewarded employees will produce a large number of low-quality units in comparison with equitably paid employees.** Employees on piece-rate pay plans can bring about equity because trading off quality of output for quantity will result in an increase in rewards with little or no increase in contributions.

inputs and outcomes to arrive at totals? When and how do the factors change over time? Regardless of these problems, equity theory has an impressive amount of research support and offers us some important insights into employee motivation.

Why Is Vroom's Expectancy Theory Considered a Comprehensive Theory of Motivation?

expectancy theory
The theory that an individual tends to act in a certain way based on the expectation that the act will be followed by a given outcome and on the attractiveness of that outcome to the individual.

The most comprehensive explanation of motivation is Victor Vroom's **expectancy theory.**[20] Though it has its critics,[21] most of the research evidence is supportive of the theory.[22]

The expectancy theory states that an individual tends to act in a certain way based on the expectation that the act will be followed by a given outcome and on the attractiveness of that outcome to the individual. It includes three variables or relationships:

> 1. **Effort-performance linkage:** the probability perceived by the individual that exerting a given amount of effort will lead to performance
> 2. **Performance-reward linkage:** the degree to which the individual believes that performing at a particular level will lead to the attainment of a desired outcome
> 3. **Attractiveness:** the importance that the individual places on the potential outcome or reward that can be achieved on the job. This considers the goals and needs of the individual[23]

While this might sound complex, it really is not that difficult to visualize. It can be summed up in the questions: How hard do I have to work to achieve a certain level of performance and can I actually achieve that level? What reward will performing at that level get me? How attractive is this reward to me and does it help achieve my goals?

Motivating Employees

Whether one has the desire to produce at any given time depends on one's particular goals and one's perception of the relative worth of performance as a path to the attainment of these goals.

How Does Expectancy Theory Work? Exhibit 12-8 shows a very simple version of the expectancy theory that expresses its major contentions. The strength of a person's motivation to perform (effort) depends on how strongly that individual believes that he or she can achieve what is being attempted. If this goal is achieved (performance), will he or she be adequately rewarded by the organization? If so, will the reward satisfy his or her individual goals? Let us consider the four steps inherent in the theory and then attempt to apply it.

First, what perceived outcomes does the job offer the employee? Outcomes may be positive: pay, security, companionship, trust, employee benefits, a chance to use talent or skills, or congenial relationships. On the other hand, employees may view the outcomes as negative: fatigue, boredom, frustration, anxiety, harsh supervision, or threat of dismissal. Reality is not relevant here; the critical issue is what the individual employee perceives the outcome to be, regardless of whether his or her perceptions are accurate.

Second, how attractive do employees consider these outcomes to be? Are they valued positively, negatively, or neutrally? This obviously is an internal issue and considers the individual's personal attitudes, personality, and needs. The individual who finds a particular outcome attractive—that is, values it positively—would rather attain it than not attain it. Others may find it negative and therefore prefer not attaining it to attaining it. Still others may be neutral.

Third, what kind of behaviour must the employee exhibit to achieve these outcomes? The outcomes are not likely to have any effect on an individual employee's performance unless the employee knows, clearly and unambiguously, what he or she must do to achieve them. For example, what is "doing well" in terms of performance appraisal? What criteria will be used to judge the employee's performance?

Fourth and last, how does the employee view his or her chances of doing what is asked? After the employee has considered his or her own competencies and ability to control those variables that will determine success, what probability does he or she place on successful attainment?[24]

How Can Expectancy Theory Be Applied? Let's use a classroom analogy as an illustration of how one can use the expectancy theory to explain motivation.

Most students prefer an instructor who tells them what is expected of them in the course. They want to know what the assignments and examinations will be like, when they are due or to be taken, and how much weight each carries in the final term grade. They also like to think that the amount of effort they exert in attending classes, taking notes, and studying will be reasonably related to the grade they will make in the course. Let us assume that you, as a student, feel this way. Consider that five weeks into a class you are really enjoying (we'll call it MNGT 301), an examination is given back to you. You studied hard for this examination, and you have consistently made As and Bs on examinations in other courses to which you have expended similar effort. The reason you work so hard is to make top grades, which you believe are important

Is being selected employee of the month important to you? Do you see it as a valuable reward? If so, then such a method can be motivational for you.

for getting a good job upon graduation. Also, you are not sure, but you might want to go on to graduate school. Again, you think grades are important for getting into a good graduate school.

Well, the results of that five-week examination are in. The class median was 74. Ten per cent of the class scored an 85 or higher and got an A. Your grade was 46; the minimum passing mark was 50. You're mad. You're frustrated. Even more, you're perplexed. How could you possibly have done so poorly on the examination when you usually score in the top range in other classes by preparing as you did for this one?

Several interesting things are immediately evident in your behaviour. Suddenly, you are no longer driven to attend MNGT 301 classes regularly. You find that you do not study for the course either. When you do attend classes, you daydream a lot—the result is an empty notebook instead of several pages of notes. One would probably be correct in describing you as "lacking in motivation" in MNGT 301. Why did your motivation level change? You know and I know, but let's explain it in expectancy terms.

If we use Exhibit 12-8 to understand this situation, we might say the following: Studying for MNGT 301 (effort) is conditioned by the resulting correct answers on the examination (performance), which will produce a high grade (reward), which will lead, in turn, to the security, prestige, and other benefits that accrue from obtaining a good job (individual goal).

The attractiveness of the outcome, which in this case is a good grade, is high. But what about the performance-reward linkage? Do you feel that the grade you received truly reflects your knowledge of the material? In other words, did the test fairly measure what you know? If the answer is yes, then this linkage is strong. If the answer is no, then at least part of the reason for your reduced motivational level is your belief that the test was not a fair measure of your performance. If the test was an essay type, maybe you believe that the instructor's grading method was poor. Was too much weight placed on a question that you thought was trivial? Maybe the instructor does not like you and was biased in grading your paper. These are examples of perceptions that influence the performance-reward linkage and your level of motivation.

Another possible demotivating force may be the effort-performance relationship. If, after you took the examination, you believe that you could not have passed it regardless of the amount of preparation you had done, then your desire to study will drop. Possibly the instructor wrote the examination under the assumption that you had a considerably broader background in the subject matter. Maybe the course had several prerequisites that you did not know about, or possibly you had the prerequisites but took them several years ago. The result is the same: You place a low value on your effort leading to answering the examination questions correctly; hence, your motivational level decreases, and you lessen your effort.

Given our classroom analogy, can we relate this to a work setting? In other words, what does expectancy theory say that can help us motivate our employees? To answer

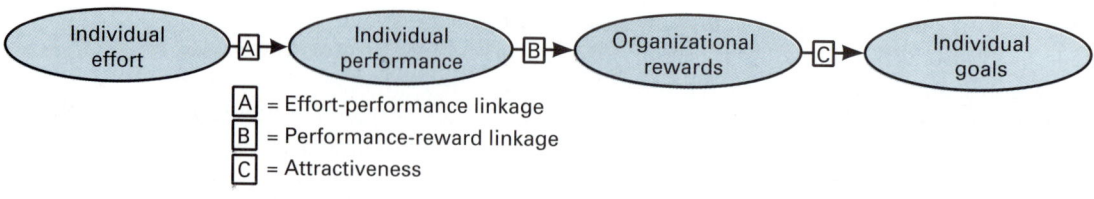

Exhibit 12-8 Simplified Expectancy Theory

Motivating Employees

that question, let's summarize some of the issues surrounding the theory. First, expectancy theory emphasizes payoffs, or rewards. As a result, managers have to believe that the rewards they offer will align with what the employee wants. As such, it is a theory based on self-interest, wherein each individual seeks to maximize his or her expected satisfaction. Second, expectancy theory stresses that managers understand why employees view certain outcomes as attractive or unattractive. They will want to reward individuals with those things they value positively. Third, the expectancy theory emphasizes expected behaviours. Do individuals know what is expected of them and how they will be appraised? Unless employees see this connection between performance and rewards, organizational goals may not be met. Finally, the theory is concerned with perceptions. What is realistic is irrelevant. An individual's own perceptions of performance, reward, and goal-satisfaction outcomes will determine his or her level of effort, not the objective outcomes themselves. Accordingly, there must be continuous feedback to align perceptions with reality.

How Can We Integrate the Contemporary Theories of Motivation?

We have presented several motivation theories in this chapter. There is a tendency, at this point, to view them independently. This is a mistake. The fact is that many of the ideas underlying the theories are complementary, and your understanding of how to motivate people is maximized when you see how the theories fit together.[25]

Exhibit 12-9 presents a model that integrates much of what we know about motivation. Its basic foundation is the simplified expectancy model shown in Exhibit 12-8. Let's work through Exhibit 12-9, beginning at the left.

The individual effort box has an arrow leading into it. This arrow flows out of the individual's goals. This goals-effort loop is meant to remind us that goals direct behaviour.

Expectancy theory predicts that an employee will exert a high level of effort if he or she perceives that there is a strong relationship between effort and performance, performance and rewards, and rewards and satisfaction of personal goals. Each of these relationships, in turn, is influenced by certain factors. For effort to lead to good performance, the individual must have the requisite ability to perform, and the performance-evaluation system that measures the individual's performance must be perceived as being fair and objective. The performance-reward relationship will be strong if the individual perceives that it is performance (rather than seniority, personal favourites, or other criteria) that is rewarded. Thus, if management has designed a reward system that is seen by employees as "paying off" for good performance, the rewards will reinforce and encourage continued good performance.

The final link in expectancy theory is the rewards-goals relationship. Need theories would come into play at this point. Motivation would be high to the degree that the rewards an individual received for his or her high performance satisfied the dominant needs consistent with his or her individual goals.

A closer look at Exhibit 12-9 will also reveal that the model considers the need for achievement and equity theories. The high achiever is not motivated by the organization's assessment of his or her performance or organizational rewards, hence the jump

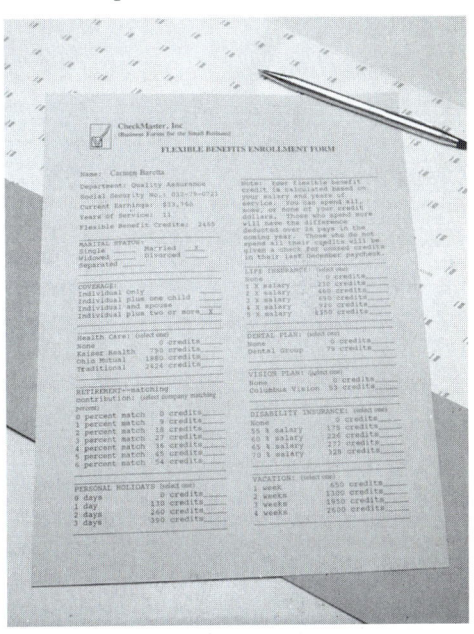

By allowing employees the opportunity to pick and choose their "rewards," flexible benefit programs can create that "something" of value for every employee.

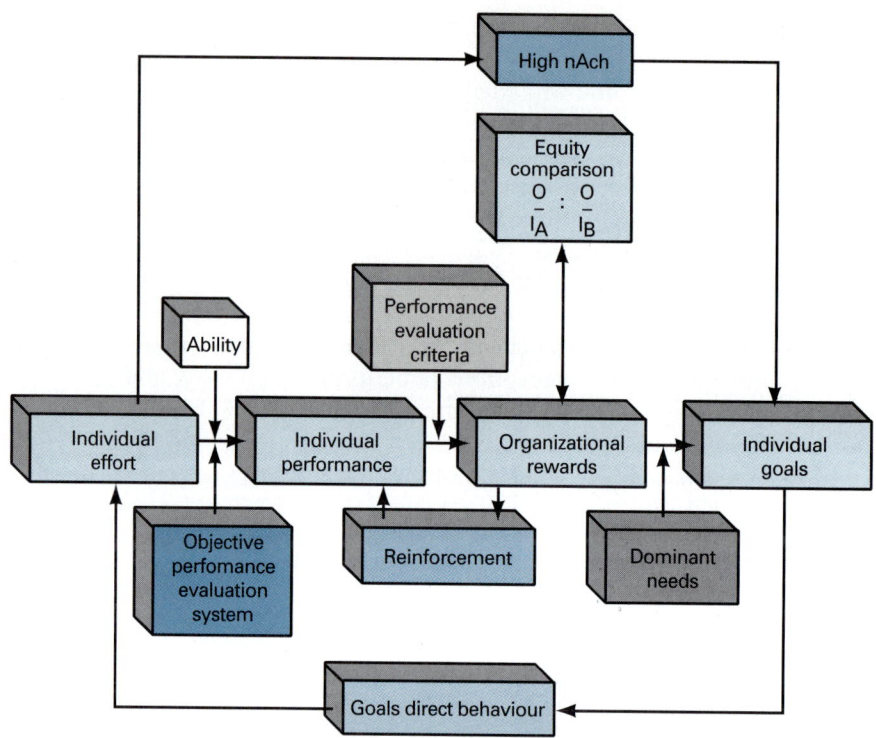

Exhibit 12-9 Integrating Theories of Motivation

from effort to individual goals for those with a high nAch. Remember that high achievers are internally driven as long as the jobs they are doing provide them with personal responsibility, feedback, and moderate risks. They are not concerned with the effort-performance, performance-rewards, or rewards-goal linkages. Finally, rewards also play the key part in equity theory. Individuals will compare the rewards (outcomes) they receive from the inputs they make with the inputs-outcomes ratio of relevant others (O/IA:O/IB), and inequities may influence the effort expended.

If you're a manager concerned with motivating your employees, what specific recommendations can you draw from this integration? While there is no simple, all-encompassing set of guidelines, we offer the following suggestions that draw on the essence of what these theories have taught us about motivating employees (see Developing Management Skills).

Are Theories of Motivation Transferable Across National Cultures?

The theories of motivation we have been studying were developed largely by U.S. psychologists and validated by studying American workers. These theories, however, need to be modified for different cultures.[26]

The self-interest concept is consistent with capitalism and the extremely high value placed on individualism in North America. Because almost all the motivation theories presented in this chapter are based on the self-interest motive, they should be applicable to organizations in such countries as Great Britain and Australia, where capitalism and individualism are highly valued. In more collectivist nations—Venezuela,

Motivating Employees

Singapore, Japan, and Mexico—the link to the organization is the individual's loyalty to the organization or society, rather than his or her self-interest. Employees in collectivist cultures should be more receptive to team-based job design, group goals, and group-performance evaluations. Reliance on the fear of being fired in such cultures is likely to be less effective, even if the laws in these countries allow managers to fire employees.

The need for achievement concept provides another example of a motivation theory with a U.S. bias. The view that a high need for achievement acts as an internal motivator presupposes the existence of two cultural characteristics: a willingness to accept a moderate degree of risk and a concern with performance. These characteristics would exclude countries with high uncertainty avoidance scores and high quality-of-life ratings. The remaining countries are exclusively Anglo-American countries such as New Zealand, South Africa, Ireland, the United States, and Canada.

Developing Management Skills

GETTING THE MOST FROM EMPLOYEES

▶ **1. Recognize individual differences.** Almost every contemporary motivation theory recognizes that employees are not homogeneous. They have different needs. They also differ in terms of attitudes, personality, and other important individual variables.

▶ **2. Match people to jobs.** There is a great deal of evidence showing the motivational benefits of carefully matching people to jobs. People who lack the necessary skills to perform successfully will be disadvantaged.

▶ **3. Use goals.** Managers should ensure that employees have hard, specific goals and feedback on how well they are doing in pursuit of those goals. In many cases, these goals should be participatively set.

▶ **4. Ensure that goals are perceived as attainable.** Regardless of whether goals are actually attainable, employees who see these goals as unattainable will reduce their effort. Managers must be sure, therefore, that employees feel confident that increased efforts can lead to performance goals.

▶ **5. Individualize rewards.** Because employees have different needs, what acts as a reinforcer for one may not for another. Managers should use their knowledge of employee differences to individualize the rewards over which they have control. Some of the more obvious rewards that managers allocate include pay, promotions, autonomy, and the opportunity to participate in goal setting and decision making.

▶ **6. Link rewards to performance.** Managers need to make rewards contingent on performance. Rewarding factors other than performance will only reinforce those other factors. Key rewards such as pay increases and promotions should be given for the attainment of employees' specific goals.

▶ **7. Check the system for equity.** Employees should perceive that rewards or outcomes are equal to the inputs given. On a simplistic level, experience, ability, effort, and other obvious inputs should explain differences in pay, responsibility, and other obvious outcomes.

▶ **8. Don't ignore money.** It's easy to get so caught up in setting goals, creating interesting jobs, and providing opportunities for participation that one forgets that money is a major reason why most people work. Thus, the allocation of performance-based wage increases, piecework bonuses, and other pay incentives is important in determining employee motivation.

Motivating a Diversified Workforce

To maximize motivation among today's diversified workforce, management needs to think in terms of flexibility (see Managers Who Made a Difference). For instance, studies tell us that men place considerably more importance on having a lot of autonomy in their jobs than do women. In contrast, the opportunity to learn, convenient work hours, and good interpersonal relations are more important to women than to men.[27] Managers need to be aware that what motivates the single mother with two dependent children who's working full time to support her family may be very different from the needs of a young, single, part-time worker or the older employee who is working to supplement his or her pension income. The following examples, which link the issue of motivation with our previous discussion of job design in Chapter 7, illustrate the importance of designing flexible work schedules and benefit programs to respond to employees' varied needs.

Ann works for Merck Pharmaceuticals. As a mother of two preschool children, she finds that the company's family-friendly benefits—day care, flextime, job sharing, flexible benefits, and personal leaves of absence—increase her commitment to her job and to Merck.

Mark also works for Merck. He is among the company's 2,000 or so employees who work part time. This Merck option allows Mark to gain valuable experience and meet his financial obligations, while at the same time allowing him to pursue his graduate studies in chemistry.

Jack is 72 years old. Because his social security check provides an inadequate income, Jack works full time at a local McDonald's. One of the franchise's hardest-working and most enthusiastic employees, he regularly praises the hamburger chain for providing him with flexible work hours and an excellent health plan that supplements Medicare.

Managers Who Made a Difference

HUBERT SAINT-ONGE AT CIBC

Hubert Saint-Onge is the head of the CIBC's leadership centre. The bank's management training centre is located on the site of the former King Ranch, north of Toronto. Here, individuals participate in highly interactive and experiential programs that focus on teamwork, leadership, and empowerment. The Foundations of Leadership, a week-long course, looks at the changing role of leaders in organizations. About 1,200 CIBC managers have attended this course.

Saint-Onge argues that training and development of people is not just for charity, or being good to people. "If an employee's attitude is low—if he doesn't feel ownership of his job—the customer knows that right away," he says. But if employees are well treated and they *do* have a sense of ownership and involvement in their jobs, that's reflected in good customer service.

Motivating Employees

Hubert Saint-Onge has an uphill struggle on his hands, but appears to be winning. The banking business has never been known for its enlightened treatment of employees. Traditionally they have relocated managers and their families at will and have ignored talented women. The structure has been based on command and control, with a strong system in place that demands conformity. Saint-Onge is trying to change that. His goal, he says, is to end training as it is generally practised—classroom-style teaching. He maintains that for a

company to become a learning organization, the responsibility for the learning must shift to the individual, with employers providing support. Much of the role of a manager will involve counselling, coaching, and supporting.

Hubert Saint-Onge was profiled by *Fortune* magazine in 1994 for his work in accounting for human assets. For instance, he suggests the value of employees may be measured by indices such as the number of new ideas generated and implemented, or their capacity for effective teamwork. Saint-Onge is bringing these and other ideas into the staid and conservative world of Canadian banking—and making a difference.[28] ▼

Summary

This Summary is organized by the chapter opening learning objectives found on page 268.

1. Motivation is the willingness to exert high levels of effort toward organizational goals, conditioned by the effort's ability to satisfy some individual need. The motivation process begins with an unsatisfied need, which creates tension and drives an individual to search for goals that, if attained, will satisfy the need and reduce the tension.

2. A need is some internal state that makes certain outcomes appear attractive.

3. The hierarchy of needs theory states that there are five needs—physiological, safety, social, esteem, and self-actualization—that individuals attempt to satisfy in a steplike progression. A substantially satisfied need no longer motivates.

4. Theory X is basically a negative view of human nature, assuming that employees dislike work, are lazy, seek to avoid responsibility, and must be coerced to perform. Theory Y is basically positive, assuming that employees are creative, seek responsibility, and can exercise self-direction.

5. The motivation-hygiene theory states that not all job factors can motivate employees. The presence

or absence of certain job characteristics, or hygiene factors, can only placate employees and not lead to satisfaction or motivation. Factors that people find intrinsically rewarding, such as achievement, recognition, responsibility, and growth, act as motivators and produce job satisfaction.

6. High achievers prefer jobs that offer personal responsibility, feedback, and moderate risks.
7. In equity theory, individuals compare their job's inputs-outcomes ratio to those of relevant others. If they perceive that they are underrewarded, their work motivation declines. When individuals perceive that they are overrewarded, they often are motivated to work harder in order to justify their pay.
8. The expectancy theory states that an individual tends to act in a certain way based on the expectation that the act will be followed by a given outcome and on the attractiveness of that outcome to the individual. Its prime components are the relationships between effort and performance, performance and rewards, and rewards and individual goals.

Review and Discussion Questions

1. What role do needs play in motivation?
2. What role would money play in (a) the hierarchy of needs theory, (b) motivation-hygiene theory, (c) equity theory, (d) expectancy theory, and (e) employees with a high nAch?
3. Contrast lower-order and higher-order needs in Maslow's need hierarchy.
4. If you accept Theory Y assumptions, how would you be likely to motivate employees?
5. Describe the three needs in the three-needs theory.
6. Would an individual with a high nAch be a good candidate for a management position? Explain.
7. What are some of the possible consequences of employees perceiving an inequity between their inputs and outcomes and those of others?
8. What difficulties do you think workforce diversity causes managers trying to use equity theory?
9. What role does perception play in (a) expectancy theory, (b) equity theory, and (c) reinforcement theory?
10. Explain the motivation implications of expectancy theory for management practice.

Self-Assessment Exercise

What Needs Are Most Important to You?

Instructions: Rank your responses for each of the following questions. The response that is most important or most true for you should receive a 5; the next should receive a 4; the next a 3; the next a 2; and the least important or least true should receive a 1.

Example

The work I like best involves:
- A __4__ Working alone.
- B __3__ A mixture of time spent with people and time spent alone.
- C __1__ Giving speeches.
- D __2__ Discussion with others.
- E __5__ Working outdoors.

1. Overall, the most important thing to me about a job is whether or not:
   - A ____ The pay is sufficient to meet my needs.
   - B ____ It provides the opportunity for fellowship and good human relations.
   - C ____ It is a secure job with good employee benefits.
   - D ____ It allows me freedom and the chance to express myself.
   - E ____ There is opportunity for advancement based on my achievements.

2. If I were to quit a job, it would probably be because:
   - A ____ It was a dangerous job, such as working with inadequate equipment or poor safety procedures.
   - B ____ Continued employment was questionable because of uncertainties in business conditions or funding sources.
   - C ____ It was a job people looked down on.

D ____ It was a one-person job, allowing little opportunity for discussion and interaction with others.
E ____ The work lacked personal meaning to me.

3. For me, the most important rewards in working are those that:
   A ____ Come from the work itself—important and challenging assignments.
   B ____ Satisfy the basic reasons why people work—good pay, a good home, and other economic needs.
   C ____ Are provided by fringe benefits—such as hospitalization insurance, time off for vacations, security for retirement, etc.
   D ____ Reflect my ability—such as being recognized for the work I do and knowing I am one of the best in my company or profession.
   E ____ Come from the human aspects of working—that is, the opportunity to make friends and to be a valued member of a team.

4. My morale would suffer most in a job in which:
   A ____ The future was unpredictable.
   B ____ Other employees received recognition, when I didn't, for doing the same quality of work.
   C ____ My co-workers were unfriendly or held grudges.
   D ____ I felt stifled and unable to grow.
   E ____ The job environment was poor—no air conditioning, inconvenient parking, insufficient space and lighting, primitive toilet facilities.

5. In deciding whether or not to accept a promotion, I would be most concerned with whether:
   A ____ The job was a source of pride and would be viewed with respect by others.
   B ____ Taking the job would constitute a gamble on my part, and I could lose more than I gained.
   C ____ The economic rewards would be favourable.
   D ____ I would like the new people I would be working with, and whether or not we would get along.
   E ____ I would be able to explore new areas and do more creative work.

6. The kind of job that brings out my best is one in which:
   A ____ There is a family spirit among employees and we all share good times.
   B ____ The working conditions—equipment, materials, and basic surroundings—are physically safe.
   C ____ Management is understanding and there is little chance of losing my job.
   D ____ I can see the returns on my work from the standpoint of personal values.
   E ____ There is recognition for my achievement.

7. I would consider changing jobs if my present position:
   A ____ Did not offer security and fringe benefits.
   B ____ Did not provide a chance to learn and grow.
   C ____ Did not provide recognition for my performance.
   D ____ Did not allow close personal contacts.
   E ____ Did not provide economic rewards.

8. The job situation that would cause the most stress to me is:
   A ____ Having a serious disagreement with my co-workers.
   B ____ Working in an unsafe environment.
   C ____ Having an unpredictable supervisor.
   D ____ Not being able to express myself.
   E ____ Not being appreciated for the quality of my work.

9. I would accept a new position if:
   A ____ The position would be a test of my potential.
   B ____ The new job would offer better pay and physical surroundings.
   C ____ The new job would be secure and offer long-term fringe benefits.
   D ____ The position would be respected by others in my organization.
   E ____ Good relationships with co-workers and business associates were probable.

10. I would work overtime if:
    A ____ The work is challenging.
    B ____ I need the extra income.
    C ____ My co-workers are also working overtime.
    D ____ I must do it to keep my job.
    E ____ The company recognizes my contribution.

Turn to page 415 for scoring directions and key.

Source: George Manning and Kent Curtis, *Human Behaviour: Why People Do What They Do* (Cincinnati, Ohio: Vista Systems/South-Western Publishing, 1988), pp. 17–20. With permission.

Class Exercise

How Can We Motivate Others?

This exercise is designed to help increase your awareness of how and why we motivate others and to help focus on the needs of those we are attempting to motivate.

Step 1: Break into groups of five to seven people. Each group member is to individually respond to the following:

Situation 1: You are the owner and president of a fifty-employee organization. Your goal is to motivate all fifty employees to their highest effort level.

Task 1: On a separate piece of paper, list the factors you would use to motivate your employees. Avoid general statements like give them a raise. Rather, be as specific as possible.

Task 2: Rank order (from highest to lowest) all the factors listed in task one above.

Situation 2: Consider now that you are one of the fifty employees who has been given input into what motivates you.

Task 3: As an employee, list those factors that would most effectively motivate you. Again, be as specific as possible.

Task 4: Rank order (from highest to lowest) those factors listed in task three above.

Step 2: Each member should share his or her prioritized lists (both lists from tasks 2 and 4 above) with the other members of the group.

Step 3: After each member has presented his or her lists, the group should respond to the following questions:

1. Are each individual's lists (task 2 and task 4) more similar or dissimilar? What does this mean to you?
2. What have you learned about how and why to motivate others and how can you apply these data?

Step 4: Each group should appoint a spokesperson to present its answers from step 3 to the class.

Source: Adapted from B.E. Smith, "Why Don't They Respond: A Motivational Experience," *Organizational Behavior Teaching Review,* Vol. X, No. 2 (1985–86), pp. 98–100.

Key Terms

Key terms are listed in the order in which they appear in the chapter.

motivation	self-actualization needs	need for achievement
need	Theory X	need for power
hierarchy of needs theory	Theory Y	need for affiliation
physiological needs	motivation-hygiene theory	equity theory
safety needs	hygiene factors	referents
social needs	motivators	expectancy theory
esteem needs	three-needs theory	

Case Application

Lincoln Electric

Lincoln Electric is a company with annual sales of over $450 million, about 2,400 employees, and a very unusual way of motivating employees. What is its business? About 90 per cent of its sales come from manufacturing arc-welding equipment and supplies.

Factory workers at Lincoln receive piece-rate wages with no guaranteed minimum hourly pay. After working for the company for two years, employees begin to participate in the year-end bonus plan. Determined by a formula that considers the company's gross profits and the employees' base piece rate and merit rating, it might be the most lucrative bonus system for factory workers in North America. The *average* size of the bonus over the last fifty-eight years has been 95.5 per cent of base wages. A handful of Lincoln factory workers make more than $100,000 a year. In recent good years, average Lincoln employees have earned about $44,000, well above the $17,000 average earnings for factory workers as a whole. But in a bad year, as in the 1982 recession, Lincoln employees' average earnings fell to $27,000—still not bad, but a significant drop from better years.

The company has a guaranteed employment policy that it put in place in 1958. Since that time, it has not laid off a single worker. During slow times, employees will accept reduced work periods. They also agree to accept work transfers, even to lower-paid jobs, if that is necessary to maintain a minimum of thirty hours of work per week.

Lincoln Electric is extremely cost- and productivity-conscious. If a worker produces a part that does not meet quality standards, he or she is not paid for the part until it is fixed. The piece-rate wage system and a highly competitive merit rating system create a high-pressure atmosphere that some workers might find stressful. But the pressure has been good for productivity. One company executive esimates that Lincoln's overall productivity is about double that of its domestic competitors. The company has earned a profit every year since the depths of the depression in the 1930s and has never missed a quarterly dividend. Lincoln has an extremely low employee turnover rate.

Questions

1. Which motivation theories discussed in this chapter, if any, do you feel Lincoln is using in motivating its employees?
2. Why does Lincoln's approach to motivating employees work so well?
3. What problems, if any, do you think this system might create for management?

Reward and Motivation

How do you reward individuals for doing a good job? How do you recognize achievement? How do you signal performance above the ordinary? We've all seen Employee of the Week/ Month/ Year programs, and if you've heard about Mary Kay Cosmetics, you'll know about her pink Cadillacs that individuals who sell above a certain level get to use. This is the world of "incentives" — gifts or benefits that aim to recognize and reward good performance. They range from items worth a few dollars or less (edible yo-yos) to trips and expensive items such as cars or furniture. In the 1970s, a Canadian investment dealer rewarded its top three salesmen with Mercedes convertibles.

In most cases, the items that individuals receive as incentives are things they could easily afford to buy if they so wished. Even the Mercedes convertibles, which sound extremely exotic (and which cost $57,000 20 years ago) were given to individuals who had all made more than a million dollars in commissions that year. So where's the incentive? A great number of Canadian companies believe there's something to it — Labatt, Imperial Oil, Xerox, The Royal Bank, Chrysler, Toyota, Campbell Soups, Kelloggs, and many others. What do the incentives achieve? Bell Canada gives its employees points for doing their jobs well. Much like tokens for gasoline or airline frequent flyer points, these can be redeemed for merchandise. Bell employees can use their accumulated points to acquire a wide variety of items from a catalogue of choices.

How do you get employees to do a good job without having to give them constant raises or financial bonuses? Few companies operate like Lincoln Electric (see the Case Application). But every organization should be concerned about getting the best out of its people, and many feel that incentives and incentive programs help achieve that goal. Many of the items centre around recognition for a job well done or for outstanding achievement. One trucking company gives a ring to drivers who have logged more than a million miles. And plaques and certificates of accomplishment are common.

Questions

1. Do incentives motivate people? How? How effective are they, in your opinion?
2. Have you, or a close friend or family member, been the recipient of an incentive reward or award? What was the recipient's reaction? How did they feel? Do you think it affected their performance?
3. Are incentive awards a substitute for salary increases? Explain your answer.
4. Given that wage increases are getting rarer by the year, will incentive awards begin to become more important? Why? What do they achieve?

Video Resource: "Incentives '94," *Venture* 479 (March 13, 1994).

13

Leadership and Supervision

Learning Objectives

WHAT WILL I BE ABLE TO DO AFTER I FINISH THIS CHAPTER?

1. **Explain the difference between managers and leaders.**
2. **Summarize the conclusions of trait theories.**
3. **Identify the two underlying leadership styles in the managerial grid.**
4. **Describe the Fiedler contingency model.**
5. **Summarize the path-goal model.**
6. **Explain when leaders may not be that important.**
7. **Identify the key characteristics of charismatic leaders.**
8. **Contrast transactional and transformational leadership.**
9. **Describe the unique characteristics of being a first-line supervisor.**
10. **Explain how the supervisor's role is changing in today's organizations.**

It's a long way from St-Jerome, Quebec, to Redmond, Washington, and you have to be one of the very best to make it. But Daniel Langlois, who grew up on a farm near St-Jerome not only made it to Redmond, but he also had the ticket paid by Bill Gates at Microsoft—with US$130 million of Microsoft stock in exchange for Langlois' company, Softimage Inc. You may not know the name Softimage, but you know some of its work because it's the company whose software created the animation in *The Mask* and *Jurassic Park*.

Daniel Langlois was awarded *Canadian Business's* Entrepreneur of the Year award in 1994. He's a leader—dedicated, visionary, disciplined, focused. His leadership ability is shown by the fact that in eight years he has been able to take Softimage from its founding in 1986 as a one-man company, to a rapidly growing and key part of giant Microsoft. Langlois was initially able to raise $350,000 from a group of Toronto investors, but not without tremendous hard work and persistence, since Canada is renowned as being a difficult place to raise venture capital. However, on the basis of that $350,000, Langlois was able to build his company's revenues to US$8.5 million by 1992, at which point he raised US$10 million with a public stock offering, and an additional US$13.6 million in 1993.[1]

Leadership is about getting others to follow. Great leaders are able to get others to accept their ideas and to put them into practice. In many cases, great ideas wither on the vine because there isn't the strength of leadership to drive them to successful implementation. Great leaders, in whatever field, are driven by vision, and Langlois is an excellent example of someone who can combine his vision with energy and drive, and, most importantly, with organization and self-discipline. Many people would see the Microsoft buy-out as the ideal ticket to retirement.

Daniel Langlois has shown what vision and focus can do by expanding his company, which developed the software for the animation in *Jurassic Park* and *The Mask*, to the point where Microsoft bought it for US$130 million.

Not Langlois. "My goal hasn't changed," he says. "I want to push the technology. I want these tools to exist. I want to create the ultimate creative environment." He can project his drive, excitement and commitment to others around him, and perhaps the ultimate proof of this is that, usually when a small company is bought out by a giant, the small one gets swallowed. High-quality staff get absorbed by the parent. But not with Softimage. Instead of taking Softimage people out of Montreal to Redmond, Microsoft people are moving the other way, and researchers and developers are being added to Softimage as rapidly as possible. Daniel Langlois, at 38, demonstrates what good leadership and dedication can achieve.

But if leadership is so important, it's only natural to ask: Are leaders born or made? What differentiates leaders from nonleaders? What can you do if you want to be seen as a leader? In this chapter we'll try to answer such questions.

Managers versus Leaders

Let's begin by clarifying the distinction between managers and leaders. Writers frequently confuse the two, although they are not necessarily the same.

Managers are appointed. They have legitimate power that allows them to reward and punish. Their ability to influence is based on the formal authority inherent in their positions. In contrast, leaders may either be appointed or emerge from within a group. Leaders can influence others to perform beyond the actions dictated by formal authority.

Should all managers be leaders? Conversely, should all leaders be managers? Because no one yet has been able to demonstrate through research or logical argument that leadership ability is a handicap to a manager, we can state that all managers should ideally be leaders. However, not all leaders necessarily have the capabilities in other managerial functions, and thus not all should hold managerial positions. The fact that an individual can influence others does not tell whether he or she can also plan, organize, and control. Given (if only ideally) that all managers should be leaders, we will pursue the subject from a managerial perspective. Therefore, **leaders** in this chapter mean those who are able to influence others and who possess managerial authority.

leaders
Those who are able to influence others and who possess managerial authority.

Trait Theories of Leadership

Ask the average person on the street what comes to mind when he or she thinks of leadership. You're likely to get a list of qualities such as intelligence, charisma, decisiveness, enthusiasm, strength, bravery, integrity, and self-confidence. These responses represent, in essence, **trait theories** of leadership. The search for traits or characteristics that differentiate leaders from nonleaders, though done in a more sophisticated manner than our on-the-street survey, dominated the early research efforts in the study of leadership.

trait theories
Theories isolating characteristics that differentiate leaders from nonleaders.

Is it possible to isolate one or more traits in individuals who are generally acknowledged to be leaders—for instance, Pierre Trudeau, Winston Churchill, Joan of Arc, Nelson Mandela, Mahatma Gandhi, Margaret Thatcher—that nonleaders do not possess? We may agree that these individuals meet our definition of a leader, but they represent individuals with utterly different characteristics. If the concept of traits was to prove valid, all leaders would have to possess specific characteristics.

Research efforts at isolating these traits resulted in a number of dead ends. Attempts failed to identify a set of traits that would always differentiate leaders from followers and effective leaders from ineffective leaders. Perhaps it was a bit optimistic to believe that a set of consistent and unique personality traits could apply across the board to all effective leaders, whether they were in charge of the Hell's Angels, Montreal Expos, Federal Express, Petro-Canada, Vancouver General Hospital, or the Anglican Church of Canada.

What traits characterize leaders like SNC-Lavalin CEO Guy Saint-Pierre? Research has identified six: drive, the desire to lead, honesty and integrity, self-confidence, intelligence, and job-related knowledge.

Exhibit 13-1 Six Traits That Differentiate Leaders from Nonleaders

Source: Shelly A. Kirkpatrick and Edwin A. Locke, "Leadership: Do Traits Really Matter?," *Academy of Management Executive,* May 1991, pp. 48–60.

▶ 1. **Drive.** Leaders exhibit a high effort level. They have a relatively high desire for achievement, they're ambitious, they have a lot of energy, they're tirelessly persistent in their activities, and they show initiative.

▶ 2. **Desire to lead.** Leaders have a strong desire to influence and lead others. They demonstrate the willingness to take responsibility.

▶ 3. **Honesty and integrity.** Leaders build trusting relationships between themselves and followers by being truthful or nondeceitful and by showing high consistency between word and deed.

▶ 4. **Self-confidence.** Followers look to leaders for an absence of self-doubt. Leaders, therefore, need to show self-confidence in order to convince followers of the rightness of goals and decisions.

▶ 5. **Intelligence.** Leaders need to be intelligent enough to gather, synthesize, and interpret large amounts of information; and to be able to create visions, solve problems, and make correct decisions.

▶ 6. **Job-relevant knowledge.** Effective leaders have a high degree of knowledge about the company, industry, and technical matters. In-depth knowledge allows leaders to make well-informed decisions and to understand the implications of those decisions.

However, attempts to identify traits consistently associated with leadership have been more successful. Six traits on which leaders are seen to differ from nonleaders include drive, the desire to lead, honesty and integrity, self-confidence, intelligence, and job-relevant knowledge.[2] These traits are briefly described in Exhibit 13-1.

Yet traits alone are not sufficient for explaining leadership. Explanations based solely on traits ignore situational factors. Possessing the appropriate traits only makes it more likely that an individual will be an effective leader. He or she still has to take the right actions. And what is right in one situation is not necessarily right for a different situation. So while there has been some resurgent interest in traits during the past decade, a major movement away from trait theories began as early as the 1940s. Leadership research from the late 1940s through the mid-1960s emphasized the preferred behavioural styles that leaders demonstrated.

Behavioural Theories of Leadership

The inability to explain leadership solely from traits led researchers to look at the behaviour that specific leaders exhibited. Researchers wondered whether there was something unique in the behaviour of effective leaders. For example, do leaders tend to be more democratic than autocratic?

behavioural theories
Theories identifying behaviours that differentiate effective from ineffective leaders.

It was hoped that not only would the **behavioural theories** approach provide more definitive answers about the nature of leadership but, if successful, would also have practical implications quite different from those of the trait approach. If trait research had been successful, it would have provided a basis for selecting the "right" people to assume formal positions in organizations requiring leadership. In contrast, if behavioural studies were to turn up critical behavioural determinants of leadership, we could train people to be leaders.

Leadership and Supervision

A number of studies looked at behavioural styles. We shall briefly review the two most popular ones: the Ohio State group and the University of Michigan group. Then we shall see how the concepts that these studies developed could be used to create a grid for looking at and appraising leadership styles.

What Was the Importance of the Ohio State Studies?

The most comprehensive and replicated of the behavioural theories resulted from research that began at Ohio State University in the late 1940s.[3] These studies sought to identify independent dimensions of leader behaviour. Beginning with over 1,000 dimensions, they eventually narrowed down the list to two categories that accounted for most of the leadership behaviour described by employees. They called these two dimensions initiating structure and consideration.

Initiating structure refers to the extent to which a leader is likely to define and structure his or her role and those of employees in the search for goal attainment. It includes behaviour that attempts to organize work, work relationships, and goals. For example, the leader who is characterized as high in initiating structure assigns group members to particular tasks, expects workers to maintain definite standards of performance, and emphasizes meeting deadlines.

Consideration is defined as the extent to which a person has job relationships characterized by mutual trust and respect for employees' ideas and feelings. A leader who is high in consideration helps employees with personal problems, is friendly and approachable, and treats all employees as equals. He or she shows concern for his or her followers' comfort, well-being, status, and satisfaction.

Extensive research based on these definitions found that a leader who is high in initiating structure and consideration (a "high-high" leader) achieved high employee performance and satisfaction more frequently than one who rated low on either consideration, initiating structure, or both. However, the high-high style did not always yield positive results. For example, leader behaviour characterized as high on initiating structure led to greater rates of grievances, absenteeism, and turnover and lower levels of job satisfaction for workers performing routine tasks. Other studies found that high consideration was negatively related to performance ratings of the leader by his or her manager. In conclusion, the Ohio State studies suggested that the high-high style generally produced positive outcomes, but enough exceptions were found to indicate that situational factors needed to be integrated into the theory (see Managers Who Made a Difference).

initiating structure
The extent to which a leader defines and structures his or her role and those of employees to attain goals.

consideration
The extent to which a person has job relationships characterized by mutual trust, respect for employees' ideas, and regard for their feelings.

What Were the Leadership Dimensions of the University of Michigan Studies?

Leadership studies undertaken at the University of Michigan's Survey Research Center, at about the same time as those being done at Ohio State, had similar research objectives: to locate behavioural characteristics of leaders that were related to performance effectiveness. The Michigan group also came up with two dimensions of leadership behaviour, which they labelled employee oriented and production oriented.[4] Leaders who were **employee oriented** were described as emphasizing interpersonal relations; they took a personal interest in the needs of their employees and accepted individual differences among members. The **production-oriented** leaders, in contrast, tended to emphasize the technical or task aspects of the job, were concerned mainly with accomplishing their group's tasks, and regarded group members as a means to that end.

employee oriented
Leadership style that emphasizes interpersonal relations.

production oriented
Leadership style that emphasizes technical aspects of the job.

Chapter 13

Managers Who Made a Difference

Guy Saint-Pierre at SNC-Lavalin

Guy Saint-Pierre could write a book entitled *Everything You Ever Wanted to Know About Leadership* if he was so inclined. He is what leadership is all about. His outstanding leadership abilities have made him highly successful in a series of major careers—in the Canadian Army where his former commanding officer, Lieutenant Colonel Al Loveridge says, "My forecast was that he would be a general if he stayed in"; as a senior executive with Acres, the international engineering firm; in politics, where he was minister of education and minister of industry and commerce in Robert Bourassa's Quebec cabinet in the 1970s; and as CEO of SNC-Lavalin, Canada's largest engineering consulting firm. He is also a highly valued director of the Royal Bank, General Motors of Canada, Purolator Courier, and Alcan. And he has applied his leadership skills successfully to areas like charities—for instance, when he was co-chairman of the charity organization, Centraide, he tripled the number of individual sponsors.

Saint-Pierre has the ability to inspire confidence in the people around him. At SNC-Lavalin he faced an enormous challenge. When he became CEO on January 10, 1989, many key executives had either left, were in the process of leaving, or were looking for opportunities to leave. Morale was low throughout the firm. The company was losing lots of money and its bankers were worried about its debt. As Saint-Pierre saw it, "The big challenge was how to motivate people, many of whom you knew would leave if they had another job offer." He met with the shell-shocked top managers and told them, "Many of you feel like prisoners on a sinking ship. If I'm here it is because I believe it will not go under." (Saint-Pierre had left the job of president and CEO of Ogilvie Mills Ltd. to come to SNC-Lavalin). "But to make that so, I need you." His remarkable ability to inspire confidence and build morale, and to communicate with people—over the year he talked with 600 employees over coffee—helped the company go from a loss of almost $33 million in 1988 to a profit of $26.2 million a year later.

Guy Saint-Pierre has learned from all his experiences. Students of leadership can learn from him. "Working for my father taught me to be precise in life. Honesty and personal integrity were more important than your bank account. From my mother I learned intellectual curiosity. She believed you were never too old to learn, and that you are your only judge. It was important to have perseverance and never give up." The army taught him the importance of communication and for "real leadership you don't need rank." "You can't be a leader unless you are able to want and see the need for change," he argues. "Second, it is always important to learn not only in your own narrow field but to be interested in the world around you." And, he says, his parents gave him another highly important ingredient for successful leadership—an "awareness that in life you can't be selfish, you have to give back somehow. How do you do that? By getting involved. And the more you get involved, the more satisfaction you get out of it." Peter Widrington, chairman of the Toronto Blue Jays and an SCC-Lavalin board member says of Saint-Pierre, "In this age of cut-throats and hard driving in business, he is just so damn civilized that it amazes you. He is urbane, level-headed and straightforward and is proof you don't need those other qualities to be effective at the top."[5]

Leadership and Supervision

The conclusions of the Michigan researchers strongly favoured leaders who were employee oriented. Employee-oriented leaders were associated with higher group productivity and higher job satisfaction. Production-oriented leaders were associated with lower group productivity and lower worker satisfaction.

What Is the Managerial Grid?

The **managerial grid** is a two-dimensional view of leadership style developed by Robert Blake and Jane Mouton.[6] They proposed a managerial grid based on the styles of "concern for people" and "concern for production," which essentially represent the Ohio State dimensions of consideration and initiating structure and the Michigan dimensions of employee orientation and production orientation.

The grid, depicted in Exhibit 13-2, has nine possible positions along each axis, creating eighty-one different positions into which a leader's style may fall. The grid does not show the results produced but rather the dominating factors in a leader's thinking in regard to getting results. That is, although there are eighty-one positions on the grid, the five key positions identified by Blake and Mouton focus on the four corners of the grid and a middle-ground area (see Exhibit 13-2).

From their findings, Blake and Mouton concluded that managers perform best using a 9,9 style. Unfortunately, the grid offers no answers to the question of what makes a manager but only a framework for conceptualizing leadership style. In fact, there is little substantive evidence to support the conclusion that a 9,9 style is most effective in all situations.[7]

managerial grid
A two-dimensional portrayal of leadership based on concerns for people and for production.

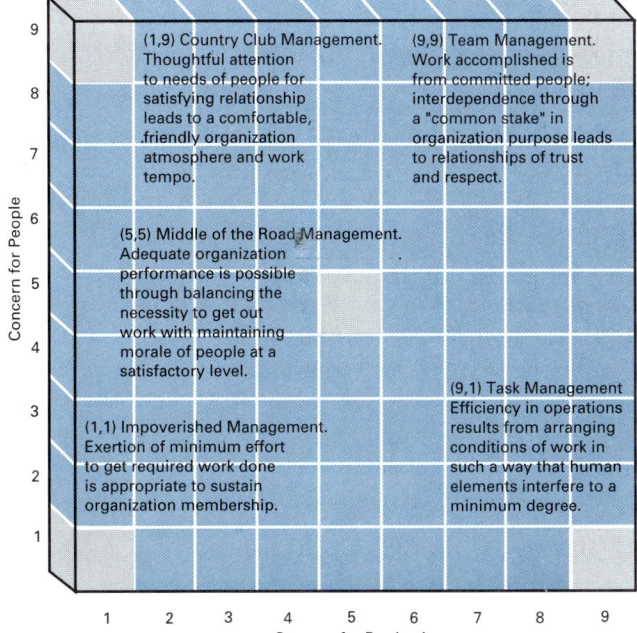

Exhibit 13-2 The Managerial Grid

Source: Reprinted by permission of *Harvard Business Review.* An exhibit from "Breakthrough in Organization Development" by Robert R. Blake, Jane S. Mouton, Louis B. Barnes, and Larry E. Greiner, November-December 1964, p. 136. Copyright © 1964 by the President and Fellows of Harvard College; all rights reserved.

What Did the Behavioural Theories Teach Us About Leadership?

We have described the most popular and important attempts to explain leadership in terms of behaviour. Obviously there were other efforts,[8] but they faced the same problem that confronted the Ohio State and Michigan researchers: they had very little success in identifying consistent relationships between patterns of leadership behaviour and successful performance. General statements could not be made because results would vary over different ranges of circumstances. What was missing was consideration of the situational factors that influence success or failure. For example, would Mother Teresa have been a great leader of the poor at the turn of the century? Would Pierre Trudeau have become the leader of Brazil, or Nelson Mandela the president of South Africa in 1960? It seems quite unlikely, yet the behavioural approaches we have described could not clarify such situational factors.

Contingency Theories of Leadership

It became increasingly clear to those studying the leadership phenomenon that predicting leadership success involved something more complex than isolating a few traits or preferable behaviours. The failure to obtain consistent results led to a new focus on situational influences. The relationship between leadership style and effectiveness suggested that under condition a, style X would be appropriate, whereas style Y would be more suitable for condition b, and style Z for condition c. But what were the conditions a, b, c, and so forth? It was one thing to say that leadership effectiveness depended on the situation and another to be able to isolate those situational conditions.

Several approaches to isolating key situational variables have proven more successful than others and, as a result, have gained wider recognition. We shall consider three of these: the Fiedler model, path-goal theory, and the leader-participation model.

What Is the Fiedler Model?

The first comprehensive contingency model for leadership was developed by Fred Fiedler.[9] The **Fiedler contingency model** proposes that effective group performance depends upon the proper match between the leader's style of interacting with his or her employees and the degree to which the situation gives control and influence to the leader. Fiedler developed the **least-preferred coworker (LPC) questionnaire** that purports to measure whether a person is task or relationship oriented. Further, he isolated three situational criteria—**leader-member relations, task structure,** and **position power**—that he believes can be manipulated to create the proper match with the behavioural orientation of the leader. In a sense the Fiedler model is an outgrowth of trait theory, since the LPC questionnaire is a simple psychological test. However, Fiedler goes significantly beyond trait and behavioural approaches by isolating situations, relating an individual's personality to the situation, and then predicting leadership effectiveness as a function of the two.

Fiedler believes a key factor in leadership success to be an individual's basic leadership style. Thus, he first tries to find out what that basic style is. Fiedler created the LPC questionnaire for this purpose. As shown in Exhibit 13-3, it contains sixteen pairs of contrasting adjectives. Respondents are asked to think of all the coworkers they have

Fiedler contingency model
The theory that effective groups depend on a proper match between a leader's style of interacting with employees and the degree to which the situation gives control and influence to the leader.

least-preferred coworker (LPC) questionnaire
A questionnaire that measures whether a person is task or relationship oriented.

leader-member relations
The degree of confidence, trust, and respect subordinates have in their leader.

task structure
The degree to which the job assignments are procedurized.

position power
The degree of influence a leader has over power variables such as hiring, firing, discipline, promotions, and salary increases.

Exhibit 13-3
Fiedler's LPC Scale

Source: From Fred E. Fiedler and Martin M. Chemers, *Leadership and Effective Management* (Glenview, IL: Scott, Foresman & Co., 1974). Reprinted by permission of authors.

	8	7	6	5	4	3	2	1	
Pleasant									Unpleasant
Friendly	8	7	6	5	4	3	2	1	Unfriendly
Rejecting	1	2	3	4	5	6	7	8	Accepting
Helpful	8	7	6	5	4	3	2	1	Frustrating
Unenthusiastic	1	2	3	4	5	6	7	8	Enthusiastic
Tense	1	2	3	4	5	6	7	8	Relaxed
Distant	1	2	3	4	5	6	7	8	Close
Cold	1	2	3	4	5	6	7	8	Warm
Cooperative	8	7	6	5	4	3	2	1	Uncooperative
Supportive	8	7	6	5	4	3	2	1	Hostile
Boring	1	2	3	4	5	6	7	8	Interesting
Quarrelsome	1	2	3	4	5	6	7	8	Harmonious
Self-assured	8	7	6	5	4	3	2	1	Hesitant
Efficient	8	7	6	5	4	3	2	1	Inefficient
Gloomy	1	2	3	4	5	6	7	8	Cheerful
Open	8	7	6	5	4	3	2	1	Guarded

ever had and to describe the one person they least enjoyed working with by rating him or her on a scale of 1 to 8 for each of the sixteen sets of adjectives. Fiedler believes that, on the basis of the respondents' answers to this LPC questionnaire, you can determine most people's basic leadership style.

If the least preferred coworker is described in relatively positive terms (a high LPC score), then the respondent is primarily interested in good personal relations with this coworker. That is, if you describe the person you are least able to work with in favourable terms, Fiedler would label you relationship oriented. In contrast, if you see the least preferred coworker in relatively unfavourable terms (a low LPC score), you are primarily interested in productivity and thus would be labeled task oriented. Using the LPC instrument, Fiedler is able to place most respondents into either of these two leadership styles (see Details on a Management Classic).

Once an individual's basic leadership style has been assessed through the LPC, it is necessary to evaluate the circumstances and match the leader with the situation. Fiedler has identified three contingency dimensions that, he argues, define the key situational factors for determining leadership effectiveness. These are leader-member relations (the degree of confidence, trust, and respect employees have in their leader); task structure (the degree to which the job assignments are structured or unstructured); and

How effective will the leader of this group be? According to the Fiedler contingency model, based on the individual's LPC, effective leadership will be contingent on the situation he leads. That is, an effective leader is one whose leadership style fits the job situation.

position power (the degree of influence a leader has over power variables such as hiring, firing, discipline, promotions, and salary increases). These situational dimensions are then evaluated. Leader-member relations are either good or poor, task structure either high or low, and position power either strong or weak. Altogether, by mixing the three contingency variables, there are potentially eight different situations or categories in which a leader could find him or herself.

It's important to note that Fiedler assumes that an individual's leadership style is fixed. This means that if a situation requires a task-oriented leader and the person in that leadership position is relationship oriented, either the situation has to be modified or the leader has to be removed and replaced if optimum effectiveness is to be achieved. Fiedler argues that leadership style is innate—you can't change your style to fit changing situations!

How Does Path-Goal Theory Operate?

Currently, one of the most respected approaches to leadership is **path-goal theory.** Developed by Robert House, path-goal theory is a contingency model of leadership that extracts key elements from the Ohio State leadership research and the expectancy theory of motivation.[10]

The essence of the theory is that it's the leader's job to assist his or her followers in attaining their goals and to provide the necessary direction and/or support to ensure that their goals are compatible with the overall objectives of the group or organization.

Details on a Management Classic

FRED FIEDLER AND THE FIEDLER CONTINGENCY MODEL OF LEADERSHIP

The Fiedler model proposes matching an individual's LPC and an assessment of the three contingency variables to achieve maximum leadership effectiveness. In his studies of over 1,200 groups, in which he compared relationship- versus task-oriented leadership styles in each of the eight situational categories, Fiedler concluded that task-oriented leaders tend to perform better in situations that were very favourable to them and in situations that were very unfavourable (see Exhibit MC13-1). Fiedler would predict that, when faced with a category I, II, III, VII, or VIII situation, task-oriented leaders perform better. Relationship-oriented leaders, however, perform better in moderately favourable situations—categories IV through VI.

Remember that according to Fiedler an individual's leadership style is fixed. Therefore, there are really only two ways in which to improve leader effectiveness. First, you can change the leader to fit the situation. For example, if a group situation rates as highly unfavourable but is currently led by a relationship-oriented manager, the group's performance could be improved by replacing that manager with one who is task oriented.

Leadership and Supervision

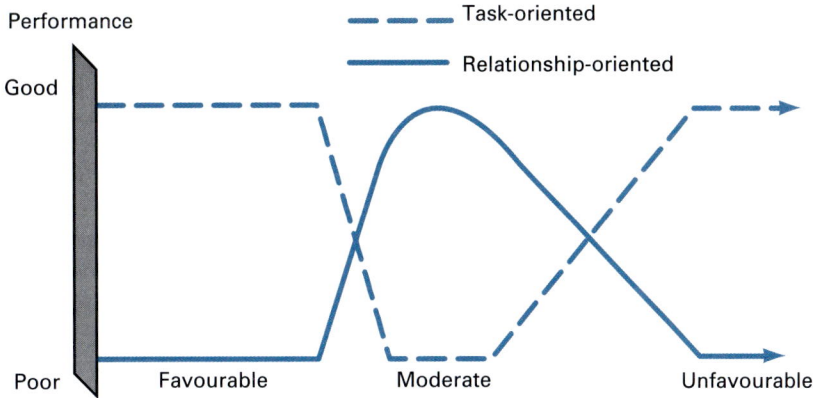

Exhibit MC13-1 The Findings of the Fiedler Model

The second alternative would be to change the situation to fit the leader. That could be done by restructuring tasks or increasing or decreasing the power that the leader has to control factors such as salary increases, promotions, and disciplinary actions.

As a whole, reviews of the major studies undertaken to test the overall validity of the Fiedler model show there is considerable evidence to support it.[11] But there are problems with the LPC and the practical use of the model that need to be addressed.[12] Nonetheless, Fiedler has made an important contribution toward understanding leadership effectiveness. His work continues to be a dominant input in the development of contingency explanations of leadership effectiveness. ▼

The term "path-goal" is derived from the belief that effective leaders clarify the path to help their followers get from where they are to the achievement of their work goals and make the journey along the path easier by reducing roadblocks and pitfalls.

According to path-goal theory, a leader's behaviour is acceptable to employees to the degree that they view it as an immediate source of satisfaction or as a means of future satisfaction. A leader's behaviour is motivational to the degree that it (1) makes employee need-satisfaction contingent on effective performance, and (2) provides the coaching, guidance, support, and rewards that are necessary for effective performance. To test these statements, House identified four leadership behaviours. The directive leader lets employees know what is expected of them, schedules work to be done, and gives specific guidance as to how to accomplish tasks. This type of leadership closely parallels the Ohio State dimension of initiating structure. The supportive leader is friendly and shows concern for the needs of employees. This type of leadership is essentially synonymous with the Ohio State dimension of consideration. The participative leader consults with employees and uses their suggestions before making a decision. The achievement-oriented leader

path-goal theory
The theory that a leader's behaviour is acceptable to employees insofar as they view it as a source of either immediate or future satisfaction.

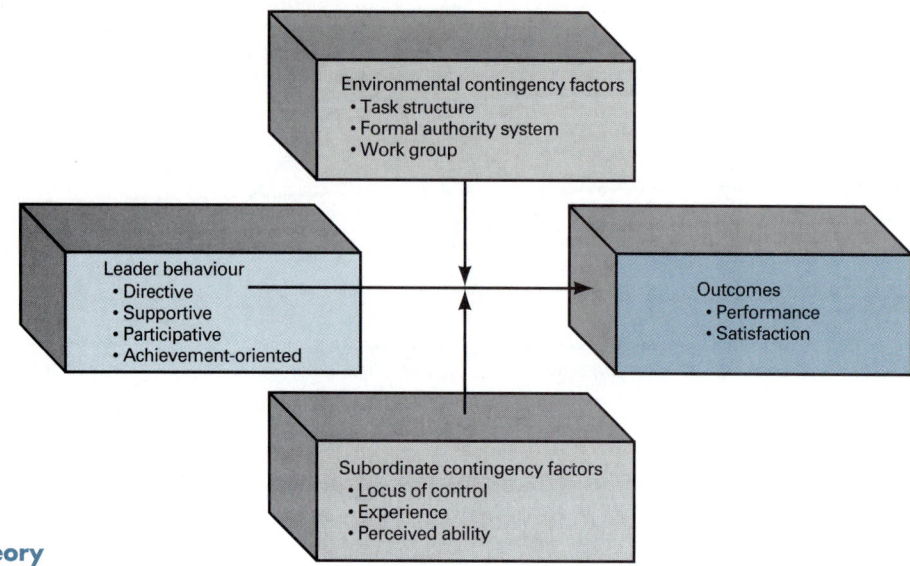

Exhibit 13-4 Path-Goal Theory

sets challenging goals and expects employees to perform at their highest level. In contrast to Fiedler's view of a leader's behaviour, House assumes that leaders are flexible. Path-goal theory implies that the same leader can display any or all of these leadership styles depending on the situation.

As Exhibit 13-4 illustrates, path-goal theory proposes two classes of situational or contingency variables that moderate the leadership behaviour-outcome relationship—those in the environment that are outside the control of the employee (task structure, the formal authority system, and the work group) and those that are part of the personal characteristics of the employee (locus of control, experience, and perceived ability). Environmental factors determine the type of leader behaviour required as a complement if subordinate outcomes are to be maximized, while personal characteristics of the subordinate determine how the environment and leader behaviour are interpreted. The theory proposes that leader behaviour will be ineffective when it is redundant with sources of environmental structure or incongruent with subordinate characteristics.

What Is the Leader-Participation Model?

leader-participation model
A leadership theory that provides a set of rules to determine the form and amount of participative decision making in different situations.

Back in 1973, Victor Vroom and Phillip Yetton developed a **leader-participation model** that related leadership behaviour and participation to decision making.[13] Recognizing that task structures have varying demands for routine and nonroutine activities, these researchers argued that leader behaviour must adjust to reflect the task structure. Vroom and Yetton's model was normative; it provided a sequential set of rules that should be followed in determining the form and amount of participation in decision making, as determined by different types of situations. The model was a decision tree incorporating seven contingencies (whose relevance could be identified by making yes or no choices) and five alternative leadership styles.

More recent work by Vroom and Arthur Jago has resulted in a revision of this model.[14] The new model retains the same five alternative leadership styles but expands the contingency variables to twelve—from the leader making the decision completely by him or herself, to sharing the problem with the group and developing a consensus decision. These are listed in Exhibit 13-5.

Leadership and Supervision

QR:	Quality Requirement:	How important is the technical quality of this decision?
CR:	Commitment Requirement:	How important is employee commitment to the decision?
LI:	Leader Information:	Do you have sufficient information to make a high-quality decision?
ST:	Problem Structure:	Is the problem well-structured?
CP:	Commitment Probability:	If you were to make this decision by yourself, is it reasonably certain that your employees would be committed to the decision?
GC:	Goal Congruence:	Do employees share the organizational goals to be attained in solving this problem?
CO:	Employee Conflict:	Is conflict among employees over preferred solutions likely?
SI:	Employee Information:	Do employees have sufficient information to make a high-quality decision?
TC:	Time Constraint:	Does a critically severe time constraint limit your ability to involve employees?
GD:	Geographical Dispersion:	Are the costs involved in bringing together geographically dispersed employees prohibitive?
MT:	Motivation Time:	How important is it to you to minimize the time it takes to make the decision?
MD:	Motivation-Development:	How important is it to you to maximize the opportunities for employee development?

Exhibit 13-5 Contingency Variables in the Revised Leader-Participation Model
Source: V.H. Vroom and A.G. Jago, *The New Leadership: Managing Participation in Organizations* (Englewood Cliffs, N.J.: Prentice Hall, Inc., 1988), pp. 111–12. With permission.

Research testing the original leader-participation model was very encouraging.[15] But unfortunately, the model is far too complex for the typical manager to use regularly. In fact, Vroom and Jago have developed a computer program to guide managers through all the decision branches in the revised model. Although we obviously cannot do justice to this model's sophistication in this discussion, the model has provided us with some solid, empirically supported insights in contingency variables of leadership. For instance, the leader-participation model confirms that leadership research should be directed at the situation rather than at the person. It probably makes more sense to talk about autocratic and participative situations rather than autocratic and participative leaders. As did House in his path-goal theory, Vroom, Yetton, and Jago argue against the notion that leader behaviour is inflexible. The leader-participation model assumes that the leader can adapt his or her style to different situations.

Is Leadership Ever Irrelevant?

In keeping with the contingency spirit, we want to conclude this section by offering this notion: The belief that some leadership style will always be effective regardless of the situation may not be true. Leadership may not always be important. Data from numerous studies demonstrate that, in many situations, any behaviours a leader exhibits are irrelevant. Certain individual, job, and organizational variables can act as "substitutes for leadership," negating the influence of the leader.[16]

For instance, characteristics of employees such as experience, training, "professional" orientation, or need for independence can neutralize the effect of leadership. These characteristics can replace the need for a leader's support or ability to create structure and reduce task ambiguity. Similarly, jobs that are inherently unambiguous and routine or that are intrinsically satisfying may place fewer demands on the leadership variable. Finally, such organizational characteristics as explicit formalized goals, rigid rules and procedures, or cohesive work groups can act in the place of formal leadership.

Canadians have made some important contributions to leadership thinking. Bill Reddin, a former professor at the University of New Brunswick developed a contingency approach to leadership in 1970 that was based on the idea that "the effectiveness of any behaviour depends on the situation in which it is used."[17] He argued that a manager must be able to read a situation in order to know how best to manage it. Effectiveness is not simply a matter of leadership style, it's a matter of using a particular style at the right time. Reddin's 3-D theory of management looks at how using a particular style of leadership in one situation can be ineffective, while using it in another situation can be effective. So leaders must have a sensitivity to the situation in which they find themselves. Reddin's theory helps to explain why leaders can turn from being highly successful to failures while still doing the same sorts of things. General George Patton is a good example—the right man for the moment, but ineffective once the need for his skills was over. IBM and General Motors both encountered huge problems because their leadership style remained constant while the situation changed around them.

Rick Roskin, a professor at Memorial University in Newfoundland has also made a significant contribution to thinking on leadership with his M.ach One theory.[18] Roskin looked at the data on which the Ohio State model was based and found that while the findings showed clusters that could be interpreted as structure and consideration, there was a lot of the basic data that remained unexplained. He examined it more closely and recognized that there was indeed a *third* type of behaviour in which managers engage: bringing together the diverse activities and outputs of the people who report to them. This is the function of *integration* and *coordination*. Roskin's model is three-dimensional. And like Reddin, he has developed a method of analyzing the situational demands of a job, which means that managers can determine the optimal leadership style behaviour for a particular job.

What characteristics does retired general Norman Schwarzkopf possess that enhance his charismatic style? The research cites several key attributes such as self-confidence, vision, articulateness, and strong convictions.

Emerging Approaches to Leadership

We conclude our review of leadership theories by presenting two emerging approaches to the subject: charismatic leadership and transactional versus transformational leadership. If there is one theme that underlies these approaches, it is that they take a more practical view of leadership than previous theories have (with the exception of trait theories, of course). That is, both approaches look again at leadership from the way the average "person on the street" does.

What Is Charismatic Leadership Theory?

charismatic leadership theory
Followers make attributions of heroic or extraordinary leadership abilities when they observe certain behaviours.

In Chapter 10, we discussed attribution theory in relation to perception. **Charismatic leadership theory** is an extension of that theory. It says that followers make attributions of heroic or extraordinary leadership abilities when they observe certain behaviours.[19] Studies on charismatic leadership have, for the most part, been directed at identifying those behaviours that differentiate charismatic leaders—the Pierre Trudeaus and Ronald Reagans of the world—from their noncharismatic counterparts.

Leadership and Supervision

Several authors have attempted to identify personal characteristics of the charismatic leader. Robert House (of path-goal fame) has identified three: extremely high confidence, dominance, and strong convictions in his or her beliefs.[20] Warren Bennis, after studying ninety of the most effective and successful leaders in the United States, found that they had four common competencies: they had a compelling vision or sense of purpose; they could communicate that vision in clear terms that their followers could readily identify with; they demonstrated consistency and focus in the pursuit of their vision; and they knew their own strengths and capitalized on them.[21] The most recent and comprehensive analysis, however, has been completed by Jay Conger and Rabindra Kanungo at McGill University.[22] Among their conclusions, they propose that charismatic leaders have an idealized goal that they want to achieve and a strong personal commitment to that goal, are perceived as unconventional, are assertive and self-confident, and are perceived as agents of radical change rather than managers of the status quo. Exhibit 13-6 summarizes the key characteristics that appear to differentiate charismatic leaders from noncharismatic ones.

What can we say about the charismatic leader's effect on his or her followers? There is an increasing body of research that shows impressive correlations between charismatic leadership and high performance and satisfaction among followers.[23] People working for charismatic leaders are motivated to exert extra work effort and, because they like their leader, express greater satisfaction.

On the contrary, charismatic leadership may not always be needed to achieve high levels of employee performance. It may be most appropriate when the follower's task has an ideological component.[24] This may explain why, when charismatic leaders surface, it is more likely to be in politics, religion, or a business firm that is introducing a radically new product or facing a life-threatening crisis. Such conditions tend to involve ideological issues. Second, charismatic leaders may be ideal for pulling an organization through a crisis but become a liability to an organization once the crisis and need for

Exhibit 13-6
Key Characteristics of Charismatic Leaders

Source: Based on Jay A. Conger and R.N. Kanungo, "Behavioral Dimensions of Charismatic Leadership," in Jay A. Conger and R.N. Kanungo, *Charismatic Leadership* (San Francisco: Jossey-Bass, 1988), p. 91.

▶ 1. **Self-confidence.** Charismatic leaders have complete confidence in their judgment and ability.
▶ 2. **Vision.** They have an idealized goal that proposes a future better than the status quo. The greater the disparity between this idealized goal and the status quo, the more likely that followers will attribute extraordinary vision to the leader.
▶ 3. **Ability to articulate the vision.** They are able to clarify and state the vision in terms that are understandable to others. This articulation demonstrates an understanding of the followers' needs and, hence, acts as a motivating force.
▶ 4. **Strong convictions about the vision.** Charismatic leaders are perceived as being strongly committed and willing to take on high personal risk, incur high costs, and engage in self-sacrifice to achieve their vision.
▶ 5. **Behaviour that is out of the ordinary.** They engage in behaviour that is perceived as being novel, unconventional, and counter to norms. When successful, these behaviours evoke surprise and admiration in followers.
▶ 6. **Appearance as a change agent.** Charismatic leaders are perceived as agents of radical change rather than as caretakers of the status quo.
▶ 7. **Environmental sensitivity.** They are able to make realistic assessments of the environmental constraints and resources needed to bring about change.

dramatic change subsides.[25] Why? Because the charismatic leader's overwhelming self-confidence often becomes problematic. He or she is unable to listen to others, becomes uncomfortable when challenged by aggressive employees, and begins to hold an unjustifiable belief in his or her "rightness" on issues.

How Do Transactional Leaders Differ From Transformational Leaders?

The second section of research we'll touch on is the recent interest in differentiating transformational leaders from transactional leaders.[26] As you'll see, because transformational leaders are also charismatic, there is some overlap between this topic and our discussion above on charismatic leadership.

Most of the leadership theories presented in this chapter—for instance, the Ohio State studies, Fiedler's model, path-goal theory, and the leader-participation model—have been addressing **transactional leaders.** These leaders guide or motivate their followers in the direction of established goals by clarifying role and task requirements. But there is another type of leader who inspires followers to transcend their own self-interests for the good of the organization and is capable of having a profound and extraordinary effect on his or her followers. These are **transformational leaders.** They pay attention to the concerns and developmental needs of individual followers; they change followers' awareness of issues by helping those followers to look at old problems in new ways; and they are able to excite, arouse, and inspire followers to put out extra effort to achieve group goals.

Transactional and transformational leadership should not be viewed as opposing approaches to getting things done.[27] Transformational leadership is built on top of transactional leadership. Transformational leadership produces levels of employee effort and performance that go beyond what would occur with a transactional approach alone. Moreover, transformational leadership is more than charisma. "The purely charismatic [leader] may want followers to adopt the charismatic's world view and go no further; the transformational leader will attempt to instill in followers the ability to question not only established views but eventually those established by the leader."[28]

The evidence supporting the superiority of transformational leadership over the transactional variety is overwhelmingly impressive (see Ethical Dilemmas in Management). For instance, a number of studies with U.S., Canadian, and German military officers found, at every level, that transformational leaders were evaluated as being more effective than their transactional counterparts.[29] Managers at Federal Express who were rated by their followers as exhibiting more transformational leadership were evaluated by their immediate supervisors as higher performers and more promotable.[30] In summary, the overall evidence indicates that transformational, as compared with transactional, leadership is more strongly correlated with lower turnover rates, higher productivity, and higher employee satisfaction.[31]

transactional leaders
Leaders who guide or motivate their followers in the direction of established goals by clarifying role and task requirements.

transformational leaders
Leaders who provide individualized consideration, intellectual stimulation, and possess charisma.

A Special Case of Leadership: First-Line Supervision

Supervision is often conveniently lumped together with all levels in the managerial hierarchy, yet this camouflages the fact that supervisors are uniquely different from all other managers. This difference, together with the growing recognition that the job of

Ethical Dilemmas in Management

IS IT UNETHICAL TO CREATE CHARISMA?

In 1993, no list of charismatic business leaders would have been complete without the names of Bill Gates, Jack Welch, and Ted Turner. They personified the contemporary idea of charisma in the corporate world. But are these men authentically charismatic figures or self-created images?

Each of these men employs a public relations firm or has public relations specialists on his staff to shape and hone his image. Bill Gates, cofounder and CEO of Microsoft, has promoted the vision of the aggressive, take-charge executive who is determined to see every software program put in every personal computer. Jack Welch relishes his reputation for reshaping General Electric by buying and selling dozens of businesses. Ted Turner has worked hard to project his "to hell with tradition" image in the popular press.

One view of these men is that they are authentically charismatic leaders whose actions and achievements have caught the fancy of the media. This view assumes that these leaders couldn't hide their charismatic qualities. It was just a matter of time before they were found out and gained the public's eye. Another view—certainly a more cynical one—proposes that these men consciously created an image that they wanted to project and then purposely went about doing things that would draw attention to, and confirm, that image. They are not inherently charismatic individuals but rather highly astute manipulators of symbols, circumstances, and the media. In support of this latter position, one can identify leaders such as Sandra Kurtzig at Ask Computer Systems, Max DePree at Herman Miller, and Chuck Knight at Emerson Electric, who are widely viewed as charismatic in their firms and industries but are relatively unknown in the popular press.

Is charismatic leadership an inherent quality within a person, a label thrust upon an individual, or a purposely and carefully moulded image? If charisma can be derived from the media, is it unethical for a person to engage in practices whose primary purposes are to create or enhance this perception? Is it unethical to create charisma? What do you think?

---

supervisor is undergoing rapid change, justifies a separate discussion. In the following pages, we will highlight these factors that make the supervisory position a special case of leadership, show how the supervisor's role suffers from ambiguous interpretations, and demonstrate how the supervisor's job is likely to change in the near term.

Why Are Supervisors Considered First-Level Managers?

The term **supervision** is often used to refer to the activity of directing the immediate activities of employees. In such a context, it can occur at all levels. However, we use a narrower perspective. We consider supervision to be a first-level management task and supervisors as first-level managers. That is, counting from the bottom of the traditional pyramid-shaped organization, they represent the first, or lowest, level in the management hierarchy.

As first-level managers, supervisors must, by definition, occupy the only level of management charged with the responsibility of directing the work of nonmanagerial employees. It is true, of course, that all managers may direct activities of their staff, but the direct responsibility of nonsupervisory managers is to work for other managers. Therefore, only supervisors are directly responsible for the daily activities of operative employees.

supervision
First-level management task of directing the activities of immediate employees.

What's Unique About Being a Supervisor?

We have already noted one of the unique characteristics of supervisors—they don't direct activities of other managers. In addition, there are specific distinctive characteristics that create problems peculiar to first-level managers. These arise from the supervisor's heavy reliance on technical expertise; having to communicate to both managers and operative employees; coping with role conflict; coping with constrained authority; and being management's representative to operative employees (see Exhibit 13-7).

How Is the Supervisor's Role Different?

Interpretations of the supervisor's role in an organization have been very inconsistent. The position has been described as everything from the "critical link" in an organization to a "necessary evil." A synthesis of five such descriptions of the supervisor's role is shown in Exhibit 13-8.[32]

Supervisors may be viewed as the key person in getting the work done. They are the hub in the communication wheel, with every crucial organizational activity related to generating the final product or service revolving around them. However, supervisors may be seen as the person in the middle. They are forced to interact with, and reconcile, the different frames of references, experiences, and needs of managers and

> 1. **Heavy reliance on technical expertise.** Supervisors are required to know the job they supervise. Unlike other managers who are heavily oriented toward planning and controlling, supervisors spend a large portion of their time leading and overseeing the activities of operative employees.
> 2. **Communicating to both managers and operative employees.** Communications is a problem at all levels in the organization. However, it is particularly a problem for supervisors. Middle- and top-level managers converse with managers both above and below them, in many cases with people who share their educational backgrounds, experiences, and needs. On the other hand, supervisors are required to communicate with two distinct groups—managers and workers. Therefore, they must be able to blend the experiences, expectations, and needs of these divergent groups.
> 3. **Coping with role conflict.** Supervisors are neither fish nor fowl. They're not operatives, and although they are officially classified as management, they are often not accepted by other managers. A supervisor may be assumed to be like any other manager, but his or her activities, status, and security are quite different.
> 4. **Coping with constrained authority.** Sixty years ago, supervisors had complete authority. In the production area, for example, the foreman was the biggest, meanest, and toughest. His word was law. Today, however, key personnel decisions are now determined by the conditions of the labour-management collective bargaining agreement or have been centralized in HRM departments.
> 5. **Management's representative.** The final problem unique to supervisors is that, to the operatives, they are *the organization*. Rules, policies, procedures, and other dictates from above are implemented at the supervisory level. So when operatives think of management, their main point of reference is their supervisors.

Exhibit 13-7 Unique Characteristics of Being a Supervisor

Leadership and Supervision

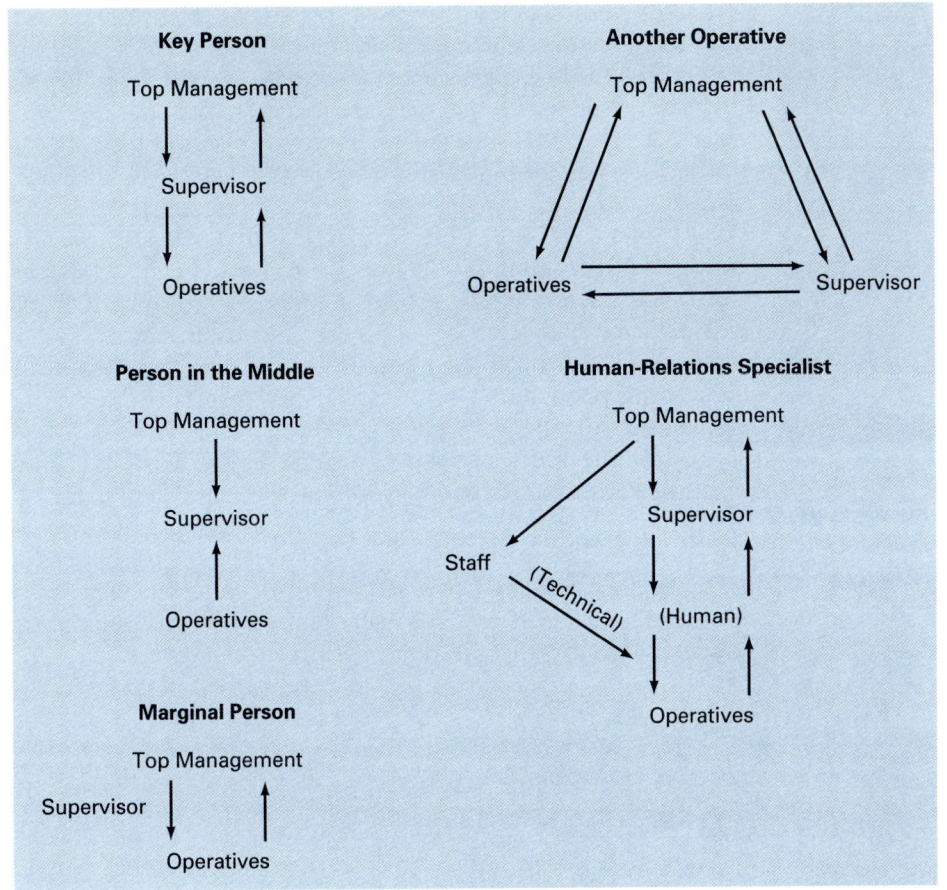

Exhibit 13-8 Different Viewpoints of the Supervisor's Role

Source: Adapted from Keith Davis, *Human Behavior at Work: Organizational Behavior*, 6th ed. (New York: McGraw-Hill, 1981), p. 142. With permission.

operative employees—thus serving as a buffer between the two groups.

At times, however, supervisors can be viewed as being marginal people. This stigma may derive from being powerless in the organizational hierarchy, left out of, or on the margin of, the principal decisions and influences that affect their unit. This marginal status is often reinforced by their being held accountable for their units' performance but with authority that is often extremely confining. For instance, they may be bypassed on union matters, which are negotiated above them, or constrained by the grievance procedure that subjects their decision to review. Such constraints, plus the abundance of rules and procedures, frequently make supervisors powerless in dealing with both operative employees and nonsupervisory managers.

A first-line supervisor's position is often regarded as one of the more difficult jobs in an organization. No longer part of the operative employee population, many first-line supervisors get caught in limbo because they are not regarded by managers as management staff either.

Technology changes, like robotics, are quickly changing the way supervisors work. Such innovations reduce the need for supervisors to directly monitor operative employees' work.

Supervisors may also be viewed as glorified operative employees. This can be reinforced because of supervisors' frequent lack of authority, implementing other people's decisions, and strictly following instructions. However, the legal interpretation since the 1940s has been that supervisors are members of the management team. Unfortunately, the way they are treated is frequently at odds with their legal status.

A final view of the supervisor's role is that of a staff specialist concerned with caring for the human or people side of the operations—a human relations specialist. They must deal with everyday problems that employees may have. As such, it can be said that supervisors get the work done best by getting along with others and by gaining cooperation and compliance from their operative employees.

It is difficult to accept any of the descriptions above as characteristic of all supervisors, but there is some truth in each of them. We have not presented these five roles in order to arrive at a universal description of the supervisor but to show the differing perceptions of the supervisor's position. The supervisor truly holds a unique position in the managerial hierarchy, one that is unlike any other management position. Of course, that position continues to change today!

How Is the Supervisor's Role Changing in Today's Organizations?

A number of forces are reshaping the supervisor's job in today's organizations. Primary among them are changing technology in the workplace, new organizational designs, and ideas about appropriate leadership styles.

What Effect Does Changing Technology Have on Supervisory Roles?

Computer-based technology is changing the work of both blue- and white-collar employees. This, in turn, is changing the supervisor's role.

More and more white-collar workers are performing clerical tasks and data analyses at a video display terminal. Supervisors of these employees are thus confronted with new challenges. They have to understand the capabilities of the software programs that their employees use in order to teach new employees and to respond to problems as they occur. They also have to deal with the increasingly difficult problems of coordinating integrated office systems. Computers are now linking data entry equipment, printers, reproduction machines, telecommunications systems, and the like. Today, when problems occur in the office, they are more difficult to identify and broader in impact than they were when various office activities were separate and independent.

Among blue-collar workers, changing technology has introduced things like robotics to assembly lines and computer-controlled production flows. In many cases, such innovations have reduced the need for supervisors to directly monitor and control operating activities.

In both offices and factories, computerized information systems will increasingly substitute for direct supervision. These systems will make it possible for management to obtain information about workers' quantity of output, quality level, ability to meet deadlines, and similar performance standards without going to their supervisors.

Leadership and Supervision

Will New Organizational Designs Eliminate the Need for Supervisors? In chapter 7, we introduced boundary-free organizations and self-managed work teams. One of the important characteristics of these groups is that they are self-governing; that is, they eliminate the need for the traditional supervisor.

There is no current evidence to suggest any imminent wholesale replacement of traditional supervised work groups with self-governing groups. However, to the degree that self-managed work teams increase in popularity, they represent a direct threat to the traditional authority of the supervisor. The supervisor's role in a self-governing group becomes predominately that of a coach and mentor responsible for developing members' roles, which many supervisors find unfamiliar (see Developing Management Skills).

Developing Management Skills

COACHING SKILLS

1. **Show genuine interest in the person as an individual, not merely as "an employee."** During times when people need assistance, they need to know you care. Give the individual your undivided attention.

2. **Listen to the employee to better understand his or her world.** Don't interrupt the employee so you can talk. Concentrate on what is being said, and if you aren't sure about something said, ask for clarification.

3. **Create a climate that contributes to a free and open exchange of ideas.** Do not judge what is being said. The minute you evaluate a statement or concern from an employee, he or she will likely "clam up."

4. **Offer help and assistance when asked.** Don't dictate to the employee what to do. If help is asked, be prepared and willing to assist.

5. **Encourage your employees by being positive and upbeat.** Nothing can "motivate" a person more than having a genuinely positive and upbeat supervisor. The "yes you can" attitude can be the strength or nudge some employees need.

6. **Focus on mistakes as learning opportunities.** We all make mistakes. Hopefully, though, we learn from them. Point out what was done incorrectly and how to develop oneself so that it won't happen again. In this way, the mistake will lead to personal growth.

7. **Reduce any obstacles that might hinder the employee from improving his or her performance.** Many variables can be contributing factors in a performance issue. For example, if the employee's computer system is outdated, and unable to speedily process the necessary statistics, no effort by the employee is likely to help. Such obstructions must be eliminated!

8. **Express to the employee the value of his or her contribution to the department's goals.** Reinforce to the employee that he or she is valuable to the department. Each employee contributes in some significant way. Sometimes this is not fully understood by the employee.

9. **Recognize and reward small improvements.** When efforts are being made by the employee, give credit. Don't expect a major turnaround overnight. It takes time and a lot of encouragement on your part. Like the saying goes, How do you eat an elephant? One bite at a time!

10. **Use a collaborative style.** Engage your employee in joint problem solving. Let him or her have a role in developing methods for correcting the problem. This increases the employee's commitment to the "new" requirements.

11. **Model the qualities that you expect from your employees.** Don't have employees do as you say, have them do as you do. In the 1990s, it's called "walking the talk." The best teacher is a good example.

How Are Supervisory Leadership Styles Changing? Old-style effective supervisors tended to be seen as hard-nosed disciplinarians who closely watched over their employees. This fit with the assumption that employees were low in intelligence, modestly skilled, and prone to goof off. It was the supervisor's job, therefore, to autocratically tell employees what to do and closely monitor their work. When performance wasn't satisfactory, supervisors were expected to take appropriate disciplinary actions.

Those assumptions no longer hold. Today's operative employees are better educated and skilled than those of previous generations. Moreover, these employees, and society as a whole, have changed their expectations of the supervisor's leadership behaviour. Supervisors are expected to exhibit a more "worker-sensitive" style. They should listen to what workers have to say and use the workers' ideas. The supervisor is now seen as a coach—the person who helps employees set goals, provides general direction for their attainment, and supports rather than intimidates. Not surprisingly, many old-line and experienced supervisors are having a difficult time accepting these changing expectations.

Summary

This Summary is organized by the chapter opening learning objectives found on page 293.

1. Managers are appointed. They have legitimate power that allows them to reward and punish. Their ability to influence is founded upon the formal authority inherent in their positions. In contrast, leaders may either be appointed or emerge from within a group. Leaders can influence others to perform beyond the actions dictated by formal authority.

2. Six traits have been found on which leaders differ from nonleaders—drive, the desire to lead, honesty and integrity, self-confidence, intelligence, and job-relevant knowledge. Yet possession of these traits is no guarantee of leadership because they ignore situational factors.

3. The managerial grid focuses on two leader styles: concern for people and concern for production.

4. Fiedler's contingency model identifies three situational variables: leader-member relations, task structure, and position power. In situations that are highly favourable or highly unfavourable, task-oriented leaders tend to perform best. In moderately favourable or unfavourable situations, relations-oriented leaders are preferred.

5. The path-goal model proposes two classes of contingency variables—those in the environment and those that are part of the personal characteristics of the subordinate. Leaders select a specific behaviour—directive, supportive, participative, or achievement-oriented—that is congruent with the demands of the environment and the characteristics of the subordinate.

6. Leaders might not be important when individual variables replace the need for a leader's support or ability to create structure and reduce task ambiguity; when jobs are unambiguous, routine, or intrinsically satisfying; or when such organizational characteristics as explicit goals, rigid rules and procedures, or cohesive work groups act in place of formal leadership.

7. Charismatic leaders are self-confident, possess a vision of a better future, have a strong belief in that vision, engage in unconventional behaviours, and are perceived as agents of radical change.

8. Transactional leaders guide their followers in the direction of established goals by clarifying role and task requirements. Transformational leaders inspire followers to transcend their own self-interests for the good of the organization and are capable of having a profound and extraordinary effect on their followers.

9. Unique characteristics of being a supervisor include not directing the activities of other managers; a heavy reliance on technical expertise; having to communicate to both managers and operative employees; coping with role conflict; coping with constrained authority; and being management representative to the employees.

10. Supervisors' roles are changing in today's organizations due to technology changes, new organizational designs, and expectations for leadership styles.

Leadership and Supervision

Review and Discussion Questions

1. "All managers should be leaders, but not all leaders should be managers." Do you agree or disagree with this statement? Support your position.
2. Discuss the strengths and weaknesses of the trait theory of leadership.
3. What is the managerial grid? Contrast its approach to leadership with that of the Ohio State and Michigan groups.
4. Is "high-high" the most effective leadership style? Explain.
5. What similarities, if any, can you find among all the behavioural theories?
6. How is a least-preferred coworker determined? What is the importance of one's LPC for the Fiedler theory of leadership?
7. What are the contingencies in the path-goal theory of leadership?
8. What is charismatic leadership? Can people learn to be charismatic leaders? Explain.
9. "Charismatic leadership is always appropriate in organizations." Do you agree or disagree? Support your position.
10. Contrast transactional and transformational leaders.
11. What is a first-line supervisor? Why is that job unique in management?
12. "First-line supervision will become tomorrow's dinosaur. With the rapid changes in American businesses, there will be little need for supervisors for tomorrow's organizations." Do you agree or disagree with this statement? Explain.

Self-Assessment Exercise

What Kind of Leader Are You?

Instructions: The following items describe aspects of leadership behaviour. Respond to each item according to the way you would be most likely to act if you were the leader of a work group. Circle whether you would be likely to behave in the described way Always (A), Frequently (F), Occasionally (O), Seldom (S), or Never (N).

If I Were the Leader of a Work Group . . .

A F O S N _____ 1. I would most likely act as the spokesperson of the group.
A F O S N _____ 2. I would encourage overtime work.
A F O S N _____ 3. I would allow members complete freedom in their work.
A F O S N _____ 4. I would encourage the use of uniform procedures.
A F O S N _____ 5. I would permit the members to use their own judgment in solving problems.
A F O S N _____ 6. I would stress being ahead of competing groups.
A F O S N _____ 7. I would speak as a representative of the group.
A F O S N _____ 8. I would needle members for greater effort.
A F O S N _____ 9. I would try out my ideas in the group.
A F O S N _____ 10. I would let the members do their work the way they think best.
A F O S N _____ 11. I would be working hard for a promotion.
A F O S N _____ 12. I would be able to tolerate postponement and uncertainty.
A F O S N _____ 13. I would speak for the group when visitors were present.
A F O S N _____ 14. I would keep the work moving at a rapid pace.
A F O S N _____ 15. I would turn the members loose on a job and let them go to it.
A F O S N _____ 16. I would settle conflicts when they occur in the group.
A F O S N _____ 17. I would get swamped by details.
A F O S N _____ 18. I would represent the group at outside meetings.
A F O S N _____ 19. I would be reluctant to allow the members any freedom of action.
A F O S N _____ 20. I would decide what shall be done and how it shall be done.
A F O S N _____ 21. I would push for increased production.

A F O S N _____ 22. I would let some members have authority that I could keep.
A F O S N _____ 23. Things would usually turn out as I predict.
A F O S N _____ 24. I would allow the group a high degree of initiative.
A F O S N _____ 25. I would assign group members to particular tasks.
A F O S N _____ 26. I would be willing to make changes.
A F O S N _____ 27. I would ask the members to work harder.
A F O S N _____ 28. I would trust the group members to exercise good judgment.
A F O S N _____ 29. I would schedule the work to be done.
A F O S N _____ 30. I would refuse to explain my actions.
A F O S N _____ 31. I would persuade others that my ideas are to their advantage.
A F O S N _____ 32. I would permit the group to set its own pace.
A F O S N _____ 33. I would urge the group to beat its previous record.
A F O S N _____ 34. I would act without consulting the group.
A F O S N _____ 35. I would ask that group members follow standard rules and regulations.

Turn to page 416 for scoring directions and key.

Source: From J. William Pfeiffer and John E. Jones, eds., *A Handbook of Structural Experiences for Human Relations Training,* Vol. 1 (San Diego, Calif.: University Associates, Inc., 1974). With permission.

Class Exercise

The Pre-Post Leadership Assessment

Objective: To compare characteristics intuitively related to leadership with leadership characteristics found in leadership theory.

Time: Part I takes approximately ten minutes.
Part II takes about twenty-five minutes.

Procedure: Part I is to be completed prior to reading Chapter 13. Identify three people (i.e., friends, relatives, previous boss, public figures, etc.) whom you consider to be outstanding leaders. For each one of these individuals, make a list of why you feel they are good leaders. Compare your lists of the three individuals. Which traits, if any, are common to all three?

Part II is to be completed after the lecture on the material in Chapter 13. Your instructor will lead the class in a discussion of leadership characteristics based on your lists developed in Part I. Students will call out what they identified and your instructor will write the traits on the chalkboard. When all students have shared their lists, class discussion will focus on the following:

1. What characteristics consistently appeared on students' lists?
2. Were these characteristics more trait oriented or behaviour oriented?
3. Under what situations were these characteristics useful?
4. What, if anything, does this exercise suggest about leadership attributes?

Key Terms

Key terms are listed in the order in which they appear in the chapter.

leaders
trait theories
behavioural theories
initiating structure
consideration
managerial grid
Fiedler contingency model
least-preferred coworker (LPC) questionnaire
leader-member relations

Leadership and Supervision

task structure
position power
path-goal theory

leader-participation model
charismatic leadership theory
transactional leaders

transformational leaders
supervision

CASE APPLICATION

Sue Reynolds

Sue Reynolds is 22 years old and will be graduating in management from Humber College at the end of the term. She has spent the past two summers working for Manufacturers Life, filling in on a number of different jobs while employees took their vacations. She has received and accepted an offer to join Manufacturers as a supervisor in the policy renewal department.

Manufacturers is a large insurance company. In the office where Sue will work, there are more than 800 employees. The company believes strongly in the personal development of its employees. This translates into a philosophy, emanating from the top executive offices, of trust and respect for all employees.

The job Sue will be assuming requires her to direct the activities of twenty-five clerks. Their jobs require little training and are highly routine. A clerk's responsibility is to ensure that renewal notices are sent on current policies, to tabulate any changes in premiums from a standardized table, and to advise the sales division if a policy is to be cancelled as a result of nonresponse to renewal notices.

Sue's group is composed of all females, ranging from nineteen to sixty-two years of age, with a median age of twenty-five. For the most part they are high school graduates with little prior working experience. The salary range for policy renewal clerks is $1,720 to $2,370 per month. Sue will be replacing a long-time employee, Mabel Fincher. Mabel is retiring after thirty-seven years, the last fourteen of which were spent as a policy renewal supervisor. Because Sue spent a few weeks in Mabel's group last summer, she is familiar with Mabel's style and knows most of the group members. She anticipates no problems from any of her soon-to-be employees, except possibly for Lillian Lantz. Lillian is well into her fifties, has been a policy renewal clerk for over a dozen years, and—as the "grand old lady"—carries a lot of weight with group members. Sue has concluded that her job could prove very difficult without Lantz's support.

Sue is determined to get her career off on the right foot. As a result, she has been doing a lot of thinking about the qualities of an effective leader.

Questions

1. What critical factors will influence Sue's success as a leader? Would these factors be the same if success were defined as group satisfaction rather than as group productivity?
2. Do you think that Sue can choose a leadership style? If so, describe the style you think would be most effective for her. If not, why?
3. What suggestions might you make to Sue to help her win over or control Lillian Lantz?

Visionary of the North

Roger Gruben is an Inuvialuit who runs a global investment fund — The Aboriginal Global Investment Corp. — worth around a quarter of a billion dollars. It owns an airline, a food company, and a food store, as well as a number of international investments. Its portfolio includes 56,000 square kilometres of land, an oil company and real estate in Vancouver.

So who is Roger Gruben? He's a man with a vision, a vision of what can be achieved in the Northwest Territories. He's been described as part politician and part businessman, and while he isn't a "formal" leader, with impressive titles and hundreds of staff, he's an example of a transformational leader, helping people look at old problems in new ways, and exciting, arousing, and inspiring others to achieve goals they would not normally have thought possible. He's full of energy and ideas, and he's always on the move, meeting with people across the country and as far afield as Hong Kong. He's restless; he's driven; he's committed; he has no business background — and he's successful.

The Inuvialuit got a $170-million land claim settlement, and Rogen Gruben has increased its worth by more than 40 per cent through investment. But his vision is not limited to managing the Inuvialuit funds; by the end of the century, native land claim settlements could total about $7 billion, and Gruben recognizes the incredible potential for pooling a large percentage of that money in an aboriginal global investment fund. His interest is in setting up something that is enduring and will help native peoples develop their economies and cultures in a sustained manner over the long term. So, as well as managing investments, Gruben is also involved in negotiating on behalf of various Inuit groups for participation in projects in the North. For instance, he has negotiated to have native firms and native people take part in the federal government's $50-million maintenance contract for the North Warning System.

The Northwest Territories will be divided in 1999, creating new entities with their own governments, structures, and cultures. But simply being created and given a new degree of independence is a long way from guaranteeing stability and long-term viability. Money alone will not ensure that the native cultures of the North remain strong, healthy, and prosperous. Leadership from a variety of sectors and people is needed. Individuals with vision and drive, like Roger Gruben, can make a very big difference.

Questions

1. Compare Roger Gruben, as a leader, with Daniel Langlois. They operate in quite different situations. How does that affect the way they need to operate to be effective?
2. If Roger Gruben were able to meet with Guy Saint-Pierre to talk about achieving some of his visions for his people, what are the three more important things they should discuss to help Gruben be effective as a leader?
3. Transformational leaders often appear to be driven. They believe deeply in what they're doing and, like Roger Gruben, at times their ideas can get ahead of the thinking of others around them. Would you like to work for one of these people? Why? Why not?

Video Resource: "Roger Gruben," *Venture* 466 (December 12, 1993).

Communication and Conflict Management

Learning Objectives

WHAT WILL I BE ABLE TO DO AFTER I FINISH THIS CHAPTER?

1. Define communication and explain why it is important to managers.
2. Describe the communication process.
3. Identify the more popular methods of communication.
4. Describe the barriers that exist to effective communication.
5. List techniques for overcoming communication barriers.
6. Define conflict.
7. Explain the three views of conflict.
8. Describe how conflict can be positive.
9. List the more popular conflict-resolution skills.
10. Describe how managers can stimulate conflict.

At 7:40 P.M. on January 25, 1990, Avianca Flight 52 was cruising at 37,000 feet above the southern New Jersey coast.[1] The aircraft had enough fuel to last nearly two hours—a healthy cushion considering the plane was less than half an hour from touchdown at New York's Kennedy Airport. Then a series of delays began. First, at 8:00, the air traffic controllers at Kennedy told the pilots on Flight 52 that they would have to circle in a holding pattern because of heavy traffic. At 8:45, the Avianca copilot advised Kennedy that they were "running low on fuel." The controller at Kennedy acknowledged the message, but the plane was not cleared to land until 9:24. In the interim, the Avianca crew relayed no information to Kennedy that an emergency was imminent, yet the cockpit crew spoke worriedly among themselves about their dwindling fuel supplies.

Flight 52's first attempt to land at 9:24 was aborted. The plane had come in too low and poor visibility made a safe landing uncertain. When the Kennedy controllers gave Flight 52's pilot new instructions for a second attempt, the crew again mentioned that they were running low on fuel, but the pilot told the controllers that the newly assigned flight path was OK. At 9:32, two of Flight 52's engines lost power. A minute later, the other two cut off. The plane, out of fuel, crashed on Long Island at 9:34. All seventy-three people on board were killed.

When investigators reviewed the cockpit tapes and talked with the controllers involved, they learned that a communication breakdown caused this tragedy. A closer look at the events of that evening help to explain why a simple message was neither clearly transmitted nor adequately received.

First, the pilots kept saying they were "running low on fuel." Traffic controllers told investigators that it is fairly common for pilots to use this phrase. In times of delay, controllers assume that everyone has a fuel problem. However, had the pilots uttered the words "fuel emergency," the controllers would have been obligated to direct the jet ahead of all others and clear it to land as soon as possible. As one controller put it, if a pilot "declares an emergency, all rules go out the window and we get the guy to the airport as quickly as possible." Unfortunately, the pilots of Flight 52 never used the word "emergency," so the people at Kennedy never understood the true nature of the pilots' problem.

Second, the vocal tone of the pilots on Flight 52 didn't convey the severity or urgency of the fuel problem to the air traffic controllers. Many of these controllers are trained to pick up subtle tones in a pilot's voice in such situations. While the crew of Flight 52

Air traffic controllers are responsible for keeping all air traffic in its proper flight routes. Doing so requires constant and precise communications.

expressed considerable concern among themselves about the fuel problem, their voice tones in communicating to Kennedy were cool and professional.

Finally, the culture and traditions of pilots and airport authorities may have made the pilot of Flight 52 reluctant to declare an emergency. A pilot's expertise and pride can be at stake in such a situation. Declaration of a formal emergency requires the pilot to complete a wealth of paperwork. Moreover, if a pilot has been found to be negligent in calculating how much fuel was needed for a flight, the Federal Aviation Administration can suspend his or her licence. These negative reinforcers strongly discourage pilots from calling an emergency.

Communication and Conflict Management

The Avianca Flight 52 disaster illustrates an important point: communication is fundamentally linked to successful performance.[2] In this chapter, we will present basic concepts in interpersonal communication. We'll explain the communication process, methods of communicating, barriers to effective communication, and ways to overcome those barriers. Additionally, we'll also use this chapter to review a basic interpersonal skill—managing conflict—in which every manager needs to become proficient.

Understanding Communication

The importance of effective communication for managers can't be overemphasized for one specific reason: everything a manager does involves communicating. Not some things, but everything! A manager can't make a decision without information. That information has to be communicated. Once a decision is made, communication must again take place. Otherwise, no one will know that a decision has been made. The best idea, the most creative suggestion, or the finest plan cannot take form without communication. Managers therefore need effective communication skills. We are not suggesting, of course, that good communication skills alone make a successful manager. We can say, however, that ineffective communication skills can lead to a continuous stream of problems for the manager.

The main purpose of communications is to get the message across the way it is intended. International symbols, such as this no smoking sign, clearly transfer meaning and understanding. As a result, effective communications occur.

What Is Communication?

Communication involves the transfer of meaning. If no information or ideas have been conveyed, communication has not taken place. The speaker who is not heard or the writer who is not read does not communicate. The philosophical question, "If a tree falls in a forest and no one hears it, does it make any noise?" must, in a communicative context, be answered negatively.

However, for communication to be successful, the meaning must be not only imparted but also understood. A letter addressed to us but written in Farsi (a language of which we are totally ignorant) cannot be considered a communication until we have it translated. **Communication** is the transferring and understanding of meaning (see Managers Who Made a Difference). Perfect communication, if such a thing were possible, would exist when a transmitted thought or idea was perceived by the receiver exactly as it was envisioned by the sender.

communication
The transferring and understanding of meaning.

Managers Who Made a Difference

BURGESS OLIVER AT NORTHERN TELECOM

Communication is an essential element in change, as Burgess Oliver, director of operations of Northern Telecom's repair and distribution centre, can attest. The day before he took over his job, the company had laid off 600 of its 800 workers and closed its manufacturing operations. Things were so bad that there had been forty bomb threats over the previous three years. Oliver's job was to increase efficiency and quality and his strategy involved the creation of self-directed teams. But he came up against the resistances that are part of any large organization that has become set in its ways.

He recognized the importance of symbols as powerful communication devices and purposely manipulated them to get his message across. One day, when he asked a supervisor to come up to his second-floor office to pick up a report, the supervisor refused. He told Oliver he'd never been allowed on the second floor. Oliver's reaction was to schedule team meetings in his office in order to signal the clear break with the company's past.

And because managers are often very worried and defensive about losing the security that their authority gives them, Oliver has adopted a technique to move them out of the way for long enough for new processes to take root. "I overload 'em," he says. "I get them out of their comfort zone and load them up with responsibilities. They're gone half the time, leaving the workers behind to run the shop." But he is not a slash-and-burn executive, trying to eliminate management positions. "I get frustrated when the boss of some plant decides to have teams and says we're going to fire five supervisors," he says. "That's asinine. You need them as business consultants because we don't have the skill sets on the teams." That's a very reassuring viewpoint and has resulted in almost no Northern Telecom managers in Oliver's division leaving because of the introduction of teams.

Oliver gets the message through, and the changes implemented, using four steps that he calls reach, teach, empower, and equip. Reaching involves getting across the message of core values like teamwork, customer service, risk-taking, and quality. Teaching focuses on skills like problem solving, conflict management, and customer service, while empowering puts teams in place and starts to get them to share responsibility for management. The final phase, equipping, gives higher-level skills such as a knowledge of marketing, understanding financial statements, and generating process flow charts.

The process works because the plant achieved a customer-satisfaction rating of 91 per cent in 1993, compared to 58 per cent in 1988. It is now the repair centre for all U.S. operations. Sales are up 12 per cent, while absenteeism is down to 2 per cent from 6 per cent. And bomb threats are down to zero.[3] ▼

Another point to keep in mind is that good communication is often erroneously defined by the communicator as agreement instead of clarity of understanding.[4] If someone disagrees with us, many of us assume that the person just didn't fully understand our position. In other words, many of us define good communication as having someone accept our views. But I can understand very clearly what you mean and not agree with what you say. In fact, when observers conclude that a lack of communication must exist because a conflict has continued for a prolonged time, a close

Communication and Conflict Management

examination often reveals that there is plenty of effective communication going on. Each fully understands the other's position. The problem is one of equating effective communication with agreement.

A final point before we move on: Our attention in this chapter will be on **interpersonal communication.** This is communication between two or more people in which the parties are treated as individuals rather than as objects. Organization-wide communication—which encompasses topics such as the development of management information systems—will be covered in our discussion of information control systems in Chapter 16.

How Does The Communication Process Work?

Before communication can take place, a purpose, expressed as a **message** to be conveyed, must exist. It passes between a source (the sender) and a receiver. The message is converted to symbolic form (called **encoding**) and passed by way of some medium (**channel**) to the receiver, who retranslates the sender's message (called **decoding**). The result is the transfer of meaning from one person to another.[5]

Exhibit 14-1 depicts the **communication process.** This model is made up of seven stages: (1) the communication source, (2) the message, (3) encoding, (4) the channel, (5) decoding, (6) the receiver, and (7) feedback. In addition, the entire process is susceptible to **noise**—that is, disturbances that interfere with the transmission of the message (depicted in Exhibit 14-1 as lightning bolts). Typical examples of noise include illegible print, telephone static, inattention by the receiver, or the background sounds of machinery on the production floor. Remember that anything that interferes with understanding—whether internal (such as the low speaking voice of the speaker/sender) or external (like the loud voices of coworkers talking at an adjoining desk)—represents noise. Noise can create distortion at any point in the communication process. Because the impact of external noise on communication effectiveness is self-evident, let's look at some potential internal sources of distortion in the communication process.

A source initiates a message by encoding a thought. Four conditions affect the encoded message: skills, attitudes, knowledge, and the social-cultural system.

If textbook authors are without the requisite skills, their message will not reach

interpersonal communication
Communication between two or more people in which the parties are treated as individuals rather than as objects.

message
A purpose to be conveyed.

encoding
Converting a message into symbols.

channel
The medium by which a message travels.

decoding
Retranslating a sender's message.

communication process
The seven stages in which meaning is transmitted and understood.

noise
Disturbances that interfere with the transmission of a message.

Exhibit 14-1 The Communication Process

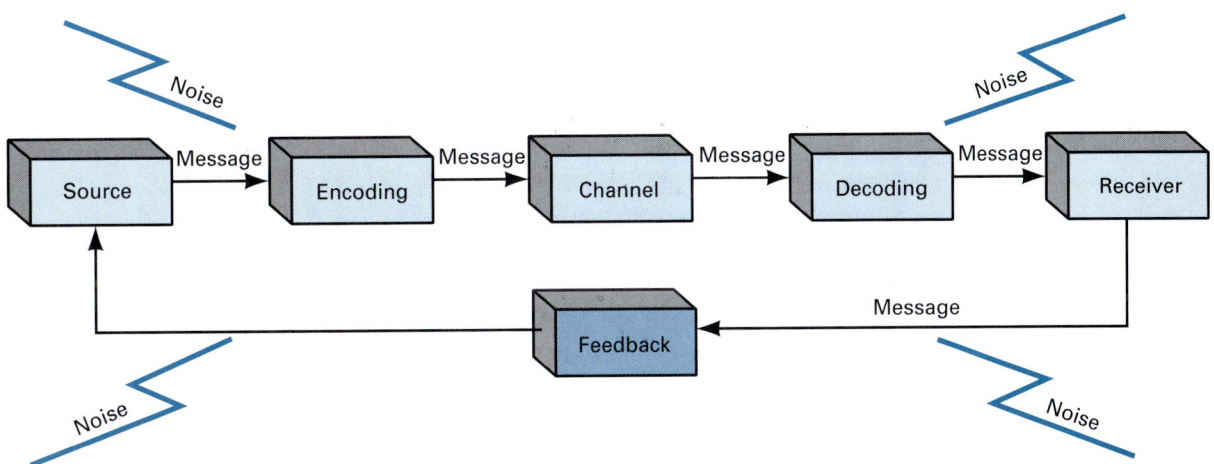

students in the form desired. Our success in communicating to you depends on our writing skills. One's total communicative success also includes speaking, reading, listening, and reasoning skills. As we discussed in Chapter 10, our attitudes influence our behaviour. We hold preformed ideas on numerous topics, and these ideas affect our communications. Furthermore, we are restricted in our communicative activity by the extent of our knowledge of a particular topic. We cannot communicate what we do not know; and should our knowledge be too extensive, it is possible that our receiver will not understand our message. Clearly, the amount of knowledge we have about a subject affects the message we seek to transfer. Finally, just as our attitudes influence our behaviour, so does our position in the social-cultural system in which we exist. Our beliefs and values (all part of our culture) act to influence us as communication sources.

How do symbols affect us? Take this mime. Through her gestures, movements, expressions, etc., we get the message.

The message itself can cause distortion in the communication process, regardless of the supporting apparatus used to convey it. Our message is the actual physical product encoded by the source. "When we speak, the speech is the message. When we write, the writing is the message. When we paint, the picture is the message. When we gesture, the movements of our arms, the expressions on our face are the message."[6] Our message is affected by the code or group of symbols we use to transfer meaning, the content of the message itself, and the decisions that the source makes in selecting and arranging both codes and content. Each of these three segments can act to distort the message.

The channel is the medium through which the message travels. It is selected by the sender. Common channels are air for the spoken word and paper for the written word. If you decide to convey to a friend something that happened to you during the day in a face-to-face conversation, you're using spoken words and gestures to transmit your message. But you have choices. A specific message—an invitation to a party, for example—can be communicated orally or in writing. In an organization, certain channels are more appropriate for certain messages. Obviously, if the building is on fire, a memo to convey the fact is inappropriate! If something is important, such as an employee's performance appraisal, a manager might want to use multiple channels—for instance, an oral review followed by a summary letter. This decreases the potential for distortion.

The receiver is the individual to whom the message is directed. But before the message can be received, the symbols in it must be translated into a form that can be understood by the receiver. This is the decoding of the message. Just as the encoder was limited by his or her skills, attitudes, knowledge, and social-cultural system, so is the receiver equally restricted. Just as the source must be skilful in writing or speaking, the receiver must be skilful in reading or listening, and both must be able to reason. A person's level of knowledge influences his or her ability to receive, just as it does his or her ability to send. Moreover, the receiver's preformed attitudes and cultural background can distort the message being transferred.

Communication and Conflict Management

The final link in the communicative process is a feedback loop. "If a communication source decodes the message that he encodes, if the message is put back into the system, we have feedback."[7] That is, feedback returns the message to the sender and provides a check on whether understanding has been achieved.

What is Oral Communication?

People communicate with each other most often by talking, or oral communication. Popular forms of oral communication include speeches, formal one-on-one and group discussions, informal discussions, and the rumour mill or grapevine.

The advantages of oral communication are quick transmission and quick feedback. A verbal message can be conveyed and a response received in a minimum amount of time. If the receiver is unsure of the message, rapid feedback allows the sender to detect the uncertainty and to correct it.

The major disadvantage of oral communication surfaces whenever a message has to be passed through a number of people. The more people who are involved, the greater the potential for distortion. Each person interprets the message in his or her own way. The message's content, when it reaches its destination, is often very different from the original. In an organization where decisions and other communiqués are verbally passed up and down the authority hierarchy, considerable opportunity exists for messages to become distorted.

Are Written Communications More Effective?

Written communications include memos, letters, organizational periodicals, bulletin boards, or any other device that transmits written words or symbols. Why would a sender choose to use written communications? Because they're permanent, tangible, and verifiable. Typically, both sender and receiver have a record of the communication. The message can be stored for an indefinite period of time. If there are questions about the content of the message, it is physically available for later reference. This is particularly important for complex or lengthy communications. For example, the marketing plan for a new product is likely to contain a number of tasks spread out over several months. By putting it in writing, those who have to initiate the plan can readily refer to it over the life of the plan. A final benefit of written communication comes from the process itself. Except in rare instances, such as when presenting a formal speech, more care is taken with the written word than with the oral word. Having to put something in writing forces a person to think more carefully about what he or she wants to convey. Therefore, written communications are more likely to be well thought out, logical, and clear.

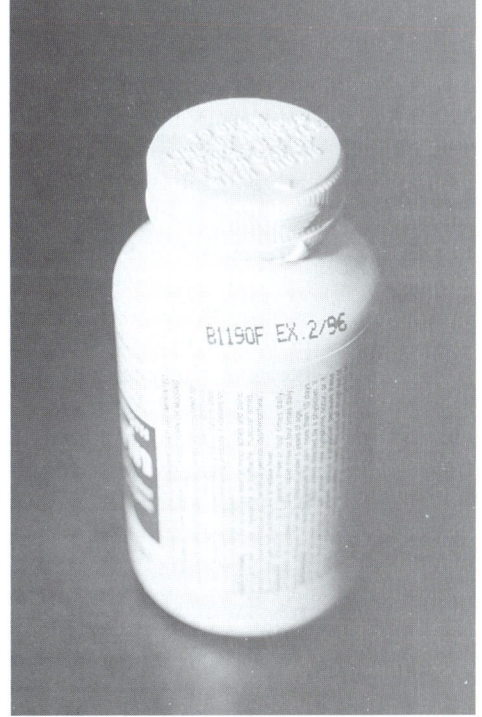

For how long will this aspirin be good? Without an expiration date on the package, we would not know if the product was still effective. Thus, written communications, like the expiration date, can be very helpful.

nonverbal communication
Communication transmitted without words.

body language
Gestures, facial configurations, and other movements of the body that convey meaning.

verbal intonation
An emphasis given to words or phrases that conveys meaning.

Of course, written messages have their drawbacks. While writing may be more precise, it also consumes a great deal more time. You could convey far more information to your college instructor in a one-hour oral exam than in a one-hour written exam. In fact, you could probably say the same thing in ten to fifteen minutes that takes you an hour to write. The other major disadvantage is feedback or lack of it. Oral communications allow the receivers to respond rapidly to what they think they hear. However, written communications do not have a built-in feedback mechanism. The result is that sending a memo is no assurance that it will be received; if it is received, there is no guarantee that the recipient will interpret it as the sender meant. The latter point is also relevant in oral communiqués, except that it's easier in such cases merely to ask the receiver to summarize what you've said. An accurate summary presents feedback evidence that the message has been received and understood.

How Do Nonverbal Cues Affect Communications?

Some of the most meaningful communications are neither spoken nor written. These are **nonverbal communications.** A loud siren or a red light at an intersection tells you something without words. A college instructor doesn't need words to know that students are bored when their eyes get glassy or they begin to read the school newspaper during class. Similarly, when papers start to rustle and notebooks begin to close, the message is clear: class time is about over. The size of a person's office and desk or the clothes a person wears also convey messages to others. However, the best-known areas of nonverbal communication are body language and verbal intonation.

Body language refers to gestures, facial configurations, and other movements of the body. A snarled face, for example, says something different from a smile. Hand motions, facial expressions, and other gestures can communicate emotions or temperaments such as aggression, fear, shyness, arrogance, joy, and anger.

Verbal intonation refers to the emphasis someone gives to words or phrases. To illustrate how intonations can change the meaning of a message, consider the student who asks the instructor a question. The instructor replies, "What do you mean by that?" The student's reaction will vary, depending on the tone of the instructor's response. A soft, smooth tone creates a different meaning from one that is abrasive and puts a strong emphasis on the last word. Most of us would view the first intonation as coming from someone who sincerely sought clarification, whereas the second suggests that the person is aggressive or defensive.

The fact that every oral communication also has a nonverbal message cannot be overemphasized. Why? Because the nonverbal component is likely to carry the greatest impact. One researcher found that 55 per cent of an oral message is derived from facial expression and physical posture, 38 per cent from verbal intonation, and only 7 per cent from the actual words used.[8] Most of us know that animals respond to how we say something rather than what we say. Apparently, people aren't much different.

Is the Wave of Communication's Future in Electronic Media?

Today we rely on a number of sophisticated electronic media to carry our communications. In addition to the more common media—the telephone and public address system—we have closed-circuit television,

Any doubt as to what this individual is expressing? Enough said. Actions do speak louder than words.

Communication and Conflict Management

voice-activated computers, xerographic reproduction, fax machines, and a host of other electronic devices that we can use in conjunction with speech or paper to create more effective communication. Maybe the fastest growing is **electronic mail.** Electronic mail allows individuals to instantaneously transmit written messages on computers that are linked with the appropriate software. Messages sit at the receiver's terminal to be read at the receiver's convenience. Electronic mail is fast and cheap and can be used to send the same message to dozens of people at the same time. Its other strengths and weaknesses generally parallel those of written communications.

Years ago, we relied on Canada Post and mail couriers for delivering our written messages. Then companies like Federal Express helped us with overnight deliveries. Now with the fax machine, documentation can quickly be sent anywhere in the world.

electronic mail
Instantaneous transmission of written messages on computers that are linked.

What Barriers Exist to Effective Communication?

In our discussion of the communication process, we noted the consistent potential for distortion. What causes such distortions? In addition to the general distortions identified in the communication process, there are other barriers to effective communication. These are presented below and are summarized in Exhibit 14-2.

Filtering is the deliberate manipulation of information to make it appear more favourable to the receiver. For example, when a manager tells his or her boss what the boss wants to hear, the manager is filtering information. The extent of filtering tends to be a function of the height of the structure and the organizational culture. The more vertical levels there are in an organization's hierarchy, the more opportunities there are for filtering. The organizational culture encourages or discourages filtering by the type of behaviour it emphasizes through rewards. The more rewards emphasize style and appearance, the more managers are motivated to alter communications in their favour.

The second barrier can be identified as selective perception. We've mentioned selective perception several times throughout this book. The receiver in the communication process selectively sees and hears communications depending on his or her needs, motivation, experience, background, and other personal characteristics. The receiver also projects his or her interests and expectations into communications in decoding them. The employment interviewer who expects a female job candidate to put family before career is likely to see that in all female candidates, regardless of whether the candidates feel that way. As we said in Chapter 10, we don't see reality; instead, we interpret what we see and call it reality (see Ethical Dilemmas in Management).

Filtering:	The deliberate manipulation of information to make it appear more favourable to the receiver.
Selective Perception:	Receiving communications based on what one selectively sees and hears depending on his or her needs, motivation, experience, background, and other personal characteristics.
Emotions:	Messages will often be interpreted differently depending on how happy or sad one is when the message is being communicated.
Language:	Words have different meanings to different people. As such, receivers will use their definition of words communicated, which may be different than what the sender intended.
Nonverbal Cues:	Body language or intonation that sends the receiver another message. When the two are not aligned, communication is distorted.

Exhibit 14-2 Barriers to Effective Communication

Ethical Dilemmas in Management

▼ IS IT UNETHICAL TO PURPOSELY DISTORT INFORMATION? ▲

The issue of ethics was introduced in Chapter 2. Since then, you've had ample time to think about this issue. Because lying is such a broad concern and so closely intertwined with interpersonal communication, this might be a good time to think again about dilemmas that managers face relating to the intentional distortion of information.

You have just seen your division's sales report for last month. Sales are down considerably. Your boss, who works 2,000 miles away in another city, is unlikely to see last month's sales figures. You're optimistic that sales will pick up this month and next so that your overall quarterly numbers will be acceptable. You also know that your boss is the type of person who hates to hear bad news. You're having a phone conversation today with your boss. He happens to ask, in passing, how last month's sales went. Do you tell him the truth?

An employee asks you about a rumour she's heard that your department and all its employees will be transferred from Vancouver to Toronto. You know the rumour to be true, but you would rather not let the information out just yet. You're fearful that it could hurt departmental morale and lead to premature resignations. What do you say to your employee?

These two incidents illustrate dilemmas that managers face relating to evading the truth, distorting facts, or lying to others.

It might not always be in a manager's best interest or that of his or her unit to provide full and complete information. In fact, a strong argument can be made for managers to purposely keep their communications vague and unclear.[9] Keeping communications fuzzy can cut down on questions, permit faster decision making, minimize objections, reduce opposition, make it easier to deny one's earlier statements, preserve the freedom to change one's mind, permit one to say no diplomatically, help to avoid confrontation and anxiety, and provide other benefits that work to the advantage of the manager.

Is it unethical to purposely distort communications to get a favourable outcome? Is distortion acceptable but lying not? What about "little white lies" that really don't hurt anybody? What do you think?

Another obstruction in communications comes from people's emotions. How the receiver feels when a message is received influences how he or she interprets it. Extreme emotions such as jubilation or depression are most likely to hinder effective communication. In such instances, we often disregard our rational and objective thinking processes and substitute emotional judgments.

Words, too, mean different things to different people. Age, education, and cultural background are three of the more obvious variables that influence the language a person uses and the definitions he or she gives to words. The language of George Will is clearly different from that of the typical high-school-educated factory worker. The latter, in fact, would undoubtedly have trouble understanding much of Will's vocabulary. In an organization, employees usually come from diverse backgrounds. And this diversity may mean that you will work with people who don't speak your language. But even if they did, our use of that language is far from uniform. A knowledge of how each of us modifies the language would minimize communication difficulties. The problem is that members in an organization usually don't know how others with whom they interact have modified the language. Senders tend to assume that their words and terms will be appropriately interpreted by the receiver. This, of course, is often incorrect and creates communication difficulties.

Communication and Conflict Management

Finally, barriers to effective communications can come from nonverbal cues. Earlier, we noted that nonverbal communication is an important way in which people convey messages to others. But nonverbal communication is almost always accompanied by oral communication. As long as the two are in agreement, they act to reinforce each other.

How Can Managers Overcome Communication Barriers?

Given these barriers to communication, what can managers do to overcome them? The following suggestions should help to make communication more effective (see also Exhibit 14-3).

The legendary sportscaster, Howard Cosell had a command of the English vocabulary that was second to none. And in his early years as an attorney, his articulate speech was quite appropriate. But was this same, eloquent speech tailored to Monday Night Football fans? For most of us, some of Howard's words never "scored."

Why Use Feedback? Many communication problems can be directly attributed to misunderstandings and inaccuracies. These problems are less likely to occur if the manager uses the feedback loop in the communication process. This feedback can be verbal or nonverbal.

If a manager asks a receiver, "Did you understand what I said?" the response represents feedback. Also, feedback should include more than yes and no answers. The manager can ask a set of questions about a message in order to determine whether or not the message was received as intended. Better yet, the manager can ask the receiver to restate the message in his or her own words. If the manager then hears what was intended, understanding and accuracy should be enhanced. Feedback also includes subtler methods than the direct asking of questions or the summarizing of messages. General comments can give a manager a sense of the receiver's reaction to a message. In addition, performance appraisals, salary reviews, and promotions represent important forms of feedback.

Of course, feedback does not have to be conveyed in words. Actions can speak

Use Feedback:	Check the accuracy of what has been communicated—or what you think you heard.
Simplify Language:	Use words that the intended audience understands.
Listen Actively:	Listen for the full meaning of the message without making premature judgments or interpretations—or thinking about what you are going to say in response.
Constrain Emotions:	Recognize when your emotions are running high. When they are, don't communicate until you have calmed down.
Watch Nonverbal:	Be aware that your actions speak louder than your words. Keep the two consistent.

Exhibit 14-3 Overcoming Barriers to Effective Communication

louder than words. The sales manager who sends out a directive to his or her staff describing a new monthly sales report that all sales personnel will need to complete receives feedback if some of the salespeople fail to turn in the new report. This feedback suggests that the sales manager needs to clarify the initial directive. Similarly, when you give a speech to a group of people, you watch their eyes and look for other nonverbal clues to tell you whether they are getting your message.

Why Should Simplified Language Be Used? Because language can be a barrier, managers should choose words and structure their messages in ways that will make those messages clear and understandable to the receiver. The manager should consider the audience to whom the message is directed so that the language will be tailored to the receivers. Remember, effective communication is achieved when a message is both received and understood. Understanding is improved by simplifying the language used in relation to the audience intended. This means, for example, that a hospital administrator should always try to communicate in clear, easily understood terms and that the language used in messages to the surgical staff should be purposely different from that used with office employees. Jargon can facilitate understanding when it is used within a group of those who know what it means, but it can cause innumerable problems when used outside that group.

Why Must We Listen Actively? When someone talks, we hear. But too often we don't listen. Listening is an active search for meaning, whereas hearing is passive. In listening, two people are thinking—the receiver and the sender.

Many of us are poor listeners. Why? Because it's difficult, and it's usually more satisfying to be on the offensive. Listening, in fact, is often more tiring than talking. It demands intellectual effort. Unlike hearing, **active listening** demands total concentration. The average person speaks at a rate of about 150 words per minute, whereas we have the capacity to listen at the rate of nearly 1,000 words per minute.[10] The difference obviously leaves idle time for the brain and opportunities for the mind to wander.

Active listening is enhanced by developing empathy with the sender—that is, by placing yourself in the sender's position. Because senders differ in attitudes, interests, needs, and expectations, empathy makes it easier to understand the actual content of a message (see Developing Management Skills). An empathic listener reserves judgment on the message's content and carefully listens to what is being said. The goal is to improve one's ability to receive the full meaning of a communication without having it distorted by premature judgments or interpretations.

Why Must We Constrain Emotions? It would be naive to assume that managers always communicate in a fully rational manner. We know that emotions can severely cloud and distort the transference of meaning. A manager who is emotionally upset over an issue is more likely to misconstrue incoming messages and fail to express his or her outgoing messages clearly and accurately. What can the manager do? The simplest answer is to desist from further communication until he or she has regained composure.

Why the Emphasis on Nonverbal Cues? If actions speak louder than words, then it's important to watch your actions to make sure that they align with and reinforce the words that go along with them. We noted that nonverbal messages carry a great deal of weight. Given this fact, the effective communicator watches his or her nonverbal cues to ensure that they too convey the desired message.

---

active listening
Listening for full meaning without making premature judgments or interpretations.

Developing Management Skills

DEVELOPING EFFECTIVE ACTIVE LISTENING SKILLS

▶ **1. Make eye contact.** How do you feel when somebody doesn't look at you when you're speaking? If you're like most people, you're likely to interpret this as aloofness or disinterest. Making eye contact with the speaker focuses your attention, reduces the likelihood that you will become distracted, and encourages the speaker.

▶ **2. Exhibit affirmative nods and appropriate facial expressions.** The effective listener shows interest in what is being said through nonverbal signals. Affirmative nods and appropriate facial expressions, when added to good eye contact, convey to the speaker that you're listening.

▶ **3. Avoid distracting actions or gestures that suggest boredom.** The other side of showing interest is avoiding actions that suggest that your mind is somewhere else. When listening, don't look at your watch, shuffle papers, play with your pencil, or engage in similar distractions. They make the speaker feel that you're bored or disinterested or indicate that you aren't fully attentive.

▶ **4. Ask questions.** The critical listener analyses what he or she hears and asks questions. This behaviour provides clarification, ensures understanding, and assures the speaker that you're listening.

▶ **5. Paraphrase using your own words.** The effective listener uses phrases such as: "What I hear you saying is..." or "Do you mean...?" Doing so is an excellent control device to check on whether you're listening carefully and to verify that what you heard is accurate.

▶ **6. Avoid interrupting the speaker.** Let the speaker complete his or her thought before you try to respond. Don't try to second-guess where the speaker's thoughts are going. When the speaker is finished, you'll know it.

▶ **7. Don't overtalk.** Most of us would rather speak our own ideas than listen to what someone else says. While talking might be more fun and silence might be uncomfortable, you can't talk and listen at the same time. The good listener recognizes this fact and doesn't overtalk.

▶ **8. Make smooth transitions between the roles of speaker and listener.** The effective listener makes transitions smoothly from speaker to listener and back to speaker. From a listening perspective this means concentrating on what a speaker has to say and practising not thinking about what you're going to say as soon as you get your chance.

Cross-Cultural Insights into Communication Processes

Interpersonal communication is not conducted in the same way around the world. For example, compare countries that place a high value on individualism (such as Canada) with countries where the emphasis is on collectivism (such as Japan).[11]

Owing to the emphasis on the individual in countries such as Canada, communication patterns there are individual oriented and rather clearly spelled out. For instance, Canadian managers rely heavily on memoranda, announcements, position papers, and other formal forms of communication to stake out their positions in intraorganizational negotiations. Supervisors in Canada often hoard secret information in an attempt to promote their own advancement and as a way of inducing their employees to accept decisions and plans. For their own protection, lower-level employees also engage in this practice.

In collectivist countries such as Japan, there is more interaction for its own sake and a more informal manner of interpersonal contact. The Japanese manager, in contrast to Canadian managers, will engage in extensive verbal consultation over an issue first and only draw up a formal document later to outline the agreement that was made. Face-to-face communication is encouraged. Additionally, open communication is an inherent part of the Japanese work setting. Work spaces are open and crowded with individuals at different levels in the work hierarchy. Canadian organizations emphasize authority, hierarchy, and formal lines of communication.

Conflict Management Skills

The ability to manage conflict is undoubtedly one of the most important skills a manager needs to possess. A study of middle- and top-level executives by the American Management Association revealed that the average manager spends approximately 20 per cent of his or her time dealing with conflict.[12] The importance of conflict management is reinforced by a survey of what topics practising managers consider most important in management development programs; conflict management was rated as being more important than decision making, leadership, or communication skills.[13] In further support of our claim, one researcher studied a group of managers and looked at twenty-five skill and personality factors to determine which, if any, were related to managerial success (defined in terms of ratings by one's boss, salary increases, and promotions).[14] Of the twenty-five measures, only one—the ability to handle conflict—was positively related to managerial success.

Traditional View:	The early approach assumed that conflict was bad and would always have a negative impact on an organization. Conflict became synonymous with violence, destruction, and irrationality. Because conflict was harmful, it was to be avoided. Management had a responsibility to rid the organization of conflict. This traditional view dominated management literature during the late nineteenth century and continued until the mid-1940s.
Human Relations View:	The human relations position argued that conflict was a natural and inevitable occurrence in all organizations. Because conflict was inevitable, the human relations approach advocated acceptance of conflict. This approach rationalized the existence of conflict; conflict cannot be eliminated, and there are times when it may even benefit the organization. The human relations view dominated conflict thinking from the late 1940s through the mid-1970s.
Interactionist View:	The current theoretical perspective on conflict is the interactionist approach. While the human relations approach accepts conflict, the interactionist approach encourages conflict on the grounds that a harmonious, peaceful, tranquil, and cooperative organization is prone to become static, apathetic, and nonresponsive to needs for change and innovation. The major contribution of the interactionist approach, therefore, is that it encourages managers to maintain an ongoing minimum level of conflict—enough to keep units viable, self-critical, and creative.

Exhibit 14-4 Three Views of Conflict

Communication and Conflict Management

What Is Conflict?

When we use the term **conflict,** we are referring to perceived incompatible differences resulting in some form of interference or opposition. Whether the differences are real or not is irrelevant. If people perceive that differences exist, then a conflict state exists. In addition, our definition includes the extremes, from subtle, indirect, and highly controlled forms of interference to overt acts such as strikes, riots, and wars.

Over the years, three differing views have evolved toward conflict in organizations[15] (see Exhibit 14-4). One argues that conflict must be avoided, that it indicates a malfunctioning within the organization. We call this the **traditional view of conflict.** A second, the **human relations view of conflict,** argues that conflict is a natural and inevitable outcome in any organization and that it need not be evil but, rather, has the potential to be a positive force in contributing to an organization's performance. The third and most recent perspective proposes not only that conflict can be a positive force in an organization but also that some conflict is absolutely necessary for an organization or units within an organization to perform effectively. We label this third approach the **interactionist view of conflict.**

Can Conflict Ever Be Positive?

The interactionist view does not propose that all conflicts are good. Rather, some conflicts support the goals of the organization; these are **functional conflicts** of a constructive form. However, some conflicts prevent an organization from achieving its goals; these are **dysfunctional conflicts** and are destructive forms.

Of course, it is one thing to argue that conflict can be valuable, but how does a manager tell whether a conflict is functional or dysfunctional? Unfortunately, the demarcation is neither clear nor precise. No one level of conflict can be adopted as acceptable or unacceptable under all conditions. The type and level of conflict that promote a healthy and positive involvement toward one department's goals may, in another department or in the same department at another time, be highly dysfunctional. Functionality or dysfunctionality, therefore, is a matter of judgment. Exhibit 14-5 illustrates the challenge facing managers. They want to create an environment within their organi-

conflict
Perceived incompatible differences that result in interference or opposition.

traditional view of conflict
The view that all conflict is bad and must be avoided.

human relations view of conflict
The view that conflict is a natural and inevitable outcome in any organization.

interactionist view of conflict
The view that some conflict is necessary for an organization to perform effectively.

functional conflicts
Conflicts that support an organization's goals.

dysfunctional conflicts
Conflicts that prevent an organization from achieving its goals.

Digital Equipment Corporation is one of an increasing number of firms that have learned the value of functional conflict. DEC openly encourages all employees "to push back against the system," and the company rewards those who do.

Exhibit 14-5 Conflict and Organizational Performance

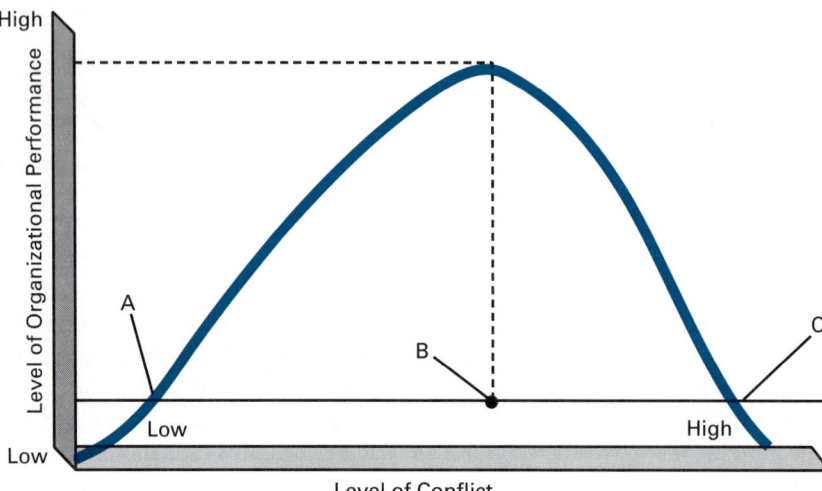

Situation	Level of Conflict	Type of Conflict	Organization's Internal Characteristics	Level of Organizational Performance
A	Low or none	Dysfunctional	Apathetic Stagnant Unresponsive to change Lack of new ideas	Low
B	Optimal	Functional	Viable Self-critical Innovative	High
C	High	Dysfunctional	Disruptive Chaotic Uncooperative	Low

zation or organizational unit in which conflict is healthy but not allowed to run to pathological extremes. Neither too little nor too much conflict is desirable. Managers should stimulate conflict to gain the full benefits of its functional properties, yet reduce its level when it becomes a disruptive force. Because we have yet to devise a sophisticated measuring instrument for assessing whether a given conflict level is functional or dysfunctional, it remains for managers to make intelligent judgments concerning whether conflict levels in their units are optimal, too high, or too low.

If conflict is dysfunctional, what can a manager do? In the following sections, we'll review conflict-resolution skills. Essentially, you need to know your basic conflict-handling style, as well as those of the conflicting parties, to understand the situation that has created the conflict and to be aware of your options.

What Is Your Underlying Conflict-Handling Style?

While most of us have the ability to vary our conflict response according to the situation, each of us has a preferred style for handling conflicts.[16] The self-assessment exercise at the end of this chapter can help you to identify your basic conflict-handling style. You might be able to change your preferred style to suit the context in which a certain

Communication and Conflict Management

conflict exists; however, your basic style tells you how you're most likely to behave and the conflict-handling approaches on which you most often rely.

Which Conflicts Do You Handle?

Not every conflict justifies your attention. Some might not be worth the effort; others might be unmanageable. Not every conflict is worth your time and effort to resolve. While avoidance might appear to be a "cop-out," it can sometimes be the most appropriate response. You can improve your overall management effectiveness, and your conflict-management skills in particular, by avoiding trivial conflicts. Choose your battles judiciously, saving your efforts for the ones that count.

Regardless of our desires, reality tells us that some conflicts are unmanageable.[17] When antagonisms are deeply rooted, when one or both parties wish to prolong a conflict, or when emotions run so high that constructive interaction is impossible, your efforts to manage the conflict are unlikely to meet with much success.

Don't be lured into the naive belief that a good manager can resolve every conflict effectively. Some aren't worth the effort. Some are outside your realm of influence. Still others may be functional and, as such, are best left alone.

Who Are the Conflict Players?

If you choose to manage a conflict situation, it's important that you take the time to get to know the players. Who is involved in the conflict? What interests does each party represent? What are each player's values, personality, feelings, and resources? Your chances of success in managing a conflict will be greatly enhanced if you can view the conflict situation through the eyes of the conflicting parties.

What Are the Sources of the Conflict?

Conflicts don't pop out of thin air. They have causes. Because your approach to resolving a conflict is likely to be determined largely by its causes, you need to determine the source of the conflict. Research indicates that while conflicts have varying causes, they can generally be separated into three categories: communication differences, structural differences, and personal differences.[18]

Communication differences are disagreements arising from semantic difficulties, misunderstandings, and noise in the communication channels. People are often quick to assume that most conflicts are caused by lack of communication but, as one author has noted, there is usually plenty of communication going on in most conflicts.[19] As we pointed out at the beginning of this chapter, the mistake many people make is equating good communication with having others agree with their views. What might at first look like an interpersonal conflict based on poor communication is usually found, upon closer analysis, to be a disagreement caused by different role requirements, unit goals, personalities, value systems, or similar factors. As a source of conflict for managers, poor communication probably gets more attention than it deserves.

As we discussed in Chapter 6, organizations are horizontally and vertically differentiated. This structural differentiation creates problems of integration. The frequent result is conflicts. Individuals disagree over goals, decision alternatives, performance criteria, and resource allocations. These conflicts are not due to poor communication or personal animosities. Rather, they are rooted in the structure of the organization itself.

The third conflict source is personal differences. Conflicts can evolve out of individual idiosyncrasies and personal value systems. The chemistry between some people

Details on a Management Classic

KENNETH W. THOMAS AND CONFLICT-HANDLING TECHNIQUES

Conflict in any organization is inevitable. Whenever you put people together and arrange them into some type of structure (formal or informal) there is a good probability that some individuals will perceive that others have negatively affected, or are about to negatively affect, something that they care about. How then do we react to deal with the conflict? The research of Kenneth W. Thomas has given us some insight.

Thomas recognized that in these conflict-laden situations, one must first determine the intention of the other party. That is, one has to speculate the other person's purpose for causing the conflict in order to respond to that behaviour. To do so, Thomas concluded that one's response will depend on his or her cooperativeness or assertiveness. Cooperativeness is the degree to which an individual attempts to rectify the conflict by satisfying the other person's concerns. On the other hand, assertiveness is the degree to which an individual will attempt to rectify the conflict to satisfy his or her concerns. Placing assertiveness on the "Y" axis and cooperativeness on the "X" axis (and ranging both from low to high), Thomas was able to identify four distinct conflict-handling techniques—plus one middle-of-the-road combination. These were competing (where one is assertive, but uncooperative); collaborating (assertive and cooperative); avoiding (unassertive and uncooperative); accommodation (unassertive, but cooperative); and compromising (mid-range on both assertiveness and cooperativeness). The question raised, then, is where should these be used?

Thomas recognized that one conflict-resolution method is not appropriate in all situations.[20] Rather, the situation itself must dictate the technique. For instance, competition is most appropriate when a quick decisive action is vital or against people who take advantage of noncompetitive behaviours. Collaboration is appropriate when one is attempting to merge insights from different people, and avoidance works well when the potential for disruption outweighs the benefits of resolving the conflict. Accommodation can assist in issues that are more important to others than yourself or where harmony and stability are important to you. Finally, compromise works well in achieving temporary settlements to complex issues or reaching a solution when time constraints dictate.

Thomas' work provided us with general guidelines for dealing with conflict. Although we know that people do change their intentions because of how they currently see the issue, or in an emotional reaction to the other individual, it appears that people do prefer one of the five techniques more often than the other four. Subsequent research supports that a person's intentions can also be predicted rather well from a combination of intellectual and personality characteristics. Thus, it may be more appropriate to view individuals from their preferred style and react accordingly. That is, when confronting a conflict situation, recognize that some people want to win it all at any cost, some want to find an optimum solution, some want to run away, others want to be obliging, and still others want to "split the difference." ▼

Communication and Conflict Management

makes it hard for them to work together. Factors such as background, education, experience, and training mould each individual into a unique personality with a particular set of values. The result is people who may be perceived by others as abrasive, untrustworthy, or strange. These personal differences can create conflict.

What Tools Can You Use to Reduce Conflict?

Managers essentially can draw upon five conflict-resolution options to reduce conflict when it is too high: avoidance, accommodation, forcing, compromise, and collaboration.[21] Each has particular strengths and weaknesses, and no one option is ideal for every situation. You should consider each a "tool" in your conflict-management "tool chest." While you might be better at using some tools than others, the skilled manager knows what each tool can do and when each is likely to be most effective (see Details on a Management Classic).

As we noted earlier, not every conflict requires an assertive action. Sometimes **avoidance**—just withdrawing from or suppressing the conflict—is the best solution. When is avoidance a desirable strategy? When the conflict is trivial, when emotions are running high and time is needed to cool them down, or when the potential disruption from a more assertive action outweighs the benefits of resolution.

The goal of **accommodation** is to maintain harmonious relationships by placing another's needs and concerns above your own. You might, for example, yield to another person's position on an issue. This option is most viable when the issue under dispute isn't that important to you or when you want to build up credits for later issues.

In **forcing**, you attempt to satisfy your own needs at the expense of the other party. In organizations this is most often illustrated by a manager using his or her formal authority to resolve a dispute. Forcing works well when you need a quick resolution on important issues where unpopular actions must be taken, and when commitment by others to your solution is not critical.

A **compromise** requires each party to give up something of value. Typically this is the approach taken by management and labour in negotiating a new labour contract. Compromise can be an optimum strategy when conflicting parties are about equal in power, when it is desirable to achieve a temporary solution to a complex issue, or when time pressures demand an expedient solution.

Collaboration is the ultimate win-win solution. All parties to the conflict seek to satisfy their interests. It is typically characterized by open and honest discussion among the parties, active listening to understand differences, and careful deliberation over a full range of alternatives to find a solution that is advantageous to all. When is collaboration the best conflict option? When time pressures are minimal, when all parties seriously want a win-win solution, and when the issue is too important to be compromised.

How Does a Manager Stimulate Conflict?

What about the other side of conflict management—situations that require managers to stimulate conflict? The notion of stimulating conflict is often difficult to accept. For almost all of us the term "conflict" has a negative

avoidance
Withdrawal from or suppression of conflict.

accommodation
Resolving conflicts by placing another's needs and concerns above one's own.

forcing
Satisfying one's own needs at the expense of another's.

compromise
A solution to conflict in which each party gives up something of value.

collaboration
Resolving conflict by seeking a solution advantageous to all parties.

The labour mediator attempts to get both labour and management to overcome their impasse. By getting to know each side's issues, values, and the like, he is in a better position to find common ground that both parties can live with.

> **1.** Are you surrounded by "yes people"?
> **2.** Are employees afraid to admit ignorance and uncertainties to you?
> **3.** Is there so much concentration by decision makers on reaching a compromise that they lose sight of values, long-term objectives, or the organization's welfare?
> **4.** Do managers believe that it is in their best interest to maintain the impression of peace and cooperation in their unit, regardless of the price?
> **5.** Is there an excessive concern by decision makers for not hurting the feelings of others?
> **6.** Do managers believe that popularity is more important for obtaining organizational rewards than competence and high performance?
> **7.** Are managers unduly enamored of obtaining consensus for their decisions?
> **8.** Do employees show unusually high resistance to change?
> **9.** Is there a lack of new ideas?
> **10.** Is there an unusually low level of employee turnover?
>
> An affirmative answer to any or all of these questions suggests the need for conflict stimulation.

Exhibit 14-6 Is Conflict Stimulation Needed?

Source: From Stephen P. Robbins, "'Conflict Management' and 'Conflict Resolution' Are Not Synonymous Terms," *California Management Review,* Winter 1978, p. 71. With permission of the regents.

connotation, and the idea of purposely creating conflict seems to be the antithesis of good management. Few of us personally enjoy being in conflict situations. Yet the evidence demonstrates that there are situations in which an increase in conflict is constructive.[22] Given this reality and the fact that there is no clear demarcation between functional and dysfunctional conflict, we have listed in Exhibit 14-6 a set of questions that might help you. While there is no definitive method for assessing the need for more conflict, an affirmative answer to one or more of the questions in Exhibit 14-6 suggests a need for conflict stimulation.

We know a lot more about resolving conflict than about stimulating it. That's only natural, because human beings have been concerned with the subject of conflict reduction for hundreds, maybe thousands, of years. The dearth of ideas on conflict-stimulation techniques reflects the very recent interest in the subject. The following are some preliminary suggestions that managers might want to utilise.[23]

The initial step in stimulating functional conflict is for managers to convey to employees the message, supported by actions, that conflict has its legitimate place. This may require changing the culture of the organization. Individuals who challenge the status quo, suggest innovative ideas, offer divergent opinions, and demonstrate original thinking need to be rewarded visibly with promotions, salary increases, and other positive reinforcers.

Politicians frequently use communication to stimulate conflict. Ministers "plant" possible policy decisions with the media through "leaks" and then assess the public reaction. This way they can test whether a tax change, a change in the health care system, welfare, unemployment, or whatever will be acceptable to the voting public. If there is a huge outcry, which the politicians judge to be representative of the voters at large in Canada, they simply deny the rumours and the policy change is either dropped from the agenda or altered.

Communication and Conflict Management

Ambiguous or threatening messages also encourage conflict. Information that a plant might close, that a department is likely to be eliminated, or that a layoff is imminent can reduce apathy, stimulate new ideas, and force reevaluation—all positive outcomes that result from increased conflict.

Another widely used method for shaking up a stagnant unit or organization is to bring in outsiders—either by hiring from outside or by internal transfer—whose backgrounds, values, attitudes, or managerial styles differ from those of present members. Many large corporations have used this technique during the last decade in filling vacancies on their boards of directors. Women, minority group members, consumer activists, and others whose backgrounds and interests differ significantly from those of the rest of the board have been purposely selected to add a fresh perspective.

We also know that structural variables are a source of conflict. It is therefore only logical that managers look to structure as a conflict-stimulation device. Centralizing decisions, realigning work groups, increasing formalization, and increasing interdependencies between units are all structural devices that disrupt the status quo and act to increase conflict levels.

Finally, one can appoint a **devil's advocate.** A devil's advocate is a person who purposely presents arguments that run counter to those proposed by the majority or against current practices. He or she plays the role of the critic, even to the point of arguing against positions with which he or she actually agrees. A devil's advocate acts as a check against groupthink and practices that have no better justification than "that's the way we've always done it around here." When thoughtfully listened to, the advocate can improve the quality of group decision making. On the other hand, others in the group often view advocates as time wasters, and their appointment is almost certain to delay any decision process.

devil's advocate
A person who purposely presents arguments that run counter to those proposed by the majority.

Summary

This Summary is organized by the chapter opening learning objectives found on page 319.

1. Communication is the transference and understanding of meaning. It is important because everything a manager does—decision making, planning, leading, and all other activities—requires that information be communicated.

2. The communication process begins with a communication source (a sender) who has a message to convey. The message is converted to symbolic form (encoding) and passed by way of a channel to the receiver, who decodes the message. To ensure accuracy, the receiver should provide the sender with feedback as a check on whether understanding has been achieved.

3. The more popular methods of communication are oral or verbal communications, written communications, nonverbal communications, and electronic media.

4. Several barriers to communications exist. They can take many forms, such as filtering, selective perception, emotions, language, and nonverbal cues.

5. Some techniques for overcoming communication barriers include using feedback, simplifying language, listening actively, constraining emotions, and watching nonverbal cues.

6. Conflict is the perceived incompatible differences that result in interference or opposition.

7. The three views of conflict are the traditional view that holds that all conflict should be avoided; the human relations view that holds that conflict is natural and inevitable in any organization; and the interactionist view that holds that some conflict is necessary for an organization to perform effectively.

8. Conflict can be positive when it leads to high levels of organizational performance that support an organization's goals.

9. The more popular conflict-resolution techniques are understanding one's conflict-handling style; determining which conflicts to handle; evaluating the conflict players; assessing the source of the conflict; and understanding the options one has for dealing with the conflict (avoidance, accommodation, forcing, compromise, or collaboration).

10. A manager can stimulate conflict by changing the organization's culture, through the use of communications, by bringing in outsiders, by restructuring the organization, or by appointing a devil's advocate.

Review and Discussion Questions

1. Why isn't effective communication synonymous with agreement?
2. Where in the communication process is distortion likely to occur?
3. "Ineffective communication is the fault of the sender." Do you agree or disagree with this statement? Support your position.
4. What are the most popular communication methods used by people in organizations?
5. Why are effective communication skills so important to a manager's success?
6. What is conflict?
7. Contrast the traditional, human relations, and interactionist views of conflict.
8. What view of conflict—traditional, human relations, or interactionist—do you think most managers have? Do you think this view is appropriate?
9. What are the five primary conflict-resolution techniques?
10. Why would a manager ever want to stimulate conflict?

Self-Assessment Exercise

Conflict-Handling Style Questionnaire

Indicate how often you do the following when you differ with someone.

When I Differ With Someone:	Usually	Sometimes	Seldom
1. I explore our differences, not backing down, but not imposing my view either.	☐	☐	☐
2. I disagree openly, then invite more discussion about our differences.	☐	☐	☐
3. I look for a mutually satisfactory solution.	☐	☐	☐
4. Rather than let the other person make a decision without my input, I make sure I am heard and also that I hear the other out.	☐	☐	☐
5. I agree to a middle ground rather than look for a completely satisfying solution.	☐	☐	☐
6. I admit I am half wrong rather than explore our differences.	☐	☐	☐
7. I have a reputation for meeting a person halfway.	☐	☐	☐
8. I expect to get out about half of what I really want to say.	☐	☐	☐
9. I give in totally rather than try to change another's opinion.	☐	☐	☐
10. I put aside any controversial aspects of an issue.	☐	☐	☐
11. I agree early on, rather than argue about a point.	☐	☐	☐
12. I give in as soon as the other party gets emotional about an issue.	☐	☐	☐
13. I try to win the other person over.	☐	☐	☐
14. I work to come out victorious, no matter what.	☐	☐	☐

Communication and Conflict Management

15. I never back away from a good argument. ☐ ☐ ☐
16. I would rather win than end up compromising. ☐ ☐ ☐

Turn to page 416 for scoring directions and key.

Source: Reprinted with the permission of Macmillan College Publishing from *Supervision: Managerial Skills for a New Era* by Thomas Von Der Embse. Copyright © 1987 by Macmillan College Publishing, Inc.

Class Exercise

Active Listening

Purpose: To reinforce that good listening skills are necessary for managers and that as communicators we can motivate listeners to actively listen.

Time Required: Approximately thirty minutes

Instructions: Most of us are pretty poor listeners. This is probably because active listening is very demanding. This exercise is specifically designed to dramatize how difficult it is to listen actively and to accurately interpret what is being said. It also points out how emotions can distort communication.

Your instructor will read you a story and ask you some follow-up questions. You'll need paper and pencil.

Source: Adopted from Bonnie L. McNeely, "A Fun Exercise in Listening: The Neglected Managerial Skill," *The Organizational Behavior Teaching Review,* Vol. XIII, No. 4 (1988–1989), pp. 126–29.

Key Terms

Key terms are listed in the order in which they appear in the chapter.

communication	body language	dysfunctional conflicts
interpersonal communication	verbal intonation	avoidance
message	electronic mail	accommodation
encoding	active listening	forcing
channel	conflict	compromise
decoding	traditional view of conflict	collaboration
communication process	human relations view of conflict	devil's advocate
noise	interactionist view of conflict	
nonverbal communication	functional conflicts	

Case Application

WordPerfect

Today's communication patterns have drastically changed. More and more of us are faced with electronic media that are designed to enhance communications effectiveness and make our lives "easier." But do such systems really support the basic premise that communication implies an understanding between two or more people?

Consider when you have had to contact an organization—especially those with 800 numbers. These companies provide toll-free lines to assist us in obtaining the information we want, whether it's ordering a product, seeking advice, or attempting to get some help with a product we purchased. And while this is a cost-savings service to customers, what do we typically find? A response that all operators are currently busy, so please hold on the line for the next available customer service representative. Then to top it off, we have to listen to "elevator music" while waiting for our turn in the queue. How dehumanizing!

WordPerfect (WP), the software company in Orem, Utah, recognized this. In their business, many people call for technical assistance, but instead of listening to electronically enhanced directions, they listen to "hold jockeys." Barbara Lee and Dave Webb share these duties. What do they do? Trained as disc jockeys, they give customers on hold a "live" person to relate to. Using sixteen monitors in their studio to determine the backup for the fifty-plus support lines that WP currently has, they create an atmosphere that entertains customers who are waiting for service. This is done by introducing and playing pop music, interspersed with "traffic update" messages that provide the caller with the "detour" they may encounter. For example, one of these two hold jockeys may announce "a three-call delay for Windows installation support," interjecting to the customer next in line that they are about to be waved through the call-jam.

One would expect an organization in the software industry to provide more automated support. But feedback from callers indicates their appreciation for this "more caller-friendly" approach. In fact, it's gotten so much praise that competitors like Lotus and Microsoft have removed some of their automated lines and hired hold jockeys.

Questions

1. Analyse how hold jockeys at WP help to enhance communications between the company and customers.
2. Considering that the electronic media is the "wave of the future," what potential barriers for effective communications does this create?
3. "Efforts at companies like WordPerfect, Lotus, and Microsoft to hire hold jockeys are reversing a trend in telephone customer service operations—going from automated systems back to people-run operations." Do you agree or disagree with this statement. Support your position.

Source: Mark D. Fefer, "Taking the Pain Out of Holding Patterns," *Fortune,* January 10, 1994, p. 20.

Red Cross and the Canadian Blood Supply

In the 1980s, Canada was rocked with the news that contaminated blood had transmitted AIDS to people across the country. Inquiries and investigations brought the facts to light. At the centre of the controversy was a profound problem of communication. The dangers had been known but not communicated. Serious lessons were to be learned.

How then, a decade later, could the Canadian Red Cross be involved in another blood scandal, this time with blood infected with hepatitis C — a disease that causes 20 per cent of people who have contracted it through transfusions to get sclerosis of the liver within five years ? A similar pattern to the AIDS-infected blood has unfolded. Anyone who received a blood transfusion prior to 1990 should have a test for hepatitis C. It is currently estimated that 85 per cent of Canada's hemopheliacs are infected.

Why, if officials knew of the danger, did they not communicate it to the public? Clearly, not all donated blood is infected with hepatitis C. The Red Cross and health care officials in Canada considered that the percentage of infected blood was low enough to constitute "an acceptable risk" and therefore decided not to tell the public. In addition, in 1986, a surrogate test was developed to detect hepatitis C, and the United States began using it right away. However, Canada did not, because the Red Cross considered that "the evidence wasn't strong enough" that the test was effective. It is now known that while the test would not have detected all infected blood, it would have screened out 85 per cent of infected cases. But for four years it was not used. Why?

There are a number of factors that contributed to the tragedy. For instance, individuals who know they will be undergoing an operation can donate their own blood and have it stored for use when they need transfusions. However, the Red Cross is geared to recruiting large numbers of general donors, and their funding is structured to support this program. They did not encourage self donations because they felt it might cause the average donor to feel blood donation was not important and therefore be less willing to donate blood regularly. It is also cheaper for the system to rely on individual donors. Compounding the problem is the fact that hospitals that wish to implement self-donation programs have to fund these from their own budgets, while it is much easier and cheaper to get blood from the Red Cross.

Questions

1. Identify the barriers to effective communication in this case. What could have been done to overcome them?
2. Was a fear of conflict one of the factors that caused the information concerning hepatitis C infection not to be clearly communicated to the public? How could this potential conflict have been used to bring about a positive outcome to the problem?
3. If you had been an official in charge of communicating the dangers of the hepatitis C situation to the public, what are the five things you would have done to make the message effective while not causing a panic or a major disruption in blood supplies?

Video Resource: "Lessons Not Learned," *Prime Time Magazine* (December 13, 1994).

15

Foundations of Control

Learning Objectives

WHAT WILL I BE ABLE TO DO AFTER I FINISH THIS CHAPTER?

1. Define control.
2. Explain why control is important.
3. Describe the control process.
4. Distinguish between the three types of control.
5. Describe the qualities of an effective control system.
6. Identify the contingency factors in the control process.
7. Explain how controls can become dysfunctional.

All day long, each working day of the week, salespeople at Frito-Lay (a division of PepsiCo) punch information into their hand-held computers.[1] At the end of each workday, these salespeople "download" the collected information into minicomputers at local sales offices or through modems in their homes. These downloaded data are then relayed to corporate headquarters. The company's CEO, Robert Beeby, will have a complete report within twenty-four hours. Information on 100 Frito-Lay product lines in 400,000 stores is available on his computer screen in easy-to-read, colour-coded charts: red means a sales drop, yellow a slowdown, and green an advance. This system allows problems to be quickly identified and corrected.

Frito-Lay's control system helped the company solve a recent problem. Sales were slumping in area supermarkets. Beeby turned on his computer, called up data, and quickly isolated the cause. A regional competitor had just introduced El Galindo, a white-corn tortilla chip. The chip was getting good word-of-mouth advertising, and store managers were giving it more shelf space than Frito's traditional Tostitos tortilla chips. Using this information, Beeby sprang into action. He immediately directed his product development people to produce a white-corn version of Tostitos. Within three months his new product was on the shelves, and his company successfully won back lost market share.

Interestingly, this control mechanism at Frito-Lay is relatively new. Before its installation, Beeby would have needed at least three months just to pinpoint the problem. But this new system gathers data daily from supermarkets, scans them for important clues about local trends, and warns executives about problems and opportunities in all of Frito-Lay's markets.

Information recorded in her hand-held computer by this Frito-Lay sales representative is transferred to company headquarters and is used to help the company meet its goals.

The Frito-Lay example illustrates what can happen when an organization has effective controls. Regardless of the thoroughness of the planning, an idea still may be poorly or improperly implemented without a satisfactory control system. Effective management, therefore, needs to consider the benefits of a well-designed control system.

What Is Control?

Control can be defined as the process of monitoring activities to ensure that they are being accomplished as planned and of correcting any significant deviations. All managers should be involved in the control function even if their units are performing as planned. Managers cannot really know whether their units are performing properly

control
The process of monitoring activities to ensure they are being accomplished as planned and of correcting any significant deviations.

until they have evaluated what activities have been done and have compared the actual performance with the desired standard.[2] An effective control system ensures that activities are completed in ways that lead to the attainment of the organization's goals. The criterion that determines the effectiveness of a control system is how well it facilitates goal achievement. The more it helps managers achieve their organization's goals, the better the control system.[3]

The Importance of Control

Planning can be done, an organization structure can be created to efficiently facilitate the achievement of objectives, and employees can be directed and motivated. Still, there is no assurance that activities are going as planned and that the goals managers are seeking are, in fact, being attained. Control is important, therefore, because it is the final link in the functional chain of management. However, the value of the control function lies predominantly in its relation to planning and delegating activities.

In Chapter 3, we described objectives as the foundation of planning. Objectives give specific direction to managers. However, just stating objectives or having employees accept your objectives is no guarantee that the necessary actions have been accomplished. The effective manager needs to follow up to ensure that the actions that others are supposed to take and the objectives they are supposed to achieve are, in fact, being taken and achieved.

The Control Process

control process
The process of measuring actual performance, comparing it against a standard, and taking managerial action to correct deviations or inadequate standards.

The **control process** consists of three separate and distinct steps: (1) measuring actual performance; (2) comparing actual performance against a standard; and (3) taking managerial action to correct deviations or inadequate standards (see Exhibit 15-1). Before we consider each step in detail, you should be aware that the control process assumes that standards of performance already exist. These standards are the specific objectives against which progress can be measured. They are created in the planning function. If managers use some variation of mutual goal setting, then objectives are, by definition, tangible, verifiable, and measurable. In such instances, these objectives are the standards against which progress is measured and compared. If "goal setting" is not practised, then standards are the specific performance indicators that management uses. Our point is that these standards are developed in the planning function; planning must precede control.

What Is Measuring?

To determine what actual performance is, a manager must acquire information about it. The first step in control, then, is measuring. Let us consider how we measure and what we measure.

How Do Managers Measure? Four common sources of information, frequently used by managers to measure actual performance, are personal observation, statistical reports, oral reports, and written reports. Each has particular strengths and

Foundations of Control

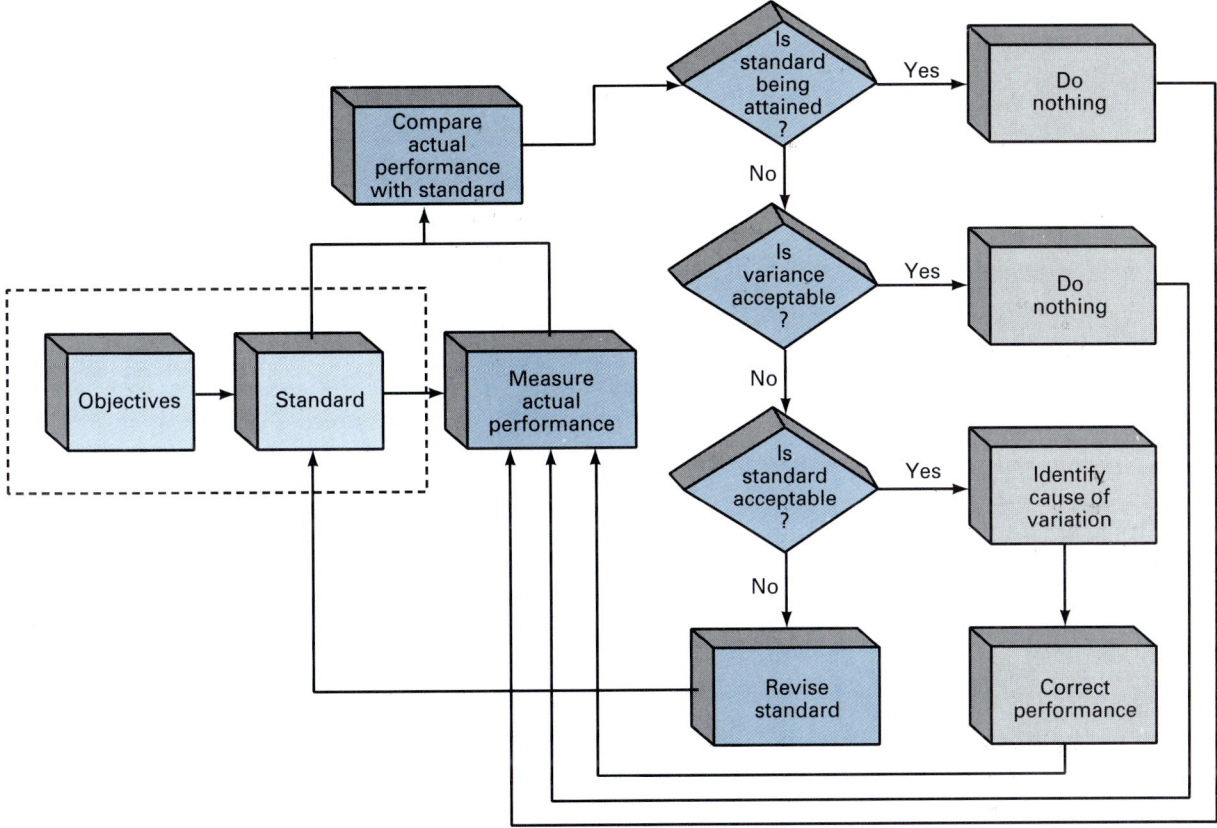

Exhibit 15-1 The Control Process

weaknesses; however, a combination of them increases both the number of input sources and the probability of receiving reliable information.

Personal observation provides firsthand, intimate knowledge of the actual activity—information that is not filtered through others. It permits intensive coverage because minor as well as major performance activities can be observed, and it provides opportunities for the manager to "read between the lines." Management-by-walking-around can pick up omissions, facial expressions, and tones of voice that may be missed by other sources. Unfortunately, in a time when quantitative information suggests objectivity, personal observation is often considered an inferior information source. It is subject to perceptual biases—what one manager sees, another might not. Personal observation also consumes a good deal of time. Finally, this method suffers from obtrusiveness. Employees might interpret a manager's overt observation as a sign of a lack of confidence in them or of mistrust.

The current wide use of computers in organizations, like Frito-Lay, has made managers rely increasingly on statistical reports for measuring actual performance. This measuring device, however, is not limited to computer outputs. It also includes graphs, bar charts, and numerical displays of any form that managers may use for assessing

> An increasing number of managers are using personal observations as a means of control. Management-by-walking-around provides a richness of information often lost in formal reports.

performance. Although statistical data are easy to visualize and effective for showing relationships, they provide limited information about an activity. Statistics report on only a few key areas and often ignore other important factors.

Information can also be acquired through oral reports—that is, through conferences, meetings, one-to-one conversations, or telephone calls. The advantages and disadvantages of this method of measuring performance are similar to those of personal observation. Although the information is filtered, it is fast, allows for feedback, and permits language expression and tone of voice, as well as words themselves, to convey meaning. Historically, one of the major drawbacks of oral reports was the problem of documenting information for later references. However, our technological capabilities have progressed in the last couple of decades to the point where oral reports can be efficiently taped and become as permanent as if they were written.

Actual performance may also be measured by written reports. As with statistical reports, they are slower yet more formal than first- or second-hand oral measures. This formality also often means greater comprehensiveness and conciseness than is found in oral reports. In addition, written reports are usually easy to catalogue and reference.

Given the varied advantages and disadvantages of each of these four measurement techniques, comprehensive control efforts by managers should use all four.

How do you measure the performance of this grade school teacher? Often, his activities are not easily quantified. Thus, his principal must determine what value he adds to the school and translate that into job standards.

What Do Managers Measure? *What* we measure is probably more critical to the control process than *how* we measure. The selection of the wrong criteria can result in serious dysfunctional consequences. Besides, what we measure determines, to a great extent, what people in the organization will attempt to excel at.[4] For example, assume your instructor has assigned a twenty-page term paper on your syllabus for this course. In the grade computation section of the syllabus, you notice that the term paper is not scored. In fact, when you ask your professor if that is a mistake, she says no; the term paper is for your own enlightenment and has no grade consequence for the course. Grades are solely a function of how well you perform on the three exams in the course. Accordingly, we can expect most, if not all, effort geared toward preparing for and taking the three exams.

For the most part, controls are directed at one of several areas: information, operations, finances, or people (we'll explore these areas in more detail in the next chapter). Some control criteria, however, are applicable to any management situation. For instance, because all managers, by definition, direct the activities of others, criteria such as employee satisfaction or turnover and absenteeism rates can be measured. Most managers have budgets for their area of responsibility set in dollar costs. Keeping costs within budget is therefore a fairly common control measure. However, any comprehensive control system needs to recognize the diversity of activities among managers. A production manager in a manufacturing plant might use measures of the quantity of units produced per day, units produced per labour hour, scrap per unit of output, or percentage of rejects returned by customers. The manager of an administrative unit in a government agency might use number of document pages typed per day, number of orders processed per hour, or average time required to process service calls. Marketing managers often use measures such as percentage of market captured, average dollar value per sale, or number of customer visits per salesperson.

Foundations of Control

The performance of some activities is difficult to measure in quantifiable terms. It is more difficult, for instance, for an administrator to measure the performance of a research chemist or an elementary school teacher than of a person who sells life insurance. But most activities can be broken down into objective segments that allow for measurement. The manager needs to determine what value a person, department, or unit contributes to the organization and then convert the contribution into standards.

Most jobs and activities can be expressed in tangible and measurable terms. When a performance indicator cannot be stated in quantifiable terms, managers should look for and use subjective measures. Certainly, subjective measures have significant limitations. Still, they are better than having no standards at all and ignoring the control function. If an activity is important, the excuse that it is difficult to measure is inadequate. In such cases, managers should use subjective performance criteria. Of course, any analysis or decisions made based on subjective criteria should recognize the limitations of the data.

How Do Managers Determine Variations Between Actual Performance and Planned Goals?

Managers determine the variation between actual performance and the standard through a process called comparing. The comparing step determines the degree of variation between actual performance and the standard. Some variation in performance can be expected in all activities; it is therefore critical to determine the acceptable **range of variation** (see Exhibit 15-2). Deviations in excess of this range become significant and receive the manager's attention. In the comparison stage, managers are particularly concerned with the size and direction of the variation. An example should help make this clearer.

Rich Tanner is sales manager for Eastern Distributors. The firm distributes imported beers in the Maritimes. Rich prepares a report during the first week of each month that describes sales for the previous month, classified by brand name. Exhibit 15-3 displays both the standard and actual sales figures (in hundreds of cases) for the month of July.

range of variation
The acceptable parameters of variance between actual performance and the standard.

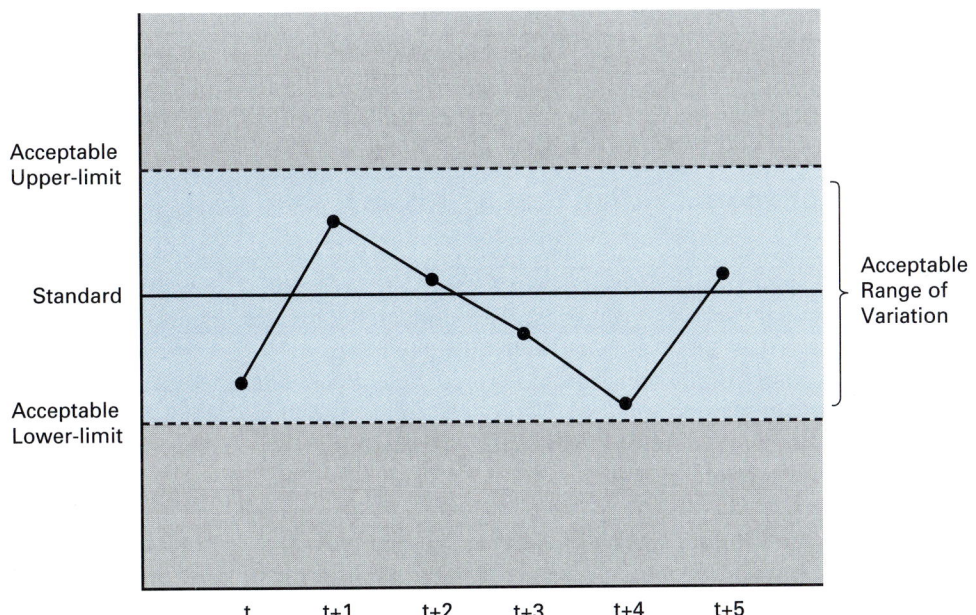

Exhibit 15-2 Defining an Acceptable Range of Variation

BRAND	STANDARD	ACTUAL	OVER (UNDER)
Heineken	1,075	913	(162)
Molson	630	634	4
Beck's	800	912	112
Moosehead	620	622	2
Labatt	540	672	132
Corona	160	140	(20)
Amstel Light	225	220	(5)
Dos Equis	80	65	(15)
Tecate	170	286	116
Total Cases	4,300	4,464	164

Exhibit 15-3 Eastern Distributors' Sales Performance for July (Hundreds of Cases)

Should Rich be concerned about the July performance? Sales were a bit higher than he had originally targeted, but does that mean that there were no significant deviations? Even though overall performance was generally quite favourable, several brands might deserve the sales manager's attention. However, the number of brands that deserve attention depends on what Rich believes to be significant. How much variation should he allow before he takes corrective action?

The deviation on several brands is very small and undoubtedly not worthy of special attention. These include Guinness and Amstel Light. Are the shortages for Corona and Dos Equis brands significant? That's a judgment Rich must make. Heineken sales were 15 per cent below his goal. This needs attention. He should look for a cause. In this case, he attributed the loss to aggressive advertising and promotion programs by the big domestic producers, Labatt and Molson. Because Heineken is the number-one selling import, it is most vulnerable to the promotion clout of the big domestic producers. If the decline in Heineken is more than a temporary slump, Rich will need to reduce his orders with the brewery and lower his inventory stock.

An error in understating sales can be as troublesome as an overstatement. For instance, is the surprising popularity of Tecate a one-month aberration, or is this brand increasing its market share? Our Eastern example illustrates that both overvariance and undervariance require managerial attention.

What Managerial Action Can Be Taken?

The third and final step in the control process is taking managerial action. Managers can choose among three courses of action: they can do nothing; they can correct the actual performance; or they can revise the standard. Because "doing nothing" is fairly self-explanatory, let's look more closely at the latter two.

If the source of the variation has been deficient performance, the manager will want to take corrective action. Examples of such corrective action might include changes in strategy, structure, compensation practices, or training programs; the redesign of jobs; or the replacement of personnel.

A manager who decides to correct actual performance has to make another decision: should he or she take immediate or basic corrective action? **Immediate corrective action** corrects problems at once and gets performance back on track. **Basic corrective action** asks how and why performance has deviated and then proceeds to

immediate corrective action
Correcting an activity at once in order to get performance back on track.

basic corrective action
Determining how and why performance has deviated and correcting the source of deviations.

Foundations of Control

correct the source of deviation. It is not unusual for managers to rationalize that they do not have the time to take basic corrective action and therefore must be content to perpetually "put out fires" with immediate corrective action. Effective managers, however, analyse deviations and, when the benefits justify it, take the time to permanently correct significant variances between standard and actual performance.

To return to our example of Eastern Distributors, Rich Tanner might take basic corrective action on the negative variance for Heineken. He might increase promotion efforts, increase the advertisement budget for this brand, or reduce future orders with the manufacturer. The action he takes will depend on his assessment of each brand's potential effectiveness.

It is also possible that the variance was a result of an unrealistic standard—that is, the goal may be too high or too low. In such cases it's the standard that needs corrective attention, not the performance. In our example, the sales manager might need to raise the standard for Tecate to reflect its increasing popularity. This frequently happens in sports when athletes adjust their performance goals upward during a season if they achieve their season goal early.

The more troublesome problem is the revising of a performance standard downward. If an employee or unit falls significantly short of reaching its target, the natural response is to shift the blame for the variance to the standard. For instance, students who make a low grade on a test often attack the grade cutoff points as too high. Rather than accept the fact that their performance was inadequate, students argue that the standards are unreasonable. Similarly, salespeople who fail to meet their monthly quota may attribute the failure to an unrealistic quota. It may be true that standards are too high, resulting in a significant variance and acting to demotivate those employees being assessed against it. But keep in mind that if employees or managers don't meet the standard, the first thing they are likely to attack is the standard itself. If you believe the standard is realistic, hold your ground. Explain your position, reaffirm to the employee or manager that you expect future performance to improve, and then take the necessary corrective action to turn that expectation into reality.

This Allen-Bradley employee is replacing a circuit board in the company's computerized production process. In doing so, he is taking corrective action.

Types of Control

Management can implement controls before an activity commences, while the activity is going on, or after the activity has been completed. The first type is called feedforward control, the second is concurrent control, and the last is feedback control (see Exhibit 15-4).

What Is Feedforward Control?

The most desirable type of control—**feedforward control**—prevents anticipated problems. It is called feedforward control because it takes place in advance of the actual activity. It is future-directed.[5] For instance, managers at Westinghouse Corporation may hire additional personnel as soon as the government announces that the firm has won a major defence contract. The hiring of personnel ahead of time prevents potential delays. The key to feedforward control, therefore, is taking managerial action before a problem occurs.

feedforward control
Control that prevents anticipated problems.

Exhibit 15-4 Types of Control

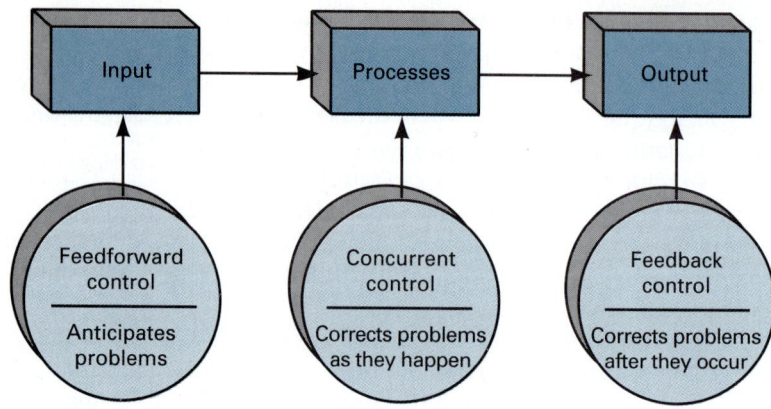

Feedforward controls are desirable because they allow management to prevent problems rather than having to cure them later. Unfortunately, these controls require timely and accurate information that is often difficult to develop. As a result, managers frequently have to use one of the other two types of control.

When Is Concurrent Control Used?

concurrent control
Control that occurs while an activity is in progress.

Concurrent control, as its name implies, takes place while an activity is in progress. When control is enacted while the work is being performed, management can correct problems before they become too costly.

The best-known form of concurrent control is direct supervision. When a manager directly oversees the actions of an employee, the manager can concurrently monitor the employee's actions and correct problems as they occur. While there is obviously some delay between the activity and the manager's corrective response, the delay is minimal. Technical equipment can be designed to include concurrent controls. Most computers, for instance, are programmed to provide operators with immediate response if an error is made. If you input the wrong command, the program's concurrent controls reject your command and may even tell you why it is wrong.

As part of Boise Cascade's quality audit process, these engineers are checking a problem that was just identified through the company's on-line computer control system.

Foundations of Control

Why Is Feedback Control So Popular?

The most popular type of control relies on feedback. The control takes place after the action. The control report that Rich Tanner used for assessing beer sales is an example of a **feedback control**.

The major drawback of this type of control is that by the time the manager has the information, the damage is already done. It's analogous to the proverbial closing the barn door after the horse has been stolen. But for many activities, feedback is the only viable type of control available.

We should note that feedback has two advantages over feedforward and concurrent control.[6] First, feedback provides managers with meaningful information on how effective their planning effort was. If feedback indicates little variance between standard and actual performance, this is evidence that planning was generally on target. If the deviation is great, a manager can use this information when formulating new plans to make them more effective. Second, feedback control can enhance employee motivation. People also want information on how well they have performed. Feedback control provides that information (see Developing Management Skills.)

feedback control
Control imposed after an action has occurred.

Developing Management Skills

▼ PROVIDING FEEDBACK ▲

► **1. Focus on specific rather than general behaviours.** Feedback should be specific rather than general. General statements are vague and provide little useful information from which the recipient can "correct" the problem.

► **2. Support negative feedback with hard data.** Tell the recipient precisely why you are being critical and on what basis you concluded that a "good job" was not completed. Hard data also help the recipient to identify where he or she erred and what behaviours should be avoided in the future.

► **3. Keep comments impersonal and job related.** Feedback, particularly the negative kind, should be descriptive rather than judgmental or evaluative. No matter how upset you are, keep the feedback job-related and never criticize someone personally because of an inappropriate action. You are censuring job-related behaviour, not the person!

► **4. Ensure the recipient has clear and full understanding of the feedback.** Feedback must be concise and complete enough so that the recipient clearly and fully understands your communications. Consistent with active listening techniques, have the recipient rephrase the content of your feedback to check whether it fully captures your meaning.

► **5. Direct the negative feedback toward behaviour that is controllable by the recipient.** Negative feedback should be directed toward behaviour that the recipient can do something about. Indicate what the recipient can do to improve the situation. This helps to take the sting out of the criticism and offers guidance to those who understand the problem but don't know how to resolve it.

This Motorola manager works with company suppliers to teach them how Motorola's control process operates. In running such seminars, and increasing supplier understanding of what Motorola wants, quality of goods supplied has increased. So, too, has there been a reduction in the suppliers' time taken to ship the parts.

Qualities of an Effective Control System

Effective control systems tend to have certain qualities in common.[7] The importance of these qualities varies with the situation, but we can generalize that the following characteristics should make a control system more effective.

▶ 1. **Accuracy.** A control system that generates inaccurate information can result in management failing to take action when it should or responding to a problem that doesn't exist. An accurate control system is reliable and produces valid data.

▶ 2. **Timeliness.** Controls should call management's attention to variations in time to prevent serious infringement on a unit's performance. The best information has little value if it is dated. Therefore, an effective control system must provide timely information.

▶ 3. **Economy.** A control system must be economically reasonable to operate. Any system of control has to justify the benefits that it gives in relation to the costs it incurs. To minimize costs, management should try to impose the least amount of control that is necessary to produce the desired results.

▶ 4. **Flexibility.** Effective controls must be flexible enough to adjust to adverse change or to take advantage of new opportunities. Few organizations face environments so stable that there is no need for flexibility. Even highly mechanistic structures require controls that can be adjusted as times and conditions change.

▶ 5. **Understandability.** Controls that cannot be understood have no value. It is sometimes necessary, therefore, to substitute less complex controls for sophisticated devices. A control system that is difficult to understand can cause unnecessary mistakes, frustrate employees, and eventually be ignored.

▶ 6. **Reasonable criteria.** Control standards must be reasonable and attainable. If they are too high or unreasonable, they no longer motivate. Because most employees don't want to risk being labelled incompetent by accusing superiors of asking too much, employees may resort to unethical or illegal shortcuts. Controls should, therefore, enforce standards that challenge and stretch people to reach higher performance levels without being demotivating or encouraging deception.

▶ 7. **Strategic placement.** Management can't control everything that goes on in an organization (see Managers Who Made a Difference). Even if it could, the benefits couldn't justify the costs. As a result, managers should place controls on those

Foundations of Control

factors that are strategic to the organization's performance. Controls should cover the critical activities, operations, and events within the organization. That is, they should focus on places where variations from standard are most likely to occur or where a variation would do the greatest harm. In a department where labour costs are $20,000 a month and postage costs are $50 a month, a 5 per cent overrun in the former is more critical than a 20 per cent overrun in the latter. Hence, we should establish controls for labour and a critical dollar allocation, whereas postage expenses would not appear to be critical.

▶ 8. **Emphasis on the exception.** Because managers can't control all activities, they should place their strategic control devices where those devices can call attention only to the exceptions. An exception system ensures that a manager is not overwhelmed by information on variations from standard. For instance, if management policy gives supervisors the authority to give annual raises up to $200 a month, approve individual expenses up to $500, and make capital expenditures up to $5,000, then only deviations above these amounts require approval from higher levels of management. These checkpoints become controls that are part of the authority constraints and free higher levels of management from reviewing routine expenditures.

Managers at the Goodyear Tire and Rubber Company would pay particular attention to the demands of suppliers of critical petroleum products used in the tire manufacturing process; officials at banks where the company has sizeable short-term loans; government regulatory agencies that grade tires and inspect facilities; security analysts at major brokerage firms who specialize in the tire and rubber industry; regional tire jobbers and distributors; and purchasing agents responsible for the acquisition of tires at Ford, Mack Truck, Caterpillar, and other vehicle manufacturers.

▶ 9. **Multiple criteria.** Managers and employees alike will seek to "look good" on the criteria that are controlled. If management controls by using a single measure such as unit profit, effort will be focused only on looking good on this standard. Multiple measures of performance decrease this narrow focus. Multiple criteria have a dual positive effect. Because they are more difficult to manipulate than a single measure, they can discourage efforts to merely look good. Additionally, because performance can rarely be objectively evaluated from a single indicator, multiple criteria make possible more accurate assessments of performance.

▶10. **Corrective action.** An effective control system not only indicates when a significant deviation from standard occurs but also suggests what action should be taken to correct the deviation. That is, it ought to both point out the problem and specify the solution. This is frequently accomplished by establishing if-then guidelines; for instance, if unit revenues drop more than 5 per cent, then unit costs should be reduced by a similar amount.

Managers Who Made a Difference

PAUL CLOUGH AT IMPERIAL PARKING

Can you make money in the parking business? You certainly don't get much glamour. But Paul Clough, president and chairman of Imperial Parking Ltd. (Impark) is changing the face of the parking business, and he's using some very sophisticated control techniques to do it. Imperial has 200,000 spaces in 1,270 lots in forty-seven cities, including cities in the U.S. such as Minneapolis and Milwaukee. Chances are that if you've driven to a Toronto Blue Jays game at the SkyDome, you may have parked in one of Imperial's lots.

No, the profit isn't startling. In 1994, Impark's gross margin was 11 per cent of sales. Although this figure was the best result for the company over five years, margins should improve because Impark's strength is tight controls and management systems. For instance, Impark parking decals have bar codes that are scanned by hand-held computers. They can track whether the owner is paid up. If

Foundations of Control

not, a notice is mailed out, and after two warnings, the car is towed away. Impark generates information quickly—which is a key to success in any business and something that the landlords for whom it manages property like. In the United States, it is installing park-yourself machines that allow management at head office to call the machine and get an up-to-the-minute report on volume, revenue, and so on. With the systems and controls in place, when Impark adds new properties, revenue increases, but fixed costs remain relatively stable—a recipe for increased profits. So even in something as apparently mundane as parking lots, effective managers like Paul Clough can make a difference.[8] ▼

Contingency Factors of Control

While the generalizations above about effective control systems provide guidelines, their validity is influenced by situational factors. These include size of the organization, position in the organization's hierarchy, degree of decentralization, organizational culture, and importance of an activity (see Exhibit 15-5).

Control systems should vary to reflect the size of the organization. A small business relies on informal and more personal control devices. Concurrent control through direct supervision is probably most cost effective. As organizations increase in size, direct supervision is likely to be supported by an expanding formal system. Very large organizations will typically have highly formalized and impersonal feedforward and feedback controls.

When personnel in a college registrar's office become overly concerned with every rule and procedure being followed rigidly, regardless of the possible negative consequences on a student's enrolment or personal life, the control imposed by the rules and procedures can become dysfunctional.

Exhibit 15-5 Contingency Factors in the Design of Control Systems

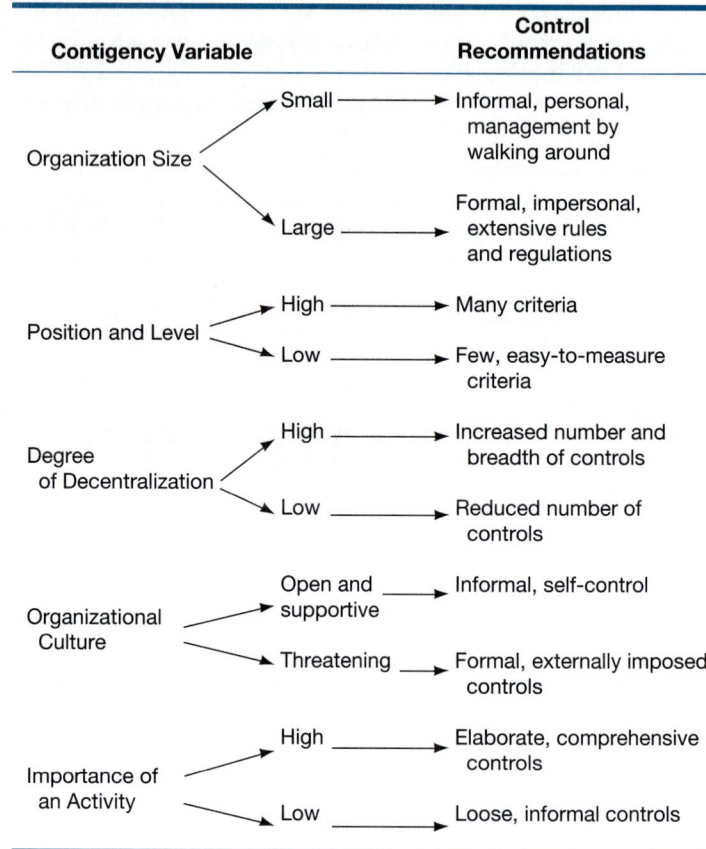

The higher one moves in the organization's hierarchy, the greater the need for multiple set of control criteria, tailored to the unit's goals. This reflects the increased ambiguity in measuring performance as a person moves up the hierarchy. Conversely, lower-level jobs have clearer definitions of performance that allow for a more narrow interpretation of job performance.

The greater the degree of decentralization, the more managers will need feedback on the performance of subordinate decision makers. Since managers who delegate authority are ultimately responsible for the actions of those to whom it is delegated, managers will want proper assurances that their employees' decisions are both effective and efficient.

The organizational culture may be one of trust, autonomy, and openness, or fear and reprisal. In the former, we can expect to find more informal self-control and, in the latter, more externally imposed and formal control systems to ensure that performance is within standards. As with leadership styles, motivation techniques, organizational structuring, conflict-management techniques, and the extent to which organizational members participate in decision making, the type and extent of controls should be consistent with the organization's culture.

Finally, the importance of an activity influences whether, and how, it will be controlled. If control is costly and the repercussions from error small, the control system is not likely to be elaborate. However, if an error can be highly damaging to the organization, extensive controls are likely to be implemented—even if the cost is high.

Adjusting Controls for National Differences

Methods of controlling people and operations can be quite different in foreign countries. For the multinational corporation, managers of foreign operations tend to be less closely controlled by the head office, if for no other reason than that distance precludes direct controls. The head office of a multinational must rely on extensive formal reports to maintain control. But collecting data that are comparable between countries introduces problems for multinationals. A company's factory in Mexico might produce the same products as its factory in Canada. The Mexican factory, however, might be much more labour intensive than its counterpart in Canada (to take advantage of low labour costs in Mexico). If headquarters' executives were to control costs by, for example, calculating labour costs per unit or output per worker, the figures would not be comparable. Therefore, distance creates a tendency to formalize controls, and technological differences often make control data uncomparable.

Technology's impact on control is most evident in comparing technologically advanced nations with more primitive countries. Organizations in technologically advanced nations such as the United States, Japan, Canada, Great Britain, Germany, and Australia use indirect control devices—particularly computer-related reports and analyses—in addition to standardized rules and direct supervision to ensure that activities are going as planned. In Tanzania, Zambia, Lebanon, and other less advanced countries, direct supervision and highly centralized decision making are the basic means of control.

Constraints on managerial corrective action may also affect managers in foreign countries. For example, laws in some countries do not allow management the options of closing plants, laying off personnel, taking money out of the country, or bringing in a new management team from outside the country.

The Dysfunctional Side of Controls

Here are actual instances of controls taken too far. Fortunately they didn't happen in Canada, but the negative aspects of what we criticize as "bureaucratic procedures" taken to the extreme are well illustrated by the examples, and we, as Canadians, are no more immune to them than any other culture. Larry Boff called the Dallas Fire Department's emergency number to get immediate help for his stepmother, who was having trouble breathing.[9] The nurse/dispatcher, Billie Myrick, spent fifteen minutes arguing with Boff because he wouldn't bring his stepmother to the phone. He told Myrick that his stepmother was in the bedroom and couldn't speak. Myrick insisted that she was required to talk to the person in question so she could determine if the situation was a true emergency. Boff insisted that his stepmother was unable to speak on the phone and pleaded with Myrick to send an ambulance. Myrick continually responded that she could not send an ambulance until she spoke to Boff's stepmother. After getting nowhere for fifteen minutes, Boff hung up the phone. His stepmother was dead.

Three managers at a big General Motors truck plant installed a secret control box in a supervisor's office to override the control panel that governed the speed of the assembly line.[10] The device allowed the managers to speed up the assembly line—a serious violation of GM's contract with the United Auto Workers. When caught, the managers explained that, while they knew that what they had done was wrong, the pressure from higher-ups to meet unrealistic production goals was so great that they felt the secret control panel was the only way they could meet their targets. As described by one manager, senior GM executives would say, "I don't care how you do it—just do it."

Did you ever notice that the people who work in the college registrar's office often don't seem to care much about students' problems? They become so fixated on ensuring that every rule is followed that they lose sight of the fact that their job is to serve students, not hassle them!

These examples illustrate what can happen when controls are inflexible or control standards are unreasonable. People lose sight of the organization's overall goals.[11] Instead of the organization running the controls, sometimes the controls run the organization.

Because any control system has imperfections, problems occur when individuals or organizational units attempt to look good exclusively in terms of the control devices. The result is dysfunctional in terms of the organization's goals. More often than not, this dysfunctionality is caused by incomplete measures of performance. If the control system evaluates only the quantity of output, people will ignore quality. Similarly, if the system measures activities rather than results, people will spend their time attempting to look good on the activity measures.

Ethical Dilemmas in Management

▼ CONTROL AND EMPLOYEES' RIGHT TO PRIVACY ▲

When do management's efforts to control the actions of its employees become an invasion of privacy? Consider two cases.[12]

Daniel Winn made nearly $9 an hour setting up machinery at Best Lock Corporation. He was fired after he testified in a relative's legal hearing that he drank socially from time to time. Unfortunately for Winn, Best Lock forbids alcohol consumption by its employees, even after work.

Employees at General Electric's Answering Center handle telephone inquiries from customers all day long. Those conversations are taped by GE and occasionally reviewed by its management.

Are either of the above practices—firing someone for drinking off the job or listening in on telephone conversations—an invasion of privacy? These questions actually touch on two larger issues: does management have the right to tell employees how they can or cannot spend their time off the job; and on the job, when does management overstep the bounds of decency and privacy by silently (even covertly) scrutinizing the behaviour of its employees?

How does management defend such practices? In the case of Best Lock, the argument essentially is based on keeping medical costs down. In recent years, corporate insurance plan premiums have risen an average of 17 per cent annually. And employees who engage in unhealthy habits—such as drinking, smoking, or overeating—file more claims. General Electric can point to U.S. government statistics estimating that six million workers are being electronically monitored on their jobs. And silent surveillance of telephone calls can be used to help employees do their jobs better. Managers can review employee performance and provide feedback that can improve the quality of the employees' work.

But once management starts regulating off-the-job behaviour, where does it stop? What about employees who eat lots of greasy food? Is that grounds for disciplinary action? Similarly, when does management's need for more information about employee performance cross over the line and interfere with a worker's right to privacy? What do you think?

To avoid being reprimanded by managers because of the control system, people can engage in behaviours that are designed solely to influence the information system's data output during a given control period. Rather than actually performing well, employees can manipulate measures to give the appearance that they are performing well. Evidence indicates that the manipulation of control data is not a random phenomenon. It depends on the importance of an activity. Organizationally important activities are more likely to make a difference in a person's rewards; therefore, there is a greater incentive to look good on these particular measures.[13] When rewards are at stake, individuals tend to manipulate data to appear in a favourable light by, for instance, distorting actual figures, emphasizing successes, and suppressing evidence of failures. On the other hand, only random errors occur when the distribution of rewards is unaffected.[14]

Our conclusion is that controls have both an up side and a down side (see Ethical Dilemmas in Management). Failure to design flexibility into a control system can create problems more severe than those the controls were implemented to prevent.

Summary

This Summary is organized by the chapter opening learning objectives found on page 344.

1. Control is the process of monitoring activities to ensure that they are being accomplished as planned and of correcting any significant deviations.
2. Control is important because it monitors whether objectives are being accomplished as planned and delegated authority is being abused.
3. In the control process, management must first have standards of performance from the objectives it formed in the planning stage. Management must then measure actual performance and compare that performance to the standards. If a variance exists between standards and performance, management must either adjust performance, adjust the standards, or do nothing, according to the situation.
4. There are three types of control: feedforward control is future-directed and prevents anticipated problems; concurrent control takes place while an activity is in progress; feedback control takes place after the activity.
5. An effective control system is accurate, timely, economical, flexible, and understandable. It uses reasonable criteria, has strategic placement, emphasizes the exception, uses multiple criteria, and suggests corrective action.
6. The contingency factors in control systems include the size of the organization; the level in the organization's hierarchy; the degree of decentralization; the organization's culture; and the importance of the activity.
7. Controls can be dysfunctional when they redirect behaviour away from an organization's goals. This can occur as a result of inflexibility or unreasonable standards. Additionally, when rewards are at stake, individuals are more likely to manipulate data so that their performance will be perceived positively.

Review and Discussion Questions

1. What is the role of control in management?
2. How are planning and control linked?
3. In Chapter 9 we discussed the white water rapids view of change. Do you think it's possible to establish and maintain effective standards and controls in this type of atmosphere?
4. Why is what is measured in the control process probably more critical to the control process than how it is measured?
5. Name four methods that managers can use to acquire information about actual performance.
6. Contrast immediate and basic corrective action.

7. What are the advantages and disadvantages of feedforward control?
8. Why is feedback control the most popular type of control?
9. What can management do to reduce the dysfunctionality of controls?
10. Do you think goal setting and TQM programs facilitate the control process? Explain your answer.

Self-Assessment Exercise

How Willing Are You to Give Up Control?

Instructions: You can get a good idea of whether you are willing to give up enough control to be effective in delegating by responding to the following items. If you have limited work experience, base your answers on what you know about yourself and your personal beliefs. Indicate the extent to which you agree or disagree by circling the number following each statement.

	Strongly Agree				Strongly Disagree
1. I'd delegate more, but the jobs I delegate never seem to get done the way I want them to be done.	5	4	3	2	1
2. I don't feel I have the time to delegate properly.	5	4	3	2	1
3. I carefully check on subordinates' work without letting them know I'd doing it, so I can correct their mistakes if necessary before they cause too many problems.	5	4	3	2	1
4. I delegate the whole job—giving the opportunity for the subordinate to complete it without any of my involvement. Then I review the result.	5	4	3	2	1
5. When I have given clear instructions and the task isn't done right, I get upset.	5	4	3	2	1
6. I feel the staff lacks the commitment that I have. So any task I delegate won't get done as well as I'd do it.	5	4	3	2	1
7. I'd delegate more, but I feel I can do the task better than the person I might delegate it to.	5	4	3	2	1
8. I'd delegate more, but if the individual I delegate the task to does an incompetent job, I'll be severely criticized.	5	4	3	2	1
9. If I were to delegate a task, my job wouldn't be nearly as much fun.	5	4	3	2	1
10. When I delegate a task, I often find that the outcome is such that I end up doing the task over again myself.	5	4	3	2	1
11. I have not really found that delegation saves any time.	5	4	3	2	1
12. I delegate a task clearly and concisely, explaining exactly how it should be accomplished.	5	4	3	2	1
13. I can't delegate as much as I'd like to because my subordinates lack the necessary experience.	5	4	3	2	1
14. I feel that when I delegate I lose control.	5	4	3	2	1
15. I would delegate more but I'm pretty much a perfectionist.	5	4	3	2	1
16. I work longer hours than I should.	5	4	3	2	1
17. I can give subordinates the routine tasks, but I feel I must do nonroutine tasks myself.	5	4	3	2	1
18. My own boss expects me to keep very close to all details of my job.	5	4	3	2	1

Turn to page 417 for scoring directions and key.

Reprinted by permission of publisher from *Management Review*, May 1982. © 1982 American Management Association, New York. All rights reserved.

Class Exercise

Paper Plane Corporation

Purpose
1. To integrate the management functions.
2. To apply planning and control concepts specifically to improve organizational performance.

Required Knowledge
Planning, organizing, and controlling concepts.

Time Required
Approximately one hour.

Instructions
Any number of groups of six participants each are used in this exercise. These groups may be directed simultaneously in the same room. Each person should have

Instructions for aircraft assembly

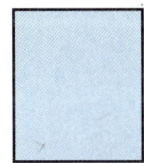 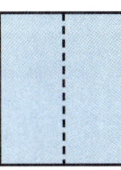
Step 1: Take a sheet of paper and fold it in half, then open it back up.

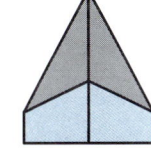 
Step 4: Fold in half.

Step 2: Fold upper corners in the middle.

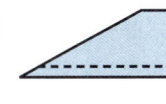 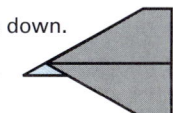
Step 5: Fold both wings down.
Step 6: Fold tail fins up.

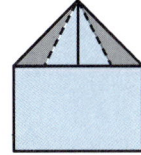 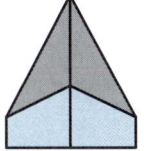 
Step 3: Fold the corners to the middle again.

Completed aircraft

Summary Sheet

Round 1:
Bid: _____ Aircraft @ $20,000.00 per aircraft = _____
Result: _____ Aircraft @ $20,000.00 per aircraft = _____
Less: $300,000.00 overhead
_____ × $3,000 cost of raw materials
_____ × $25,000 penalty
Profit: _____

Round 2:
Bid: _____ Aircraft @ $20,000.00 per aircraft = _____
Result: _____ Aircraft @ $20,000.00 per aircraft = _____
Less: $300,000.00 overhead
_____ × $3,000 cost of raw materials
_____ × $25,000 penalty
Profit: _____

Round 3:
Bid: _____ Aircraft @ $20,000.00 per aircraft = _____
Result: _____ Aircraft @ $20,000.00 per aircraft = _____
Less: $300,000.00 overhead
_____ × $3,000 cost of raw materials
_____ × $25,000 penalty
Profit: _____

Exhibit CE15-1 Paper Plane Corporation: Data Sheet

Source: Based on an exercise in James H. Donnelly, Jr., James L. Gibson, and John M. Ivancevich. *Fundamentals of Management*, 8th ed. (Burr Ridge, IL: Irwin, 1992), pp. 285–89. With permission.

assembly instructions (Exhibit CE15-1) and a summary sheet, plus ample stacks of paper (8-1/2 by 11 inches). The physical setting should be a room that is large enough that individual groups of six can work without interference from other groups. A working space should be provided for each group.

- The participants are doing an exercise in production methodology.
- Each group must work independently of the other groups.
- Each group will choose a manager and an inspector, and the remaining participants will be employees.
- The objective is to make paper airplanes in the most profitable manner possible.
- The facilitator will give the signal to start. This is a ten-minute, timed event utilizing competition among the groups.
- After the first round, each group should report its production and profits to the entire group. Each group reports the manner in which it planned, organized, and controlled for the production of the paper airplanes. This same procedure is followed for as many rounds as there is time.

Your group is the complete workforce for Paper Plane Corporation. Established in 1943, Paper Plane has led the market in paper plane production. Currently under new management, the company is contracting to make aircraft for the U.S. Air Force. You must establish a plan and organization to produce these aircraft. You must make your contract with the Air Force under the following conditions:

1. The Air Force will pay $20,000 per airplane.
2. The aircraft must pass a strict inspection.
3. A penalty of $25,000 per airplane will be subtracted for failure to meet the production requirements.
4. Labour and other overhead will be computed at $300,000.
5. Cost of materials will be $3,000 per bid plane. If you bid for ten but make only eight, you must pay the cost of materials for those you failed to make or that did not pass inspection.

Key Terms

Key terms are listed in the order in which they appear in the chapter.

| control | range of variation | basic corrective action | concurrent control |
| control process | immediate corrective action | feedforward control | feedback control |

Case Application

Mayor Barnes

"I took office six weeks ago," the new mayor began, "and I'll be honest—I haven't the slightest idea of what is going on in my district. What surprises me the most, I guess, is that things are as bad as I'd been saying in my campaign speeches."

The mayor of this community of 100,000 people continued, "I was a business executive for nearly thirty years before retiring to this community. I know how things are supposed to be! And one thing I know for sure is that if you're going to operate an organization properly, you've got to have decent information on what's happening. That information just isn't here. For instance, I don't know how much of this year's budget each department has spent, and neither do they. Monthly expense reports are issued at least six months after the month ends. Can you believe it—getting a report on February's expenses in August. What can you do about it then? But that's the good news. The bad news is that there are no mechanisms in the system to tell me how well departments are performing. I don't know if waste collection is being done, never mind whether it's being done effectively and efficiently. The same goes for the police and fire protection, snow removal, health care, recreational facilities, and so on. The only feedback I get is nasty phone calls when someone has a complaint. The problem is immense. I really don't know where to begin."

Questions

1. If you were the mayor, what questions would you be asking?
2. Describe the type of feedforward, concurrent, and feedback controls you would instal if you were the mayor.

Is Franchising the Shortcut to Success?

In Canada, 40 per cent of retail dollars are spent in franchises — in clothing shops, food outlets, dry cleaners, video stores, photographic stores, muffler shops, etc. The list goes on and on. In many cases, entry into a franchise business is simple: pay the fee and get into business. No experience is required, and you get to take part of the more than $90 million spent in franchise outlets each year.

The advantages of becoming a franchisee in a well-run franchise like McDonalds, The Body Shop, or Moto Photo is that there is a lot of support, you enter a ready-made operation, the franchiser has conducted market research concerning the location of the outlet, market size, growth potential, competition, and so on. You also get to share the brand name and image and share in the overall advertising to support that brand name. The disadvantages occur when the franchiser does not provide support services, has not done the research, and has built in a number of conditions that tie the franchisee into deals that are not in his or her best interest. John Sotos, a lawyer who is knowledgeable about franchises and franchising, estimates that about a third of franchisers make their money by selling and reselling to franchisees, and not from revenues gained from the operation of the business. Only Alberta has laws that require franchisers to tell potential franchisees what they are getting before they buy. Otherwise, the industry is unregulated.

Facts about the franchising industry are hard to find, but Ted Dixon, who publishes a directory of franchise chains in North America, disputes the industry claim that 80 per cent of franchises are successful. A U.S. study, although small, indicated that franchise businesses failed more frequently than independent businesses during the recent recession. Is this an industry that should come under some sort of government or other controls?

Questions

1. If you were to recommend controls on the franchise business in Canada, what would they be? Bear in mind that the function of controls is to help, not hinder, and the definition of control is the process of monitoring activities to ensure they are being accomplished as planned, and then correcting any significant deviations as they occur.
2. Apply the criteria of effective control systems to the controls that you recommended in question 1, and rate your proposal on a scale of 1 to 10 against each of the criteria.
3. What contingency factors should be built into any system for controlling franchising?

Video Resource: "Franchising," *Venture* 482 (April 3, 1994).

16

Control Tools and Techniques

Learning Objectives

WHAT WILL I BE ABLE TO DO AFTER I FINISH THIS CHAPTER?

1. **Explain the purpose of a management information system (MIS).**
2. **Differentiate between data and information.**
3. **Describe how an MIS affects decision making.**
4. **Explain the role of information systems in control.**
5. **Define the role of the transformation process in operations management.**
6. **Explain the relationship between cost centres, direct costs, and indirect costs.**
7. **Identify three approaches to maintenance control.**
8. **Contrast TQM and quality control.**
9. **Distinguish between external and internal audits.**
10. **Explain how cost-benefit analysis can improve financial control.**
11. **Identify six performance appraisal methods.**
12. **Explain the "hot-stove" rule of discipline.**

The trucking industry is often volatile. Severe competition, high capital start-up costs, and customers who constantly look for bargain transportation prices and substitutes make this one of the riskier ventures in which to invest. Couple that with a 10 per cent company failure rate each year, and you have a recipe for potential turmoil. So what would you think of an individual who one day decides to get into the trucking business—entering this highly competitive environment without the slightest idea of how the industry functions? Glutton for punishment? Maybe so, but Bill Ward of OTR Express felt that his lack of experience was in fact his advantage—simply because he didn't know how other trucking companies operated.[1] Rather, he got into this business with one rig, a Macintosh computer system, and a lot of data processing savvy.

OTR Express has brought the high-tech world to a low-tech industry. Ward's computers control everything from which customers may have the most profitable freight to haul that day, where each of the company's 230 trucks are located at any given time, to how much each rig costs to operate. You might say, Ward's information system is providing some calm to a very erratic business.

Through his information system, Ward is able to "chart, track, and measure" almost all facets of his company's operations. For example, one aspect of that system is to treat each rig as a cost centre. That is, the driver is the "manager" of the unit, and each truck is treated as a separate business—complete with its own financial statements.

In the trucking business, the key to success is keeping the trailers filled and on the road. OTR, through its extensive trend and scheduling analysis, knows when any particular customer may be shipping. Accordingly, it always has a rig coming into a region when another load is expected. Doing so means that the truck won't have to return empty. To help keep costs down—which in this business is a competitive advantage—OTR also tracks the cheapest labour and parts costs with respect to truck maintenance. Then, knowing routine maintenance schedules for the rigs, Ward is able to schedule a specific truck to carry freight to that region—then get its preventive repairs. Furthermore, OTR spends several million dollars a year on diesel fuel. But, by carefully analysing

Bill Ward, cofounder of OTR Express, uses a sophisticated control system for each of the company's trucks. By looking at each rig and its driver as a cost centre, OTR is better able to track costs and identify profits from their operations.

past routes travelled and strategically placing several company-owned fuel depots around the country, OTR has reduced its fuel costs by as much as 15 cents per gallon. When you consider that his trucks drive more than 22 million miles each year, that 15 cents per gallon savings becomes significant.

Ward's careful attention to the data has paid off. OTR's net profit margin is one of the highest in the business, its average trip is more than double that of its competitors, and it enjoys more than a 40 per cent reduction in empty trucks on the road than most of its competitors. Through it all, this inexperienced trucker, with a computer, has witnessed more than a 400 per cent growth in sales over the past five years.

Technologically advanced systems such as this one at Dell Computer handle customer requests efficiently. Cassye Ewald (pictured) takes an order. By having production schedules at her disposal, Cassye is able to tell the customer that his specifically designed computer will be delivered within five working days.

In this chapter, we want to take a closer look at control tools and techniques. Specifically, we want to address four primary areas that require effective controls: information, operations, finances, and employee behaviour.

Today's organizations are information-processing "machines." With new technologies available to managers like Bill Ward, they need to understand how to best use this information and to ensure organizational activities are proceeding as planned. With the greater importance placed on efficiency, effectiveness, and productivity, managers must develop well-designed operating systems and tight controls to survive in the global village. In addition, managers need to monitor the financial side of the organization to ensure budgets and costs are kept in line. Finally, since achieving organizational objectives greatly depends on management's ability to effectively utilize people, it makes good sense to understand the control mechanisms available for monitoring their performance.

Information Control Systems

How does management control the rapid, ongoing information about all the major activities in the organization? And how are the techniques for controlling and using this information changing the way managers manage? In this section, we'll address these two issues.

What Is a Management Information System (MIS)?

management information system (MIS)
A system that provides management with needed information on a regular basis.

While there is no universally agreed-upon definition for a **management information system (MIS),** we'll define the term as a system used to provide management with needed information on a regular basis.[2] In theory, this system can be manual or computer based, although all current discussions, including ours, focuses on computer-supported applications.

The term "system" in MIS implies order, arrangement, and purpose. Further, an MIS focuses specifically on providing management with information, not merely data. These two points are important and require elaboration.

A library provides a good analogy. Although it can contain millions of volumes, a library doesn't do users much good if they can't find what they want quickly. That's

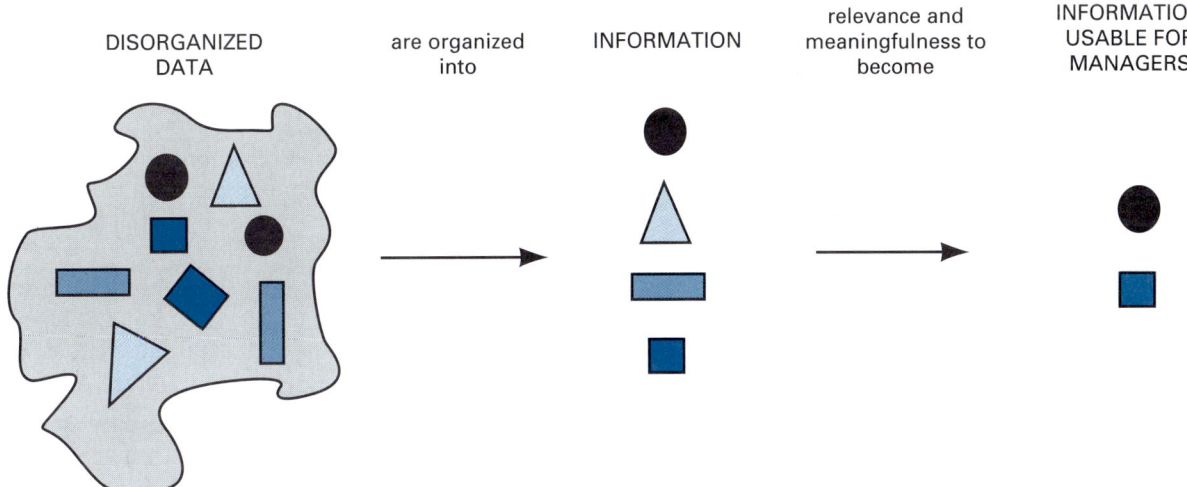

Exhibit 16-1 How MIS Makes Data Usable

why libraries spend a lot of time cataloguing their collections and ensuring that volumes are returned to their proper locations. Organizations today are like well-stocked libraries. There is no lack of data. There is, however, a lack of ability to process those data so that the right information is available to the right person when he or she needs it.[3] A library is almost useless if it has the book you want, but either you can't find it or the library takes a week to retrieve it from storage. An MIS, on the other hand, has organized data in some meaningful way and can access the information in a reasonable amount of time. **Data** are raw, unanalysed facts, such as numbers, names, or quantities. But as data, these facts are relatively useless to managers.[4] When data are analysed and processed, they become **information.** An MIS collects data and turns them into relevant information for managers to use. Exhibit 16-1 summarizes these observations.

data
Raw, unanalysed facts.

information
Analysed and processed data.

end-user
The person who uses information and assumes responsibility for its control.

Why Are End-Users Replacing Centralized Systems?

MIS has come a long way in the last four-plus decades. Most of this progress is a direct result of improvements in computing power. The trend has been toward smaller, faster, and cheaper technology. For example, in 1946, there was one computer in the United States. It weighed 30 tons and had 18,000 vacuum tubes and 70,000 resistors. The computing power that in 1966 took a roomful of equipment and cost $15 million is available today on a $10 microprocessor chip that's only a quarter of an inch square.[5] The results of technological advancements have fostered the decentralization of information control—meaning that managers are now becoming **end-users.**

When a manager becomes an end-user, he or she takes responsibility for information control (also see

Is this the picture of the war room at the Pentagon? No! It's EDS's command post, its MIS centre. This centre provides data support and computer information to the organization's worldwide operations.

Ethical Dilemmas in Management).[6] It is no longer delegated to some other department or staff assistant. As an end-user, managers have to become knowledgeable about their own needs and the systems that are available to meet those needs—and to accept responsibility for their systems' failures. Accordingly, if they don't have the information they want, there is no one to blame but themselves.

Managers have come to realize that they now have a better information base from which to make more timely decisions and improve managerial control. By developing their computer skills and judiciously selecting the right software, managers are able to get the exact information they want, literally in seconds.

A final outcome of today's MIS is the creation and implementation of mechanisms to link end-users. By means of an interactive **network,** a manager's computer can communicate with other computers.[7] That is, the user of a personal computer can communicate with other personal computers, turn the computer into a terminal and gain access to an organization's mainframe system, share the use of expensive printers, and tap into outside databases.

network
Linking computers so that they can communicate with each other.

How Can MIS Enhance Planning?

As we discussed in Chapter 3, managers seek to develop organizationwide strategies that will give them an advantage over their competition. We talked about gaining a competitive advantage through strategies such as being the cost leader in a given market or by carefully differentiating your product from that of the competition. In recent years, managers at a number of organizations have realized that information systems can be used as a tool to give their firms a competitive advantage.[8] Wal-Mart stores, for example, capitalized on information technology to become the world's largest retailer.[9] A satellite communications system allows it to track inventory and handle accounting and payments. It can also electronically place orders with suppliers. And 1,500 of its vendors can access Wal-Mart's point-of-sale terminals to track sales of their products and resupply a Wal-Mart store before merchandise runs out. Another 3,800 vendors get

If you got on an airplane with this computer, you would have to buy several tickets. Seriously, what once required the power of a mainframe system like this IBM ES/9000 can now be handled with a laptop personal computer. Employees can be more efficient, have better and continuous computer access wherever they go, and the person sitting in the seat behind them isn't crowded out!

Ethical Dilemmas in Management

▼ **WHAT'S WRONG WITH PIRATING SOFTWARE?** ▲

The court officers and lawyers walked into the Milan headquarters of Montedison, Italy's chemical giant. Employees at computer work stations were ordered to step away from their keyboards while the investigators punched in commands to test the programs. Their suspicions were confirmed. The employees were using pirated copies of Lotus 1-2-3, the popular spreadsheet program.

The duplicating of software programs has become a widespread practice. It's been estimated that in the United States about 40 per cent of all software used is pirated,[10] cheating software developers of approximately $1.5 billion. Go worldwide, and that number increases upward to $12 billion a year to software pirates. Yet almost all of these duplicated programs are protected by copyright law. Copying them is punishable by fines of up to $100,000 and five years in jail. How is it, then, that this lawbreaking has become such a common practice? Part of the answer is due to cultural differences. A lot of piracy occurs in places like Hong Kong and Singapore, where copyright laws don't apply and sharing rather than protecting creative work is the norm. In the United States, employees and managers who pirate software defend their behaviour by giving such answers as: "Everybody does it!" "I won't get caught!" "The law isn't enforced!" "No one really loses!" or "Our departmental budget isn't large enough to handle buying dozens of copies of the same program!"

Contrast software to other forms of intellectual property. Ask the same employees who copy software if it is similarly acceptable to steal a book from the library or a tape from a video store. Most are quick to condemn such practices. However, some think that there's nothing wrong with checking out a video, making a copy, and returning it—despite the copyright statement at the beginning of the tape that specifically states that the act of copying that tape is in violation of the law.

Is reproducing copyrighted software ever an acceptable practice? Is it wrong for employees of a corporation to do it but permissible for struggling college students? What do you think?

---

daily sales data directly from Wal-Mart stores. This system has been a major factor in making Wal-Mart the low-cost operator in its industry.

Once an information system has been put in place and management gains a leg up on its competition, the trick—as with any competitive advantage—is to sustain that advantage. Kmart, for instance, has recently invested in an information system that seeks to duplicate the one at Wal-Mart. Similarly, Federal Express was able to deliver packages faster and with more detailed tracking than could its competition for many years because it was the first to computerize the process completely. But as UPS, Canada Post, and other competitors introduced comparable systems, Federal Express's on-time delivery advantage based on its MIS all but disappeared. So while MIS can provide a competitive edge, that edge is not permanent. The system must be regularly modified and updated if it is to give an organization a sustainable advantage.

What Effect Does MIS Have on Decision Making?

We know that managers rely on information to make decisions. Because a sophisticated MIS significantly alters the quantity and quality of information (see Managers Who Made a Difference), as well as the speed with which it can be obtained, an effective MIS will improve management's decision-making capability.[11]

These UPS employees use a special package tracking system to offer their customers guarantees on delivery times.

The effect will be seen in establishing the need for a decision, in the development and evaluation of alternatives, and in the final selection of the best alternative. On-line, real-time systems allow managers to identify problems almost as they occur. Gone are the long delays between the appearance of a serious discrepancy and a manager's ability to find out about it. Easy access to large databases allows managers to look things up or get to the facts without either going to other people or digging through piles of paper. This reduces a manager's dependence on others for data and makes fact gathering far more efficient. Today's manager can identify alternatives quickly, evaluate those alternatives posing a series of what-if questions based on financial data, and finally select the best alternative on the basis of answers to those questions.

Managers Who Made a Difference

ROBERT CULLEN AT MOUNT SINAI HOSPITAL

A hospital like Mount Sinai in Toronto needs a constant flow of medical supplies. It buys about 600 different medical and surgical items from sixty vendors, which meant that sixty deliveries had to arrive at the hospital, many of them at the same time. That can amount to major traffic congestion at the delivery doors, making it impossible for a hospital in a downtown location like Mount Sinai to consider a traditional just-in-time inventory system with each of its suppliers. So it did what most Canadian hospitals do—it stocked all the myriad items needed in the daily running of a hospital and bore the cost of doing that as part of its annual budget.

Staffing a department to handle supplies—ordering them, paying for them, maintaining inventory control of them, tracking them, handling them, etc.—cost Mount Sinai about $5 million a year. Medical and surgical supplies account for about $6 million of the overall supplies budget. Under the old system of buying, inventorying, and transferring to various departrments, some items in the hospital could be handled as many as 20 times before being used on a patient. That is, until Robert Cullen, the hospital's director of materials management, had a better solution.

The solution was to find a single sourcing agent for medical and surgical supplies—Livingston Healthcare Services Inc., of Oakville, Ontario. What Livingston does is take orders, by user department or work station, pack them, and deliver them the same day directly to the part of the hospital where they are used. Of course, technology is needed to make the system work. First, all items are bar-coded. A clerk scans the inventory at each work station daily and feeds the information into a computer, which assembles the data and transmits an order to Livingston. Livingston then packs boxes of supplies for each work station and delivers them that night to the hospital, with each box labelled with its final destination.

The hospital's inventory is now much smaller, but controls in the system can indicate where materials are elsewhere in the hospital if one work station should somehow run out. And if there is a real pinch, Livingston can deliver in one hour. Materials costs are also controlled through a process whereby Mount Sinai puts its annual needs for each item out to tender, with the understanding that items are to be delivered to Livingston Healthcare. In 1993, Mount Sinai saved $200,000 with the program. The hospital has also freed up 5,000 square feet of space, which, at $150 a foot, means that the hospital could expand its facilities without paying $750,000 for the new space. With increasing pressure on the cost of health care, making a difference will focus more and more on solutions of this kind.[12] ▼

How Does MIS Affect an Organization's Structure?

When organizations introduce sophisticated, computer-based management information systems, they are changing the technology component of organizational structure (see Chapter 6). For instance, a computer-based MIS lessens the need to depend on direct supervision and staff reports as control mechanisms. A senior executive can monitor what's occurring on the shop floor or in the accounts payable department by simply pushing a few keys on his or her desk terminal. And such changes in technology have a very real effect on the organization's structure. For instance, traditional departmental boundaries are becoming less confining as networks cut across departments, divisions, geographic locations, and levels in the organization. But the most evident change is probably that MIS is making organizations flatter and more organic.[13]

Managers can now handle more employees. Why? Because computer control substitutes for personal supervision. As a result, there are wider spans of control and fewer levels in the organization. The need for staff support is also reduced with an MIS. By being an end-user, managers can obtain information directly. Thus, large staff support groups, which traditionally compiled, tabulated, and analysed data, become redundant.[14] Both forces—wider spans and reduced staff—lead to flatter organizations.

One of the more interesting phenomena created by sophisticated information systems is that they have allowed management to make organizations more organic without any loss in control.[15] Management can lessen formalization and become more decentralized—thus making their organizations more organic—without giving up control. How? MIS substitutes computer control for rules and decision discretion. Computer technology rapidly informs top managers of the consequences of any decision and allows them to take corrective action if the decision is not to their liking. Thus, there's the appearance of decentralization without any commensurate loss of control.

Does MIS Change Communication Patterns in Organizations?

Improvements in information technology—specifically, progress made in MIS that has enhanced our ability to gather, synthesize, organize, monitor, and disseminate information—are significantly changing the way communication takes place in organizations.[16] Traditional discussions of organizational communication focused on upward and downward communication. The primary flow of formal communication was vertical. The MIS, however, permits more lateral and diagonal communication on a formal basis.

Employees using internal networks can get their work done more efficiently by jumping levels in the organization and avoiding the obstacles involved in "going through channels." The direct accessing of data, rather than the traditional sequential passing of data up and down the hierarchy, also decreases the historical problem of distortion and filtering of information. The breaking down of sequential communication patterns allows managers to formally monitor information across the organization that previously was limited to informal channels like the grapevine.

What Effect Does MIS Have on Controlling?

Inherent in the control function is a manager's need to assess how the work is being performed and compare those data with the plan. MIS makes it possible to obtain more complete and accurate information in the measuring phase of controlling. Furthermore, the sophistication of the system may also permit managers to focus precisely on what they want to know. For example, suppose a manager at Hershey-Pasta wants to confirm that the long-noodle spaghetti production is on schedule to fill a major grocery chain order for San Georgio #9 that is to be shipped by 4:00 P.M. that day. By entering the MIS system and directing the inquiry to the computer controlling the long-noodle production run, she can obtain the specific information she needs. Accordingly, MIS assists managers in obtaining timely information about workers' quantity of output, quality level, and other performance data. And because the data are directly assessed, many of the potential distortions that may arise when information is obtained "through channels" are avoided.

But accurate, timely, and complete information is only half of the issue here. With controlling, when a significant variance is determined, managers must take some action. By obtaining the precise information one seeks, and having it faster, a manager can correct a problem sooner. Thus, MIS enables managers to be more efficient and more effective in the controlling function.

Operations Controls

In this section, we want to focus on the importance of efficiency and productivity in the operations' side of the organization. Effective control systems allow organizations to produce higher-quality products and services at prices that meet or beat those of their rivals.

transformation process
The process through which an organization produces goods or services.

What Is the Transformation Process?

All organizations produce goods or services—through a means called the **transformation process.** Exhibit 16-2 portrays, in a very simplified fashion, the

Control Tools and Techniques

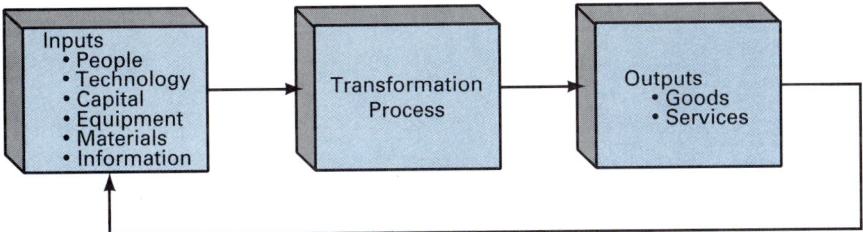

Exhibit 16-2 The Transformation Process

fact that every organization has an operations system that creates value by transforming inputs into outputs. The system takes inputs—people, capital, equipment, materials—and transforms them into desired finished goods and services.

The transformation process is readily applicable to the manufacturing process. But what about in a service organization—like a university? University administrators bring together instructors, books, journals, audio-visual materials, and similar resources to transform "unenlightened" students into educated and skilled individuals. Our conclusion: the transformation process is as relevant to service organizations as to those in manufacturing. The study and application of this transformation process to organizations is called **operations management**.

Because organizational survival may very well rest on how successful operations management is, managers need to develop control techniques to monitor their productive processes. We will focus our discussion on four primary operations subsystems: cost controls, inventories, maintenance, and quality controls.

How Can Managers Control Costs?

An automobile industry analyst has compared the U.S. and Japanese approaches to cost control: "The Japanese regard cost control as something you wake up every morning and do. Americans have always thought of it as a project. You cut costs 20 per cent and say: 'Whew! That's over.' We can't afford to think that way anymore."[17]

U.S. managers have often treated cost control as an occasional crusade that is initiated and controlled by the accounting staff. Accountants establish cost standards per unit, and if deviations occur, management looks for the cause. Have material prices increased? Is labour being used efficiently? Do employees need additional training? Cost control, nonetheless, needs to play a central part in the design of an operating system, and it needs to be a continuing concern of every manager.

Many organizations have adopted the **cost-centre approach** to controlling costs. Work areas, departments, or plants are identified as distinct cost centres, and their managers are held responsible for the cost performance of these units. Any unit's total costs are made up of two types of costs: direct and indirect. **Direct costs** are costs incurred in proportion to the output of a particular good or service. Labour and materials typically fall into this category. On the other hand, indirect costs are largely unaffected by changes in output. Insurance expenses and the salaries of staff personnel are examples of typical indirect costs. This direct-indirect distinction is important. While cost-centre managers are held responsible for all direct costs in their units, **indirect costs** are not necessarily within their control. However, because all costs are controllable at some level in the organization, top managers should identify where the control lies and hold lower managers accountable for costs under their control.[18]

operations management
The design, operation, and control of the transformation process that converts resources into finished goods and services.

cost-centre approach
Managers are held responsible for costs within their unit.

direct costs
Costs incurred in proportion to the output of a particular good or service.

indirect costs
Costs that are largely unaffected by changes in output.

Computer-aided design allows manufacturers to create and view a model in a fraction of the time it would have taken to prepare a preproduction sample for customer inspection. That translates into significant cost savings.

How Can Managers Minimize Purchasing Costs?

It has been said that human beings are what they eat. Metaphorically, the same applies to organizations. Their processes and outputs depend on the inputs they "eat." It's difficult to make quality products out of inferior inputs. Gas-station operators depend on a regular and dependable inflow of certain octane-rated gasolines from their suppliers in order to meet their customers' demands. If the gas isn't there, they can't sell it. If the gasoline is below the specified octane rating, customers may be dissatisfied and take their business elsewhere. Management must therefore monitor the delivery, performance, quality, quantity, and price of inputs from suppliers. Purchasing control seeks to ensure availability, acceptable quality, continued reliable sources, and, at the same time, reduced costs.

What can managers do to facilitate control of inputs? They need to gather information on the dates and conditions in which supplies arrive. They need to gather data about the quality of supplies and the compatibility of those supplies with operations processes. Finally, they need to obtain data on supplier price performance. Are the prices of the delivered goods the same as those quoted when the order was placed?

This information can be used to rate suppliers, identify problem suppliers, and guide management in choosing future suppliers. Trends can be detected. Suppliers can be evaluated, for instance, on responsiveness, service, reliability, and competitiveness.

Why Should an Organization Build Close Links with Suppliers? A rapidly growing trend in manufacturing is turning suppliers into partners.[19] Instead of using ten or twelve vendors and forcing them to compete against each other to gain the firm's business, manufacturers are using only two or three vendors and working closely with them to improve efficiency and quality.

Motorola, for instance, sends its design-and-manufacturing engineers to suppliers to help with any problems.[20] Other firms now routinely send inspection teams to rate suppliers' operations. They're assessing these suppliers' manufacturing and

Control Tools and Techniques

delivery techniques, statistical process controls that identify causes of defects, and ability to handle data electronically. Companies in Canada and around the world are doing what has long been a tradition in Japan—that is, they are developing long-term relationships with suppliers. As collaborators and partners, rather than adversaries, firms are finding that they can achieve better quality of inputs, fewer defects, and lower costs. Furthermore, when problems arise with suppliers, open communication channels facilitate quick resolutions.

What is the Economic Order Quantity Model? One of the best-known techniques for mathematically deriving the optimum quantity for a purchase order is the **economic order quantity model (EOQ)** (see Exhibit 16-3). The EOQ model seeks to balance four costs involved in ordering and carrying inventory: the purchase costs (purchase price plus delivery charges less discounts); the ordering costs (paperwork, follow-up, inspection when the item arrives, and other processing costs); carrying costs (money tied up in inventory, storage, insurance, taxes, and so forth); and stockout costs (profits foregone from orders lost, the cost of reestablishing goodwill, and additional expenses incurred to expedite late shipments). When these four costs are known, the model identifies the optimal order size for each purchase. Readers interested in the detailed mathematics of the EOQ model are encouraged to research the model in a current production/operations management textbook.

economic order quantity model (EOQ)
A technique for balancing purchase, ordering, carrying, and stockout costs to derive the optimum quantity for a purchase order.

What Are Inventory Ordering Systems? In many chequebooks, after you use up about 80 per cent of the cheques, you find a reorder form included among the few that remain; it reminds you that it's time to reorder. This is an example of a **fixed-point reordering system.** At some pre-established point in the operations process, the system is designed to "flag" the fact that the inventory needs to be replenished. The flag is triggered when the inventory reaches a certain point or the safety stock level (see Exhibit 16-4).

fixed-point reordering system
A system that "flags" the fact that inventory needs to be replenished when it reaches a certain level.

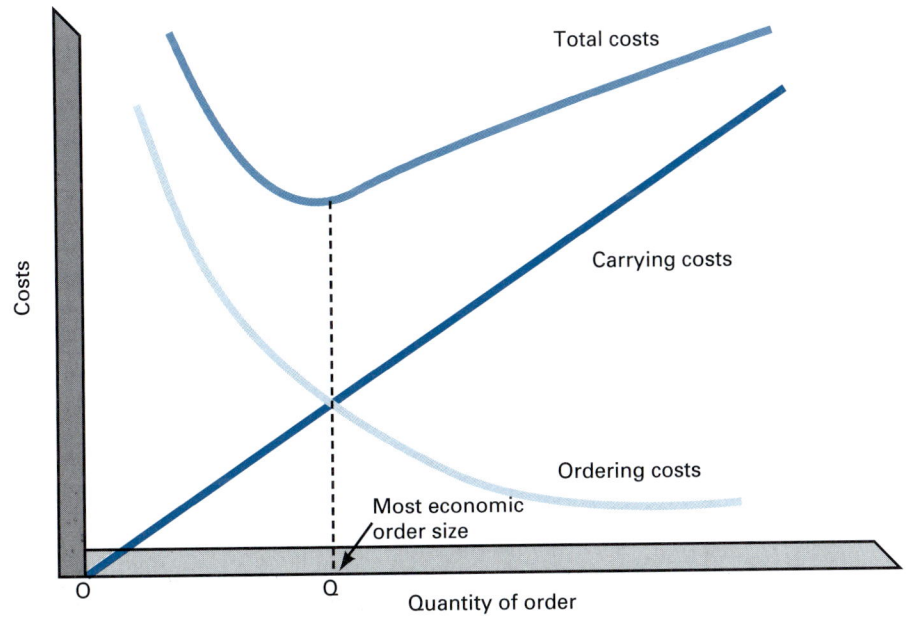

Exhibit 16-3 Determining the Most Economic Order Quantity

fixed-interval reordering system
A system that uses time as the determining factor for reviewing and reordering inventory items.

Another common inventory system is the **fixed-interval reordering system.** The fixed-interval system uses time as the determining factor for inventory control. At a predetermined time—say, once a week or every ninety days—the inventory is counted, and an order is placed for the number of items necessary to bring the inventory back to the desired level. The desired level is established so that if demand and ordering lead time are average, consumption will draw the inventory down to zero (or some safety lead time can be added) just as the next order arrives. This system may have some transportation economies and quantity discount economies over the fixed-point system. For example, it may allow us to consolidate orders from one supplier if we review all the items we purchase from this source at the same time. This is not possible in the fixed-point reordering system.

What Is a Just-In-Time Inventory Practice? It's arguably the fastest-growing control technique for minimizing inventory costs. It's called the **just-in-time inventory (JIT).** With JIT, inventory items arrive when they are needed in the production process instead of being stored in stock. The ultimate goal of JIT is to have only enough inventory on hand to complete the day's work—reducing a company's inventory, and its associated costs to zero.

just-in-time inventory (JIT)
A system in which inventory items arrive when they are needed in the production process instead of being stored in stock.

JIT attempts to eliminate raw material inventories by coordinating production and supply deliveries precisely. When the system works as designed, it results in a number of positive benefits for a manufacturer. These include reduced inventories, reduced setup time, better work flow, shorter manufacturing time, less space consumption, and even higher quality. Of course, suppliers who can be depended on to deliver quality materials on time must be found. Because there are no inventories, there is no slack in the system to absorb defective materials or delays in shipment.

What Is Maintenance Control?

Delivering goods or services in an efficient and effective manner requires operating systems with high equipment utilization and a minimum amount of downtime. Therefore,

Exhibit 16-4 Inventory Cycle with Safety Stock

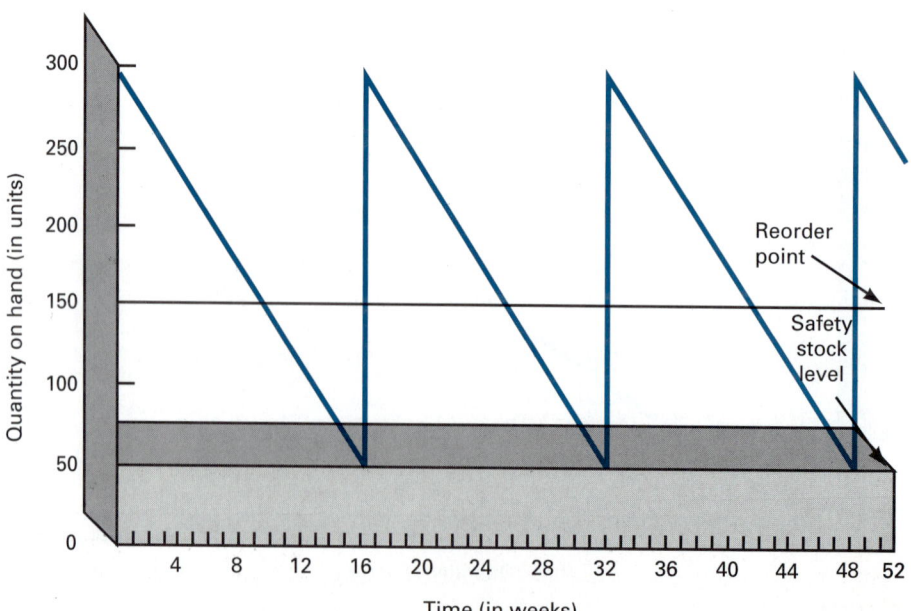

Control Tools and Techniques

managers need to be concerned with maintenance control. The importance of maintenance control, however, depends on the process technology used. For example, if a standardized assembly line process breaks down, it can affect hundreds of employees. On an automobile or dishwasher assembly line, it's not unusual for a serious breakdown on one machine to bring an entire plant to a halt. In contrast, most systems using more general-purpose and redundant processes have less interdependency between activities; therefore, a machine breakdown is likely to have less of an impact. Nevertheless, an equipment breakdown—like an inventory stockout—may mean higher costs, delayed deliveries, or lost sales.

There are three approaches to maintenance control.[21] **Preventive maintenance** is performed before a breakdown occurs. **Remedial maintenance** is a complete overhaul, replacement, or repair of the equipment when it breaks down. **Conditional maintenance** refers to overhaul or repair in response to an inspection and measurement of the equipment's state. When British Airways tears down its planes' engines every 1,000 hours, it is engaging in preventive maintenance. When it inspects the planes' tires every twenty-four hours and changes them when conditions warrant it, it is performing conditional maintenance. Finally, if British Airways' operations policy is to repair lavatory equipment on board its planes only after the equipment breaks down, then it is using remedial maintenance practices.

How often do you change the oil in your car? If you do it according to the manufacturer's recommended scheduled intervals, you are performing preventive maintenance to avoid major engine problems later on. As the Fram ad goes, "You can pay a little now, or pay a lot later."

The British Airways example points out that the type of maintenance control depends on the costs of a breakdown. The greater the cost in terms of money, time, liability, or increased loss of goodwill, the greater the benefits from preventive maintenance.

Maintenance control should also be considered in the design of equipment. If downtime is highly inconvenient or costly, reliability can be increased by designing redundancy into the equipment. Nuclear power plants, for example, have elaborate backup systems built in. Similarly, equipment can be designed to facilitate fast or low-cost maintenance. Equipment that has fewer parts has fewer things to go wrong. High-failure items can also be placed in locations that are easily accessible or in independent modular units that can be quickly removed and replaced. Cable-television operators follow these guidelines. Breakdowns infuriate customers, so when they occur, management wants to be able to correct them quickly. Speed is facilitated by centralizing equipment in easy-access locations and making extensive use of modular units. If a piece of equipment fails, the whole module of which it is a part can be pulled or replaced in just a few minutes. Television service is resumed rapidly, and the pulled modular unit can be taken to the shop and repaired without time pressures.

preventive maintenance
Maintenance performed before a breakdown occurs.

remedial maintenance
Maintenance that calls for the overhaul, replacement, or repair of equipment when it breaks down.

conditional maintenance
Maintenance that calls for an overhaul or repair in response to an inspection.

Are TQM and Quality Control the Same Thing?

We've discussed total quality management throughout this book, describing it as a comprehensive, customer-focused program to continuously improve the quality of the organization's processes, products, and services. While TQM emphasizes actions to prevent mistakes, **quality control** emphasizes identifying mistakes that may have already occurred.

quality control
Ensuring that what is produced meets some pre-established standard.

These Daewoo Company employees perform several inspections of railroad cars at their Korea plant to ensure that no defects exist. This is all part of the company's quality control program.

acceptance sampling
A quality control procedure in which a sample is taken and a decision to accept or reject a whole lot is based on a calculation of sample risk error.

process control
A quality control procedure in which sampling is done during the transformation process to determine whether the process itself is under control.

attribute sampling
A quality control technique that classifies items as acceptable or unacceptable on the basis of a comparison to a standard.

variable sampling
A quality control technique in which a measurement is taken to determine how much an item varies from the standard.

So what do we mean by quality control? It refers to monitoring quality—weight, strength, consistency, colour, taste, reliability, finish, or any one of a myriad of characteristics—to ensure that it meets some pre-established standard. Quality control will probably be needed at one or more points beginning with the receipt of inputs. It will continue with work in process and all steps up to the final product. Assessments at intermediate stages of the transformation process typically are part of quality control. Early detection of a defective part or process can save the cost of further work on the item.

In imposing quality control, managers should begin by asking whether they expect to examine 100 per cent of the items or whether a sample can be used. The inspection of each item makes sense if the cost of continuous evaluation is very low or if the consequences of a statistical error are very high (as in the manufacture of a drug used in open-heart surgery). Statistical samples are usually less costly, and sometimes they are the only viable option. For example, if the quality test destroys the product—as happens with bombs or flashbulbs—then sampling has to be utilized. There are two categories of statistical quality control procedures: acceptance sampling and process control. **Acceptance sampling** refers to the evaluation of purchased or manufactured materials or products that already exist. A sample is taken; then the decision to accept or reject the whole lot is based on a calculation of sample risk error. **Process control** refers to sampling items during the transformation process to see whether the transformation process itself is under control.

A final consideration in quality control relates to whether the test is done by examining attributes or variables. The inspection and classification of items as acceptable or unacceptable is called **attribute sampling.** An inspector compares the items against some standard and rates their quality as acceptable or not acceptable. In contrast, **variable sampling** involves taking a measurement to determine how much an item varies from the standard. It involves a range rather than a dichotomy. Management typically identifies the standard and an acceptable deviation. Any sample that measures within the range is accepted, and those outside are rejected.

Before we leave the issue of quality control, there is an important issue before us. That is, who's really responsible for increasing the quality of our goods and services produced? We know that quality is a function of both operations and people variables. Of course, management needs to focus on both.

A lot of our discussion above has focused on the "operations" side. Management must ensure that it has a productive transformation process. From the people side, techniques we have discussed in previous chapters should be considered. Empowerment, management by objectives, team-based work groups, and equitable pay systems are examples of people-oriented approaches toward quality enhancement. But much of the

Control Tools and Techniques

> 1. Plan for the long-term future, not for next month or next year.
> 2. Never be complacent concerning the quality of your product.
> 3. Establish statistical control over your production processes and require your suppliers to do so as well.
> 4. Deal with the fewest number of suppliers—the best ones, of course.
> 5. Find out whether your problems are confined to particular parts of the production process or stem from the overall process itself.
> 6. Train workers for the job that you are asking them to perform.
> 7. Raise the quality of your line supervisors.
> 8. Drive out fear.
> 9. Encourage departments to work closely together rather than to concentrate on departmental or divisional distinctions.
> 10. Do not be sucked into adopting strictly numerical goals, including the widely popular formula of "zero defect."
> 11. Require your workers to do quality work, not just to be at their stations from 9 to 5.
> 12. Train your employees to understand statistical methods.
> 13. Train your employees in new skills as the need arises.
> 14. Make top managers responsible for implementing these principles.

Exhibit 16-5 Deming's Fourteen Points for Improving Quality
Source: W. Edwards Deming, "Improvement of Quality and Productivity Through Action by Management," *National Productivity Review,* Winter 1981–82, pp. 12–22. With permission. Copyright 1981 by Executive Enterprises, Inc., 22 West 21st St., New York, N.Y. 10010-6904. All rights reserved.

people side of the equation focuses on operative employees—those actually performing the work. The late management consultant and quality expert W. Edwards Deming, however, shifted that primary responsibility to managers. Exhibit 16-5 outlines Deming's fourteen points for improving quality.

A closer look at Exhibit 16-5 reveals Deming's understanding of the interplay between people and operations. High quality cannot come solely from good "people management." Rather, the truly effective organization will maximize quality and ultimately productivity by successfully integrating people into the overall operations system. This can explain, for instance, why in one recent year U.S. companies spent $17 billion on computers and new process-control equipment.[22] Increased capital investment will make facilities more modern and efficient.

Financial Controls

In Chapter 4, we introduced budgets as both a planning and control device. Now, we turn to financial analyses, which serve as feedback controls. We know that investors and stock analysts regularly use an organization's financial documents to assess its worth. These same documents can be analysed by managers as internal controls, which include ratio analyses, audits, cost-benefit analysis, and activity-based accounting.

What Are the More Popular Ratio Analyses?

Managers often want to examine their organization's balance and income statements to analyse key ratios; that is, comparing two significant figures from the financial statements and expressing them as a percentage or ratio. This practice allows managers to compare current financial performance with that of previous periods and against other organizations in the same industry. Some of the more useful ratios evaluate liquidity, leverage, operations, and profitability.

What Are Liquidity Ratios? Liquidity is a measure of the organization's ability to convert assets into cash in order that debts can be met. The most popular liquidity ratios are the current ratio and the acid test ratio.

The **current ratio** is defined as the organization's current assets divided by its current liabilities. Although there is no magic number that is considered safe, the accountant's rule of thumb for the current ratio is 2:1. A significantly higher ratio usually suggests that management is not getting the best return on its assets. A ratio at or below 1:1 indicates potential difficulty in meeting short-term obligations (accounts payable, interest payments, salaries, taxes, and so forth).

The **acid test ratio** is the same as the current ratio except that current assets are reduced by the dollar value of inventory held. When inventories turn slowly, or are difficult to sell, the acid test ratio may more accurately represent the organization's true liquidity. That is, a high current ratio that is heavily based on an inventory that is difficult to sell overstates the organization's true liquidity. Accordingly, accountants typically consider an acid test ratio of 1:1 to be reasonable.

What Are Leverage Ratios? Leverage refers to the use of borrowed funds to operate and expand an organization. The advantage of leverage occurs when funds can be used to earn a rate of return well above the cost of those funds. For instance, if management can borrow money at 7 per cent and can earn 12 per cent on it internally, it makes good sense to borrow. But there are risks to overleveraging. The interest on the debt can be a drain on the organization's cash resources and can, at the extreme, drive an organization into bankruptcy. The objective, therefore, is to use debt wisely. Leverage ratios such as **debt-to-assets ratio** (computed by dividing total debt by total assets) or the **times-interest-earned ratio** (computed as profits before taxes divided by total interest charges) can help managers control debt levels.

What Are Operating Ratios? Operating ratios describe how efficiently management is using the organization's resources. Probably the most popular operating ratios are inventory turnover and total assets turnover.

The **inventory turnover ratio** is defined as revenue divided by inventory. The higher the ratio, the more efficiently inventory assets are being used. Revenue divided by total assets represents an organization's **total assets turnover ratio.** It measures how much assets are needed to generate the organization's revenue. The fewer assets used to achieve a given level of revenue, the more efficiently management is using the organization's total assets.

What Are Profitability Ratios? Profit-making organizations want to measure their effectiveness and efficiency. Profitability ratios serve such a purpose. The better known of these are profit-margin-on-revenues and return-on-investment ratios.

Managers of organizations that have a variety of products want to put their efforts into those products that are most profitable. The **profit-margin-on-revenues ratio,**

---

current ratio
An organization's current assets divided by its current liabilities.

acid test ratio
An organization's current assets, minus inventories, divided by its current liabilities.

leverage
Refers to the use of borrowed funds to operate and expand an organization.

debt-to-assets ratio
Total debt divided by total assets.

times-interest-earned ratio
Profits before taxes divided by total interest charges.

inventory turnover ratio
Revenue divided by total inventory.

total assets turnover ratio
Revenue divided by total assets.

profit-margin-on-revenues ratio
Net profit after taxes divided by total revenues.

Control Tools and Techniques

This internal staff auditor is reviewing company financial statements for accuracy. As an internal auditor, he will also review operations to ensure they, too, are functioning according to plans.

computed as net profit after taxes divided by total revenues, is a measure of profits per dollar revenues.

One of the most widely used measures of a business firm's profitability is the **return-on-investment ratio.** It's calculated by multiplying [revenues/investments] times [profit/revenues]. This percentage recognizes that absolute profits must be placed in the context of assets required to generate those profits.

return-on-investment ratio
[Revenues/investments] times [profit/revenues].

What Are Audits? An **audit** is a formal verification of an organization's accounts, records, operating activities, or performance. It is essentially designed to check an organization's control mechanisms. Audits can generally be characterized as either external or internal.

audit
Formal verification of an organization's financial statements.

What's the Difference Between External and Internal Audits? An **external audit** is a verification of an organization's financial statements by an outside and independent accounting firm. The organization creates its own financial statements using its own accountants. The external auditor's job then is to review the various accounts on the financial statements with respect to their accuracy and conformity with generally accepted accounting practices.

The **internal audit,** as its name implies, is done by an organization's own financial or accounting staff. It encompasses verifying the financial statements, just as the external audit, but additionally includes an evaluation of the organization's operations, procedures, and policies, plus any recommendations for improvement.

external audit
Formal verification of an organization's financial statements by an outside and independent source.

internal audit
Evaluation of an organization's financial statements, processes, operations, procedures, and policies by internal financial staff members.

How Can Internal Audits Be Useful as a Managerial Control Tool? Internal audits go beyond verifying financial statements. They seek to uncover inefficiencies in the organization's processes and suggest actions for their corrections. Specifically, managers can use internal audits to identify problems and ensure organizational activities are progressing as planned. For example, in our discussion of PERT networks in Chapter 4, we discussed the need to place controls on critical activities. Internal audits, in a like fashion, key into similar activities, to ensure the processes are operating as needed. These preventive measures, then, can be implemented before a major "breakdown" is experienced.

What Role Does Cost-Benefit Analysis Play in Control?

Some organizational activities do not lend themselves to objective financial evaluation techniques. Rather, they compare costs against objectives and use the result to

cost-benefit analysis
Evaluating an activity where costs are known, but where the standard against which these costs must be compared is ambiguous or difficult to measure.

prioritize and evaluate activities. When managers perform this activity, we say they are conducting a **cost-benefit analysis.** Cost-benefit analysis is useful when the amount of costs is known, but the standard against which these costs must be compared is ambiguous or difficult to measure. This is particularly the case, for example, when evaluating the effectiveness of such programs as defence projects, welfare programs, or educational systems. Cost-benefit expresses all the relevant benefits that accrue from an activity in the common denominator of money, so that they can be added together and their costs subtracted. This helps managers to determine if funds spent by their organizations on a number of activities are achieving benefits in excess of the amount spent.

Cost-benefit analysis is probably more applicable and effective as an informal measuring concept than as a formal control technique. The reason for this is that it is difficult to objectively quantify subjective qualitative factors. Thus, cost-benefit gives no final answer as to whether a program or activity is "justified" or "good," or whether it should be expanded or contracted. Rather, it merely suggests how well an activity is operating when viewed in a specific manner.

What Is Activity-Based Accounting?

activity-based accounting (ABC)
An accounting procedure whereby costs are allocated based on activities performed and resources used.

Activity-based accounting (ABC) is an accounting procedure whereby costs for producing a good or service are allocated based on the "activities performed and resources employed."[23] That is, the purpose of ABC is to reflect production costs more accurately. It is gaining an increasingly wide following in all types of business and not-for-profit organizations.

For instance, consider the operating room costs at a regional hospital associated with two medical procedures—tonsillectomy and heart bypass surgeries. Indeed, the latter operation is the more serious one. But what should the heart bypass operating room cost be in relation to that of the tonsillectomy? If hospital records show that a tonsillectomy is a one-hour operation, and the heart bypass a two-hour procedure, should the operating room charge be twice as much for the heart operation? Probably not. Why? Because the heart bypass requires that much more medical equipment be used. For example, a heart and lung machine, which keeps the patient breathing and blood circulating during the bypass surgery, is not used in tonsillectomies. There will also be extra costs associated with more medical apparatus and supplies. Accordingly, a simple "two-times" pricing mechanism may not reflect the true costs.

The concept of ABC is relatively simple. Allocate costs based solely on usage! Instead of spreading costs evenly or on a percentage basis to jobs as more traditional accounting methods utilize, ABC focuses on the specific costs incurred in the production of a good or service and charges them directly to the task. Thus, the tonsillectomy patient won't be charged a flat rate that overstates the costs of the operation. In this manner, organizations, like hospitals, are better able to set accurate prices, which ultimately could lead to the development of a competitive advantage.

Behavioural Controls

Managers accomplish things by working through other people. They need and depend on employees to achieve their unit goals. It's important, therefore, for managers to get their employees to behave in ways that management considers desirable. But how do managers ensure that employees are performing as they are supposed to? In organizations,

Control Tools and Techniques

the formal means of assessing the work of employees is through a systematic performance appraisal process.

What Is a Performance Appraisal?

Performance appraisal is a process of evaluating individuals' work performance in order to arrive at objective human resource decisions. Organizations use performance appraisals to make a number of employee decisions like pay increases, training needs, as well as providing documentation to support termination decisions. Consequently, they serve as control mechanisms.

Undoubtedly, performance appraisals are important. But how do you evaluate an employee's performance? That is, what are the specific techniques for appraisal? We have listed them in Exhibit 16-6.[24]

The **written essay** requires no complex forms or extensive training to complete. However, a "good" or "bad" appraisal may be determined as much by the evaluator's writing skill as by the employee's actual level of performance. The use of **critical incidents** focuses the evaluator's attention on those critical or key behaviours that separate effective from ineffective job performance. The appraiser writes down little anecdotes that describe what the employee did that was especially effective or ineffective. The key here is that only specific behaviours are cited, not vaguely defined personality traits. One of the oldest and most popular methods of appraisal is **graphic rating scales.** This method lists a set of performance factors such as quantity and quality of work, job knowledge, cooperation, loyalty, attendance, honesty, and initiative. The evaluator then goes down the list and rates each on an incremental scale. Finally, an approach that has received a great deal of attention in recent years involves **behaviourally anchored rating scales (BARS).**[25] These scales combine major elements from the critical incident and graphic rating scale approaches: the appraiser rates an employee according to items along a numerical scale, but the items are examples of actual behaviour on a given job rather than general descriptions or traits.

Should We Compare People to One Another Instead of Against Some Set Standards? The methods identified above have one thing in common. They require us to evaluate employees based on how well their performance matches established

performance appraisal
The evaluation of an individual's work performance in order to arrive at objective personnel decisions.

written essay
A performance appraisal technique in which an evaluator writes out a description of an employee's strengths, weaknesses, past performance, and potential and then makes suggestions for improvement.

critical incidents
A performance appraisal technique in which an evaluator lists key behaviours that separate effective from ineffective job performance.

graphic rating scales
A performance appraisal technique in which an evaluator rates a set of performance factors on an incremental scale.

behaviourally anchored rating scales (BARS)
A performance appraisal technique in which an evaluator rates employees on specific job behaviours derived from performance dimensions.

METHOD	ADVANTAGE	DISADVANTAGE
Written Essay	Simple to use	Evaluation of writer's ability as opposed to actual performance
Critical Incidents	Rich examples behaviourally based	Time consuming; lack quantification
Graphic Rating Scales	Provide quantitative data; less time-consuming	Do not provide depth of job behaviour assessed
BARS	Focus on specific and measurable job behaviours	Time-consuming; difficulty in developing measures
Multiperson	Compares employees to one another	Unwieldy with large number of employees
MBO	Focuses on end goals; results-oriented	Time-consuming

Exhibit 16-6 Performance Appraisal Methods Advantages and Disadvantages

This manager is writing an appraisal essay for one of her employees. Such a method allows the manager to describe in detail an employee's strengths, weaknesses, past performance, and areas for improvement.

multiperson comparison
A performance appraisal technique in which individuals are compared to one another.

group order ranking
A performance appraisal approach that groups employees into ordered classifications.

individual ranking
A performance appraisal approach that ranks employees in order from highest to lowest.

paired comparison
A performance appraisal approach in which each employee is compared to every other employee and rated as either the superior or weaker member of the pair.

or absolute criteria. **Multiperson comparisons,** on the other hand, compare one person's performance to that of one or more individuals. Thus, it is a relative, not an absolute, measuring device. The three most popular uses of this method are group order ranking, individual ranking, and paired comparison.

The **group order ranking** requires the evaluator to place employees into a particular classification such as "top one-fifth" or "second one-fifth." When this method is used to appraise employees, managers rank all their employees. If a rater has twenty employees, only four can be in the top fifth, and, of course, four must be relegated to the bottom fifth. The **individual ranking** approach requires the evaluator merely to list the employees in order from highest to lowest. Only one can be "best." In an appraisal of thirty employees, the difference between the first and second employee is assumed to be the same as that between the twenty-first and twenty-second. Even though some employees may be closely grouped, there can be no ties. In the **paired comparison** approach, each employee is compared to every other employee in the comparison group and rated as either the superior or weaker member of the pair. After all paired comparisons are made, each employee is assigned a summary ranking based on the number of superior scores he or she achieved. While this approach ensures that each employee is compared against every other, it can become unwieldy when large numbers of employees are being assessed.

Isn't MBO an Appraisal Approach, too? We previously introduced management by objectives during our discussion of planning in Chapter 3. MBO, however, is also a mechanism for appraising performance. In fact, it is the preferred method for assessing managers and professional employees.[26]

With MBO, employees are evaluated by how well they accomplish a specific set of objectives that have been determined to be critical in the successful completion of their jobs. As you'll remember from our discussion in Chapter 3, these objectives need to be tangible, verifiable, and measurable.

MBO's popularity among managerial personnel is probably due to its focus on end goals. Managers tend to emphasize such results-oriented outcomes as profit, sales, and costs. This emphasis aligns with MBO's concern with quantitative measures of performance. Because MBO emphasizes ends rather than means, this appraisal method allows managers the discretion to choose the best path for achieving their goals.

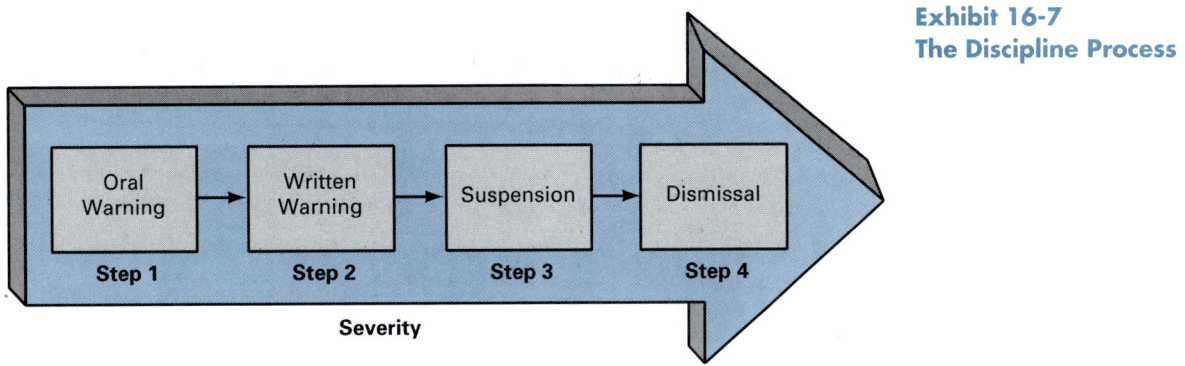

Exhibit 16-7
The Discipline Process

What Is Discipline?

So far our discussion on behavioural controls has focused on the performance appraisal process. And while that is the dominant form of behavioural control, we need to ask ourselves an important question: if we find that an employee cannot perform in a satisfactory manner (even with our coaching) or, worse, violates organizational rules or policies, what can a manager do? In such cases, the manager may have no other recourse than to take the employee through the disciplinary process.

What specifically do we mean when we use the term **discipline**? It refers to actions taken by a manager to enforce the organization's standards and regulations. It generally follows a typical sequence of four steps: oral warning, written warning, suspension, and dismissal (see Exhibit 16-7). This progressive order, however, may be circumvented if the behaviour variance is extremely severe. For example, stealing or attacking another employee with intent to inflict serious harm may result in an immediate suspension or dismissal. Regardless of any action taken, discipline should be fair and consistent. The punishment should fit the "crime," similar violations should be treated in a like manner, and discipline should follow the "hot-stove" rule.

The **"hot stove" rule** is a frequently cited set of principles that can guide you in effectively disciplining an employee.[27] The name comes from the similarities between touching a hot stove and administering discipline. Both are painful, but the analogy goes further. When you touch a hot stove, you get an immediate response. The burn you receive is instantaneous, leaving no doubt in your mind about the relation between cause and effect. You have ample warning. You know what happens if you touch a hot stove. Furthermore, the result is consistent. Every time you touch a hot stove, you get the same result—you get burned. Finally, the result is impersonal. Regardless of who you are, if you touch a hot stove, you will be burned (see Developing Management Skills).

discipline
Actions taken by a manager to enforce the organization's standards and regulations.

"hot stove" rule
Discipline should immediately follow an infraction, provide ample warning, be consistent, and impersonal.

Are There Substitutes for Direct Behavioural Control?

The likelihood that an employee's performance will prove unsatisfactory and require direct managerial control is moderated by several factors. Exhibit 16-8 illustrates that an effective selection process, acceptance of the organization's culture, a high degree of formalization, and employee training will all reduce the probability that an employee's actual performance will deviate from the performance standard. These subtle, but powerful, indirect control mechanisms substitute for the more overt forms of direct control.[28]

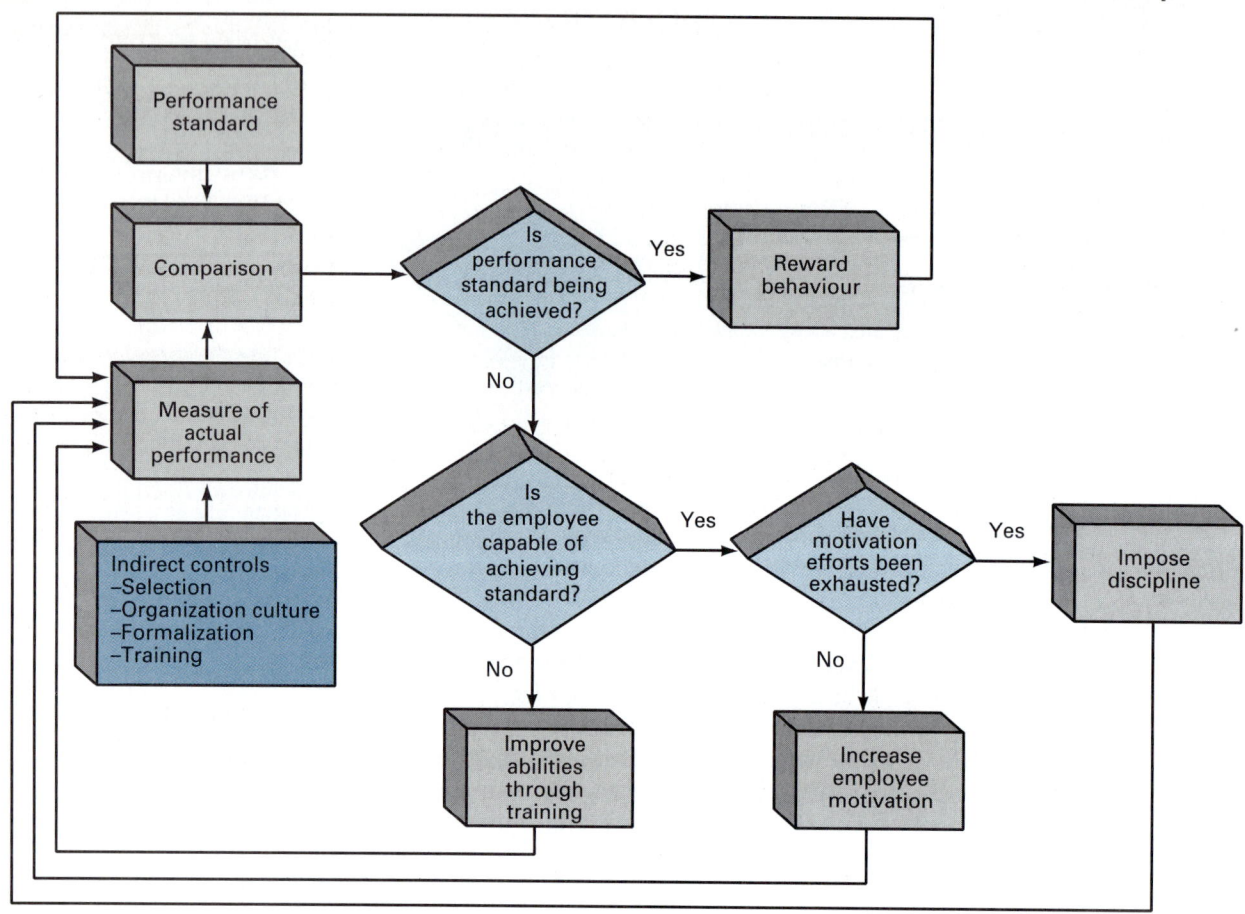

Exhibit 16-8 The Behavioural Control Process

How Can the Selection Process Substitute for Behavioural Control? As we discussed in Chapter 8, managers do not choose employees at random. Rather, job applicants are processed through a series of selection devices to differentiate those who are likely to be successful performers from those who won't. Accordingly, an effective selection process should be designed to determine if job candidates "fit" into the organization. Fit, here, implies not only the ability to do the job but also the personality, work habits, and attitudes that the organization desires. Consequently, selection should be recognized as one of the most widely used techniques by which management can control employee behaviour. That is, the selection process should screen out those who think and act in ways that management considers undesirable or inappropriate for successful performance.

In What Ways Does an Organization's Culture Substitute for Behavioural Control? The more that employees accept the values and norms of the organization's culture, the greater the likelihood that their behaviour will conform to that which management desires. Organizational culture, to the degree to which it is accepted by

Developing Management Skills

DISCIPLINING EMPLOYEES

1. **Before you accuse anyone, do your homework.** If you didn't personally see the infraction, investigate to determine what happened. Document date, time, place, individual involved, mitigating circumstances, and the like.

2. **Ensure ample warning was provided.** Before any formal action is taken, be sure you've provided the employee with reasonable previous warnings and that those warnings have been documented.

3. **Act in a timely fashion.** When you become aware of an infraction, and it has been supported by your investigation, do something, and do it quickly.

4. **Conduct the discipline session in private.** Praise employees in public, but keep punishment private. Public reprimands embarrass and humiliate the employee and may not lead to the behaviour change you desire.

5. **Adopt a calm and serious tone.** Administering discipline should not be facilitated in a loose, informal, and relaxed manner. Avoid anger or other emotional responses, and convey your comments in a calm and serious tone.

6. **Be specific about the problem.** Define the violation in exact terms instead of citing ambiguous regulations. Explain why the behaviour cannot continue by showing how it affects the employee's job performance, the unit's effectiveness, and the employee's colleagues.

7. **Keep it impersonal.** Focus on the employee's behaviour, not the employee. The discussion should be on objective information, not some subjective or evaluative statement.

8. **Get the employee's side of the story.** Due process demands that you give the employee the opportunity to explain his or her position regarding what happened. If significant deviations occur, you may need to do more investigating. Active listening is critical here to ensure you have all the relevant facts.

9. **Keep control of the discussion.** Disciplining an employee, by definition, is an authority-based act. You are enforcing the organization's standards and regulations. Yes, ask the employee for his or her side of the story and get the facts. But don't let the employee interrupt you or divert you from your objective.

10. **Agree on how mistakes can be prevented next time.** Discipline should include guidance and direction for correcting the problem. Have the employee draft a step-by-step plan to change the problem behaviour. Then set a timetable, with follow-up meetings in which progress can be evaluated.

employees, acts to constrain and control their behaviour. Since employees who don't accept the organization's culture are not likely to stay employed long, culture is a relevant influence on all continuing employees.

To What Extent Does Formalization Substitute for Behavioural Control?
Management provides most employees with a job description to clarify what their job encompasses, who they are responsible to, and what is and is not within their authority. This document formalizes behaviour and, of course, also controls behaviour. Since employees modify their behaviour to align with their job description, the job description acts as a control device. Furthermore, since management defines each individual's job description, management controls employee behaviour through it.

The job description, however, is not the only dimension of formalization that acts as a constraint on employee behaviour. Rules, procedures, and policies are other formalized controls.

How Can Employee Orientation and Training Substitute for Behavioural Control? When management provides employees with training, its intention is to instil in them preferred work behaviours and attitudes. This may be most obvious during a new employee's orientation.

New employees are often required to undergo a brief orientation program to familiarize them with the organization's objectives, history, philosophy, and rules. In many cases, this is followed by specific job training. The stated efforts of these orientation and training efforts are typically to help the new employee adjust to his or her new job. Another way of looking at this, however, is that orientation and training help to mould and eventually control the employee's behaviour.

Summary

This Summary is organized by the chapter opening learning objectives found on page 366.

1. The purpose of an MIS is to provide managers with accurate and current information for decision making and control.
2. Data are raw, unanalysed facts. Information is data that have been organized into a usable form.
3. An MIS significantly alters the speed, quantity, and quality of information from which managers will make a decision. With an MIS, managers can identify problems more quickly, gather appropriate facts more efficiently, test alternatives through what-if questions, and select the best alternative-based answers to those questions.
4. An MIS makes it possible to obtain more complete and accurate information in the measuring phase of controlling. It also permits managers to focus precisely on what they want to know.
5. Operations management takes inputs, including people and materials, and then acts on them by transforming them into finished goods and services. This applies in service organizations as well as in manufacturing firms.
6. A cost centre is a unit in which managers are held responsible for all associated costs. These costs incurred are direct (costs incurred in proportion to the output of a particular good or service) or indirect (costs that are largely unaffected by changes in output). In a cost centre, managers are generally held responsible for all direct costs, but not the indirect costs that are not within their control.
7. The three types of maintenance control are preventive, remedial, and conditional. Preventive maintenance is performed before a breakdown occurs. Remedial maintenance is performed when the equipment breaks down. Conditional maintenance is a response to an inspection.
8. Total quality management emphasizes actions that an organization can take to prevent mistakes from happening. Quality control emphasizes identifying mistakes that may have already occurred in the production of goods and services.
9. An external audit is a verification of an organization's financial statements by an outside and independent accounting firm. An internal audit is performed by an organization's own financial staff. It also verifies financial data but additionally includes an evaluation of the organization's operations, procedures, and policies.
10. A cost-benefit analysis is a tool for evaluating the benefits from activities whose benefits are ambiguous or subjective. It expresses all relevant benefits of an activity in the common term of money so they can be added together and their costs subtracted.
11. Six performance appraisal methods are (a) written essays—written descriptions of an employee's strengths, weaknesses, past performance, potential, and areas in need of improvement; (b) critical incidents—lists of key behaviours that separate effective from ineffective job performances; (c) graphic rating scales—ratings of performance factors on an incremental scale; (d) BARS—rating employees on performance factors derived from performance dimensions of the job; (e) multiperson comparisons—comparing individual employees against one

Control Tools and Techniques

another; and (f) objectives—evaluating employees against tangible, verifiable, and measurable objectives.

12. The "hot-stove" rule of disciplining proposes that effective discipline should be equivalent to touching a hot stove. The response should be immediate, there should be ample warning, and enforcement of rules should be consistent and impersonal.

Review and Discussion Questions

1. How can an MIS assist a manager in the control function?
2. In what ways is information a unique resource for organizations? Give examples.
3. How can an MIS create a flatter organization while simultaneously giving managers more control over the organization's operations?
4. Does the use of MIS empower all employees, all managers, or only a select few individuals in the organization? Discuss.
5. What is the transformation process?
6. Contrast acceptance sampling and process control.
7. Which is more critical for success in organizations—total quality management or quality control? Support your position.
8. What are the more popular financial ratios and how are they calculated?
9. "Cost-benefit analysis is better than no analysis at all. If the data are subjective and do lend themselves to objective analyses, cost-benefit provides at least a 'good enough' response." Do you agree or disagree with the statement? Explain.
10. What qualities would characterize an effective disciplinary process?

Self-Assessment Exercise

Testing Your Understanding of Computers

The following questionnaire has been developed to determine your computer understanding. For each definition in Column A (three questions to a segment), choose the term from Column B (five possible choices) that appropriately matches.

Column A Definitions	Column B Terms
___ 1. Has four functional parts: input, processing, storage (programs and data), and output. ___ 2. Performs the mathematic operations and any comparisons required. ___ 3. Physical parts of a computer.	A. Arithmetic/logical unit B. Computer system C. CPU D. Firmware E. Hardware
___ 4. Standard method of representing a character with a number inside the computer. ___ 5. The base 2 numbering system that uses digits 0 and 1. ___ 6. Number system that uses the ten digits 0 through 9 and the six letters A through F to represent values in base 16.	A. Alphanumeric B. ASCII C. Binary D. Hexadecimal E. Numeric data
___ 7. Technique for opening folders with a mouse. ___ 8. Technique for moving an icon with a mouse. ___ 9. Pointer similar to arrows.	A. Double-clicking B. Dragging C. Highlighting D. I-beam E. Scroll bar

_____ 10. A read-only memory whose contents are alterable by electrical means.
_____ 11. Internal memory that is erased when the computer's power is shut off.
_____ 12. Time it takes to find data stored externally.

A. Access
B. Clockrate
C. Memory
D. PROM
E. RAM

_____ 13. Number of characters printed per horizontal inch of space.
_____ 14. Set of characters in one typeface, style, and size.
_____ 15. Narrows the spacing between letters.

A. Font
B. Kerning
C. Leading
D. Pitch
E. Points

_____ 16. Operator that describes the quality that connects two data or expressions such as greater than, less than, or equal to.
_____ 17. Messages the user sends to the computer that make it perform specific operations.
_____ 18. The ability to run more than one program at one time without interrupting the execution of another program.

A. Commands
B. Distributed
C. Execute
D. Multitasking
E. Relational operator

_____ 19. Place to enlarge or shrink a window.
_____ 20. Place documents are saved.
_____ 21. Place you are typing.

A. Active window
B. Dialog box
C. Folders
D. Record box
E. Zoom box

_____ 22. A term that refers to memory in which data or software is lost when the computer is turned off.
_____ 23. Program that moves the read/write head to a section of the disk that has no data.
_____ 24. Read/write comes into contact with the disk's surface.

A. Crash
B. Erasable
C. Pack
D. Park
E. Volatile

_____ 25. The smallest piece of data that can be recognized by computers.
_____ 26. Basic unit of measure of computer's storage
_____ 27. Placed in a microcomputer to take the burden of manipulating numbers off the CPU.

A. Bit
B. Byte
C. Chip
D. Control unit
E. Coprocessor

_____ 28. Program that translates the mnemonics and symbols of low-level language into the opcodes and operands of machine language.
_____ 29. Software that translates a whole program into machine language.
_____ 30. Language designed so that machines and human beings can interact easily.

A. Assembler
B. Compiler
C. Interpreter
D. Natural
E. Pascal

Turn to page 417 for scoring directions and key.

Source: Based on the "Computer Literacy Questionnaire," developed by Floyd Brock and Wayne Thomsen, Department of Management/MIS, University of Nevada at Las Vegas. With permission.

Class Exercise

Financial Controls

The purpose of this exercise is to provide you with an opportunity to calculate financial ratios given typical financial statements of companies. Using the information from the statements below, individually calculate the following: current ratio, acid test ratio, debt-to-assets ratio, times-interest-earned ratio, inventory turnover ratio, total assets turnover ratio, profit-margin-on-revenues ratio, and return-on-investment ratio. You may want to refer to pages 382–83 in this chapter for the formulas used in calculating these ratios.

Control Tools and Techniques

When you have completed your calculations, get into groups of four to five individuals. Compare your ratios. If differences exist, recalculate them until each group member has the same number. Then, with your group, determine what these ratios mean. For example, if you were deciding to invest in one of the two companies listed in the financial statements, which one would you choose? Why? When all groups have made these determinations, your professor will ask each group to share its results and support for its decision.

BALANCE SHEET

ASSETS	WOLLENBURG MEDIA INC. (000s omitted)	CMT RESEARCH INTERNATIONAL (000s omitted)
Current Assets		
Cash	4,123	71,000
Market Securities (short-term investments)	4,236	-0-
Receivables, net	6,331	137,000
Inventories	5,840	202,000
Prepaid Expenses	3,830	16,000
Total Current Assets	24,360	426,000
Net Property, etc.	35,330	159,000
Investments (long-term)	23,346	10,005
Other Assets	10,493	19,460
TOTAL ASSETS	93,529	614,465
LIABILITIES AND STOCKHOLDER EQUITY		
Current Liabilities		
Notes Payable	1,244	16,438
Accounts Payable	13,851	159,219
Other Liabilities	5,822	30,343
Total Current Liabilities	20,917	206,000
Long-Term Debt	22,195	119,000
Capital Lease Obligations	24,296	20,548
Deferred Income	2,211	9,917
Stockholder Equity	23,910	259,000
TOTAL LIABILITIES AND EQUITY	93,529	614,465

INCOME STATEMENT	(000s omitted)	(000s omitted)
Total Revenue	148,889	462,000
Cost of Products Sold	(114,335)	(229,000)
Administrative Costs	(23,475)	(136,000)
Total Costs	(137,810)	(365,000)
Earnings from Operations	11,079	97,000
Interest Expense	(5,771)	(21,000)
Earnings Before Taxes	5,308	76,000
Income Taxes	(1,713)	(30,000)
Net Income (Earnings)	3,595	46,000

Source: Adapted from Charles T. Horngren and Walter T. Harrison, Jr., *Accounting* (Englewood Cliffs, N.J.: Prentice-Hall, Inc., 1989), pp. 762–77. Used with permission.

Key Terms

Key terms are listed in the order in which they appear in the chapter.

management information system (MIS)
data
information
end-user
network
transformation process
operations management
cost-centre approach
direct costs
indirect costs
economic order quantity model (EOQ)
fixed-point reordering system
fixed-interval reordering system
just-in-time inventory (JIT)
preventive maintenance
remedial maintenance
conditional maintenance
quality control
acceptance sampling
process control
attribute sampling
variable sampling
current ratio
acid test ratio
leverage
debt-to-assets ratio
times-interest-earned ratio
inventory turnover ratio
total assets turnover ratio
profit-margin-on-revenues ratio
return-on-investment ratio
audit
external audit
internal audit
cost-benefit analysis
activity-based accounting (ABC)
performance appraisal
written essay
critical incidents
graphic rating scales
behaviourally anchored rating scales (BARS)
multiperson comparison
group order ranking
individual ranking
paired comparison
discipline
"hot stove" rule

Case Application

Harley-Davidson

In the mid-1970s, North America was going wild over motorcycles. Harley-Davidson, then owned by AMF Corporation, responded by nearly tripling production to 75,000 units annually over a four-year period. Along with this growth, however, came problems. Engineering and design of Harleys had become dated. Quality had deteriorated so much that more than half the cycles coming off the assembly line had missing parts, and dealers had to fix them before they could be sold. Harleys leaked oil, vibrated badly, and couldn't match the performance of the flawlessly built Japanese bikes. Hard-core Harley enthusiasts were willing to tolerate these inconveniences, but newcomers had no such devotion and bought Japanese bikes.

In 1973, Harley had 75 per cent of the super-heavyweight market. By 1980, its market share had plummeted to less than 25 per cent. AMF was fast losing confidence in Harley and sold the company in 1981 to a group of Harley executives.

Harley's new owner-managers introduced a number of new products, redesigned and updated their basic product line, and greatly improved the company's marketing programs. However, none of these actions would have meant much if Harley hadn't dramatically revised its production and operations practices. The new managers visited Honda's assembly plant in Marysville, Ohio, and realized what they were up against. In response, they initiated a number of changes on Harley's production floor. A new inventory system was introduced that eliminated the mountains of costly inventory parts. Management redesigned the entire production system, closely involving employees in planning and working out the details. Workers were taught statistical techniques for monitoring and controlling the quality of their own work. Harley's management even worked with its suppliers—as has long been done by Japanese manufacturers—to help them adopt the same efficiency and quality-improvement techniques that Harley had instituted in its plants.

Harley's management succeeded in pulling off one of America's most celebrated turnarounds. On the verge of bankruptcy in the early 1980s, ten years later Harley's share of the super-heavyweight market was almost 65 per cent. The company was losing money in 1982, but now it's highly profitable.

Questions

1. What TQM concepts did Harley utilize as part of its turnaround?
2. What specific types of controls did Harley-Davidson implement? How do you think each of these controls contributed to Harley's turnaround?
3. What lessons can be drawn from Harley that might help a company, like General Motors, that has seen its market share eroded?

Source: "On the Road Again," ABC News *20/20,* January 25, 1991.

Software Sells at Home

How important is performance measurement in an organization? Perhaps it depends on what performance you're measuring, and perhaps it depends on what you define as performance. Autoskill is an Ottawa-based company founded by two neuro-psychologists, Christina Fiedorowicz and Ron Trites. Their research into reading disabilities led them to develop software that helped people to overcome these disabilities. Their interest is in helping school children, and their focus for the company was to sell to schools. Their software teaches people how to read, and since education takes place outside school as well as in it, there is also a very large potential home market.

Like all new businesses, Autoskill needed financing to get started, and it was able to attract a group of investors. But, for Christina and Ron, the investors created a problem. The objective of investment is profit return. Investors talk about profitability ratios, return on investment, and cost controls. Often founders talk about the thing that got them into the business in the first place — their love of what they do. Who is right? Which way should a company go?

Autoskill built itself to sales of $2 million, but hit a brick wall in its efforts to grow through sales to schools. One of the difficulties arose from the budget cutbacks in education: schools simply don't have much money to spend any more. The effectiveness of the Autoskill software as an educational tool aid simply wasn't enough. So the investors began to put pressure on Christina and Ron to develop a product for the home market. Eventually, when results from school sales failed to meet expectations, a change took place. Ron was removed as chairman of the board and replaced by a principal investor, and Christina resigned as president, but remained on the board. A new CEO was brought in to focus Autoskill on the home education market. A professional manager, he described the company, as he found it, as being in chaos, with no clear vision or focus, and he set about implementing controls over cash, costs, and activities.

Questions

1. How could you apply the behavioural control process to the people problem at Autoskill? Would it help to clarify the issues?
2. How important is profit? Does a company have to grow and increase its profits? When is enough enough? Take the views of a company founder and of an investor.

Video Resource: "Autoskill," *Venture* 515 (November 20, 1994).

APPENDIX: THE EVOLUTION OF MANAGEMENT

United Parcel Service (UPS) employs 150,000 people and delivers an average of nine million packages a day to locations in 180 countries. To achieve its claim of "running the tightest ship in the shipping business," UPS's management methodically trains its employees in how to do their jobs as efficiently as possible. For instance, consider the job of a delivery driver.[1]

Industrial engineers at UPS have time-studied each driver's route and set standards for each delivery, stop, and pickup. These engineers have recorded every second taken up by stoplights, traffic, detours, doorbells, walkways, stairways, and coffee breaks. Even bathroom stops are put into the standards. All of this is then fed into company computers to provide detailed time standards for every driver, every day.

To meet their objective of 130 deliveries and pickups each day, drivers must follow the engineers' procedures exactly. As they approach a delivery stop, drivers shed their seat belts, toot their horns, and cut their engines. In one seamless motion, they are required to yank up their emergency brakes and push their gearshifts into first. They're now ready for takeoff after their deliveries. The drivers slide to the ground with their clipboards under their right arms and their packages in their left hands. Their keys, teeth up, are in their right hands. They take one look at the package to fix the address in their minds. Then they walk to the customer's door at the prescribed three-feet-per-second and knock first to avoid lost seconds searching for the doorbell. After making the delivery, they do the paperwork on the way back to the truck.

Does this rigid time scheduling seem obsessive? Maybe. Does it make for high efficiency? You bet! Productivity experts describe UPS as one of the most efficient companies anywhere. As a case in point, Federal Express averages only 80 stops a day versus the UPS average of 130. And all of this seems to positively influence UPS's bottom line. Although the company is privately held, it is widely recognized as being highly profitable.

The purpose of this appendix is to demonstrate that a knowledge of management history can help you to understand theory and practice as they are today. This appendix will introduce you to the origins of many contemporary management concepts and demonstrate how they have evolved to reflect the changing needs of organizations and society as a whole.

Historical Background

Organized activities that are overseen by people responsible for planning, organizing, leading, and controlling activities have existed for thousands of years. The Egyptian pyramids and the Great Wall of China are current evidence that projects of tremendous scope, employing tens of thousands of people, were undertaken well before modern times. The pyramids are a particularly interesting example. The construction of a single pyramid occupied over 100,000 people for twenty years.[2] Who told each worker what he was supposed to do? Who ensured that there would be enough stones at the site to keep workers busy? The answer to questions such as these is management. The Roman Catholic Church also represents an interesting example of the practice of management. The current structure of the church was essentially established in the second century A.D. At that time, its objectives and doctrines were more rigorously defined. Final authority was centralized in Rome. A simple authority hierarchy was created, which has remained basically unchanged for nearly 2,000 years.

These examples from the past demonstrate that organizations have been with us for thousands of years and that management has been practised for an equivalent period. However, it has been only in the past several hundred years, particularly in the last century, that management has undergone systematic investigation, acquired a common body of knowledge, and become a formal discipline for study.

What Was Adam Smith's Contribution to the Field of Management?

Adam Smith's name is more typically cited in economics courses for his contributions to classical economic doctrine, but his discussion in *The Wealth of Nations*, published in 1776, included a brilliant argument on the economic advantages that organizations and society would reap from the division of labour. He used the pin-manufacturing industry for his examples. Smith noted that ten individuals, each doing a specialized task, could produce about 48,000 pins a day among them. However, if each were working separately and independently, those ten workers would be lucky to make 200—or even ten—pins in one day.

Smith concluded that division of labour increased productivity by increasing each worker's skill and dexterity, by saving time that is commonly lost in changing tasks, and by the creation of labour-saving inventions and machinery. The wide popularity today of job specialization—in service jobs like teaching and medicine as well as on assembly lines in automobile plants—is undoubtedly due to the economic advantages cited over 200 years ago by Adam Smith.

How Did the Industrial Revolution Influence Management Practices?

Industrial Revolution
The advent of machine power, mass production, and efficient transportation.

Possibly the most important pre-twentieth-century influence on management was the **Industrial Revolution.** Begun in the eighteenth century in Great Britain, the revolution had crossed the Atlantic to America by the end of the Civil War. Machine power was rapidly being substituted for human power. This, in turn, made it more economical to manufacture goods in factories. The advent of machine power, mass production, the reduced transportation costs that followed the rapid expansion of the railways, and almost no governmental regulation also fostered the development of big organizations. John D. Rockefeller was putting together the Standard Oil monopoly, Andrew Carnegie was gaining control of two-thirds of the steel industry, and similar entrepreneurs were creating other large businesses that would require formalized management practices. The need for a formal theory to guide managers in running their organizations had arrived. However, it was not until the early 1900s that the first major step toward developing such a theory occurred.

A Period of Diversity

The first half of this century was a period of diversity in management thought. Scientific management looked at the field from the perspective of how to improve the productivity of operative personnel. The general administrative theorists were concerned with the overall organization and how to make it more effective. One group of writers and researchers emphasized the human resource or "people side" of management, while another group focused on developing and applying quantitative models.

In the following sections we'll present the contributions of these four approaches. Keep in mind that each is concerned with the same "animal"; the differences reflect the backgrounds and interests of the writers.

Scientific Management

If one had to pinpoint the year that modern management theory was born, one could make a strong case for 1911. This was the year that Frederick Winslow Taylor's *Principles of Scientific Management*[3] was published. Its contents would become widely accepted by managers throughout the world. The book described the theory of **scientific management**—the use of the scientific method to define the "one best way" for a job to be done. The studies conducted before and after the book's publication would establish Taylor as the father of scientific management.

scientific management
The use of the scientific method to define the "one best way" for a job to be done.

What Contributions Did Frederick Taylor Make?

Frederick Taylor did most of his work at the Midvale and Bethlehem Steel companies in Pennsylvania. As a mechanical engineer with a Quaker-Puritan background, he was consistently appalled at the inefficiency of workers. Employees used vastly different techniques to do the same job. Also, they were prone to "take it easy" on the job; Taylor believed that worker output was only about one-third of what was possible. Therefore, he set out to correct the situation by applying the scientific method to jobs on the shop floor. He spent more than two decades pursuing with a passion the "one best way" for each job to be done.

It's important to understand what Taylor saw at Midvale Steel that aroused his determination to improve the way things were done in the plant. At the time, there were no clear concepts of worker and management responsibilities. Virtually no effective work

Exhibit A-1 Taylor's Four Principles of Management

> 1. Develop a science for each element of an individual's work, which replaces the old rule-of-thumb method.
> 2. Scientifically select and then train, teach, and develop the worker. (Previously, workers chose their own work and trained themselves as best they could.)
> 3. Heartily cooperate with the workers so as to ensure that all work is done in accordance with the principles of the science that has been developed.
> 4. Divide work and responsibility almost equally between management and workers. Management takes over all work for which it is better fitted than the workers. (Previously, almost all the work and the greater part of the responsibility were thrown upon the workers.)

standards existed. Workers purposely worked at a slow pace. Management decisions were of the "seat-of-the-pants" nature, based on hunch and intuition. Workers were placed on jobs with little or no concern for matching their abilities and aptitudes with the tasks they were required to do. Most important, management and workers considered themselves to be in continual conflict. Rather than cooperating to their mutual benefit, they perceived their relationship as a zero-sum game—any gain by one would be at the expense of the other.

Taylor sought to create a mental revolution among both the workers and management by defining clear guidelines for improving production efficiency. He defined four principles of management, listed in Exhibit A-1; he argued that following these principles would result in the prosperity of both management and workers. Workers would earn more pay, and management more profits. The current application of these principles at United Parcel Service continues to provide some support for Taylor's expectations. UPS delivery drivers earn over $18 an hour. With overtime, they average better than $50,000 a year.[4] At the same time, management is able to generate consistently high profits.

Building on principle one, Taylor was able to define the one best way for doing each job. He could then, after selecting the right people for the job, train them to do it precisely in this one best way. To motivate workers, he favoured incentive wage plans. Overall, Taylor achieved consistent improvements in productivity in the range of 200 per cent or more. He reaffirmed the role of managers to plan and control and that of workers to perform as they were instructed. The *Principles of Scientific Management,* as well as other papers that Taylor wrote and presented, spread his ideas not only in the United States but also in France, Germany, Russia, and Japan. (Learn more about Frederick Taylor and scientific management in Details on a Management Classic.)

Who Else, Besides Taylor, Were Major Contributors to Scientific Management?

Taylor's ideas inspired others to study and develop methods of scientific management. His most prominent disciples were Frank and Lillian Gilbreth.

A construction contractor by background, Frank Gilbreth gave up his contracting career in 1912 to study scientific management after hearing Taylor speak at a professional meeting. Along with his wife Lillian, a psychologist, he studied work arrangements to eliminate wasteful hand-and-body motions. The Gilbreths also experimented

Details on a Management Classic

FREDERICK TAYLOR

Probably the most widely cited example of scientific management is Taylor's pig iron experiment. Workers loaded "pigs" of iron weighing 92 pounds onto rail cars. Their average daily output was 12.5 tons. Taylor believed that by scientifically analysing the job to determine the one best way to load pig iron, the output could be increased to between 47 and 48 tons per day.

Taylor began his experiment by looking for a physically strong subject who placed a high value on the dollar. The individual Taylor chose was a big, strong Dutch immigrant, whom he called Schmidt. Schmidt, like the other loaders, earned $1.15 a day, which even at the turn of the century was barely enough for a person to survive on. As the following quotation from Taylor's book demonstrates, Taylor used money—the opportunity to make $1.85 a day—as the primary means to get workers like Schmidt to do exactly as they were told:

> "Schmidt, are you a high-priced man?" "Vell, I don't know vat you mean." "Oh, yes you do. What I want to know is whether you are a high-priced man or not." "Vell, I don't know vat you mean." "Oh, come now, you answer my questions. What I want to find out is whether you are a high-priced man or one of these cheap fellows here. What I want to know is whether you want to earn $1.85 a day or whether you are satisfied with $1.15, just the same as all those cheap fellows are getting." "Did I vant $1.85 a day? Vas dot a high-priced man? Vell, yes, I vas a high-priced man."[5]

Using money to motivate Schmidt, Taylor went about having him load the pig irons, alternating various job factors to see what impact the changes had on Schmidt's daily output. For instance, on some days Schmidt would lift the pig irons by bending his knees, whereas on other days he would keep his legs straight and use his back. He experimented with rest periods, walking speed, carrying positions, and other variables. After a long period of scientifically trying various combinations of procedures, techniques, and tools, Taylor succeeded in obtaining the level of productivity he thought possible. By putting the right person on the job with the correct tools and equipment, by having the worker follow his instructions exactly, and by motivating the worker through the economic incentive of a significantly higher daily wage, Taylor was able to reach his 48-ton objective. ▼

in the design and use of the proper tools and equipment for optimizing work performance.[6] Frank Gilbreth is probably best known for his experiments in reducing the number of motions in bricklaying.

The Gilbreths were among the first to use motion picture films to study hand-and-body motions. They devised a microchronometer that recorded time to 1/2,000 second, placed it in the field of study being photographed, and thus determined how long a worker spent enacting each motion. Wasted motions missed by the naked eye could be identified and eliminated. The Gilbreths also devised a classification scheme to label seventeen basic hand motions—such as "search," "select," "grasp," "hold"—which they called **therbligs** ("Gilbreth" spelled backward with the "th" transposed). This allowed the Gilbreths a more precise way of analysing the exact elements of any worker's hand movements.

therbligs
A classification scheme for labelling seventeen basic hand motions.

Another notable associate of Taylor at Midvale and Bethlehem Steel was a young engineer named Henry L. Gantt. Like Taylor and the Gilbreths, Gantt sought to increase worker efficiency through scientific investigation. But he extended some of Taylor's original ideas and added a few of his own. For instance, Gantt devised an incentive system that gave workers a bonus for completing their jobs in less time than the allowed standard. He also introduced a bonus for foremen to be paid for each worker who made the standard plus an extra bonus if all the workers under the foreman made it. In so doing, Gantt expanded the scope of scientific management to encompass the work of managers as well as that of operatives.

However, Gantt is probably most noted for creating a graphic bar chart that could be used by managers as a scheduling device for planning and controlling work (see Chapter 4). The Gantt chart showed the relationship between work planned and completed on one axis and time elapsed on the other.

Why Did Scientific Management Receive So Much Attention?

Many of the guidelines Taylor and others devised for improving production efficiency appear to us today to be common sense. For instance, one can say that it should have been obvious to managers in those days that workers should be carefully screened, selected, and trained before being put into a job.

To understand the importance of scientific management, you have to consider the times in which Taylor, the Gilbreths, and Gantt lived. The standard of living was low. Production was highly labour intensive. Midvale Steel, at the turn of the century, may have employed twenty or thirty workers who did nothing but load pig iron onto rail cars. Today, their entire daily tonnage could probably be done in several hours by one person with a hydraulic lift truck. But they didn't have such mechanical devices. Similarly, the breakthroughs the Gilbreths achieved in bricklaying are meaningful only when you recognize that most quality buildings at that time were constructed of brick, that land was cheap, and that the major cost of a plant or home was the cost of the materials (bricks) and the labour cost to lay them.

General Administrative Theorists

general administrative theorists
Writers who developed general theories of what managers do and what constitutes good management practice.

classical theorists
The term used to describe the scientific management theorists and general administrative theorists.

Another group of writers looked at the subject of management but focused on the entire organization. We call them the **general administrative theorists.** They are important for developing more general theories of what managers do and what constitutes good management practice. Because their writings set the framework for many of our contemporary ideas on management and organization, this group and the scientific management group are frequently referred to as **classical theorists.** The most prominent of the general administrative theorists were Henri Fayol and Max Weber.

What Did Henri Fayol and Max Weber Contribute to Management Thought?

We mentioned Henri Fayol in Chapter 1 for having designated management as a universal set of functions, specifically planning, organizing, commanding, coordinating, and controlling. Because his writings were important, let's take a more careful look at what he had to say.[7]

The Evolution of Management

Fayol wrote during the same time as Taylor. However, whereas Taylor was concerned with management at the shop level (or what we today would describe as the job of a supervisor) and used the scientific method, Fayol's attention was directed at the activities of all managers, and he wrote from personal experience. Taylor was a scientist. Fayol, the managing director of a large French coal-mining firm, was a practitioner.

Fayol described the practice of management as something distinct from accounting, finance, production, distribution, and other typical business functions. He argued that management was an activity common to all human undertakings in business, in government, and even in the home. He then proceeded to state fourteen principles of management—fundamental or universal truths—that could be taught in schools and universities. These principles are shown in Exhibit A-2.

Exhibit A-2 Fayol's Fourteen Principles of Management

▶ 1. **Division of Work.** This principle is the same as Adam Smith's "division of labour." Specialization increases output by making employees more efficient.
▶ 2. **Authority.** Managers must be able to give orders. Authority gives them this right. Along with authority, however, goes responsibility. Wherever authority is exercised, responsibility arises.
▶ 3. **Discipline.** Employees must obey and respect the rules that govern the organization. Good discipline is the result of effective leadership, a clear understanding between management and workers regarding the organization's rules, and the judicious use of penalties for infractions of the rules.
▶ 4. **Unity of Command.** Every employee should receive orders from only one superior.
▶ 5. **Unity of Direction.** Each group of organizational activities that has the same objective should be directed by one manager using one plan.
▶ 6. **Subordination of Individual Interests to the General Interest.** The interests of any one employee or group of employees should not take precedence over the interests of the organization as a whole.
▶ 7. **Remuneration.** Workers must be paid a fair wage for their services.
▶ 8. **Centralization.** Centralization refers to the degree to which subordinates are involved in decision making. Whether decision making is centralized (to management) or decentralized (to subordinates) is a question of proper proportion. The task is to find the optimum degree of centralization for each situation.
▶ 9. **Scalar Chain.** The line of authority from top management to the lowest ranks represents the scalar chain. Communications should follow this chain. However, if following the chain creates delays, cross-communications can be allowed if agreed to by all parties and superiors are kept informed.
▶ 10. **Order.** People and materials should be in the right place at the right time.
▶ 11. **Equity.** Managers should be kind and fair to their subordinates.
▶ 12. **Stability of Tenure of Personnel.** High employee turnover is inefficient. Management should provide orderly personnel planning and ensure that replacements are available to fill vacancies.
▶ 13. **Initiative.** Employees who are allowed to originate and carry out plans will exert high levels of effort.
▶ 14. **Esprit de Corps.** Promoting team spirit will build harmony and unity within the organization.

Exhibit A-3 Weber's Ideal Bureaucracy

> 1. **Division of labour.** Jobs are broken down into simple, routine, and well-defined tasks.
> 2. **Authority Hierarchy.** Offices or positions are organized in a hierarchy, each lower one being controlled and supervised by a higher one.
> 3. **Formal Selection.** All organizational members are to be selected on the basis of technical qualifications demonstrated by training, education, or formal examination.
> 4. **Formal Rules and Regulations.** To ensure uniformity and to regulate the actions of employees, managers must depend heavily on formal organizational rules.
> 5. **Impersonality.** Rules and controls are applied uniformly, avoiding involvement with personalities and personal preferences of employees.
> 6. **Career Orientation.** Managers are professional officials rather than owners of the units they manage. They work for fixed salaries and pursue their careers within the organization.

Max Weber (pronounced Vay-ber) was a German sociologist. Writing in the early part of this century, Weber developed a theory of authority structures and described organizational activity based on authority relations.[8] He described an ideal type of organization that he called a bureaucracy. It was a system characterized by division of labour, a clearly defined hierarchy, detailed rules and regulations, and impersonal relationships. Weber recognized that this "ideal bureaucracy" didn't exist in reality but, rather, represented a selective reconstruction of the real world. He meant it as a basis for theorizing about work and how work could be done in large groups. His theory became the design prototype for many of today's large organizations. The detailed features of Weber's ideal bureaucratic structure are outlined in Exhibit A-3.

What Were the General Administrative Theorists' Contributions to Management Practice?

A number of our current ideas and practices in management can be directly traced to the contributions of the general administrative theorists. For instance, the functional view of the manager's job owes its origin to Henri Fayol. Also, while many of his principles may not be universally applicable to the wide variety of organizations that exist today, they became a frame of reference against which many current concepts have evolved.

Weber's bureaucracy was an attempt to formulate an ideal model around which organizations could be designed. It was a response to the abuses that Weber saw going on within organizations. Weber believed that his model could remove the ambiguity, inefficiencies, and patronage that characterized most organizations at that time. While not as popular as it was a decade ago, many of bureaucracy's components are still inherent in large organizations today.

Human Resource Approach

Managers get things done by working with people. This explains why some writers and researchers have chosen to look at management by focusing on the organization's human resources. Much of what currently makes up the field of personnel or human resource management, as well as contemporary views on motivation and leadership, has come out of the work of those we have categorized as being part of the **human resource approach** to management.

Who Were Some Early Advocates of the Human Resources Approach?

While there were undoubtedly a number of people in the nineteenth and early part of the twentieth century who recognized the importance of the human factor to an organization's success, four individuals stand out as early advocates of the human resource approach. They were Hugo Munsterberg, Mary Parker Follett, Chester Barnard, and Elton Mayo.

For What Is Hugo Munsterberg Best Known?

Hugo Munsterberg created the field of industrial psychology—the scientific study of individuals at work to maximize their productivity and adjustment. His text, *Psychology and Industrial Efficiency,* was published in 1913. In it, he argued for the scientific study of human behaviour to identify general patterns and to explain individual differences. Munsterberg suggested the use of psychological tests to improve employee selection, the value of learning theory in the development of training methods, and the study of human behaviour in order to understand what techniques are most effective for motivating workers. Interestingly, he saw a link between scientific management and industrial psychology. Both sought increased efficiency through scientific work analyses and through better alignment of individual skills and abilities with the demands of various jobs. Much of our current knowledge of selection techniques, employee training, job design, and motivation is built on the work of Munsterberg.

What Contributions Did Mary Parker Follett Make to Management?

One of the earliest writers to recognize that organizations could be viewed from the perspective of individual and group behaviour was Mary Parker Follett.[9] A transitionalist writing in the time of scientific management but proposing more people-oriented ideas, Follett was a social philosopher. However, her ideas had clear implications for management practice. Follett thought that organizations should be based on a group ethic rather than individualism. Individual potential, she argued, remained only potential until released through group association. The manager's job was to harmonize and coordinate group efforts. Managers and workers should view themselves as partners—as part of a common group. As such, managers should rely more on their expertise and knowledge to lead subordinates than on the formal authority of their position. Her humanistic ideas influenced the way we look at motivation, leadership, power, and authority.

Who Was Chester Barnard?

A transitionalist like Follett, Chester Barnard's ideas bridged classical and human resource viewpoints. Like Fayol, Barnard was a practitioner—he was president of New Jersey Bell Telephone Company. He had read Weber and was influenced by his writings. But unlike Weber, who had an impersonal view of organizations, Barnard saw organizations as social systems that require human cooperation. He expressed his views in his book, *The Functions of the Executive,*[10] published in 1938.

human resource approach
The study of management that focuses on human behaviour.

traditional view of authority
The view that authority comes from above.

acceptance view of authority
The theory that authority comes from the willingness of subordinates to accept it.

Hawthorne studies
A series of studies during the 1920s and 1930s that provided new insights into group norms and behaviour.

Barnard believed that organizations were made up of people who have interacting social relationships. The manager's major roles were to communicate and stimulate subordinates to high levels of effort. A major part of an organization's success, as Barnard saw it, depended on obtaining cooperation from its employees. Barnard also argued that success depended on maintaining good relations with people and institutions outside the organization with whom the organization regularly interacted. Barnard is also important for his enlightened ideas on authority. The dominant or **traditional view of authority** at the time he wrote was that a superior's right to exact compliance from subordinates develops at the top and moves down through an organization. Barnard offered a contrasting position, arguing that authority comes from below. The **acceptance view of authority** proposed that authority comes from the willingness of subordinates to accept it. According to Barnard, there can be no such thing as persons of authority, but only persons to whom authority is addressed.

What Were the Hawthorne Studies?

Without question, the most important contribution to the human resource approach to management came out of the **Hawthorne studies** undertaken at the Western Electric Company's Hawthorne Works in Cicero, Illinois. Scholars generally agree that the Hawthorne studies had a dramatic impact on the direction of management thought. Elton Mayo, a Harvard professor, concluded that behaviour and sentiments were closely related, that group influences significantly affected individual behaviour, that group standards established individual worker output, and that money was less a factor in determining output than were group standards, group sentiments, and security. These conclusions led to a new emphasis on the human factor in the functioning of organizations and the attainment of their goals. They also led to increased paternalism by management. (For further information on the Hawthorne studies, see Details on a Management Classic.)

Why Was the Human Relations Movement Important to Management History?

Another group within the human resource approach is important to management history for its unflinching commitment to making management practices more humane. Members of the human relations movement uniformly believed in the importance of employee satisfaction—a satisfied worker was believed to be a productive worker. For the most part, names associated with this movement—Dale Carnegie, Abraham Maslow, and Douglas McGregor—were individuals whose views were shaped more by their personal philosophies than by substantive research evidence.

Dale Carnegie is often overlooked by management scholars, but his ideas and teachings have had an enormous effect on management practice. His book, *How to Win Friends and Influence People*,[13] was read by millions in the 1930s, 1940s, and 1950s. In addition, during this same period, tens of thousands of managers and aspiring managers attended his management speeches and seminars. What was the theme of Carnegie's book and lectures? Essentially, he said that the way to success was through winning the cooperation of others.[14]

Abraham Maslow, a humanistic psychologist, proposed a theoretical hierarchy of five needs: physiological, safety, social, esteem, and self-actualization.[15] In terms of motivation, Maslow argued that each step in the hierarchy must be satisfied before the next can be activated, and that once a need was substantially satisfied it no longer motivated behaviour.

Details on a Management Classic

HAWTHORNE STUDIES

These studies, originally begun in 1924 but eventually expanded and carried through the early 1930s, were initially devised by Western Electric industrial engineers to examine the effect of various illumination levels on worker productivity. Both control and experimental groups were established. The experimental group was presented with varying illumination intensities, while the control group worked under a constant intensity. The engineers had expected individual output to be directly related to the intensity of light. However, they found that as the light level was increased in the experimental group, output for both groups rose. To the surprise of the engineers, as the light level was dropped in the experimental group, productivity continued to increase in both groups. In fact, a productivity decrease was observed in the experimental group only when the light intensity had been reduced to that of moonlight. The engineers concluded that illumination intensity was not directly related to group productivity, but they could not explain the behaviour they had witnessed.

In 1927, the Western Electric engineers asked Elton Mayo and his associates to join the study as consultants. Thus began a relationship that would last through 1932 and encompass numerous experiments covering the redesign of jobs, changes in the lengths of the workday and workweek, the introduction of rest periods, and individual versus group wage plans.[11] For example, one experiment was designed to evaluate the effect of a group piecework incentive pay system on group productivity. The results indicated that the incentive plan had less effect on workers' output than did group pressure and acceptance and the concomitant security. Social norms or standards of the group, therefore, were concluded to be the key determinants of individual work behaviour.

The Hawthorne studies have not been without critics. Attacks have been made on procedures, analyses of the findings, and the conclusions drawn.[12] However, from a historical standpoint, it is of little importance whether the studies were academically sound or their conclusions justified. What is important is that they stimulated an interest in human factors. The Hawthorne studies went a long way in changing the dominant view at the time that people were no different than machines; that is, you put them on the shop floor, cranked in the inputs, and they produced a known quantity of outputs. ▼

Douglas McGregor is best known for his formulation of two sets of assumptions—Theory X and Theory Y—about human nature.[16] Briefly, Theory X presents an essentially negative view of people. It assumes that they have little ambition, dislike work, want to avoid responsibility, and need to be closely directed to work effectively. On the other hand, Theory Y offers a positive view. It assumes that people can exercise self-direction, accept responsibility, and consider work to be as natural as rest or play. McGregor believed that Theory Y assumptions best captured the true nature of workers and should guide management practice.

What Was the Common Thread That Linked Advocates of the Human Relations Movement?

The common thread that united human relations supporters, including Carnegie, Maslow, and McGregor, was an unshakable optimism about people's capabilities. They believed strongly in their cause and were inflexible in their beliefs, even when faced with contradictory evidence. No amount of contrary experience or research evidence would alter their views. Of course, in spite of this lack of objectivity, advocates of the human relations movement had a definite influence on management theory and practice.

Who Were the Behavioural Science Theorists?

One final category within the human resource approach encompasses a group of psychologists and sociologists who relied on the scientific method for the studying of organizational behaviour. Unlike the theorists of the human relations movement, individuals like Fred Fiedler, Victor Vroom, Frederick Herzberg, Edwin Locke, David McClelland, Richard Hackman, Jeffrey Pfeffer, Kenneth Thomas, and Charles Perrow engaged in objective research of human behaviour in organizations. They carefully attempted to keep their personal beliefs out of their work. They sought to develop rigorous research designs that could be replicated by other behavioural scientists. In so doing, they hoped to build a science of organizational behaviour.

What Can Be Concluded from the Human Resource Contributors?

Both scientific management and the general administrative theorists viewed organizations as machines. Managers were the engineers. They ensured that the inputs were available and that the machine was properly maintained. Any failure by the employee to generate the desired output was viewed as an engineering problem: it was time to redesign the job or grease the machine by offering the employee an incentive wage plan. After all, who wouldn't work harder for a few more dollars? Apparently, a lot of people! UPS, which we earlier described as being a modern-day proponent of scientific management principles, has pushed a number of its drivers so hard that they quit. As one driver put it, "They squeeze every ounce out of you. You're always in a hurry, and you can't work relaxed."[17] Contributors to the human resources approach forced managers in many organizations to reassess the simplistic machine-model view.

The Quantitative Approach

We close our discussion of the period of diversity with a review of quantitative contributions to the study of management. This approach has also been labelled as operations research or management science.

The quantitative approach to management evolved out of the development of mathematical and statistical solutions to military problems during World War II. For instance, when the British confronted the problem of how to get the maximum effectiveness from their limited aircraft capability against the massive forces of the Germans, they turned to their mathematicians to devise an optimum allocation model. Similarly, U.S. antisubmarine warfare teams used operations research techniques to improve the odds of survival for Allied convoys crossing the North Atlantic and for

The Evolution of Management

selecting the optimal depth-charge patterns for aircraft and surface vessel attacks on German U-boats.

After the war, many of the quantitative techniques that had been applied to military problems were moved into the business sector. One group of military officers, labelled the "Whiz Kids," joined Ford Motor Company in the mid-1940s and immediately began using statistical devices to improve decision making at Ford. Two of the most famous Whiz Kids were Robert McNamara and Charles "Tex" Thornton. McNamara rose to the presidency of Ford and then became U.S. Secretary of Defence. At the Department of Defence, he sought to quantify resource allocation decisions in the Pentagon through cost-benefit analyses. He concluded his career as head of the World Bank. Tex Thornton founded the billion-dollar conglomerate Litton Industries, again relying on quantitative techniques to make acquisition and allocation decisions.

What Are the Quantitative Techniques and How Have They Contributed to Current Management Practice?

The quantitative approach to management includes applications of statistics, optimization models, information models, and computer simulations. Linear programming, for instance, is a technique that managers can use to improve resource allocation choices. Work scheduling can be made more efficient as a result of critical-path scheduling analysis. Decisions on determining the optimum inventory levels a firm should maintain have been significantly influenced by the economic order quantity model.

How Has the Quantitative Approach Contributed to Management Practice?

The quantitative approach has contributed most directly to management decision making, particularly to planning and control decisions. Without denigrating the contribution of the quantitative approach, it should be noted that it has never gained the influence on management practice that the human resource approach has. This is undoubtedly due to a number of factors: many managers are unfamiliar with the quantitative tools; behavioural problems are more widespread and visible; and most students and managers can relate better to real, day-to-day people problems in organizations, such as motivating subordinates and reducing conflicts, than to the more abstract activity of constructing quantitative models.

Key Terms

Key terms are listed in the order in which they appear in the appendix.

Industrial Revolution
scientific management
therbligs
general administrative theorists
classical theorists
human resource approach
traditional view of authority
acceptance view of authority
Hawthorne studies

SCORING KEYS FOR SELF-ASSESSMENT EXERCISES

Chapter 1 • How Strong Is Your Motivation to Manage in a Large Organization?

Total your circled numbers. Your score will fall somewhere between 7 and 49. Arbitrary norms for comparison are: Scores of 7-21 = relatively low motivation to manage; 22-34 = moderate; 35-49 = relatively high.

Chapter 2 • What Are Your Personal Value Preferences? (Self-Assessment)

These eighteen values have been labelled as instrumental values, which means they represent beliefs about near-term modes of conduct. Research studies have found that different groups have different ranked preferences. The following represent the highest ranked and lowest ranked values from three groups: 345 graduates of a university's executive MBA program; a sample of 1,000 members from a steelworkers' union local; and a diverse set of 234 community activists.

	Executives	Unions	Activists
Top five responses:			
1.	Honest	Responsible	Honest
2.	Responsible	Honest	Helpful
3.	Capable	Courageous	Courageous
4.	Ambitious	Independent	Responsible
5.	Independent	Capable	Capable

	Executives	Unions	Activists
Bottom five responses:			
14.	Helpful	Helpful	Ambitious
15.	Polite	Cheerful	Self-controlled
16.	Cheerful	Intellectual	Polite
17.	Clean	Forgiving	Clean
18.	Obedient	Imaginative	Obedient

What were your top five and bottom five responses? How do they compare with the three groups above?

Chapter 2 • The International Culture Quiz (Class Exercise)

The correct answers are:

1. a   2. b   3. e (Portuguese)   4. b   5. d
6. a   7. d   8. d   9. b   10. b

Scores of eight correct answers or more indicate that you are relatively knowledgeable about customs, practices, and facts regarding different countries. Scores of four correct answers or less suggest considerable room for expanding your knowledge of other people and lands.

Chapter 3 • Are You a Good Planner?

According to the author of this questionnaire, the "perfect" planner would have answered:

1. Yes   2. No   3. Yes   4. Yes
5. Yes   6. Yes   7. Yes   8. No

Chapter 4 • Are You an Entrepreneur?

Total your score for the twenty-two characteristics. Your score will fall between +44 and −44. The higher your positive score, the more you share traits common to highly successful entrepreneurs.

Chapter 5 • What's Your Intuitive Ability?

Total the number of "a" responses circled for questions 1, 3, 5, 6, 11; enter the score here [A =   ]. Total the number of "b" responses for questions 2, 4, 7, 8, 9, 10, 12; enter the score here [B =   ]. Add your "a" and "b" scores and enter the sum here [A + B =   ].

This is your intuitive score. The highest possible intuitive score is 12; the lowest is 0. The author of this scale states that traditional analytical techniques "are not as useful as they once were for guiding major decisions. . . . If you hope to be better prepared for tomorrow, then it only seems logical to pay some attention to the use and development of intuitive skills for decision making." (Source: Weston H. Agor, AIM Survey (El Paso, TX: ENFP Enterprises, 1989), Part I.)

Chapter 6 • How Power Oriented Are You?

This test is designed to compute your Machiavellian (Mach) score. To obtain your score, add the number you have checked on questions 1, 3, 4, 5, 9, and 10. For the other four questions, reverse the numbers you have checked: 5 becomes 1, 4 is 2, 2 is 4, 1 is 5. Total your ten numbers to find your score. The National Opinion Research Center, which used this short form of the scale in a random sample of American adults, found that the national average was 25.

The results of research using the Mach test found that men are generally more Machiavellian than women; older adults tend to have lower Mach scores than younger adults; and high-Machs tend to be in professions that emphasize the control and manipulation of individuals—for example, managers, lawyers, psychiatrists, and behavioural scientists.

Scoring Keys for Self-Assessment Exercises

Chapter 7 • Is an Enriched Job for You? (Self-Assessment)

This exercise is designed to assess the degree to which you desire complex, challenging work. A high need for growth suggests that you are more likely to experience the desired psychological states in the job characteristics model when you have an enriched job. This twelve-item questionnaire taps the degree to which you have a strong versus weak desire to obtain growth satisfaction from your work. Each item on the questionnaire yields a score from 1 to 7 (that is, "Strongly prefer A" is scored 1; "Neutral" is scored 4; and "Strongly prefer B" is scored 7). To obtain your individual growth need strength score, average the twelve items as follows:

#1, #2, #7, #8, #11, #12 (direct scoring)
#3, #4, #5, #6, #9, #10 (reverse scoring)

Average scores for typical respondents are close to the midpoint of 4. Research indicates that if you score high on this measure, you will respond positively to an enriched job. Conversely, if you score low, you will tend not to find enriched jobs satisfying or motivating.

Chapter 7 • What Kind of Organization Design Do You Want to Work For? (Class Exercise)

For items 5, 6, 7, and 9, score as follows:

Strongly agree	= +2
Agree	= +1
Uncertain	= –0
Disagree	= –1
Strongly disagree	= –2

For items 1, 2, 3, 4, 8, and 10, reverse the score (Strongly agree = –2, and so on). Add up your total. Your score will fall somewhere between +20 and –20. What does your score mean? The higher your score (positive), the more comfortable you'll be in a formal, stable, rule-oriented, and structured culture. This is synonymous with large corporations in stable environments and government agencies. Negative scores indicate a preference for small, innovative, flexible, team-oriented cultures that are more likely to be found in research units or small businesses.

Chapter 8 • How Do You Define Life Success?

This questionnaire taps six dimensions of life success. These are the achievement of status and wealth; contribution to society; good family relationships; personal fulfilment; professional fulfilment; and security.

Calculate your scores as follows:

The STATUS/WEALTH SCORE is found by adding responses to items:

____ ____ ____ ____ ____ ____ ____ ____ ____ /8 = ____
1   7   12   16   24   26   34   36   Total

The CONTRIBUTION TO SOCIETY SCORE is found by adding responses to items:

____ ____ ____ ____ ____ ____ ____ ____ ____ /8 = ____
6   15   18   22   33   35   39   42   Total

The FAMILY RELATIONSHIPS SCORE is found by adding responses to items:

____ ____ ____ ____ ____ ____ ____ ____ /8 = ____
 3   8   10   11   20   25   31   41   Total

The PERSONAL FULFILMENT SCORE is found by adding responses to items:

____ ____ ____ ____ ____ ____ ____ ____ /8 = ____
 2   14   17   23   27   29   38   40   Total

The PROFESSIONAL FULFILMENT SCORE is found by adding responses to items:

____ ____ ____ ____ ____ /5 = ____
 5   13   21   32   37   Total

The SECURITY SCORE is found by adding responses to items:

____ ____ ____ ____ ____ /5 = ____
 4   9   19   28   30   Total

You can compare your scores with the following norms based on surveys of managers:

	Females (n = 439)	Males (n = 317)
Status/Wealth	3.48	3.65
Social Contribution	4.04	4.07
Family Relationships	4.44	4.28
Personal Fulfilment	4.60	4.43
Professional Fulfilment	4.21	4.15
Security	4.30	4.21

Chapter 9 • How Ready Are You for Managing in a Turbulent World?

Score 4 points for each A, 3 for each B, 2 for each C, 1 for each D, and 0 for each E. Compute the total, divide by 24, and round to one decimal place. While the results are not intended to be more than suggestive, the higher your score, the more comfortable you seem to be with change. The test's author suggests analysing scores as if they were grade point averages. In this way, a 4.0 average is an A, a 2.0 is a C, and scores below 1.0 flunk. Using replies from nearly 500 MBA students and young managers, the range of scores was found to be narrow—between 1.0 and 2.2. The average score was between 1.5 and 1.6—a D+/C− sort of grade!

Chapter 10 • Who Controls Your Life?

This exercise is designed to measure your locus of control. Give yourself 1 point for each of the following selections: 1B, 2A, 3A, 4B, 5B, 6A, 7A, 8A, 9B, and 10A. Scores can be interpreted as follows:

8-10	=	Moderate internal locus of control
6-7	=	Moderate internal locus of control
5	=	Mixed
3-4	=	Moderate external locus of control
1-2	=	High external locus of control

Scoring Keys for Self-Assessment Exercises   **415**

The higher your internal score, the more you believe that you control your own destiny. The higher your external score, the more you believe that what happens to you in your life is due to luck or chance.

Chapter 11 • How Trustworthy Are You?

Add up your total score. It will be somewhere between 8 and 80. What does your score mean?

65-80	=	High trustworthiness
24-64	=	Moderate trustworthiness
8-23	=	Low trustworthiness

Chapter 12 • What Needs Are Most Important to You?

Place the values you gave A, B, C, D, and E for each question in the spaces provided in the scoring key. Notice that the letters are not always in the same place for each question. Then add up each column and obtain a total score for each of the motivation levels.

Scoring Key

Question					
Question 1	A	C	B	E	D
Question 2	A	B	D	C	E
Question 3	B	C	E	D	A
Question 4	E	A	C	B	D
Question 5	C	B	D	A	E
Question 6	B	C	A	E	D
Question 7	E	A	D	C	B
Question 8	B	C	A	E	D
Question 9	B	C	E	D	A
Question 10	B	D	C	E	A
TOTAL SCORE					
	I	II	III	IV	V
	MOTIVATION LEVELS				

The five motivation levels are as follows:

Level I: Physiological needs   Level IV: Esteem needs
Level II: Safety needs   Level V: Self-actualization needs
Level III: Social needs

Those levels that received the highest scores are the most important needs identified by you in your work. The lowest show those needs that have been relatively well satisfied or that have been deemphasized by you at this time.

Chapter 13 • What Kind of Leader Are You?

To find your leadership style,

1. Circle the item numbers for items 8, 12, 17, 18, 19, 30, 34, and 35.
2. Write a "1" in front of the circled items to which you responded S (seldom) or N (never).
3. Write a "1" in front of items not circled to which you responded A (always) or F (frequently).
4. Circle the "1s" which you have written in front of the following items: 3, 5, 8, 10, 15, 18, 19, 22, 24, 26, 28, 30, 32, 34, and 35.
5. Count the circled "1s." This is your score for concern for people. Record the score.
6. Count the uncircled "1s." This is your score for concern for task. Record this number.
7. Now refer to the diagram. Find your score on the concern for task dimension on the left-hand arrow. Next, move to the right-hand arrow and find your score on the concern for people dimension. Draw a straight line that intersects the two scores. The point at which that line crosses the shared leadership arrow indicates your score on that dimension.

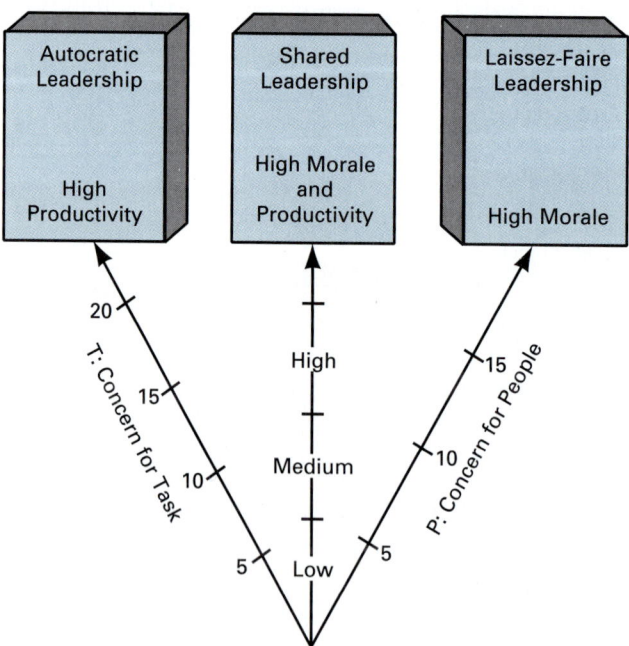

Chapter 14 • Conflict-Handling Style Questionnaire

Total your choices as follows: give yourself 5 points for "Often"; 3 points for "Sometimes"; and 1 point for "Never." Then total them for each set of statements, grouped as follows:

Scoring Keys for Self-Assessment Exercises

Set A: items 13-16   Set B: items 9-12
Set C: items 5-8   Set D: items 1-4

Treat each set separately. A score of 17 or above on any set is considered high; scores of 12 to 16 are moderately high; scores of 8 to 11 are moderately low; and scores of 7 or less are considered low. Sets A, B, C, and D represent different conflict-resolution strategies:

- A = Forcing/domination: I win, you lose.
- B = Accommodation: I lose, you win.
- C = Compromise: Both you and I win some and lose some.
- D = Collaboration: I win, you win.

Everyone has a basic underlying conflict-handling style. Your score on this exercise indicates the strategies you rely on most.

Chapter 15 • How Willing Are You to Give Up Control?

Add up your total score for the eighteen items. Your score can be interpreted as follows:

- 72-90 points = Ineffective delegation
- 54-71 points = Delegation habits need substantial improvement
- 36-53 points = You still have room to improve
- 18-35 points = Superior delegation

Chapter 16 • Testing Your Understanding of Computers

The correct answers are as follows:

1. B	2. A	3. E	4. B	5. C	6. D
7. A	8. B	9. D	10. D	11. E	12. A
13. D	14. A	15. B	16. E	17. A	18. D
19. E	20. C	21. A	22. E	23. D	24. A
25. A	26. B	27. E	28. A	29. B	30. D

Arbitrary cutoffs suggest:

- 25-30 correct = High literacy
- 20-24 correct = Considerable computer knowledge
- 15-19 correct = Some computer knowledge
- 10-14 correct = Modest computer knowledge
- 0-9 correct   = Very little knowledge of computers

ENDNOTES

Chapter 1

1. Geoffrey Rowan, "How Software Star Solved Service Slips," *The Globe & Mail,* December 13, 1994.
2. U.S. Bureau of the Census, *Statistical Abstracts of the United States: 1993,* 113th ed. (Washington, D.C.: Government Printing Office, 1993), p. 405.
3. Henri Fayol, *Industrial and General Administration* (Paris: Dunod, 1916).
4. Harold Koontz and Cyril O'Donnell, *Principles of Management: An Analysis of Managerial Functions* (New York: McGraw-Hill, 1955).
5. For a comprehensive review of this question, see Colin P. Hales, "What Do Managers Do? A Critical Review of the Evidence," *Journal of Management Studies,* January 1986, pp. 88–115.
6. Henry Mintzberg, *The Nature of Managerial Work* (New York: Harper & Row, 1973).
7. Fred Luthans, Stuart A. Rosenkrantz, and Harry W. Hennessey, "What Do Successful Managers Really Do? An Observation Study of Managerial Activities," *Journal of Applied Behavioral Science,* Vol. 21, No. 3 (1985), pp. 255–70; Fred Luthans, "Successful vs. Effective Real Managers," *Academy of Management Executive,* May 1988, pp. 127–32; Fred Luthans, Richard M. Hodgetts, and Stuart A. Rosenkrantz, *Real Managers* (Cambridge, Mass.: Ballinger Publishing, 1988); and Fred Luthans, Dianne H.B. Welsh, and Lewis A. Taylor III, "A Descriptive Model of Managerial Effectiveness," *Group & Organization Studies,* June 1988, pp. 148–62.
8. See, for example, Larry D. Alexander, "The Effect Level in the Hierarchy and Functional Area Have on the Extent Mintzberg's Roles Are Required by Managerial Jobs," *Academy of Management Proceedings,* 1979, pp. 186–89; Alan W. Lau and Cynthia M. Pavett, "The Nature of Managerial Work: A Comparison of Public and Private Sector Managers," *Group and Organization Studies,* December 1980, pp. 453–66; Morgan W. McCall, Jr., and C.A. Segrist, *In Pursuit of the Manager's Job: Building on Mintzberg,* Technical Report No. 14 (Greensboro, N.C.: Center for Creative Leadership, 1980); Cynthia M. Pavett and Alan W. Lau, "Managerial Work: The Influence of Hierarchical Level and Functional Specialty," *Academy of Management Journal,* March 1983, pp. 170–77; Hales, "What Do Managers Do? A Critical Review of the Evidence;" Allen I. Kraut, Patricia R. Pedigo, D. Douglas McKenna, and Marvin D. Dunnette, "The Role of the Manager: What's Really Important in Different Management Jobs," *Academy of Management Executive,* November 1989, pp. 286–93; and Mark J. Martinko and William L. Gardner, "Structured Observation of Managerial Work: A Replication and Synthesis," *Journal of Management Studies,* May 1990, pp. 330–57.
9. Pavett and Lau, "Managerial Work: The Influence of Hierarchical Level and Functional Specialty."
10. Stephen J. Carroll and Dennis A. Gillen, "Are the Classical Management Functions Useful in Describing Managerial Work?" *Academy of Management Review,* January 1987, p. 48.
11. See, for example, Harold Koontz, "Commentary on the Management Theory Jungle—Nearly Two Decades Later," in Harold Koontz, Cyril O'Donnell, and Heintz Weihrich, eds., *Management: A Book of Readings,* 6th ed. (New York: McGraw-Hill, 1984), pp. 10–14; and Carroll and Gillen, "Are the Classical Management Functions Useful in Describing Managerial Work?" pp. 38–51.
12. Koontz, "Commentary on the Management

Theory Jungle—Nearly Two Decades Later"; and Peter Allan, "Managers at Work: A Large-Scale Study of the Managerial Job in New York City Government," *Academy of Management Journal,* September 1981, pp. 613–19.

13. Robert L. Katz, "Skills of an Effective Administrator," *Harvard Business Review,* September–October, 1974, pp. 90–102.

14. See, for example, James W. Driscoll, Gary Cowger, and Robert Egan, "Private Managers and Public Myths—Public Managers and Private Myths," *Sloan Management Review,* Fall 1979, pp. 53–57; David Rogers, "Managing in the Public and Private Sectors: Similarities and Differences," *Management Review,* May 1981, pp. 48–54; Graham Allison, "Public and Private Management: Are They Fundamentally Alike in All Unimportant Respects?" in F.S. Lane, ed., *Current Issues in Public Administration,* 2nd ed. (New York: St. Martin's Press, 1982); Douglas Yates, Jr., *The Politics of Management* (San Francisco: Jossey-Bass, 1985), pp. 12–39; J. Norman Baldwin, "Public vs. Private: Not That Different, Not That Consequential," *Public Personnel Management,* Summer 1987, pp. 181–91; and Hal G. Rainey, "Public Management: Recent Research on the Political Context and Managerial Roles, Structures, and Behaviors," *Journal of Management,* June 1989, pp. 229–50.

15. U.S. Small Business Administration, *The State of Small Business: A Report of the President* (Washington, D.C.: GPO, 1986), p. x; "As Exports Rise, Big Companies Rev Up Hiring," *Business Week,* April 11, 1988, p. 91; "The 1990 Guide to Small Business," U.S. News & World Report, October 23, 1989; and T. Pouschine and M. Kripalani, "I Got Tired of Forcing Myself to Go to the Office," *Forbes,* May 25, 1992, pp. 104–14.

16. Joseph G.P. Paolillo, "The Manager's Self-Assessments of Managerial Roles: Small vs. Large Firms," *American Journal of Small Business,* January–March 1984, pp. 58–64.

17. See, for example, Gerald d'Amboise and Marie Muldowney, "Management Theory for Small Business: Attempts and Requirements," *Academy of Management Review,* April 1988, pp. 226–40.

18. Amanda Lang, "Honour Thy Grandfather," *Report on Business,* June 1995.

19. Harold Koontz, "The Management Theory Jungle," *Journal of the Academy of Management,* December 1961, pp. 174–88.

20. Harold Koontz, ed., *Toward a Unified Theory of Management* (New York: McGraw-Hill, 1964).

21. See, for example, Louis W. Fry and Deborah A. Smith, "Congruence, Contingency, and Theory Building," *Academy of Management Review,* January 1987, pp. 117–32.

Chapter 2

1. Thomas A. Stewart, "Reengineering: The Hot New Managing Tool," *Fortune,* August 23, 1993, p. 41–48.

2. Ibid.

3. Ibid.

4. Robert H. Miles, *Macro Organizational Behavior* (Santa Monica, Calif.: Goodyear Publishing, 1980), p. 195.

5. Geert Hofstede, *Culture's Consequences: International Differences in Work-Related Values* (Beverly Hills, CA: Sage Publications, 1980), pp. 25–6; and Geert Hofstede, "The Cultural Relativity of Organizational Practices and Theories," *Journal of International Business Studies,* Fall 1983, pp. 75–89.

6. Ibid.

7. Hofstede called this last dimension masculinity-femininity. We've changed it because of the strong sexist connotation in his choice of terms.

8. Robert D. Hisrich, "Entrepreneurship/Intrapreneurship," *American Psychologist,* February 1990, p. 218.

9. See, for instance, Thomas M. Begley and David P. Boyd, "A Comparison of Entrepreneurs and Managers of Small Business Firms," *Journal of Management,* Spring 1987, pp. 99–108.

10. Peter F. Drucker, *Innovation and Entrepreneurship* (New York: Harper & Row, 1985).

11. Karl H. Vesper, *New Venture Strategies* (Englewood Cliffs, N.J.: Prentice-Hall, 1980), p. 14.

12. Gary W. Loveman and John J. Gabarro, "The Managerial Implications of Changing Work Force Demographics: A Scoping Study," *Human Resource Management* (Spring 1991), pp. 7–29.

13. See, for example, Bob Krone, "Total Quality Management: An American Odyssey," *Bureaucrat,* Fall 1990, pp. 35–38; Andrea Gabor, *The Man Who Discovered Quality* (New York: Random House, 1990); Jim Clemmer, "How Total Is Your Quality Management?" *Canadian Business Review,* Spring 1991, pp. 38–41; and Marshall Sashkin and Kenneth J. Kiser, *Total Quality Management* (Seabrook, Md.: Ducochon Press, 1991).

14. Albert C. Hyde, "Rescuing Quality Management from TQM," *Bureaucrat,* Winter 1990–91, p. 16.

15. Archie B. Carroll, "A Three-Dimensional Con-

ceptual Model of Corporate Performance," *Academy of Management Review,* October 1979, p. 499.
16. Robert Bott, "Everyday Ethics," *Report on Business,* April 1995.
17. See, for example, Rogene A. Buchholz, *Essentials of Public Policy for Management,* 2nd. ed (Englewood Cliffs, N.J.: Prentice-Hall, Inc., 1990)
18. See S. Prakash Sethi, "A Conceptual Framework for Environmental Analysis of Social Issues and Evaluation of Business Response Patterns," *Academy of Management Review,* January 1979, pp. 68–74.
19. See, for example, Donna J. Wood, "Corporate Social Performance Revisited," *Academy of Management Review,* October 1991, pp. 703–8.
20. Daniel Stoffman, "The Big Clean-up," *Report on Business,* April 1995.
21. See, for example, Michele Galen, "Out of the Shadows," *Business Week,* October 28, 1991, pp. 30–31; and Joann S. Lublin, "Sexual Harassment Is Topping Agenda in Many Executive Education Programs," *Wall Street Journal,* December 2, 1991, p. B1.
22. Alanna Mitchell, "Harassment Risk High, Study says," *The Globe & Mail,* December 15, 1994.
23. Ibid.
24. Thomas A. Stewart, "Reengineering: The Hot New Managing Tool," *Fortune,* August 23, 1993, pp. 41–48.
25. Ibid., pp. 41–43.
26. Ibid., p.42.
27. See Kenneth W. Thomas and Betty A. Velthouse, "Cognitive Elements of Empowerment: An 'Interpretive' Model of Intrinsic Task Motivation," *Academy of Management Review,* October 1990, pp. 666–81.
28. See S. Dentzer, "The Vanishing Dream," *U.S. News & World Report,* April 22, 1992, pp. 39–43; and Aaron Bernstein, "The Global Economy: Who Gets Hurt," *Business Week,* August 10, 1992, pp. 48–53.
29. Archie B. Carroll, *Social Responsibility of Management* (Chicago: Science Research Associates, 1984), p. 13.
30. Keith Davis and William C. Frederick, *Business and Society: Management, Public Policy, Ethics,* 5th. ed (New York: McGraw-Hill, 1984), p. 76.
31. Gerald F. Cavanagh, Dennis J. Moberg, and Manuel Valasquez, "The Ethics of Organizational Politics," *Academy of Management Journal,* June 1981, pp. 363–74. See F. Neil Brady, "Rules for Making Exceptions to Rules," *Academy of Management Review,* July 1987, pp. 436–44 for an argument that the theory of justice is redundant with the prior two theories.
32. Brian Dumaine, "Exporting Jobs and Ethics," *Fortune,* October 5, 1992, p. 10.
33. See, for example, M. Cash Mathews, "Codes of Ethics: Organizational Behavior and Misbehavior," in William C. Frederick and Lee E. Preston, eds., *Business Ethics: Research Issues and Empirical Studies* (Greenwich, Conn.: JAI Press, 1990), pp. 99–122.
34. Cited in Catherine Fredman, "Nationwide Examination of Corporate Consciences," *Working Woman,* December 1991, p. 39.
35. Paul Richter, "Big Business Puts Ethics in Spotlight," *Los Angeles Times,* June 19, 1986, p. 29.

Chapter 3

1. Merle MacIsaac, "Cup Victories," *The Globe & Mail,* February 13, 1995.
2. See, for example, John A. Pearce II, K. Keith Robbins, and Richard B. Robinson, Jr., "The Impact of Grand Strategy and Planning Formality on Financial Performance," *Strategic Management Journal,* March–April 1987, pp. 125–34; Lawrence C. Rhyne, "Contrasting Planning Systems in High, Medium, and Low Performance Companies," *Journal of Management Studies,* July 1987, pp. 363–85; Richard Brahm and Charles B. Brahm, "Formal Planning and Organizational Performance: Assessing Emerging Empirical Research Trends," paper presented at the National Academy of Management Conference, New Orleans, August 1987; John A. Pearce II, Elizabeth B. Freeman, and Richard B. Robinson, Jr., "The Tenuous Link between Formal Strategic Planning and Financial Performance," *Academy of Management Review,* October 1987, pp. 658–75; and Deepak K. Sinha, "The Contribution of Formal Planning to Decisions," *Strategic Management Journal,* October 1990, pp. 479–92.
3. Russell Ackoff, "A Concept of Corporate Planning," *Long Range Planning,* September 1970, p. 3.
4. Michael B. McCaskey, "A Contingency Approach to Planning: Planning With Goals and Planning Without Goals," *Academy of Management Journal,* June 1974, pp. 281–91.
5. Several of these factors were suggested by J. Scott Armstrong, "The Value of Formal Planning for Strategic Decisions: Review of Empirical Research," *Strategic Management Journal,* July–September 1982, pp. 197–211; and Rudi K. Bresser and Ronald C. Bishop, "Dysfunctional Effects of Formal Planning: Two Theoretical

Explanations," *Academy of Management Review,* October 1983, pp. 588–99.
6. Richard F. Vancil, "The Accuracy of Long–Range Planning," *Harvard Business Review,* September–October 1970, p. 99.
7. Pam Carroll, "Freedom," *Success,* June 1990, pp. 44–45.
8. The concept is generally attributed to Peter F. Drucker, *The Practice of Management* (New York: Harper & Row, 1954).
9. See, for example, Edwin A. Locke, "Toward a Theory of Task Motivation and Incentives," *Organizational Behavior and Human Performance,* May 1968, pp. 157–89; Edwin A. Locke, Karyl N. Shaw, Lise M. Saari, and Gary P. Latham, "Goal Setting and Task Performance: 1969–1980," *Psychological Bulletin,* July 1981, pp. 125–52; Mark E. Tubbs, "Goal Setting: A Meta-Analytic Examination of the Empirical Evidence," *Journal of Applied Psychology,* August 1986, pp. 474–83; Anthony J. Mento, R. P. Steel, and R. J. Karren, "A Meta-Analytic Study of the Effects of Goal Setting on Task Performance: 1966–1984," *Organizational Behavior and Human Decision Processes,* February 1987, pp. 52–83; and Edwin A. Locke and Gary P. Latham, *A Theory of Goal Setting and Task Performance* (Englewood Cliffs, N.J.: Prentice-Hall, 1990).
10. See, for example, Gary P. Latham and Lise M. Saari, "The Effects of Holding Goal Difficulty Constant on Assigned and Participatively Set Goals," *Academy of Management Journal,* March 1979, pp. 163–68; Miriam Erez, P. Christopher Earley, and Charles L. Hulin, "The Impact of Participation on Goal Acceptance and Performance: A Two–Step Model," *Academy of Management Journal,* March 1985, pp. 50–66; and Gary P. Latham, Miriam Erez, and Edwin A. Locke, "Resolving Scientific Disputes by the Joint Design of Crucial Experiments by the Antagonists: Application to the Erez–Latham Dispute Regarding Participation in Goal Setting," *Journal of Applied Psychology,* November 1988, pp. 753–72.
11. Gary P. Latham, Terence R. Mitchell, and Dennis L. Dossett, "Importance of Participative Goal Setting and Anticipated Rewards on Goal Difficulty and Job Performance," *Journal of Applied Psychology,* April 1978, pp. 163–71.
12. Robert Rodgers and John E. Hunter, "Impact of Management by Objectives on Organizational Productivity," *Journal of Applied Psychology,* April 1991, pp. 322–36.
13. See for example, Larry J. Rosenberg and Charles D. Schewe, "Strategic Planning: Fulfilling the Promise," *Business Horizons,* July–August, 1985, pp. 54–62; and Walter Kiechel III, "Corporate Strategy for the 1990s," *Fortune,* February 29, 1989, pp. 34–42.
14. "A Solid Strategy Helps Companies' Growth," *Nation's Business,* October 1990, p. 10.
15. "Colleges Undergo Reassessment," *Time,* April 14, 1992, p. 81.
16. N. Venkatraman and John E. Prescott, "Environment–Strategy Coalignment: An Empirical Test of Its Performance Implications," *Strategic Management Journal,* January 1990, pp. 1–23.
17. See Susan E. Jackson and Jane E. Dutton, "Discerning Threats and Opportunities," *Administrative Science Quarterly,* September 1988, pp. 370–87.
18. See, for example, Jay B. Barney, "Organizational Culture: Can It Be a Source of Sustained Competitive Advantage?" *Academy of Management Review,* July 1986, pp. 656–65; Christian Scholz, "Corporate Culture and Strategy—The Problem of Strategic Fit," *Long Range Planning,* August 1987, pp. 78–87; Sebastian Green, "Understanding Corporate Culture and Its Relation to Strategy," *International Studies of Management and Organization,* Summer 1988, pp. 6–28; Toyohiro Kono, "Corporate Culture and Long–Range Planning," *Long Range Planning,* August 1990, pp. 9–19; and C. Marlene Fiol, "Managing Culture as a Competitive Resource: An Identity–Based View of Sustainable Competitive Advantage," *Journal of Management,* March 1991, pp. 191–211.
19. See, for example, Michael E. Porter, *Competitive Strategy: Techniques for Analyzing Industries and Competitors* (New York: Free Press, 1980); Michael E. Porter, *Competitive Advantage: Creating and Sustaining Superior Performance* (New York: Free Press, 1985); Gregory G. Dess and Peter S. Davis, "Porter's (1980) Generic Strategies as Determinants of Strategic Group Membership and Organizational Performance," *Academy of Management Journal,* September 1984, pp. 467–88; Gregory G. Dess and Peter S. Davis, "Porter's (1980) Generic Strategies and Performance: An Empirical Examination with American Data—Part I: Testing Porter," *Organization Studies,* No. 1, 1986, pp. 37–55; Gregory G. Dess and Peter S. Davis, "Porter's (1980) Generic Strategies and Performance: An Empirical Examination with American Data—Part II: Performance Implications," *Organization Studies,* No. 3, 1986, pp. 255–61; Michael E. Porter,

"From Competitive Advantage to Corporate Strategy," *Harvard Business Review,* May–June 1987, pp. 43–59; Alan I. Murray, "A Contingency View of Porter's 'Generic Strategies,' <KC–6>," *Academy of Management Review,* July 1988, pp. 390–400; Charles W.L. Hill, "Differentiation versus Low Cost or Differentiation and Low Cost: A Contingency Framework," *Academy of Management Review,* July 1988, pp. 401–12; Ingolf Bamberger, "Developing Competitive Advantage in Small and Medium-Sized Firms," *Long Range Planning,* October 1989, pp. 80–88; and Michael E. Porter, "Know Your Place," *Inc.,* September 1991, pp. 90–93.

20. Dean M. Schroeder and Alan G. Robinson, "America's Most Successful Export to Japan: Continuous Improvement Programs," *Sloan Management Review,* Spring 1991, pp. 67–81; and Richard J. Schonenberger, "Is Strategy Strategic? Impact of Total Quality Management on Strategy," *Academy of Management Executive,* August 1992, pp. 80–87.

21. Celine Bak, "Lessons From the Veterans of TQM," *Canadian Business Review,* Winter 1992. Reprinted with permission, The Conference Board of Canada.

22. Banning Kent Lary, "An 'Instinct' For Computer Success," *Nation's Business,* April 1991, pp. 46–48; Hal Lancaster and Michael Allen, "Dell Computer Battles Its Rivals with a Lean Machine," *Wall Street Journal,* March 30, 1992, p. B3; Peter H. Lewis, "Michael Dell Says He's More Than Ready for a Good Fight," *New York Times,* July 5, 1992, p. F12 and Julie Pitta, "Why Dell Is a Survivor," *Forbes,* October 12, 1992, pp. 82–91.

23. Wendy Stueck, "The Making of a Screen Star," *The Globe & Mail,* January 23, 1995.

24. See, for example, J. Barton Cunningham and Joe Lischeron, "Defining Entrepreneurship," *Journal of Small Business Management,* January 1991, pp. 45–61.

25. Adapted from Howard H. Stevenson, M.J. Roberts, and H.I. Grousbeck, *New Business Ventures and the Entrepreneur* (Homewood, Ill.: Irwin, 1989).

26. See, for instance, Thomas M. Begley and David P. Boyd, "A Comparison of Entrepreneurs and Managers of Small Business Firms," *Journal of Management,* Spring 1987, pp. 99–108.

27. John A. Hornaday, "Research about Living Entrepreneurs," in Calvin A. Kent, Donald L. Sexton, and Karl H. Vesper, eds., *Encyclopedia of Entrepreneurship* (Englewood Cliffs, N.J.: Prentice-Hall, 1982), p. 28.

28. Robert H. Brockhaus, Sr., "The Psychology of the Entrepreneur," in Kent, Sexton, and Vesper (eds.), *Encyclopedia of Entrepreneurship,* pp. 41–49.

Chapter 4

1. Andrew Tanzer, "Studying at the Feet of the Masters, *Forbes,* May 10, 1993, p. 43.

2. John Diffenbach, "Corporate Environmental Analysis in Large U.S. Corporations," *Long Range Planning,* June 1983, pp. 107–16; Subhash C. Jain, "Environmental Scanning in U.S. Corporations," *Long Range Planning,* April 1984, pp. 117–28; Leonard M. Fuld, Monitoring the Competition (New York: John Wiley & Sons, 1988); and Elmer H. Burack and Nicholas J. Mathys, "Environmental Scanning Improves Strategic Planning," *Personnel Administrator,* April 1989, pp. 82–87.

3. William L. Renfro and James L. Morrison, "Detecting Signals of Change," *Futurist,* August 1984, p. 49.

4. Benjamin Gilad, "The Role of Organized Competitive Intelligence in Corporate Strategy," *Columbia Journal of World Business,* Winter 1989, pp. 29–35; Betsy D. Gelb, Mary Jane Saxton, George M. Zinkhan, and Nancy D. Albers, "Competitive Intelligence: Insights from Executives," *Business Horizons,* January–February 1991, pp. 43–47; Leonard Fuld, "A Recipe for Business Intelligence," *Journal of Business Strategy,* January–February 1991, pp. 12–17; Gary B. Roush, "A Program for Sharing Corporate Intelligence," *Journal of Business Strategy,* January–February 1991, pp. 4–7; and Richard S. Teitelbaum, "The New Role for Intelligence," *Fortune,* November 2, 1992, pp. 104–7.

5. Robichaux, "'Competitor Intelligence': A Grapevine to Rivals' Secrets."

6. Mark Stevenson, "Waste Not," *Canadian Business,* January 1994. Reprinted by permission. Copyright 1995.

7. Robert Matas, "Fierce Contest has Retailers Using Guerilla Tactics," *The Globe & Mail,* December 30, 1994.

8. Manuel Werner, "Planning for Uncertain Futures: Building Commitment through Scenario Planning," *Business Horizons,* May–June 1990, pp. 55–58.

9. This section is based on Bruce Brocka and M. Suzanne Brocka, *Quality Management* (Homewood, Ill.: Business One Irwin, 1992), pp. 231–36; George A. Weimer, "Benchmarking Maps the Route to Quality," *Industry Week,* July 20, 1992, pp. 54–55; Jeremy Main, "How to Steal the Best Ideas Around," *Fortune,*

October 19, 1992, pp. 102–6; and Howard Rothman, "You Need Not Be Big to Benchmark," *Nation's Business,* December 1992, pp. 64–65.
10. Linda J. Shinn and M. Sue Sturgeon, "Budgeting from Ground Zero," *Association Management,* September 1990, pp. 45–58.
11. Peter A. Pyhrr, "Zero–Based Budgeting," *Harvard Business Review,* November–December 1970, pp. 111–18.
12. Virendra S. Sherlekar and Burton V. Dean, "An Evaluation of the Initial Year of Zero–Based Budgeting in the Federal Government," *Management Science,* August 1980, pp. 750–72.
13. John V. Pearson and Ray J. Michael, "Zero–Based Budgeting: A Technique for Planned Organizational Decline," *Long Range Planning,* June 1981, pp. 68–76.
14. See Harold E. Fearon, William A. Ruch, Vincent G. Reuter, C. David Wieters, and Ross R. Reck, *Fundamentals of Production/Operations Management,* 3rd ed. (St. Paul, Minn.: West Publishing, 1986), p. 97.
15. See, for example, Sarah Stiansen, "Breaking Even," *Success,* November 1988, p. 16.
16. Stephen E. Barndt and Davis W. Carvey, *Essentials of Operations Management* (Englewood Cliffs, N.J.: Prentice-Hall, 1982), p. 134.

Chapter 5

1. Nicole Parton, "Clubs Doing the Right Thing," *The Vancouver Sun,* May 19, 1995.
2. William Pounds, "The Process of Problem Finding," *Industrial Management Review,* Fall 1969, pp. 1–19.
3. Roger J. Volkema, "Problem Formulation: Its Portrayal in the Texts," *Organizational Behavior Teaching Review,* Vol. 11, No. 3 (1986–87), pp. 113–26.
4. See Herbert A. Simon, "Rationality in Psychology and Economics," *Journal of Business,* October 1986, pp. 209–24; and Ann Langley, "In Search of Rationality: The Purposes Behind the Use of Formal Analysis in Organizations," *Administrative Science Quarterly,* December 1989, pp. 598–631.
5. Fremont A. Shull, Jr., Andre L. Delbecq, and Larry L. Cummings, *Organizational Decision Making* (New York: McGraw-Hill, 1970), p. 151.
6. A few of the more enlightening of these would include Michael D. Cohen, James G. March, and Johan P. Olsen, "A Garbage Can Model of Organizational Choice," *Administrative Science Quarterly,* March 1972, pp. 1–25; Henry Mintzberg, Duru Raisinghani, and Andre Theoret, "The Structure of 'Unstructured' Decision Processes," *Administrative Science Quarterly,* June 1976, pp. 246–75; Karl E. Weick, *The Social Psychology of Organizing,* rev. ed. (Reading, Mass.: Addison-Wesley, 1979); Anna Grandori, "A Prescriptive Contingency View of Organizational Decision Making," *Administrative Science Quarterly,* June 1984, pp. 192–209; and Paul C. Nutt, "Types of Organizational Decision Processes," *Administrative Science Quarterly,* September 1984, pp. 414–50.
7. James G. March, "Decision-Making Perspective: Decisions in Organizations and Theories of Choice," in Andrew H. Van de Ven and William F. Joyce, eds., *Perspectives on Organization Design and Behavior* (New York: Wiley–Interscience, 1981), pp. 232–33.
8. See Neil McK. Agnew and John L. Brown, "Bounded Rationality: Fallible Decisions in Unbounded Decision Space," *Behavioral Science,* July 1986, pp. 148–61; Bruce E. Kaufman, "A New Theory of Satisficing," *Journal of Behavioral Economics,* Spring 1990, pp. 35–51; and David R.A. Skidd, "Revisiting Bounded Rationality," *Journal of Management Inquiry,* December 1992, pp. 343–47.
9. H.A. Simon, *Administrative Behavior,* 3rd ed. (New York: Free Press, 1976).
10. Based on Karen Lowry Miller and Hiromi Uchida, "The Boomers Take Over in Japan," *Business Week,* October 25, 1993, p. 129.
11. Michael Salter, "Full Throttle," *Report on Business,* April 1995.
12. "This Meeting Will Come to Order," *Time,* December 6, 1985.
13. Irving L. Janis, *Victims of Groupthink* (Boston: Houghton Mifflin, 1972).
14. Irving L. Janis, *Groupthink* (Boston: Houghton Mifflin, 1982); C.R. Leana, "A Partial Test of Janis' Groupthink Model: Effects of Group Cohesiveness and Leader Behavior on Defective Decision Making," *Journal of Management,* Spring 1985, pp. 5–17; and G. Morehead and J.R. Montanari, "An Empirical Investigation of the Groupthink Phenomenon," *Human Relations,* May 1986, pp. 399–410.
15. Andre L. Delbecq, Andrew H. Van de Ven, and David H. Gustafson, *Group Techniques for Program Planning and A Guide to Nominal and Delphi Processes* (Glenview, Ill.: Scott, Foresman, 1975).
16. See, for example, Timothy W. Costello and Sheldon S. Zalkind, eds., *Psychology in Administration: A Research Orientation* (Englewood Cliffs, N.J.: Prentice-Hall, 1963), pp. 429–30; Robert A.

Cooke and John A. Kernaghan, "Estimating the Difference between Group versus Individual Performance on Problem-Solving Tasks," *Group and Organization Studies,* September 1987, pp. 319–42; and Larry K. Michaelsen, Warren E. Watson, and Robert H. Black, "A Realistic Test of Individual versus Group Consensus Decision Making," *Journal of Applied Psychology,* October 1989, pp. 834–39.

17. Shull, Delbecq, and Cummings, *Organizational Decision Making,* p. 151.
18. A.F. Osborn, *Applied Imagination: Principles and Procedures of Creative Thinking* (New York: Scribners, 1941).
19. The following discussion is based on Andre L. Delbecq, A.H. Van de Ven, and D.H. Gustafson, *Group Techniques for Program Planning: A Guide to Nominal and Delphi Processes* (Glenview, Ill.: Scott, Foresman, 1975).
20. See A.R. Dennis, J.F. George, L.M. Jessup, J.F. Nunamaker, Jr., and D.R. Vogel, "Information Technology to Support Group Work," *MIS Quarterly,* December 1988, pp. 591–619; D.W. Straub and R.A. Beauclair, "Current and Future Uses of Group Decision Support System Technology: Report on a Recent Empirical Study," *Journal of Management Information Systems,* Summer 1988, pp. 101–16; J. Bartimo, "At These Shouting Matches, No One Says a Word," *Business Week,* June 11, 1990, p. 78; and M.S. Poole, M. Holmes, and G. DeSanctis, "Conflict Management in a Computer-Supported Meeting Environment," *Management Science,* August 1991, pp. 926–53.
21. See William M. Bulkeley, "<EI0.2>'Computerizing' Dull Meetings Is Touted As an Antidote to the Mouth That Bored," *Wall Street Journal,* January 28, 1992, p. B1.
22. This section is substantially based on Ellen P. Jackofsky, John W. Slocum, Jr., and Sara J. McQuaid, "Cultural Values and the CEO: Alluring Companions?" *Academy of Management Executive,* February 1988, pp. 39–49.

Chapter 6

1. Tim Richman, "Reorganizing for Growth," *INC.*, January 1991, pp. 110–11.
2. Sally Ritchie, "Life in the Fast Lane," *The Globe & Mail,* June 8, 1993.
3. Stephen P. Robbins, *Organization Theory: Structure, Design, and Applications,* 3rd ed. (Englewood Cliffs, N.J.: Prentice-Hall, 1990), Chapter 4.
4. Charles Perrow, *Complex Organizations: A Critical Essay* (Glenview, Ill.: Scott, Foresman, 1972), p. 59. See also Robbins, *Organization Theory: Structure, Design and Applications,* pp. 312–14.
5. See, for instance, Brian S. Moskal, "Supervisors, Begone!" *Industry Week,* June 20, 1988, p. 32; and Gregory A. Patterson, "Auto Assembly Lines Enter a New Era," *Wall Street Journal,* December 28, 1988, p. A–2.
6. The matrix organization is an obvious example of an organization design that breaks the unity of command. See, for instance, David I. Cleland, ed., *Matrix Management Systems Handbook* (New York: Van Nostrand Reinhold, 1984); and Erik W. Larson and David H. Gobeli, "Matrix Management: Contradictions and Insights," *California Management Review,* Summer 1987, pp. 126–38.
7. Stanley Milgram, *Obedience to Authority* (New York, NY: Harper & Row, 1974).
8. See, for instance, David Kipnis, *The Powerholders* (Chicago: University of Chicago Press, 1976); Jeffrey Pfeffer, *Power in Organizations* (Marshfield, Mass.: Pitman Publishing, 1981); Henry Mintzberg, *Power In and Around Organizations* (Englewood Cliffs, N.J.: Prentice-Hall, 1983); and David W. Ewing, "Do It My Way or You're Fired": *Employee Rights and the Changing Role of Management Prerogatives* (New York: John Wiley, 1983).
9. Steven N. Brenner and Early A. Molander, "Is the Ethics of Business Changing?" *Harvard Business Review,* January-February 1977, pp. 57–71.
10. Herbert C. Kelman and Lee H. Lawrence, "American Response to the Trial of Lt. William L. Calley," *Psychology Today,* June 1972, pp. 41–45, 78–81.
11. See John R.P. French, Jr. and Bertram Raven, "The Bases of Social Power," in Dorwin Cartwright and A.F. Zander, eds., *Group Dynamics: Research and Theory* (New York: Harper & Row, 1960), pp. 607–23; Philip M. Podsakoff and Chester A. Schreisheim, "Field Studies of French and Raven's Bases of Power: Critique, Reanalysis, and Suggestions for Future Research," *Psychological Bulletin,* May 1985, pp. 387–411; Ramesh K. Shukla, "Influence of Power Bases in Organizational Decision Making: A Contingency Model," *Decision Sciences,* July 1982, pp. 450–70; Dean E. Frost and Anthony J. Stahelski, "The Systematic Measurement of French and Raven's Bases of Social Power in Workgroups," *Journal of Applied Social Psychology,* April 1988, pp. 375–89; and Timothy

R. Hinkin and Chester A. Schriesheim, "Development and Application of New Scales to Measure the French and Raven (1959) Bases of Social Power," *Journal of Applied Psychology,* August 1989, pp. 561–67.
12. Lyndall Urwick, *The Elements of Administration* (New York: Harper & Row, 1944), pp. 52–53.
13. Quoted in Jim Braham, "Money Talks," *Industry Week,* April 17, 1989, p. 23.
14. John S. McClenahen, "Managing More People in the '90s," *Industry Week,* March 20, 1989, p. 30.
15. David Van Fleet, "Span of Management Research and Issues," *Academy of Management Journal,* September 1983, pp. 546–52.
16. John H. Sheridan, "Sizing Up Corporate Staffs," *Industry Week,* November 21, 1988, p. 47.
17. Tom Burns and G.M. Stalker, *The Management of Innovation* (London: Taristock, 1961).
18. Alfred D. Chandler, Jr., *Strategy and Structure: Chapters in the History of the Industrial Enterprise* (Cambridge, Mass.: MIT Press, 1962).
19. See, for instance, Raymond E. Miles and Charles C. Snow, *Organizational Strategy, Structure, and Process* (New York: McGraw-Hill, 1978); and Herman L. Boschken, "Strategy and Structure: Reconceiving the Relationship," *Journal of Management,* March 1990, pp. 135–50.
20. See, for instance, Peter M. Blau and Richard A. Schoenherr, *The Structure of Organizations* (New York: Basic Books, 1971); D.S. Pugh, "The Aston Program of Research: Retrospect and Prospect," in A.H. Van de Ven and W.F. Joyce, eds., *Perspectives on Organization Design and Behavior* (New York: John Wiley, 1981), pp. 135–66; and R.Z. Gooding and J. A. Wagner III, "A Meta-Analytic Review of the Relationship between Size and Performance: The Productivity and Efficiency of Organizations and Their Subunits," *Administrative Science Quarterly,* December 1985, pp. 462–81.
21. C. Chet Miller, William H. Glick, Yau–De Wang, and George Huber, "Understanding Technology–Structure Relationships: Theory Development and Meta-Analytic Theory Testing," *Academy of Management Journal,* June 1991, pp. 370–99.
22. Joan Woodward, *Industrial Organization: Theory and Practice* (London: Oxford University Press, 1965); and Charles Perrow, *Organizational Analysis: A Sociological Perspective* (Belmont, Calif.: Wadsworth, 1970).
23. Donald Gerwin, "Relationships between Structure and Technology," in P.C. Nystrom and W.H. Starbuck, eds., *Handbook of Organizational Design,* Vol. 2 (New York: Oxford University Press, 1981), pp. 3–38; and Denise M. Rousseau and R.A. Cooke, "Technology and Structure: The Concrete, Abstract, and Activity Systems of Organizations," *Journal of Management,* Fall-Winter 1984, pp. 345–61.
24. See Robbins, *Organization Theory: Structure, Design, and Applications,* pp. 210–32.
25. Brian Dumaine, "Payoff from the New Management," *Fortune,* December 13, 1993, pp. 103–10.
26. Ilan Vertinsky, David K. Tse, Donald A. Wehrung, and Kam–hon Lee, "Organizational Design and Management Norms: A Comparative Study of Managers' Perceptions in the People's Republic of China, Hong Kong, and Canada," *Journal of Management,* December 1990, pp. 853–67.
27. Geert Hofstede, "Motivation, Leadership, and Organization: Do American Theories Apply Abroad?" *Organizational Dynamics,* Summer 1980, p. 60.

Chapter 7

1. Brian Christmas, "Allied Forces," *The Globe & Mail,* March 6, 1995.
2. Robin Stuart-Kotze and Donald Rumball, *The State of Small Business and Entrepreneurship in Atlantic Canada—1993,* (Moncton, N.B.: ACOA, 1993).
3. U.S. Small Business Administration, *The State of Small Business: A Report of the President* (Washington, DC: GPO, 1986).
4. Henry Mintzberg, *Structure in Fives: Designing Effective Organizations* (Englewood Cliffs, N.J.: Prentice-Hall, 1983), p. 157.
5. See, for instance, Jay Galbraith, "Matrix Organization Designs: How to Combine Functional and Project Forms," *Business Horizons,* February 1971, pp. 29–40; and Lawton R. Burns, "Matrix Management in Hospitals: Testing Theories of Structure and Development," *Administrative Science Quarterly,* September 1989, pp. 349–68.
6. Carla Rapoport, "A Tough Swede Invades the U.S.," *Fortune,* June 29, 1992, pp. 76–79.
7. See, for example, Neal E. Boudette, "Networks to Dismantle Old Structures," *Industry Week,* January 16, 1989, pp. 27–31; Walter W. Powell, "Neither Market Nor Hierarchy: Network Forms of Organization," in B.M. Staw and L.L. Cummings, eds., *Research in Organizational Behavior,*

Vol. 12 (Greenwich, Conn.: JAI Press, 1990), pp. 295–336; and Michael Selz, "Small Companies Thrive by Taking Over Some Specialized Tasks for Big Concerns," *Wall Street Journal,* September 11, 1991, p. B1.
8. Barnard Wysocki, Jr., "Cross–Border Alliances Become Favorite Way to Crack New Markets," *Wall Street Journal,* March 26, 1990, p. A1.
9. William J. Altier, "Task Forces: An Effective Management Tool," *Sloan Management Review,* Spring 1986, pp. 69–76.
10. Ronald Henkoff, "Getting Beyond Downsizing," *Fortune,* January 10, 1994, pp. 58–62.
11. Ibid.
12. John A. Byrne, "The Horizontal Corporation," *Business Week,* December 20, 1993, pp. 76–81.
13. Ibid.
14. Ibid.
15. Ibid.
16. Thomas A. Stewart. "Welcome to the Revolution," *Fortune,* December 13, 1993, p. 66; and Noel M. Tichey, "Revolutionize Your Company," *Fortune,* December 13, 1993, pp. 114–18.
17. "A Master Class of Radical Change," *Fortune,* December 13, 1993, p. 83; and Byrne, "The Horizontal Corporation," p. 78.
18. "A Master Class of Radical Change," p. 83.
19. Ibid., p. 88.
20. Byrne, "The Horizontal Corporation," p. 76.
21. Ibid.
22. Ibid., p. 80.
23. Ibid.
24. Ronald Henkoff, "Make Your Office More Productive," *Fortune,* February 25, 1991, p. 84.
25. Ibid.
26. Linda Smircich, "Concepts of Culture and Organizational Analysis," *Administrative Science Quarterly,* September 1983, p. 339.
27. Alice M. Sapienza, "Believing Is Seeing: How Culture Influences the Decisions Top Managers Make," in Ralph H. Kilmann et. al., eds., *Gaining Control of the Corporate Culture* (San Francisco: Jossey-Bass, 1985), p. 68.
28. Based on Geert Hofstede, B. Neuijen, D.D. Ohayv, and G. Sanders, "Measuring Organizational Culture: A Qualitative and Quantitative Study Across Twenty Cases," *Administrative Science Quarterly,* June 1990, pp. 286–316; and Charles A. O'Reilly III, J. Chatman, and D.F. Caldwell, "People and Organizational Culture: A Profile Comparison Approach to Assessing Person–Organization Fit," *Academy of Management Journal,* September 1991, pp. 487–516.
29. Donald C. Hambrick and Sidney Finkelstein, "Managerial Discretion: A Bridge between Polar Views of Organizational Outcomes," in L.L. Cummings and B.M. Staw, eds., *Research in Organizational Behavior,* Vol. 9 (Greenwich, Conn.: JAI Press, 1987), pp. 384–85.
30. See, for example, Ricky W. Griffin, "Toward an Integrated Theory of Task Design," in Cummings and Staw, eds., *Research in Organizational Behavior,* pp. 79–120; and Michael Campion, "Interdisciplinary Approaches to Job Design: A Constructive Replication with Extensions," *Journal of Applied Psychology,* August 1988, pp. 467–81.
31. J. Richard Hackman and Greg R. Oldham, "Development of the Job Diagnostic Survey," *Journal of Applied Psychology,* April 1975, pp. 159–70.
32. Ibid.
33. J. Richard Hackman, "Work Design," in J. Richard Hackman and J. Lloyd Suttle, eds., *Improving Life at Work* (Glenview, Ill.: Scott, Foresman, 1977), p. 129.
34. General support for the JCM is reported in Yitzhak Fried and Gerald R. Ferris, "The Validity of the Job Characteristics Model: A Review and Meta-Analysis," *Personnel Psychology,* Summer 1987, pp. 287–322.
35. Ibid.
36. Hackman, "Work Design," pp. 136–40.

Chapter 8

1. Bruce Little, *The Globe & Mail,* May 18, 1993.
2. Elmer H. Burack, "Corporate Business and Human Resource Planning Practices: Strategic Issues and Concerns," *Organizational Dynamics,* Summer 1986, pp. 73–87.
3. David A. De Cenzo and Stephen P. Robbins, *Human Resource Management: Concepts and Practices,* 4th ed. (New York: John Wiley and Sons, Inc., 1994), p. 136.
4. Thomas J. Bergmann and M. S. Taylor, "College Recruitment: What Attracts Students to Organizations?" *Personnel,* May–June 1984, pp. 34–46.
5. Judith R. Gordon, *Human Resource Management: A Practical Approach* (Boston: Allyn and Bacon, 1986), p. 170.
6. See, for example, Jean Powell Kirnan, John A. Farley, and Kurt F. Geisinger, "The Relationship between Recruiting Source, Applicant Quality, and Hire Performance: An Analysis by Sex, Ethnicity, and Age," *Personnel Psychology,* Summer 1989, pp. 293–308.
7. Joseph Spiers, "Upper Middle Class Woes," *For-

tune, December 27, 1993, p. 80.
8. See, for example, Leonard Greenhalgh, Anne T. Lawrence, and Robert I. Sutton, "Determinants of Work Force Reduction Strategies in Declining Organizations," *Academy of Management Review,* April 1988, pp. 241–54.
9. James Parker, "Truce Tames Chemical Warfare," *The Globe & Mail,* January 17, 1995.
10. James J. Asher, "The Biographical Item: Can It Be Improved?" *Personnel Psychology,* Summer 1972, p. 266.
11. George W. England, *Development and Use of Weighted Application Blanks,* rev. ed. (Minneapolis: Industrial Relations Center, University of Minnesota, 1971).
12. John Aberth, "Pre–Employment Testing Is Losing Favor," *Personnel Journal,* September 1986, pp. 96–104.
13. Chris Lee, "Testing Makes a Comeback," *Training,* December 1988, pp. 49–59.
14. Ibid., p. 50.
15. Edwin E. Ghiselli, "The Validity of Aptitude Tests in Personnel Selection," *Personnel Psychology,* Winter 1973, p. 475.
16. G. Grimsley and H.F. Jarrett, "The Relation of Managerial Achievement to Test Measures Obtained in the Employment Situation: Methodology and Results," *Personnel Psychology,* Spring 1973, pp. 31–48; and Abraham K. Korman, "The Prediction of Managerial Performance: A Review," *Personnel Psychology,* Summer 1968, pp. 295–322.
17. See "Resume Falsehoods," *Boardroom Reports,* May 1, 1989, p. 15; and Joan E. Rigdon, "Deceptive Resumes Can Be Door–Openers But Can Become an Employee's Undoing," *Wall Street Journal,* June 17, 1992, p. B1.
18. Robert L. Dipboye, *Selection Interviews: Process Perspectives* (Cincinnati, Ohio: South–Western Publishing, 1992), p. 6.
19. See, for instance, Richard D. Arvey and James E. Campion, "The Employment Interview: A Summary and Review of Recent Research," *Personnel Psychology,* Summer 1982, pp. 281–322; and Michael M. Harris, "Reconsidering the Employment Interview: A Review of Recent Literature and Suggestions for Future Research," *Personnel Psychology,* Winter 1989, pp. 691–726.
20. Dipboye, *Selection Interviews,* p. 180.
21. See, for instance, Eugene C. Mayfield in Neal Schmitt, "Social and Situational Determinants of Interview Decisions: Implications for Employment Interview," *Personnel Psychology,* Spring 1976, p. 81; Arvey and Campion, "The Employment Interview"; Milton D. Hakel, "Employment Interview," in K.M. Rowland and G.R. Ferris, eds., *Personnel Management: New Perspectives* (Boston: Allyn and Bacon, 1982), pp. 129–55; Edward C. Webster, *The Employment Interview: A Social Judgment Process* (Schomberg, Ontario: S.I.P. Publications, 1982), Harris, "Reconsidering the Employment Interview"; and Amanda Peek Phillips and Robert L. Dipboye, "Correlational Tests of Predictions from a Process Model of the Interview," *Journal of Applied Psychology,* February 1989, pp. 41–52.
22. De Cenzo and Robbins, *Human Resource Management,* pp. 208–9.
23. See Irwin L. Goldstein, "The Application Blank: How Honest Are the Responses?" *Journal of Applied Psychology,* October 1971, pp. 491–92; and Winifred Yu, "Firms Tighten Resume Checks of Applicants," *Wall Street Journal,* August 20, 1985, p. 27.
24. Paul M. Muchinsky, "The Use of Reference Reports in Personnel Selection: A Review and Evaluation," *Journal of Occupational Psychology,* April 1979, pp. 287–97; and R.R. Reilly and G.T. Chao, "Validity and Fairness of Some Alternative Employee Selection Procedures," *Personnel Psychology,* Spring 1982, pp. 1–62.
25. Cited in "If You Can't Say Something Nice...," *Wall Street Journal,* March 4, 1988, p. 25.
26. Mayfield in Schmitt, "Social and Situational Determinants of Interview Decisions."
27. Mark E. Mendenhall, E. Dunbar, and Gary R. Oddou, "Expatriate Selection, *Training,* and Career-Pathing: A Review and Critique," *Human Resource Management,* Spring 1987, pp. 331–45.
28. Cited in "The Five Factors That Make for Airline Accidents," *Fortune,* May 22, 1989, p. 80.
29. Donald E. Super and Douglas T. Hall, "Career Development: Exploration and Planning," in Mark R. Rosenzweig and Lyman W. Porter, eds., *Annual Review of Psychology,* Vol. 29 (Palo Alto, Calif.: Annual Reviews, 1978), p. 334.
30. See, for instance, Elmer H. Burack, "The Sphinx's Riddle: Life and Career Cycles," *Training and Development Journal,* April 1984, pp. 53–61; and Douglas T. Hall and Associates, *Career Development in Organizations* (San Francisco: Jossey-Bass, 1986).
31. James A. Breaugh, "Realistic Job Previews: A Critical Appraisal and Future Research Directions," *Academy of Management Review,* October 1983, pp. 612–19; and Steven L. Premack and John P. Wanous, "A Meta-Analysis of Realistic

Job Preview Experiments," *Journal of Applied Psychology,* November 1985, pp. 706–19.
32. See, for example, Michael A. Verespej, "Partnership in the Trenches," *Industry Week,* October 17, 1988, pp. 56–64; and "Unions and Management Are in a Family Way," *U.S. News & World Report,* June 12, 1989, p. 24.
33. See, for example, S.L. Premack and J.P. Wanous, "A Meta-Analysis of Realistic Job Preview Experiments," *Journal of Applied Psychology,* November 1985, pp. 706–20.
34. Robert Bolt, "True Grit," *Report on Business,* May 1995.
35. The idea for this class exercise was directly influenced by the class exercise in De Cenzo and Robbins, *Human Resource Management,* pp. 149–50.

Chapter 9

1. Mick Lowe, "Steel Resolve," *The Financial Post Magazine,* April 1995.
2. Timothy Pritchard, "Peace Breaks Out on the Shop Floor," *The Globe & Mail,* July 6, 1993.
3. The idea for these metaphors came from Peter B. Vaill, *Managing as a Performing Art: New Ideas for a World of Chaotic Change* (San Francisco: Jossey-Bass, 1989).
4. Kurt Lewin, *Field Theory in Social Science* (New York: Harper & Row, 1951).
5. See, for instance, Tom Peters, *Thriving on Chaos* (New York: Alfred A. Knopf, 1987).
6. L. Coch and J.R.P French, Jr., "Overcoming Resistance to Change," *Human Relations,* Vol. 1, No. 4 (1948), pp. 512–32.
7. Jennifer Wells, "We Can Get It For You Wholesale," *Report on Business,* March 1995.
8. Peters, *Thriving on Chaos,* p. 3.
9. Ibid.
10. See, for example, Barry M. Staw, "Counterforces to Change," in Paul S. Goodman, and Associates, eds., *Change in Organizations* (San Francisco, Calif.: Jossey-Bass Publishers, 1982), pp. 87–121.
11. John P. Kotter and Leonard A. Schlesinger, "Choosing Strategies for Change," *Harvard Business Review,* March–April 1979, pp. 107–9.
12. Ibid., pp. 106–14.
13. Dan Ciampa, T*otal Quality: A User's Guide for Implementation* (Reading, Mass.: Addison-Wesley, 1992), pp. 100–104.
14. Keith H. Hammonds, "Where Did We Go Wrong?," *Business Week,* Quality 1991 Special Issue, p. 38.
15. See, for example, K. Kelly, "3M Run Scared? Forget About It," *Business Week,* September 16, 1991, pp. 59–62; and R. Mitchell, "Masters of Innovation," *Business Week,* April 10, 1989, p. 58.
16. These definitions are based on Teresa M. Amabile, "A Model of Creativity and Innovation in Organizations," in B.M. Staw and L.L. Cummings, eds., *Research in Organizational Behavior,* Vol. 10 (Greenwich, Conn.: JAI Press, 1988), p. 126.
17. Fariborz Damanpour, "Organizational Innovation: A Meta-Analysis of Effects of Determinants and Moderators," *Academy of Management Journal,* September 1991, pp. 555–90.
18. Peter R. Monge, Michael D. Cozzens, and Noshir S. Contractor, "Communication and Motivational Predictors of the Dynamics of Organizational Innovation," *Organization Science,* May 1992, pp. 250–74.
19. See, for instance, Amabile, "A Model of Creativity and Innovation in Organizations," p. 147; Michael Tushman and David Nadler, "Organizing for Innovation," California Management Review, Spring 1986, pp. 74–92; Rosabeth Moss Kanter, "When a Thousand Flowers Bloom: Structural, Collective, and Social Conditions for Innovation in Organization," in Staw and Cummings, eds., *Research in Organizational Behavior,* Vol. 10, pp. 169–211; and Gareth Morgan, "Endangered Species: New Ideas," *Business Month,* April 1989, pp. 75–77.
20. This dilemma is based on Kevin Kelly, "When a Rival's Trade Secret Crosses Your Desk . . . ," *Business Week,* May 20, 1991, p. 48.
21. J.M. Howell and C.A. Higgins, "Champions of Change," *Business Quarterly,* Spring 1990, pp. 31–32.

Chapter 10

1. Based on Myrna Hellerman, "Giving Executives a Field Day," *Working Woman,* March 1992, pp. 37–40.
2. S.J. Breckler, "Empirical Validation of Affect, Behavior, and Cognition as Distinct Components of Attitude," *Journal of Personality and Social Psychology,* May 1984, pp. 1191–1205.
3. Paul P. Brooke, Jr., Daniel W. Russell, and James L. Price, "Discriminant Validation of Measures of Job Satisfaction, Job Involvement, and Organizational Commitment," *Journal of Applied Psychology,* May 1988, pp. 139–45.
4. Icek Ajzen and Martin Fishbein, *Understanding Attitudes and Predicting Behavior* (Englewood Cliffs, N.J.: Prentice-Hall, 1980).
5. Leon Festinger, *A Theory of Cognitive Dissonance* (Stanford, Calif.: Stanford University Press, 1957).

6. Ibid.
7. Victor H. Vroom, *Work and Motivation* (New York: John Wiley, 1964); and M.T. Iaffaldano and P.M. Muchinsky, "Job Satisfaction and Job Performance: A Meta-Analysis," *Psychological Bulletin,* March 1985, pp. 251–73.
8. Julian B. Rotter, "Generalized Expectancies for Internal versus External Control of Reinforcement," *Psychological Monographs,* Vol. 80, No. 609 (1966).
9. See, for example, Jean B. Herman, "Are Situational Contingencies Limiting Job Attitude–Job Performance Relationship?" *Organizational Behavior and Human Performance,* October 1973, pp. 208–24; M.M. Petty, Gail W. McGee, and Jerry W. Cavender, "A Meta-Analysis of the Relationships between Individual Job Satisfaction and Individual Performance," *Academy of Management Review,* October 1984, pp. 712–21; Charles N. Greene, "The Satisfaction-Performance Controversy," *Business Horizons,* February 1972, pp. 31–41; Edward E. Lawler III, *Motivation and Organizations* (Monterey, Calif.: Brooks/Cole, 1973).
10. See, for instance, Dennis W. Organ and Charles N. Greene, "Role Ambiguity, Locus of Control, and Work Satisfaction," *Journal of Applied Psychology,* February 1974, pp. 101–02; and Terence R. Mitchell, Charles M. Smyser, and Stan E. Weed, "Locus of Control: Supervision and Work Satisfaction," *Academy of Management Journal,* September 1975, pp. 623–31.
11. T. Adorno et al., *The Authoritarian Personality* (New York: Harper & Brothers, 1950).
12. Harrison Gough, "Personality and Personality Assessment," in Marvin D. Dunnette, ed., *Handbook of Industrial and Organizational Psychology* (Skokie, Ill.: Rand McNally, 1976), p. 579.
13. R.G. Vleeming, "Machiavellianism: A Preliminary Review," *Psychological Reports,* February 1979, pp. 295–310.
14. Based on Joel Brockner, *Self–Esteem at Work* (Lexington, Mass.: Lexington Books, 1988), Chapters 1-4.
15. See M. Snyder, *Public Appearances/Private Realities: The Psychology of Self-Monitoring* (New York: W.H. Freeman, 1987).
16. John Heinzl, *Report on Business,* April 1995.
17. R.N. Taylor and M.D. Dunnette, "Influence of Dogmatism, Risk-Taking Propensity, and Intelligence on Decision-Making Strategies for a Sample of Industrial Managers," *Journal of Applied Psychology,* August 1974, pp. 420–23.
18. Ann J. Nelson, "Get a Life," *Working Woman,* November 1993, p. 57–58.
19. Irving L. Janis and Leon Mann, *Decision Making: A Psychological Analysis of Conflict, Choice, and Commitment* (New York: Free Press, 1977).
20. N. Kogan and M.A. Wallach, "Group Risk Taking as a Function of Members' Anxiety and Defensiveness," *Journal of Personality,* March 1967, pp. 50–63.
21. John L. Holland, *Making Vocational Choices: A Theory of Vocational Personalities and Work Environments,* 2nd ed. (Englewood Cliffs, N.J.: Prentice-Hall, 1985).
22. See, for example, A.R. Spokane, "A Review of Research on Person-Environment Congruence in Holland's Theory of Careers," *Journal of Vocational Behavior,* June 1985, pp. 306–43; and D. Brown, "The Status of Holland's Theory of Career Choice," *Career Development Journal,* September 1987, pp. 13–23.
23. H.H. Kelley, "Attribution in Social Interaction," in E. Jones et al., eds., *Behavior* (Morristown, N.J.: General Learning Press, 1972).
24. See A.G. Miller and T. Lawson, "The Effect of an Informational Option on the Fundamental Attribution Error," *Personality and Social Psychology Bulletin,* June 1989, pp. 194–204.
25. B.F. Skinner, *Contingencies of Reinforcement* (East Norwalk, Conn.: Appleton-Century-Crofts, 1971).
26. Ibid.
27. A. Bandura, *Social Learning Theory* (Englewood Cliffs, N.J.: Prentice-Hall, 1977).
28. The idea for this exercise came from Jeffrey Gandz and Jane M. Howell, "Confronting Sex Role Stereotypes: The Janis/Jack Jerome Cases," *Organizational Behavior Teaching Review,* Vol. XIII, No. 4 (1988–1989), pp. 103–11.
29. Jennifer Wells, "Winning Colours," *Report on Business,* July 1992.

Chapter 11

1. Martin Dickson, "Back to the Future", *The Financial Times,* May 30, 1994.
2. Solomon E. Asch, "Effects of Group Pressure upon the Modification and Distortion of Judgments," in *Groups, Leadership and Men,* ed. Harold Guetzkow (Pittsburgh: Carnegie Press, 1951), pp. 177–90.
3. See, for instance, E.J. Thomas and C.F. Fink, "Effects of Group Size," *Psychological Bulletin,* July 1963, pp. 371–84; and Marvin E. Shaw, *Group Dynamics: The Psychology of Small Group Behavior,* 3rd ed. (New York: McGraw-Hill, 1981).

4. See Robert Albanese and David D. Van Fleet, "Rational Behavior in Groups: The Free-Riding Tendency," *Academy of Management Review,* April 1985, pp. 244–55.
5. See, for example, L. Berkowitz, "Group Standards, Cohesiveness, and Productivity," *Human Relations,* November 1954, pp. 509–19.
6. Stanley E. Seashore, *Group Cohesiveness in the Industrial Work Group* (Ann Arbor: University of Michigan, Survey Research Center, 1954).
7. Based on Eric Sundstrom, Kenneth P. DeMeuse, and David Futrell, "Work Teams," *American Psychologist,* February 1990, p. 120; and Carl E. Larson and Frank M.J. LaFasto, *TeamWork* (Newbury Park, Calif.: Sage Publications, 1992).
8. Brian Dumaine, "Payoff from the New Management," *Fortune,* December 13, 1993, pp. 103–110.
9. Merle MacIsaac, "Born Again Basket Case," *Canadian Business,* May 1993.
10. See Sundstrom, DeMeuse, and Futrell, "Work Teams"; Larson and LaFasto, *TeamWork;* J. Richard Hackman, ed., *Groups That Work (and Those That Don't)* (San Francisco: Jossey-Bass, 1990); and Dean W. Tjosvold and Mary M. Tjosvold, *Leading the Team Organization* (New York: Lexington Books, 1991).
11. Adapted from Fernando Bartolome, "Nobody Trusts the Boss Completely—Now What?" *Harvard Business Review,* March–April 1989, pp. 135–42.
12. Larson and LaFasto, *TeamWork,* p. 75.
13. Bob Krone, "Total Quality Management: An American Odyssey," *Bureaucrat,* Fall 1990, p. 37.
14. Timothy Pritchard, "The Solid State Factory," *The Globe & Mail,* September 1992.

Chapter 12

1. Michael P. Cronin, "No More Clock Watchers," *Inc.,* February 1994, p. 83.
2. Ralph Katerberg and Gary J. Blau, "An Examination of Level and Direction of Effort and Job Performance," *Academy of Management Journal,* June 1983, pp. 249–57.
3. Abraham Maslow, *Motivation and Personality* (New York: Harper & Row, 1954).
4. See, for example, Edward E. Lawler, III, and J. Lloyd Suttle, "A Causal Correlational Test of the Need Hierarchy Concept," *Organizational Behavior and Human Performance,* April 1972, pp. 265–87; and Douglas T. Hall and Khalil E. Nongaim, "An Examination of Maslow's Need Hierarchy in an Organizational Setting," *Organizational Behavior and Human Performance,* February 1968, pp. 12–35.
5. Douglas McGregor, *The Human Side of Enterprise* (New York: McGraw-Hill, 1960).
6. Frederick Herzberg, Bernard Mausner, and Barbara Snyderman, *The Motivation to Work* (New York: John Wiley, 1959); and Frederick Herzberg, *The Managerial Choice: To Be Effective or To Be Human,* rev. ed. (Salt Lake City: Olympus, 1982).
7. See, for instance, Michael E. Gordon, Norman M. Pryor, and Bob V. Harris, "An Examination of Scaling Bias in Herzberg's Theory of Job Satisfaction," *Organizational Behavior and Human Performance,* February 1974, pp. 106–21; Edwin A. Locke and Roman J. Whiting, "Sources of Satisfaction and Dissatisfaction Among Solid Waste Management Employees," *Journal of Applied Psychology,* April 1974, pp. 145–56; and John B. Miner, *Theories of Organizational Behavior* (Hinsdale, Ill.: Dryden Press, 1980), pp. 76–105.
8. David C. McClelland and David G. Winter, *Motivating Economic Achievement* (New York: Free Press, 1969).
9. McClelland, *Power: The Inner Experience;* David C. McClelland and David H. Burnham, "Power Is the Great Motivator," *Harvard Business Review,* March-April 1976, pp. 100–10.
10. "McClelland: An Advocate of Power," *International Management,* July 1975, pp. 27–29.
11. David Miron and David C. McClelland, "The Impact of Achievement Motivation Training on Small Businesses," *California Management Review,* Summer 1979, pp. 13–28.
12. David C. McClelland, *The Achieving Society* (New York: Van Nostrand Reinhold, 1961); John W. Atkinson and Joel O. Raynor, *Motivation and Achievement* (Washington, D.C.: Winston, 1974); and David C. McClelland, *Power: The Inner Experience* (New York: Irvington, 1975).
13. McClelland, *The Achieving Society.*
14. J. Stacey Adams, "Inequity in Social Exchanges," in Leonard Berkowitz, ed., *Advances in Experimental Social Psychology,* Vol. 2 (New York: Academic Press, 1965), pp. 267–300.
15. "Buzz," *The Globe & Mail,* December 30, 1994.
16. Paul S. Goodman, "An Examination of Referents Used in the Evaluation of Pay," *Organizational Behavior and Human Performance,* October 1974, pp. 170–95; Simcha Ronen, "Equity Perception in Multiple Comparisons: A Field Study," *Human Relations,* April 1986, pp. 333–46; R.W. Scholl, E.A. Cooper, and J.F. McKenna, "Referent Selection in Determining

Equity Perception: Differential Effects on Behavioral and Attitudinal Outcomes," *Personnel Psychology,* Spring 1987, pp. 113–27; and Carol T. Kulik and Maureen L. Ambrose, "Personal and Situational Determinants of Referent Choice," *Academy of Management Review,* April 1992, pp. 212–37.
17. Paul S. Goodman and A. Friedman, "An Examination of Adams' Theory of Inequity," *Administrative Science Quarterly,* September 1971, pp. 271–88.
18. See, for example, Michael R. Carrell, "A Longitudinal Field Assessment of Employee Perceptions of Equitable Treatment," *Organizational Behavior and Human Performance,* February 1978, pp. 108–18; Robert G. Lord and Jeffrey A. Hohenfeld, "Longitudinal Field Assessment of Equity Effects on the Performance of Major League Baseball Players," *Journal of Applied Psychology,* February 1979, pp. 19–26; and John E. Dittrich and Michael R. Carrell, "Organizational Equity Perceptions, Employee Job Satisfaction, and Departmental Absence and Turnover Rates," *Organizational Behavior and Human Performance,* August 1979, pp. 29–40.
19. Paul S. Goodman, "Social Comparison Process in Organizations," in B.M. Staw and G.R. Salancik, eds., *New Directions in Organizational Behavior* (Chicago: St. Clair, 1977), pp. 97–132.
20. Victor H. Vroom, *Work and Motivation* (New York: John Wiley, 1964).
21. See, for example, Herbert G. Heneman, III, and Donald P. Schwab, "Evaluation of Research on Expectancy Theory Prediction of Employee Performance," *Psychological Bulletin,* July 1972, pp. 1–9; and Leon Reinharth and Mahmoud Wahba, "Expectancy Theory as a Predictor of Work Motivation, Effort Expenditure, and Job Performance," *Academy of Management Journal,* September 1975, pp. 502–37.
22. See, for example, Victor H. Vroom, "Organizational Choice: A Study of Pre-and-Postdecision Processes," *Organizational Behavior and Human Performance,* April 1966, pp. 212–25; and Lyman W. Porter and Edward E. Lawler, III, *Managerial Attitudes and Performance* (Homewood, Ill.: Richard D. Irwin, 1968).
23. Among academicians these three variables are typically referred to as valence, instrumentality, and expectancy, respectively.
24. This four-step discussion was adapted from K. F. Taylor, "A Valence–Expectancy Approach to Work Motivation," *Personnel Practice Bulletin,* June 1974, pp. 142–48.
25. See, for instance, Marc Siegall, "The Simplistic Five: An Integrative Framework For Teaching Motivation," *Organizational Behavior Teaching Review,* Vol. 12, No. 4 (1987–88), pp. 141–43.
26. Geert Hofstede, "Motivation, Leadership, and Organizations: Do American Theories Apply Abroad?" *Organizational Dynamics,* Summer 1980, p. 55; and cited in J. Greenwald, "Workers: Risks and Rewards," *Time,* April 15, 1991, p. 42.
27. Itzhak Harpaz, "The Importance of Work Goals: An International Perspective," *Journal of International Business Studies,* First Quarter 1990, pp. 75–93.
28. Gordon Pitts, "The Vision of Saint Hubert," *The Globe & Mail,* May 30, 1995.

Chapter 13

1. Merle MacIsaac, "Wizard of Awe," *Canadian Business,* December 1994.
2. See Shelly A. Kirkpatrick and Edwin A. Locke, "Leadership: Do Traits Matter?" *Academy of Management Executive,* May 1991, pp. 48–60.
3. Ralph M. Stogdill and Alvin E. Coons, eds., *Leader Behavior: Its Description and Measurement,* Research Monograph No. 88 (Columbus: Ohio State University, Bureau of Business Research, 1951). For an updated literature review of the Ohio State research, see Steven Kerr, Chester A. Schriesheim, Charles J. Murphy, and Ralph M. Stogdill, "Toward a Contingency Theory of Leadership Based upon the Consideration and Initiating Structure Literature," *Organizational Behavior and Human Performance,* August 1974, pp. 62–82; and Bruce M. Fisher, "Consideration and Initiating Structure and Their Relationships with Leader Effectiveness: A Meta-Analysis," in F. Hoy, ed., *Proceedings of the 48th Annual Academy of Management Conference,* Anaheim, Calif., 1988, pp. 201–5.
4. R. Kahn and D. Katz, "Leadership Practices in Relation to Productivity and Morale," in D. Cartwright and A. Zander, eds., *Group Dynamics: Research and Theory,* 2nd ed. (Elmsford, N.Y.: Row, Paterson, 1960).
5. Kathryn Leger, "CEO of the Year: Guy Saint-Pierre," *The Financial Post Magazine,* November 1994.
6. Robert R. Blake and Jane S. Mouton, *The Managerial Grid III* (Houston: Gulf Publishing, 1984).
7. L.L. Larson, J.G. Hunt, and R.N. Osborn, "The Great Hi-Hi Leader Behavior Myth: A Lesson from Occam's Razor," *Academy of Management*

Journal, December 1976, pp. 628–41; and Paul C. Nystrom, "Managers and the Hi-Hi Leader Myth," *Academy of Management Journal,* June 1978, pp. 325–31.

8. See, for example, the three styles—autocratic, participative, and laissez-faire—proposed by Kurt Lewin and Ronald Lippitt, "An Experimental Approach to the Study of Autocracy and Democracy: A Preliminary Note," *Sociometry,* No. 1, (1938), 292–380; or the 3–D theory proposed by William J. Reddin, *Managerial Effectiveness* (New York: McGraw-Hill, 1970).

9. Fred E. Fiedler, *A Theory of Leadership Effectiveness* (New York: McGraw-Hill, 1967).

10. Robert J. House, "A Path-Goal Theory of Leader Effectiveness," *Administrative Science Quarterly,* September 1971, pp. 321–38; Robert J. House and Terence R. Mitchell, "Path-Goal Theory of Leadership," *Journal of Contemporary Business,* Autumn 1974, p. 86; and Robert J. House, "Retrospective Comment," in Louis E. Boone and Donald D. Bowen, eds., *The Great Writings in Management and Organizational Behavior,* 2nd ed. (New York: Random House, 1987), pp. 354–64.

11. Lawrence H. Peters, D.D. Hartke, and J.T. Pholmann, "Fiedler's Contingency Theory of Leadership: An Application of the Meta-Analysis Procedures of Schmidt and Hunter," *Psychological Bulletin,* March 1985, pp. 274–85.

12. See, for instance, Robert W. Rice, "Psychometric Properties of the Esteem for the Least Preferred Co-worker (LPC) Scale," *Academy of Management Review,* January 1978, pp. 106–18; and Chester A. Schriesheim, B.D. Bannister, and W.H. Money, "Psychometric Properties of the LPC Scale: An Extension of Rice's Review," *Academy of Management Review,* April 1979, pp. 287–90.

13. Victor H. Vroom and Phillip W. Yetton, *Leadership and Decision-Making* (Pittsburgh: University of Pittsburgh Press, 1973).

14. Victor H. Vroom and Arthur G. Jago, *The New Leadership: Managing Participation in Organizations* (Englewood Cliffs, N.J.: Prentice-Hall, 1988). See especially Chapter 8.

15. See, for example, R.H. George Field, "A Test of the Vroom-Yetton Normative Model of Leadership," *Journal of Applied Psychology,* October 1982, pp. 523–32; Carrie R. Leana, "Power Relinquishment versus Power Sharing: Theoretical Clarification and Empirical Comparison of Delegation and Participation," *Journal of Applied Psychology,* May 1987, pp. 228–33; Jennifer T. Ettling and Arthur G. Jago, "Participation Under Conditions of Conflict: More on the Validity of the Vroom-Yetton Model," *Journal of Management Studies,* January 1988, pp. 73–83; and R.H. George Field and Robert J. House, "A Test of the Vroom-Yetton Model Using Manager and Subordinate Reports," *Journal of Applied Psychology,* June 1990, pp. 362–66.

16. Steven Kerr and John M. Jermier, "Substitutes for Leadership: Their Meaning and Measurement," *Organizational Behavior and Human Performance,* December 1978, pp. 375–403; Jon P. Howell and Peter W. Dorfman, "Substitutes for Leadership: Test of a Construct," *Academy of Management Journal,* December 1981, pp. 714–28; Peter W. Howard and William F. Joyce, "Substitutes for Leadership: A Statistical Refinement," paper presented at the 42nd Annual Academy of Management Conference, New York, August 1982; Jon P. Howell, Peter W. Dorfman, and Steven Kerr, "Leadership and Substitutes for Leadership," *Journal of Applied Behavioral Science,* Vol. 22, No. 1 (1986), pp. 29–46; and Jon P. Howell, D.E. Bowen, Peter W. Dorfman, Steven Kerr, and Philip M. Podsakoff, "Substitutes for Leadership: Effective Alternatives to Ineffective Leadership," *Organizational Dynamics,* Summer 1990, pp. 21–38.

17. W.J. Reddin, *Managerial Effectiveness,* (New York: McGraw-Hill, 1967).

18. Rick Roskin and Robin Stuart-Kotze, *Success Guide to Managerial Achievement,* (Reston, VA: Reston, 1983).

19. Jay C. Conger and R.N. Kanungo, "Behavioral Dimensions of Charismatic Leadership," in J.A. Conger, R.N. Kanungo and Associates, *Charismatic Leadership* (San Francisco: Jossey-Bass, 1988), p. 79.

20. Robert J. House, "A 1976 Theory of Charismatic Leadership," in J.G. Hunt and L.L. Larson, eds., *Leadership: The Cutting Edge* (Carbondale: Southern Illinois University Press, 1977), pp. 189–207.

21. Warren Bennis, "The 4 Competencies of Leadership," *Training and Development Journal,* August 1984, pp. 15–19.

22. Conger and Kanungo, "Behavioral Dimensions of Charismatic Leadership," pp. 78–97.

23. Robert J. House, J. Woycke, and E.M. Fodor, "Charismatic and Noncharismatic Leaders: Differences in Behavior and Effectiveness," in Conger and Kanungo, *Charismatic Leadership,* pp. 103–04.

24. House, "A 1976 Theory of Charismatic Leadership."

25. D. Machan, "The Charisma Merchants," *Forbes,*

January 23, 1989, pp. 100–101.
26. See James M. Burns, *Leadership* (New York: Harper & Row, 1978); B.M. Bass, *Leadership and Performance Beyond Expectations* (New York: Free Press, 1985); and B.M. Bass, "From Transactional to Transformational Leadership: Learning to Share the Vision," *Organizational Dynamics,* Winter 1990, pp. 19–31.
27. B.M. Bass, "Leadership: Good, Better, Best," *Organizational Dynamics,* Winter 1985, pp. 26–40; and J. Seltzer and B.M. Bass, "Transformational Leadership: Beyond Initiation and Consideration," *Journal of Management,* December 1990, pp. 693–703.
28. B.J. Avolio and B.M. Bass, "Transformational Leadership, Charisma and Beyond," working paper, School of Management, State University of New York, Binghamton, 1985, p. 14.
29. Cited in B.M. Bass and B.J. Avolio, "Developing Transformational Leadership: 1992 and Beyond," *Journal of European Industrial Training,* January 1990, p. 23.
30. J.J. Hater and B.M. Bass, "Supervisors' Evaluation and Subordinates' Perceptions of Transformational and Transactional Leadership," *Journal of Applied Psychology,* November 1988, pp. 695–702.
31. Bass and Avolio, "Developing Transformational Leadership."
32. Keith Davis, *Human Behavior at Work: Organizational Behavior,* 6th ed. (New York: McGraw-Hill, 1981), pp. 141–44.

Chapter 14

1. Story based on J. Cusman, "Avianca Flight 52: The Delays That Ended in Disaster," *New York Times* (February 5, 1990), p. B–1; and E. Weiner, "Right Word Is Crucial in Air Control," *New York Times* (January 29, 1990), p. B–5.
2. Larry E. Penley, Elmore R. Alexander, I. Edward Jernigan, and Catherine I. Henwood, "Communication Abilities of Managers: The Relationship to Performance," *Journal of Management,* March 1991, pp. 57–76.
3. John Southerst, "Now Everyone Can Be a Boss," *Canadian Business,* May 1994.
4. Charlotte Olmstead Kursh, "The Benefits of Poor Communication," *Psychoanalytic Review,* Summer–Fall 1971, pp. 189–208.
5. David K. Berlo, *The Process of Communication* (New York: Holt, Rinehart, & Winston, 1960), pp. 30–32.
6. Ibid., p. 54.
7. Ibid., p. 103.
8. Albert Mehrabian, "Communication Without Words," *Psychology Today,* September 1968, pp. 53–55.
9. Robert J. Graham, "Understanding the Benefits of Poor Communication," *Interfaces,* June 1981, pp. 80–82.
10. T.D. Lewis and G. H. Graham, "Six Ways to Improve Your Communications Skills," *Internal Auditor* (May 1988), p. 25.
11. Based on Shoukry D. Saleh, "Relational Orientation and Organizational Functioning: A Cross-Cultural Perspective," *Canadian Journal of Administrative Sciences* (September 1987), pp. 276–93.
12. Kenneth W. Thomas and Warren H. Schmidt, "A Survey of Managerial Interests with Respect to Conflict," *Academy of Management Journal,* June 1976, pp. 315–18.
13. Ibid.
14. J. Graves, "Successful Management and Organizational Mugging," in J. Papp, ed., *New Directions in Human Resource Management* (Englewood Cliffs, N.J.: Prentice-Hall, 1978).
15. This section is adapted from Stephen P. Robbins, *Managing Organizational Conflict: A Nontraditional Approach* (Englewood Cliffs, N.J.: Prentice-Hall, 1974), pp. 11–14.
16. Ralph H. Kilmann and Kenneth W. Thomas, "Developing a Forced-Choice Measure of Conflict Handling Behavior: The MODE Instrument," *Educational and Psychological Measurement,* Summer 1977, pp. 309–25.
17. Leonard Greenhalgh, "Managing Conflict," *Sloan Management Review,* Summer 1986, pp. 45–51.
18. Robbins, *Managing Organizational Conflict,* pp. 31–55.
19. Charlotte O. Kursh, "The Benefits of Poor Communication," *The Psychoanalytic Review,* Summer–Fall 1971, pp. 189–208.
20. This section is drawn from K.W. Thomas, "Toward Multidimensional Values in Teaching: The Example of Conflict Behaviors," *Academy of Management Review* (July 1977), p. 487.
21. Kenneth W. Thomas, "Conflict and Conflict Management," in Marvin Dunnette, ed., *Handbook of Industrial and Organizational Psychology* (Chicago: Rand McNally, 1976), pp. 889–935.
22. See, for instance, Dean Tjosvold and David W. Johnson, *Productive Conflict Management Perspectives for Organizations* (New York: Irvington Publishers, 1983).
23. Robbins, *Managing Organizational Conflict,* pp. 78–89.

Endnotes

Chapter 15

1. Jeffrey Rothfeder and Jim Bartimo, "How Software Is Making Food Sales a Piece of Cake," *Business Week,* July 2, 1990, pp. 54–55.
2. Kenneth A. Merchant, "The Control Function of Management," *Sloan Management Review,* Summer 1982, pp. 43–55.
3. Eric Flamholtz, "Organizational Control Systems as a Managerial Tool," *California Management Review,* Winter 1979, p. 55.
4. Steven Kerr, "On the Folly of Rewarding A, While Hoping for B," *Academy of Management Journal,* December 1975, pp. 769–83.
5. Harold Koontz and Robert W. Bradspies, "Managing Through Feedforward Control," *Business Horizons,* June 1972, pp. 25–36.
6. William H. Newman, *Constructive Control: Design and Use of Control Systems* (Englewood Cliffs, N.J.: Prentice-Hall, 1975), p. 33.
7. Ibid.
8. Gordon Pitts, "From Potholes to Profits," *The Globe & Mail,* April 4, 1995.
9. Based on a tape recording made by the Dallas Fire Department and made available under the Texas Open Records Act.
10. Cited in Archie B. Carroll, "In Search of the Moral Manager," *Business Horizons,* March–April 1987, p. 7.
11. See, for instance, Bernard J. Jaworski and S. Mark Young, "Dysfunctional Behavior and Management Control: An Empirical Study of Marketing Managers," *Accounting, Organizations and Society,* January 1992, pp. 17–35.
12. This is based on Zachary Schiller and Walecia Konrad, "If You Light Up on Sunday, Don't Come In on Monday," *Business Week,* August 26, 1991, pp. 68–72; and G. Bylinsky, "How Companies Spy on Employees," *Fortune,* November 4, 1991, pp. 131–40.
13. Edward E. Lawler III and John Grant Rhode, *Information and Control in Organizations* (Santa Monica, Calif.: Goodyear, 1976), p. 108.
14. James D. Thompson, *Organizations in Action* (New York: McGraw-Hill, 1967), p. 124.

Chapter 16

1. Edward O. Well, "Riding the High-Tech Highway," *Inc.,* March 1993, pp. 72–84.
2. John T. Small and William B. Lee, "In Search of an MIS," *MSU Business Topics,* Autumn 1975, pp. 47–55.
3. Herbert A. Simon, *Administrative Behavior,* 3rd ed. (New York: Free Press, 1976), p. 294.
4. John C. Carter and Fred N. Silverman, "Establishing an MIS," *Journal of Systems Management,* January 1980, p. 15.
5. See W. David Gardner and Joseph Kelly, "Technology: A Price/Performance Game," *Dun's Review,* August 1981, pp. 66–68; "Computers: The New Look," *Business Week,* November 30, 1987, pp. 112–23; and William M. Bulkeley, "PC Networks Begin to Oust Mainframes in Some Companies," *Wall Street Journal,* May 23, 1990, pp. A1, A13.
6. See Steven A. Stanton, "End-User Computing: Power to the People," *Journal of Information Systems Management,* Summer 1988, pp. 79–81; and Glen L. Boyer and Dale McKinnon, "End-User Computing Is Here to Stay," *Supervisory Management,* October 1989, pp. 17–22.
7. See, for example, David Kirkpatrick, "Here Comes the Payoff from PCs," *Fortune,* March 23, 1992, pp. 93–102.
8. See, for instance, John C. Henderson and Michael E. Treacy, "Managing End-User Computing for Competitive Advantage," *Sloan Management Review,* Winter 1986, pp. 2–14; Peter Coy, "The New Realism in Office Systems," *Business Week,* June 15, 1992, p. 128–33; and Myron Magnet, "Who's Winning the Information Revolution," *Fortune,* November 30, 1992, pp. 110–17.
9. "Cutting Out the Middleman," *Forbes,* January 6, 1992, p. 169.
10. Justin Martin, "Freeze, It's the Cyber Fuzz!" *Fortune,* May 2, 1994, pp. 14–15.
11. See, for instance, Stephen W. Quickel, "Management Joins the Computer Age," *Business Month,* May 1989, pp. 42–46; and George P. Huber, "A Theory of the Effects of Advanced Information Technology on Organizational Design, Intelligence, and Decision Making," *Academy of Management Review,* January 1990, pp. 47–71.
12. Bruce Little, "Stock Answers," *The Globe & Mail,* June 6, 1995.
13. Lynda M. Applegate, James I. Cash, Jr., and D. Quinn Mills, "Information Technology and Tomorrow's Manager," *Harvard Business Review,* November–December 1988, pp. 128–36.
14. Joseph H. Boyett and Henry P. Conn, *Workplace 2000* (New York: Dutton, 1991), p. 25.
15. Ibid.
16. This section is based on Richard C. Huseman and Edward W. Miles, "Organizational Communication in the Information Age: Implications of Computer-Based Systems," *Journal of Management,* Summer 1988, pp. 181–204.

17. Cited in *Fortune,* October 28, 1985, p. 47.
18. Stephen E. Barndt and Davis W. Carvey, *Essentials of Operations Management* (Englewood Cliffs, N.J.: Prentice-Hall, 1982), p. 112.
19. Joel Dreyfuss, "Shaping Up Your Suppliers," *Fortune,* April 10, 1989, pp. 116–22; and Thomas M. Rohan, "Supplier-Customer Links Multiplying," *Industry Week,* April 17, 1989, p. 20.
20. Rohan, "Supplier-Customer Links Multiplying."
21. Richard B. Chase and Nicholas J. Aquilano, *Production and Operations Management: A Life–Cycle Approach,* 3rd ed. (Homewood, Ill.: Irwin, 1981), pp. 551–52.
22. "The Productivity Paradox," *Business Week,* June 6, 1988, p. 100.
23. Jim Thomas, "As Easy as ABC," *Chilton's Distribution,* January 1994, p. 40.
24. See, for example, David A. De Cenzo and Stephen P. Robbins, *Human Resource Management,* 4th ed. (New York: John Wiley and Sons, 1994), pp. 385–393.
25. BARS have not been without critics. See, for example, Luis R. Gomez–Mejia, "Evaluating Employee Performance: Does the Appraisal Instrument Make a Difference?" *Journal of Organizational Behavior Management,* Winter 1988, pp. 155–71.
26. Robert D. Bretz, Jr., George T. Milkovich, and Walter Read, "The Current State of Performance Appraisal Research and Practice: Concerns, Directions, and Implications," *Journal of Management,* June 1992, p. 331.
27. Douglas McGregor, "Hot Stove Rules of Discipline," in George Strauss and Leonard Sayles, eds., *Personnel: The Human Problems of Management* (Englewood Cliffs, N.J.: Prentice-Hall, 1967).
28. It has been argued that indirect control mechanisms are most appropriate in organic structures. See Steven Kerr and John W. Slocum, Jr., "Controlling the Performance of People in Organizations," in Paul C. Nystrom and William H. Starbuck, eds., *Handbook of Organizational Design,* Vol. 2 (New York, NY: Oxford University Press, 1981), pp. 128–30.

Appendix

1. Based on Daniel Machalaba, "United Parcel Service Gets Deliveries Done by Driving Its Workers," *Wall Street Journal,* April 22, 1986, pp. 1, 26; and Michael Skratulia, "Scientific Management: A Case Study of the United Parcel Service," a research paper prepared under the supervision of Professor Stephen P. Robbins, San Diego State University, 1990.
2. Claude S. George, Jr., *The History of Management Thought,* 2nd ed. (Englewood Cliffs, N.J.: Prentice-Hall, 1972), p. 4.
3. Frederick W. Taylor, *Principles of Scientific Management* (New York: Harper and Brothers, 1911).
4. Machalaba, "United Parcel Service Gets Deliveries Done by Driving Its Workers"; and Skratulia, "Scientific Management."
5. Taylor, *Principles of Scientific Management.*
6. See, for example, Frank B. Gilbreth, *Motion Study* (New York: D. Van Nostrand, 1911); and Frank B. Gilbreth and Lillian M. Gilbreth, *Fatigue Study* (New York: Sturgis and Walton Co., 1916).
7. Henri Fayol, *Industrial and General Administration* (Paris: Dunod, 1916).
8. Max Weber, *The Theory of Social and Economic Organizations,* ed. Talcott Parsons, trans. A.M Henderson and Talcott Parsons (New York: Free Press, 1947).
9. Mary Parker Follett, *The New State: Group Organization the Solution of Popular Government* (London: Longmans, Green and Co., 1918).
10. Chester Barnard, *The Functions of the Executive* (Cambridge, Mass.: Harvard University Press, 1938).
11. Elton Mayo, *The Human Problems of an Industrial Civilization* (New York: Macmillan, 1933); and Fritz J. Roethlisberger and William J. Dickson, *Management and the Worker* (Cambridge, Mass.: Harvard University Press, 1939).
12. See, for example, Alex Carey, "The Hawthorne Studies: A Radical Criticism," *American Sociological Review,* June 1967, pp. 403–16; Richard H. Franke and James Kaul, "The Hawthorne Experiments: First Statistical Interpretations," *American Sociological Review,* October 1978, pp. 623–43; Berkeley Rice, "The Hawthorne Defect: Persistence of a Flawed Theory," *Psychology Today,* February 1982, pp. 70–74; Jeffrey A. Sonnenfeld, "Shedding Light on the Hawthorne Studies," *Journal of Occupational Behavior,* April 1985, pp. 111–30; and Stephen R. G. Jones, "Worker Interdependence and Output: The Hawthorne Studies Reevaluated," *American Sociological Review,* April 1990, pp. 176–90.
13. Dale Carnegie, *How to Win Friends and Influence People* (New York: Simon & Schuster, 1936).
14. Daniel A. Wren, *The Evolution of Management Thought,* 3rd ed. (New York: John Wiley & Sons, 1987), p. 422.
15. Abraham Maslow, *Motivation and Personality* (New York: Harper & Row, 1954).
16. Douglas McGregor, *The Human Side of Enterprise* (New York: McGraw-Hill, 1960).
17. Machalaba, "United Parcel Service Gets Deliveries Done by Driving Its Workers," p 1.

GLOSSARY

The number in parentheses following each term indicates the chapter in which the term is defined.

acceptance sampling (16) A quality control procedure in which a sample is taken and a decision to accept or reject a whole lot is based on a calculation of sample risk error.

acceptance view of authority (A) The theory that authority comes from the willingness of subordinates to accept it.

accommodation (14) Resolving conflicts by placing another's needs and concerns above one's own.

acid test ratio (16) An organization's current assets, minus inventories, divided by its current liabilities.

active listening (14) Listening for full meaning without making premature judgments or interpretations.

activities (4) The time or resources needed to progress from one event to another in a PERT network.

activity-based accounting ABC (16) An accounting procedure whereby costs are allocated based on activities performed and resources used.

adhocracy (6) A structure that is low in complexity, formalization, and centralization (organic).

affective component of an attitude (10) The emotional or feeling segment of an attitude.

affirmative action programs (8) Programs that enhance the organizational status of members of protected groups.

assessment centres (8) Places in which job candidates undergo performance simulation tests that evaluate managerial potential.

assumed similarity (10) The belief that others are like yourself.

attitudes (10) Evaluative statements concerning objects, people, or events.

attitude surveys (10) Eliciting responses from employees through questionnaires about how they feel about their jobs, work groups, supervisors, and/or the organization.

attribute sampling (16) A quality control technique that classifies items as acceptable or unacceptable on the basis of comparison to a standard.

attribution theory (10) A theory used to develop explanations of how we judge people differently depending on the meaning we attribute to a given behaviour.

audit (16) Formal verification of an organization's financial statements.

authoritarianism (10) A measure of a person's belief that there should be status and power differences among people in organizations.

authority (6) The rights inherent in a managerial position to give orders and expect them to be obeyed.

autonomy (7) The degree to which a job provides substantial freedom, independence, and discretion to an individual in scheduling and carrying out his or her work.

avoidance (14) Withdrawal from or suppression of conflict.

basic corrective action (15) Determining how and why performance has deviated and correcting the source of deviations.

behaviour (10) The actions of people.

behavioural component of an attitude (10) An intention to behave in a certain way toward someone or something.

behaviourally anchored rating scales (BARS) (16) A performance appraisal technique in which an evaluator rates employees on specific job behaviours derived from performance dimensions.

behavioural science theorists (A) Psychologists and sociologists who relied on the scientific method for the study of organizational behaviour.

behavioural theories (13) Theories identifying behaviours that differentiate effective from ineffective leaders.

benchmarking (4) The search for the best practices among competitors or noncompetitors that leads to their superior performance.

bi-modal workforce (2) Employees tend to perform either low-skilled service jobs for near-minimum wage or high-skilled, well-paying jobs.

body language (14) Gestures, facial configurations, and other movements of the body that convey meaning.

bona fide occupational qualifications (BFOQ) (8) A criterion such as sex, age, or national origin may be used as a basis for hiring if it can be clearly demonstrated to be job related.

bounded rationality (5) Behaviour that is rational within the parameters of a simplified model that captures the essential features of a problem.

brainstorming (5) An idea-generating process that encourages alternatives while withholding criticism.

break-even analysis (4) A technique for identifying the point at which total revenue is just sufficient to cover total costs.

budget (4) A numerical plan for allocating resources to specific activities.

bureaucracy (6) A form of organization marked by division of labour, hierarchy, rules and regulations, and impersonal relationships (mechanistic).

career (8) The sequence of positions occupied by a person during the course of a lifetime.

chain of command (6) The flow of authority from the top to the bottom of an organization.

change (9) An alteration in structure, technology, or people.

change agents (9) People who act as catalysts and manage the change process.

channel (14) The medium by which a message travels.

charismatic leadership theory (13) Followers make attributions of heroic or extraordinary leadership abilities when they observe certain behaviours.

classical theorists (A) The term used to describe the scientific management theorists and general administrative theorists.

closed systems (1) Systems that are neither influenced by nor interact with their environment.

coach (2) A manager who motivates, empowers, and encourages his or her employees.

code of ethics (2) A formal statement of an organization's primary values and the ethical rules it expects its employees to follow.

cognitive component of an attitude (10) The beliefs, opinions, knowledge, or information held by a person.

cognitive dissonance (10) Any incompatibility between two or more attitudes or between behaviour and attitudes.

collaboration (14) Resolving conflict by seeking a solution advantageous to all parties.

collective bargaining (8) A process for negotiating a union contract and for administrating the contract after it has been negotiated.

collectivism (2) A cultural dimension in which people expect others in their group to look after them and protect them when they are in trouble.

commitment concept (3) Plans should extend far enough to see through current commitments.

committee structure (7) A structure that brings together a range of individuals from across functional lines to deal with problems.

communication (14) The transferring and understanding of meaning.

communication process (14) The seven stages in which meaning is transmitted and understood.

competitor intelligence (4) Environmental scanning activity that seeks to identify who competitors are, what they're doing, and how their actions will affect the focus organization.

compromise (14) A solution to conflict in which each party gives up something of value.

conceptual skills (1) A manager's ability to coordinate the organization's interests and activities.

Glossary

concurrent control (15) Control that occurs while an activity is in progress.

conditional maintenance (16) Maintenance that calls for an overhaul or repair in response to an inspection.

conflict (14) Perceived incompatible differences that result in interference or opposition.

consideration (13) The extent to which a person has job relationships characterized by mutual trust, respect for subordinates' ideas, and regard for their feelings.

contingency approach (1) Recognizing and responding to situational variables as they arise.

control (15) The process of monitoring activities to ensure they are being accomplished as planned and of correcting any significant deviations.

control process (15) The process of measuring actual performance, comparing it against a standard, and taking managerial action to correct deviations or inadequate standards.

controlling (1) Monitoring activities to ensure that they are being accomplished as planned and correcting any significant deviations.

core process (7) A basic focus of the business.

cost-leadership strategy (3) The strategy an organization follows when it wants to be the lowest-cost producer in its industry.

cost-benefit analysis (16) Evaluating an activity where costs are known, but where the standard against which these costs must be compared is ambiguous or difficult to measure.

cost-centre approach (16) Managers are held responsible for costs within their unit.

creativity (9) The ability to combine ideas in a unique way or to make unusual associations between ideas.

critical incidents (16) A performance appraisal technique in which an evaluator lists key behaviours that separate effective from ineffective job performance.

critical path (4) The longest sequence of activities in a PERT network.

cultural environments (2) The attitudes and perspectives shared by individuals from a specific culture, or country, that shape their behaviour and the way they see the world.

current ratio (16) An organization's current assets divided by its current liabilities.

customer departmentalization (6) Grouping activities on the basis of common customers.

data (16) Raw, unanalysed facts.

debt-to-assets ratio (16) Total debt divided by total assets.

decision criteria (5) Criteria that define what is relevant in a decision.

decision-making process (5) A set of eight steps that include identifying a problem, selecting an alternative, and evaluating the decision's effectiveness.

decisional roles (1) Roles that include those of entrepreneur, disturbance handler, resource allocator, and negotiator.

decline career stage (8) The final phase in one's career, usually marked by retirement.

decoding (14) Retranslating a sender's message.

decruitment (8) Techniques for reducing the labour supply within an organization.

Delphi technique (5) A group decision-making technique in which members never meet face to face.

devil's advocate (14) A person who purposely presents arguments that run counter to those proposed by the majority.

differentiation strategy (3) The strategy a firm follows when it wants to be unique in its industry along dimensions widely valued by buyers.

direct costs (16) Costs incurred in proportion to the output of a particular good or service.

directional plans (3) Flexible plans that set out general guidelines.

discipline (16) Actions taken by a manager to enforce the organization's standards and regulations.

distinctive competence (3) The unique skills and resources that determine the organization's competitive weapons.

divisional structure (7) An organization structure made up of autonomous, self-contained units.

division of labour (6) The breakdown of jobs into narrow, repetitive tasks.

downsizing (2) An activity in an organization designed to create a more efficient operation through extensive layoffs.

dysfunctional conflicts (14) Conflicts that prevent an organization from achieving its goals.

economic order quantity model (EOQ) (16) A technique for balancing purchase, ordering, carrying, and stockout costs to derive the optimum quantity for a purchase order.

effectiveness (1) Doing the right thing. Goal attainment.

efficiency (1) Doing the thing right. Concerned with the relationship between inputs and outputs, seeks to minimize resource costs.

electronic mail (14) Instantaneous transmission of written messages on computers that are linked.

electronic meetings (5) Decision-making groups that interact by way of linked computers.

empowerment (2) Increasing the decision-making discretion of workers.

encoding (14) Converting a message into symbols.

end-user (16) The person who uses information and assumes responsibility for its control.

entrepreneurs (2) A manager who is confident in his or her abilities, seizes innovative opportunities, and capitalizes on surprises.

entrepreneurship (3) A process by which individuals pursue opportunities, fulfilling needs and wants through innovation, without regard to the resources they currently control.

environment (2) Outside institutions or forces that potentially affect an organization's performance.

equity theory (12) The theory that an employee compares his or her job's inputs = outcomes ratio to that of relevant others and then corrects any inequity.

establishment career stage (8) A period in which one begins to search for work. It includes getting one's first job.

esteem needs (12) Internal factors such as self-respect, autonomy, and achievement; and external factors such as status, recognition, and attention.

ethics (2) Rules or principles that define right and wrong conduct.

events (4) End points that represent the completion of major activities in a PERT network.

expectancy theory (12) The theory that an individual tends to act in a certain way based on the expectation that the act will be followed by a given outcome and on the attractiveness of that outcome to the individual.

exploration career stage (8) A career stage that usually ends in one's mid-20s as one makes the transition from school to work.

external audit (16) Formal verification of an organization's financial statements by an outside and independent source.

feedback (7) The degree to which carrying out the work activities required by a job results in an individual's obtaining direct and clear information about the effectiveness of his or her performance.

feedback control (15) Control imposed after an action has occurred.

feedforward control (15) Control that prevents anticipated problems.

Fiedler contingency model (13) The theory that effective groups depend on a proper match between a leader's style of interacting with subordinates and the degree to which the situation gives control and influence to the leader.

first-line managers (1) Supervisors; the level of management that directs the work of operative employees.

fixed-interval reordering system (16) A system that uses time as the determining factor for reviewing and reordering inventory items.

fixed-point reordering system (16) A system that "flags" the fact that inventory needs to be replenished when it reaches a certain level.

focus strategy (3) The strategy a company follows when it pursues a cost or differentiation advantage in a narrow industry segment.

forcing (14) Satisfying one's own needs at the expense of another's.

functional conflicts (14) Conflicts that support an organization's goals.

functional departmentalization (6) Grouping activities by functions performed.

fixed-interval reordering system (16) A system that uses time as the determining factor for reviewing and reordering inventory items.

fundamental attribution error (10) The tendency to underestimate the influence of external factors and overestimate the influence of internal factors when making judgments about the behaviour of others.

fundamental structure (7) A design that groups similar or related occupational specialties together.

Gantt chart (4) A graphic bar chart that shows the relationship between work planned and

Glossary

completed on one axis and time elapsed on the other.

general administrative theorists (A) Writers who developed general theories of what managers do and what constitutes good management practice.

geographic departmentalization (6) Grouping activities on the basis of territory.

global village (2) The production and marketing of goods and services worldwide.

graphic rating scales (16) A performance appraisal technique in which an evaluator rates a set of performance factors on an incremental scale.

group (11) Two or more interacting and interdependent individuals who come together to achieve particular objectives.

group order ranking (16) A performance appraisal approach that groups employees into ordered classifications.

groupthink (5) The withholding by group members of different views in order to appear in agreement.

halo effect (10) A general impression of an individual based on a single characteristic.

Hawthorne studies (A) A series of studies during the 1920s and 1930s that provided new insights into group norms and behaviour.

hierarchy of needs theory (12) Maslow's theory that there is a hierarchy of five human needs: physiological, safety, social, esteem, and self-actualization. As each need is substantially satisfied, the next becomes dominant.

horizontal organization (7) An organization design option characterized by very flat structures.

"hot stove" rule (16) Discipline should immediately follow an infraction, provide ample warning, be consistent, and impersonal.

human relations view of conflict (14) The view that conflict is a natural and inevitable outcome in any organization.

human resources approach (A) The study of management that focuses on human behaviour.

human resource management (8) Function in management concerned with getting, training, motivating, and keeping employees.

human skills (1) A manager's ability to work with people.

hygiene factors (12) Factors that eliminate dissatisfaction.

ill-structured problems (5) New problems in which information is ambiguous or incomplete.

immediate corrective action (15) Correcting an activity at once in order to get performance back on track.

implementation (5) Conveying a decision to those affected and getting their commitment to it.

incremental budget (4) A budget that allocates funds to departments according to allocations in the previous period.

indirect costs (16) Costs that are largely unaffected by changes in output.

individualism (2) A cultural dimension in which people are supposed to look after their own interests and those of their immediate family.

individual ranking (16) A performance appraisal approach that ranks employees in order from highest to lowest.

Industrial Revolution (A) The advent of machine power, mass production, and efficient transportation.

information (16) Analysed and processed data.

informational roles (1) Roles that include monitor, disseminator, and spokesperson activities.

initiating structure (13) The extent to which a leader defines and structures his or her role and those of subordinates to attain goals.

innovation (9) The process of taking a creative idea and turning it into a useful product, service, or method of operation.

interactionist view of conflict (14) The view that some conflict is necessary for an organization to perform effectively.

internal audit (16) Evaluation of an organization's financial statements, processes, operations, procedures, and policies by internal financial staff members.

interpersonal communication (14) Communication between two or more people in which the parties are treated as individuals rather than as objects.

interpersonal roles (1) Roles that include figurehead, leader, and liaison activities.

intrapreneurship (2) Creating the entrepreneurial spirit in a large organization.

inventory turnover ratio (16) Revenue divided by total inventory.

job analysis (8) An assessment that defines jobs and the behaviours necessary to perform them.

job characteristics model (JCM)(7) A framework for analysing and designing jobs; identifies five primary job characteristics, their interrelationships, and impact on outcome variables.

job description (8) A written statement of what a jobholder does, how it is done, and why it is done.

job design (7) The way in which tasks are combined to form complete jobs.

job involvement (10) The degree to which an employee identifies with his or her job, actively participates in it, and considers his or her job performance important to his or her self-worth.

job satisfaction (10) A person's general attitude toward his or her job.

job specification (8) A statement of the minimum acceptable qualifications that an incumbent must possess to perform a given job successfully.

just-in-time inventory (JIT) (16) A system in which inventory items arrive when they are needed in the production process instead of being stored in stock.

labour-management relations (8) The formal interactions between unions and an organization's management.

labour union (8) An organization that represents workers and seeks to protect their interests through collective bargaining.

late career stage (8) A period in which one is no longer learning about his or her job, nor is it expected that he or she should be trying to outdo his or her levels of performance from previous years.

leader-member relations (13) The degree of confidence, trust, and respect subordinates have in their leader.

leader-participation model (13) A leadership theory that provides a set of rules to determine the form and amount of participative decision making in different situations.

leaders (13) Those who are able to influence others and who possess managerial authority.

leading (1) Includes motivating subordinates, directing others, selecting the most effective communication channels, and resolving conflicts.

learning (10) Any relatively permanent change in behaviour that occurs as a result of experience.

least-preferred coworker (LPC) questionnaire (13) A questionnaire that measures whether a person is task or relationship oriented.

leverage (16) Refers to the use of borrowed funds to operate and expand an organization.

linear programming (4) A mathematical technique that solves resource allocation problems.

line authority (6) The authority that entitles a manager to direct the work of a subordinate.

load chart (4) A modified Gantt chart that schedules capacity by work stations.

locus of control (10) A personality attribute that measures the degree to which people believe they are masters of their own fate.

long-term plans (3) Plans that extend beyond five years.

Machiavellianism (10) A measure of the degree to which people are pragmatic, maintain emotional distance, and believe that ends can justify means.

management (1) The process of getting activities completed efficiently with and through other people.

management by objectives (MBO)(3) A system in which specific performance objectives are jointly determined by subordinates and their superiors, progress toward objectives is periodically reviewed, and rewards are allocated on the basis of this progress.

management functions (1) Planning, organizing, leading, and controlling.

management information system (MIS) (16) A system that provides management with needed information on a regular basis.

management roles (1) Specific categories of managerial behaviour.

managerial grid (13) A two-dimensional portrayal of leadership based on concerns for people and for production.

managers (1) Individuals in an organization who direct the activities of others.

matrix structure (7) A structural design that assigns specialists from functional departments to work on one or more projects that are led by a project manager.

mechanistic organization (6) A structure that is high in complexity, formalization, and centralization (bureaucracy).

message (14) A purpose to be conveyed.

Glossary

mid-career stage (8) A period marked by continuous improvement in performance, levelling off in performance, or beginning to deteriorate in performance.

mission (3) The purpose of an organization.

motivation (12) The willingness to exert high levels of effort to reach organizational goals, conditioned by the effort's ability to satisfy some individual need.

motivation-hygiene theory (12) The theory that intrinsic factors are related to job satisfaction, while extrinsic factors are associated with dissatisfaction.

motivators (12) Factors that increase job satisfaction.

multinational corporations (MNC) (2) Companies that maintain significant operations in more than one country simultaneously but manage them all from one base in a home country.

multiperson comparison (16) A performance appraisal technique in which individuals are compared to one another.

need (12) An internal state that makes certain outcomes appear attractive.

need for achievement (12) The drive to excel, to achieve in relation to a set of standards, to strive to succeed.

need for affiliation (12) The desire for friendly and close interpersonal relationships.

need for power (12) The need to make others behave in a way that they would not have behaved otherwise.

network (16) Linking computers so that they can communicate with each other.

network structure (7) A small centralized organization that relies on other organizations to perform its basic business functions on a contract basis.

noise (14) Disturbances that interfere with the transmission of a message.

nominal group technique (5) A decision-making technique in which group members are physically present but operate independently.

nonprogrammed decisions (5) Unique and nonrecurring decisions that require a custom-made solution.

nonverbal communication (14) Communication transmitted without words.

norms (11) Acceptable standards shared by a group's members.

open systems (1) Dynamic systems that interact with and respond to their environment.

operant conditioning (10) A type of conditioning in which desired voluntary behaviour leads to a reward or prevents a punishment.

operational plans (3) Plans that specify details of how overall objectives are to be achieved.

operations management (16) The design, operation, and control of the transformation process that converts resources into finished goods and services.

operatives (1) People who work directly on a job or task and have no responsibility for overseeing the work of others.

organic organization (6) A structure that is low in complexity, formalization, and centralization (adhocracy).

organization (1) A systematic arrangement of people to accomplish some specific purpose.

organizational behaviour (10) The study of the actions of people at work.

organizational commitment (10) An employee's orientation toward the organization in terms of his or her loyalty to, identification with, and involvement in the organization.

organization culture (7) A system of shared meaning within an organization that determines, in a large degree, how employees act.

organization structure (6) An organization's framework as expressed by its degree of complexity, formalization, and centralization.

organizing (1) Determining what tasks are to be done, who is to do them, how the tasks are to be grouped, who reports to whom, and where decisions are to be made.

orientation (8) The introduction of a new employee into his or her job and the organization.

paired comparison (16) A performance appraisal approach in which each employee is compared to every other employee and rated as either the superior or weaker member of the pair.

path-goal theory (13) The theory that a leader's behaviour is acceptable to subordinates insofar as they view it as a source of either immediate or future satisfaction.

perception (10) The process of organizing and

interpreting sensory impressions in order to give meaning to the environment.

performance appraisal (16) The evaluation of an individual's work performance in order to arrive at objective personnel decisions.

personality (10) A combination of psychological traits that classifies a person.

PERT network (4) A flowchartlike diagram showing the sequence of activities needed to complete a project and the time or costs associated with each.

physiological needs (12) Basic food, drink, shelter, and sexual needs.

planning (1) Includes defining goals, establishing strategy, and developing plans to coordinate activities.

policy (5) A guide that establishes parameters for making decisions.

political skills (1) A manager's ability to build a power base.

position power (13) The degree of influence a leader has over power variables such as hiring, firing, discipline, promotions, and salary increases.

power (6) The capacity to influence decisions.

power distance (2) A cultural measure of the extent to which a society accepts the unequal distribution of power in institutions and organizations.

preventive maintenance (16) Maintenance performed before a breakdown occurs.

problem (5) A discrepancy between an existing and a desired state of affairs.

procedure (5) A series of interrelated sequential steps that can be used to respond to a structured problem.

process approach (1) Management performs the functions of planning, organizing, leading, and controlling.

process control (16) A quality control procedure in which sampling is done during the transformation process to determine whether the process itself is under control.

process departmentalization (6) Grouping activities on the basis of product or customer flow.

product departmentalization (6) Grouping activities by product line.

profit-margin-on-revenues ratio (16) Net profit after taxes divided by total revenues.

Program Evaluation and Review Technique (PERT) (4) A technique for scheduling complicated projects comprising many activities, some of which are interdependent.

programmed decision (5) A repetitive decision that can be handled by a routine approach.

qualitative forecasting (4) Uses the judgment and opinions of knowledgeable individuals to predict future outcomes.

quality circles (11) Work groups that meet regularly to discuss, investigate, and correct quality problems.

quality control (16) Ensuring that what is produced meets some pre-established standard.

quality of life (2) A national cultural attribute that reflects the emphasis placed upon relationships and concern for others.

quantitative approach (A) The use of quantitative techniques to improve decision making.

quantitative forecasting (4) Applies a set of mathematical rules to a series of past data to predict future outcomes.

quantity of life (2) A national cultural attribute describing the extent to which societal values are characterized by assertiveness and materialism.

queuing theory (4) A technique that balances the cost of having a waiting line against the cost of service to maintain that line.

range of variation (15) The acceptable parameters of variance between actual performance and the standard.

rational (5) Describes choices that are consistent and value-maximizing within specified constraints.

realistic job preview (8) Exposing job candidates to both negative and positive information about a job and an organization.

recruitment (8) The process of locating, identifying, and attracting capable applicants.

reengineering (2) Radical, quantum change in the organization.

referents (12) The persons, systems, or selves against which individuals compare themselves to assess equity.

reliability (8) The ability of a selection device to measure the same thing consistently.

remedial maintenance (16) Maintenance that calls for the overhaul, replacement, or repair of equipment when it breaks down.

Glossary

responsibility (6) An obligation to perform assigned activities.

return-on-investment ratio (16) [Revenues/investments] times [profit/revenues].

revenue forecasting (4) Predicting future revenues.

risk taking (10) The willingness to take chances.

role (11) A set of behaviour patterns expected of someone occupying a given position in a social unit.

rule (5) An explicit statement that tells managers what they ought or ought not to do.

safety needs (12) A person's needs for security and protection from physical and emotional harm.

scenario (3) A consistent view of what the future is likely to be.

scheduling (4) A listing of necessary activities, their order of accomplishment, who is to do each, and time needed to complete them.

scientific management (A) The use of the scientific method to define the "one best way" for a job to be done.

selection process (8) The process of screening job applicants to ensure that the most appropriate candidates are hired.

selectivity (10) The process by which people assimilate certain bits and pieces of what they observe, depending on their interests, background, experience, and attitudes.

self-actualization needs (12) A person's drive to become what he or she is capable of becoming.

self-esteem (10) An individual's degree of like or dislike for him or herself.

self-monitoring (10) A personality trait that measures an individual's ability to adjust his or her behaviour to external, situational factors.

self-serving bias (10) The tendency for individuals to attribute their own successes to internal factors while putting the blame for failures on external factors.

sexual harassment (2) Behaviour marked by sexually suggestive remarks, unwanted touching and sexual advances, requests for sexual favours, or other verbal or physical conduct of a sexual nature.

shaping behaviour (10) Systematically reinforcing each successive step that moves an individual closer to the desired response.

short-term plans (3) Plans that cover less than one year.

simple structure (7) An organization that is low in complexity and formalization but high in centralization.

skill variety (7) The degree to which a job includes a variety of activities that call for a number of different skills and talents.

slack time (4) The difference between the critical path time and the time of all other paths.

small business (1) An independently owned and operated, profit-seeking enterprise having fewer than 500 employees.

social learning theory (10) People can learn through observation and direct experience.

social needs (12) A person's needs for affection, belongingness, acceptance, and friendship.

social obligation (2) The obligation of a business to meet its economic and legal responsibilities.

social responsiveness (2) The capacity of a firm to adapt to changing societal conditions.

social responsibility (2) An obligation, beyond that required by the law and economics, for a firm to pursue long-term goals that are good for society.

span of control (6) The number of subordinates a manager can direct efficiently and effectively.

specific plans (3) Plans that are clearly defined and leave no room for interpretation.

staff authority (6) Authority that supports, assists, and advises holders of line authority.

status (11) A prestige grading, position, or rank within a group.

stereotyping (10) Judging a person on the basis of one's perception of a group to which he or she belongs.

strategic alliance (7) Joint partnerships between two or more firms that are created to gain a competitive advantage in a market.

strategic human resource planning (8) The process by which management ensures that it has the right personnel, who are capable of completing those tasks that help the organization reach its objectives.

strategic management process (3) A nine-step process encompassing strategic planning, implementation, and evaluation.

strategic plans (3) Plans that are organization-wide, establish overall objectives, and position an organization in terms of its environment.

strong culture (7) Organizations in which the key values are intensely held and widely shared.

supervision (13) First-level management task of directing the activities of immediate employees.

systems approach (1) A theory that sees an organization as a set of interrelated and interdependent parts.

task force structure (7) A temporary structure created to accomplish a specific, well-defined, complex task that requires the involvement of personnel from a number of organizational subunits.

task identity (7) The degree to which a job requires completion of a whole and identifiable piece of work.

task significance (7) The degree to which a job has a substantial impact on the lives or work of other people.

task structure (13) The degree to which the job assignments are procedurized.

technical skills (1) A manager's ability to use procedures and techniques of a specialized field.

Theory X (12) The assumption that employees dislike work, are lazy, seek to avoid responsibility, and must be coerced to perform.

Theory Y (12) The assumption that employees are creative, seek responsibility, and can exercise self-direction.

therbligs (A) A classification scheme for labelling seventeen basic hand motions.

three-needs theory (12) The needs for achievement, power, and affiliation are major motives in work.

times-interest-earned ratio (16) Profits before taxes divided by total interest charges.

total assets turnover ratio (16) Revenue divided by total assets.

total quality management (TQM) (2) A philosophy of management that is driven by customer needs and expectations.

traditional view of authority (A) The view that authority comes from above.

traditional view of conflict (14) The view that all conflict is bad and must be avoided.

trait theories (13) Theories isolating characteristics that differentiate leaders from nonleaders.

transactional leaders (13) Leaders who guide or motivate their followers in the direction of established goals by clarifying role and task requirements.

transformational leaders (13) Leaders who provide individualized consideration, intellectual stimulation, and possess charisma.

transformation process (16) The process through which an organization produces goods or services.

transnational corporation (TNC)(2) A company that maintains significant operations in more than one country simultaneously and decentralizes decision making in each operation to the local country.

uncertainty avoidance (2) A cultural measure of the degree to which people tolerate risk and unconventional behaviour.

unity of command (6) The principle that a subordinate should have one, and only one, superior to whom he or she is directly responsible.

validity (8) The proven relationship that exists between a selection device and some relevant criterion.

variable sampling (16) A quality control technique in which a measurement is taken to determine how much an item varies from the standard.

verbal intonation (14) An emphasis given to words or phrases that conveys meaning.

well-structured problems (5) Straightforward, familiar, easily defined problems.

work sampling (8) A personnel selection device in which job applicants are presented with a miniature replica of a job and are asked to perform tasks central to that job.

workforce diversity (2) Employees in organizations are heterogeneous in terms of gender, race, ethnicity, or other characteristics.

work teams (11) Formal groups made up of interdependent individuals, responsible for the attainment of a goal.

written essay (16) A performance appraisal technique in which an evaluator writes out a description of an employee's strengths, weaknesses, past performance, and potential and then makes suggestions for improvement.

zero-based budgeting (ZBB) (4) A system in which budget requests start from scratch, regardless of previous appropriations.

ILLUSTRATION CREDITS

Chapter 1
2 Paul Hoeffler/Courtesy Delrina **3** Canadawide Features Service **4** Mike Greenlar/Business Week, 10/4/93, p. 56 **7** Michael L. Abramson **9** Courtesy Bell Canada **11** Andy Sacks/Tony Stone Images **13** David Fields **15** (top) Caroline Parsons/Aria Pictures, Tokyo **15** (bottom) Courtesy Hollinger **17** Courtesy Bombardier Inc., Sea-Doo/Ski-Doo Division

Chapter 2
26 Courtesy Union Carbide Corporation **28** Courtesy Ford **34** Larry Ford **35** Danny Turner **39** Shonna Valeska **40** Patrick Fordham **41** Donal Holway **43** Teri Stratford **45** Brian Smith **47** Bill Luster/Time Picture Services

Chapter 3
55 John Davis **56** Paul Nightingale/Gamma-Liaison **60** Phil Huber/Black Star **61** Courtesy Johnson & Dean, Inc. **64** Brownie Harris/Courtesy GE **65** Courtesy Panasonic **68** Courtesy Marks & Spencer **69** Ann States/SABA **73** Bob Daemmrich

Chapter 4
79 Joan Boivin **80** Riclafe/Sipa Press **81** Bochsler Photographic/Courtesy Philip Environmental Inc. **82** Charles Gupton/Uniphoto **84** Courtesy Volkswagen Canada **88** FPG/Masterfile **90** AP/Wide World Photos **92** Courtesy Kinko's Service Corporation **94** Uniphoto

Chapter 5
102 Bob Carroll **103** Teri Stratford **104** Llewellyn/Uniphoto **110** The Photo Works/Monkmeyer Press **111** Caroline Parsons/Aria Pictures, Tokyo **113** Michael Abramson **117** Katherine Lambert

Chapter 6
125 Courtesy CMP Publications **128** Tim Barnwell/Stock Boston, Inc. **129** Courtesy U.S. Army **136** John Abbott Photography **138** Spar Aerospace/NASA **139** Courtesy Texas Instruments, Inc. **140** Courtesy Allison Engine Co. **142** James Schnepf

Chapter 7
149 Neil Graham **150** Bob Carroll **153** Courtesy Buick **154** Courtesy ABB Inc. **156** (top) Brownie Harris/The Stock Market **156** (bottom) Bob Sacha **160** Courtesy Ryder Truck Rental Canada Inc. **165** David Strick/Onyx

Chapter 8
174 Honeywell Limited **178** Four by Five **181** Courtesy Saskatoon Chemicals Ltd. **186** Jeremy Jones **189** Shaun van Steyn/Uniphoto **190** Mike Surowiak/Tony Stone Images **191** Prentice Hall Archives **196** Taro Yamasaki

Chapter 9
204 Courtesy Algoma Steel Inc. **206** Courtesy Fishery Products International Limited **209** David Stoecklein/Stock Market **211** Bob Carroll **212** Bob Daemmrich/Stock Boston, Inc. **215** Courtesy Intel **216** Colin Patey, The Waterford Hospital

Chapter 10
225 Courtesy Hyatt Hotels Corp. **237** Bob Carroll **240** Tim Brown/Tony Stone Images **241** Globe Photos

Chapter 11
249 Courtesy 3M Canada Inc. **251** Paul H. Henning/Uniphoto **252** David M. Grossman/Photo Researchers **254** Karen Leeds/The Stock Market **255** Deloitte & Touche **257** C. Archambault **260** Kevin Horan **262** Courtesy Ford Motor Co.

Chapter 12
269 Courtesy Roppe Corp. **270** Canadian Sport Images/Ted Grant **271** Bettmann **275** Ken Karp **281** Kathleen Bellesiles **283** Teri Stratford **287** Neil Graham

Illustration Credits

Chapter 13
294 Image Actuelle/Publiphoto **295** Kirdi/Ponopresse **298** Courtesy SNC-Lavalin Group Inc. **302** Janet Gill/Tony Stone Images **306** Ferry/Van der Stockt/Gamma-Liaison, Inc. **311** David Ximeno Tejada/Tony Stone Images **312** Chrysler

Chapter 14
320 Harrington/Masterfile **322** Courtesy Northern Telecom Inc. **324** Matthew McVay/Stock Boston, Inc. **325** Brady/Monkmeyer Press **326** Tony Henshaw/Tony Stone Images **327** Sharp Electronics Corporation **329**, AP/Wide World Photos **333** Bryce Flynn/Picture Group **337** CAW/CANADA

Chapter 15
345 Reid Horn **347** John Coletti/Uniphoto **348** Arthur Tilley/FPG International **351** James Schnepf **352** John Madere **354** Michael Abramson **355** Courtesy The Goodyear Tire and Rubber Company **356** Ahearne/The Globe and Mail **357** Bob Carroll

Chapter 16
367 Dan Pearce **368** Ed Kashi **369** John Madere **370** IBM **372** (top) Andrew Garn **372** (bottom) Henry Feather, courtesy of Mount Sinai Hospital **376** Levenson/Tony Stone Images **379** Teri Stratford **380** Paul Chesley **383** Bob Carroll **386** Bob Carroll

INDEX

A
A&B Sound, 81—82
Aboriginal Global Investment Corporation, 318
Acceptance view of authority, 406
Accept errors, 182
Access to Information Act, 177
Accommodation, in conflict reduction, 337
Acid test ratio, 382
Acres, 298
Active listening, 277—78
Activities, as component of PERT, 89, 90—92
Activity-based accounting (ABC), 384
Acton Rubber Plant, 100
Adam, Everett E., Jr., 99
Adams, J. Stacey, 277—78
Adhocracy, 139
Advertisements, for recruitment, 180
Aerospace industry, 112, 141, 184
Affective component of attitudes, 227
Affirmative action programs, 177
Agor, Weston H., 120
AIDS, and donated blood supply, 343
Air Canada, 15, 24, 32
Air Jordan athletic shoes, 122
Airline industry, 209
Alcan, 30, 298
Alfa Romeo, 66
Algoma Steel, 204, 207
Allen-Bradley, 73, 351
Aloro Foods, 27
Ambiguity, acceptance of, 218
Ambiguous responsibility, 114
American Airlines, 209
AMF Corp., 394
Amoco Production Co., 163
AMP of Canada Ltd., 71
Anglican Church of Canada, 295
Annis, Barbara, 247
Apple Computer, 112, 158
Application form, 183, 188
Arcola, Saskatchewan, 267
Arthur Andersen, accountants, 14—15
Artistic personality, 234, 235
Asch, Solomon, 252—53, 261
ASEA Corporation, 154
Assembly line, 172, 398
Assessment, of employees, 178—79
Assessment centres, 184—85, 188
Assumed similarity, 239
AT&T, 42
Attentional processes, in social learning theory, 241
Attitude, 227—31
Attitude surveys, 230
Attribution theory, 237—38
 fundamental errors of, 238
Attrition, as means of decruitment, 180

Audits, 383
Authoritarianism, 231
Authority, 129—36, 405
 acceptance view, 406
 classic view, 129, 132
 compared to power, 134—36
 contemporary view, 132
 traditional view, 406
Authorization card, 194
Automotive industry, 36, 52
Autonomy, and JCM, 167
Autoskill, 396
Avianca Flight 52 disaster, 320, 321
Avoidance
 in conflict reduction, 337
 of uncertainty, 33, 243
Axworthy, Lloyd, 202

B
Background investigation, 186
Ball, Ken, 256—57
Bank of Montreal, 278
Bank of Nova Scotia, 27, 278
Bankruptcy, 67
Bark, Basil, 232
Barnard, Chester, 405
Barnes, Louis B., 299
Barnevik, Percy, 154
Barrett, Matthew, 278
Barriers, to communication, 327—30
BARS, 385
Basic corrective action, 350—51
Beaudoin, Laurent, 17
Beaudoin, Pierre, 17
Beeby, Robert, 345
Behaviour, defined, 225
Behavioural component of attitudes, 227
Behavioural controls, 384—90
 and organizational culture, 387
 and orientation, 390
 and selection, 387—88
 substitutes for, 387—90
 and training, 390
Behaviourally anchored rating scales, 385
Behavioural Science Systems Ltd, 156
Behavioural science theories of leadership, 296—300, 408
Bell Canada, 9, 32, 292
Bell & Howell Co., 27
Bell Northern Research Ltd., 159
Benchmarking, 83—84
Bennis, Warren, 307
Berard, Andre, 278
Bethlehem Steel, 399, 402
BFOQ, 177
BIAC, 16
Big Box stores, 102, 233
Bi-modal work force, 45
Binney & Smith (Canada), 246

Birmingham, Bruce, 278
Black, Conrad, 15
Black & Decker Canada, 66, 138
Blake, Robert R., 299
BMW, 206
Body language, 326
Body Shop, 16, 102, 365
Boff, Larry, 359
Boise Cascade, 352
Bombardier Inc., 17, 84, 112, 152
Bona fide occupational qualifications, 177
Boniferro, Steve, 204
Boundary-free organization, 159, 160
Bounded rationality, 108, 109
Bourassa, Robert, 298
Brackhaus, Karl, 72, 73
Brainstorming, 116—17
Break-even analysis, 92—93
 as planning tool, 93
Brisebois, Diane, 102
British Airways, 209, 379
Brock, Floyd, 392
Brooks athletic footwear, 122
Brown-Boveri, 154
Budgets, 85—88
 incremental, 86
 types, 85
 zero-based, 86—88
Buick Century, 104—106
Bureaucracy, 127, 139, 142, 147, 404
Burger King, 28, 82

C
Cable News Network (CNN), 27
Calm-waters metaphor of change, 208—209
Campbell Soup Co., 292
Canada Dry Beverages, 30
Canadair, 112
Canada Labour Code, 177
Canada Post, 371
Canadarm, 138, 141
Canadian Airlines, 24, 209
Canadian Armed Forces, 32
Canadian Auto Workers, 207
Canadian Breweries, 16, 27
Canadian Broadcasting Corporation, 152
Canadian Business, 294
Canadian Business Review, 72
Canadian Imperial Bank of Commerce, 247, 278, 286
Canadian Medical Association, 3
Canadian Red Cross, 343
Canadian Tire, 123
Canary Wharf, 56, 77, 206
Capital expenditure budget, 85
Career development, 190—92
Career stages, 191—92
Cargill Ltd., 71—72

449

Carnegie, Andrew, 399
Carnegie, Dale, 406, 408
Carroll, S.J., 12
Cash budget, 85
Caterpillar, 355
Cavanaugh, Gerald F., 48
CBS, 27
Centraide, 298
Centralization, 126, 143
Chain of command, 131
Champy, James, 172
Chandler, Alfred, 140
Change, 42—43, 205—207, 213—14
 and continuous incremental improvement, 214
 incremental, 42—43
 internal forces, 207
 and manager's job, 205, 207
 metaphors for, 208—209
 organizational, 211—13
 process, 208—209
 quantum, 42—43
 and reengineering, 214
 resistance to, 212—13
 restraining forces, 208
 and technology, 205—206
 and TQM, 213—14
Change agents, 207
Channel, for communication, 323, 324
Channel Tunnel (England to France), 112
Chapter 11, and bankruptcy protection, 67
Charismatic leadership, 306—308, 309
Chevrolet Cavalier, 104—106
Chevrolet Lumina, 84
Christie, R., 145
Chrysler Canada, 30, 36, 52, 66, 192—93, 207, 292
Chrysler LHS, 52
Chung, K.H., 221
Churchill, Winston, 295
Chusmir, Leonard H., 199
Classical management writers, 126—27
Classical theorists, 126—27, 402
Classic Casuals, 150
Classic management studies. *See* Management classics
Classroom lectures, in on-the-job training, 190
Cleghorn, John, 278
Clorox, 45
Closed systems, 18
Clough, Paul, 356—57
CMP Publications, 125
Coach, manager as, 44—45
Coch, L., 210
Cochran, Philip L., 41
Coercive power, 135
Cognitive component of attitudes, 227
Cognitive dissonance theory, 228, 229
Cohesiveness, 255, 256
Collaboration, in conflict reduction, 337
Collective bargaining, 194—95
Collectivism, 33, 143, 260, 331—32
Columbia Records, 82
Command groups, 250

Commitment concept, 60
Committee structure, 158—59
Communication, 247
 barriers, 327—30
 defined, 321
 interpersonal, 323
 as management activity, 9
 and MIS, 374
 and national culture, 331—32
 purpose, 323
 and symbols, 322, 324
 and teams, 259
Comparisons, in control process, 346
Comper, Tony, 278
Competition, global, 26, 31
Competitive advantage, 71
Competitor intelligence, 80—81, 84
Complexity, of organization structure, 128
Compromise, in conflict reduction, 337
Computer networks, 368—69
Computer simulations, 409
Conceptual skills, 12
Concurrent control, 352, 357
Conditional maintenance, 379
Conference Board of Canada, 189
Conflict, 332—39
 and organizational structure, 335, 339
 players in, 335
 reduction tools, 337
 sources of, 335, 337
 stimulating, 337—39
 views of, 332
Conflict-handling styles, 334—35
Conflict management, 332—39
Conformity, 252, 253, 261
Conger, Jay, 306—7
Connaught Laboratories Ltd., 30
Consideration, 297
Consumers Packaging, 263
Continental Airlines, 209
Contingency approach
 to organization design, 138—39
Contingency variables, 19—20, 302, 305
Continuous improvement, 36, 43, 196, 214
 and change, 214
 and TQM, 36
Control
 and audits, 383
 and comparing for performance appraisal, 349—50
 and contingency factors, 357—58
 and cost-benefit analysis, 383—84
 defined, 345—46
 dysfunctional, 359—60
 importance of, 346
 and managerial action, 350—51
 and MIS, 374
 and national differences, 359
 and organization culture, 388
 and planning, 345
 process of, 347—48
 and small business, 357
 types of, 351—53
Control data, manipulation of, 361
Controlling, as management function, 6

Control system, qualities of, 354—56
Conventional personality, 234—35
Coordination, as management task, 306
Core process, 159—60, 161
Corrective action, 350—51
Cosell, Howard, 329
Cost-benefit analysis, 383—84, 396
Cost-centre approach, 375
Cost control, 375—76
Cost-leadership strategy, 68, 69
Country club management, 299
Courville, Leon, 278
Crayola, 246
Creativity, 215
Criteria, in decision-making, 104, 105, 108, 109
Critical incident, as technique of performance appraisal, 385
Critical path, 89—90
Cross-functional teams, 250, 260
Cross-training, 246
Crystal Pepsi, 103
Cuba, 31
Cuban Missile Crisis, 115
Cullen, Robert, 372—73
Cultural diversity, 47—48
Cultural environments, 32
Cultural variables, 32—33
Culture
 and decision-making, 108
 and decison-making, 118—19
 and innovation, 218
 and organization structure, 143
Current ratio, 382
Currie, Richard, 15
Curtis, Kent, 289
Customer, as focus of TQM, 36, 71
Customer departmentalization, 137
Customer evaluation, 83
Czech Republic, 31, 147

D
Daewoo Co., 380
Dallas Cowboys, 35
Dallas Fire Department, 389
Data, 369
Data Point, 64
Davis, Keith, 39
Dawe, Peter, 216
Debt-to-asset ratio, 382
Decentralization, of information control, 369—70, 373
Decisional roles, 8—9
Decision criteria, 104
 weighted, 104, 105—106
Decision effectiveness, evaluation of, 106
Decision implementation, 106
Decision-making, 102
 criteria, 104
 and MIS, 371—72
 and national culture, 118—19
 process, 103
Decision outcomes, in selection, 182
Decision packages, in ZBB, 86—87
Decisions
 by groups, 113—18
 nonprogrammed, 112, 113

Index

and organization level, 112—13
programmed, 110—13
and types of problems, 112—13
Decline, as career stage, 191
Decoding, of communication, 323
Decruitment, 179—80, 200
Dell, Michael, 72
Dell Computer Corporation, 72, 368
Delphi technique, 117, 118
Delrina Inc., 2, 9
Deming, W. Edwards, 35—36, 39, 381
  fourteen points for quality improvement, 381
Departmentalization, 136—38
  classic view, 136—37
  contemporary view, 138
Derlan Industries, 125
Devil's advocate, 339
Differentiation strategy, 68, 69, 70
Digital Equipment Corp. (DEC), 112, 333
Direct costs, 375
Directional plans, 57, 59
Discipline, 387—88
Discrimination, 177
Disney World, 189
Disseminator role, 8
Distortion, of information, 324, 325, 328
Disturbance handler role, 8—9
Diversity
  cultural, 47—48
  and human resource management, 195—96
  of skills, 127—29
  of training, 47
  in the work force, 26, 35, 111, 195—96
Divisional structure, 152—53
  strengths and weaknesses, 153
Division of labour, 127—29, 404
Dixon, Ted, 365
Dodge automobile, 30
Dofasco Inc., 33, 204
Dominion Stores, 27
Domino's Pizza, 206
Donnelly, James H., Jr., 363
Dow Corning, 67
Downsizing, 32—34, 172
Drake Personnel Services, 131
Dress code, 252
Drew, Richard, 249
Driving forces, toward change, 208
Drucker, Peter, 34, 63
Dubord, Paul, 51
Du Pont Corporation, 30, 140, 152, 159
Dynapro System Inc., 72, 73
Dysfunctional conflicts, 333, 334

E

Early retirement, as form of decruitment, 180
Earth Buddy, 123
Eastern Airlines, 209
Eastern Europe, 29, 31
Eastman Chemical Company, 161
Eastman Kodak, 34
Ebert, Ronald J., 99
Econometric models, 83

Economic indicators, 83
Economic order quantity model, 377, 409
EDS, 369
Effectiveness, 5
Efficiency, 5
Effort-performance linkage, in expectancy theory, 280
Eisner, Michael, 278
Electronic mail, 327
Electronic meeting, 117—18
ELI Eco Logic Inc., 40
Eller, Martha E., 42
E-mail, 327
Emotions, 328
Employee assessment, 177—78
Employee leasing, in recruitment, 180
Employee-oriented leader, 297, 299
Employee referrals, in recruitment, 179, 180
Employee training, 188—90
Empowerment, 36, 44, 380
  and redesigning jobs, 45
  and TQM, 36
  of workers, 36, 44, 249
Encoding, 323
End user, 369—70, 373
Enterprising personality, 234—35
Entrepreneur role, 8—9
Entrepreneurs, 34, 72—74
  characteristics, 73—74
  compared to managers, 74
  and small business, 34
Entrepreneurship, 72, 73
  and strategic planning, 72
Environment, 38
  cultural, 32
  and cultural variables, 32—33
  flexibility, 47
  general, 28
  global, 30—32
  and management, 27—34
  specific, 28
  stability, 47
  and structure, 141
Environmental protection, 40, 81
Environmental scanning, 80
Environmental waste management, 81
EOQ, 377, 409
Equity theory, 277, 279
  propositions, 279
Esprit clothing, 157
Establishment, as career stage, 191
Esteem needs, 272
Ethics
  code, 47
  defined, 46
  differing views of, 46—47, 48
Ethics situations
  agreeing with the boss, 261
  CEO compensation, 278
  competitor intelligence, 84
  competitor's trade secrets, 218
  creating charisma, 309
  creative resume writing, 184
  decision-making and social responsibility, 108

distorting information, 328
employee rights and control, 360
following orders, 133
going bankrupt, 67
matrix structure's effect on employees, 163
shaping behaviour and manipulation, 242—43
software piracy, 371
European Union, 27, 31
Evaluation, of decision effectiveness, 106
Events, as component of PERT, 89
Ewald, Cassye, 368
Expectancy theory, 280—83
  application, 281—82
Expense budget, 85
Expert power, 135
Exploration, as career stage, 191
External audit, 383
Extinction, and shaping behaviours, 243

F

Fax machines, 327
Fayol, Henry, 5, 6, 402—403
  principles, 403
Federal Express, 72, 156, 295, 327, 397
Feedback, 62, 63, 329—30
  in communication process, 323, 325
  and JCM, 167—68
Feedback control, 353, 357
Feedforward control, 351—52, 357
Fefer, Mark D., 342
Festinger, Leon, 228, 229, 244
Fiat automobile, 30
Fiedler, Fred, 300—303
Fiedler Contingency Model for leadership, 300—305
Fiedorowicz, Christina, 396
Figurehead role, 7, 8
Films and videos, used in training, 190
Filtering, of information, 327, 348, 374
Filtering down effect, of strategic planning, 71
Financial controls, 381—84
Firing, as means of decruitment, 180
First Canadian Place, 77
First-line managers, 3, 4, 59, 309. See also Supervision
First-line supervision, 308—12
First Nations people, 196
Fishery Products International, 206
Fixed budget, 85
Fixed-interval reordering system, 378
Fixed-point reordering system, 377
Flexibility, of environment, 47
  compared with stability, 47
Flood, Al, 278
Flynn, Walter J., 42
Focus factories, 71
Focus strategy, 68, 69
Follett, Mary Parker, 405
Following orders, 130
Forcing, in conflict reduction, 337
Ford Electronics Manufacturing, 266
Ford Escort, 104—106
Ford Motor Company, 29, 30, 36, 38,

52, 84, 178, 262, 263
Ford Taurus, 84
Forecasting techniques, 83
Forecasts, 82—83
Formalization, 126, 143, 387, 389
Fortune magazine, 287
Forzani, John, 232—33
Forzani's Locker Room, 233
Foundations of Leadership course, 286
Fracassi, Allen, 80, 81
Fracassi, Philip, 80, 81
Franchises, 365
Frederick, William C., 39, 50
French, John R.P., Jr., 134, 210
Frito-Lay, 345, 347
Frost, Peter, 98
Fuji, 27
Fujitsu Ltd., 111
Fuji-Xerox, 84
Functional conflicts, 333—34
Functional departmentalization, 136
Functional structure, 151—52
Fundamental attribution error, 238
Future Shop, 81

G

Gallo Wines, 69
Gandhi, Mahatma, 295
Gantt, Henry L., 88, 402
Gantt chart, 88, 402
Gates, William, 294, 309
Gateway 2000, 27
Geis, F.L., 145
General administrative theorists, 399, 402—404, 409
General Electric, 33, 47, 54, 66, 135, 136, 159, 160, 230, 360
General Motors, 16, 27, 29, 32, 36, 52, 140, 152, 153, 164—65, 172, 306, 359
Geographic departmentalization, 137
Geo Prism automobile, 104—106
George Weston Ltd., 15
Germany, 27, 31
Getty Oil, 67
Gilbreth, Frank, 400—402
Gilbreth, Lillian, 400—402
Giordano Holdings Ltd., 79
Global assignments, 187
Global village, 28—29
Goals
 relationship to performance, 63
 setting, 70
 and teams, 55, 254
Goal specificity, 62
Godsoe, Peter, 27, 278
Goodyear Tire and Rubber Co., 80, 355
Government regulation, 38
Goza, Barbara K., 22
Grafix Terminal, 72
Grand Banks, 206
Graphic rating scales, 385
Greene, Charles N., 99
Greiner, Larry E., 299
Group
 defined, 250
 reasons for joining, 250—51
Group behaviour, and size, 254

Group cohesiveness, 256
Group decision-making, 114—18
 advantages and disadvantages, 113—14
 effectiveness, 114—16
 improving of, 116—18
Group order ranking, 386
Gruben, Roger, 318
Grupo Financiero Inverlat SA, 27
GTE, 26, 43

H

Hackman, J. Richard, 167, 170, 408
Hall, D.T., 191
Hallett, Douglas, 39, 40
Halo effect, 239—40
Haner, Mike, 181
Haney, W.V., 121
Harary, Ronnen, 123
Harley-Davidson, 394—95
Harris, Hollis, 15
Harrison, Walter T., Jr., 393
Hartley, Leonard Darryl, 225
Hartley, Robert F., 122
Harvard Graduate School of Business, 68
Harwood Manufacturing Company, 210
Hawthorne Studies, 406, 407
Hazardous waste management, 40, 81
Heitman, Lee, 147
Hell's Angels, 295
Hepatitis C, and donated blood supply, 343
Hershey Foods Corporation, 152—53
Hershey-Pasta, 374
Herzberg, Frederick, 273—75, 408
Hewlett-Packard, 112, 164—65
Hierarchy, in organization, 127
Hierarchy of needs theory, 271—72
Hill, Anita, 40
Hisrich, Robert, 74
Hitchcock, Bob, 81—82
Hodgetts, Richard M., 11
Hofstede, Geert, 32, 33
Hold jockeys, 342
Holland, John L, 234—35, 244
Hollinger Inc., 15
Honda, 30, 84
Honda Accord, 30, 84
Honda Civic, 104—106
Honeywell Ltd., 174
Hopkins, Al, 204
Hopkins, David, 51
Horizontal structure, 159—62
Horngren, Charles T., 393
Hot stove rule, 387
House, Robert, 302, 303, 307
Hudson Bay Company, 157
Human relations management, 399, 406—408
Human relations view of conflict, 333, 334
Human resource approach to management, 404—408
Human resource inventory, 177
Human resource management, 9—10, 175
 and environmental factors, 176—77
 process, 175—76
Human resource planning, strategic,

177—78
Human resources, 51
 and innovation, 215—18
Human skills, 12
Humber College, 28
Hungary, 31
Hunsaker, J.S., 266
Hunsaker, P.L., 266
Husky Oil, 30
Hyatt Hotels, 225
Hygiene factors, 275
Hyundai Excel automobile, 104—106

I

IBM, 16, 27, 32, 34, 72, 112, 117, 165, 217, 370
Ill-structured problems, 110, 112, 113
Imperial Oil, 37, 138, 256—57, 292
Imperial Parking Ltd. (Impark), 356—57
Implementation, of decisions, 106
Impoverished management, 299
Incentives, 292
Income
 of Canadian CEOs, 15, 278
 of managers, 15—16
Incremental budgets, 86
Incremental change, 42—43
Independent contractors, in recruitment, 180
Indirect costs, 375
Individual differences, as contingency variable, 20
Individualism, 33, 260, 331, 405
Individual ranking, in performance appraisal, 386
Industrial psychology, 405
Industrial Revolution, 398—99
Infiniti automobile, 206
Information, 369
 decentralization, 369
Informational roles, 7, 8
Information control systems, 368—74
Information models, 409
Ingram company, 211
Initiating structure, 297
Innovation, 215—19
 fostering, 217—19
 and human resources, 219
 and organizational culture, 218
 and structure, 217
Insider-outsider transition, 188, 195
Integrated work teams, and job design, 166
Integration, as management task, 306
Intel, 69, 215, 217
Interactionist view of conflict, 332, 333
Internal audit, 383
Internal forces, toward change, 207
Internal search, in recruitment, 180
International assignments, 187
International culture
 and personality, 235—36
 and teams, 260
International Machinists and Aerospace Workers (union), 266
International management, 28—32, 143
 and CEO pay, 278
 and communications, 331—32

Index

and culture, 118—19
and decision-making, 118—19
and motivation, 284—85
Interpersonal communication, 323
Interpersonal roles, 7, 8
Interviews, 184—85, 188
Intrapreneurship, 34—35
Inuit people, 318
Inventory ordering systems, 377—78
Inventory turnover ratio, 382
Investigative personality, 234—35
Ivancevich, John M., 363

J
Jago, A.G., 303, 305
Jaguar automobile, 30
JCM, 166—68
Jerdee, T.H., 12
Jet Propulsion Lab, 156
Jick, Todd, 98
JIT inventory practice, 378
Joan of Arc, 295
Job, matching personality, 234—35
Job analysis, 177—78
Job characteristics model (JCM), 166—68
Job description, 178
Job design, 166—68, 405
and work teams, 166
Job enlargement, 166
Job enrichment, 166, 275
Job involvement, and attitude, 227
Job rotation, 166
and on-the-job training, 190
Job satisfaction, 273
and attitude, 227
Job sharing, in decruitment, 180
Job specialization, 166, 398
Job specification, 178
John Labatt Ltd., 27, 292
Johnson and Johnson Inc., 33, 218
Johnson-George, Cynthia, 265
Jones, Gordon, 55
Jones, John E., 316
Jones, Sonia, 55
Jordan, Michael, 122
Judgments, distortion in, 238—39
Jurassic Park, 294
Jury of opinion, 83
Just-in-time inventory practice, 174, 378

K
Kane, Joe, 147
Kanungo, Rabindra N., 307
Katz, Robert L., 12
Kay, Mary, 27, 69, 165
Kelleher, Herb, 60
Kellogg Co. Inc., 292
Keon, Clifford M., 42
Kidd, Robert, 15
Kikuta, Yasuyo, 111
Kirkpatrick, Shelly A., 296
Kluge, Holger, 278
K Mart, 123, 371
Korthals, Robert, 278
Kwinter, Monte, 77

L
Labatt, 27, 292
Labour-management relations, 181, 192—95, 223
Labour unions, 181, 192—94
Lai, Jimmy, 79
Langfeld, Mark, 267
Langlois, Daniel, 294
Language, 327, 328
simplified, 329, 330
Late career stage, 191
Laumann, Silken, 270
Layoffs, in decruitment, 180
Leader-member relations, 300—302
Leader-participation model, 304—305
Leader role, 7, 8
Leaders
achievement-oriented, 303—304
defined, 295
directive, 303
participative, 303
relationship-oriented, 302
supportive, 303
task-oriented, 302
transactional, 308
transformational, 308
Leadership, 294—308, 405
behavioural theories, 296—300, 303
changes in style, 314
charismatic, 306—308
contingency theories, 300—305
irrelevance of, 305—306
trait theories, 295—96
Leading, as management function, 6
Learjet, 112
Learning, 240—42
Learning for Life (employee education program), 174
Least-preferred coworker, 300—303
questionnaire, 300
Leeds, Gerry, 125
Leeds, Lilo, 125
Legitimate power, 135
Lesley, Elizabeth, 76
Level in organization, and decisions, 112
Leverage ratio, 382
Lewin, Kurt, 208—209
Lexus automobile, 206
Liaison role, 7, 8
Life cycle, of organization, 58—60
Life insurance industry, 80
Linear programming, 93—94, 409
Line authority, 131
Liquidity ratio, 382
Litton Industries, 409
Livingston Healthcare Services Inc., 373
Liz Claiborne, 157
L.L. Bean, 69
Loblaw Cos. Ltd., 15, 27
Locke, Edwin A., 296, 408
Long-term plans, 56, 57, 88
Loveridge, Lt.-Col. Al, 298
Loyalty, and teams, 259
Luthans, Fred, 9, 11, 20
Lying, as ethical issue, 328

M
Machiavelli, Niccolo, 232
Machiavellianism, 232
M.ach One theory, 306
Mack Truck, 355
MacMillan, John, 174
MacMillan Bloedel, 223
Magna International, 39, 84, 165
Mahoney, T.A., 12
Maintenance control, 378—79
Management
defined, 5
roles, 7—9
study of, 16
Management by objectives, 61—63, 386
Management classics
bounded rationality (Simon), 109
cognitive dissonance (Festinger), 228—29
conflict handling techniques (Thomas), 336
contingency model (Fiedler), 302—3
cultural variables (Hofstede), 32—33
generic strategies (Porter), 69
group conformity (Asch), 133
groupthink (Janis), 115
Hawthorne Studies, 407
ideal organization structure (Weber), 127
job characteristics model (Hackman/Oldham), 167
managers' roles (Mintzberg), 10
realistic job previews (Wanous), 192, 193
resistance to change (Coch/French), 216
scientific management (Taylor), 399, 400, 401
three needs theory (McClelland), 276—77
zero-based budgeting (Texas Instruments), 86—87
Management functions, 5—6
Management skills
building a power base, 135
building team trust, 259
coaching skills, 313
conducting a meeting, 116
effective listening, 331
empowering employees, 151
goal setting, 70
interviewing, 187
overcoming resistance to change, 213
preventing sexual harassment charges, 42
providing feedback, 353
time management, 96
Managerial action, in control process, 350—51
Managerial grid, 299
Managers
as agents of change, 207
as cheerleaders, 45
classification, 4
as coaches, 44, 287
compared to entrepreneurs, 74
income, 15

Mandela, Nelson, 295, 300
Manning, George, 289
Maritime Telegraph and Telephone, 157
Marks & Spencer, 66, 68
Marx, Robert, 98
Mary Kay Cosmetics, 27, 69, 165, 292
Maslow, Abraham, 271—72, 408
Massey-Ferguson, 16
Matrix structure, 154—56
Matsushita, Konosuke, 54
Matsushita company, 54
Matthias, Rebecca, 13
Mayo, Elton, 405, 406, 407
Maytag, 69
MBO, 61—63
  and performance appraisal, 386
MCA Records, 82
McCain Foods, 16
McClelland, David, 275—77, 408
McCurry, Bob, 273
McDonald's Corp. (restaurants), 7, 28, 286, 365
McDonnell Douglas, 263
McGregor, Douglas, 272, 407, 408
McGuire, Joseph M., 39
McKnight, William, 249
McLennan, John, 9
McNamara, Robert, 409
McNeely, Bonnie L, 341
Measurement, in TQM, 36
Measuring, in control process, 346—49
Mechanistic organization, 139, 158
Megatrends, 156
Megginson, L.C., 221
Melting pot, 35
Merck Pharmaceuticals, 16, 286
Merisol company, 211
Message, in communication, 323—24
Metal Recovery Industries, 81
Mexico, 31, 359
Michelin, 80
Microsoft, 33, 294
Midcareer stage, 191
Middle managers, 3, 4, 59
Middle-of-the-road management, 299
Midvale Steel, 399, 402
Milgram, Stanley, 130
Minolta, 27, 117
Mintzberg, Henry, 7—9, 10, 20, 24
MIS, 368—74
  and communication, 374
  and control, 374
  and decision-making, 371—72
  and organization structure, 373
  and planning, 370—71
Mission, of organization, 65
Mitsubishi Motor Corp., 31
Mizuno, Masoto, 15
MNCs, 30
Moberg, Dennis J., 48
Monitor role, 7—8
Monsen, Joseph R., Jr., 39
Montreal Expos baseball team, 295
Monty, Jean, 278
Moore, Jim, 2, 6, 9
Mosard, Gil, 263
Mother's Work Inc., 13

Mother Teresa, 300
Motivating potential score (MPS), 167
Motivation, 45—46, 167, 270—92, 400, 405
  defined, 270
  and diversity, 286
  and feedback, 353
  integrated perspective, 283—84
  and national culture, 284—85
  process, 270—71
  and rewards, 292
  and teams, 260
  theories, 271—77
Motivation hygiene theory, 272—75
Motivators, 275
Moto Photo, 365
Motorized consumer products group (MCPG), 17
Motorola, 16, 85, 159, 354, 376
Motor reproduction processes, in social learning theory, 241—42
Mount Sinai Hospital, Toronto, 372—73
Mouton, Jane S., 299
Multilin, 125
Multinational corporations, 30
Multiperson comparisons, 385, 386
Munsterberg, Hugo, 405
Muscat, Austin, 123
Muscat, Michelle, 123
Mutual Benefit Life Insurance, 26, 43

N
nAch, 275, 276, 277
nAff, 276, 277
NAFTA, 31, 52, 206
Naisbitt, James, 156
National Bank, 278
National culture, and decision-making, 118—19
National Transport Agency (NTA), 24
Need
  for achievement, 275—77
  for affiliation, 275—77
  and motivation, 271
  for power, 275—77
Needs, hierarchy of, 271—72
Negative reinforcement, and shaping behaviours, 243
Negotiation, labour-management, 194—95
Negotiator role, 8—9
Nestle's, 30, 31
Network, linking end users of information, 369
Networking, 9—10
Newall, Ted, 278
New Balance athletic footwear, 122
New Jersey Bell Telephone Company, 405
Nike athletic footwear, 122, 156, 157
Nissan Canada, 66
Nissan Maxima automobile, 84
Noise, in communication, 323—24
Nominal group technique, 117, 118
Nonprogrammed decisions, 112, 113
Nonverbal communication, 326
Nonverbal cues, 327, 329
Norms, 252, 253

North American Free Trade Agreement, 31, 52, 206
Northern Telecom, 278, 322
North Warning System, 318
Not-for-profit organization, 12—13, 65
Nova Corp., 278
nPow, 276, 277
Nucor, 33

O
Office Depot, 103
Official Languages Act, 177
Ogilvie Mills Ltd., 298
Ohio State University leadership studies, 297, 302, 306
Oil and gas industry, 80
Oldham, Greg R., 167, 170
Oliver, Burgess, 321—2
Olympia and York Developments Ltd., 56, 77
Ontario Electronics Ltd. (OEL), 228
Open systems, 18, 218
Operant conditioning, 240—41
Operational plans, 56, 57
Operation ratio, 382
Operations control, 374—81
Operations management, 375
Operatives, 381
  defined, 3, 4
Optimization models, 409
Oral communication, 325, 326
Oral reports, in performance appraisal, 346, 348
Organic organization, 139
Organization
  defined, 3
  goals, 3
  life cycle, 58—60
  people, 3
  purposes, 3
  structure, 3—4
Organizational behaviour, 225—27
  goals in, 226—27
Organizational change, 211—13
Organizational commitment, 227
Organizational strategy, 64, 68
Organization culture
  and behavioural control, 388—89
  characteristics, 164
  and structure, 163—65
Organization design
  contingency approach of, 138—41
  design concepts, 126
  design options, 162
  and supervision, 313
  traditional, 150—53
Organization structure, 3, 126
  and contingencies, 20
  and MIS, 373
  and reengineering, 172
  and size, 141
Organizing, as management function, 6
Orientation, 188—89, 195
  and behavioural control, 390
Osborne Computer, 112
OTR Express, 367
Outsider-insider transition, 188, 195

Index

P

Paired comparisons, in performance appraisal, 386
Pan Am, 209
Panasonic, 54, 65
Paolillo, Joseph G., 14
Parker, Barbara, 199
Participative decision-making, 62
Participative goal setting, 63
Patey, Colin, 216, 217
Path-goal theory of leadership, 302—304
Patton, General George, 306
PCBs, 40
Peninsula Farm, 55
Pennzoil, 67
People Express, 209, 211
PepsiCo, 103, 161, 345
Perception, 236—40
Performance
  and planning, 56
  relationship to goals, 63
Performance appraisal, 348—49, 385—86
  criteria, 348—49
  and MBO, 56, 386
  methods, 385—86
Performance feedback, 62
Performance objectives, 62
Performance-reward linkage, in expectancy theory, 280—82
Performance simulation tests, 184
Perrigo, L., 61
Perrow, Charles, 408
Personality
  and authoritarianism, 231—32
  and behaviour, 231
  defined, 231
  and job matching, 234—35
  and locus of control, 231
  and Machiavellianism, 232
  and national culture, 235—36
  and risk taking, 234
  and self-esteem, 232
  and self-monitoring, 233
Personal observation, in performance appraisal, 346, 347
Personnel Decisions Inc., 183
PERT
  components, 89—90
  and control, 383
  network, 89, 91
  as planning tool, 89—92
Peters, Tom, 135, 211
Peterson, Monte, 142
Petro-Canada, 295
Pfeffer, Jeffrey, 408
Pfeiffer, J. William, 316
Phelps Dodge Mining, 118
Philip Environmental, 81
Physical examination, 186, 188
Physiological needs, 271—72
Pizza Hut, 206
Planning
  and contingencies, 58—61
  and control, 345
  and decision-making, 102, 103
  defined, 54—55
  as management function, 6
  and MIS, 370—71
  and organization life cycle, 58—60
  and performance, 56
  purposes, 56
  and uncertainty, 60
Plans, types of, 56—57, 59
Plymouth Satellite automobile, 52
Poco Petroleums, 80
Poland, 31
Polaris submarine missile system, 89, 90
Policy, 114
Political skills, 12
Politics, and decision-making, 108
Pollack, Ted, 75
Porter, Michael, 68—69
Position power, 300, 302
Positive reinforcement, and shaping behaviours, 243
Power, 123—34, 256, 405
  and decision-making, 108
  types of, 135
Power distance, 32—33, 143, 236
Pratt & Whitney Canada Ltd., 71
Predictors, selection devices as, 188
Preston, L.E., 50
Price-Costco, 102, 233
Price Waterhouse, 14—15
Prime Time Magazine, 343
Privacy Act, 177
Private employment agencies, for recruitment, 180
Problem identification, 103, 105
Problems
  and decisions, 112—13
Procedure, 110—11
Process approach, 16—17
Process control, 380
Process departmentalization, 138
Process reengineering, 172
Procter & Gamble, 39, 108
Product departmentalization, 137
Production-oriented leader, 297, 298
Productivity, 397, 398, 400
Profitability ratio, 382—83
Profit budget, 85
Profit-margin-on-revenues ratio, 382—83
Profits, 38
Program Evaluation and Review Technique (PERT), 89—92
Programmed decisions, 110—13
Public employment agencies, for recruitment, 180
Pulp and paper industry, 223
Puma athletic footwear, 122
Punishment, and shaping behaviours, 243
Purolator Courier, 298

Q

Qantas Airlines, 209
Qualitative forecasts, 83
Quality, as principle of TQM, 36, 71
Quality circles, 263—64
Quality control, 249, 379—81
  groups, 36
  and TQM, 36
Quality of life, 33
Quantitative approach to management, 408—409
Quantitative forecasts, 83
Quantity of life, 33
Queuing theory, 94—96

R

Rabie, Anton, 123
Radler, David, 15
Range of variation, in performance appraisal, 349
Ransom, Cindy, 45
Rapoport, Sandra E., 42
Ratio analysis, 382—83
Rational decision-making, 107—109
Rationality
  bounded, 108, 109
  defined, 107
Raven, Bertram, 134
Realistic job preview, 192—93
Realistic personality, 234—35
Recruitment, 179—80
Reddin, Bill, 306
Redesign, of work process, 32—33. *See also* Job design
Reduced work week, in decruitment, 180
Reengineering, 26, 32—33, 42—43, 172, 214
Reference checks, 186, 188
Referent, 277, 279
Referent power, 135
Referrals, in recruitment, 179, 180
Regression models, 83
Reichmann brothers, 77, 206
Reinforcement processes, in social learning theory, 242
Reject erors, 182
Reliability, 182
Remedial maintenance, 379
Remington company, 30
Resistance to change, 212—13
Resource allocator role, 8—9
Responsibility, 37—39, 129—30
Responsiveness, 37—39
Restraining forces, and change, 208
Restructuring, and change, 207
Retail Council of Canada, 102
Retention processes, in social learning theory, 242
Return-on-investment ratio, 396
Revenue budgets, 85
Revenue forecasts, 82
Revlon, 27
Reward power, 135
Reynolds Metals, 135
Richman, Tom, 148
Rights view of ethics, 48
Risk taking, 234
RJP, 192, 193
RnR The Walking Store, 233
Robbins, Stephen P., 266, 338
Rockefeller, John D., 399
Roles

defined, 251
  of management, 7—10
Roman Catholic Church, 73, 207, 398
Romania, 31
Roppe Corporation, 269
Rosenkrantz, Stuart A., 11
Roskin, Rick, 306
Rothmans Inc., 30
Rotter, Julian B., 245
Royal Bank, 278, 292, 298
Royal Dutch/Shell, 30
Rubbermaid, 138
Rule, 111
Ryder Systems, 160

S

Safety needs, 271, 272
Saint-Pierre, Guy, 298
Sales force composition, 82
Santa Fe development, Mexico City, 77
Sara Lee, 82
Saskatoon Chemicals Ltd., 181
Saturn company, 260
Scanning, environmental, 80
Scenario, 82
Scheduling, 88, 89
School placements, in recruitment, 180
Schulmeyer, Gerhard, 154
Schwarzkopf, Norman, 307
Scientific management, 44, 399—402, 408
Scotchgard coating, 215
Sea-Doo/Ski-Doo, 17
Sears, 27, 135, 140, 206
Seiko, 5
Selection, 180—88, 405
  and behavioural control, 387, 388
  and decision outcomes, 182
  devices as predictors, 188
  process, 180—82
Selective perception, 327
Selectivity, 239
Self-actualization needs, 272
Self-directed work teams, 249
Self-esteem, 232, 250
Self-managed work teams, 250
  and job design, 166
Self-monitoring, and personality, 233
Self-serving bias, 238
Sexual harassment, 40—42
Shaping behaviour, 242—43
Shell Oil, 30
Shoe and boot industry, 100
Short Brothers, 112
Short-term plans, 56, 57
SHRP, 177—79
Siemens Group, 30
Silicone breast implants, 67
Simon, Herbert, 109
Simple structure, 150—51
Simplified models, in bounded rationality, 108, 109
Simulation exercises, in training, 190
Singer company, 30
Size, and group behaviour, 254—55
Skill diversity, 127—28
Skill variety, and JCM, 167

Skinner, B.F., 240—41
Skyfreight, 24
Slack time, 92
Slovakia, 31
Small business
  and control, 357
  defined, 13
  and entrepreneurs, 34
  management of, 13—14
Smith, Adam, 389
Smith, B.E., 290
Smith, Frederick, 72
Smith, Norman R., 21
SNC-Lavalin, 298
Social learning theory, 241—42
Social needs, 272
Social norms, 39, 407
Social obligation, 37, 39
Social personality, 234—35
Social responsibility, 37—42
  arguments for and against, 38
  compared to social responsiveness, 37, 39
  in decision-making, 108
  defined, 37
Social responsiveness, 37, 39, 41
  compared to social responsibility, 37, 39
Softimage Inc., 294
Software development, 396
Software Support Professional Association, 2
Sony Corp., 3
Soros, George, 77
Sotos, John, 365
Southwest Airlines, 60, 69
Span of control, 134—35, 373
Spar Aerospace, 141, 184
Specific environment, 28
Specific plans, 56, 57—58
Spokesperson role, 8
Sport Check, 233
Sports Authority, 233
Sports Experts, 233
Sports lottery, 27
Sportsmart, 233
Stability, of environment, 47
  compared to flexibility, 47
Staff authority, 131—32
Standardization, 127
Standard Oil, 140, 399
Starbuck's stores, 102
StarKist tuna, 39
Statistical quality control, 380
Statistical reports, in performance appraisal, 347, 348—49
Status, 254
Steelcase Canada Ltd., 71
Stegora, Philip A., 218
Stelco, 33
Stereotyping, 239
Stouffers, 69
Strategic human resource planning, 181
Strategic management process, 64—71
  steps in, 64—65
Strategic planning, 57
Strategic plans, 57

Strategy
  and structure, 140
  and TQM, 71—72
Strategy formulation, 68—69
Strayer, Jacqueline, 42
Strengths, weaknesses, opportunities, threats (SWOT), 67
Stronach, Frank, 165
Structure
  and control, 357, 358
  and environment, 141
  and innovation, 217
  and organization culture, 163—64
  and organization size, 141
  and strategy, 140
  and technology, 141
Substitution effect, 83
Supervision, 308—14, 352
  and leadership style, 314
  and organizational design, 313
  and technology, 312, 373
Supervisors, 4
  changing roles, 310—14
  as first-level managers, 309—10
  unique characteristics, 310
Supportive climate, for teams, 260
Swaney, William, 61
SWOT analysis, 67
Symbols, and communication, 322, 324
Syncrude Canada Ltd., 195—96
Systems approach, 18—19

T

Talker, Michael, 24
Tannen, Deborah, 247
Task force, 158, 250, 260
Task identity, and JCM, 167
Task significance, and JCM, 167
Task structure, 300—2
Taylor, Alan, 278
Taylor, Frederick, 86, 399—401, 402, 403
  four principles of management, 400
Team management, 299
Teams, 249, 380. *See also* Work teams
  as challenge for managers, 260—61
  common characteristics, 258—60
  and communication, 259, 322
  cross-functional, 250, 260
  and goals, 258, 259, 260, 262
  and loyalty, 259
  and national culture, 260—61
  overcoming obstacles, 262
  and quality circles, 263—64
  reason for using, 257—58
  self-directed, 249
  and supportive climate, 260
  and TQM, 263
  and trust, 259
Technical skills, 12
Technological forecasts, 82—88
Technology
  and change, 205, 206
  and structure, 141
  and supervision, 312
Temporary help services, in recruitment, 180
Tengelmann supermarkets, 27

Index

Testing, as employee selection device, 183
Texaco Canada Ltd., 67
Thatcher, Margaret, 295
The Bay, 206
The Globe and Mail, 278
The Mask, 294
Theory of justice view of ethics, 48
Theory X, in motivation studies, 273—74, 407
Theory Y, in motivation studies, 273—74, 407
Therbligs, 401
Thermos company, 142, 256
Thomas, Clarence, 40
Thomas, Dave, 72
Thomas, Kenneth W., 336, 408
Thompson, Richard, 278
Thomsen, Wayne, 392
Thornton, Charles "Tex," 409
360-degree employee review system, 136, 160
3M Company, 33, 215, 218, 249
Three needs theory, 275—77
Tidlund, Mary, 267
Tiger athletic footwear, 122
Time-series analysis, 83
Times-interest-earned ratio, 382
TNCs, 30—31
Tolerance, 218
Tonin, Guido
Top managers, 3, 59
Topps Trading Cards, 76
Toronto Blue Jays baseball team, 3, 298, 356
Toronto-Dominion Bank, 278
Total assets turnover ratio, 382
Total quality management. *See* TQM
Toyota, 27, 29, 66, 273, 292
Toys "R" Us, 16
TQM, 35—36, 174
  and change, 213—14
  characteristics, 36
  and strategy, 71—72
  and structure design, 162—63
  and teams, 263—64
  and training, 214
Trade secrets, 218
Trading alliances, 31
Traditional management, 9
Traditional organization options, 150—53
Traditional view of conflict, 332
Training, 405
  and behavioural control, 390
  classroom lectures, 190
  in diversity consciousness, 47
  films and videos, 190

job rotation, 190
methods, 190
simulation exercises, 190
understudy assignment, 190
vestibule, 192
Traits, of leaders, 308
Trait theories of leadership, 295—96
Transactional leaders, 308
Transfers, in decruitment, 180
Transformational leaders, 308
Transformation process, 374—75
Transnational corporations, 30—31
Transport Canada, 24
Trites, Ron, 396
Trucking business, 367
Trudeau, Pierre, 29, 295, 300
Trust, and teams, 259, 261, 262
Turner, Ted, 309

U
U-Haul, 160
Uncertainty
  and contingencies, 20
  and planning, 60
Uncertainty avoidance, 33, 143
Understudy assignment, in on-the-job training, 190
Unilever Canada, 30
Union Carbide Corp., 26, 43
Union Gas, 30
Unions, 187, 192—95, 223
United Auto Workers, 359
Unity of command, 129
University of Michigan leadership studies, 297, 299
University of Toronto, 28
UPS, 371, 372, 397, 400, 408
Utilitarian view of ethics, 48

V
Vaill, Peter B., 221
Valasquez, Manual, 48
Validity, 182—83
Vancouver General Hospital, 295
Varadi, Ben, 123
Variable budget, 85
Variables, cultural, 32—33
Variable sampling, 380
Venture (Canadian Broadcasting Corporation), 24, 52, 77, 100, 147, 172, 202, 247, 267, 292, 318, 365, 396
Verbal communication, 325
Verbal intonation, 326
Verteuil, Peter de, 81
Vestibule training, 190
Vietnam War, 115
Voice-activated computers, 327
Voice mail, 327
Volkswagen, 84

Von Der Embse, Thomas, 341
Vroom, Victor, 280, 304—5, 408

Wal-Mart Corporation, 3, 16, 27, 33, 69, 135, 370—71
Walt Disney Co., 278
Wang Laboratories, 67
Wartick, Steven L., 41
Waterford Hospital, St. John's, Newfoundland, 84, 216
Watson, Thomas, 165
Waxman Resources, 81
Webb, David, 342
Weber, Max, 127, 404, 405
Weighted application, 183
Weights, on decision-making criteria, 104—105
Welch, Jack, 136, 309
Well-structured problems, 111, 112
Wendy's Restaurants, 3, 72
Western Electric, 406
Weston, Galen, 15
Weyerhaeuser Canada Ltd., 181
Whirlpool, 113
White-water rapids metaphor of change, 209
Whiz Kids, 409
Widrington, Peter, 298
Williston Wildcatters Oil Corp., 267
Women, and social responsibility, 41
Woods, Maureen, 42
Woodward, Joan, 141
WordPerfect, 341—42
Work force, 35, 40—41
  diversity in, 26, 35
Work process redesign, 32—34. *See also* Job design
Work sampling, 184, 185, 188
Work teams, 143, 166, 174, 380. *See also* teams
World Bank, 409
Written communication, 325
Written essay, in performance appraisal, 385
Written reports, in performance appraisal, 346, 348
Written tests, 183, 188

X
Xerox, 4, 51, 84, 292

Y
Yetton, Phillip, 303, 305

Z
Zellers Inc., 123
Zenith company, 31
Zero-based budgeting (ZBB), 86—88
Zlin Aerospace, 147